The Roman Question

Arthur and Odo Russell at the ages of 17 and 13. Lithograph by Kriehuber

THE
ROMAN QUESTION

Extracts from the despatches
of Odo Russell from Rome
1858 - 1870

EDITED BY
NOEL BLAKISTON

LONDON
CHAPMAN AND HALL
37 ESSEX STREET · WC2

First published in 1962
© *1962 Noel Blakiston*
Printed in Great Britain by
The Shenval Press Ltd
London, Hertford and Harlow
Catalogue number 4217/4

Illustrations

Acknowledgments

I am most grateful to Lord Ampthill for permission to publish despatches and letters of his grandfather, and to Lord Clarendon for permission to examine, and publish from, the Clarendon Papers.

Plates 4, 9, 11, 12, 15, 30 are reproduced by permission of Radio Times Hulton Picture Library; plates 6, 7, 8 (the original lent by Earl Mountbatten of Burma), 21, 23, 25, 26, 27 by permission of the National Portrait Gallery; plates 10, 20a, 24, 28, 29 by permission of the *Bibliothèque Nationale*. Plate 14 is reproduced by courtesy of the Duc de Guiche; plate 16 by courtesy of Miss Flora Russell; plate 19 by courtesy of Miss Gwen Williams; plate 20b by courtesy of G. Laterza & Figli; the despatch on pages 154-155 is crown copyright and is reproduced by permission of the P.R.O.

Introduction

Odo Russell, the author of the despatches here printed, was the third
of the three sons of Lord William Russell and his wife Elizabeth Anne,
daughter of the Hon John Theophilus Rawdon, brother of the Marquis of Hastings. Lord William, whose marriage took place in 1817,
was second son of the 6th Duke of Bedford and elder brother of Lord
John Russell. Entering the army in 1806 as a cornet in the 1st Dragoons,
he served as aide-de-camp to the Duke of Wellington in the Peninsula.
Having retired from the army on half pay in 1828, he became a diplomat. In 1832 he was sent on a special mission to Portugal and from 1835
to 1841 was Ambassador in Berlin. He died at the age of fifty-six in
1846.

Of his three sons, the eldest, Hastings, born in 1819, succeeded to
the dukedom of Bedford in 1872 and died in 1891. The second, Arthur
(b. 1825, d. 1892), was a philosopher and *savant*. For 28 years, from
1857 to 1885, he was Liberal Member of Parliament for Tavistock. The
third, Odo, was born in Florence on 20 February 1829. He early
followed his father into the diplomatic service, becoming attaché to the
Embassy in Vienna at the age of twenty. He served in the Foreign
Office under Palmerston and Granville (1850-52), and was later posted
to Paris (1853), Constantinople (1854), Washington (1857) and Rome
(November 1858 to July 1870). He was then transferred to the Foreign
Office, to be sent in November 1870 on a special mission to Bismarck
at Versailles. On 16 October 1871 he was appointed Ambassador in
Berlin where he died on 25 August 1884. On 7 March 1881 he had been
created Baron Ampthill.

The three boys, Hastings, Arthur and Odo, were educated mainly
abroad, in Austria and Germany, by tutors. The name of a M. Drocourt
survives, their French instructor, to whom they were much attached
and whom they would visit, in later life, when passing through Paris.
The company of their brilliant mother, moreover, must have been an
education in itself. For Lady William was an exceedingly intellectual

woman and a great buyer of books. Her library included the classics not only of Greece and Rome but of the principal modern European languages, the pages cut and often marked with annotations in her large, emphatic hand.

Away from academic grooves, the education of the boys was broad and international. Here it must be said that I am referring mainly to Arthur and Odo, who were very much closer to one another than either was to Hastings. There is evidence that Hastings reacted against the intellectual atmosphere and was disposed to regard his younger brothers, particularly Arthur, as pedantic and professorial. The reaction continued when he himself had a son to educate. Lady William gave her grandson, Sackville, then aged thirteen, a copy (presumably in English) of Herodotus. Arthur, staying with his brother at Endsleigh in July 1865, wrote to his mother:

> Sackville is much interested with your Herodotus. I make him tell me the stories at dinner. He comes of his own accord to make me read French tragedies with him, which he seems to enjoy. His father and mother are much distressed at his tastes and say he will evidently become a prig.

Odo Russell's culture then was cosmopolitan; but it certainly had a German bias. He never learned to think in Italian, as, to judge from the frequent German words and phrases in his private letters, he evidently thought in German. It is clear that at the beginning of his Italian mission he had no command at all of the Italian language. Approaching Rome in December 1858, accompanied by an Italian travelling servant, Giuseppe Tartini, he wrote from Florence:

> What a lovely place Florence is! A paradise inhabited by devils in the shape of police and *douaniers*! At the gate of every town they stop you and want your passport and God knows what. I should have been most uncomfortable without a servant who knew the people and the language. I did not care to go to Pisa, but Tartini would not *auslassen* and forced me to stop there. He was right and I was delighted. I made up my mind as to what I thought good, bad or indifferent and was vastly pleased on reading over Murray's Handbook that I had been well guided by instinct and had been able to feel correctly.

Not many weeks after his arrival in Rome, Odo Russell's name

appears in Gregorovius' Journal, where he is simply described as
'of German education'.[1] He undoubtedly had a Teutonic thirst for
knowledge.

My interest for ancient, more especially Greek history, he wrote to
his mother from Constantinople in 1856,

> is growing very great and my attempts to satisfy my curiosity
> and *wissbegier* do not succeed to my satisfaction. I want to read and
> learn and do not know how to set about it. I have read all I could get
> hold of and I study Bouillet day and night and the other books of
> reference you gave me. Books of reference have become a necessity
> of life for me and dictionaries are my consolation. I want your advice
> and assistance. Tell me how to set about it and point out a course of
> reading for ancient history.

And a month later, after some books had arrived:

> I did not read but I *devoured* Xenophon's *Anabasis*, and sat up the
> whole night to do so. You could not have chosen better. It has given
> me the satisfaction I was wanting and the insight I longed for. Pray
> send me more books *de votre façon*. I want history, facts, truth, life,
> and can no longer toil through novels. It is ancient history, the
> history of the country I am living in, that I thirst after. Grote will
> not do yet. You were right. I am still too ignorant and require pre-
> paration. Baron Prokesh and Mr Newton[2] of Mytilene have had
> much influence on me and naturally also the classical ground I live
> on. I have entered upon Aischylos but the German is difficult and
> hard to *auffassen*, so that I must take time and read *bedächtig*.

A few months later, in the spring of 1857, he wrote from his new
post, Washington:

> I am reading all I can on America and I take unusual interest in it,
> and often when I feel puzzled about English names and various

---

[1] Gregorovius, *Roman Journals*, 2 April 1859.

[2] Mr, later Sir, Charles Thomas Newton entered the British Museum in 1840.
In 1852 he became Vice-Consul at Mytilene and in 1852-53 was acting Consul
at Rhodes. He was responsible for the excavation of the Mausoleum at Halicar-
nassus. From 10 June 1859 to 16 January 1861 he was Consul in Rome. He then
became Keeper of Greek and Roman Antiquities in the British Museum. On 27
April 1861 he married Mary, daughter of Joseph Severn, who succeeded him as
Consul in Rome.

references to things I don't know, I wish you were in the next room
that I might go and ask you to explain.

And again:

> I am reading a great deal now. It is the only thing I care for, my
> books and my fireside. My colleagues and society bore me to death
> and I avoid them like the plague. My books are all unpacked and
> form a most excellent library. I refer 100 times a day to the *Conver-
> sations Lexicon*, which is a treasure. In short, the *Ernst des Lebens* is
> breaking out upon me like flowers in May and the burden is often
> heavy, pleasant as it may appear. The *education of my own mind* is
> the thought uppermost in my daily existence and all I ask for is *Time*
> to carry it out.

Odo Russell's education was a matter of interest not only to himself
and to his mother, but to his brother, Arthur. In acknowledging a
letter from Odo on 23 April 1859, Arthur wrote:

> You say 'I hope we *will* preserve the strictest neutrality', instead of
> '*shall*'. I do hope you are more careful of these things in your
> despatches, which will ere long be before the world in the Blue
> Books.

And two months later:

> Three extracts of your despatches have been published and Baba (i.e
> the eldest brother, Hastings) and I have severely scrutinized them.
> They are in a strange un-English style, but with no faults of gram-
> mar. Here and there I should omit and alter a word. As your business
> is to write, you should study to do it well and the only way is to read
> often, daily, some of the great writers of English prose. Pray do so!

And again:

> Instead of the *Times*, you should study Gibbon, Macaulay, Addison,
> Johnson, Southey, for their style. By frequent perusal you uncon-
> sciously imbue their locutions.

The advice was heeded. On 10 February 1860 Odo Russell wrote to
his mother from Rome:

> Macaulay's Essay on Macchiavelli has given me rare delight. Do you

know it well? One can read it several times with satisfaction. I read a little Macaulay every night before going to sleep, to improve my English, and like him more and more. Tell Atty (i.e. Arthur).

Arthur was an educational force in Odo's life that made itself felt not only by correspondence. For he would visit his brother, even in his most distant posts, and stay with him for many weeks. Readers of the manuscript of Odo Russell's despatches from Rome will know when Arthur has come to stay, for the bold, clear hand of the younger brother is replaced by that of the elder, equally bold and clear, who helped in writing out the fair copies, as, no doubt, he had helped in the composition of the despatches. Arthur's visits were always an inspiration to Odo.

'Rome absorbs him altogether,' Odo wrote to his mother, 'and he is very learned already in Ancient and Mediaeval Rome, which is useful and pleasant to me as I learn much from him. . . . He leaves me tomorrow. I have enjoyed his civilizing conversation, which springs from his aesthetic mind, more than words can tell, and I shall feel his absence dreadfully.'

If an impression of pedantry is emerging, it is certainly unjustified in respect of Odo. 'Odo,' wrote Mrs Sarah Austin, when he was twenty-five, 'is very different from Arthur, but charming—a poet—full of *esprit*, and entirely without fatuity or pride.'[1] There is universal testimony to his charm and gaiety. Two at least of the surviving photographs of him from his Roman days show him taking part in amateur theatricals. In the English colony, Mrs Lockwood is mentioned in his letters as an organizer of such entertainments. Also, 'the Roman Princesses are talking much about getting up some plays, but they make two conditions, one and all (including the *Neri* such as Princess Chigi Campagnano), 1st. They will not act *with* any of the Frenchmen, 2nd. They will not act *without* me—*sine qua non*.'

Odo Russell, says de Cesare,[2] was much appreciated on account of his wit, but more so for presenting the Roman ladies with the latest thing in hats sent out by his orders from London.

He had a good tenor voice, which he took the trouble to train. In

[1] Janet Ross, *Three Generations of Englishwomen* (1888), Vol. II, p. 11.
[2] R. de Cesare, *The Last Days of Papal Rome* (1909), p. 82. This book is a translation, and abbreviation, of de Cesare's two volumes, *Roma e lo Stato del Papa dal ritorno di Pio IX al XX settembre*.

Vienna his master was Salvi, who, he wrote to his mother on 17
December 1851,

> is very severe about not singing anything but scales as you wish. He
> answers altogether quite to your description of your old singing-
> masters. *None* of his scholars have ever known him to allow that they
> sang anything at all well, and his continual satire and ridicule and
> imitating your faults by singing thro' the nose and pretending to
> have a hot potato in his mouth, make him very unpleasant and
> provoking to anyone who has any sort of vanity about his singing.
> This is luckily not the case with me, and I feel that he is teaching me
> that I have unknown powers and faculties in my voice.

His interest in music was in no way confined to his own vocal performance. 'My greatest enjoyment,' he wrote from Carlsbad in 1856,
'and it is indeed a very great one to me, is classical music – Mozart,
Beethoven, Onslow,[1] Schubert, etc. We have organised a *Streich
quartett*, with Labitzky, Ortel, Lang etc., and I now fully appreciate
and understand the beauties of classical music.'

In Rome, where his singing master was Alari, his voice was in much
demand. 'Goyon[2] and his wife *m'aiment beaucoup*,' he wrote on 13
March 1860. 'He is constantly showing me small attentions and yesterday she renewed her attack upon me about coming to warble a duet
with her at her house.' A week later he reported that 'she sang rather
false at times but seemed delighted at *our* performance'. By 1867, however, he wrote, 'I never sing *dans le monde* now, for it bores me. People
tormented me too much about it and I have been obliged to become
uncivil – nevertheless they never cease to ask.'

There were occasions when he could not, had he wished it, refuse to
sing. In November 1863, while on leave, he stayed with the Prince of
Wales at Sandringham. 'Last night I was asked to sing and the Princess
of Wales accompanied me, reading the accompaniments at first sight.
She then played Danish melodies and then the Prince and I sang Santa
Lucia etc.' On another occasion, staying with Lord Clarendon at the
Grove, Watford,

> I was asked to sing and the Queen[3] who was playing at whist in
> another room, got up and rushed to the piano, and payed me won-

[1] Georges Onslow (1784-1852), composer, of Clermont-Ferrand.
[2] The commander of the French garrison in Rome.
[3] Of Holland.

derful compliments, and as everybody rose in confusion it was a real *coup de théâtre*. Lyons said that only Orpheus had been known to attract others by his music to follow him but even he had not moved Queens to leave their whist, etc., etc.

Odo Russell was popular with children, a characteristic that on one occasion caused a certain strain between himself and his chief in Washington.[1]

Some days ago, Lady Napier's drawing rooms being full of ladies and visitors, the children were sent for to be admired by the crowd. The four boys were kissed and slobbered by the ladies and then, with a view to enchant the already delighted parents, they were asked: 'Well, my sweet dears, who do you love best in the world, Papa or Mamma?' Breathless silence! The parents were already enjoying in anticipation the happiness of hearing the love of their children publicly proclaimed. Everyone was preparing to sympathise and declare the children to be little angels descended from heaven, when – oh horror! – the four little boys answered in chorus, 'we love Mr Russell best in the world, then Mamma and then Papa!' This incident has been repeated all over the district of Columbia and grieves poor My Lady, who looks at me with jealous eyes.

Odo Russell, like his brothers, was much interested in animals, both from a companionable and a scientific point of view. He might well have a snake in his pocket while he was talking to you. 'Pray do me the favour when you come here,' he would write to his mother, 'to bring me a small family of white rats.'

My little white doves are recovering the shaking of the journey and are eating and drinking with great appetite.

Tell Mitchel that I sent a case of Reptilia to him containing: 2 *Calopeltis Leopardina*, 3 *Hierophis Viridiflavus*, 1 *Jamenis Aesculapii*, 3 *Trop. Natrix, varietas Mumorum* and 4 *Lacerta chloronotus*. The *Leopardinas* are beautiful and the '*Eschklapp*'[2] a fine specimen. I am very rich just now in living Reptilia, that give me much pleasure.

---

[1] Lord Napier.
[2] Presumably 'Äskulap', the German name for the Aesculapian snake.

Would you do me the favour to get me a few fancy eggs — bantams, ducks, geese, cassowary — from Buckland or the Zoological or any London dealer, and ask Buckland how they should be packed not to kill the germ or principle of life and then send me a few in a box by Messenger any other Monday. My object is to ascertain whether eggs can be travelled without killing life, so that even if you can only send half a dozen, I should be grateful. Uncle John's Japanese fowls I like for instance.

One of my wild plans is to do for the Lakes of Albano and Nemi, what Hudson has done for Maggiore and Como, namely to introduce the trout, salmon and other useful fish.

Miss Diana Russell, a niece of Odo Russell, tells me that 'one year a natural history shop in Berlin was selling off and Uncle Odo just couldn't resist buying, and box after boxful of animals arrived at the Ridgeway' (the house of Arthur Russell in Surrey). 'Out of one, when opened, ran six little crocodiles, all over the lawn.'

In stature Odo Russell was short and inclined to stoutness. He had no beard when he arrived in Rome but speaks in a letter of 22 September 1859 of having recently grown one. It seems to have remained with him continuously for the rest of his life. In the view of Walburga, Lady Paget, he was 'the image of a German professor'.[1]

His health was robust, though his liver caused him trouble. At the early age of twenty-seven, he took a cure at Carlsbad, a place to which he was already much attached. And the following summer he wrote from Niagara, which he was visiting with Arthur,

I have an idea that if I could take one more cure at Carlsbad such as the one in November last, I would do my liver *everlasting* good. I am forced to think a good deal about my liver here because so many people suffer from it and it pains me oftener than in other places.

His arrival in Rome seems to have had a beneficial effect upon his health, in spite of the time he had to spend at his desk, being not provided by the Foreign Office with any clerical assistance whatever. Indeed, apart from Arthur's occasional help, the burden of the great deal of writing he had to do was not alleviated until his marriage with Lord Clarendon's daughter. 'I hope you approve of my new secretary,' he

[1] Walburga, Lady Paget: *The Linings of Life*, Vol. I, p. 125.

then wrote to her father at the Foreign Office. On 6 November 1860, he wrote to his mother:

> I am making the most of my present post – and I can put my hand on my breast and say in conscience that I lose no time, perhaps even I ought to allow myself more exercise. But as I feel quite happy without it, I hope it is not so necessary for my constitution as was thought. I have *taught* myself to eat very little. I have entirely given up wine and beer. Water and coffee and tea are my only drinks and by this frugal existence I am gradually enabled to sleep less and work more. The whole tendency of my existence is to find the means of satisfying a glowing ambition which is now at the bottom of all my thoughts, hopes and longings. I have all this time derived great comfort and benefit from Pantaleoni.[1] He comes *every day* without exception to me to read the papers, and he has made at the same time a careful study of my health and doctors me and watches me, and certainly *unberufen* he has freed me from my old palpitations and congestions and has enabled me to work more than I ever could before.

And again on 19 November:

> Pantaloon every day calls on me like clockwork to read the papers and look after me. I think it a comfort and a luxury to have a medical friend whom one sees every day. The more I see of Pantaloon the better I like him. He is wonderfully well informed and intelligent.

Nobody can ever have been better adapted than Odo Russell to a diplomatic career, both by temperament and by family background. The son of a diplomat, he found himself for many years addressing his despatches to his uncle and then to his father-in-law at the Foreign Office. Urbane and good-humoured, he moved easily in the most various company, from Cardinals[2] to anti-clerical liberals,[3] from

[1] Dr Pantaleoni, who was to play a certain part on the diplomatic stage, as appears in the despatches.
[2] Cardinal Pentini, for example, with whom O.R. was very friendly (de Cesare, p. 320). During the Vatican Council O.R. was constantly in the company of Manning.
[3] Gregorovius, for instance, whose attitude to the Roman scene was in many ways similar to that of O.R., or those middle class liberals mentioned in the despatch of 21 March 1860, who came to say goodbye to O.R. on their way to exile.

princes[1] to professors.[2] He was well aware how limited were the horizons of most diplomats. 'As I advance in years and in experience in my profession,' he wrote to his mother in 1860, 'I am much struck by the general and distressing imbecillity of the diplomatists.' For Odo Russell the 'lower orders' did not exist simply by hearsay.

> You did me an *immense service*, he told his mother, when you so wisely allowed me in my young days to associate frankly with the Carlsbad tradespeople, for it has given me a practical insight into the *honest* portion of the working classes, which are totally unknown to the class I live in and belong to, and who only judge of them by some w----s and sharpers they have been deceived by. Hundreds of times I have been able to apply the experience sucked in at Carlsbad to the wants and requirements of the working classes of other countries and in the end my impressions have proved more correct than those of my fellow dips. Therefore don't mind if stupid asses reproach you with the liberty you gave your little boys, for it has left fresh, wholesome and true impressions which will serve me as a man through life.

Born into a Whig family, Odo Russell lived in a generation in which the old appellation was being replaced, not quite automatically, by the new word, Liberal. Odo Russell, like his uncle John, was undoubtedly one of those who advanced with the times. He believed in democratic institutions, the spread of education, and the benefits that scientific discoveries can bestow. He was not troubled by a conflict of religion and science. How could truth and the enlargement of knowledge be in conflict? When Lady William in the early sixties became a Catholic, her

---

[1] 'The Roman Princes,' he wrote in Nov. 1859, 'are wondrous civil. I see a great deal of Borgheses, Piombinos, Salviatis, Soras, Fianos, Santa Croces, etc.' Then there was the Princess Rospigliosi *alias* 'Roast-pigliosi'. 'She has now,' wrote O.R. in 1863, 'managed to quarrel with most of the respectable Roman families, and is obliged to invite foreigners, English and American, to fill her drawing room. I will mention the following *habitués* of her palazzo, the Storys, the Monks, the Peters (Virginian girls), the St Albans, the Adeanes, the Buxtons, the Caldwells etc. Now for the friends who have quarrelled with her, Duca and Duchessa Grazioli, Malatestas, Sermonetas, Fianos, Calabrinis, Troiles, Del Dragos, Piancianis, Origos etc. All of us who have broken with her go by the name of the *Confederati*.' O.R.'s conquest of the *beau monde* could not be more decisively expressed than in the sentence, 'the Colonnas crush me with civilities'.

[2] Such as Friedmann, Gervinus or Bergenroth.

sons did not follow her. Indeed, they seem to have paid little attention to the matter. Nor does she appear to have tried to convert them. Mrs Story, wife of the American sculptor, said of her religion:[1]

> She had more than once spoken to me of her having lately embraced the Catholic faith [1862]. Her earliest religious impressions had come to her at Vienna, where her father was English Ambassador.[2] She was left almost entirely to the guidance of a French governess, who, as a strong Catholic, carried her at the most impressionable age to the ceremonies of that Church, which produced a deep effect on her young mind. The impression then received revived in after years and sustained and controlled her under the stress of sorrow and illness. She was at the same time never narrow or violent in her faith, and when once Mrs H., in her presence, began to use arguments to convert *me*, Lady William reproved her and said 'Don't meddle with her beliefs; they are what she needs, probably better than any you can supply.' Again, at a time when she was really ill, and I was with her and a Monsignore was announced, she wrote on a slip of her queer paper and handed it to me: 'Tell them not to let him come in. I will *not* see him.' No such 'good' Catholic could have been, in short, more easy — which converts so rarely are; and she was buried not in Catholic ground, but at Chenies with her husband's folk.

Mrs Story has left the following impression of Lady William:

> 'As we had a great friend in Lord Odo, he made us acquainted with his mother as soon as she arrived in Rome, and from that moment grew up one of the most intimate and interesting friendships of our life. Lady William was full of all good things, heart and head. I learnt from her much of the philosophy of life, and her lessons are never forgotten. Full of gifts, accomplishment and knowledge, she was yet wholly without pedantry, and was extraordinarily wise about the world without being at all of it. Her ideas and feelings were all noble. After her carriage accident in Rome, by which her leg was broken, I sat by her bedside during long visits, for she could even

[1] *William Wetmore Story*, by Henry James, 1957 (originally published 1903), Vol. 2, p. 194.

[2] This is an error. The Hon John Rawdon was a soldier who had lost a leg at the battle of Brandywine in America. Caught on the continent at the recommencement of war with France in 1803, he spent his winters in Vienna and the summers in the Veneto until his death in 1808.

then talk and carry me back to old and wonderful days. She had been for years, abroad and in England, at Court and at home, the centre of everything that was distinguished and wise and witty. The devotion of her sons, especially of her best-loved Odo, was perfect; Odo ministered to her wants with the tenderness of a woman, watched her and took care of her as if she had been his child. Her own care of the three and of their education had been beyond praise; they had been her sole companions during her widowhood; she had studied with them and for them, taught them Latin and Greek and everything she had learned or *could* learn. She was a linguist of the first order, so that when one listened to her different facilities one scarcely knew which to think the greatest. An old fashioned disciplinarian as to manners and customs, she (while their intimate and best friend) exacted from her boys the utmost consideration and deference; often when they were young, keeping them standing in her presence and sometimes obliging them to haul their hats off even when driving with her. By whatever means employed, she had absolutely gained their confidence and devotion; it was a relationship unlike any I have seen in other sons.'

The English representative who arrived in Rome at the end of 1858, though he was not yet thirty years old, had had nearly ten years' experience of the world of diplomacy. Not the least of his diplomatic achievements had been to succeed, where many had failed, in establishing a happy *modus vivendi* with that difficult man, Lord Stratford de Redcliffe, his chief in Constantinople, familiarly known as the Great Eltschi.[1] Already in 1852 the great Ambassador, passing through Vienna on his way from Constantinople to London, had made an impression on young Odo Russell. 'It is long since I have gazed upon so clever a face,' Russell wrote to his mother.

He had not been many weeks in his post on the Bosphorus before he sent his mother, on 10 January 1855, a character sketch of Lord Stratford:

> The more I see of Lord Stratford, the more I must admire his good qualities. He belongs to that set of old men that exist no longer. He is full of high principles, the effect of a purely classical education and the *umgang* in his youth with great men. All his actions are effects of

[1] The Turkish word for Ambassador.

his principles and of a strong attachment to his native land. In small things he is passionate; he gets into a rage about nothing. He is full of misplaced suspicion. He boils over like a kettle, but quiets down very quickly and then he is ashamed of his fury and sorry for it. He expects *entire* submission. He is full of *great virtues*. His affections and hatreds are strong. He is warm hearted and *exceedingly generous about money*. His mind is polished like one of Mr Günther's boxes. His conversation is most fascinating and improving, but not as brilliant and varied as yours. German and French literature and modern writing in general are unknown to him. Altogether he is one of those superior natures made to command and not always understood by the rabble, from being high principled, conscientious, warm hearted and clear headed. He has behaved very handsomely to me. He sent for me on New Year's Day and said, 'I have given you time to look about you. Now listen and answer me sincerely and frankly.' He then told me all he had suffered from his subordinates for many years past. He told me that he had long wished to have to deal with a gentleman, that my appointment had given him pleasure, that I had been praised to him by Lord Clarendon, Lord Westmorland and Lord Cowley, and others, that he wished to give me much work and to employ me in confidential and delicate matters, but that his temper was bad, that he got into a passion and could not help it, and he wished me to consider whether I had sufficient patience to bear with him, if so he would always keep me by him for secret work and feel thankful if I would show great patience and always *perfect frankness* and sincerity.

Odo Russell showed himself equal to the demands made upon him. Eight months later he wrote:

I was firmly resolved, on coming out here, to do all in my power and to leave no means untried to be as useful to Lord Stratford as I had tried to be to my former chiefs. I had little hope of succeeding, for old men like Hammond, Mellish, Lord Cowley, General Rose, etc., had found it impossible, and had all told me so. I beat about for a long time in the dark, but my resolution was always before me and I worked hard to understand him and to serve him. Little did I expect that my success was to be even greater than what I had bargained for. In one of my last letters I told you that Count Pisani, after 30 years' service had been made to resign his direction of the Chancellerie and that I was placed over his head. It was an unpleasant crisis, but I fancy I have conciliated the Count.

I know the Eltschi's character and we get on admirably. He tells me everything he is about to do. His most secret thoughts are known to me. The worst of it is that I am now a *necessity* to Lord Stratford and that I have not an hour to myself.

By last messenger, he signed *eleven* despatches I had composed without changing one word in the drafts.

After recording Odo Russell's success in the Embassy at Constantinople, let us here insert two tributes to his Roman despatches from even more important personages than the Eltschi. On 14 March 1859 Arthur Russell wrote to his brother:

I met Disraeli walking to the House who instantly took my arm. He has done this before and it makes me very shy for when we get to the House members stare awfully. But what I wanted to say is this: he told me he often had occasion to see your despatches and approved highly of them and of all you had done at Rome.

And on 24 April 1869 Odo wrote to Arthur:

I cannot tell you how pleased and gratified I am at a letter from Gladstone to Lord Clarendon, analysing my despatches just after reading them under the impulse of the moment. It begins thus: 'My dear C. Whenever there is an Odo in the box, satisfaction instantly predominates. I think Odo has the true idea of the Roman Court etc.' To have caught the eye of the great man is very satisfactory. To know that my despatches in the F.O. red box attract his attention is immensely encouraging.

Odo Russell was not appointed to Rome as an officially accredited agent to the Vatican. Protestant England would not have permitted such an appointment. When he first went there he was regarded as detached from the mission to Tuscany, and his despatches, like those of Lyons before him, were directed to the English minister in Florence. When that mission came to an end on 24 March 1860, he was attached to the mission in Naples and, after the termination some months later of that also, he reported directly to the Foreign Office. Though technically a mere spectator of the diplomatic scene, he was for all practical purposes (except in certain matters of diplomatic ceremonial) the English representative at the Vatican. He was received by the Pope and had constant access to Antonelli, the Cardinal Secretary of State. Though he had a poor opinion of the intelligence of the one and of the honesty of the other, he was on the best of terms with both His Holiness and His Eminence. The genial smile, the warm handshake, the '*caro mio Russell*', with which these amiable personages received him, at once threw a bridge across the great gulf that separated them, the gulf, as it seemed to him, between the nineteenth and the thirteenth century.

He quickly fell in love with his work in Rome. His correspondence is that of a happy man, leading the fullest of lives. 'I hope and pray,' he wrote to his uncle on 11 March 1863, 'you will be able to put off the evil hour of appointing me Secretary of Embassy.'

> I don't care, he went on, being thrown back a few years in my profession. I don't ask for money or for rank, but I do beg and pray not to be taken from a mission full of historical interest and useful labour during a period when the Roman question is uppermost in men's minds, and for the loss of which no secretaryship of Embassy, small mission or thousands of pounds could compensate me. I am in nobody's way, since I interfere with nobody's promotion in the profession, and I ask for nothing but what I already have. So pray, my dear uncle, leave me here as long as you possibly can.

When, in fact, a year later, he was offered a secretaryship at Constantinople, he declined it.

His first impressions of Rome, however, had been unfavourable. Arriving on 20 December 1858, he had at length found a room at the *Hotel de Londres*, where the Granvilles also were staying. The streets of Rome struck him that first day as 'small, dark, dirty and dull'. With his friend Cartwright, he then set about looking for an apartment for himself and his mother, who was coming to live with him till the following spring. Rooms were found at No. 13 via Mario de'Fiori, 'clean and very airy, a rare thing to obtain at present in Rome', and from there he wrote a week later to his mother:

> You do not lose anything by staying a little longer in Paris, for this is a stinking hole. I observe that everybody is so *exceedingly* fond of Rome that I suppose I must *end* by feeling like them. At present I am still at a loss to make out what it is that fascinates people to such an extraordinary extent in a stinking, dirty, comfortless place,

inhabited by a race of chimpanzees cheating a legion of English from morning till night.

After the first few days we hear no more of such talk.

In September 1859 he moved to the Casa Zucchari, 64 via Sistina. 'The house is situated close to the Trinita di Monte and the Pincio is close at hand – my windows look all over Rome – and it is out of the way of Roman stinks. Queen Christina of Sweden lived in it, Claude Lorraine painted in my rooms, and Zucchari the painter once owned it. Nicholas Poussin lived next door. In short it is a historical house.' It is not clear how long he lodged in this house. In a letter to his uncle of 7 July 1860, he speaks of a summer apartment in the palazzo Doria, near piazza Venezia. Certainly, on returning to Rome from his leave in December 1863, he took 'a very nice little apartment' at 52 via Frattina. In the autumn of 1864 he moved into the Palazzo Chigi where he remained till the end of his residence in Rome.

His servant, called in the letters 'Cocky Nazzareno' or 'The Nazarene', was evidently a character. He claimed to have been a secret agent of the Emperor Napoleon III before the latter became Emperor and gave curious accounts of him as a young man in Rome. Cocky belonged to the National or Cavour party but did not believe in United Italy. He thought, in 1859, that Murat would replace the King of the Sicilies. 'Cocky, you see, is a political character and I conclude a spy of the Roman Police – but that they all are, so *que faire?* He serves me well and keeps my clothes clean, so I had better keep him on.'

'Cocky must be on the best terms with the brigands for he has begged and entreated of me to offer no resistance if I am attacked but to give up my money, and he promises he will get it all back through the police next day. But he says if I resist they will run a long knife into me and then run away.' One asks whether Cocky perhaps was one of those undisclosed sources of information that enabled Odo Russell to write so circumstantially in his despatches about brigandage.

An anecdote about another servant must not be omitted. It is told by Arthur Russell:

Odo was walking down the Corso in Rome and met a procession of Capuchin friars. Suddenly one of them left the ranks, betraying symptoms of deep emotion, and endeavoured to grasp and kiss my brother's hand, who struggled to resist until the Capuchin succeeded in pressing reverently the end of his coat tail to his lips. '*Monsieur*

ne se souvient plus de moi?' asked the friar. 'I am Deodati, the Eltchi's
servant, and have often had the honour of serving Your Excellency
at Pera and Therapia.' He then went on to relate that after Lord
Stratford left the Embassy, he had returned to Naples, his native
place and found that none of his family or of his old friends survived,
and he then decided, as he felt too old to seek service again, to enter
the church *'pour me mortifiquer avant ma mort'*, as he expressed it.
He then plunged his hand into his cowl, behind his head, and produced the certificate the Ambassador had given him. Since then,
whenever he met the Capuchin, Odo used to shake hands and converse with him, and decline to satisfy the curiosity of his colleagues,
who were perplexed by this unusual familiarity. *'C'est probablement
un de vos espions,'* said the Secretary of the French Embassy, a little
irritated by their mysterious relations.

The French secretary, in whose memoirs Russell is often mentioned,
has left the following sketch of him:[1]

Odo Russell, élevé en France, comme le baron de Meyendorff, a
autant d'esprit, mais beaucoup plus de tenue que ce dernier. Fort
bien vu de tous dans la société romaine, homme du monde, aimable et
séduisant, il ne néglige aucune coterie. Accueilli avec distinction chez
les princes et les amis les plus dévoués du Saint-Siège, il est égale-
ment lié avec les membres du parti d'action, du comité italien de
Rome, dont il écoute très complaisamment les confidences et auquel
il sert, disait-on, d'intermédiaire. Le cardinal et le Pape n'ignorent
pas le singulier rôle que joue Odo Russell auprès de leurs ennemis,
mais le pauvre gouvernement pontifical s'il se debarrassait d'Odo
Russell tomberait sur un adversaire plus dangéreux et sur un agent
plus actif et plus perfide encore. Vivant à Rome comme un simple
touriste, en voyageur épris de ce séjour, Russell n'a aucun caractère
diplomatique reconnu; il voit néanmoins souvent le Saint-Père, mais
surtout le cardinal Antonelli.

Another diplomatic colleague, Schlözer, secretary of the Prussian
legation at Rome, spoke with admiration of Odo Russell, *dieser kluge
Engländer*, who contrived to be in touch with the Piedmontese authorities and with the secret societies in Rome, while at the same time a

---

[1] H. A. d'Ideville: *Journal d'un diplomate en Italie*, 1862-1866 (Paris, 1873),
p. 42.

welcome visitor to ex-King Francis II and to the Holy Father, with
the latter of whom he was on terms of positive affection (*zärtlichkeit*).
In a letter of 3 February 1868 Schlözer observes that Odo Russell and
Liszt formed the basis of his own life in Rome.[1]

De Cesare confirms the descriptions of Russell's charm and origin-
ality. He was, he says, a person of extraordinary geniality. With the
great white top-hat that he wore on his enormous head in summer,
with his jovial face and his flowing beard and his gold spectacles, he
was a most striking figure. He spoke Italian well, though with a marked
English accent, and liked to attempt the Neapolitan and Roman dia-
lects, with the most amusing results. He was mad about music, had a
passion for snakes, loved Rome and was a most original character.[2]

A domestic event of the first importance in Odo Russell's life took
place at the beginning of 1868. In December 1867 Lord and Lady
Clarendon arrived in Rome with their daughter Lady Emily Villiers.
On 30 January following, His Lordship wrote to Hammond, Permanent Under Secretary of the Foreign Office:[3]

> We do not wish the subject mentioned for another day or two, but
> writing to an old friend like yourself I can't make a secret of Odo
> having just proposed to and been accepted by Emily. It is an attach-
> ment of some standing on his part. In a worldly point of view it is
> of course not a good marriage, as it will be poverty and expatriation,
> but I think she will be *quite happy* with him and that is all her mother
> and I care about as we are neither greedy nor ambitious for our

[1] K. von Schlözer: *Römische Briefe*, 1864-1869 (1913).

[2] R. de Cesare: *Roma e lo Stato del Papa dal ritorno di Pio IX al xx settembre*,
Vol. 2, p. 35.

Il Russell era uomo di straordinario genialità. Vestiva in qualunque stagione
abiti larghi; in estate piantava sull'enorme testa un cappellone bianco a cilindro,
e con la sua faccia gioviale, la fluente barba e gli occhiali d'oro, era veramente
una figura caratteristica e distinta. Parlava bene l'Italiano, quantunque con accento
marcamente inglese, e pretendeva di parlare il napoletano e il romanesco, nei cui
dialetti riusciva esilarantissimo. Amava le compagnie allegre e le recitazioni
filodrammatiche; era pazzo per la musica, cantava da tenore, e sostenne la parte
di Gennaro della L. Borgia nel teatrino del maestro Alari in via delle Cappelle.
Aveva la passione dei serpi, e prima di prender moglie ne allevava parecchi in
casa sua. Abitava palazzo Chigi, e villeggiava a l'Ariccia, o a Frascati. Era un
entusiasta di Roma, e un originale di gran talento e amico del cardinale Pentini,
del duca di Sermoneta, dei Castellani, dell'abate Pappalettere, e dei principali
membri del Comitato Nazionale.

[3] Hammond Papers, P.R.O., F.O. 391/4.

children. He is clever and as likely as any one else in his stagnant profession to advance, and he is one of the most thoroughly amiable men I ever knew. Such a son as he is must make a good husband.

And again, on 13 February:

The more I see of Odo, the more I think him abounding in all the qualities calculated to make a woman happy and Lady C. and I are almost as delighted as Emily herself with her choice.

Thus Odo Russell, at the age of thirty-nine, obtained a wife – and a secretary.

Hard worked though he was, Odo Russell was not, of course, the only English representative in Rome. There were also the Consuls. The occupant of the post of Consular Agent at Rome when Russell arrived there was John Freeborn. They did not, however, have many months to work together as Freeborn died in the spring of 1859. On 22 May of that year Cardinal Antonelli told Russell that it had been a matter of great regret to the Papal Government that the late Mr Freeborn had identified himself so strongly with the revolutionary party in 1848, a circumstance which had done injury to all personal relations between the Consul and the Papal authorities. 'Tell Lord Malmesbury,' he said, 'that we shall be happy to receive anyone His Lordship desires to appoint as successor to Mr Freeborn, and we do not care whether he is a Protestant or a Roman Catholick, but we do attach great importance to one thing, namely, that he should prove to be an *honest man*.'

The person at length appointed was the scholar Charles Newton, already mentioned as having been known to Odo Russell in Constantinople. He was named, with Papal approval, full Consul. 'I am delighted he has come,' Russell wrote to his mother at the New Year, 1860, 'and expect much pleasure from his society.' By 24 February, however, he was writing:

I cannot get Newton the new Consul to act for himself. He persists in throwing everything on me, saying that he is yet new to the place and still in want of advice. This is very irksome and I have told him so today. He must learn to be *selbständig*. I have given two months of *daily* advice, and what would he have done had I not been here? I have already given him an exceptional position in society. He is received almost everywhere and he must gradually learn to do for

himself. I cannot and will not continue to do the dirty work of the
Consulate to afford him the literary leisure he says he must have.
I want some leisure myself for reading and every man must attend
to his department.

And three weeks later:

I like Newton very much, but he is an odd man, he cannot live without constant admiration and incense, and in politics reminds me
much of Lord Napier. He is very touchy and always fancies men
are not sufficiently civil to him, and is convinced that all the women
are in love with him and wanting to marry him. I have made him
understand that I won't do the Consular work, but on the other
hand he wishes much to take the political work out of my hands, as
he is ambitious and wishes naturally to get into diplomacy and bid
adieu to Consulates. I told him to do as he pleased, as his political
despatches in no way interfered with mine, but to his astonishment
he finds that neither the Dips nor the Cardinals and Monsignores
will talk politics to him, so he now fancies I have put them up to
not doing so. He will gradually settle down to his own department
and his archaeological studies and I have no doubt he will be very
happy and contented in Rome. He is full of pleasant, interesting and
useful qualities and I am glad to have him here and enjoy his society.
I have learned much and hope to learn much more from him.

Newton's despatches were indeed ambitious. His descriptions of a
demonstration in the Corso or of the aberrations of the Irish Brigade
were as long and vivid as Odo Russell's own; and on one occasion at
least the French Ambassador talked politics freely with him. 'The
Italians,' Gramont told him *inter alia*, 'have never shown any indication
to fight except among themselves, when they know the foe not to be
formidable.'[1]

But Newton did not settle down to his own department. 'Betwixt
you and me,' Odo Russell told his mother on 6 November 1860, 'the
Consulate is *de facto* under me, for Newton won't take a step without
talking it over for hours with me.' Just a year after his arrival in Rome
Newton left to take up an appointment in the British Museum. He was
replaced in the Consulate on 5 March 1861 by his father-in-law, Joseph
Severn, the artist, famous as the friend and companion, during his last
months, of Keats.

[1] F.O. 43/80B. 16 October 1860.

Though it was a Foreign Office rule that no Consul on his first appointment should be more than fifty years of age, Severn was in his sixty-eighth year. It was true that he did not seem his age and people meeting him in Rome in the sixties sometimes supposed that it was his father who had been Keats' friend.[1] From the point of view of Odo Russell the new Consul was no better than his predecessor.

> Our Consul, Mr Severn, wrote Russell a few weeks after the appointment, is a good natured goose, utterly unfit and unqualified for his post. I have now saved him out of four very serious scrapes which would have cost him his post. But sooner or later he will get into trouble and will have to be removed, for he is too old and too silly to learn his business. I can't understand how such an appointment could have been risked by the F.O. I pity the poor man for he is so very anxious to do well. If H.M. Government appoint me to the command of a ship of war, they must not be surprized if I run her ashore and go to the bottom. The Consular Service requires training and experience as the Army and Navy do. Poor Mr Severn is *a trouble* instead of *an assistance* to me.

Though Odo Russell's apprehensions of trouble were borne out by events, Severn in fact held his post for eleven years, and, for all his indiscretion, must have accomplished a great deal of good work on behalf of those of his compatriots who needed official help. At the beginning of his third year as Consul, he was appointed, with the consent of Lord Russell and Cardinal Antonelli, Consul acting for the Kingdom of Italy in Rome. So at a time when feelings were strained to the uttermost, he was the only mediator between Rome and Turin. He had a strong sense of his own importance, of the unique position he held in Rome. ''Tis at the same time the most felicitous position,' he wrote on 12 November 1864.[2] 'For while I have all the power of an Ambassador, yet I have no etiquette to keep up and go about my painting in the true artistic style.' To judge from Severn's private letters that have been printed, you would hardly guess that there was anyone in Rome with whom he shared the duties of representing his country.

His copious despatches, signed in a hand that became ever more shaky with rheumatism, give a vivid picture of the problems that forced themselves upon the Consul, or with which he chose to meddle. There

[1] Sheila Birkenhead: *Against Oblivion; the life of Joseph Severn.*
[2] Birkenhead, op. cit.

was the case of Lieutenant Allan Bathurst, a convert and *protégé* of Monsignor Talbot, who, 'became suddenly insane on Monday last and developed a violent reaction of Protestantism and Liberalism. It was evident that he had gone mad from the over excitement of his late conversion and his horror at the insight it had presented as regards the Court and the state of the Roman people.' He was moved from the villa of his cousin, the Dowager Countess of Castle Stuart, to a home in Perugia.

There were murders and robberies in the Corso; there were the complications caused by mixed marriages. There was the case of twenty-two year old Miss Larkworthy, who eloped with the penniless Cavalier Hector Cumbo, a Knight of Malta, from her aunt's villa at Frascati. When, after four days, they were found, Cumbo was imprisoned and Miss Larkworthy put in a convent, where Severn succeeded in having a two hours' interview with her. He found that she had changed her religion in expectation of making a marriage. The matter was referred to Cardinal Antonelli who consented that the aunt should take her niece away unmarried, on the understanding that she did not interefere with Miss Larkworthy's new religion.

Severn's good nature was rewarded by a sharp reprimand from the Foreign Office. 'You should not have interfered in such a case as that of Miss Larkworthy, where the lady is of full age and chooses her religion and her husband of her own free will.' The last word in this case was, however, with Severn. 'Subsequent results,' he wrote, 'have changed the whole aspect of the affair. The young lady in the convent turned round against both her assumed religion and her projected husband. On my pressing the Cardinal Vicar to decide about her conversion, he again examined the young lady's soul and, finding it a "dead waste", at last consented to my restoring her to her family.' (It appears that Miss Larkworthy's change of heart had been the result of her interview with Severn.) 'She left Rome with her family, well content that she had given up the religion and the husband. I trust Your Lordship may consider that I rescued the lady from a cruel destiny of marriage without money and religion without truth.'

Then there was Daniel Douglas Home, who was expelled from Rome for spiritualistic practices and for other reasons; and the Revd David Williamson and the Revd Robert Lewis, two Scottish clergymen, who had been holding Protestant prayer meetings in their rooms; and various Protestant missionaries who had distributed tracts and bibles.

1. Odo Russell at the age of 18. Lithograph by Kriehuber

2. Odo Russell

There was Mr Napier Speir, who won an Anglo-Roman steeple-chase in 1865, wearing a green jacket and red waistcoat and white belt, the prohibited nationalistic colours. 'This occasioned the wildest enthusiasm in the Roman people.' The authorities gave Speir twenty-four hours to leave Rome. 'As the affair had now assumed a very serious political aspect, I submitted the question to Mr Odo Russell, if it would not be best that he should advise with Cardinal Antonelli as to the propriety of suspending this outrageous order. And this Mr Russell did with admirable skill.' The Cardinal reluctantly consented that Mr Speir should leave, at his pleasure, in a week.

There was Miss Agnes Burke, a young English lady of eighteen, who took it into her head to leave her old friend and protectress, Mrs Ramsden, and to go and live alone in the Corso where she received visits from a Roman gentleman. (No single woman was allowed to live alone in Rome.) Severn consulted Odo Russell and they agreed that 'as it was a case of simply morality', they should not try to prevent the authorities acting as they thought fit. Miss Burke was so frightened by the visit of some gendarmes that she returned to Mrs Ramsden.

Then there was the question of the English church. On 15 January 1864 Severn wrote to Lord Russell:

I have the honour to inform Your Lordship of the solution of a difficulty about the English church (now situated outside the walls of Rome). A number of English visitors this year, who cannot find seats in the overfilled church having applied to me to receive them into my house for the performance of divine service, I at once consulted the Governor of Rome, who assured me privately that I could not venture to do it, for the Anglo-Roman converts about the Pope would be sure to persecute me and try to endanger my Consular privileges. Also Mr Odo Russell wished me to refuse. But as I felt that my personal refusal might be somewhat ungracious and even be misconstrued into my favouring the Papal Ministers, I felt it expedient to refer the difficulty to Cardinal Antonelli. His Eminence refused the request but directed me to an easy way of enlarging our present church and all parties are at last satisfied by two morning services. This question at first took rather a serious form inasmuch as the English Protestants were accused of striving to introduce their church altogether into Rome. The affair having been variously reported with much party feeling, I have taken the liberty of stating it fairly to Your Lordship.

Here again Severn's good intentions earned a rebuke:

> Lord Russell cannot but think it was rather imprudent to appeal to the Papal Government for permission to open a second British chapel in Rome, when by the simple expedient of increasing the number of services in the existing chapel, as has now been done, full accommodation could be provided for the wants of the British visitors. At all events, as the chapel is not under the control of H.M. Govt., it would be better for H.M. Consul to abstain from any communication with the Papal Govt., and though Lord Russell is willing to give you credit for having meant well, he thinks that you as H.M. Consul should not interfere in future with the Papal Govt., in a matter in regard to which that Govt. is known to be very susceptible.

Some further straight words from the Foreign Office were directed to Severn at the end of 1866, when Lord Stanley was Foreign Secretary. The departure of the French troops from Rome had been almost completed, and various British subjects had applied to the Consul for protection in the disorders which were expected. Severn wrote for instructions as to his behaviour.

> Mr Severn, runs the F.O. minute, is so impressed with the idea of his own importance that it would be almost dangerous to give him instructions other than to be guided by the advice of Mr Odo Russell, whom he should be desired to consult as to his proceedings. This might be told him in civil but unmistakeable terms.

A submissive answer was at once returned to this communication:

> I beg to assure Your Lordship that I consult Mr Odo Russell on almost every occasion and I consider it a great privilege to be thus permitted to avail myself of his excellent judgement and experience.

Severn was a resilient character, who did not lose heart under domestic sorrows, the death of his loved wife and of his daughter, Mary, Newton's wife. 'Poor Newton!' wrote Arthur Russell, on the latter occasion. 'What will become of him, naturally of a desponding condition of mind as he is? Old Severn, her father, is not a man who can feel much or long.'

By the time Odo Russell left Rome, in the middle of 1870, it was

clear to the departing diplomat that old Severn could not carry on unaided. On 21 September 1870 he wrote a memorandum in the Foreign
Office:[1]

> It would be desirable under present circumstances to appoint an un-
> paid Vice-Consul to Mr Severn's Consulate at Rome. Mr Severn's
> great age and bad health compel him occasionally to go to the baths
> of Tolfa and during his absence the necessity for the presence at
> Rome of a Vice-Consul has been very much felt by British subjects.
> Mr Severn was only appointed in 1861 at the request of the Prince
> Consort and by the advice of Baron Bunsen. If he had been longer
> in the service he might have been pensioned with advantage to the
> public but not to himself, for dismissal from the service would be
> sending him to the workhouse.

After a very few weeks, however, of having Severn as a colleague, Mr
Jervoise, Russell's successor at Rome,[2] wrote, on 27 October 1870, a
powerful protest to the Foreign Office about the Consul's ways. Severn
took on far more than he ought. One of the extravagant things he had
done was to put an announcement in the newspapers that any foreigners
proceeding from Rome to Malta should be furnished with a letter from
him, Severn.

Hammond was for dismissing Severn. Lord Granville, who was now
the Foreign Secretary, asked Odo Russell for his opinion. 'Patiently
listened to,' wrote the letter, 'judiciously advised, kindly treated and
carefully managed, Severn became a willing, useful and even energetic
agent during the ten years we worked together in Rome, and I regret
a decision which must lead the poor old man to the workhouse. I
should have thought a severe reprimand sufficient.'

Odo Russell then was set to write the severe reprimand. Lord Granville's minute thereon for Hammond reads: 'I have ticked Odo's draft
and concur that I have done a wrong but a pleasant thing.' So Severn
was allowed to hold his post for another fifteen months.

Russell's despatches call for little elucidation. They tell their story
simply and clearly; and the main story was indeed a momentous one.
The twelve years of Odo Russell's sojourn in Rome witnessed the
creation of the new Italy and, with it, the collapse of the Pope's

[1] F.O. 43/111.
[2] H.S.C.C. Jervoise had been temporarily attached to O.R. since February
1870.

B

Temporal Power. Had his mission lasted a few weeks longer, it would have fallen to him to report the extinction thereof.

Unwilling, after his experiences in 1848-9, and still more after those of 1859-60, to compromise with the modern world, the Pope depended for the maintenance of his temporal dominion on the armed protection of the French Emperor. The embarrassments of the Eldest Son of the Church in his *rôle* of Protector (*'l'occupation de Roma sera la faute de mon règne'*), his vacillations and the rage they caused at the Vatican, such are the themes of the English envoy. And Russell's opinion, reiterated again and again in the despatches and frankly expressed to the Holy Father himself,[1] was that the Spiritual Power would be far stronger without the Temporal millstone round the neck of the Papacy. Has not history in fact confirmed this opinion?

The tide might indeed be said to have turned, in this sense, before Russell left Rome. For the Oecumenical Council, whose proceedings he reported so ably, was an overwhelming triumph for the Vatican. If Pius IX was worsted by liberalism in temporal matters, he had at least put liberal churchmanship most decisively in its place.

However much of a simpleton the Supreme Pontiff may appear in Russell's despatches – and the expression 'second childhood' is used – the English envoy undoubtedly had a certain respect, as well as affection, for the stubborn, genial, old man. When the French Ambassador, in a published despatch, attributed 'a weak, silly and undignified part' to his Holiness in conversation with Odo Russell, the latter was stung to retort. 'Anyone who knows Pope Pius IX,' he wrote to his uncle on 26 January 1863, 'however much he may differ in opinions, must admit that his character is firm and independent, his heart charitable and benevolent, and his mind clear and logical, and that he means what he says.'

For the Pio Nono who came out of the Vatican Council with such flying colours, Odo Russell had a proper regard. A year before the meeting of the Council he had been quite sure what the result would be. 'Whatever may be said to the contrary on high authority,' he wrote to his father-in-law on 16 December 1868, 'I do not myself believe that any single bishop or any number of conspiring bishops can sustain an individual or independent opinion under the paternal wings of the Vatican if the Pope commands obedience.' Such was his belief and he stuck to it throughout the meetings of the Council. 'Nothing,' wrote

[1] See the account of his audience of 26 July 1862.

Arthur Russell to his mother from Rome on 21 January 1870, 'nothing will shake Odo's confidence in the ultimate success of the Pope. Acton, Cartwright and Sir Rowland Blennerhasset seem quite angry with him about it.'

It was Odo Russell, however, who was proved right. On 30 May 1870 Lord Clarendon wrote to him:

> The moral of the whole tale is that you have been right from the beginning and have steadily maintained against all comers that the Pope would have his own way.

To have prophesied correctly about the issue of the Council did not, however, in itself make Russell, as Purcell describes him,[1] 'an ardent supporter of Papal Infallibility'. Nor does Russell's statement in a letter to Manning[2] that it was his 'conviction that the Definition is necessary to the very existence of the Pope's future authority' in itself mean that he thought the Definition a good thing. Readers of the despatches and private letters that follow will hardly feel that, in an absolute sense, he did. That he thought it unwise for the English government to try to prevent what neither it nor the French government nor any other government was going to be able to prevent, is another matter.

Readers also will be able to form their own opinion of Strachey's picture of 'poor Mr Russell' caught in Manning's 'spider's web of delicate and clinging diplomacy'.[3] The image will perhaps remind them of Gregorovius' sketch of Manning at the time of the Council:[4]

> Sat near Manning at Arnim's last evening and closely observed the fanatic; a little grey man, looking as if encompassed by cobwebs. A certain Count Hahn kissed with mystic reverence the hand which he extended in the manner of an elderly courtesan, accustomed to such acts of homage. Was filled with disgust at a scene of the kind; but it shows the power of the priesthood over the weaklings, who are their tools, and who slink about in society as colporteurs of darkness, men of the twilight, incapable of bearing the full glare of day.

[1] E. S. Purcell: *Life of Cardinal Manning*, Vol. II, p. 433. See also E. C. Butler: *The Vatican Council* (1930), Vol. II, p. 10. 'Russell was not a Catholic, but his mother was, and he was wholly sympathetic with the ideas of the Majority.'
[2] Purcell, Vol. II, p. 440.
[3] Lytton Strachey: *Eminent Victorians: Manning*.
[4] Gregorovius: *Roman Journals*, 6 February 1870.

Odo Russell showed no such distaste for 'the fanatic'. His letters prove
again and again that, while remaining decisively outside the fold, he
took great pains to understand the Catholic point of view and to cultivate English Catholics in Rome.[1] What other diplomat of the time, one
wonders, would have done a course of reading, as Russell did, to
qualify himself to report on the Vatican Council?[2] Such industry, however, he considered a part of his job. The influence of his mother can
perhaps be exaggerated in this connection; his mother, to whom he
wrote, not many months after her conversion, about a certain Cardinal
he had been visiting, 'I have no doubt that like all the rest of them who
compose this Holy Church he is a d----d rascal, but at least he is a civil
one.'

Now Manning was exceedingly civil. Quite apart from the mutual
advantage of the diplomatic exchanges that took place in their walks on
the Pincio, it seems that he and Odo Russell genuinely enjoyed each
other's company. In a letter of congratulation to Manning on becoming
a Cardinal, Russell wrote from Berlin in 1875: 'Without entering into
the questions now raging in Europe, I would venture to remind Your
Eminence of the calm and peaceful manner in which we discussed them
under the pines and cypresses of Villa Ludovisi and along the ancient
walls of dear old Rome. . . . How much I should like to resume those
walks from Via Tritone at 3 p.m.'[3]

Russell had a great respect for the power of the Roman church. He
believed at the same time that this power would be least likely to get
out of hand if it was treated with the most generous toleration. When
later he was in Berlin, he was much shocked by Bismarck's attack on
the church. 'The Roman Church,' he wrote to Lord Derby on 4 March
1874,[4] 'has always derived strength from persecution but is impotent
against the power of freedom and its blessings.' And again, on 1 April

---

[1] e.g. to his mother, 22 February 1863, 'To make myself popular with the
English Catholics, I have accepted a small part in Mrs Plowden's private
theatricals.'

[2] See letter to Manning, printed by Purcell, asking for 'the name of any work,
book, pamphlet, speech, etc., that could be useful to me'. It is a singular fact that
O.R. says nothing in his letters to Clarendon of Manning's application to the
Vatican (mentioned by Purcell) to be released from his oath of secrecy in order
to inform O.R. correctly of the proceedings of the Council.

[3] Manning Papers.

[4] F.O. 64/802 No. 108. Quoted in Winifred Taffs: *Ambassador to Bismarck,
Lord Odo Russell*, 1938, p. 30.

1874,[1] 'The Pope had made his Church ridiculous by the proclamation of the Immaculate Conception, of the Syllabus and of his own Infallibility, but these dogmas were of interest only to the faithful and in no way concerned or stood in the way of those who chose to ignore them. . . . Bismarck's anti-church policy has compelled the German bishops to rally round the Pope and suffer martyrdom for discipline's, obedience's and example's sake, and the church that was ridiculous is becoming interesting to the religious and conservative population of Europe.' When, therefore, Odo Russell declared to Lord Clarendon on 24 January 1870, 'I adhere to my conviction that humanity will gain more in the end by the dogmatic definition of Papal Infallibility than by the contrary'; and on 22 February, 'I cannot help thinking that a clearly defined position between the Papacy and the civilized world will prove more beneficial to humanity in the end than the half measures of the opportunists who wish to preserve the benefit of the doubt'; and when thus his attitude towards the central issue of the Vatican Council coincided with Manning's, it is clear that the reasons of the diplomat were worlds apart from those of the archbishop. Is it so clear which was caught in the other's web? Odo Russell, as Shane Leslie observes, was playing a double game.'[2]

An anecdote relates that the English Catholics in Rome complained to the Pope of his friendship with the Protestant Odo Russell. 'But,' Pio Nono answered, 'he is a very bad Protestant.'

A happy view of Odo Russell in Rome, at the time of the Council, is given by his brother, Arthur, in a letter to their mother:

Odo's position in Rome is really very pleasing. He is quite as great as any accredited Ambassador and has far more reputation. His palace is as fine as theirs, though he has no liveried lacqueys. As he sees many priests and monks of all nations, he knows better than the real Ambassadors what is going on, who can only associate with great people. It is really curious to see that the Austrian and Prussian, though they dislike the humiliation, are always reduced to come to him when they want to write home by their messengers. This is the happiest period of his life, a unique moment in history, and he is young enough to enjoy his position and his success.

[1] F.O. 64/803 No. 149. Quoted ibid., p. 31.
[2] Shane Leslie: *Henry Edward Manning* (1921), p. 222. This book makes use of Odo Russell's despatches.

In conclusion, let us quote his own modest estimate of his achievement at Rome, written, a few days before he departed in July 1870, to the new Foreign Secretary, Lord Granville:[1]

> I think I may fairly say that you will find our unofficial relations with Rome as satisfactory as they can well be and the Pope better disposed on the whole towards Her Majesty's Government than towards any other power in the world. This is perhaps not saying very much, but still it is better than the contrary.

[1] P.R.O. 30/29/84.

ENGLISH MINISTRIES 1858-70

Prime Ministers		*Foreign Secretaries*
1858	Earl of Derby	Earl of Malmesbury
June 1859	Viscount Palmerston	Lord John Russell (Earl Russell, 30 July 1861)
Nov. 1865	Earl Russell	Earl of Clarendon
June 1866	Earl of Derby	Lord Stanley
Feb. 1868	B. Disraeli	Lord Stanley
Dec. 1868	W. E. Gladstone	Earl of Clarendon (d. 27 June 1870).
		Earl Granville

Documents

1. Public Record Office.
   Foreign Office, General Correspondence, Italian States and Rome
   (F.O. 43).
   Foreign Office, Clarendon Papers (F.O. 361).
   Foreign Office, Cowley Papers (F.O. 519).
   Foreign Office, Hammond Papers (F.O. 391).
   Russell Papers (P.R.O. 33/22).
   Granville Papers (P.R.O. 30/29).

2. Bodleian Library, Oxford.
   Clarendon Papers, C. 487 and C. 475.

3. Private Russell family papers, used mainly in the Introduction;
   in which also there is a single quotation from the Manning papers,
   kept at the Presbytery of St Mary of the Angels, Moorhouse
   Road, London, W2, for which I am grateful to Father A. Chapeau.

The documents here printed perhaps do not amount to more than a
quarter of the written matter sent from Rome by O.R. to the Foreign
Office. The selection has been made with a view primarily to the light
that the despatches throw upon Italian history. Many subjects, therefore, on which O.R. wrote at length are hardly or not at all mentioned
in this volume. These include the Roman Catholic movement among
Bulgarians, the ecclesiastical affairs of Malta, Mexico, Poland and
Portugal, Spanish affairs, the relations of the Vatican and Prussia, and
such matters as cattle disease or the condition of English workmen
engaged on the construction of a bridge at Velletri. Moreover, so
drastic has the cutting been in order to squeeze the material into a single
volume, that much has been omitted even with regard to some subjects,
such as brigandage and Fenianism, about which a good deal has been
included.

It will be observed that O.R. was normally absent on leave from
about the end of July till the late autumn, even as late as December. He

was thus at times absent from his post during important Italian events. It did not, for example, fall to him to report the Mentana campaign in the autumn of 1867.

The spelling has been anglicized in the case of certain words — embarcation, encrease, dignatary, enduce, appartment. Many eccentricities and inconsistencies, however, remain, both in spelling and in the use of capital letters. The punctuation has been adapted to the printed page. O.R.'s usual way of ending a sentence was by means of a comma, followed by a dash. For this a full stop has been substituted.

Unpublished material in the Public Record Office in which Crown Copyright is reserved is printed by permission of the Controller of H.M. Stationery Office.

Officially Printed Despatches

The following despatches are printed, in whole or in part:

1. In House of Commons Sessional Papers.

    1859. Nos. 28, 31, 34, 46, 47, 54 and 70 (1860 Vol. XXXII).
    1859. Nos. 88, 105 and 106 (1860 Vol. LXVIII).
    1860. Nos. 12, 47 and 49 (1860 Vol. LXVII).
    1860. Nos. 68, 106, 108, 119, 125, 128, 131, 141, 148, 156, 159, 164 and 170 (1861 Vol. LXVII).
    1862. Nos. 108 and 118 (1863 Vol. LXXV).
    1862. No. 115 } (1863 Vol. LXXIV).
    1863. No. 7

2. In House of Lords Sessional Papers.

    1859. Nos. 88, 105, 106 } (1860 Vol. XX).
    1860. Nos. 12 47, 49
    1860. Nos. 68, 106, 108, 119, 125, 128, 131, 141, 148, 156, 159, 164 and 170 (1861 Vol. XIX).
    1862. Nos. 108, 115 and 118 } (1863 Vol. XXVII).
    1863. No. 7

3. In Foreign Office Confidential Print (P.R.O., F.O. 425).

    1859. Nos. 28, 31 (F.O. 425/51); 40 (52); 46-7, 54, 57-8, 65, 70 (53); 105-7 (55); 120 (57); 127-30, 134, 137-8, 140, 146-8, 150 (58).
    1860. Nos. 1, 3-6 (58); 12 (59); 19, 20, 24, 26, 28, 31-3, 35-7, 39-41, 44-5, 47, 49-52, 54-5, 58-60 (60); 66, 68 (61); 100, 102-11, 114-5, 119, 122, 124-9, 131-4, 137-42, 145-50, 152, 156-60 (62); 161, 163-4, 168-72, 174, 176-81, 185 (63); 186-90, 192-5, 197-200 (64).
    1861. Nos. 1-4, 6, 7, 9-14, 17-23, 25-8, 31-3, 35, 37, 39, 40, 44-5, 47, 49, 56-9, 66-8, 70-2, 74-5 (64).
    1867. Nos. 62-3, telegram of 19 November, 64-6, 68-74, 76, 78, 80-2, 84, 86 (87).

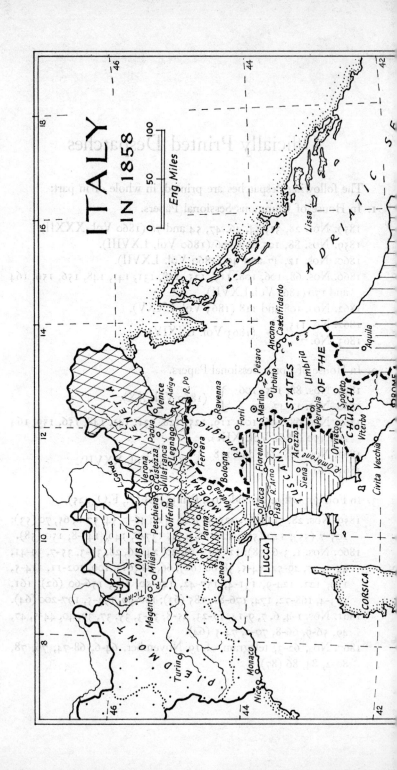

ITALY
IN 1858

Eng. Miles
0   50   100

ADRIATIC SEA

Lissa

VENETIA

VENICE
R. Adige
Verona
Padua
Custozza
Villafranca
Legnago
R. Po
Ravenna
Forli
S. Marino
Romagna
Rimini

LOMBARDY

Magenta
Milan
Peschiera
Solferino
Ticino
L. Garda

Turino

PIEDMONT

Nice

Monaco

CORSICA

Genoa

PARMA

MODENA

Bologna
Modena
R. Reno

Ferrara

Lucca
Pisa
R. Arno
Florence
R. Ombrone

TUSCANY

Arezzo
Siena

LUCCA

Pesaro
Ancona
Urbino
Castelfidardo

Perugia
Umbria

STATES

OF THE

CHURCH

Orvieto
Viterbo
Spoleto

Civita Vecchia

ROME

Aquila

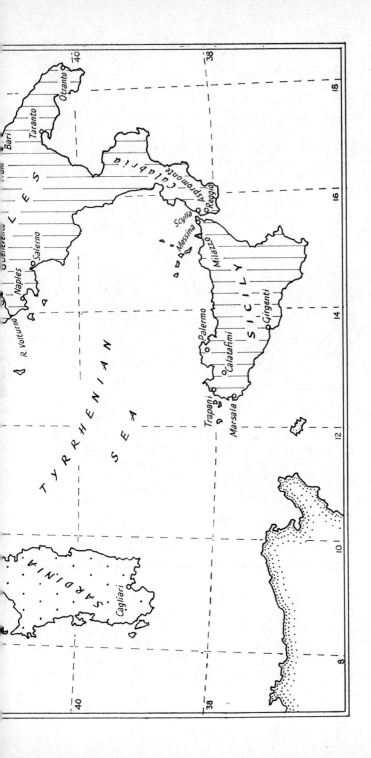

The Despatches

1 [F.O. 43/68]   *Rome, 23 Dec. 1858*

No. 2

O.R. to Edwin Corbett [Chargé d'Affaires of the English Mission at Florence]

Cardinal Antonelli, to whom I had previously sent a letter of introduction from Lord Lyons,[1] received me yesterday afternoon at the Vatican. His Eminence showed me the utmost kindness and cordiality of manner. He had communicated Lord Lyons' letter to the Pope and His Holiness had expressed a wish to see me as soon as the present festivals were over. No one, the Cardinal said, could regret the departure of Lord Lyons, for whom he entertained the highest regard and friendship, more than he did, that in compliance with the wishes expressed in His Lordship's letter it would give him sincere pleasure to continue with me those cordial and confidential relations which had existed between him and Lord Lyons, and that although only two days in the week were appointed for receiving the Diplomatic Body at the Vatican, he begged I would come at any time that suited me best as he would always be glad to see me.

I thanked Cardinal Antonelli in the warmest terms for all he had said and for the cordiality of his manner and after some further conversation I rose to take my leave, but His Eminence with great courtesy insisted on accompanying me to the entrance hall of his apartments.

2 [F.O. 43/70]   *Rome, 14 Jan. 1859*

No. 1. Most Confidential
O.R. to E.C.

I had the honour of being received by the Pope at a private audience this morning at the Vatican. No one else was present. His Holiness, whose manner towards me was most kind and benevolent, said:

'You are appointed to succeed a very good man for whom I felt great affection and I regret that he has left Rome. You may be as good as he was and we shall become friends, but I do not know you yet and Mr Lyons I had known for many years. He is going to America I hear and he will find the Americans far more difficult to deal with than us.

'I am much gratified to hear that the Prince of Wales is likely to visit Rome, and Her Majesty, I feel sure, has done well to allow him to

[1] O.R.'s predecessor at Rome.

prosecute his studies here. It will be an honour to me to receive him at the Vatican and I beg that you will confer with Cardinal Antonelli as to the best means of making the Prince's visit here useful and pleasant. We are anxious that all his wishes should be attended to that he may preserve a pleasant recollection of Rome in the future. Alas, so many erroneous impressions exist about this country that I hope you will not judge of us too rashly. We are advised to make reforms and it is not understood that those very reforms which would consist in giving this country a government of laymen would make it cease to exist. It is called "States of the Church" (*Etâts de l'Eglise*) and that is what it must remain. It is true, I have lately appointed a layman to a post formerly held by an ecclesiastic, and I may do so again occasionally, but, however small we may be, we cannot yield to outer pressure and this country must be administered by men of the Church. For my part I shall fulfil my duties according to my conscience and should governments and events turn against me they cannot make me yield. I shall go with the faithful to the Catacombs as did the Christians of the early Centuries and there await the will of the Supreme Being, for I dread no human power upon earth and fear nothing but God.'

'But Holy Father,' I said, 'you speak as if some great danger threatened Rome. Is there any cause for apprehension?'

'Have you not heard,' His Holiness answered, 'that great excitement prevails throughout Italy? The state of Lombardy is deplorable. Evil spirits are at work even in my dominions and the late speech of the King of Sardinia is calculated to inflame the minds of all the revolutionary men of Italy. It is true, he says he will observe existing treaties, but that will scarcely counterbalance the effect produced by other portions of his speech. News has also reached me of an extensive amnesty granted by the King of Naples. He did not yield to outer pressure and he was right. But now, on the occasion of the marriage of his son, an act of clemency on his part is well advised.'

'Is it true,' I said, 'that political prisoners are included in that amnesty?'

'Yes,' His Holiness answered, 'I saw the name of Settembrini and I think also of that other man in whom your Government took so much interest, his name begins with a P if I remember rightly. . . .'

'Poerio?' I suggested.

'That is the name,' the Pope continued, 'and I fancy that all the other political prisoners will be released. They are to be sent to Cadiz at the expense of the King, they are to be clothed and to receive some money I believe and after that arrangements have been made with the Minister of the United States to have them conveyed to that country. They are to be exiled for life. I hope this event may have the effect of making your Government and that of France renew diplomatic relations with Naples.[1] I always regretted that rupture, but the King was right not to yield to outer pressure. It is lucky,' the Pope ended with a smile, 'that Lord Palmerston is not in office, he was too fond of interfering in the concerns of foreign countries and the present crisis would just have suited him. *Addio Caro*,' the Pope then said and dismissed me with his blessing.

I then, according to usage, called on Cardinal Antonelli and recounted to him what had passed. He confirmed all the Pope had said but denied that there was any very serious cause for immediate apprehension of any general disturbance of the peace of Italy.

3   [F.O. 43/70]   *Rome, 15 Jan. 1859*

No. 2
O.R. to E.C.

Ever since my arrival in Rome I have observed in the general tone of conversation a remarkable degree of excitement, when Italian affairs are discussed, which, according to the political creed of the persons present, manifests itself in hope or in apprehension. A vague idea seems afloat that Italian interests must shortly be uppermost in the minds of the leading Governments of Europe, and that the Emperor Napoleon is about to espouse a cause, which England is said to have forsaken.

These fears and apprehensions, hopes and national longings, have greatly increased and been strengthened by the words lately addressed to the Austrian Ambassador at Paris, on New Year's day by the Emperor of the French, by the growing disaffection and consequent increase of Austrian troops in Lombardy, by the speech of the King of Sardinia at the opening of the Chambers, and by the amnesty granted to his political prisoners by the Neapolitan King, an act attributed more to fear than to clemency.

I am not able to judge whether any real importance attaches to this

---

[1] After repeated remonstrances with the King of Naples on his tyrannical government, the English and French Governments broke off diplomatic relations on 28 October 1856. They were resumed on 14 June 1859.

state of feeling, which certainly extends to all classes of the population of Rome, and I should not take the liberty of calling your attention to it, were it not for the fact that all persons competent to give an opinion on such matters unite in asserting that no similar state of political excitement has agitated the people of Rome since the year 1848.

4   [F.O. 43/70]   *Rome, 15 Jan. 1859*
No. 3
O.R. to E.C.

The Revd Doctor Manning has arrived here rather suddenly and unexpectedly from London and is to spend part of the winter in Rome.

It is said that some differences have arisen between Cardinal Wiseman and the Chapter with respect to the administration and application of their funds and that Doctor Manning has been deputed by the former to advocate his cause at the Propaganda.

5   [F.O. 43/70]   *Rome, 21 Jan. 1859*
No. 7
O.R. to E.C.

I had occasion to see Cardinal Antonelli today, and in the course of conversation His Eminence expressed to me in the strongest terms his anxious hope that the Governments of England and France would soon be induced to renew diplomatic relations with the King of Naples. 'Such a measure,' he said, 'would go a long way in calming the disturbed spirits of Italy, and would, more particularly at this moment, have a most beneficial effect throughout the country.'

6   [F.O. 43/70]   *Rome, 28 Jan. 1859*
No. 8. Confidential
O.R. to E.C.

Cardinal Antonelli, on whom I called this morning, pointed to some dispatches on his writing table and said he was happy to inform me that most satisfactory reports had just reached him from all parts of the Papal States respecting the general tranquillity of the population. Carnival was progressing quietly in the Provinces and he saw no reason to fear any disturbance of the peace at present, indeed if he might use the term, the people were almost too quiet for Italians.

I answered that I was glad to hear it and that I knew Her Majesty's Government had learnt with satisfaction that the Pope had been able to protest against the augmentation of Austrian forces in the Legations.[1]

The Cardinal replied: 'I will tell you in strict confidence what occurred. Some time ago the French Ambassador showed me a letter from his consul announcing the arrival of nearly two thousand Austrian troops at Ancona. The details were so minute and the Duc de Gramont's[2] language so positive that I was myself misled and even His Holiness the Pope for some days believed this report. I therefore sent at once for the Austrian Ambassador and demanded explanations, saying, that his Government were at liberty to act as they pleased in the fortress of Ferrara but that as regarded the Legations in general I had a right to be consulted first. There were plenty of troops at my disposal near Rome with which to strengthen the garrison at Ancona if I thought necessary to do so, and I was surprised to hear that troops had been landed there without my permission. . . .

'Count Colloredo,[3] however, knew nothing whatever about the matter and it was only quite lately that I learnt the truth, namely, that about sixty men, absent on leave, and belonging to the garrison of Ancona, had returned there to complete their regiments, and further that the repairs made to a portion of the fortifications had greatly contributed to mislead the French Consul.'

'Could Your Eminence not ascertain the truth at once by telegraph?' I inquired.

'Not easily,' the Cardinal replied, 'I rather feared creating unnecessary excitement by asking questions and showing ignorance at Rome respecting the proceedings of the Austrian Government at Ancona.

'Your Eminence,' I said, 'will pardon me a question, but could so simple a proceeding on the part of the Roman Government as that of inquiring by telegraph, in cypher, whether the Austrian garrison at Ancona was being increased, produce any alarming excitement?'

'You do not yet know how inflammable the Italian mind is,' said Cardinal Antonelli, 'moreover the general state of feeling a few days ago was not as good as it is now, and great caution was necessary not to

[1] The Papal provinces of Bologna, Ferrara, Forli and Ravenna, administered by Legates.
[2] French Ambassador in Rome.   [3] Austrian Ambassador in Rome.

give rise to further alarm. But now that the people of France have shown themselves so decidedly in favour of peace I can again return to the accomplishment of my favourite scheme, namely, the withdrawal of the French garrison to Civita Vecchia. For their presence here is in my opinion quite unnecessary and I have plenty of Papal troops at my disposal to maintain order at Rome. To remove the excuse put forward that there is not room enough at Civita Vecchia, I have ordered the construction of provisional wooden barracks capable of holding several thousand men at Civita Vecchia. The drawings and ground plans have already been submitted to me and the works will be commenced at once I hope. The French can then gradually evacuate Rome and take up their quarters at Civita Vecchia and I think a more satisfactory state of things will thereby be inaugurated in the dominions of the Pope.'

'It is gratifying,' I said, 'to hear such good accounts from Your Eminence for when I had the honour of being admitted to the presence of the Pope, on the 14th instant, His Holiness took a very gloomy view of affairs, which Your Eminence then seemed in great measure to share.'

'We were all more alarmed than was necessary,' the Cardinal answered very cheerfully, 'Rome is always full of false and contradictory reports, for although we have not like you the liberty of the press, we have the liberty of speech in the highest degree. Do not therefore ever hesitate to call on me when you want to hear the truth or know the real state of things. Take my advice, apply to no one else, for I will always tell you as much of the truth as I happen to know myself.'

[*At the beginning of February the Prince of Wales, travelling incognito as Baron Renfrew, visited Rome. O.R. describes his cordial reception by the Pope.*]

7 [F.O. 43/70]   *Rome, 22 Feb. 1859*

No. 21 [Recites Telegram]
O.R. to Earl of Malmesbury [Foreign Secretary]

The Cardinal desires me to inform Your Lordship confidentially that the condition of the Papal States is so satisfactory that he has demanded, in the name of the Pope, the early and complete withdrawal of the French and Austrian troops from the Papal States, and that their complete evacuation and the fulfilment of this request now rests with the Gov^ts. of France and Austria.

8 [F.O. 43/70]   *Wednesday, 23 Feb. 1859*

No. 22 [Recites Telegram]
Earl of M. to O.R.

Express the great satisfaction of H.M. Gov^t. at the Cardinal's request
for the withdrawal of troops. It would be of great use to us for the
maintenance of peace and for the Cardinal's object if he would allow
me to state in Parliament that he has done so or meant to do so, as
Lord Palmerston is on Friday going to attack the Cardinal's policy and
that of Her Majesty's Government in Italy.

9 [F.O. 43/70]   *Rome, 24 Feb. 1859*

No. 25 [Recites Telegram]
O.R. to Earl of M.

Your Lordship is at liberty to state in Parliament the facts reported by
me, but the Cardinal begs you will not say they come direct from him
and will remember that we have no official relations with Rome.

The request for the withdrawal of troops is official, earnest and sincere. France and Austria, he assures me, can confirm it to Your Lordship. His Eminence has protested against the increase of the garrison
unexpectedly proposed by the French Government.

[*On 25 February Lord Palmerston referred in the House of Commons to
the danger to peace caused by the presence of French and Austrian troops
in the Roman States. The Chancellor of the Exchequer (Disraeli) said in
reply that there was reason to believe that these troops would soon be
evacuated.*]

10 [F.O. 43/70]   *Rome, 8 March 1859*

No. 28. Confidential
O.R. to Earl of M.

Your Lordship learnt from my telegrams that the Papal Government
had demanded the early and complete evacuation of the Papal States
by the French and Austrian troops and it is well known that the two
Imperial Governments have declared their readiness to comply with
the wishes of the Pope. It is now my duty to give your Lordship some
account of what has passed since for the more complete information of
Her Majesty's Government.

Although the propriety of taking the above mentioned step had often been considered and discussed by the Cardinal Secretary of State and the Pope had written an autograph letter from Bologna last year to the Emperor of the French about it, the demand for the withdrawal of the troops of occupation had never been made officially.

The first debate on Italy at the opening of Parliament, the Emperor's speech and the general tone of the press has deeply wounded the sensitive heart of Pope Pius IX. He complained in bitter terms that Europe was unjust towards him and the best argument he found in defence of his Government was the often repeated exclamation: 'What have foreign tourists to complain of, who pass the winter in Rome? Is not everything done to satisfy and amuse them and why therefore do they say my Government is bad? My people are satisfied and quiet and the taxation is lower than in any other Italian State and if only the French troops would withdraw from Rome the world would soon perceive that my people are contented.'

While His Holiness was thus complaining to everyone he saw, 300 French soldiers were unexpectedly landed at Civita Vecchia and a requisition was made for further barrack room for nearly twelve hundred more.

The Cardinal, surprized and alarmed, protested and called upon the French Ambassador to stop the further embarkation of these men at Marseilles. It was done, but not without some hesitation I believe, and when explanations were called for, the Cardinal said that having repeatedly of late declared he could do without the aid of foreign troops in Rome, it would be inconsistent in him, in the face of that declaration, to accept an increase of the garrison and it would be best in his opinion if the occupation ceased altogether.

The French Ambassador asked whether he was to consider the Cardinal's language as an official request for the recall of the troops. The Cardinal begged His Excellency to do so and added that a similar request would be made to the Austrian Ambassador that very day.

Your Lordship knows what followed. The official request was communicated by telegraph to Paris and Vienna, and in due course the evacuation agreed to.

Nearly a fortnight has elapsed since these events, but up to this day no written official note embodying the request of the Papal Government has been transmitted from the Vatican to the two Imperial Embassies.

The reasons assigned to me for this delay are: the great importance of the document and the time required for its composition and consideration. . . .

Meanwhile a meeting of Cardinals took place at the Vatican on Friday and the Pope is reported to have told them that he must now put his trust in God, for the French Gov^t· had forsaken him. He did not intend they should withdraw their protecting forces from his dominions altogether. He had merely meant that if their departure could prevent war and bloodshed he was ready to trust in Providence and do without them. . . .

In a few hours the report of this speech was all over Rome, and the numerous enemies of Cardinal Antonelli were particularly active in making it known to everyone.

I have reason to believe that the Duc de Gramont asked the Cardinal this morning what foundation there was to this strange report, but His Eminence soon found means to explain it all away saying that nothing whatever was changed, since he had agreed with His Holiness to ask for the evacuation of the Papal States and that the official Note, embodying the request, would be communicated to the Embassies on Saturday next.

While the Duc de Gramont and Count Colloredo emphatically deny that any date has yet been fixed upon for the departure of the troops, the French authorities including the Commander in Chief, General Count Goyon, talk openly of their preparations for departure and most of them seem to think that there will not be a French soldier left in Italy by the beginning of May.

I fancy I perceive some soreness on the part of the Ambassadors at the rather abrupt manner in which the demand for the total evacuation of the Papal territories was made. They do not, however, seem to apprehend any disturbances when the troops have left, nor does Cardinal Antonelli, who continues to assert that the condition of the Holy See was never more satisfactory than at the present moment.

The laity in general seem anxiously to desire the withdrawal of the troops of occupation and the only party that shews signs of fear and apprehension is that portion of the Clergy most hostile to the Cardinal's Government and the pleasure-seeking members of the Roman aristocracy.

Your Lordship knows best how desirable it is, and more especially at this moment, to free Italy from foreign occupation. With every

desire for peace the principal object of disgust to public opinion in
Europe is the long protracted presence of French and Austrian troops
in the Papal States. It would be idle in me to dwell upon the subject.

11 [F.O. 43/70]   *Rome, 15 March 1859*

No. 31. Confidential
O.R. to Earl of M.

I called this morning on Cardinal Antonelli and said: Your Eminence
is already aware that Lord Cowley[1] was sent to Vienna by Her
Majesty's Government who earnestly desire the maintenance of peace
in Europe, to ascertain whether the relations between France and
Austria could be put on a better footing. Now Her Majesty's Government consider three points essential to the maintenance of peace in
Italy:

    1st. That Austria should bind herself not to attack Sardinia, and
    2nd. That she should concert with France on the best and safest
           manner of evacuating the Pope's territory.

Here the Cardinal interrupted me and said: 'Austria can have no
difficulty in agreeing to the first point for she never had the slightest
intention or desire to attack Sardinia.'

'Respecting the second point she has no choice. I have, as you
already know, addressed an official Note to the Ambassadors of France
and Austria in which I ask for the withdrawal of the troops of occupation in the name of the Pope and I have requested they would so do
in the course of the present year.'

'And at what season,' I asked, 'will the Papal Government be prepared to let them withdraw, in what manner are they to commence, and
what forces will be substituted for the maintenance of order when they
are gone?'

The Cardinal replied, 'They will be able to leave us before the close
of the year, the sooner the better I think, I cannot myself say exactly
in what month, but my plan is now to request the two Governments to
cause their troops to be gradually withdrawn so that we may get
accustomed to do with smaller garrisons. It is a bad system in my
opinion to habituate populations to a larger number of troops than are
really needed, and by a gradual reduction of the garrisons the contrast

[1] English Ambassador in Paris, 1852 to 1867.

will be less felt when we are left to our own resources. Their place will
be supplied by our own troops and by a new battalion of riflemen
which I am organizing. Orders have been sent to recruit in Switzerland
and knowing the love those mountaineers bear to the rifle I have myself
chosen that arm for the new corps, so as to ensure success. They will
be stationed at Sinigaglia in the first instance, there to be instructed and
organized. Our army when complete is to consist of nearly eighteen
thousand men.'

I said, 'As Your Eminence has anticipated, Austria agreed to the first
points. I now come to the

3rd. That Austria should advize and support Reforms in the Papal
       States on the basis she proposed in 1856 and 1857.

Her Majesty's Government have told Austria, France and Sardinia
that they are persuaded that Reforms would tend both to the benefit of
the Roman people and to the security of the Papal Authority, but as a
Protestant power England does not desire to take the initiative or to
appear in the first line. Still for the sake of peace and consequently, as
Your Eminence must yourself admit, for the sake of conservative
principles, Her Majesty's Government earnestly hope to see the Papal
Government adopt such measures as will ensure the full support of
public opinion in Europe and remove all causes or pretexts for revolution and war.'

The Cardinal shrugged his shoulders and said with some hesitation,
'I do not remember any plan for reforms in the Pope's dominions
proposed you say in 1856 or 1857.'

'Your Eminence will remember,' I said, 'that the subject was brought
before the Congress of Paris in March 1856.'

'I have no recollection of it whatever,' replied Cardinal Antonelli.

'Then Your Eminence may possibly remember certain conversations
on the subject of Reforms which took place between yourself and Lord
Lyons when he returned from Paris to Rome at Lord Clarendon's
request?'

'Yes,' said His Eminence, 'I do remember those conversations
perfectly, but all I can say on the subject is this. We have our laws and
it is our duty to maintain and execute those laws. The promises made
by the Pope at Gaeta will be strictly carried out. It is true, that the
municipal elections and certain administrative subdivisions in the
Legations are not yet in force, and the cause of this delay must be

sought in the past state of the country and the presence of foreign troops. . . .'

The Cardinal paused and shewed no inclination to go beyond what he had already said, so I next endeavoured to elicit his opinion respecting the treaties between Austria, Parma and Modena of 1847.

He at once told me he had already received information that Mr Scarlett[1] was advizing those duchies to take the initiative and relieve Austria of her obligations towards them. He added with some bitterness that he thought Governments had a right to make treaties with their neighbours for their own safety and protection without the interference of the rest of Europe. Had England not separate treaties with many powers, had she not one with Portugal? etc., etc. Then returning to his usual cordial tone he continued, 'The danger I fear most for Italy and indeed for Europe is the conduct of the Sardinian Government. Their agents are all over the country organizing the revolutionary party, which unhappily exists everywhere. In the event of an outbreak, the Piedmontese will protect and head the movement. They have already committed themselves so far that they cannot deviate from their course without ruin to themselves. They are bringing Italy on the verge of dangers which Divine Providence alone can avert.'

I replied, 'It is those very dangers that Her Majesty's Government is deeply convinced could be removed through the agency of peaceful diplomacy, by timely reforms and measures calculated to preserve the sympathies of the Italian people for their respective Governments. You admit yourself the existence of a powerful revolutionary party which is rapidly enlisting those sympathies for King Victor Emmanuel. So long as the people of Italy see no hope of progressive development at home they must ever turn a longing heart to their more prosperous neighbour. Her Majesty's Government, in tendering their good offices to the Governments unhappily at variance with each other, have but one object at heart, peace and order, happiness to the people and security to their Governments and in this great work they beseech Your Eminence to lend an able and powerful hand.'

'We are convinced of the good intentions of Her Majesty's Government,' said the Cardinal pressing both my hands with great cordiality. I waited but he would say no more, then I thanked him and left the room.

---

[1] Peter Campbell Scarlett, English Minister in Florence.

From various conversations I have had with the Cardinal Secretary of State, with the Ambassadors of France and Austria, the Russian Minister and many others I can clearly perceive that in their private and individual opinion the present crisis in Italy will blow over like the former ones, leaving the condition of the Holy See unchanged, and the 'Status Quo' in full bloom. A little patience, they think, and a financial crash will break the influence of Piedmont, then all will return to its former tranquillity.

Since 1815 Administrative Reforms have been periodically recommended to the Popes. In 1832 Austria herself took the lead. Your Lordship best knows with what effect and with what result.

The Papal Government well know that the Church of Rome cannot be shaken by foreign Governments, that the Protestant powers cannot interfere directly or indirectly with their internal or external, temporal or spiritual affairs, and that in moments of danger the Catholic powers, whose armies have ever been at the disposal of the Holy See, can never refuse their protection to the Papacy.

And what prospect then have the subjects of the Pope of seeing their hopes and aspirations realized, whether for good or for evil, so long as their despotic rulers can look with calm and perfect security to the future?

On the other hand, Your Lordship is aware that the leaders of the National party in Italy say, 'We ask not for the interference of foreign powers in our behalf, we ask only for their neutrality. Let the great powers of Europe bind themselves by treaty not to interfere singly or separately in the internal development of Italy. Let them all unite as the one protecting power, and not Austria or France alone. Grant us the same privileges as those extended to the Danubian principalities. Give us the same chances Piedmont has enjoyed, and then, no longer at the mercy of foreign bayonets, we can settle our own internal affairs ourselves, and gradually lead Italy to the pathway of progressive development.'

Such, My Lord, are the two leading ideas I have observed in Rome. The principal changes in the public mind since 1848 appear to be these, first, that Piedmont affords the national party a *Leader*, and the nucleus of a national army, which did not exist before, and therefore a greater prospect of success, and 2nd. that France has become the friend, while England has joined Austria as the enemy of Italian freedom and independence.

12   [f.o. 43/70]   *Rome, 2 April 1859*

No. 34

O.R. to Earl of M.

The proposed Congress for the settlement of Italian Affairs is at present uppermost in everyone's mind at Rome. The conditions under which it is to meet seem more or less known to diplomacy. I had occasion to speak to the Ambassadors of France and Austria and to the Ministers of Prussia, Belgium, Naples and Sardinia who all agreed in thinking that the Government of the Pope as well as the King of Naples would decline the invitations of the five powers to send Representatives to the Congress if they were not to have a voice in its decisions.

Yesterday morning I sought an interview with the Cardinal Secretary of State and His Eminence volunteered to enter upon the subject. The result of his remarks at the end of a long conversation was this:

He considered the Congress proposed by Russia for the settlement of Italian affairs as quite uncalled for, and he doubted whether such interference with the internal affairs of smaller countries by the great European Powers was justifiable and in accordance with the Law of Nations. The Governments of Italy had not asked for advice and therefore he was at a loss to know what would be discussed by the five powers in Congress. If they were going to take the views of Piedmont and its adherents in Italy into consideration, then Congress simply promoted discontent, encouraged rebellion and became a revolutionary organ.

The '*Indépendance Belge*' has compared the plan of admitting representatives of the Italian Governments '*sous titre consultatif*' to the plan adopted at the London Conferences for the establishment of the Kingdoms of Holland and Belgium, but that comparison was false. Belgium was in a state of rebellion and asked for a Government. Italy was not in a state of rebellion and her Governments asked for nothing. If invited by France or Austria to send a representative the Pope would decline. His Holiness could take no notice of the proposed Congress.

13   [f.o. 43/70]   *Rome, 2 April 1859*

No. 35

O.R. to Earl of M.

Monsieur de Martino, the Neapolitan Chargé d'Affaires, was instructed by his King to inform the Papal Government that in the event of the five powers inviting the Governments of Italy to send representatives to the proposed Congress, His Majesty intended to decline the invitation and he hoped the Government of the Pope would do the same thing.

To this course of proceeding, I am informed, His Holiness entirely agreed, but beyond that I have not been able to obtain any details as to what passed between the two Governments.

14 [F.O. 43/70]   *Rome, 9 April 1859*
No. 38. Confidential
O.R. to Earl of M.

Your Lordship learnt from my dispatch No. 34 that the Papal Government would not send a representative to the proposed Congress of the five powers.

The Ambassadors of France and Austria both agree in thinking that there are no conditions under which the Pope could be induced to do so, and public report goes so far in Rome as to assert that His Holiness will make a formal protest against the said Congress.

Conceiving it my duty to make every effort in my power in the interest of peace I proceeded to the Vatican and said to Cardinal Antonelli:

'Her Majesty's Government deeply regret to hear from me that Your Eminence does not admit the propriety of sending a representative to be heard and to advize at the proposed Congress. They have no wish to impose, but only to recommend, such measures as may ensure the peace of Europe. They wish to do so through the Governments of Italy and their sole object is to avert a war of opinion and national hatred with which Europe is now threatened, and Your Eminence by refusing your powerful co-operation is heaping fuel upon the fire which may shortly burst forth in Italy. In calling on you today I bring you a new proof of the desire which animates Her Majesty's Government to maintain peace and order in Europe. Her Majesty's Government, you know it, represent the Conservative principle in England, and therefore also abroad, and we now learn by the telegraph that they are ready to make another great effort in the interest of the policy they represent. Her Majesty has consented to the dissolution of Parliament to enable Government to carry out their home and foreign policy in the spirit already known to Your Eminence.'

Cardinal Antonelli replied: 'We sincerely acknowledge the good intentions of Her Majesty's Government and hope they may continue long to govern England, but, as I have said before, the proposed Congress is uncalled for, and not desired by the Governments of Italy. The Great Powers want to settle the so called 'Italian Question', and what is the Italian Question? It is simply the desire of Piedmont to extend her dominion in Italy. That question need not exist at all if the Great Powers will simply ignore it. Piedmont by restless intrigue has forced it upon their notice, and the peace of Europe is far more likely to be disturbed by the importance given to Piedmontese policy through the medium of a Congress than by totally ignoring their unfounded complaints.

The Papal Government has shewn that it requires no assistance from without, by demanding the withdrawal of foreign troops. That being done, the Powers of Europe have no right to interfere with us. The Pope has never asked for the advice of any foreign Government, does not require it, and will never accept it, and therefore His Holiness will not send a Representative to appear at the bar of a self constituted tribunal such as the proposed Congress is.'

I replied, 'I cannot agree with Your Eminence. History teaches us that the Papacy has often required the intervention of foreign powers. In 1832 you tolerated it, and in 1849 you asked for it, and without going further back, for the last ten years the temporal power of the Pope owes its existence in Europe to foreign bayonets alone. Why then suddenly inaugurate a new policy and refuse the friendly advice and aid which the Great Powers offer in the interest of a general and lasting peace?'

Cardinal Antonelli listened to me with benevolent patience and then said: 'Simply because we do not require it and because we conceive that the cause of peace will be better served in Italy by not creating artificially, a question which, in reality, does not exist.'

'Then,' said I, 'how do you intend to meet a popular outbreak which is imminent, and how will you deal with the endless contingencies and complications daily arising, that can only find their solution in war and bloodshed, if the Congress, unaided by those whom it concerns, cannot fulfil its object?'

'Our destinies are in the hands of God, in Him let us confide, beyond that I can say no more,' replied Cardinal Antonelli and he extended his hand to me to wish me good bye.

I rose, bowed and left the room.

15 [F.O. 43/70]   *Rome, 16 April 1859*

No. 40

O.R. to Earl of M.

The French Ambassador presented yesterday an official Note from his
Government to Cardinal Antonelli containing a formal invitation to
the Congress of the five powers for the settlement of Italian affairs.

This Note, I am assured, is couched in the strongest terms, a most
earnest appeal is made to the Pope to send a Representative to the
Congress and every argument is used to shew how much the peace of
Europe depends on the present policy of the Papal Government. . . .

I am told that this Note is long, well argued and very able, but I
regret to inform Your Lordship that Cardinal Antonelli replied to the
Duc de Gramont with the same arguments and in the same terms as
those I submitted to Your Lordship in my dispatches Nos. 34 and 38.

Monsieur de Gramont declined to accept a definitive refusal from
the Cardinal to attend the Congress until the Note had been submitted
to the Pope, and before leaving His Eminence, after a long argument,
the Ambassador enquired in what manner the Papal Government, if
unrepresented at the Congress would signify their protest against such
measures proposed by the Congress as might appear objectionable to
the Pope?

Cardinal Antonelli is said to have replied that since the Papal
Government could take no notice one way or the other of the Congress, which he called a self-constituted tribunal, it was a matter of
perfect indifference to the Pope what might be debated or resolved by
the five powers in Congress assembled.

16 [F.O. 43/70]   *Rome, 26 April 1859*

No. 46

O.R. to Earl of M.

On Easter Sunday when the French Ambassador and General Count
Goyon left St Peter's they were loudly cheered, from the steps of the
Basilica to the Fort of St Angelo, by the Roman population with cries
of '*Vive l'Empereur*', '*vive la France*' and '*Vive l'Italie*'.

On the same night the leaders of this demonstration in favour of the
French Emperor were arrested by order of Cardinal Antonelli. They
were all respectable men of the middle classes.

Notwithstanding this measure a second demonstration of a similar nature took place on Monday night under the windows of Count Goyon.

The French Ambassador remonstrated with the Cardinal Secretary of State on the severity of his proceedings against men who had simply given vent to their sympathies for the army of occupation and the Emperor Napoleon, and in consequence the prisoners were set at liberty but not until it had been agreed that the French Commander in Chief should issue the enclosed proclamation to the people of Rome.

[*Printed Proclamation in French and Italian forbidding demonstrations.*]

17 [F.O. 43/70]   *Rome, 27 April 1859*

No. 47
O.R. to Earl of M.

I had the honor to inform Your Lordship by telegraph that the Austrian Government had landed two thousand men at Ancona on the 26 instant.

Great annoyance was felt at the Vatican at this unexpected proceeding and Cardinal Antonelli sent for Count Colloredo to demand explanations and protest against an increase of Austrian troops in the Papal States.

The reply sent from Vienna was to this effect:

That the additional two thousand men sent to Ancona only completed the garrison of that city and must not be considered as an increase of the Austrian army of occupation, at the same time it was in contemplation to reduce the garrison of Bologna by an equal number of troops.

The Pope not feeling quite satisfied with this explanation caused Cardinal Antonelli to address a note yesterday to the Embassies of France and Austria, saying, 'that it was the wish and intention of His Holiness to maintain the strictest neutrality during the coming events, that the armies of France and Austria had been allowed to occupy the Papal States for the sole purpose of maintaining peace and order and that he solemnly protested against the Holy See being made a scene of contest and bloodshed in the impending War.'

[*On 27 April war was declared between Sardinia and Austria.*]

3. Arthur Russell

4. Pope Pius IX

18 [F.O. 43/71]   *Rome, 17 May 1859*

No. 54

O.R. to Earl of M.

Cardinal Antonelli told me today that the Austrian Gov^t. had thrown the responsibility of the arbitrary acts of their garrison at Ancona on the military authorities there, who had not clearly understood the declaration of neutrality of the Pope. That declaration was now practically accepted and understood by the cabinet of Vienna and he thought the inhabitants of Ancona would no longer be annoyed by the unnecessary energy of the Austrian soldiers.

He had been much gratified by the repeated assurances from France that no event in the future should interfere with the peace and quiet of Rome and that the personal security of the Pope was earnestly desired by the French Emperor. His Majesty had addressed autograph letters to His Holiness and to General Goyon to that effect.

The presence of the French garrison had again become necessary since the Papal troops were misled through Sardinian influence and Sardinian agents, cases of desertion and disaffection occurred daily, and it might soon be impossible to prevent the whole of the Italian regiments from joining the Piedmontese Army.

His Eminence ended by observing that besides a strict neutrality the Papal Government was practically compelled to ignore the events that threatened Italy.

19 [F.O. 43/71]   *Rome, 19 May 1859*

No. 57

O.R. to Earl of M.

Cardinal Antonelli, whose naturally excellent spirits now forsake him altogether when he speaks of the present war, assured me that while he did not apprehend any disturbance or interruption of the neutrality the Pope desired to maintain during the present conflict, he greatly feared the Government of Naples would be dragged into the war. He believed Sardinia was about to send a Plenipotentiary to Naples to invite the King to join the national cause and in the event of a refusal to do so, it would be easy for the Piedmontese Government to act at Naples as they had acted at Florence, for the army was Piedmontese to a man,

c

and indeed, as he had told me before, the Papal army was animated by the same spirit. It was therefore difficult to foresee what would happen after the King's death.

The apprehensions of Cardinal Antonelli were to a certain degree confirmed to me later by the Sardinian Chargé d'Affaires and other persons well versed in Count Cavour's policy.

The French Embassy, however, disclaimed all knowledge of the Count's plans at Naples.

20 [F.O. 43/71]   *Rome, 19 May 1859*

No. 58
O.R. to Earl of M.

The measures taken by the French authorities to maintain the tranquillity of Rome, to secure the safety of the Pope and the neutrality of his Government, the moderation of their language to Cardinal Antonelli respecting the proceedings of the Austrian garrison at Ancona, and the friendly advice given to prevent a breach of the Pope's neutrality endangered by those arbitrary proceedings, certainly deserve the highest commendation and do the French Government the greatest credit. There can be no doubt that it is of importance to the cause of Piedmont and France in Italy that the Pope should have no reason to complain of them before the Roman Catholick world.

Any open leaning towards or public expression of sympathy for Austria on the part of the Pope might prove prejudicial to the powers allied against her, and it is therefore natural to conclude that every cause of complaint will be carefully withheld or removed from His Holiness and every exertion will be made to maintain peace and order in Rome for the present.

The Pope's flight to Gaeta has also not been forgotten, and it is well known that His Holiness would willingly accept the secret and pressing invitation of Queen Isabella of Spain to reside in her states until the crisis in Italy is over, if he could but escape the vigilant eye of his French protectors, and it may therefore in truth be said that while the warmest assurances of friendship and respect are almost daily sent to His Holiness from France, while everything is done to ensure his neutrality and good will, the Pope, *de facto*, is a prisoner of the Emperor of the French.

21 [F.O. 43/71] *Rome, 22 May 1859*

No. 62. Confidential
O.R. to Earl of M.

In speaking with Cardinal Antonelli about the death of Mr Freeborn,
Her Majesty's Consular Agent in Rome, His Eminence said to me that
it had been a matter of great regret to the Papal Government that Mr
Freeborn had identified himself so strongly with the revolutionary
party in 1848, a circumstance which had done injury to all personal
relations between the Consul and the Papal authorities.

'Tell Lord Malmesbury,' His Eminence said, 'that we shall be happy
to receive anyone His Lordship desires to appoint as successor to Mr
Freeborn and sincerely wish to entertain the best relations with the new
Consular agent, and we do not care whether he is a Protestant or a
Roman Catholic, but we do attach great importance to one thing,
namely, that he should prove to be an *honest man*. Tell Lord Malmesbury we have the fullest confidence in His Lordship's choice.'

[*Endorsed in pencil by Malmesbury:* H.M.G. will be careful to appoint
a man of respectable character and who will not interfere with politics.]

22 [F.O. 43/71] *Rome, 25 May 1859*

No. 65. Secret
O.R. to Earl of M.

Yesterday morning Count Della Minerva[1] communicated a dispatch
he had received from Count Cavour, dated May 16th, to Cardinal
Antonelli, by which the Sardinian Government decline to accept the
Pope's declaration of neutrality unconditionally and without reserve.

Count Cavour while acknowledging the Pope's wishes in terms of
high respect, argues that Sardinia, not having troops in the Papal
States like France and Austria, is in a different position altogether and
cannot bind herself, if certain contingencies arise, to respect the Pope's
territory. It may, for instance, become impossible to allow the Austrians to continue in their present position in the Legations, if they take
advantage of it as a basis of operation against the allied armies. The
whole of the country lying between Ancona and the Po is occupied by
them. It is in their power to send provisions from the Papal States to
Lombardy, to impede the operations about to be undertaken from

[1] Sardinian Chargé d'Affaires in Rome.

Tuscany through Modena, and under such circumstances it might become necessary to drive them out of the Papal States. Count Cavour declares, however, that only the most urgent necessity would compel Sardinia to enter the Pope's dominions as it is their anxious desire to pay all respect to the wishes of His Holiness, and he hopes the Papal Government will duly appreciate the reasons for which he cannot accept their declaration of neutrality unconditionally and without reserve.

Cardinal Antonelli replied that France having accepted their neutrality he thought Sardinia as her ally was bound to do the same. The Austrians had also accepted it and they occupied the Pope's dominions like the French, as protectors. He could therefore not allow them to be interfered with, and if Sardinia refused to accept this view of the case he was in duty bound to say to Austria: 'We can afford you no guarantee for your safety in the Holy See if our neutrality is not respected by your enemies, so you had better retire and evacuate the Papal States.'

The French Ambassador, who returned on Sunday last from Genoa, next saw Cardinal Antonelli and His Eminence called upon him to use his influence to make Sardinia follow the same policy as her French ally.

The Duc de Gramont replied that he had nothing to do with Count Cavour's instructions to Count Della Minerva, but that France in accepting the Pope's neutrality fully expected Austria on her part to do so honestly and without reserve. Instead of that she was treating Ancona and the Legations like a conquered country, she was ill using the inhabitants, she was raising fortifications and destroying valuable property and she was exporting a vast amount of provisions from the Pope's dominions to Lombardy. He had acted with patience and moderation and had given full time to the Cardinal to protest against their conduct and protect the subjects of the Pope, but the Austrians had to this day not altered their arbitrary course. It therefore became his duty to address an official note to the Pope's Gov^t· specifying the conditions and reserves under which his Government could accept the neutrality of His Holiness.

Monsieur de Gramont has since sent this note to the Vatican. He says in it that the Emperor will guarantee the tranquillity and safety of every part of the Papal States occupied by French soldiers, but if the Austrians increase their forces in the Legations, operate against the allied armies or send reinforcements and provisions from thence to Lombardy it may become necessary to resort to such measures as will render their presence there harmless to the allies.

I saw Cardinal Antonelli yesterday and found him deeply alarmed and agitated. He gave me a full account of what had passed and said he regretted he had not communicated to me the note addressed by him to the foreign Legations at Rome announcing the Pope's desire for neutrality during the present conflict.

'Unfortunately we have no official relations with you,' he continued, 'but nevertheless I will send you a copy of the note confidentially for communication to Lord Malmesbury. His Lordship, I am sure, will feel how awkward and difficult our present position is. We insist on our neutrality but we have not the means to enforce it if foreign Governments will not respect the wishes of the Pope.

'Naples may want to send troops through these dominions. We can only protest, we can do no more. The best policy for Naples would be to seek a close alliance with England and perhaps her influence might yet save Southern Italy, but you will see the whole of Italy revolutionized and inflamed ere long to serve the purposes of Sardinia. Nothing can prevent it. The Legations will be invaded under some pretext or other and in that case the Austrians had better retire and evacuate so as not to make the Holy See a field of battle and bloodshed.

'Do you know, there is a great advantage, *mon cher Russell*, in your unofficial position here, we can speak more freely to each other, I can say things to you I could not say to your colleagues.

'Now I cannot conceal from you that all this is evidently a preconcerted plan between Sardinia and France. The former takes the lead, the latter follows to establish an excuse and very shortly Prince Napoleon[1] will occupy Bologna, and then our Austrian troops in the Legations will simply become a large body of French prisoners.'

Cardinal Antonelli continued in this strain for a long time. I had never seen him so much alarmed before, and he thanked me with great warmth when I promised to report faithfully, all he had told me, to Your Lordship.

23 [F.O. 43/71]   *Rome, 28 May 1859*

No. 69
O.R. to Earl of M.

... I will endeavour to make a sketch of the present state of things in Rome.

[1] Prince Jérome Napoleon, cousin of Napoleon III, known as Plon Plon.

War declared, France gave every proof of her desire to maintain peace and order in Rome and to secure the safety of the Pope. The instructions to that effect from Paris and the measures taken at Rome did great credit to the French authorities, and praise is also due to them for their moderation when the arbitrary course pursued by the Austrians at Ancona afforded ample cause for complaint.

The Pope's declaration of neutrality was accepted without reserve by France. At the same time the leaders of the National party openly declared that they had positive orders from Count Cavour to prevent an outburst in their ranks and to avoid everything that could interfere with the peace and tranquillity of the Pope, or the orders of the French Emperor.

In short so much was done to ensure the tranquillity of Rome and the safety of the Pope that His Holiness has, practically speaking, become a prisoner of the French. . . .

The Pope entrusts the exercise of his temporal power to Cardinal Antonelli and Cardinal Antonelli in his heart is, I believe, a sincere partizan of Austria.

Unfortunately for him he endeavoured to excuse her conduct at Ancona and to declare that the new fortifications were thought desirable by the Pope's Government and that a sum of 6,000 Scudi p.a. should be paid towards their execution.

Immediately after his return from headquarters at Genoa, the French Ambassador at once assumed a more dictatorial tone and Cardinal Antonelli was made distinctly to feel that he had but two courses to follow, either to be French, or to resign.

Sardinia then very unexpectedly refused to accept unconditionally the neutrality declared by the Pope and was at once followed and backed up by France. . . .

This move will enable France and Sardinia to attack Austria in the Legations whenever they feel prepared to do so. It is known that they will have the full assistance of the people who have long been ripe for revolution.

The Austrian party in Rome is small and ill guided, it is chiefly confined to the aristocracy of the Roman Church. The Austrian Embassy seems powerless, helpless and forsaken and complains loudly of the weakness of the Papal Gov[t]

The partizans of France are everywhere, they no longer conceal their sympathies and hatreds. They speak boldly and without reserve. The

Roman Princes have contributed money and the other classes send soldiers to the national war. The power of Count Cavour over the minds and hearts of the Roman subjects is beyond all belief. A word from him will be sufficient to revolutionize the Legations. Cardinal Antonelli expects that word will soon be uttered. The hatred to the Priests is controlled by the presence of French troops.

England is also hated. She is supposed to have a secret alliance with Austria and the poor benighted Romans say they hope she will be chastized by France for having forsaken the cause of Italian freedom and independence.

The more moderate and enlightened Romans conceal their fears as to the future in saying: 'Whatever happens, things cannot be worse than they are now, and any change must after all be for the better.'

In conclusion it may therefore be said that the influence of Sardinia and the power of France are increasing, while the cause of Austria and the Government of the Pope become weaker day after day.

With respect to the probable course of events in this Capital, it may, I think, be confidently asserted that the French authorities will make every effort to keep the peace in Rome and with every prospect of success. Seconded by Piedmontese influence order can easily be expected wherever French soldiers are stationed.

With regard to the Provinces occupied by Austria the case is different. Well informed people assert that the Legations will rise and together with the Italian regiments of the Papal army, will join the Tuscan movement, when they receive orders from Turin to do so, and finally it is believed that Cardinal Antonelli will continue in office so long as he obeys the orders of France, but not a day longer.

[*Endorsed in pencil by Malmesbury*: Important. Assuming this description of Italy to be correct what chance is there of arresting the war?]

24 [F.O. 43/71]   *Rome, 29 May 1859*

No. 70
O.R. to Earl of M.

Just as I am leaving my house to start for Naples, a messenger from the Vatican places the accompanying Note from Cardinal Antonelli in my hands. It is the Note addressed by His Eminence to all the foreign Legations here declaring the Pope's intention to maintain the strictest neutrality during the present war. . . .

25 [F.O. 43/71]   *Naples, 6 June 1859*

No. 72

O.R. to Earl of M.

I hear from Rome that the Sardinian Chargé d'Affaires, Count Della
Minerva, on the 3rd instant, read a dispatch addressed to him by Count
Cavour, to Cardinal Antonelli stating that the Sardinian Government
considered the fortifications which the Austrians were now raising at
Ancona, as a breach of the Pope's neutrality they had formerly engaged
to respect in that city.

The Cardinal replied that those fortifications were for local purposes
only and their construction had been sanctioned by the Pope's Government. They were of no military importance whatever in the present
war and he could therefore not accept Count Cavour's objection to
their construction and completion. At the same time His Eminence
requested Count Della Minerva to inform his Government that cases
of desertion from the Pontifical army were increasing to an alarming
extent in consequence of the encouragement the men received from
Piedmont and the reception they met with at the hands of the Sardinian
agents on crossing the Tuscan frontier, and to state that he deeply
deplored the course adopted in this matter by the Government of
Sardinia.

Count Della Minerva said he would convey Cardinal Antonelli's
answer and observations to Count Cavour.

[*On 18 June O.R. returned from Naples to Rome.*]

26 [F.O. 43/71]   *Rome, 21 June 1859*

No. 74

O.R. to Earl of M.

. . . On the 11th instant the Austrian troops of occupation received
orders from Verona to evacuate the Legations, and on the 12th they
departed without previous notice to the Papal authorities and proceeded in hurried marches to Ferrara. The immediate result at Bologna
and Ravenna was a rising of the people, the establishment of provisional
governments by the municipal authorities and a declaration that
the dictatorship should be offered to King Victor Emmanuel and an
active part taken in the war of independence. The Cardinals Legate of

both cities fled, the former to Ferrara, the latter to Loretto. The example given by Bologna, Ravenna and Perugia has been rapidly followed by Imola, Faenza, Rimini, Cesena, Forli, Fossombrone, Fano, Fuligno and Ancona. Sinigaglia, Macerata, Viterbo and the other cities are expected to declare themselves at once and all have united in offering themselves to the King of Sardinia.

At the meeting of the Sacred College called forth by these events Cardinals Antonelli and De Pietro alone advocated the propriety of requesting the French Government to extend their present military occupation to those parts of the Holy See which had been evacuated by the Austrians and thereby to maintain order in the rebellious cities, but their advice did not prevail and the measures taken for the present by the Papal Government, to meet this crisis are very limited. Some Swiss regiments have been sent to Perugia and Ancona, and a 'Circular' Note has been addressed by the Cardinal Secretary of State to the foreign representatives in Rome, copy of which I have just received from His Eminence [enclosed]. . . .

Monsieur de Gramont, the French Ambassador, condemns and deplores this popular rising in the Legations in the strongest possible terms.

27 [P.R.O. 30/22/111]   *F.O. 23 June 1859*

Private
Lord John Russell[1] to O.R.

It is of great importance to me in this office that I should get accurate and intelligent accounts of what is going on at Rome, and I am happy to think I can depend upon you for that purpose.

I am sorry to see by the telegram received this morning that the Pope has been setting his Swiss wolves upon his poor sheep at Perugia. Such an act is sure to increase the ill will and animosity of his Roman subjects. But the most important question is to know how the Emperor N. will view the insurrections that are going on in the Roman States. If he protects them, how can he keep his word to the Pope? and if he suppresses them by force how can he retain his title of Liberator of Italy?

---

[1] The Conservative Government fell on 11 June. Malmesbury was succeeded at the Foreign Office by Russell.

I shall be glad to learn from you what Cardinal Antonelli says with respect to Romagna, Perugia and Rome itself. You will of course always repeat that England is unable to give any advice. . . .

28 [F.O. 43/71]   *Rome, 24 June 1859*
No. 76
O.R. to Earl of M.

The Pope sent Signor Latanzi, a lawyer of repute, to Perugia for the purpose of admonishing the inhabitants to return to their duties and surrender to the legitimate authority of His Holiness. Unfortunately while Signor Latanzi was still negotiating with the provisional Government and before his mission was over, Colonel Schmidt at the head of about four thousand Swiss troops, who had been sent from Rome for that purpose, attacked the town on the 20th instant.

The Perugians at once broke off the negotiations entered into with Latanzi and though insufficiently armed made a desperate resistance. After three hours combat and considerable losses they were compelled to yield to the Swiss. These latter are reported to have lost two Captains, one Lieutenant and about sixty men killed and wounded.

I regret to inform Your Lordship that the Papal soldiers after entering the town acted with cruel ferocity. They shot everyone they could find and entering private houses pillaged and murdered their peaceful inmates including old men and helpless women, nine of whom were mothers.

A highly respectable American family (Mr Perkins of Boston with his wife, mother, sister and niece) were dining at the Hotel de France in Perugia at the time of the invasion and saw the innkeeper and a waiter murdered by the soldiers under their own eyes. The innkeeper's wife was able to escape with the American ladies and concealed them in a remote part of the building where they remained for fourteen hours, but, meanwhile, the whole of their property was pillaged by the Swiss soldiers. Many reports of similar acts of cruelty are circulating in Rome and have produced a most painful impression for several very respectable Perugians have been killed like the master of the Hotel de France.

The Pope has promoted Colonel Schmidt to the rank of Brigadier General.

29 [F.O. 43/71] *Rome, 1 July 1859*

No. 80

O.R. to Lord John Russell

Cardinal Antonelli told me this morning that he hoped I had not believed the exaggerated accounts which were circulating in Rome respecting the conduct of the Papal soldiers at Perugia. The revolutionary party, at the instigation of Piedmont, were ever at work to poison the minds of the Roman people.

I replied that I well knew what value could be placed on public reports in Rome, but that nevertheless I had seen letters from persons who had been present at the siege of Perugia and in whom I could place implicit reliance, giving a heartrending account of the ferocious behaviour of the Swiss, even after the city was in their power, and I could not doubt that they had murdered, pillaged, burnt houses and committed other outrages. These acts, I said, were the more to be regretted because they increased the ill will and animosity of the Pope's subjects.

The Cardinal replied that revolutions must be put down and bloodshed was the natural consequence of such a conflict, the Papal troops had met with great resistance and had lost two of their officers, besides which they had been fired upon by the Perugians out of the windows of their houses and the fury of the soldiers could not well be controlled at first, which was after all but natural. General Schmidt who was an excellent officer had in consequence consigned his men to barracks for a day and perfect tranquillity now reigned at Perugia. His Eminence intended to publish a report of the Perugia Affair which would prove how much the conduct of the soldiers had been exaggerated. Unfortunately the leaders had escaped to Tuscany and could not therefore be brought to trial. He had, however, great satisfaction in telling me that Ancona and all the cities on this side of La Cattolica[1] had now submitted to the Papal authority. Forli, Ravenna, Bologna and Ferrara remained still to be conquered, and the task was not an easy one, first, because the Pope had not troops enough, and, secondly, because, if they advanced, their retreat might be cut off by a second rising of the conquered provinces. The arrival of the Sardinian squadron in the Adriatic might be the signal for a general outbreak in the Adriatic

[1] Halfway between Rimini and Pesaro, on the border of Romagna and the Marches.

provinces, and he had therefore resolved to take no further steps for
the present, but to await events before deciding on the attack of
Bologna, Ravenna and Ferrara.

I enquired whether he intended to ask for French co-operation?

His Eminence said, No, he did not, he could not expose himself to
a second refusal on their part, for he had originally applied to General
Goyon with respect to Perugia, because he felt sure the Perugians
would have yielded at once to French troops in consequence of the
great sympathies the Emperor Napoleon now enjoyed in Italy. General
Goyon had replied he could not spare any of the garrison of Rome at
present and could do nothing without direct orders from the Emperor.
Under these circumstances His Eminence would not ask again for
French co-operation.

Meanwhile, the King of Sardinia, while he publicly declined to accept
the dictatorship of the Legations, had sent a Commissioner and some
officers to Bologna and it was the intention of His Holiness to demand
explanations of the Sardinian Government respecting an act which was
in direct contradiction with the declarations of King Victor Emmanuel.

I enquired what His Eminence thought of the present state of Rome?

The French force, he replied, was sufficient to ensure order in and
about Rome and safety to the Pope, and he knew that General Goyon
had the most stringent orders from the Emperor to that effect. Great
vigilance however was necessary everywhere for unfortunately the
revolutionary influence of Piedmont could be traced in every portion
of the Holy See.

30 [F.O. 43/71]   *Rome, 1 July 1859*

No. 81. Secret
O.R. to Lord J.R.

A question which naturally rises into importance at the present moment
is, how the Emperor of the French will view the insurrections which
are going on in the Roman States? If he protects them how can he keep
his word to the Pope, and if he suppresses them by force how can he
retain his title as Liberator of Italy?

The Emperor Napoleon has repeatedly promised the Pope to protect
his person and to ensure his safety in Rome, but the French military

authorities here have declined to interfere at Perugia and have shewn a decided determination not to interfere in the Legations or any portion of the Papal States which is not already occupied by them, besides which they encourage the Papal Government to act with its own means, so that, while the French soldier associates and fraternizes with the citizen of Rome, the odium which necessarily accompanies acts of violent repression falls, in the eyes of his people, solely on the Pope.

The effect of this policy is self-evident. The moral influence of the Pope on his subjects is becoming weaker, and the hatred to his Government stronger, every day, throughout the Holy See, so that at present the temporal power of the Pope demands solely on French bayonets and the will of the Emperor. On the other hand the Pope's influence over the Roman Catholic clergy of France is, I am told, so great that His Majesty could not afford to quarrel with His Holiness at present. . . .

Immediately after the late revolutionary movement in the Papal States, the French Ambassador applied to the Emperor at headquarters for instructions, and His Majesty replied to the Duc de Gramont by telegraph and in cypher. The contents of this reply have been kept strictly secret in Rome. A person, however, in possession of a copy of the decyphered letter, read it to me in the strictest confidence, but could not allow me to take a copy of it.

I endeavoured to put it on paper from memory, and my informant to whom I afterwards read my version of this letter assured me that it was 'quite correct'.

It is herewith submitted for Your Lordship's confidential information and I earnestly request that the contents both of His Majesty's letter to Monsieur de Gramont and of this despatch may be kept *strictly secret*, otherwise my sources of information in Rome might be seriously injured.

[Memorandum of a letter from the Emperor Napoleon III to the Duc de Gramont dated, Cavriana, Imperial Headquarters, June 25th 1859.]

I wish you to offer some advice on my part to the subjects of the Pope.

There can exist no contradiction between my words and my actions. I wish for the independence of Italy, but I must maintain the authority of the Pope in which one hundred and fifty millions of consciences are interested; and I am firmly resolved to maintain order in Rome.

When foreign influence and foreign preponderance have been driven from Italy, the established Governments can no longer resist the legitimate wishes of their people, and for my part, I know of no religion incompatible with liberty and honor. While on the one hand I refuse to recognize the separation of the Legations, on the other hand I cannot but appreciate an act which places twenty thousand men at my disposal. But should the revolution, crossing the Appenines, approach there where my soldiers are stationed, I could not tolerate it for one moment, and you will tell those men, with whom I otherwise sympathize, to be careful not to pursue a course which would necessarily compel my troops to acts of repression.

Neither revolution, nor insurrection nor isolated demonstrations can improve the condition of this Country.

I cannot, for my part, settle the affairs of Italy alone and by myself.

The Great Powers will claim their part in the discussions, which will follow the war, for the settlement of the equilibrium of Europe. And if God gives us victory and when treaties are being discussed then shall I defend, where they are founded, the legitimate wishes and just demands of the people of Italy with all the warmth and sincere interest with which I feel them. I shall be foremost in your cause when the moment for settlement arrives.

Be tranquil until then!

31 [F.O. 43/71]   *Rome, 7 July 1859*

No. 82
O.R. to Lord J.R.

In obedience to Your Lordship's instruction I expressed to Cardinal Antonelli the painful impression which the atrocities perpetrated by the Swiss soldiers at Perugia had caused in England, and I stated that Her Majesty's Government took for granted that His Holiness was ignorant of the butcheries committed by his troops when he gave an order for the promotion of their commander.

Cardinal Antonelli replied that, as he had told me before those acts had been grossly exaggerated by the Piedmontese party who were at the bottom of the whole insurrectionary movement in the Papal States, that it was the duty of every Government to put down revolutions whenever they broke out (had not England done so lately in India?) and that Colonel Schmidt who had commanded the siege of Perugia was one of the best officers the Pope had and fully deserved his promotion to the rank of Brigadier General conferred on him by the Pope for his valuable services. General Schmidt had met with great resistance at Perugia, his men after entering the streets had been fired upon out of the windows of the houses. He had lost three officers and ten men, and was he not to put down the rebels as they deserved it? Why, Napoleon I, when his troops were fired upon out of the windows of the houses of a town in the Papal States, had condemned that town to be burnt to the ground and a medal commemorating this act could be seen in the collections of the Vatican.

'Of course,' His Eminence continued, 'we deplored the necessity to employ force and we feel for those who have suffered. An American family whose property was taken by the soldiers will be fully compensated by the Papal Government. But on the other hand the moral effect produced by the conduct of our troops at Perugia has proved most beneficial, for Ancona and all the other towns we sent detachments to, submitted without resistance. Unfortunately we have not troops enough to enter the Legations at present and retake Bologna, Ferrara and Ravenna.'

I replied to His Eminence 'that the right to put down armed insurrections was incontestable but it was the manner in which it had been done at Perugia that I deplored. The troops had attacked the town unexpectedly, they had murdered, pillaged and burnt houses, and their conduct had been approved. Why had they not summoned the town to surrender and given the inhabitants time to reconsider the position they had placed themselves in?'

Cardinal Antonelli replied that France, Austria and all the other Governments represented at Rome had congratulated the Papal Government on the conduct of their troops, and he again assured me that there was great exaggeration in all that had been said and published about Perugia and he referred me for correct information to the Official account in the *Giornale di Roma*.

On leaving His Eminence I repeated what I had said on a former occasion, namely that I feared the real moral effect produced was to increase the ill-will and animosity of the Pope's subjects against the Government of His Holiness and for that reason I thought the events at Perugia were to be deeply regretted.

[*After the defeat of the Austrians at Magenta and Solferino, Napoleon III, to the great disappointment of the Italians, concluded an armistice*

with the Austrians on 11 July at Villofranca. By this agreement it was
proposed that an Italian Confederation should be formed under the presi-
dency of the Pope. Lombardy was ceded to Napoleon (and by him to
Victor Emmanuel). Venetia, for which the Italians had hoped, was to
remain Austrian but be part of the Confederation. The Grand Duke of
Tuscany and the Duke of Modena, who had fled, were to return. The Pope
was to be pressed to introduce certain reforms in his State. The terms of
this agreement were confirmed on 10 November at the Treaty of Zurich.]

32 [F.O. 43/71]   *Rome, 14 July 1859*
No. 88
O.R. to Lord J.R.

Cardinal Antonelli told me that considering the conduct of the King
of Sardinia with respect to Bologna and the Legations he did not see
how the Papal Government could do otherwise than break off diplomatic relations with the Piedmontese Government. The King of
Sardinia had declined the dictatorship of the Legations offered to him
by the Bolognese, but he had, nevertheless, sent a Commissioner,
several officers and a body of Piedmontese troops to Bologna. As yet
no explanation of this extraordinary breach of the neutrality of the
Pope's dominions had been given, and a note addressed by His Eminence, on the subject to the Sardinian Chargé d'Affaires had remained
unanswered. Count Della Minerva's passports were ready and he
would have sent them to him forthwith had the Count not assured His
Eminence that Count Cavour's absence from Turin had delayed the
answer to that note.

Another reason for which he had not sent Count Della Minerva his
passports was the receipt of a telegram by the French Ambassador
from the Emperor Napoleon begging the Pope to take no steps against
the King of Sardinia until the arrival of an explanatory letter from His
Imperial Majesty to the Duc de Gramont respecting the policy of
Sardinia in the Legations. It was, however, not likely that any explanation of such proceedings could prove satisfactory to His Holiness and
the total rupture of diplomatic intercourse with Sardinia would shortly
be an 'accomplished fact'.

I enquired of His Eminence whether there was any truth in the report
that the Pope contemplated pronouncing the 'Major Excommunication' against King Victor Emmanuel?

The Cardinal replied that in the hearts of all good and pious Catholics His Majesty was already excommunicated, that the 'Major Excommunication' had not been put in practice since the Middle Ages, not even against Napoleon I and although some persons were favourable to the measure in the present instance he had advised against it. The only spiritual weapon the Pope would employ against the King of Sardinia was the late allocution.

I next told His Eminence that it was very generally believed that the Pope would ask for Spanish or Neapolitan troops to assist him in recovering the Legations.

Cardinal Antonelli assured me this report was unfounded and for obvious reasons: the Pope could not expose his allies, while assisting him, to find themselves at war with Sardinia. The Legations were *de facto* in the power of Sardinia and the deputations sent to offer them to the King had been well received by the French Emperor at headquarters. In consequence it was the intention of His Eminence to address a formal demand to the French Government through the Papal Nuncio at Paris, which would be to this effect:

The Papal Government were preparing measures which would enable them sooner or later to recover the Legations and for this reason the Holy Father desired to be distinctly informed whether, when his troops were about to attack and reconquer the lawful property of the Holy See he should find himself at war with Sardinia and her present ally the Emperor of the French?

A categorical reply from France to this question would enable the Government of the Pope to judge more clearly of the future. Meanwhile, he would send me the formal and official protest addressed to the courts of Europe for communication to my Government, and he begged I would tell Lord John Russell when I wrote to His Lordship that the Papal Government hoped for the friendly assistance of Her Majesty's Government when the question of the frontiers of the Holy See and of the temporal rights of the Pope were discussed before an European Congress.

33 [P.R.O. 30/22/75]   *Rome, 16 July 1859*

Private

O.R. to Lord J.R.

... Your orders shall be strictly attended to and I will write as often

as I can so as to give you full accounts of Roman affairs. Lord Malmesbury told me to write as little as possible, now I will write often and
as copiously as you desire. We know only little here as yet about this
sudden and unexpected peace, but the greatest discontent prevails at the
idea of an Italian Confederation under the presidency of the Pope. At
the Vatican they seem startled and don't know what to make of it. But
we are sure to be quiet so long as the French soldiers are here. When
they retire, God help us!....

34 [F.O. 43/71]   *Rome, 17 July 1859*

No. 89. Secret
O.R. to Lord J.R.

Some days since a letter from the 'Pontifical Antichamber' directed
to *'Signor Odone Russell, Agente Officioso di Sua Majesta Britannica'*
informed me that His Holiness the Pope desired to see me. In consequence I proceeded to the Vatican and was ushered into the presence
of His Holiness by Monsignor Talbot,[1] the *Cameriere* in waiting, who
immediately withdrew and I remained alone with the Pope.

His Holiness welcomed me with his usual benevolence and good
humour. He seemed very gay and spoke with more than customary
frankness, so much so indeed, that I have felt some hesitation as to the
propriety of submitting what passed between us to Your Lordship.
But after mature reflection I think it best you should be in possession
of an accurate and conscientious account of the sentiments of His Holiness in the present important juncture of affairs.

'*Caro mio* Russell,' the Pope said, 'you have been so long at Naples
that I was already thinking of sending after you to bring you back.
We do not like you to leave us, and the more so as I have heard you
were attached to the mission of Mr Elliot who is a son of Lord Minto,[2]
and if he entertains the same political views as his father he is a dangerous man to the peace of Italy. Now I knew Lord Minto here and
altho' he may be a very good man, I do not think him a man of any

---

[1] Monsignor George Talbot, an English convert, *pendant près de vingt ans le
confident et le favori le plus intime de Pie IX, auquel it était lui-même attaché corps
et âme* (Aubert: *Le Pontificat de Pie IX*, p. 284).

[2] Earl Minto (1782-1859) had gone on a special mission to Italy in 1847, one
of the objects of which had been to persuade the reactionary rulers to introduce
reforms.

capacity and his doctrines were calculated to bring on the ruin of Italy.'

I replied, 'I cannot agree with your Holiness for I consider Lord Minto to be a very clever man, whose honest, sound and liberal views, had they been listened to, might have prevented the crisis which is now convulsing Italy.'

The Pope said, 'Well of course you belong to his party, but *poveri noi*, what is to become of us with your uncle and Lord Palmerston at the head of affairs in England? They have always sympathized with the turbulent spirits of Italy and their accession to power will greatly increase the hopes of the Piedmontese party. Indeed I well know what the English Government want; they want to see the Pope deprived of his temporal power.'

I replied, 'Again I regret to find Your Holiness so entirely mistaken with respect to the policy of England. We derive great happiness from our free institutions and we would be glad to see our neighbours in Europe as happy and as prosperous as we are, but we have no wish to interfere with the internal concerns of other nations or to give advice, without being asked for it, least of all as a Protestant power would *we* think of interfering, one way or the other, with the Government of Your Holiness.'

The Pope said: 'I do not doubt the good intentions of England, but unfortunately you do not understand this country and your example is dangerous to the Italian minds. Your speeches in Parliament excite them, and you fancy because Constitutional liberties and institutions suit you that they must suit all the world. Now the Italians are a dissatisfied, interfering, turbulent, and intriguing race, they can never learn to govern themselves. It is impossible. Only see how they follow Sardinia in all she tells them to do simply because they love intrigue and revolution, whilst in reality they do not know what they want. A hotheaded people like the Italians require a firm and just Government to guide and take care of them and Italy might have continued tranquil and contented had not the ambition of Sardinia led her to revolutionize the whole country. The Grand Duke of Tuscany, for instance, is an excellent and just man and nevertheless at the instigation of Piedmont he was turned out of the country and for no earthly purpose. I suppose you have read Monsieur About's book about Rome? Well, all he says is untrue, pure calumny and it would be easy for me to have it all refuted, but he is not really worthy of such an honor. His book, I see, has been translated into English and I have no doubt it will be much read and believed in England. Such books and our refugees mislead your countrymen and I often wonder at the language your statesmen hold about us in the Houses of Parliament. I always read their speeches. Lord Palmerston, Lord John Russell and Mr Gladstone do not know us, but when I think how kindly and hospitably Lord Granville was received at Rome last winter and then read the extraordinary speech he made last February about us I think the gout he suffered from here must have gone to his head when he reached England and I wonder how Her Majesty the Queen could send for him to form a Government![1] Then again Mr Gladstone, who allowed himself to be deceived about the Neapolitan prisoners. He does not know us and Italy. And Mr Cobden, I knew him in 1847, he is always in favor of peace and he must be very fond of animals for when he came here from Spain he wanted me to write to that country and put a stop to bullfights, a very good man, but I do not know his views about Italy. And Lord Stratford de Redcliffe, do you think he will be employed again? He seemed so anxious to get a place. Mr Disraeli was my friend, I regret him. But tell me, "*caro mio* Russell", if you are a prophet, how all this war and fuss is to end?'

I replied, 'Your Holiness has better claims to being a prophet than I have, and I sincerely hope all this may end well for Italy, but as regards the present and the past I must again say that I deeply regret to see Your Holiness misconceive the honest views and sincere sympathies of the statesmen you have named, for the welfare of Italy. They would like to see Italy independent, prosperous, progressing and contented and able to take care of herself without foreign troops. Your Holiness has done me the honor to speak freely and openly with me. Permit me to do the same, and ask Your Holiness what England must think when she sees the temporal power of Your Holiness imposed upon three millions of people by the constant presence of French and Austrian bayonets? And when after ten years of occupation the Austrians withdraw suddenly, there is at once an insurrection throughout the country; and if the French were to leave Rome it is generally acknowledged that a revolution would compel Your Holiness to seek refuge in some foreign country. At the same time when the troops of Your Holiness

---

[1] On 3 February, in answer to the Queen's speech, Lord Granville had said, 'the entire lay population of the Papal Dominions are, almost to a man, hostile to the government under which they now live,' and more in the same vein. *Hansard*.

are employed as at Perugia, the Government is too weak to control them, they pillage and murder and instead of investigating their conduct, the excesses committed by them are publicly rewarded!'

The Pope smiled, paused, took a pinch of snuff and then said good humouredly:

'Although I am not a prophet I know one thing; this war will be followed by an European Congress and a Congress about Italian affairs is even worse for us than war. There will be changes in Italy, but mark my words, whatever those changes are, the Pope will ever be the Pope, whether he dwells in the Vatican or lives concealed in the Catacombs.

Lastly I will give you some advice. Prepare and take care of yourselves in England for I am quite certain the French Emperor intends sooner or later to attack you.'

The Pope then beckoned to me to approach and making the sign of the Cross he gave me his blessing in Latin, then with both his hands he took one of mine, pressed it and said with great warmth: 'Be our friend in the hour of need!'

[*Endorsed in pencil by Lord John:* Very curious.]

35 [F.O. 43/71]   *Rome, 18 July 1859*

No. 91

O.R. to Lord J.R.

The Pope has declined to give an opinion one way or the other with respect to the telegraphic announcement that His Holiness was to have the honorary Presidency of an Italian Confederation. All things considered, however, it may be conjectured that the Vatican is not unfavorable to the idea, the more so as it seems to have been sanctioned by Austria. The appointment of Baron Hübner as Austrian Ambassador to the Court of Rome and the departure of Count Colloredo to attend a Congress on Italian affairs at Zurich has also given great satisfaction to the Papal authorities. They look forward with ardent hope to a return of Austrian influence in the Papal States and Baron Hubner's appointment is hailed as the first step to that end.

On the other hand the announcement of peace has created a most painful impression on the minds of the Roman population. They think their cause abandoned and betrayed by France and the old sympathies for England which had vanished since the beginning of the year have returned with extraordinary suddenness. They loathe Austria and the temporal dominion of the Pope, and were it not for the vigilant care of the French military authorities the Pope and his Government would not last 24 hours in Rome.

36 [F.O. 43/71]   *Rome, 22 July 1859*

No. 94
O.R. to Lord J.R.

The Cardinal Secretary of State, who is also Minister of War, told me yesterday that at the beginning of the year the Papal army numbered about 8000 men: 2500 had deserted to join the Piedmontese army so that the army of His Holiness was now reduced to about 5500 men. His Eminence was organizing new regiments and recruitment was carried on with great energy so as to bring the Papal army to its normal condition which was 14,000 men.

This was to be effected by the end of the year and Cardinal Antonelli assured me that he sincerely hoped he could by that time insist on the withdrawal of the French army of occupation from Rome and Civita Vecchia — a measure he now had more than ever at heart. The French Government had obtained from King Victor Emmanuel the recall of Marquis d'Azeglio from Bologna. The next step, he hoped, would be the withdrawal of the Piedmontese troops from the Legations, and once they were free, His Eminence forsaw no difficulty in attacking and reconquering those rebellious provinces. At the request of the Emperor he had given up the idea of breaking off diplomatic relations with Sardinia and in return he expected France would keep order on this side of the Appenines while the Papal troops effected the submission of the Legations.

Cardinal Antonelli seemed very sanguine as to the success of these measures. Perhaps His Eminence is not aware that the Emperors' positive orders to General Goyon at the commencement of the war were to maintain order in and about Rome, but in no way to interfere in any other portion of the Papal States.

I have also positive information that secret negotiations have been pending between the Court of Rome and the Spanish Government by which the latter have promised a contingent to the Pope whenever His Holiness should ask for assistance.

Your Lordship may be certain that cost what it will the Pope is firmly determined not to lose the Legations.

37 [F.O. 43/71]   *Rome, 22 July 1859*

No. 97
O.R. to Lord J.R.

Monsieur de Menneval, an officer on the Emperor Napoleon's staff, arrived here some days ago with letters from His Imperial Majesty to the Pope and to the Duc de Gramont. Great secrecy is observed with regard to the contents of these letters, and many exaggerated rumours are afloat respecting the advice the Emperor is supposed to give the Pope. I am, however, in a position to submit to your Lordship an outline of this letter to His Holiness.

The Emperor assures the Pope in the warmest terms of his dutiful devotion to the Holy Father and of his anxious desire to promote the cause of religion and to improve the condition of Italy. He thinks this can best be done by a system of administrative reform throughout the country and the establishment of an Italian Confederation under the honorary Presidency of the Pope. He is prepared under certain conditions to see the Dukes of Tuscany and Modena reinstated, but he makes no mention of the Duchess of Parma. He wishes the Legations to have a separate government with a free and independent administration of their own internal affairs, but to remain under the nominal '*Suzeraineté*' of the Pope, and as regards Rome and the rest of the Papal States he wishes his plan of reform of the 1st of July 1857 to be adopted by His Holiness. . . .

The Pope is favorable to the idea of an Italian Confederation, and is not disinclined to certain mild administrative reforms in his own States, but whether he is prepared to adopt the whole of the French plan is, I conceive, very doubtful.

Anything tending to weaken his authority in the Legations, he will not listen to, and ever since the events of 1848 the idea of a secular government is distasteful to him in the highest degree.

Cardinal Antonelli is still all powerful with the Pope but he may find it difficult to maintain his position at the head of the Government if His Holiness enters upon the pathway of Reform. Whether rightly or wrongly, His Eminence is hated by all classes of the population, by the Roman aristocracy and by the entire Clergy who accuse him of being the author of almost every evil under the sun. His dismissal from office would be the most popular act with which the Pope could inaugurate his Presidency over confederated Italy, but the Cardinal is fond of power and may possibly make concessions to the spirit of the age. Indeed, yesterday, I perceived the first symptoms of it when His Eminence assured me that the idea of an Italian Confederation filled him with 'national pride and enthusiasm'.

Meanwhile public report mentions Cardinal de Pietro, who was nine years Papal Nuncio at Lisbon, as the most likely successor to Cardinal Antonelli.

38   [F.O. 43/71]   *Rome, 27 July 1859*

No. 98
O.R. to Lord J.R.

With reference to my dispatch No. 97 of the 22nd instant respecting the letter addressed by the Emperor Napoleon to the Pope, recommending certain reforms in the administration of the Papal States I learn that His Holiness has declared his readiness to adopt in part the advice of His Imperial Majesty, that he has no objection to an increase of laymen in his Government but that he never can admit the principle of a separate selfworking administration for the Legations. . . .

To this the Emperor has replied that the Legations are *de facto* no longer under the rule of His Holiness. To govern them he must have them, and the army of the Pope, about six thousand strong, is not in a condition to meet the army of volunteers at present in the Legations which amounts to ten thousand men. Having driven the Austrians out of Italy it is the duty of France towards Europe to withdraw her army of occupation from Rome and His Holiness had better therefore at once adopt a system of government which will enable him to maintain himself in his own country.

The Pope has replied that the French army may go when it pleases for he has made an arrangement with Spain which will place thirty thousand men at his disposal whenever he wants them.

The negotiations between the two governments have progressed thus far, but since the Cardinal Secretary of State is considered to be the chief impediment to the concessions expected from the Pope it is probable that the French Embassy here will use all its influence to get His Eminence removed from office, and the Roman population who are in a state of great and hopeless dejection look forward with doubt and anxiety to the downfall of Cardinal Antonelli.

39 [F.O. 43/71]   *Rome, 30 July 1859*

No. 99
O.R. to Lord J.R.

Lt Colonel de Menneval returned to Paris some days ago with a letter from the Pope and dispatches from the Duc de Gramont to the Emperor. The Pope's letter was sealed, but the Ambassador's dispatches reported the favorable manner in which His Holiness had received the Emperor's advice respecting reforms in the Papal States.

Yesterday morning the Ambassador received a telegram from Count Walewsky to the effect 'that Mr de Menneval had arrived in Paris, the Ambassador's report was satisfactory but the sealed letter was a mockery (*dérisoire*), and that Monsr de Gramont was to proceed to Paris without delay.'

This telegram not being in cypher was at once known all over Rome and created the greatest sensation. It was said that the Pope evidently did not seriously intend to reform his administration, while on the other hand the Emperor still took compassion on the Romans and wished to do something for them, and the Cardinal Secretary of State was accused of having persuaded the Pope to retract what he had promised in the first instance to the French Ambassador.

At 7 o'clock yesterday evening the Duc de Gramont had an audience of the Pope which the French authorities declare to have been satisfactory, and tomorrow morning the Ambassador leaves Rome for Paris.

All is in suspense and it is difficult for the moment to give Your Lordship any more detailed account of present circumstances or future prospects in regard to French policy in Rome.

40 [P.R.O. 30/22/75]   *Rome, 30 July 1859*

Private
O.R. to Lord J.R.

Pharaoh's heart is hardened! Pio Nono regrets the concessions he made to the wonders performed by the Emperor in the land of Lombardy and if he can succeed in promising and *procrastinating* at present, he will do nothing in the future for the three millions of individuals doomed to be his slaves. As in the case of Napoleon I the Pope will prove an insurmountable difficulty to the policy of Napoleon III and I am more than ever convinced that no satisfactory settlement of Italian affairs is possible so long as the temporal power of the Pope is tolerated in the Peninsula. However, there it is, and there it will remain, until some day or other it will die a victim to its own internal corruption. . . .

41 [F.O. 43/71]   *Rome, 30 July 1859*

No. 100
O.R. to Lord J.R.

It is almost impossible to give Your Lordship any correct account of what is doing in the Legations. . . . Cardinal Antonelli told me yesterday that a large body of volunteers was marching upon Pesaro, that in case of attack the Papal troops could only act on the defensive at present, but that he had every reason to hope that disorder and disunion in the rebel camp would come to the assistance of the Papal cause. . . .

The progress of recruitment for the Papal army was unfortunately rather slow, but the Pope received many letters from Ireland offering him any amount of soldiers for his army. He foresaw, however, two reasons against organizing Irish regiments: *1st* the cheapness of wine in Italy which might prove fatal to the Irishman, and, *2ndly* the laws of England which might involve the Pope in difficulties with Her Majesty's Government if he accepted the offers made by these Irish volunteers. In consequence he had no intention of accepting them.

I replied that his judgement of the difficulties was perfectly correct.

42 [F.O. 43/72]   *Rome, 5 September 1859*

No. 101
O.R. to Lord J.R.

. . . The members of the Diplomatic Body are all in the country, the new Austrian Ambassador, Baron de Bach, is expected by the end of the month and the Duc de Gramont who returned to Rome some days since has only once been able to see the Pope in consequence of the protracted illness of His Holiness.

The Sovereign Pontiff, I am sorry to inform your Lordship, was tormented by the itching of a small pimple on his left leg, and, as Cardinal Antonelli tells me, could not be prevailed upon to leave it alone. His Holiness scratched it until it became a large sore or ulcer. The intense heat acting upon the wound brought on inflammation and the Holy Father was thereby compelled to remain in a reclining position for a fortnight, on the first instant fever set in, and His Holiness has not been able to leave his bed since. This morning, however, I am happy to say, His Holiness was a good deal better.

Cardinal Antonelli, who received me with the utmost kindness and cordiality this morning told me that nothing could be done so long as the Pope was unable to attend to business. . . .

43 [F.O. 43/72]   *Rome, 10 September 1859*

No. 105. Confidential
O.R. to Lord J.R.

I told Cardinal Antonelli that the affairs of Italy were far too much disturbed to allow H.M. Government to give any final opinion in respect to them without communication with the other Great Powers of Europe; that our habits and opinions induced us to think the people of any country were the best judges of the institutions under which they lived and that the readiness of the people of Romagna to rise, when the weight of foreign troops was removed, afforded to our minds a presumption against the administration of the Papal Legates, and I ended by saying that although in judging of a foreign country H.M. Government might be entirely mistaken it appeared to them that a layman appointed by the Pope from the most able, enlightened and popular of his lay subjects as governor for life of the Legations and Marches with Representative Councils would seem to H.M. Government to afford the best chances of maintaining the Pope's temporal sovereignty.

Cardinal Antonelli replied that he always expected the Great Powers would think a general congress necessary for the settlement of Italian affairs. The present crisis had been created by Sardinia and nourished by the armed interference of France. A general congress appeared almost unavoidable. No doubt the people of England were the best judges of their own institutions, but that could not with equal truth be said of the Italians. They were an impulsive, hot blooded, licentious, improvident race who loved disorder for disorder's sake, and were ever ready to sacrifice interest to amusement. They were children who required guidance. Without going any further back in history, he thought the troubles of 1848 sufficiently proved his assertion.

As to the rising in Romagna, it could not be regarded as the expression of the will of the majority by anyone who really knew that country. It was effected by Piedmontese agents who had for some years past been constantly at work in Northern and Central Italy revolutionizing the country in the interest of Sardinia. The great majority hated the present state of things, he had every proof that they only desired to see the Pope's authority established there as speedily as possible and the whole population would join the Papal troops the moment they advanced to rescue the people from their Sardinian oppressors. Unfortunately at present this could not be done without danger to the rest of the Papal States. The Pope's army was not strong enough yet to leave a garrison in the Marches while advancing into the Legations and the Tuscans taking advantage of the absence of Papal troops on the Tuscan frontier might feel tempted to march through the Papal States towards the Kingdom of Naples and revolutionize the people of the Abruzzi, as His Eminence has reason to fear was the desire of generals Fanti and Garibaldi.

With respect to the plan for a lay governor of the Legations and Marches with Representative Councils already proposed to the Pope by the French Government, he could only repeat what His Holiness has said to the Duc de Gramont, namely that he would never admit of a separate government for any portion of his states. . . .

Cardinal Antonelli wound up by telling me with considerable satisfaction that the Duc de Gramont having communicated the Pope's answer to the French Government, His Excellency had at once received instructions from Paris to assure His Holiness that the Emperor of the French had merely submitted the above plan to the Pope's consideration at the instigation of the Bolognese without attaching any importance whatever to it himself, and His Majesty therefore begged the subject might be dropped.

44 [F.O. 43/72]   *Rome, 10 September 1859*

No. 106
O.R. to Lord J.R.

I have had several conversations with the Duc de Gramont on the subject of the administration of the temporal sovereignty of the Pope. His Excellency is convinced of the urgent necessity for administrative reform in the Pope's dominions and as Your Lordship is already aware has submitted a plan to that effect to His Holiness on the part of the Emperor of the French.

Until the Pope's health is sufficiently restored to admit of his attending to business no answer will be returned to the French propositions and the Duc has declined any argumentative or speculative conversation with Cardinal Antonelli on the subject until the Pope is prepared to return a positive and definitive answer to the French Government....

45 [P.R.O. 30/22/75] *Rome, 16 September 1859*

Private
O.R. to Lord J.R.

The following is an account of the impression I gathered on my journey to Rome via Paris, Turin and Florence. I found Lord Cowley, who received me in the kindest possible manner, full of confidence in the Emperor Napoleon and in his desire to maintain the alliance with England. He did not think His Majesty had any fixed plan or policy in regard to Italy but he believed in his sincere desire to re-establish the power of the Dukes. This desire Lord Cowley evidently shares for he believes it is the only way to secure *Constitutionalism* to Central Italy, and he seems to place implicit trust in the good faith of the Dukes (towards their people) who will feel themselves bound by the conditions of their return. I humbly beg leave to differ from Lord Cowley in this point. He forgets that those Dukes are imbued with Austrian convictions and look upon constitutional principles and popular representation as wicked and the work of the Devil. In Austria, religion and politics are closely connected and their religion condemns all manner of liberty. In their opinion inconvenient oaths are not binding, the Pope can suspend an oath, as for instance he proposed to do for the late King of Naples in 1848. Besides which the Pope will always be glad to lend a hand towards the destruction of political liberty in Italy. I can see no guarantee for the future liberty, progress and peace of Central Italy in the return of those Austrian Archdukes. I was surprized to observe how great was Lord Cowley's belief and trust in the Emperor. On what it is founded, I know not! Lord Cowley and many other persons inimical to Italian freedom, such as Prince Metternich, the Duc de Gramont and others, told me the Emperor Napoleon had been sadly disappointed in the Italians, who had proved to be helpless cowards, for he had taken 20,000 rifles to Italy to arm the volunteers and had only been able to dispose of 7,000. To this I naturally observed that it struck me the Italians had done far better than join the general massacre for they had expressed their wishes in a calm dignified manner and had acted with praiseworthy moderation, and good sense without violence or blood- shed. Indeed I did not see that they could answer His Majesty's procla- mation at Milan calling upon them to be soldiers and then free citizens etc., etc., more effectively, for when H.M. had ceased to fight they had proclaimed and almost established their freedom. In Paris I saw the friend of my youth Prince Richard Metternich, the new Austrian Ambassador, and I found him, like Lord Cowley, strangely under the influence of the French Emperor, who had succeeded in persuading him that no one regretted more than he did having undertaken the Italian war, that he had been deceived and led into it by '*des intrigants*' and he now wished to set himself right again by a close alliance with Austria etc., etc., and so we may expect to see the tenderest of alliances blossom out of the Zurich Conferences between France and Austria. In France I met everywhere with a desire for war with England and all the Austrians I have spoken to cannot conceal their burning wish to see us soundly beaten and humiliated by France. It was really quite re- freshing to get back into Piedmont where I met again with a whole- some breeze of freedom and good sense. Sir James Hudson[1] was most anxious and ready to assist me. He thinks the National and constitu- tional cause so closely connected in Italy that they can no longer be separated. They will henceforward go hand in hand whether Count Cavour be alive or dead, who did not instill his own views into his countrymen but adapted his policy to the wishes of the nation etc. Everywhere in Italy I found a deep distrust of France and her Emperor, French influence declining and English sympathies reviving. In Tus- cany I met with a degree of unity and public spirit that quite amazed me. Surely these Italians have not yet sunk so low as is the fashion to believe. Their desire for annexation to Piedmont is solely dictated by a national desire to strengthen the latter against Austrian encroachment and they feel the necessity of sacrificing their Tuscan nationality to the welfare of united Italy. Is not this the result of true patriotism coupled to the knowledge of what they really wish and want? Corbett is very active and conscientious and his reports must be both correct and useful, besides which he is a liberal minded man, and ready to listen

[1] English Minister to Sardinia, strongly in favour of the cause of Italian Nationalism.

to every side of a question before he condemns anyone, as Scarlett and Lord Normanby[1] were wont to do. There are plenty of French agents in Central Italy working the interests of Prince Napoleon. Who they are sent by I know not; the Italians seem to think they are Mazzinians in disguise. In Rome I found the Pope ill and under the influence of profound irritation against the Emperor Napoleon and his Ambassador the Duc de Gramont and firmly determined to turn a deaf ear to the voice of freedom, reform and moderation. Both His Holiness and Cardinal Antonelli persist in wishing to repeat the butcheries of Perugia in the Legations and an army is being rapidly gathered together for that purpose. The French Emperor threatens to withdraw his army early next spring, not before, and so long as French bayonets maintain order in Rome it is difficult to speak positively of the public spirit and true aspirations of the Romans, but I have little doubt that once left to themselves they would soon compel the Pope to secularize his Government or fly to more orthodox climes. There is an awful absence of true religious feeling in the Pope's dominions which sooner or later (I speak of centuries) must turn into open hostility against the Roman Catholic Church. At present it amounts to indifference, but in years to come, the want of some pure religion will again be felt by the Romans as it was by the heathens in the early centuries of Christianity. . . .

46 [F.O. 43/72]   *Rome, 16 September 1859*

No. 107
O.R. to Lord J.R.

Cardinal Antonelli informed me this morning that he was well satisfied with the news he received from the Legations, the people were getting daily more disgusted with the terrorism exercised over them by the agents of Sardinia and heartily wished to return to their lawful sovereign, the Pope. . . .

The Papal army was daily increasing and the Swiss soldiers enlisted on their way from Naples to the north seemed animated with the most excellent military spirit. All now tended to make His Eminence hope that the Papal army would ere long be able to commence operations in the Legations, and the more so as the article published in the *Moniteur* of the 9th instant respecting the Duchies, which had been telegraphed by Count Walewsky to Gramont for communication to

[1] English Minister to Tuscany, 1854 to 1858.

the Roman authorities, left no doubt in his mind that an alliance between France and Austria would soon bring the 'Italian Complication' to a satisfactory solution.

I have never seen Cardinal Antonelli so cheerful or more hopeful of success, and all I see and hear impresses me with a painful belief that all hope of a peaceful and conciliatory policy in regard to the Legations is at an end and that the success of the butcheries of Perugia has instilled a military ardour into His Holiness the Pope and His Eminence Cardinal Antonelli, which appears to me as ill-judged and misplaced as it is revengeful and bloodthirsty.

47 [F.O. 43/72]   Rome, 28 September 1859
No. 108
O.R. to Lord J.R.

Baron Bach, the new Austrian Ambassador, arrived in Rome on the 24th. The Austrian embassy, while expressing a strong conviction in favor of administrative reforms in the Papal States, has not joined the French embassy in recommending the Emperor Napoleon's plan of reform to the Pope's government. The Austrian embassy seems to consider a representative form of government as totally unsuited to the States of the Church and any experiment that way as dangerous to their internal peace. They think the written laws of the Papal States (unfortunately existing on paper only) good and calculated to ensure the happiness of the Pope's subjects, if only the Papal authorities could be prevailed upon to adhere to them and put them in practice. The best thing, therefore, the Pope could do for the welfare of his subjects in the estimation of the Austrian embassy in Rome, would be to insist on the practical and sincere application of the existing laws and to abolish the gross abuses which have gradually and clandestinely taken their place in the administration of the Holy See.

48 [F.O. 43/72]   Rome, 1 October 1859
No. 112
O.R. to Lord J.R.

... The Pope still holds out a prospect of reforming the abuses of his temporal power and the French ambassador still awaits some substantial proof of the Pope's earnest to adopt the plan of reforms recommended

5. Cardinal Antonelli

6. Lord Malmesbury

to His Holiness by his imperial master. Yet no edict or public document has appeared to calm the anxious expectations of the Romans. It would almost appear as if the Pope wished to drive a bargain with the devoted son of the Roman Catholic Church. 'Give me back my lost Legations and in return I will proclaim to the world that I have adopted your plan for reforming my temporal government.' But the French Emperor has declined to interfere in the Legations and the Pope withholds the desired reforms.

Meanwhile it has been decided to send the Sardinian Chargé d'Affaires, Count della Minerva, his passports and to break off all diplomatic relations with Piedmont in consequence of King Victor Emmanuel's speech to the Bolognese deputation.

Great alarm has been felt at the Vatican at the presence of General Garibaldi at Rimini. At the suggestion of Cardinal Antonelli, who expects General Garibaldi will invade the Marches and extend his operations along the Abruzzi, the Neapolitan Government are to send troops to the frontiers of the Papal States, and although General Kalbermatten is in favor of attacking Garibaldi at once from Pesaro, the Cardinal has directed him to act on the defensive only. The troops at present under General Kalbermatten's orders amount to about 8000 men. . . .

49 [F.O. 43/72]   *Rome, 4 October 1859*

No. 114
O.R. to Lord J.R.

. . . The Sardinian Chargé d'Affaires received a note on the 2nd instant enclosing his passports. The principal cause assigned for this long expected rupture is the speech of the Sardinian King to the deputation offering him the Legations. The event is much talked of and among some of the higher dignitaries of the church it is not very generally approved.

On the other hand the National or Piedmontese party think it the best thing that could happen to them. They say the odium of the rupture will fall upon the Pope's government and strengthen the sympathies for King Victor Emmanuel who will reap the advantage from it of having his hands free to deal with ecclesiastical matters without reference to the Pope, a circumstance which is expected to be very popular in central and northern Italy. . . .

D

50 [F.O. 43/72]   *Rome, 8 October 1859*

No. 115
O.R. to Lord J.R.

For the last three days hundreds of young Romans have been, from
morning till night, pouring into the house of the Sardinian Chargé
d'Affaires to leave their cards and thereby to express their adhesion to
the policy of Sardinia. French gendarmes are stationed along the street
to keep order and to advise everyone who stands still for a moment to
go home quietly and without delay.

General Goyon having announced his intention to suppress any
public demonstration, as Your Lordship will see from the enclosed
order of the day, the members of the National party chose the only way
left them to give vent to their feelings and sympathies without coming
into contact with the gallant general or the Roman police.

Count Della Minerva who leaves tomorrow has been much hurt by
the assertion contained in General Goyon's order of the day that he
had asked for this puerile demonstration and has protested against the
insinuation in a letter to the Duc de Gramont.

The French Ambassador is still anxiously awaiting the decisions of
the Pope in regard to reforms, while His Holiness has sought refuge at
Castel Gandolfo, there to consider the propriety of reforming his
temporal government or not. . . .

51 [F.O. 43/72]   *Rome, 10 October 1859*

No. 116
O.R. to Lord J.R.

. . . For some days past, as Your Lordship is already aware, some
thousand visiting cards had been left at the Sardinian Legation, which
were brought there, according to the report of the French police, by
about three hundred individuals in the pay of Sardinia. These cards
which have greatly occupied the attention of the French authorities
were printed on red, green and white pasteboard (the National colours)
and did not all give the name of the bearer. They were addressed to the
Sardinian representative and bore the mysterious letters P.V., meaning
according to some, '*Prospero Viaggio*' but according to others '*Pro
Voto*'. Be that as it may the stationer of the Piazza Colonna who
printed them having declared his inability to give up the name of the

conspirators by whom they were ordered has been thrown into prison, there to expiate his crime.

Sunday afternoon was fixed by Count della Minerva for his departure, and, in consequence, the leaders of the liberal party were summoned by the Roman police on Saturday night and told that they should be held responsible for the events of the following day.

Other precautionary measures were taken by the Roman authorities but they were superfluous for General de Goyon had declared that no demonstration should take place in Rome and that the Holy Father should not be insulted in the presence of a French army, and it must be stated that the gallant General was true to his word.

As the sun rose upon the eventful day he was already himself giving orders for the disposal of his forces and ready to face any danger. Soldiers and gendarmes were stationed at every street in the Campo Marzo, the vias Ripetta, Corso, Babuino, Borgognona, Condotti, della Croce etc., etc., the piazzas di Spagna and del Popolo as well as the Pincian Hill and a part of the road to Florence as far as Ponte Mole were lined with pickets of French soldiers to whom *ball cartridges* had been served out on the previous night. Policemen in plain clothes watched the Post Office and the coffee houses, gendarmes the doors of private houses. In short Rome bore a most martial appearance and certainly the French force under arms might have resisted the attack of an Austrian army.

Meanwhile the Romans in Sunday attire, numbering about twenty thousand, flocked into the streets, and if we are to believe the reports of the police, had actually bought up all the flowers to be had in Rome for the purpose of throwing them to the Sardinian Chargé d'Affaires on his passage down the Corso to Piazza del Popolo. It is even believed that some of these conspirators had concealed national flags in their houses to wave them out of the windows as a last farewell to the parting representative of the only liberal government in Italy, and many carried audacity so far as to contemplate taking off their hats as he drove past them!

It is difficult to say how much of these evil machinations might have been carried into effect had not a providential circumstance afforded General de Goyon a most complete triumph over the enemies of public peace and order. One of the windows of the General's apartment in the Palazzo Ruspoli commanded an entire view of the Via Borgognona in which the Sardinian Chargé d'Affaires lived. Here the General took up his post of observation and gave his orders out of the window in the hour of danger. Before even his secret agents had reported the departure of the Postchaise from the Post Office stables, he saw it with his own eyes halt before the enemies' door and at once ordered one of his aide-de-camps with a body guard of gendarmes on horseback to surround it and escort Count della Minerva outside the walls of Rome, at the same time directing him to pass through the Piazza di Spagna and Babuino so as to thwart the hopes and dangerous intentions of the expectant population in the Corso. Unfortunately Count della Minerva would not submit to this military escort and stoutly declined leaving Rome if not allowed the undivided enjoyment of his Postchaise. So General de Goyon from his window found himself compelled to withdraw the order, much to the irreverent amusement of the gaping mob.

At last the dreaded moment of danger to Popedom arrived and the Representative of Sardinia was seen to step into his carriage. Preceded by the General's aide-de-camp in a one horse cab, he drove through the Piazza de Spagna and along the Babuino, the French soldiers barring the passage of every street behind him so as to prevent the people from rushing after his carriage. The Porta del Popolo had been carefully closed all day and was now opened to let him pass and closed again until all danger was over. At Ponte Mole he was joined by an escort of gendarmes who, relieved at every station, accompanied him to the Tuscan frontier.

I deeply regret to state that notwithstanding the energy, wisdom and good taste with which order was manifested in Rome on this day so fraught with danger, the French official police reports announce that eight individuals could not be prevented from taking off their hats to the Postchaise, five within the walls of Rome and three on the highroad to Florence.

The conspirators now revenge themselves on General de Goyon by saying that their sole object having been to display the sympathies Piedmont commands in Rome, they can only thank the General for having proved to the world how formidable their numbers must be since it required such a tremendous military force to keep them from throwing flowers or waving their hats to the Sardinian representative.

Perhaps General de Goyon, inspired by the *Moniteur*, may be thought to have waged war for '*an idea*' only, but certain it is that he displayed great energy and that the honors of the day devolve on him alone, for the French Ambassador was not in Rome, being compelled

by an unforeseen *complication* to attend to two dinners, one at 2 p.m.
with the Pope at Albano and the other at his villa at Frascati at 5 p.m.

The moral to be deduced from these events is, that Popedom owes
the continuance of its temporal existence, in the present age, to the
protecting power of foreign bayonets and that the Romans if they were
allowed the free expression of their political instincts would follow the
example of their brethren in the north and vote for annexation to
Piedmont.

52 [F.O. 43/72]   *Rome, 15 October 1859*

No. 117

O.R. to Lord J.R.

At last the Government of the Pope has returned a straightforward and
positive answer to the French Government in regard to the plan for
reforms recommended by them to His Holiness.

The Duc de Gramont addressed a private letter to Cardinal Antonelli stating that he could no longer accept the policy of procrastination
which had been practised upon him ever since his return from Paris
and that his Imperial Master desired to know whether his well-meant
advice would be followed or not.

Cardinal Antonelli replied that until the Legations returned to their
lawful sovereign the Pope, nothing could be done in Rome or the rest
of the Papal States in the shape of administrative reforms and His
Eminence requests the French Government to have patience until the
States of the Church are in their normal condition when the subject of
reforms can again be taken into serious consideration by His Holiness.

This answer was certainly not expected by the French Ambassador
whose position and influence, backed by a French army of occupation
certainly seemed to warrant the complete success of French policy in
Rome. Nevertheless, after ten years of undivided power in Rome, the
Emperor Napoleon must acknowledge that his policy has been defeated
by Pius IX, whose agents are busily employed in rousing the religious
indignation of the people of France through the powerful influence of
their Bishops and Priests.

So complete is the discomfiture of French influence that the Emperor
has even failed in obtaining the nomination of certain French Bishops
to Cardinalships from the Pope, and the efforts of the French Embassy
to bring about the dismissal of Cardinal Antonelli and the appointment

of Cardinal De Pietro who was expected to be more docile have fallen hopelessly to the ground.

The Pope is said to complain in very unmeasured language of the 'treachery' of the Emperor Napoleon who wrote him letters full of promise and devotion during the war and who will not assist him now to get back his lost Legations. On the other hand he seems to expect much from Austria whose present Ambassador, Baron de Bach was one of the most active promoters of the Concordat, and although the new Protestant laws in Austria have caused distress and anguish of mind at the Vatican, yet it is hoped and believed that they are merely intended to pacify provisionally the dissatisfied spirits of the Empire and like the famous 'Motu Proprio' of Portici are not intended ever to be carried out.

53 [P.R.O. 30/22/75]   *Rome, 15 October 1859*

Private
O.R. to Lord J.R.

Our Dips. in Rome are somewhat at a loss to find something to write about. The Papal Government devotes itself to the *dolce far niente* while the Pope is giving small dinners to his admirers at Castel Gandolfo. Gramont lives in the country shooting skylarks which he calls *gibier*. Bach conceals himself from the eyes of the world and has spoken to no other Dip but myself. Your speech at Aberdeen has made him profoundly unhappy, he thinks you are an *Idealogue*, but the excesses committed at Parma the other day have somewhat cheered him up, he thinks they may lead to a wholesome reaction which he ardently desires. The smaller herd of Dips know nothing and consequently look mysterious. Your speech, which has been read *with enthusiasm* by the Liberals, has greatly distressed the governing powers. I think it has done real good here in every way, for our policy has been much misrepresented *by our Allies* as well as by the Austrians and it was very desirable to know what you really thought and intended. General Goyon made a fool of himself when the Sardinian Chargé d'Affaires left Rome and it is expected the Emperor will blow him up about it. Gramont who hates Goyon quite as much as Goyon hates Gramont is secretly delighted. The Papal authorities are annoyed at Goyon's proceedings and now that they are taking an anti-French line do not even take the trouble to conceal it. They are dead tired of French protection and sigh for Austrian influence and supremacy. . . .

54 [F.O. 43/72]   *Rome, 22 October 1859*

No. 118
O.R. to Lord J.R.

. . . The Duc de Gramont's letter although marked 'Private' is in
reality a very able State Document, in which the well meant advice of
the Emperor, the urgent necessity for reforms and the danger incurred
if not attended to by His Holiness, are set forth with manly frankness,
benevolent honesty, and unanswerable logic.

The effect produced by this letter on the Papal Government was to
place a written assurance in the Ambassador's hands that the Emperor's
advice was accepted. The Cardinal's answer was courteous: 'The Pope,'
he said, 'would not hesitate to promulgate the reforms already agreed
upon in principle with the French Government the moment the Legations again acknowledged his lawful sovereignty over them, not before' — and in conclusion His Eminence authorized in the name of the
Pope the communication of the contents of his letter, through the
agency of the French Government, to the European Powers, England
being specified in the first instance.

55 [F.O. 43/72]   *Rome, 18 November 1859*

No. 121
O.R. to Lord J.R.

The Neapolitan troops at present stationed on the frontiers of the
Pope's dominions are estimated by the Papal authorities at nearly
twenty thousand men.

A secret agreement is said to exist between the Pope and the King of
Naples dated on 14 October last by which the latter is at liberty to enter
the Papal territory and attack General Garibaldi whenever he sees fit,
but it is not thought likely that either the King or Garibaldi will take
the initiative.

The accounts received from Pesaro respecting the Papal troops are
not very favorable. They are reported to be an ill disciplined medley of
foreign adventurers, who inspire their officers with little confidence and
throw terror among the inhabitants.

The population of the Marches is more than ever desirous of joining
their northern brethren and shaking off the temporal authority of the
Pope and should Garibaldi invade those Provinces he will meet with

friends and sympathy everywhere and be greeted as the liberator of a people who have already groaned too long under the degrading rule of Popedom.

56 [F.O. 43/72]   *Rome, 18 November 1859*

No. 122

O.R. to Lord J.R.

The French ambassador has at last obtained an *official* note from the Cardinal Secretary of State in which His Eminence states that the Pope abides by his declaration that he will 'promulgate the reforms discussed between Cardinal Antonelli and the Duc de Gramont whenever order shall have been reestablished in the States of the Church'.

The Duke obtained this note with considerable difficulty from the Cardinal who resorted to various subterfuges before he would consent to write it.

The French Ambassador attaches importance to this *official* declaration which he thinks will be communicated from Paris to the European Powers and will give general satisfaction. But I cannot for my part see anything else in it than a variation of the numerous pledges already so often given by the Papal Government to the Catholic Powers, and it remains to be seen how much longer the Emperor will consent to be befooled by the Pope.

57 [P.R.O. 30/22/75]   *Rome, 19 November 1859*

Private

O.R. to Lord J.R.

. . . Thanks for your advice about my Minerva dispatch. I will be serious in future. . . .

The Austrian and French Embassies in Rome have become more ultramontane, despotic and anti-Italian than ever. At present the chief characteristics of the French authorities here are: hatred and contempt of Piedmont in particular and the Italians in general and loyal indignation at the struggle for freedom in Central Italy. The Austrian Embassy shares these views most heartily, pretends to be perfectly passive, but Monsieur Bach secretly supports Antonelli against French policy whenever administrative reforms are recommended. Forgetful of the war and the famous Milan proclamation, they throw the whole blame of the present disturbed state of Italy upon the pernicious example of England and the encouragement given to revolutionary principles by Her Majesty's Government. Piedmont is but an instrument in the hands of England, England is to be blamed for everything, England is the curse of Europe! Your presence at the F.O. in these conjunctures is looked upon as particularly unfortunate. If it were not for you, order might speedily be restored in Italy. France and Austria might come to an understanding, but you are sure to urge your fantastic notions that Princes have duties as well as rights, that it is wrong to break one's oath, that justice should be done and other wild theories. . . .

On the other hand the liberal party look to you and to you alone, as their last hope. No one cares for the reforms recommended by Gramont for they are believed to be utterly inadequate to the real wants of the Papal States and no one believes they will ever be executed. The priests and their friends think them unnecessary and dangerous, and the people care for nothing but the total abolition of the Pope's temporal sovereignty. While Gramont pompously proclaimed the success of his negotiation and announced the immediate publication of the reforms recommended by France, the Papal Govt. managed to give him nothing but a promise that reforms should be promulgated when order had been reestablished in the States of the Church. The policy of France has hereby met with a severe check at the hands of the Pope, and Gramont's position has become exceedingly disagreeable in Rome. In consequence he has received orders from Paris to drop all further allusions to reforms and the Romagna and to soothe and pacify the Pope by conciliatory and reactionary language so that the Emperor and the Holy Father may meet as good friends when the Great Powers go into Congress. In vain Gramont endeavours to persuade his colleagues that His Majesty is highly satisfied with the *triumph* of his policy in Rome. It is but too evident that the Emperor has not yet proved a match for the Pope. As regards Pio Nono he is as you know a Pope of the Middle Ages. The late events have rendered him exceedingly irritable, he has taken a profound dislike to the French Emperor, to his policy and to his Ambassador. He takes every opportunity of abusing His Majesty, calls him a traitor and a liar because he does not fulfil promises made in his private letters during the war and accuses him of secretly encouraging and supporting the revolution in the Legations and in Central Italy. Antonelli with whom I have had some curious and confidential conversations, has confirmed these impressions and the priests immediately surrounding the Pope hold exactly the same language. Antonelli says that the Emperor of the French will soon prove to be a European nuisance, that he has already succeeded in frightening all the Great Powers, and that he will gradually carry out a thoroughly Napoleonic policy in Italy. His first intention was to place young Murat on the throne of Naples, but the Tuscan movement which was unexpected made him relinquish this idea and he thought it easier to place Prince Napoleon on the throne of Etruria, then finding Central Italy against him, he left her to herself, and is again turning his attention to the chances of a Bonaparte at Naples. The great object he has in view at the approaching Congress is the abrogation of the Treaties of 1815 and in due course of time the revival of the title of King of Rome for the Prince Imperial, a prospect which seems greatly to annoy His Eminence. Antonelli and the *Papalini* dwell fondly on the invasion of England by the Emperor, partly because they would like to see us in a scrape from a religious point of view, and partly because they think from a political point of view that we are more likely in the end to upset him than any other Power. Neither the Pope nor his ministers believe in the withdrawal of the French garrison and the feeling of personal security this conviction gives them precludes all hope of improvement in the temporal administration of Rome, the consequence of which must be an everlasting occupation by foreign troops. In obedience to your instructions I have supported and shall continue to support Gramont and the French, that is, of course, so far as Whiggism and conscience will allow of my doing so. Antonelli will probably go himself to Congress.

58   [F.O. 43/72]   *Rome, 23 November 1859*

No. 128
O.R. to Lord J.R.

Observing in Count Walewsky's 'Circular' of the 5th instant to the Diplomatic Agents of the French Emperor the following passage:

Déja le Gouvernement de l'Empereur a l'assurance que le Saint Père n'attend qu'un moment opportun pour faire connâitre les réformes dont il est décidé à doter ses Etats et qui auront pour effet, en assurant au pays une administration généralement laique, de lui donner les garanties d'une meilleure distribution de la justice et d'un côntrole de la gestion des finances au moyen d'une assemblée élective.

I thought it desirable to avail myself of so favourable an opportunity to seek a conversation with Cardinal Antonelli on the subject of Reforms, which being based upon the official language of the French Government as published in the *Moniteur* might tend to acquaint Your Lordship with the precise nature of the intentions of the Court of Rome and with the true relations at present existing between the Emperor Napoleon and Pope Pius IX.

I therefore called on Cardinal Antonelli and having read to him the above mentioned extract, I said that it gave me great satisfaction as I felt sure that the measures therein alluded to would tend to establish those relations of mutual confidence between the Pope and his subjects which past events had rent asunder.

The Cardinal replied: 'The language of Count Walewsky's "Circular" is not sufficiently precise and may easily lead to misinterpretation and I have found it necessary to say so to the French Ambassador. As I have told you before, the Pope has always wished to grant Reforms to his subjects. His attempts to do so in 1848 met with ingratitude, and if his last concessions embodied in the *"Motu proprio"* of Gaeta have not been carried out, if many excellent measures are still on paper and not in practice, it is simply owing to the prelonged occupation of Rome and the States of the Church by foreign troops whose presence practically paralized the action of the Papal Government. We ardently desire the withdrawal of foreign troops from the Pope's Dominions and we hope ere long to have an army strong enough to maintain order without foreign aid. The enemies of order and of the Papal authority are few in number, they are chiefly composed of Piedmontese agents and an army of 18,000 men will be sufficient for all home purposes. When order has been re-established, when the Legations are again under the Pope's sovereignty, when the army of occupation has been withdrawn, the Holy Father will be free to carry out the Reforms he has already granted to his subjects, Reforms which have been promulgated in principle in the *"Motu proprio"* of Gaeta.'

I here observed to His Eminence that Count Walewsky mentioned an assurance received by the Government of the Emperor from the Pope that the Reforms His Holiness intended to confer upon his States would assure a generally lay government to the country, a measure which did not appear to me to be contained in the '*Motu Proprio*' of Gaeta.

'The language of the "Circular" is too vague,' the Cardinal repeated, 'let us endeavour to analize what is meant by a lay government. The lay element preponderates in the Papal administration, for it is not the cloth that constitutes the priest, and many of the officials and Monsignore's you see in priestly attire, when attending to their duties, have wives and children at home and are laymen like yourself. There are not above one hundred priests in the Papal Government, and only the other day the Holy Father observed to me that if he were on his deathbed not one single member of his Cabinet could administer the holy Sacrament to him. Persons unacquainted with the nature of our Government fancy that every individual who wears black, purple or red stockings must be a priest. This is an absurd mistake. Our lay officials and many of our lawyers wear the gown because it is the uniform of our Court and when the French Government call upon us to secularize the Papal administration, they are simply making war upon our uniform. The French Emperor might just as well advize Her Majesty's Government to abolish the wigs of your judges. We have sometimes appointed men who did not wear the robes as Governors of our Provinces but the population have generally petitioned for priests as they are preferred to laymen.'

Cardinal Antonelli then continued to cite a large number of Monsignore's who were married or could marry and who were laymen since they had not taken the vows and ended by repeating his assurance that the lay element largely preponderated in the Papal administration.

I next enquired in what manner the better distribution of justice mentioned by Count Walewsky was to be accomplished?

'The French Government,' Cardinal Antonelli replied, 'call upon us to adopt the Code Napoléon. This is a question which very naturally affects our national vanity. Did not Rome, did not our ancestors found the laws which govern the civilized world and is not the Code Napoléon simply the result of the Laws of Justinian? Rome still has men enough fully equal to the task of revising and codifying our laws, we need not ask foreigners to return to us what we gave them in days gone by and it is our intention to appoint a commission for the revision of our laws and if possible for their codification. . . .'

'What is going to be done,' I said, 'to ensure the better control over the financial department to which Count Walewsky makes allusion and in what manner is the elective assembly to be constituted?'

The Cardinal said: 'We have already as you know a financial *Consulta* elected by the municipalities of the Roman States, which is about to assemble in a few days. Its labours will probably last three months. I do not think we can have a better control over our finances than that afforded by this *Consulta*, elected on an entirely popular basis and I foresee little need to change its constitution. Within the last twenty years the expenses of the Papal administration have increased nearly fivefold and will continue to increase the more we add to our administrative establishment. The Pope would really not be justified if he saddled the country with a senate composed of 40 members as proposed by the Government of the Emperor. 20 would be sufficient for all our wants and would cost the country just half. Our states are small and we cannot burden them with an expenditure which our income could never meet. All these details are so simple, so rational and easy to comprehend that our plenipotentiary at the projected Congress can find no difficulty in explaining them to the representatives of the Great Powers should he be called upon to do so.'

I enquired what result His Eminence expected from the deliberations of the proposed congress and what success he predicted to the plan of an Italian Confederation suggested at Villa Franca by the French Emperor.

'We can only regret,' the Cardinal Secretary of State replied, 'that a congress should have become necessary from the effects of the late war. The French Emperor having gone so far might have gone a little further and settled some of the difficulties raised by his armed intervention in favor of Piedmont, instead of declarations in the *Moniteur*. By his moral influence alone and without firing a shot, he might have brought the Dukes back to their states and restored the Legations to the Pope, but for some unknown reason he prefers a congress, and we have at present no other course open to us than to go and plead our cause before the great European Powers who cannot fail to appreciate its justice. As to the Italian Confederation, it is a beautiful idea and no man has studied the question more than myself. It originated in 1846 with the Pope and in obedience to His Holiness's orders I made it a subject of special investigation. The advantage of a Customs Union with uniform measured coin and a net of railways would be incalculable for Italy, but the obstacle to a Confederation must be sought in the impossibility to establish a sincere union between the people and their governments, and how can Naples, Tuscany and Austria live on terms of friendship with Piedmont, who is ever at work to set the People against their Rulers? And again, how is Austria to behave as a

member of both the Italian and Germanic Confederations, should the
two powers ever go to war with each other? The Pope as head of the
Church can never declare war against any power and though member
of a Confederation can never be otherwise than neutral, and if as head
of the Italian Confederation his political powers are to be extended, he
must insist on many changes in the internal arrangements of the States
under his protectorate, for his new temporal power cannot admit of his
forgetting his spiritual duties. In short the difficulties appear almost
insurmountable but His Holiness is ready to accept the Protectorate if
the Confederation can be organized.'

59 [P.R.O. 30/22/111]   *F.O. 26 November 1859*

Private
Lord J.R. to O.R.

Your accounts of Roman affairs are very interesting. I don't expect
that the Pope and Cardinal Antonelli will ever have their darling
Austrians back again, so they must do as well as they can with the
French, and if that does not suit them, they must put up with
Garibaldi. . . .

60 [F.O. 43/72]   *Rome, 5 December 1859*

No. 130
O.R. to Lord J.R.

The French Ambassador, on the part of his Government, communicated this morning to the Cardinal Secretary of State the official invitation to the proposed congress. The place of meeting is not mentioned
but the time is fixed for 5th January next.

   The Cardinal accepted the invitation in the name of the Pope. The
Austrian Ambassador has received no instructions as yet on this subject
but His Excellency expects a messenger from Vienna on Friday next
who is probably the bearer of the invitation. There is reason to think
that Austria has been secretly advizing the Pope to adopt the following
course of action in regard to the congress.

   1st. To repudiate all attempts on the part of the Great Powers to
interfere with the administration of the Holy See and to claim for the

Italian States which are to form the projected Confederation the sole right of settling their internal affairs themselves.

2ndly. That the Pope should secretly and in his own name invite the lesser Catholick Powers, Spain, Portugal and Naples, to support the policy of Austria as well as the limits she desires to put to the deliberations of congress.

Cardinal Antonelli, I am informed, has already spoken confidentially in this sense to the representatives of Naples, Spain and Portugal. It is generally expected that His Eminence will proceed himself to the congress.

61 [F.O. 43/72]   *Rome, 10 December 1859*

No. 138. Most Confidential
O.R. to Lord J.R.

Ever since the Pope's illness in September last, His Holiness has been subject to great irritability, which is vented indiscriminately before those who approach his presence in acrimonious invectives against the Emperor Napoleon and his Ambassador in Rome.

It would perhaps be more reverent to pass in silence over the temporal infirmities of the Spiritual Father of the Roman Church, were they not likely at the present juncture to lead to serious political consequences, consequences which become daily more apparent as they cast ridicule on the French authority in Rome and must evoke opposition at Paris, and as everyone here must view with regret the schism they engender between the Vatican and the French Embassy. Not only is the excellent advice offered by France to the Court of Rome entirely disregarded, but it suffices for the Duc de Gramont to express a wish and he is sure to see it thwarted, so that His Excellency's position has become painful and difficult in the extreme.

A few instances are hereby submitted for Your Lordship's information.

The French Government enjoy the privilege of nominating a French Cardinal. Monsieur de Gramont has used every exertion to obtain the Papal sanction to the Imperial choice, but the Pope has indefinitely postponed the convocation of a Consistory to avoid the appearance of fulfilling the Emperor's wishes.

Mr Santangeli, a Roman gentleman, has been imprisoned without apparent cause and is detained, nobody knows where, without trial or hearing. Monsr de Gramont and General de Goyon at the solicitation of Mr Santangeli's friends and relations have done their utmost to obtain justice for the unfortunate gentleman, but, as it now appears, without a chance of success. . . .

Monsignor Sapeto, a missionary in the service of France, was sent by the Emperor on a religious mission to Abyssinia and passed through Rome to solicit the Pope's blessing, but the Holy Father refused to grant it and forbade in angry language the acceptance of a religious mission from the 'unworthy' elder son of the Church. Monsignor Sapeto, however, who is a Sardinian and who enjoys a high reputation as a missionary and a Christian, although he will not bow to the new dogma of the Immaculate Conception, has set out on his holy errand without the Pope's blessing.

To every Frenchman who obtains an audience of the Pope His Holiness makes it a point to give solemn assurances that he is bound by no promise of reforms to the Emperor Napoleon, and since the publication of an article to that effect in the official Roman Gazette at the Pope's own desire, the interviews between the French Ambassador and His Holiness have become so unsatisfactory that His Excellency has resolved to avoid them altogether.

The Pope had determined to send Cardinal Antonelli to the Congress at Paris, but since the Emperor Napoleon has intimated through his Ambassador that no Plenipotentiary could be more acceptable than His Eminence, the Sovereign Pontiff has changed his mind.

I cease, not to weary Your Lordship with details. But before concluding I must still cite a curious instance of Papal policy. When it had been resolved at the Vatican to stimulate the spirits of the Catholic world in favor of the Pope's Temporal Power, a learned Benedictine, who enjoys His Holiness's full confidence, was selected for the task and sent in plain clothes to organize the Episcopal Pastorals which have lately stirred the faithful in various parts of Europe. On his return he had an audience of the Pope and I happened to meet him soon after he had left the Vatican. In the course of a long conversation I enquired what would be the result if the measures thus taken failed to bring the Romagna back to their lawful sovereign.

'I will tell you,' replied the Benedictine, 'the Pope is fully determined if the Emperor Napoleon does not restore the Legations to him to use the power he has over the French clergy, and France will soon be made too hot to hold His Majesty much longer.'

62 [P.R.O. 30/22/111] *F.O. 12 December 1859*

Private

Lord J.R. to O.R.

Things are approaching their end, tho' very slowly. The Emperor N. says he will ask the Pope to consent to the separation of Romagna, and I imagine will take no denial. That is to say, if the Pope refuses, as he is sure to do, Buoncompagni and Farini will rule without his Papal benediction. The French troops will stay till the settlement of the affairs of Italy. How long this may be no one can tell. But the Emperor has by this means a powerful club in his hand.

Gramont does not seem to represent the opinions of his master — perhaps he only represents Walewski which is quite a different thing. Walewski is bent upon having an Austrian Archduke at Florence, which he will hardly accomplish.

In the meantime you have only to listen and report. I have a great respect for the virtues of Pius IX and hope he may be left undisturbed at Rome, but he must not seek to govern three millions of people for their perpetual misery, even though the pride of the Church may require it. In fact Italy has outgrown the Papacy. The Pope would be a saint at Madrid, Valencia or Majorca. In Italy he is only an anachronism.

63 [F.O. 43/72] *Rome, 15 December 1859*

No. 140. Confidential

O.R. to Lord J.R.

The Sovereign Pontiff had determined not to send Cardinal Antonelli to the Congress at Paris and two other Plenipotentiaries had been already selected when Baron de Bach informed His Holiness that the Austrian Government particularly desired that Cardinal Antonelli should be present at the proposed deliberations and that Count de Rechberg[1] would not go himself if His Eminence were not appointed to represent the States of the Church.

Knowing the reluctance which the Cardinal Secretary of State entertains to being present at the Congress of Paris, the Pope convened the Sacred Council which in this case was represented by eight Cardinals, viz. De Pietro, Patrizi, Altieri, Ferretti, De la Genga, Santucci, Marini and Mertel and consulted them as to whom they thought he ought to send to Paris. Their Eminences unanimously agreed that no one could

[1] Austrian Foreign Secretary.

better represent the interests of the Holy See than Cardinal Antonelli, and they suggested that the Under-Secretary of State, Monsignor Berardi, should take his place so long as the Congress lasted.

In consequence the Pope has instructed His Eminence to proceed to Paris and at present his departure is fixed for the 28th inst. There can be no doubt that Cardinal Antonelli does not appreciate the honor thus conferred upon him.

64 [F.O. 43/72]   *Rome, 17 December 1859*

No. 143
O.R. to Lord J.R.

The financial *Consulta* met a few days since as I had the honor to state in my previous correspondence. The constitution of this body is already known to Your Lordship. Established in 1850 after the abrogation of the constitution of 1848 it is partly composed of members selected by the Pope from candidates proposed by the provincial municipalities and partly of members named directly by His Holiness, who reserves an unlimited control and appoints a Cardinal to preside over its deliberations.

Cardinal Savelli, the President, and the Members of the *Consulta* proceeded according to usage to the Vatican to do homage to the Pope and to announce the opening of their deliberations, which as Your Lordship is aware are always secret. The Cardinal President had been furnished with a short complimentary speech, which, also according to usage, is previously prepared at the Vatican and submitted for the approval of His Holiness and when delivered is intended to represent a free expression of opinion on the part of the *Consulta*. But Cardinal Savelli, who is a Corsican, did not confine himself to the speech the Pope was prepared to listen to and said that it was his painful duty to call His Holiness's attention to the fact that the object of the *Consulta* had been defeated, that financial operations had been undertaken by the Government and money spent without consulting the *Consulta*. If this continued they were a useless body of men and their present meeting was without object, for how could they thus be held answerable for the financial embarrassments which he thought would soon threaten the Papal Government? Who was to furnish the immense sums expended on an army, the organization of which never seemed to advance, who was answerable for the mysterious sale of the railway concessions and how could the unlimited sale of *Consolidati* be justified, when the fatal effect of such a measure had only the other day been witnessed at Vienna?

Cardinal Savelli would perhaps have said more, had not the Pope after interrupting him three times commanded him to be silent and broken up the audience with angry words and angry gestures while the *Consulta* withdrew in confusion.

The next morning Cardinal Savelli was dismissed by the Pope, and Cardinal Altieri appointed President of the Financial *Consulta* in his stead, the members of which were advized to beg the Pope's pardon for what had occurred. This they accordingly did with every assurance that they had not been prepared for their President's indiscretion and that they feared his mind must have suffered from the effects of an illness he labored under last year.

This incident has created considerable sensation in Rome as also the dismissal of Cardinal Tosti from the governorship of the prison of San Michele for disrespectful language to Cardinal Antonelli whom he most insolently reminded of his alleged relationship to the notorious brigand of Sonino, Gasparoni.

65 [F.O. 43/72]   *Rome, 20 December 1859*

No. 144. Secret
O.R. to Lord J.R.

While the recent policy of France in Italy has estranged the Pope and the Roman hierarchy from her, the natural alliance and old friendship between the Holy See and Austria has been gradually and secretly rekindled. The sudden flight of the Austrian garrison from the Legations in June last, which caused the loss of those provinces, has been forgiven and Austria atones for her late involuntary neglect of the Papal power by furnishing men to the Papal army, and advice through her Ambassador, whose connection with the introduction of the Concordat gives him unusual claims to the confidence of the Church.

Although the negotiations between the Palace of Venice and the Vatican are veiled in mystery, although Baron Bach affects an appearance of complete inaction, yet those negotiations have not been so well concealed as to render all knowledge of them unattainable and the following outline of the preconcerted policy of Austria and Rome at the Congress of Paris will in the main, I think, be found correct.

Austria's first object is to regain her lost influence in Italy. The Pope shares this desire, and Austria proposes a joint plan of action, to which His Holiness is to invite the co-operation of Naples, Spain and Portugal, while Austria assures that she is already certain of Russia and Sweden.

The invitation to Congress bears a twofold object: the Pacification and the Independence of Italy. These ends Austria proposes to obtain through the restoration of the Duchies and the Romagna to their legitimate rulers, and through the establishment of an Italian Confederation as settled at Villa Franca.

In consequence it is proposed that the Roman and Austrian Plenipotentiaries shall proceed in the following order:

1. To insist on confining the deliberations of Congress to the basis established by the Treaty of Zurich.
2. To insist on the recognition of the Sovereign Rights of the Dukes and of the Pope.
3. To insist, as a consequence, that the Representatives of the Dukes shall immediately be called to assist at the Congress.
4. The revolutionary governments of central Italy to be informed of this decision and if it be not at once submitted to by them, that the Congress shall consult on the best measures of coercion.
5. That an Italian Confederation be established in principle by the Congress, on the plan of the German Confederation, but that all conditions and details be referred to a subsequent Congress or Conference which, being exclusively composed of the Italian Powers shall alone have the right to discuss and settle their affairs.
6. The future welfare of Italy being only possible through the re-establishment of order and respect to sacred and legitimate authority, the Congress shall proclaim the absolute independence of every state as regards its internal administration.
7. The establishment of a Confederation on the above basis once confirmed, the task of the Congress will be accomplished and all further details relating to the Confederation shall be made over to the subsequent conferences composed of the Italian states exclusively.
8. In the event of these points not being carried the Papal Plenipotentiary shall protest and withdraw.

The Papal Government and their Austrian advizers are however most sanguine of success and the chief points for the consideration of the subsequent Conference have been settled as follows:

1. To insist on the thorough independence of each separate state from foreign influence or interference.

2. To keep in view the principles best calculated to secure the autonomy of each member of the Confederation unimpaired.

3. To limit the discussions in these subsequent conferences exclusively to the mode of establishing the Confederation and above all to exclude all allusion to reforms or concessions, these latter being declared matters solely of local interest.

4. To limit the connection of the Holy See with the Confederation to a Customs Union and an uniform system of money, weights and measures.

5. To propose Bologna as the seat of the Federal Government.

6. The Naval and Military organization to be uniform and the numbers of forces of each state to be regulated by the Federal Government.

7. The recruitment of the federal army to be in the proportion of one per cent of the population.

8. The commanders of the garrisons of Ancona and Civita Vecchia to be appointed by the Pope and changed every six months.

9. In the case of invasion all the states to unite for defence, not so, however, if internal order be disturbed. In this case Sardinia would be bound to intervene solely in Western Tuscany and in Parma, Venetia in the Eastern Provinces of the Holy See and in Modena, and Naples in the Western Provinces of the Holy See and in Southern Tuscany.

10. In the event of war, the Pope would place his votes at the disposal of any other member of the Confederation he would be pleased to select.

11. The number of votes in the Federal Government to be allotted as follows: The Pope 3, Sardinia 3, Naples 3, Venetia 2, Tuscany 2, Parma 1, Modena 1, Total 15.

These are the essential points of the Austro-Papal agreement which contains in all 34 articles. But a remarkable secret article is appended to the Draft of Instructions, which runs as follows: 'In the event of the Conference not agreeing to the continuance of the present form of each separate government and advizing the adoption of a uniform system, the Plenipotentiaries are to vote for the form of government at present established in France, in which case Piedmont shall be called upon to modify and restrain her present institutions and make them similar to those of France and of the other Italian states forming the Confederation.'

Such, My Lord, is the substance of the cunning policy which Austria and Rome propose to advocate at the Congress, and which is calculated

to place the fate of the Italian People once more into their hands and at
their mercy.

I refrain from all comment, for Your Lordship is best able to feel the
importance of this scheme, and to judge of its chances of success at the
Congress of Paris.

66 [F.O. 43/72]   *Rome, 28 December 1859*

No. 147
O.R. to Lord J.R.

At the time of the first victories of Napoleon and Victor Emmanuel
over the Austrians in Lombardy, the Romans determined to present
two swords of honor to their Majesties as a token of gratitude for the
anticipated liberation of Italy. Although the subscription was limited
to a franc a head, a large sum was immediately gathered and the execution of the swords was entrusted to the eminent artist and jeweller
Castellani. They are now completed and pronounced by all competent
judges to be works of rare beauty and irreproachable taste, and Prince
Gabrieli, who is connected by family ties with the Bonapartes, has been
chosen to convey them to Paris and Turin and to present them to their
Majesties in the name of the people of Rome.

Before starting, Prince Gabrieli, having applied for his passports,
thought it best to adopt the most open course and called on the
Cardinal Secretary of State to communicate the object of his journey.
Cardinal Antonelli, however, refused the passports, declaring in the
name of the Government that the presentation of these swords by the
subjects of the Pope would be considered as a hostile demonstration by
His Holiness.

67 [F.O. 43/72]   *Rome, 30 December 1859*

No. 148
O.R. to Lord J.R.

Cardinal Wiseman has arrived in Rome and taken up his quarters
at the English College. His Eminence has been met here by Bishops
Errington, Ullathorne, Roskell, Monsignor Searle and Dr Juin, Bishop
of Brisbane in New South Wales. Other English and Irish Bishops are

expected and the large concourse of foreign priesthood already assembled in Rome indicates that the Pope is dealing out instructions to his flock intended to meet the difficulties which threaten the Holy See. . . .

The Pastoral Letters dictated from Rome to the Bishops of France have not kindled the religious enthusiasm they were intended to evoke, and the reserved and mysterious policy of the Emperor Napoleon in regard to the Legations has deeply alarmed the Curia Romana. The Catholic Powers in general have disappointed and disheartened Pope Pius IX by not shewing more zeal in effecting the restoration of the Romagna, but on the other hand His Holiness has lately declared himself deeply touched by the sympathy his cause has met with in Ireland.

It had been piously hoped that by directing the Irish priesthood to cause their flocks to give full utterance to their feelings towards England, Her Majesty's Government might have been terrified into taking violent measures of repression against the friends of the Pope, which might have added some new names to the 'Roman Martyrology'.

The failure of all these hopes has caused surprize sorrow and vexation at the Vatican.

The whole aspect of affairs at Rome, the attitude assumed by the entire Hierarchy, tends to prove that the instructions to the Roman clergy in foreign countries now emanating from the Vatican are imbued with a troublesome, spiteful and revolutionary spirit which is scarcely calculated to win the sympathies of foreign governments in favor of the Papacy.

68 [F.O. 43/72]   Rome, 31 December 1859

No. 150
O.R. to Lord J.R.

It would be difficult to convey a correct account to Your Lordship of the immense and general excitement produced in Rome by the publication at Paris of the pamphlet entitled *Le Pape et le Congrès*, the authorship of which is confidently attributed by the Romans to the Emperor Napoleon. . . .

[*In this famous pamphlet, it was more or less assumed that the Pope would have to sacrifice a good deal of his temporal power.*]

69 [F.O. 43/76]   *Rome, 1 January 1860*

No. 1

O.R. to Lord J.R.

General Count de Goyon, attended by his staff, waited this morning
on the Pope to felicitate His Holiness according to usage, on the beginning of a New Year. After the customary homages, the General
added 'that if the garrison of Rome had been denied the advantage of
sharing with their comrades the glories of the late war, they found
consolation in remembering that they had stood in the field in honour
of Catholicism.'

The Pope replied: 'During the past years your visits to me were ever
a subject of consolation, but this year it offers a double consolation to
see the French Army participate in the exceptional position of the Holy
See. Your assurances of devotion and affection are a very great consolation to me. I pray that God will bless the army, that portion stationed
in Rome and all the army in the French Empire. Prostrate before the
Almighty, I pray that He will bless the French nation. I throw myself
at the feet of the God of Mercy and I pray that He will send grace and
light to the Head of the Nation, that he may have the courage to condemn those perverse principles contained in a pamphlet lately published, which are not in harmony with the Church and which are a
monument of hypocrisy and of ignoble contradictions. I hope, nay, I
am sure that the Emperor will receive the light of God to condemn the
principles contained in that pamphlet. I may add that I have in my
possession letters which the Emperor wrote to me and which are in
contradiction with those principles. With this certainty and under this
condition I bless him, I bless his august Consort, the Prince Imperial
and with him the whole Nation.'

The above version of the Pope's speech has been obtained from the
best sources and I need hardly add that this conditional benediction of
the Emperor by the Pope has caused great annoyance to the French
authorities, both civil and military, in Rome.

70 [F.O. 43/76]   *Rome, 4 January 1860*

No. 4

O.R. to Lord J.R.

I called yesterday on the Cardinal Secretary of State in order to learn the opinion of the Papal Government on the pamphlet lately published in Paris, *Le Pape et le Congrès*.

'We know not,' Cardinal Antonelli said, 'and care not who is the author of that pamphlet, but since the government of the Emperor saw fit to take measures against the circulation of the charges of the French Bishops to the clergy of their dioceses and against the Catholic newspapers who were writing in favor of the Pope, I have deemed it my duty to demand of the French Ambassador here, since Count Walewsky was unable to give a satisfactory explanation to our Nuncio at Paris, how the publication of a pamphlet directed against the Pope and the Holy See could have been permitted by the French Government. As to the principles contained in that pamphlet, they are revolutionary and dangerous to the peace of Europe, for where, I ask, is a system to end, which advocates taking the lawful property of one person to give it to another and which totally ignores the principles of equity and of international law. The European powers must feel this quite as much as the government of His Holiness for their rights can be equally questioned any day. The policy of the Pope is unchangeable for it is subject only to the holy laws of religion and the sacred principles of justice. When Napoleon I wanted to carry out the Continental blockade, the Pope resisted him, not because he had any reason to be satisfied with the policy of England but simply because the course Napoleon proposed was unjust, and Pius VII allowed himself to be dragged into exile and kept a prisoner in France but he never swerved from the paths of justice and religion. The Pope does not belong to himself, he belongs to the Catholicks of England, Ireland, France, Germany, Austria, Spain, Portugal, to the Catholicks of all the world and to God whose Vicar he is on Earth. He cannot choose between one course and the other. His line of action lies clearly before him and he cannot mistake it. The Catholicks of the whole world will speak out when he is in distress and will not forsake him, but far be it from us to wish the subjects of foreign Sovereigns to assume a hostile attitude towards their governments, when their Holy Father is threatened with injustice. We infinitely prefer to suffer ourselves than to see others suffer. We can wait and bear with patience and humility the trials God sees fit to send us and like to suffer for others, but come what may we cannot deviate from the course prescribed to us by our Lord Jesus Christ. If the Pope himself were to say to me: prepare the cession of the Romagna, I should resign my charge into his hands and say: Holy Father! Neither you nor

I, nor anyone else has a right to do it. We are in God's hands, let His will, not ours, be done. The Church can never cede any portion of her states, nor indeed can any of those changes in Central Italy be tolerated, the peace of Europe is at an end if we depart from the principles of legitimacy and submit to the reign of terror and brute force, with which we are now threatened. The Pope for one can never give way, he will let himself be persecuted, martyrized, and will die for the glory of God, but mortal man shall not make him give way.'

Cardinal Antonelli spoke with warmth and an appearance of deep conviction, but cheerfully and without signs of alarm or apprehension.

71 [F.O. 43/76]   *Rome, 5 January 1860*

No. 5. Secret
O.R. to Lord J.R.

The pamphlet *Le Pape et le Congrès* has spread joy among the laity and grief among the priesthood of Rome. The somewhat humiliating position which the author of the pamphlet would assign to the Romans has been corrected by their politicians in the following ingenious manner. 'Rome being the seat of the Federal Government,' they say, 'let the *Civis Romanus*, instead of being only a proud idea, become a reality and imply the rights of citizenship throughout the Italian Confederation, so that Roman talent alone may not de debarred from aspiring to serve the country.'

Cardinal Antonelli's views may be said to represent the feelings of the majority of the priesthood in Rome, with regard to the pamphlet. The position of the French Embassy and military authorities has naturally become very awkward and their language reserved. Although the Papal government and their friends are preparing to make a desperate stand against the ideas contained in the pamphlet, the Austrian Ambassador, Baron Bach, thinks it necessary to keep them up to the mark by the following arguments: 'If the Treaty of Villa Franca is not carried out according to the Austrian interpretation (i.e. the restoration of Duchies and Legations), a most dangerous example will be given to the Revolutionists in Austria. The misfortunes of Austria must necessarily reflect upon the Holy See. The Pope will be left entirely at the mercy of France *"et cantabit Gallus in ecclesia Petri"*. The only power that can endanger the position of the Emperor Napoleon in France is the Pope through the French clergy. The only motives that actuate the Emperor Napoleon are those of private interest. Therefore let the Pope put forward all his power and influence to turn the private interests of the Emperor in favor of the Pope.' In what manner this power is to be exercised in France has not yet been decided, but some of the schemes discussed illustrate the helplessness of Pius IX and his advizers.

The Pope wanted to excommunicate the French Emperor, but Cardinal Antonelli opposed the extravagant plan, saying there was no ground to justify so strong a measure. Then it was suggested by Cardinal De Pietro that the Pope should ask for a Neapolitan man of war, sail for Marseilles, proceed in triumph to Paris, and there admonish the rebellious Emperor to repent and humble himself before the Church, and if this could not be done, that Cardinal Antonelli, arrived with the full powers of Legate *a latere*, should proceed on a similar mission to France. It was next proposed that all means should be employed to get up an effectual counter-revolution in the interest of the Pope and of the Grand Dukes in Central Italy. Finally it was hoped that if the Roman Catholick members of Parliament would contribute their influence towards bringing about a change of her Majesty's present advizers, a Conservative government might be found more favorable to Austrian or Conservative interests in Italy.

I will not weary Your Lordship any further with these idle schemes, suffice it to say that at present the Papacy is in a helpless and desponding condition.

72 [F.O. 43/76]   *Rome, 7 January 1860*

No. 7

O.R. to Lord J.R.

At a moment when Cardinal Antonelli, who for the last ten years has swayed the temporal power of the Papacy, is about to take his seat in the Councils of Europe, I have thought that a short biographical notice of His Eminence might not be unwelcome to Her Majesty's representatives at the Congress of Paris.

Domenico Antonelli, the Cardinal's father was a native of Sonino, a village in the province of Frosinone, who acquired by his intelligent services the protection of the Pellegrinis, the oldest and wealthiest family of the district. Benedict Pellegrini, the head of the family, having been captured by brigands in 1807 and only released on a heavy ran-

som, took a natural antipathy to the neighbourhood and withdrew to
Rome, where he settled, confiding the administration of his estates to
the intelligent zeal of Domenico Antonelli, who soon found opportunities of increasing his own fortune by lucky speculation. He had,
some years before, had occasion to assist several dignitaries of the
Church, on their flight from Rome, during the French Wars of
1798-99. Among them was Monsignor Saluzzo, who later became
Cardinal and in 1817 President of the Congregation 'del buon Gov-
erno'. Cardinal Saluzzo, mindful of his past services, conceded to
Domenico Antonelli several lucrative undertakings, and the construction of a road, for which he contracted, was alone said to have increased
his capital by 50 or 60,000 scudi. His increasing business led him to
quit Sonino and settle at Terracina, where his wealth, his intelligence
and the protection he enjoyed in high quarters, secured him the consideration of the whole neighbourhood. Domenico Antonelli had five
sons and three daughters, whom he brought up with severe discipline.
Philip and Gregorio assisted their father in the management of his
extensive business and Giacomo was destined to enter the Church and
put to board with a priest, who being attached to the service of the
Court inhabited the Vatican. Giacomo studied at the *Collegium
Romanum* and was noted for his laborious and regular habits. He
graduated and was provided by his father with the property qualifica-
tion necessary to attain the *Prelatura* and the title of Monsignore. It
has been fixed at 1500 scudi p.a. by a decree of Alexander VII but on
this occasion it was graciously lowered by special favour of the Pope.
Monsignor Antonelli was now qualified to enter the service of the
State and was appointed assessor of the Criminal Court and soon after
promoted delegate of the Province of Orvieto and later delegate of the
Province of Viterbo. The arrest, for political offences, of several of the
principal inhabitants of that town, which had been conducted under
his auspices, made a prolonged residence in the province unpleasant,
and he was removed by the government to the Delegation of Macerata.

At that time two Secretaries of State presided over the Pope's
Government. Cardinal Lambruschini was Secretary for foreign and
Cardinal Mattei for home affairs. The inactivity and indecision of
Monsignor Roberto, Under Secretary to the latter Cardinal, having
excited general complaint, the delegate of Macerata, whose energy had
attracted the attention of the Government, was appointed Under Secretary in his stead. He lodged at the Vatican where his manners and his

intelligence won the favour of Pope Gregory, who soon transacted business with the active Under Secretary in preference to the infirm Cardinal. Cardinal Mattei, in consequence, promoted him to the office of Treasurer General. Gregory XVI died shortly after. Pius IX at the commencement of his Pontificate was unfavourable to the new Treasurer, because he conceded too many advantageous financial transactions to his brother Philippo Antonelli. Numerous and active intrigues were set on foot to displace him. The Pope to remove him from his office, raised him to the dignity of Cardinal and the high praise which Pius IX bestowed on him in the ensuing allocution, excited some surprise at the time. The events of 1848 had rapidly consumed the services of the two Secretaries of State, Cardinals Gizzi and Bofondi, when a government combined of lay and ecclesiastic members was attempted, in which Cardinal Antonelli accepted the offices of Secretary of State and President of the Council at a moment when no member of the Sacred College envied the dignity. The war party, however, objected to an ecclesiastic holding these high offices and Cardinal Antonelli, yielding to a riot, resigned with his colleagues. After the ephemeral governments of Cardinal Orioli and Cardinal Ferretti, Mr Rossi was called to establish a parliamentary government and Cardinal Soglia was named Secretary of State. Monsignor Pallavicini, the Majordomo, having resigned, Cardinal Antonelli was appointed in his stead with title of Prefect of the Apostolic Palaces and the advantage of constant access to the Pope's person. After the flight of the Sovereign Pontiff from Rome, Cardinal Antonelli left the City in disguise and joined the Pope at Gaeta, who there appointed him Pro-Secretary of State, confirming him Secretary of State in 1852 on his return to the Vatican. Since then he has been the object of general, bitter and unceasing hatred. The disappointment and discontent which a long political crisis inevitably breeds are all vented upon him, because respect enshrines the sacred person of the Pontiff. His youth irritates the venerable members of the Sacred College, his low origin annoys the patrician families, his firmness exasperates the liberal party, his commanding position excites the envy of all. Both he and his brother, the governor of the Pontifical Bank, have largely increased their private fortunes. Their success is little calculated to soothe the public envy, and calumnious anecdotes are repeated and readily believed. I may advert to another more remote cause of the Cardinal's unpopularity among the party he serves. There is a large democratic element in the absolute government of the

Church. Here, as in the United States, where speculations on the possible successor of the President, follow immediately upon his election, impatience for place and preferment, hope of personal changes in the government and conjectures on the Pope's health, from a large portion of ecclesiastical conversation. The Pope and the Cardinal are both unusually young, and the small prospects of change irritate the impatience of a host of expectant place hunters. Notwithstanding the general cry for the Secretary of State's removal, the public voice points to no favourite, whom it would fain see in his place, though Cardinal Viale Prela and Cardinal De Pietro are sometimes mentioned as competent to discharge the duties of his important office. The former has been Nuncio at Vienna and is now Legate at Bologna, the second has been Nuncio in Portugal.

Cardinal Antonelli has received the education of a Roman prelate. He has never left Italy and is very slightly acquainted with the affairs of other countries. But great natural parts, laborious habits, a logical mind, insinuating manners, animated conversation and the experience of diplomatic drawing-rooms amply supply the shortcomings of his education. He has complete control over the amiable but weak mind of Pius IX and has now reached the highest honours the Church can bestow, for it is the intention of His Holiness in the event of Cardinal Antonelli proceeding to Paris to name him Legate *a latere*. Three kinds of Legates are known to Roman Canon law: *Legati missi, legati ex officio* (or *nati*) and *legati a latere*. The *legatio a latere* is a temporary dignity only conferred upon extraordinary occasions. The *Legatus a latere* represents the sacred person of the Pope, is preceded in all his movements by a crucifix, and is a direct emanation from the Vicar of Christ, to whom the French clergy will have to do homage in the person of Cardinal Antonelli. I am assured that his dignity will raise him too high to suffer of his taking a personal share in the business of the Congress.

73 [P.R.O. 30/22/75]   *Rome, 7 January 1860*

Private
O.R. to Lord J.R.

... Mr Bowyer, M.P.[1] (who has been very active at the Vatican and

---

[1] George Bowyer (1811-83), Member of Parliament 1852-68, became a Catholic in 1850. On 1 July 1860 he succeeded to a baronetcy.

constantly with the Pope and Antonelli) leaves tomorrow for London His judgement is highly thought of at the Vatican and he goes home with his retaining fee in the shape of the Grand X of St Gregory the Great. Both he and Cardinal Wiseman, I understand, say that Lord Palmerston is a far less fanatical Protestant than you are and if you could be induced to leave his government, the Pope's prospects would improve. They would, however, improve still more could the Irish Members bring about a complete change of government as the Conservatives will be found more favorable to Austria and the restoration of the *status quo* in Italy. So says Mr Bowyer!

74   [F.O. 43/76]   *Rome, 8 January 1860*
No. 8
O.R. to Lord J.R.

The apparent tranquillity which reigns in the kingdom of Naples, the energetic suppression of the mutiny of the Swiss troops and the general principles which actuate the Government of King Francis II have commanded the respect as well as the sympathies of the less fortunate Government of Pope Pius IX. Assurances of friendship and promises of assistance have led His Holiness to believe that he could reckon with certainty in the hour of need on the active interference of his respected neighbour, and now that the attitude assumed by France has induced the Papal Government to appeal to the sympathies of the Catholic world, they have thought it advisable to consult with Naples so as to ascertain the amount of active assistance they could reckon upon. The answer received from the Government of the two Sicilies has proved a deep disappointment to the Sovereign Pontiff for although the assurances of devotion are renewed in the strongest terms the Government of the King declare their inability to afford material assistance or protection to the Pope. 1st. because they foresee the necessity of keeping the whole of their military forces at home, and 2ndly, because they do not feel themselves justified in running the risks of a quarrel with other Powers stronger than themselves.

75   [P.R.O. 30/22/75]   *Rome, 21 January 1860*
Private and secret
O.R. to Lord J.R.

Cardinal Antonelli, who is always very civil and kind to me, lately

asked me after demonstrations of increasing cordiality what I thought
of the Emperor's offer to guarantee the integrity of the remaining
possessions of the Holy See as expressed in his letter to the Pope, published in the *Moniteur*. I replied that I did not doubt His Majesty's good
faith, but that I had no knowledge of the intentions of Her Majesty's
Government on the subject. My own private conviction, however, was
that England would not be a party to any new treaty engagements to
guarantee the possessions of any foreign Sovereign. We thought the
governed were the best judges of the form of government which suited
them and that it was the duty of all Governments to establish relations
of mutual confidence with their subjects. His Eminence observed that
this was '*une politique peu généreuse*' and next enquired what we
thought of the right of asylum, and after beating about the bush for
some time, he asked whether we had any ships of our navy near Civita
Vecchia. I pretended not to understand until he became more explicit
and asked me whether I thought Her Majesty's Government would
afford the Pope personal protection should he require it. I replied that
we granted asylum to everyone who sought it in England and that if a
foreign sovereign applied to us for personal protection on board one of
our ships, we would undoubtedly grant it. His Eminence thanked me
and a few days later he took me aside and told me in a low whisper that
he had communicated our conversation to the Pope, who desired him
to thank me for the '*bonnes dispositions*' I attributed to my Government; that His Holiness was at present well protected by the French
and firmly determined not to quit Rome, but in these critical times it
was difficult to foresee how far the Emperor might go, and it was therefore a comfort to the Holy Father to think that the strong arm of
England would afford him personal protection if things came to the
worst. I said that I would communicate the Pope's message to you, as I
had previously only spoken as a private individual and on my own
responsibility. He again thanked me and begged that what had passed
might remain between us.

76 [F.O. 43/76]   *Rome, 28 January 1860*

No. 16
O.R. to Lord J.R.

Cardinal Patrizi sometime since drew up a loyal address to the Pope to
which he endeavoured to obtain the signatures of the Roman aristoc-

7. Lord John Russell

8. Lord Palmerston. Painting by F. Cruikshank

racy. The families directly connected with the Government signed with some hesitation, whilst the independent members of the nobility all declined doing so, amongst these latter the most prominent were the Caetanis, Dorias, Massimos, Rignanos, Piombinos, Fianos, Soras, Torlonias, Rospigliosis, Gallicanos, Bandini, Giustinianis, Odeschalchis, Gabrielis, Piancianis, Buoncompagnis etc., etc. Amongst those who signed the address were the Borgheses, Orsinis, Anticis, Gavottis, Lavaggis, eight Cavaletti, eight Chigis, six Capranicas, sixty Guardie Nobili etc., etc., in all one hundred and thirty signatures. The address is herewith enclosed in original and translation. The Vatican frowned upon the bold men who had dared to imply by their silence that they were not entirely satisfied with the temporal administration of the Papal States, and the whole affair was talked of until it produced excitement in the streets of Rome.

On Sunday evening 22nd instant, as the French military band was marching down the Corso, they were followed by about three thousand persons who cheered as they passed under General de Goyon's windows, '*Viva La Francia! Viva l'Italia, Viva l'Imperatore e Viva Vittorio Emmanuele!*' They repeated these cries as they walked along, after which they retired peacefully to their homes, where they were soon followed by the Roman police and many of them arrested and thrown into prison, there to remain in all probability for many months, without trial or hearing.

The next morning General Count de Goyon issued the enclosed order of the day and for the remainder of the week strong patrols paraded the streets and at night the theatres were surrounded by French troops to intimidate the disturbers of the public peace, but Rome has remained profoundly quiet ever since. The Roman police attribute this demonstration to Mazzinian agents.

77 [F.O. 43/76]   *Rome, 30 January 1860*

No. 17
O.R. to Lord J.R.

The official part of the *Giornale di Roma* of to-day, announces that Cardinal Wiseman, 'Archbishop of Westminster', has presented two addresses to the Pope, one signed by the Roman Catholic clergy of England and the other by fourteen thousand English Roman Catholics expressive of their devotion to His Holiness.

E

78 [F.O. 43/76]   *Rome, 31 January 1860*

No. 19. Secret
O.R. to Lord J.R.

It is customary for the diplomatic body to congratulate the Pope on the commencement of the New Year, but the British Agent, not being officially accredited and therefore not admitted to share the same privileges, is usually honoured with a private audience of His Holiness some time after the official ceremony has taken place.

The order having been communicated to me I proceeded to the Vatican and thanked the Sovereign Pontiff for thus permitting me to offer him my best wishes for the New Year. The Pope received me in his usual benevolent and cheerful manner and I remained upwards of an hour and a half alone in conversation with His Holiness, who after many kind enquiries about myself seemed anxious to clear up various questions respecting the rebellion in India, the Ionian Islands, the Suez Canal, party feeling in England and Ireland, our laws and administration, our foreign relations and the state of our colonies etc., etc., on all of which I was sorry to find that the Sovereign Pontiff had but very superficial and incorrect views. I endeavoured therefore to the best of my knowledge to answer all the questions put to me by His Holiness and to destroy the erroneous and envenomed impressions he entertains respecting the statesmen and the policy of England, but I fear with very little success. It is right, however, that I should state that the Pope made two exceptions in the course of conversation and spoke in very high terms of Mr Bowyer M.P. and the Marquess of Normanby. In answering His Holiness's enquiries respecting the nature of our administration I dwelt with warmth on the blessings of free institutions and self government which were productive of confidence between the people and their authorities and animated all with loyalty to the Sovereign, but the Pope merely observed that we English were unlike other people and that what suited us would not suit anyone else. . . . His Holiness passed to the Ecclesiastical Titles Bill and the Bishop of Liverpool, observing with a good humoured smile that he did not know whether it was permitted to give the Bishop his title in my presence. Then he spoke of the Volunteer movement in England and expressed a wish to enlist some Irish soldiers for his own army if he could do so without giving annoyance to Her Majesty the Queen. All Europe he thought would want soldiers next spring and he requested me to talk the matter over with Cardinal Antonelli. After a long and desultory conversation His Holiness said with sudden warmth: 'You know the pamphlet *le Pape et le Congrès* and you know my answer to Goyon and all that followed? I do not know whether that pamphlet was written by the Emperor Napoleon or not, but I do know that he has forbidden my Bishops to speak and has taken violent measures against the Catholic newspapers who wrote in favour of the Papacy but he has taken no steps to prevent the extensive circulation of that pamphlet. But the truth is the French Emperor is now entirely in the hands of England. You are making use of him to carry out your policy, but that will not prevent him from turning against you too some day, and I do not think you have many friends in Europe to take your part when that moment comes, for even Austria who was your natural ally has been alienated from you by the hostility you have shown to the Papacy.'

I could not allow these erroneous views to be uttered unnoticed and begging His Holiness to grant me a hearing I explained in plain but respectful language that England had no wish whatever to interfere with the Pope's spiritual power with which she had nothing to do one way or the other. As to his temporal government, we thought in common with the other European powers that it might be greatly improved and exercised in such manner as to establish relations of mutual confidence between the Government and the people and ensure thereby the future prosperity and welfare of the Papal States. We might regret that His Holiness had not followed the excellent advice tendered by France for the improvement of his temporal administration but we never contemplated any direct or indirect interference between himself and his subjects however much we might wish for the prosperity of our fellow creatures.

The Pope, who had listened to me with unusual patience, interrupted me to say: 'It is not in Italy that the seeds of discontent and revolt are to be sought, but in the example of England, the speeches of her public men, and the policy of Lord Palmerston. What advantage England derives from his policy I am unable to comprehend, but I will say one thing in his favour, he is not against the Roman Catholicks, he has no inimical feeling towards them, whilst our bitterest enemy, and I will say so even before you, is Lord John Russell. His dislike to the Papacy and to the Catholic religion is so violent that he seems to tremble all over with hatred ["*trembler de haine*"] when he speaks against us. Why, I do not know, but I do know that it is so.'

The Pope was working himself into one of those passions he has lately been so often subject to, so I interposed:

'Your Holiness has been misled and misinformed by mischievous people. No man has done more for religious liberty in England, no man has more sincerely laboured for the welfare and independence of your co-religionists, and yet no man has met with blacker ingratitude from the Roman Catholics than Lord John Russell.' The Pope said with greater warmth, 'After all it matters little what people say and do, no earthly power can destroy or even harm the Pope. You may all combine with the man who rules at present in France, to change the existing order of things, but the Catholicks of the whole world will speak and God will protect his Vicar on earth. All that is done now is temporary and transitory, and the wicked will be punished, but the Papacy is of God and therefore everlasting.'

His Holiness spoke a good deal more but gradually became quite calm again and having made some further observations full of kindness, good humour and benevolent interest about myself, he told me I might ask to see him whenever I liked and dismissed me with the customary blessing.

I left the Sovereign Pontiff and went according to usage to pay my respects to the Cardinal Secretary of State and report what had passed. After thanking Cardinal Antonelli for the gracious reception I had met with at the hands of the Sovereign Pontiff I told him how much I had regretted to find that His Holiness had conceived such erroneous impressions with regard to the policy of the statesmen of England. Cardinal Antonelli replied: 'The Pope has been naturally much vexed by the late events, but as I was saying only yesterday to His Holiness, England represents a distinct national policy which is different from any other in the world, and her statesmen in carrying out that policy are merely doing their duty to their country as I am doing my duty to the Catholic world to whom the Papacy and the Holy See belong, in carrying out the orders of the Holy Father. In all the dealings I have had with you, your statements have been correct and we have been able to rely on them with perfect confidence, however much we may have disagreed with the policy of England in Italy. The Pope knows that, but what is he to say to the conduct of France towards us, which has been full of promise and deception and the ends of which are at present as mysterious as they are incalculable in the future? Where is all this to end? If France continues to change her rulers and her system of government as constantly as she has done for the last century she will become a living threat to the peace of the world and the other great Powers may possibly one of these days seriously consider the necessity of carrying General Blucher's plan into execution, namely, the division of France among themselves.'

I replied that such a plan appeared to me as wild and as practically impossible as it was morally iniquitous, but Cardinal Antonelli observed to me that we were all in the hands of God and must submit to His will with patience and humility.

79 [F.O. 43/76]   *Rome, 31 January 1860*

No. 20
O.R. to Lord J.R.

As I have more than once had the honour to state to Your Lordship, it is to the newspapers of England, France and Piedmont that we must look as the sole means of obtaining information with regard to what is passing in Italy even at fifty miles distance from Rome. Not only are all letters sent by post opened and read and in many instances delivered unsealed to their addresses, but they are even confiscated or destroyed and the correspondents placed under '*surveillance*' if their contents are unpalatable to the Papal Authorities. Parents anxious about their children, husbands about their wives and friends about each other have occasionally contrived to send authentic accounts about the state of feeling in the provinces to their relatives in Rome, in microscopic writing concealed in the heel of a *Contadino's* boot or in the harness of a *Mercante di Campagna's* horse.

Occasionally also a passing traveller recounts what he has seen and heard, but successive authentic information about the Marches and Umbria is not to be obtained in Rome. I presume your Lordship receives ample reports from Her Majesty's Vice-Consul at Ancona respecting the arrival of Austrian soldiers, the attempted demonstrations of sympathy for the Emperor Napoleon, and the general state of feeling in the Marches, which from all we can learn is tending more and more towards annexation to the neighbouring Romagna or rather to Piedmont, no small difficulty considering the insufficient amount of arms at their command and the daily increasing numbers of the Papal soldiery. From Umbria we learn similar accounts, the desire to join Tuscany is becoming more ardent and is more clearly expressed as the danger of being once more left to the tender mercies of the Papacy threatens those unfortunate subjects of His Holiness. If the wishes of the majority in the provinces can be judged by the wishes of the majority in Rome there is no doubt that, were the free expression of their will allowed them, they would at once proclaim the annexation of the states of the Church to Central Italy under the government of King Victor Emmanuel.

[On 10 February 1860 O.R. wrote to his mother: 'Everybody complains about lost letters and delays. I received yesterday 4 letters all at a time from Atty of the 2nd, 3rd, 4th and 5th. Where they have been all this time I cannot make out, but I doubt not that Eminenz Toni and Nine Pins have been reading them at breakfast with great interest and delight.']

80   [P.R.O. 30/22/75]   Rome, 31 January 1860

Private
O.R. to Lord J.R.

... Cavour's accession to power and the Queen's speech have been severe blows to the Vatican. Both were unexpected here and it will take then some time to recover. I fancy that Gramont in urging them at the Vatican to ask for the Congress so as to facilitate the establishment of a Central Italian Kingdom which he tells them would be better for them than annexation, but he preaches to deaf ears and stone walls. They will no longer listen to the advice of the 'Eldest Son'. ...

81   [F.O. 43/76]   Rome, 4 February 1860

No. 24
O.R. to Lord J.R.

The French Ambassador has had long and repeated conferences with the Cardinal Secretary of State, the object of which was to obtain the cession of the Romagna from the Pope. The first proposition, namely the appointment of a lay governor and a separate administration for the legations having been repeatedly refused, as your Lordship already knows, Monsieur de Gramont pressed Cardinal Antonelli to cause the Pope to insist on the meeting of the Congress that the question of those lost provinces might be debated. 'If Congress did not meet,' the Duke argued, 'the annexation policy of Piedmont would remain triumphant and the propositions of France at Villa Franca for a confederation under the presidency of the Pope would be for ever lost. England was urging on Piedmont to annex, and establish herself, while France in the interest of the Papacy desired a Central Italian kingdom. A congress would impede the progress of Piedmont, and an appeal to universal suffrage would undoubtedly produce a Central Italian kingdom and His Excellency therefore implored of Cardinal Antonelli to induce the Pope to ask for the Congress, in his own as well as the interest of Catholic France struggling against the intrigues of Protestant England.' These arguments produced no effect on the Sovereign Pontiff, whose faith in the policy of the eldest son of the Church seems deeply shaken.

The French Ambassador next proposed that the Grand Duke of Tuscany should be reinstated and appointed Vicar of the Pope for the Romagna for a limited number of years, but the Cardinal would not even listen to this proposition. Finally Monsieur de Gramont said that since the Pope declined to save his own property, would he at least sanction the new state of things and accept territorial compensation for the Romagna? Monsieur de Gramont gave His Holiness the choice between a part of Tuscany, a section of the kingdom of Naples, a portion of Sicily, or the whole of the island of Sardinia.

These extraordinary propositions, which have greatly surprised the foreign representatives in Rome, were peremptorily rejected by Cardinal Antonelli in the name of his Sovereign, saying that he knew not by what right the Ambassador of France was disposing of the territory of other Sovereigns. The Pope claimed his own property and rights and nothing else. His Holiness was ready to accept the policy of non-intervention in Italy proposed by France and England but he expected it to be complete and extended to his dominions also, and he felt sure, once the agents and soldiers of Sardinia had been withdrawn from the Romagna and the people left to themselves so that he could make use of all the means at his disposal as Head of the Catholic Church to recognize those provinces, that they would again submit to his authority speedily and joyfully.

In justice to the Government of the Emperor Napoleon I must say that Monsieur de Gramont declared these propositions to have originated with himself and not to have been sent to him from Paris, nevertheless he solemnly promised the Emperor's adherence to them.

82 [F.O. 43/76]   *Rome, 17 February 1860*

No. 28
O.R. to Lord J.R.

I learn that the Pope in writing privately to the Catholic sovereigns on
New Year's Day also wrote a letter to King Victor Emmanuel reminding His Majesty of his duties to the Church. The King's answer is said
to have been received on the 14th instant and it is represented to me as
being couched in respectful language although the proposals it contains
have been a new cause of irritation to His Holiness. King Victor
Emmanuel after the usual profession of devotion to the Head of the
Roman Church, declares that he is compelled by the force of events to
act as he does, he entreats of the Pope to co-operate with him towards
the future welfare of Italy and since the Romagna is unavoidably lost
to the Holy See he begs of His Holiness to grant him permission to
accept those provinces and further suggests that the work of regeneration would be complete if the Pope would make over Umbria and the
Marches to the new kingdom of Northern and Central Italy. The
Sovereign Pontiff answered this letter on the day it was received and
after reminding His Majesty once more of his duties to the Church the
Pope threatens the King with the thunders of the Vatican in the event
of further acts of disobedience. A good deal of mystery has been observed with respect to these two letters and the above account is all I
have been able to ascertain as yet from an authentic source with respect
to them.

83 [F.O. 43/76]   *Rome, 22 February 1860*

No. 31
O.R. to Lord J.R.

The Romans are constantly seeking opportunities to show their disapprobation of the Papal Government and their sympathy for the
national cause in Central Italy. As it was understood that following the
line of carriages in the Corso during Carnival hours was a demonstration of loyalty to the Sovereign Pontiff, the national party determined
to absent themselves altogether from the Corso and to express their
sympathy for liberty by driving and walking quietly along the road of
Porta Pia. The number of Liberals increased every day, while the
people in the Corso diminished and the police became alarmed. At last

it was thought necessary to send gendarmes to watch the movement and authorities at the gates of Rome reported that upwards of twenty-six thousand persons had joined in their pacific demonstration. To counteract it, the government hired carriages and sent poor people in fancy dresses to the Corso who by buffooning and pelting each other with flowers and *confetti* were to give proof of their loyal devotion to the Papacy. Notwithstanding, however, the exertions of the faithful, the Corso looked dreary and deserted. But the Pope, who in the palace of the Vatican was listening with profound irritation to the report of the misdeeds of his subjects, determined to inflict a severe lesson upon them and recollecting the trick played upon the inhabitants of Mantua by an Austrian general in 1848, he gave orders to close all the gates of Rome simultaneously so as to compel the miscreants to spend the night out in the Campagna.

Fortunately, however, for them, three of the gates are kept by the French military authorities and the orders of His Holiness could not be executed. But the resources of the Papacy are without end. So the Pope ordered the Headsman to be put into a carriage, conducted to the Porta Pia and there made to walk up and down, protected by gendarmes in plain clothes, among his disloyal subjects so as to make them feel what society they were fit for in his estimation. The Pope well knew what he was doing and the Romans were frantic. The horror entertained by them of the Headsman is such that he is not allowed by law to cross the bridges of the Tiber and is confined to a single street in the Borgo where he lives. His appearance in the town would inevitably lead to insults. The Romans were so excited by this singular occurrence that General de Goyon feared some disturbance and not knowing by whom the order had been given to convey the Papal Headsman to Porta Pia, he wished to have the over-zealous official who might have been guilty of so much imprudence reprimanded by his own government. After some investigation the truth came out and the matter was at once hushed up, the French authorities not wishing the Pope's name to be publicly mixed up in it. . . .

84 [P.R.O. 30/22/111]   *5 March 1860*

Private
Lord J.R. to O.R.

I have no time to write but must thank you for your agreeable account of your interview with the Pope. Poor man! He is sadly mistaken about me; I have fought all my life for Catholic privileges, but not for priestly government by any church.

85 [P.R.O. 30/22/75]   *Rome, 6 March 1860*
Private
O.R. to Lord J.R.

... the Pope persists in his obstinate course and says that nothing can satisfy Religion but the *Status quo ante bellum*. Some people think his mind is going, he says and does odd things at times. His craze about the Immaculate Virgin is becoming quite alarming. ...

86 [F.O. 43/76]   *Rome, 13 March 1860*
No. 35
O.R. to Lord J.R.

A confidential communication has been made by the French Ambassador to the Pope and although His Holiness, Cardinal Antonelli and the Duc de Gramont engaged to keep the secret the Holy Father could not resist the temptation of confiding it in strict confidence to a favorite Cardinal, who told it under the seal of secrecy to a Roman princess who whispered it to all her friends. Since then I have been enabled to verify the truth of the reports which had reached me and your Lordship can place full reliance on the following statement.

The Emperor Napoleon informs the Pope through the Duc de Gramont that the moment is approaching when he will be obliged to withdraw his troops from Rome. He cannot wish to see His Holiness exposed to useless dangers and he therefore proposes that the King of Naples should be invited to garrison Rome, in which case the Emperor engages to guarantee His Majesty's troops against foreign attack. This arrangement, the Emperor observes, has the advantage of leaving Italy entirely to the Italians and he proposes Neapolitan regiments as he thinks the Pope will prefer them to Sardinian troops. Although the Pope has not objected to the communication of these proposals to the King of Naples, he has not returned a direct answer to the French Ambassador as to the manner in which he views them, but there is no doubt that His Holiness and Cardinal Antonelli would be heartily glad to get rid of the French troops of occupation if they only knew how to do without them. ...

87 [F.O. 43/76]   *Rome, 16 March 1860*
No. 36
O.R. to Lord J.R.

The Duc de Gramont has this day communicated a dispatch, received
from Monsieur Thouvenel to Cardinal Antonelli stating that the Imperial Government having in vain offered advice and assistance to the
Pope and having in vain counselled King Victor Emmanuel to follow
a more moderate course in Central Italy, the Emperor Napoleon could
no longer be held responsible for the consequences of a policy he condemns as dangerous to the interests of the Papacy as well to those of
Italy in general. Whatever those consequences be, the responsibility
must fall on those who have chosen to incur them. His Majesty can no
longer interfere, and while his troops will still continue for the present
to protect the sacred person of the Pope, the Emperor washes his hands
of all further responsibility.

88 [F.O. 43/76]   *Rome, 16 March 1860*
No. 37. Confidential
O.R. to Lord J.R.

The Cardinal Secretary of State told me the other day that he was not
much satisfied with the progress of the recruitment for the Papal army,
not more than fifteen hundred men had yet been obtained from foreign
countries and he regretted to say that he did not meet with much
assistance of encouragement from foreign governments, several having
raised objections which impeded the progress of recruitment and the
Papal army increased but very slowly. His Eminence ended by telling me
in strict confidence that he might obtain any amount of men from France
and that he had applied to the French Government for permission to
recruit there, but that he had met with a peremptory refusal.

'If the Emperor is in earnest about withdrawing his garrison from
Rome,' the Cardinal observed, 'why does he thus impede the progress
and formation of our army?'

89 [F.O. 43/76]   *Rome, 16 March 1860*
No. 39
O.R. to Lord J.R.

As I have already had the honour to inform your Lordship the Romans are indulging in a series of puerile demonstrations by which they express their objections to the Papal rule. One cannot, however, but feel surprized at the admirable discipline which prevails amongst them. The order was given not to smoke and not an Italian was to be seen in the streets, excepting the Papal gendarmes, with a cigar in his mouth. When they thought the Government had been sufficiently vexed, they recommenced smoking on a given day but ceased to play in the Papal Lottery, which occasioned a serious loss to the revenue. Now an order has been issued to wear a bunch of violets in the buttonhole. Small and unimportant as these demonstrations are they fulfil their object and not only vex and irritate the Papal party but also greatly annoy the French military authorities who cannot succeed in preventing them.

It is much to be feared that they may some day lead to bloodshed in the streets of Rome.

90 [F.O. 43/76]   *Rome, 20 March 1860*

No. 41
O.R. to Lord J.R.

Yesterday being St Joseph's day a crowd of people assembled at about 6 o'clock p.m. in the Corso and Piazza Colonna and gave out that they were celebrating the feast of Joseph Garibaldi's patron saint. They were in Sunday attire with violets in their buttonholes and totally unarmed. The police called upon them to disperse, angry words it appears passed between them, the Pontifical gendarmes then arrested two men called Barberi, brothers, and tanners by profession, the people hissed the gendarmes, and some French officers who were in the crowd interfered and advized the people to be calm and the police to be less brutal in the execution of their duties. But the people continued to hiss and Captain Gorde in obedience to previous and general orders received from General Count de Goyon proceeded with a body of French soldiers stationed near there to clear the Piazza Colonna, which was accomplished by them quietly and with the butt end of their muskets while the people thus pushed back crowded into the Corso. The French soldiers who had been followed by a body of from fourteen to twenty-five Pontifical gendarmes on foot and four on horseback, then returned to their guard house, when the Pontifical gendarmes suddenly drawing their swords charged the people in the Corso cutting down indiscriminately everyone they could reach, some of them even rushing into the coffee-houses and open doorways and cutting and slashing at the terrified population. They proceeded in their wild and brutal course from the Piazza Colonna to the Piazza del Popolo where they entered their barracks, leaving about one hundred and fifty wounded people in the Corso and adjacent streets. Amongst these latter were two French officers in plain clothes, an old German artist, some women and children and several gentlemen of the Roman society as well as foreign visitors (French, Belgian, German and American), but up to this moment I am happy to say that I have not heard of any British subject being injured. Although myself a witness to part of this unaccountable affair I refrain from further details and only give the broad facts, until I have been able to consult authentic sources, so as to do injury to no one.

The Romans are in a state of profound alarm and agitation, many arrests are being made, five gentlemen have been banished, but the French officers and soldiers whose humane and intelligent conduct under such trying circumstances has been beyond all praise proclaim their indignation in the strongest terms.

Meanwhile the Pontifical gendarmes have been lauded and thanked for their energetic conduct by the Papal Government.

91 [P.R.O. 30/22/75]   *Rome, 20 March 1860*

Private
O.R. to Lord J.R.

. . . I am at a loss to make out whether the French Emperor really wishes to withdraw his troops from Rome or whether he is trying to make the Pope ask him to leave them there. Antonelli is convinced he has not the slightest intention of ever withdrawing them from Rome and the Pope revenges himself on the undutiful son of the Church by abusing him in the strongest terms to his officers or indeed to any Frenchman he speaks to. Gramont told me that if this abuse continued he would be compelled to complain *officially* to Cardinal Antonelli about it. The Pope has confided to his friends that he is directed in the policy he pursues by St Philomena, who appears to him in the night and tells him that his policy is the policy of God. *Poor man!* . . .

92 [F.O. 43/76]   *Rome, 21 March 1860*

No. 42

O.R. to Lord J.R.

Five Roman gentlemen belonging to the middle class, Messrs Mastri-
cola, Feri, Titoni, St Angeli and Silvestrelli were summoned to the
police office on the 19th instant at 11 a.m. and told that they were
banished from the Papal States for '*State Reasons*'. They were allowed
24 hours to prepare for departure, and although treated with civility
they were denied all explanations with respect to the causes which led
to the sentence of banishment. They requested to be accused and tried
but were informed that they had to conform to the sentence or submit
to be conveyed to the frontier by Papal gendarmes. In consequence
they proceeded on the 20th instant by Civita Vecchia and Leghorn to
Florence, leaving their wives and children for the present in Rome.
These gentlemen are known to be partizans of the Piedmontese or
National Party and were suspected of urging on the Roman people to
demonstrations against the Papal Government. They deny the truth of
this accusation.

I happened to be acquainted with some of these gentlemen, and after
calling on the French Ambassador to take leave of His Excellency they
also did me the honor to call a few hours before their departure to bid
me good-bye. They expressed themselves in terms of the deepest gratitude for the policy pursued by Her Majesty's Government in Italy
and hoped they might soon be able to return to Rome under more
favorable circumstances. Not wishing to commit myself one way or
the other I simply thanked them for their visit and observed that I
could scarcely pity them or look upon them as exiles since their government had merely sentenced them to travel from Italy despotic to Italy
free and happy. They thanked me with considerable emotion and
departed.

93 [F.O. 43/76]   *Rome, 3 April 1860*

No. 48

O.R. to Lord J.R.

Cardinal Antonelli told me this morning that General Lamoricière[1] had

---

[1] Lamoricière had served in the North African wars. Since the establishment
of the empire he had lived in exile in Belgium.

arrived last night in Rome and had offered his services to the Pope, which His Holiness had accepted. No previous arrangement had been made and the Emperor Napoleon's sanction had yet to be obtained from Paris. Monsieur de Gramont did not think it would be withheld. It was intended to give the entire command of the Papal army to the General with a view to its completion and reorganization and His Eminence expressed a hope that under the auspices of so eminent a general the Papal army would soon be able to relieve the French Garrison in Rome.

94   [P.R.O. 30/22/75]   *Rome, 7 April 1860*

Private
O.R. to Lord J.R.

Mr Henry Elliot has given you an account of the deep game played by the French Government at Naples with respect to the proposed occupation of the Marches by Neapolitan troops. It strikes me that they are playing a game equally deep in Rome, the object of which would be to render the relations between the Romans and the Papal Government morally and physically intolerable. Ever since the departure of Count della Minerva, the Sardinian Minister, when Goyon marched at the head of a formidable army to combat imaginary dangers in the streets of Rome, a system of constant vexation has been kept up, the object of which seems to be to exasperate the people and bring on a conflict in the streets, so as to give the French troops an excuse for remaining and perhaps even of taking the duties of the Roman police into their own hands. I am convinced that the row we had in the Corso on the 19th was secretly got up by the French authorities. I *know* that the French are secretly advizing the Papal Government to exile various Roman gentlemen known for liberal opinions. Seven have already received their passports and more are to be turned out in a few days. Goyon confided to me in the strictest confidence that he would be glad to see the Romans act on the offensive as it would give him an apportunity to shew his strength by an energetic suppression of a street row, but as he observed with great regret, 'these Italians are too cunning and at present too well disciplined *pour se laisser prendre*'. I asked him what he hoped to gain by shooting at an unarmed population in the streets and he replied that it would show the Italians, who had not followed the Emperor's advice in Central Italy, that at least *l'Armée Française* would have it all her own way in Rome. However, what Goyon says does not matter much. But Gramont in a confidential hour told me under the seal of secrecy that he thought the only way to settle the Roman difficulty was to double the garrison, take the police and local administration out of the hands of the priests, reorganize Rome and at the end of a year hand it over (that is the administration) to the Pope so thoroughly repaired that he could do it no harm, and then withdraw the French garrison for ever from the Eternal City. This Gramont says ought to have been done in 1849, while H.H. was at Gaeta, and he thinks a favourable moment to make up for lost time may shortly turn up. Unfortunately Gramont's imagination runs away with him and it is very difficult to know whether he thinks what he says, besides which his temper is soured by the constant failures he has experienced in prosecuting his reform policy at the Vatican. The French Embassy made a great show of anger and resistance when the Pope appointed General Lamoricière to the chief command of the Papal army without the Emperor's permission, but they were secretly delighted and since then the Emperor has sent his sanction to the measure by telegraph. Antonelli is evidently against the employment of the General, but he was overruled by an intriguing prelate and confidential friend of His Holiness, Monsignor de Mérode, who is a distant relation of General Lamoricière. I think the General will be followed by several young Frenchmen, Legitimists, who are going to offer their services to the Pope. The Duke of Modena is going to sell his army, 4,000 men, at present stationed in Venetia, to the Pope, which with the present Papal force amounting to 17,000 men, will make an army of 21,000.

95 [F.O. 43/76]   *Rome, 12 April 1860*
No. 59
O.R. to Lord J.R.

While the streets of Rome are filled by day and by night with patrols composed of Papal gendarmes and French soldiers, the police are equally active in the houses and homes of the population. The persons and clothes of the working classes and the books, desks, papers and correspondences of the middle-classes are subjected to a searching investigation by the Sbirri and the victims are often condemned to imprisonment or to exile. The Post Office who are unusually active in opening the letters of the Pope's subjects also profess to discover much treasonable correspondence. As at Naples a system of 'terror' is gradually being established which it is fancied will embue the Pope's subjects with greater loyalty. Signor Righetti, a wealthy Roman gentleman of the middle class, who professed liberal views, had his papers and private correspondence seized the other day and his house occupied by the Sbirri and gendarmes for five hours. They admitted that they had found nothing of importance but nevertheless he was banished and ordered to leave Rome, his house and his family in 24 hours.

Monsieur Bovet, the correspondent of the *Journal des Débats*, a gentleman who had resided 8 years unmolested in Rome has also received orders to depart in consequence of his too truthful account in the *Débats* of the charge of the gendarmerie in the Corso on the 19th of March last.

Further banishments are talked of, and on the whole it must be admitted, that if the Papal Government are bent upon their present course, exile is certainly the mildest form of punishment they can well inflict upon the Pope's subjects.

96 [P.R.O. 30/22/75] *Rome, 17 April 1860*

Private
O.R. to Lord J.R.

There is a party forming round the Pope of Ultra Catholics who want to turn out Cardinal Antonelli, because they think him too moderate, both in political and religious matters, and because they fancy he may stand in the way of General Lamoricière, through whom they expect to see the Romagna attacked and retaken for the Pope. The man they look to for the post of Secretary of State is Cardinal Viale Prela, who was many years Nuncio at Vienna, and the office of Minister of War, now held by Cardinal Antonelli, they would willingly give to Monsignor de Mérode (a Belgian Chamberlain of the Pope, formerly in the army and volunteer for some years in Algeria where he saw active service), who was sent to bring Lamoricière to Rome and who is a personal friend of the General. I think myself the Pope will stick to Cardinal Antonelli for whom he entertains great personal friendship and regard, but I should not wonder if the Cardinal relinquished the War Department in favour of Mérode. The French Ambassador would be equally glad to turn out Antonelli if he could get him replaced by Cardinal De Pietro who is supposed to be devoted to French interests, but whatever

changes may take place in the Papal Administration, I do not think the
Pope's present policy will be much affected thereby. Cardinal Antonelli
is also supported by Austria and Naples, two ideal Governments in the
eyes of His Holiness, and the hostility of the French Ambassador to his
Eminence can only contribute to strengthen his position at the Vatican.
I saw Cardinal Antonelli this morning and found him gay and pleasant
as usual, but he had no news to give me and only dwelt for a long time
on his great desire to get rid of the French garrison as soon as Gen.
Lamoricière has organised an army of 25,000 men.

97 [F.O. 43/76]   *Rome, 18 April 1860*

No. 61
O.R. to Lord J.R.

The Pope has appointed his Belgian chamberlain, Monsignor de
Mérode, to the post of 'Pro Minister of Arms' (war department). One
of the many offices held of late years by the Cardinal Secretary of State.
The official announcement of this appointment is contained in the
Giornale di Roma of to-day. Cardinal Antonelli in mentioning the fact
to me said that the increased activity of the War Office in consequence
of the appointment of General de Lamoricière rendered it necessary for
him to relinquish a department to which he could not at present give
his whole attention and Monsignor de Mérode had been selected by the
Pope, because he had been a soldier and had fought in Algeria under
General de Lamoricière who was his friend and relation and because the
General did not know the Italian language whilst the new War Secretary was well acquainted both with French and Italian.

His Eminence expressed the anxious hope that the great abilities and
energies of General de Lamoricière and the zeal of Monsignor de
Mérode would soon enable the Pope to dispense with the services of
the French garrison.

98 [P.R.O. 30/22/75]   *Rome, 1 May 1860*

Private
O.R. to Lord J.R.

I have literally nothing wherewith to trouble you to-day. I have called
on my diplomatic friends and have found them idle and their Chancel-
leries deserted. Baron Bach had detained his messenger in Rome for

another week having nothing to say, the Duc de Gramont was planning a day at the quails and Cardinal Antonelli, ever cheerful and pleasant, finding I had no news to give him talked for an hour about his flower garden and the fish of the Lake of Albano. His Eminence confided to me that his real vocation in life was the study of Nature, more especially Botany and Geology, that he hated politics and power and he prayed that Providence might relieve him of his duties to the Papacy. Some English prelates who surround the Pope told me with grim delight that the first effects of the Excommunication were beginning to shew, and that the death of Signor Quaglia, first President of the Piedmontese Chambers would be followed by other instances and manifestations of Divine wrath. The foreign priesthood seem most rabid, the Italian priests as far as I can judge think the Excommunication uncalled for, illegal and unwise. There is but little faith amongst them and they don't like to see the Pope surrounded by foreign prelates and chamberlains and converts preferred to Italians. These foreigners who never leave the Pope by day or by night and to whom the presence of General de Lamoriciére and the promotion of Mérode has given courage and energy, are intriguing to upset Cardinal Antonelli, whom they think too moderate in matters of religion; and the Italian clergy who cordially hated Antonelli are perhaps coming round to him a little because they dread to see the Pope give way to foreign influence which is odious to their national feeling. Hence a growing dislike and mistrust in the smaller Roman clergy to Lamoricière who they fear may become a supporter of the Montalembert school in Rome, viz., strict religious observance and a liberal and enlightened administration. But their fears are scarcely founded, for the Pope is too much attached to Antonelli to do without him, and Antonelli far too cunning to allow himself to be done by a Frenchman in the long run. Lamoricière is expected back in Rome in a few days when we shall hear what he expects doing in the Marches. . . . It is confidently reported that he expects a large body of Irishmen who are to come to Rome disguised as pilgrims and who are to enlist as fast as they arrive. . . .

Thanks for attaching me to Naples. It has given great satisfaction at the Vatican, as I expected.

[*With the disappearance on 24 March of the English mission to Florence, after Tuscany, by a plebiscite, had voted for annexation to Sardinia, O.R. was attached to the legation at Naples.*]

99 [F.O. 43/77]   *Rome, 10 May 1860*

No. 65
O.R. to Lord J.R.

I enquired of the Cardinal Secretary of State what truth there was in the report that the Papal Government expected one thousand Irish recruits at Ancona by way of Belgium and Trieste. His Eminence replied that since the War Department was no longer under his control the formation of the Papal army was entirely in the hands of General de Lamoricière and he was not thoroughly acquainted with all the measures taken by his Excellency but he believed the General reckoned on obtaining about one thousand Irishmen for the Papal army. They came of their own free will to Italy and enlisted here. Nothing would induce the Papal Government to attempt enlistments in Ireland, they had too much respect for the laws of other countries, and since it was prohibited to enlist in the Papal States for foreign armies, the Pope respected in other states the laws he wished to see respected in his own dominions. His Holiness was constantly receiving letters from Irish gentlemen offering to bring him from three to five thousand men at any time, but the Sovereign Pontiff had always declined to entertain such offers. His Eminence did not for many reasons think it desirable to have a large number of Irish soldiers in the Papal army, but the question at present was to form an army sufficiently strong for all police purposes in the Papal States, so as to make the French occupation cease altogether and free the Papacy from all foreign intervention and he most sincerely hoped and believed that for the sake of this long desired and much discussed object, Her Majesty's Government would generously throw no impediments in the way of such of her Roman Catholic subjects, who, of their own free will, proceeded to Rome to offer their services to the Pope.

100 [F.O. 43/77]   *Rome, 11 May 1860*

No. 66
O.R. to Lord J.R.

Negotiations have been pending between the French Ambassador and the Cardinal Secretary of State respecting the withdrawal of the French garrison from Rome. The Pope was positive on two points: 1st that the evacuation should take place as early as possible and 2nd that no French troops should remain at Civita Vecchia, His Holiness wishing the evacuation to be complete. General de Lamoricière declared that with twenty thousand men he could keep order in the Holy See, so the Cardinal and the Ambassador having discussed the details and compared drafts they finally this morning exchanged Notes, the Duc de Gramont agreeing on the part of the Emperor that the evacuation should be complete, should commence on 1st of June by the departure of the 20th Regiment and should be accomplished by the end of the month of August, while Cardinal Antonelli in the name of His Holiness accepted these conditions and thanked the Emperor for the protection he had afforded the Pope for the last twelve years.

101 [P.R.O. 30/22/75]   *Rome, 12 May 1860*

Private
O.R. to Lord J.R.

... It is very much to be hoped that no impediments will be thrown in the way of recruitment for the Papal army, so that the French army may *really* withdraw altogether and the Temporal Power of the Pope rest solely on its own merits. For that reason also I felt that you have uttered the words of wisdom in the House of Commons when you declined to lay any papers whatever respecting the Papal States and Papal Administration before Parliament. I am so deeply convinced that we ought to maintain the strictest silence respecting everything doing at present in the Holy See, that we ought carefully to avoid every kind of official publication respecting the Pope's temporal and spiritual power and that we ought to leave His Holiness and the Eldest son of the Church to fight it out between themselves, that I most sincerely hope and pray Her Majesty's Government may be able to adhere to the policy laid down by you on the 3rd inst. In the present case silences will be power in the future. Garibaldi (and his followers) is very much dreaded here and at Naples. His name is said to be sufficient to convulse the Country whenever he appears as a National Warrior, but at present it must be admitted that the Romans seem content to watch with pride and satisfaction the progress made by their brethren in the north.

[*On 13 May Garibaldi and the Thousand landed in Sicily.*]

102 [P.R.O. 30/22/111]　　　　　　　　　　　*14 May 1860*

Private
Lord J.R. to O.R.

... If you find your health requires change, you may go off to Naples
or Castellamare at any time, and pay a visit to the monks of Monte
Cassino by the way. Garibaldi I expect will not succeed.

103 [F.O. 43/77]　　　　　　　　　　　　　*Rome, 15 May 1860*

No. 68
O.R. to Lord J.R.

I asked Cardinal Antonelli whether the Roman Government contemplated any attack on Tuscany or Romagna. His Eminence replied,
'Certainly not, the Pope entertains no aggresive intentions and if he did
he has no army to carry them out. Through the exertions of General de
Lamoricière and Monsignore de Mérode, we hope to have an army of
20,000 men by the time the French troops of occupation are withdrawn,
which will be by the end of August, and 20,000 men, we hope, will be
sufficient to maintain order in the Papal States if we are not attacked by
General Garibaldi or King Victor Emmanuel. In these hard times we
must be grateful if we have strength to keep order in the country and
the Papal army is after all merely another name for the Papal police.
When the French troops are gone, the revolutionary party will make
every attempt to upset the present order of things and Rome and
Naples will be equally threatened by enemies at home and enemies
abroad. The success which has crowned the grasping policy of Piedmont may lead her government to push her revolutionary conquests
still further in the South and as neither France nor England seem inclined to arrest her progress, we must be prepared to defend our rights
and act on the defensive, but happen what may we will never be the
aggressive party.'

104 [F.O. 43/77]　　　　　　　　　　　　　*Rome, 15 May 1860*

No. 69
O.R. to Lord J.R.

Intelligence reached the Papal Government yesterday that parties of
filibusters were collecting at Orbetello, Radicoffane and other places

on the Tuscan frontier, that some had arrived at Montalto on the coast and that they had been joined on the night of the 12th instant by a portion of the garrisons of Florence and Leghorn. General de Lamoricière, who returned from Ancona two days ago at once despatched ten companies (about 1,200 men) and a small battery by rail to Civita Vecchia, with orders to march to Cornetto and Toscanella. He ordered part of the garrison of Viterbo to march to Valentano and Acquapendente, and the troops stationed at Perugia were directed to occupy Ficulle and Citta della Pieve, by which means a line of defence is established between Perugia and Civita Vecchia.

In conversation with Cardinal Antonelli this morning I learnt that the Papal Government believed these filibusters intended to force their way to the Abruzzi, through the Papal States, perhaps by way of Terni, there to form the nucleus of General Garibaldi's army, who is supposed to be in Tuscany directing this movement.

105 [F.O. 43/77] *Rome, 17 May 1860*
No. 70
O.R. to Lord J.R.

The landing of General Garibaldi in Sicily was not expected by the Papal Government. Up to the night of the 15th they fully believed he had placed himself at the head of the filibustering party which made its appearance on the Tuscan frontier between Orbetello and Radicoffane, and which occasioned the movement of Pontifical troops along the frontier of the Papal States. They believed his departure to be a blind and that some of his followers were to be sacrificed in Sicily to deceive the Neapolitan and Papal authorities and to enable him to reach the Abruzzi through the Papal States from whence they fancied he intended to operate immediately upon Naples. The expedition to Sicily appeared to them too audacious to be possible and the terror his name now strikes in the hearts of some and the hopes it raises in others shows but too clearly the animosity governed and government still feel to each other in the Holy See. It is also worthy of note that while the Papal Government was deceived respecting the real intentions of Garibaldi, the signature of the Convention between the French and Roman Governments regulating the withdrawal of the French garrison by the end of August was so suddenly carried by the Duc de Gramont that neither General de Goyon nor General de Lamoricière knew that it had been discussed until after it was signed, and both seem now to consider it premature and involving danger to the peace of the Papal States. Cardinal Antonelli and Monsignor Berardi would willingly have counselled the Pope to put off the evil hour, but His Holiness who has long suffered from a state of political over excitement declared he greatly preferred the risks of a struggle with the revolutionary party to the continuance of the Protectorate of a Sovereign whose very name had become hateful to him. So much for the gratitude of Popes.

106 [F.O. 43/77]   *Rome, 26 May 1860*

No. 71
O.R. to Lord J.R.

Colonel Pimodan, a French gentleman who had long served in the Austrian army, but at present aide-de-camp to General de Lamoricière, and who had reached Montefiascone with part of the Papal troops despatched from Rome to meet the filibusters that threatened the frontiers, proceeded on the 19th instant to Latera and having learnt that the 'Garibaldini' had already left that town for 'le Grotte', he followed them at the head of about sixty mounted gendarmes. On reaching Le Grotte, Colonel Pimodan found the Garibaldini dispersed about the town in the *trattorias* and coffee-houses. He ordered his men to charge and a sharp contest ensued. The streets being narrow and paved the horses suffered a good deal on the hard stones, and the men were fired at and pelted from the windows with articles of furniture, plates, glasses, stones bricks, etc. Finally Colonel Pimodan having lost two men killed and three wounded, including Lieut Cacchi and seven horses, and finding that the Garibaldini who were about two hundred strong maintained their ground in 'Le Grotte' by throwing up barricades, he thought it best to retreat upon Valentano and await reinforcements.

The Colonel reports that the filibusters lost nine men killed and about five and twenty wounded, and on the following day the remainder of them returned to Tuscany. Their whole force is estimated at about four hundred men. At Valentano, Colonel Pimodan met the 2nd battalion of Pontifical Cacciatori and marched at once in the middle of the night upon San Lorenzo, where he expected to meet the Garibaldini again, this hope was however not realized, but unfortunately for the Pontifical forces, a soldier having inadvertently fired off his musket, the Cacciatori fancied they were attacked by the fili-busters and began to fire upon each other in the dark. Before the mistake could be cleared up Major Corelli, Lieut Gornez and five men were killed and about eighty wounded. This unfortunate affair has not been quite explained. Some people believe the Italian soldiers wanted to join the 'Garibaldini' and were fired upon by the foreign soldiers of His Holiness. My own belief is that the accident was simply the effect of a panic but certain it is that the Cacciatori have protested in a body against the command of Colonel Pimodan and have declined to serve under his orders. In consequence General de Lamoricière started on the 23rd instant for Viterbo, where he has now concentrated a force of 3,000 infantry, 150 cavalry and 6 cannon. The artillery was so little pre-pared for active service that the field pieces had to be conveyed with posthorses to Viterbo, changing at every station and occasionally up-setting in the ditches along the postroad.

At Acquapendente the Papal officials seized with a panic ran away in a body and cannot be found anywhere. A new set of them has been sent from Rome to fill the vacant posts. Cardinal Antonelli has appealed to the French Government through the Nuncio at Paris to request their interference at Turin with a hope that the Piedmontese Government will disarm the filibusters and take measures to protect the frontiers. Meanwhile Austrian men-of-war are expected to protect the coasts of the Papal dominions.

The French authorities deserve high praise for the manner in which they maintain order in Rome.

A witty *Italian* Monsignore with whom I have had some conversa-tion on the present state of affairs observed to me that if the French had already left Rome, the Pope would have been compelled to follow them, in consequence of the invasion of his States by a mere handful of filibusters.

'His Holiness and Cardinal Antonelli,' the Monsignore continued, 'are forming German, Swiss, Belgian, French, Austrian, Irish and other foreign legions wherewith to support the edifice of the Church. They build on sand unfortunately so long as they have not the support of the nation. It is the old story of the Tower of Babel; the soldiers unable to understand the languages dividing the army which is to save us, are already beginning to quarrel, shoot and kill each other. Let us pray that all this may not be followed by a second deluge.'

107 [P.R.O. 30/22/75]   *Rome, 1 June 1860*

Private

O.R. to Lord J.R.

... I have many pressing invitations to Italian country houses, and as I am very curious to know more about Italian life, I mean to make excursions of one, two or even three days after the departure of the messenger, so as to satisfy my curiosity, benefit my health and see my kind friends. I am deeply interested in all I see, do and hear, in all I learn and all I feel. I am very happy and only hope you may be sufficiently satisfied with me to leave me at my present post, until this great Italian question is settled one way or the other. I am preparing a report on the general state of affairs and parties in Rome, which gives me much trouble as I am anxious it should prove true, and useful to you in the future. I labour conscientiously, but it takes much time and experience to understand Rome and the Romans. Garibaldi's success in Sicily has excited the population here to such a degree that Goyon has been obliged to put on double patrols day and night. The taking of Palermo has made the Vatican tremble. What the Pope and Antonelli fear most at present is that the King of Naples yielding to *una grande paura* should make concessions to his subjects to save his throne, in which case Rome could no longer resist the pressure of public opinion. No one in Rome believes in the departure of the French. Can the Emperor withdraw his troops with good grace when the Pope is surrounded with dangers of every kind? Will he dare do so in the face of Catholic France? The Pope most heartily wishes them at the D . . . l, for he fancies his appeal to the Catholic world for men and money will answer all purposes in the future, but the priests in general who fear for their skin would not be sorry to see them remain. If Italy is really to be left to settle her own affairs, they ought to depart so soon as Lamoricière has found an army of 20,000 foreign adventurers. And then let us see how the Pope will settle his difficulties with the Italians. I can see no other settlement of the Roman Question, since all advice, all assistance and all protection have been lost on Pio Nono. As a temporal sovereign, as an Italian prince, he is answerable to the Italian nation for the miseries he has inflicted on them. Let the Pope therefore settle the temporal question with Italy, and as to the Spiritual question, let the Catholic world settle it with the Pope.

108 [F.O. 43/77]   *Rome, 5 June 1860*

No. 79
O.R. to Lord J.R.

A council of ministers was held yesterday at the Vatican to discuss the
increased and increasing expenses of the Pontifical army. The Pope
said that he was resolved to assist General de Lamoricière in completing
the task he had undertaken, as he wished above all things to dispense
with the French occupation of Rome; that he had received letters from
three Catholic Sovereigns promising him pecuniary assistance and that
he should not hesitate to accept that assistance when the interests of the
Holy See required it, besides that he had full confidence in the Catholic
world who would not forsake the Papacy in the hour of need. He did
not fear the enemies of Religion for he was protected by the Immaculate Virgin. Those enemies were well known to him, they sought to
deprive him of his throne. And at this moment His Holiness struck the
chair he was sitting on with his hand and bursting forth in great anger
he spoke with vehement animosity against the Emperor Napoleon.
Having got somewhat calmer His Holiness proceeded to say that he
had proofs that the population of the lost provinces of Romagna
desired to return to him, and that the soldiers of King Victor Emmanuel
animated by true religion would one and all refuse to fight against the
soldiers of the Pope, these were facts that afforded him great consolation, and when he thought of the violent and sacrilegious course pursued by the Piedmontese Government against Cardinal Corsi, the
Bishop of Pisa, he felt that iniquity could not be carried further, that a
change must be near at hand and that the worst of the crisis to which
Religion and the Papacy had been subjected was over. He looked forward confidently to better times. Thus ended the financial Council of
the Vatican. These details were obtained from authentic sources.

109 [F.O. 43/77]   *Rome, 7 June 1860*

No. 80. [Recites Telegram]
O.R. to Lord J.R.

Rome, June 7th. De Martino, the Neapolitan Minister at Rome, leaves
to-morrow on a mission from the King of Naples, to Paris and London.
His Sicilian Majesty wishes to know on what conditions his kingdom
would be guaranteed to him.

110 [P.R.O. 30/22/75]   *Rome, 7 June 1860*

Private
O.R. to Lord J.R.

. . .Commendatore De Martino besides being a very intelligent man has
many great and good qualities, he is perfectly truthful and straightforward, honest and sincere, and his word is as good as gold. A liberal
at heart he has never hesitated to assert his principles both to his
Sovereign and to the Pope and everyone who knows him respects him
for his loyal conduct and disinterested services. He owes everything to
the Royal family of Naples, and having a warm and grateful heart he is
determined to serve them to the last, nevertheless he is fully alive to
their faults and deplores them. De Martino is at present in very low
spirits. He well knows the King will disavow him, if convenient, and he
looks upon his mission as almost useless for he told me he had consulted with the most moderate and enlightened of the liberal party at
Naples and that one and all replied: 'We want no concessions, we ask
nothing of the King, it is too late, let him be driven from the country,
Garibaldi is at hand, and soon we will all be united and be Italians.' The
extraordinary change that had come over the Neapolitans under the
present reign of terror, he said, amazed him, for the policy pursued by
the Court had actually produced a strong desire for annexation to
Piedmont. The Pope is having prayers and masses read for the Emperor
of Austria to strengthen him in his resistance. The other day the young
King of Naples was seized with such a panic that he telegraphed five
times in 24 hours for the Pope's blessing. Cardinal Antonelli through
whom the application had to be made, sent the three last blessings without reference to His Holiness, saying that he was duly authorized to do
so. The converts are awfully scandalized at this proceeding. . . .

111 [F.O. 43/77]   *Rome, 8 June 1860*

No. 82
O.R. to Lord J.R.

The French Legitimists who have entered the Pope's army made much
show of their political feelings and yesterday while assembled in the
garden of the *Caffè Nuovo* in the Palazzo Ruspoli and under General de
Goyon's windows they became very noisy and drank to the success of
legitimacy in France with loud cries of '*Vive Henri V!*'

I am assured that General de Lamoricière intends to reprimand them and forbid all similar demonstrations for the future.

112 [F.O. 43/77]   *Rome, 9 June 1860*
No. 83. Confidential
O.R. to Lord J.R.

It appears that General de Lamoricière, foreseeing the difficulties that he may have to contend with in the event of the French garrison being withdrawn from Rome, has submitted the following proposition to the Pope. In the first instance, he says, that as his army will not exceed five and twenty thousand men for the whole of the Papal States and the increasing desire for an Italian Union necessitates a strong force in the provinces, the garrison of Rome will necessarily be small. In the event of a rising of the people he intends instantly to apply measures of coercion so energetic that the Romans will, he declares, never attempt resistance again. But to ensure the perfect safety of the Sovereign Pontiff it would be necessary for His Holiness to remove to Ancona. There General de Lamoricière says, he can surround him with fortifications and a force that will ensure efficient protection, and the vicinity of Austria would greatly add to his security and to his resources.

The Pope has declared in answer to the General's plan that under all circumstances he is fully determined not to leave Rome, as he prefers the death of a martyr to the repetition of the blunder he committed in going to Gaeta in 1849.

113 [F.O. 43/77]   *Rome, 23 June 1860*
No. 89
O.R. to Lord J.R.

The greatest dissatisfaction prevails amongst the Irish recruits of the Pope and the Irish priests sent from Macerata to pacify them, instead of preaching submission have taken the part of their countrymen and declare they have been unfairly treated by the Papal military authorities. In consequence they have all been ordered to Rome to be placed under the immediate orders of General de Lamoricière. As far as I can learn they are treated exactly in the same manner as all the other foreigners who enlist in the Pope's army. No difference is made, I believe, but these poor deluded men, relying on the golden promises of their priests at home, have found their own hopes and expectations deceived. In the first instance they say they were promised two shillings a day, instead of which they receive five *bajocchis* (about fourpence). 2ndly, they expected to be commanded by Irish officers. 3rd, they expected to form a Legion and wear a special uniform and 4th, they complain of their beds, food, barracks, everything in short, and the men who were enlisted as officers have been reduced to the ranks on arriving at Macerata. As they became very riotous at one time and set fire to their barracks, gendarmes were sent to keep them in order, but they declared they would murder any foreign officers who attempted to command them.

Wherever they have been, the subjects of the Pope have had to complain of their behaviour and at Macerata the authorities declared they preferred even a Spanish garrison to an Irish one.

I must again repeat that General de Lamoricière, who is most kind to his soldiers, seems very well disposed towards them, and in all probability the true cause of their present disappointment must be attributed in great measure to the exaggerated promises and expectations held out to them by their priests in Ireland, and it must also in truth be said that the Irish priests in Rome who surround them, are most zealous in their behalf and minister both to their spiritual and bodily comforts.

114   [F.O. 43/77]   *Rome, 26 June 1860*
No. 90. Secret
O.R. to Lord J.R.

The Pope considers Cardinal Wiseman as the best authority on English politics, and his Eminence has always assured His Holiness that sooner or later there would be a great war between England and France which would prove beneficial to the interests of the Church, whatever way it ended. If England were victorious, the Pope would get rid of the Emperor Napoleon with whom His Holiness has no reason to be satisfied, but if on the other hand France were victorious, His Imperial Majesty would concede a Roman Catholic administration to Great Britain, and once relieved of the heretical thraldom of her Protestant statesmen she would rapidly return to the bosom of the Mother Church. The prospects are very comforting to the Pope who devoutly assures his favourites that such a war would be a great blessing. To me these views appeared so monstrous that I could not get myself to believe they really formed part of Cardinal Wiseman's convictions. I there-

fore called on his Eminence, with whom I am well acquainted, and
engaged him in a conversation on the future of the Papacy. He was at
first reserved, but gradually warmed up, as I respectfully opposed his
views, and finally he developed the theories already submitted above
to your Lordship. He went even so far as to tell me in strict confidence
that he knew the Emperor Napoleon had sounded the Roman Catholics
of England and had held out promises and prospects of Catholic supremacy to them, to ensure their co-operation when he should deem the
moment propitious for the invasion of Great Britain. I protested against
these insinuations and declared my firm belief that our Roman Catholics were Englishmen before they were anything else and would resist
foreign invasion like true Britons. Cardinal Wiseman replied that he
agreed with me as matters stood at present, but that some years ago the
position of our Roman Catholics was very different and that the power
and influence of religion were often under-rated by our statesmen. The
Church had means of knowing things to which diplomacy could not
have access and he knew that the Emperor Napoleon was gradually
preparing for the invasion of England. Indeed the present Congress at
Baden[1] was intended to cement a coalition against her. I assured his
Eminence that I was a firm believer in the Alliance between England
and France and could not therefore share his views. As to the civil
and religious position of our Roman Catholics in England, I said, it
was incomparably better in every respect than that of the very subjects
of the Pope.

Cardinal Wiseman admitted that education was defective in the
Papal States and that the existing laws were not always properly enforced. On my begging of him therefore to explain to me, for my
private information, what measures he considered necessary to ensure
the perfect contentment of our Roman Catholic brethren at home he
promised he would explain their grievances and requirements to me
some other day.

115 [F.O. 43/77]   *Rome, 28 June 1860*
No. 93
O.R. to Lord J.R.

On the 20th instant, being the annual *festa* of the town of Frosinone,

[1] Congress of the Emperor Napoleon, the Prince Regent of Prussia and the
German Kings and Princes.

the population assembled after Vespers on the market place to witness
the drawing of a *Tombola*. Two men happened to quarrel, the gendarmes instead of simply arresting the offenders, charged the whole
unoffending population with drawn swords, as they did in the Corso
at Rome on the 19th March last.

The younger people who could run were pressed by the gendarmes
on horseback against the wall on the other side of which was a deep
ditch and in jumping over to escape the swords of the Papal police they
were badly hurt and bruised, whilst the old people, women and children
who could not escape were wounded by the swords and trampled upon
by the horses of the heroes of the Corso. One hundred and forty seven
persons were wounded in all. As on former occasions the gendarmes
have been handsomely rewarded and lauded for their bravery and
devotion to the Pope. I enquired of the authorities here for what reason
the gendarmes were encouraged and rewarded after these repeated acts
of wanton brutality, for it was self evident that this wholesale system of
punishment could not contribute much towards conciliating the population. I was told that it was necessary to intimidate them occasionally
so as to remind them of the power of government. Some days since a
detachment of these gendarmes who had also been on duty at *le Grotte*
returned to Rome. The police sent some thirty or forty Sbirri in plain
clothes to the Porta del Popolo to meet them and cheer these valiant
defenders of the Papacy, and the next day the *Giornale di Roma*
announced in pompous language that the gendarmes had been spon-
taneously cheered by thousands of loyal subjects of the Pope.

So low is the Papal government obliged to stoop to throw sand into
the eyes of the faithful.

116 [P.R.O. 30/22/75]   *Rome, 29 June 1860*

Private
O.R. to Lord J.R.

... The concessions made by the King of Naples have greatly incensed
the Vatican and disappointed the national party who have now but one
wish and one idea all over Southern Italy, and that is the establishment
of a great united Italy under Victor Emmanuel. Nothing else will satisfy
them at present and if they had a free vote they would annex themselves
with an *overwhelming majority* to Piedmont. At this moment the withdrawal of the French garrison from Rome would be very shortly

9. The Emperor Napoleon III

10. General de Lamoricière

followed by the complete overthrow of the temporal power of the Pope, and I cannot conceal my deep conviction that the sooner the Pope's temporal power is abolished, the better for Italy and Humanity in general.

117 [F.O. 43/77]   *Rome, 3 July 1860*

No. 96
O.R. to Lord J.R.

I had some conversation this morning with the Cardinal Secretary of State respecting the new policy of the King of Naples. His Eminence was of opinion that the Italians were not able to bear representative institutions, that a minority would never learn to submit quietly to a majority unless the executive could employ coercion and that the young King would therefore find it impossible to govern with a Constitution such as that of 1848 which had now been pressed upon him by his new advizers. And as to these latter he did not give them more than two months in office. Their programme was far too liberal, a reaction was inevitable. As regarded Rome he did not apprehend any disturbances. The French garrison would maintain order, and General de Lamoricière could keep the peace in the provinces.

I enquired whether the French garrison was still expected to return to France in the course of the autumn, but his Eminence with a smile replied that in confidence he did not believe the French garrison would be withdrawn from Rome so long as the Emperor Napoleon reigned in France.

118 [F.O. 43/77]   *Rome, 3 July 1860*

No. 97
O.R. to Lord J.R.

General de Lamoricière has decided to form two great camps at Pesaro and at Spoleto and is to start himself for the latter place to-night. The Papal regiments in Rome are all to be removed and the Eternal City to be left entirely under the care of the French garrison. This measure has been rendered necessary by the constant quarrels, jealousies and rivalries of the Papal and French officers. . . .

As I have often said before it is impossible to speak too highly of the

F

admirable discipline and bearing of the French army and of the conciliatory and civilized manners both of the officers and men under General de Goyon's orders. They are liked and respected by every class of society in Rome. I cannot say as much of the Papal army....

119 [P.R.O. 30/22/75]   *Rome, 7 July 1860*

Private
O.R. to Lord J.R.

... In imitation of Lord Lyons I pass my summer in Rome which is more convenient than Frascati or Albano for business, besides which the expense of two establishments is more than I can afford. My summer apartment here in Rome in the Palazzo Doria, Piazza di Venezia, is delightfully cool, and Rome being empty I find time to read more than in winter. Lord Lyons limited his acquaintance to a very few houses of the aristocracy, but I have endeavoured to know interesting people in all classes of society so as to be better informed on all things connected with Rome, and I also know many influential priests and dignitaries of the Church who are not generally accessible to foreigners. I have endeavoured to know as many English and Irish priests as possible so as to conciliate them and learn what they want and what they complain of, and I must say that everybody I know is so kind and good to me that I have every reason to feel grateful for the good will I meet everywhere. Altogether I feel very happy. If ever you could find time to give me a little advice as to how I might improve myself and would point out my failings and shortcomings to me I should really feel deeply grateful to you. I am very ambitious and wish to work for the good of my country and if possible the glory of my family. You have accomplished the task and are adding to it daily; shew me how to imitate you and how to follow your footsteps. God knows, good will to toil and labour is not wanting, but the natural capacities are wanting I fear. Every day shows me how much I have to learn and how ignorant I am of many necessary things. I feel a little advice from you might do me a vast deal of good, forgive me therefore if by thus laying open my innermost soul before you, I chance to bore you, but do not misunderstand me — it is self-improvement, development I seek. As far as my profession goes I am so happy that I wish to remain here, as I am, as long as possible, for Rome is for me the best school in the

world at present. I can learn more here in every way than I could elsewhere and I avail myself to my present opportunities to the best of my
abilities.

120   [F.O. 43/77]   *Rome, 10 July 1860*

No. 100
O.R. to Lord J.R.

The Irish recruits of the Pope amount now to about thirteen hundred,
and the enlistment in Ireland has been stopped. They continue to be
very riotous and disorderly and are a source of constant trouble and
annoyance to the Papal authorities. . . . They are a wild set of fellows
who seem to enjoy a rare amount of exuberant spirits. Here at Rome
a good many of them have called at the British Consulate complaining
that they had been deceived in Ireland by every kind of promise, that
they had never enlisted but had simply come to look for work and were
now compelled to enter the Papal army against their will, and they
claimed to be sent home to Ireland at the expense of Her Majesty's
Government. . . .

   I called on Cardinal Antonelli and told him that although I had no
instructions to do so, I wished privately and on my own account to call
his attention to the complaints made by Her Majesty's subjects in the
Pope's service and to enquire of him whether anything could be done
to render them more satisfied with their present condition. His Eminence replied that he was glad I mentioned the subject to him since he
wished to tell me that he had given orders to send home all those who
since their arrival in the Papal States objected to serve in the Papal
army, that the Pope only sought volunteers and wished no one to serve
him against his own free will. All those, therefore, who asked to go
home would be sent back to Ireland at the expense of the Papal
Government, and those who wished to remain were treated with great
kindness by General de Lamoricière who had taken a fancy to their fine
military appearance. . . . His Eminence related many anecdotes about
the excesses they had committed, and said he now understood why I
had eight months ago so strongly urged him not to form an Irish
Legion, that the Pope as well as himself had not known the Irish
character to be so energetic and that he could also now appreciate the
difficulties experienced by the British Government in dealing with
Ireland etc., etc. . . .

121 [F.O. 43/77]   *Rome, 12 July 1860*

No. 103. Secret

O.R. to Lord J.R.

The diplomatic body had their annual audience of the Pope, on the anniversary of his accession to the Pontificate, on the 21st ultimo, and I was also admitted to that honor this morning. Cardinal Altieri, the Pontifical Cammerlengo, was with His Holiness and I waited in the anti chamber until he withdrew accompanied by the Monsignor Chamberlain on duty, when the door of the Pope's sitting room remaining open I heard the mild and benevolent voice of His Holiness calling me: '*Favorisca, caro mio Russell*' he said as I entered. After several kind enquiries respecting myself, the Pope spoke about the weather and the crops which he said were very promising. A little more rain only was wanting to ripen the Indian corn, on which the Italian peasantry of the South depended for their daily existence. In the north of Italy the peasantry were what he supposed we would call more civilized in England, that is, they were no longer satisfied with the food of their forefathers, Indian corn did not suffice, they wanted bread and meat and other luxuries as yet unknown to their brethren in the south. But happily the crops were good all over Italy while they were bad in the rest of Europe.

'God sends us a good harvest that we may not forget Him,' the Pope continued, and with a deep sigh he added, 'Otherwise and in all other things He has abandoned us. We pray in vain, He does not hear us and our enemies are allowed to triumph over us. But the Papacy has had severer trials than the present one and the Pope knows how to suffer, to wait and to hope. The day will come when the Church will triumph again over her enemies. I fully understand now that we are in a crisis which must develop itself to the end. We cannot arrest its progress and the duty of the Pope is to wait, defend the rights of the Church and not give way to his enemies so long as it pleases God to send us these trials. The Italians are not a bad people but they are easily led astray by foreign agents who revolutionize the country for their own wicked purposes. When they have suffered more they will repent and return to us. Happy is England to have a real national existence which can produce that admirable Volunteer movement in the hour of danger, I have lately read about in the newspaper.'

I here observed to His Holiness that such movements depended on the amount of confidence a People felt in their national institutions and in their Government, which made it their obvious interest to defend and preserve those institutions. The Italians had ever shown themselves ready to sacrifice their lives in an almost hopeless national struggle against their foreign oppressors. Why should they not do so for their Rulers and Governments if they could obtain what they aspired to, namely popular institutions and a national existence which it would be in their interest to live and die for? The task of Italian governments was facilitated by the fact that they had to deal with a warm hearted, highly gifted and intelligent people who loved their country better than their lives. That task was to establish such institutions as would call forth the affections and the confidence of the governed for the government. Was not that the secret of the sympathies Italy bore to King Victor Emmanuel? It was impossible to suppose that Piedmontese agents and money could have produced the present national movement in Italy, and any Italian prince could have commanded the sympathies of the nation who had in earnest held out the prospect of a national existence under popular institutions.

'You are mistaken,' the Pope said, 'if you take the present crisis in Italy for a national one. What is being done now will all be undone again in time. Piedmont is an instrument in the hands of the Emperor Napoleon, who thinks it his duty to carry out the ideas of his uncle. What his ultimate objects are I know not, but whatever he establishes will end with him as the Kingdom of his uncle ended with the Empire. The Grand Dukes or their heirs will return to their dominions and the rights of the Papacy are everlasting. I went to the Romagna in 1857 and, believe me, the true affections of the Romagnoles are for me, they have faith, and would return to me at once if they were not terrorized by foreign agents like the rest of Northern Italy. It is absurd to talk of non-intervention in Italy so long as Piedmontese agents infest the Romagna and the Duchies. Let them be withdrawn and the votes of the true majority will be for their legitimate sovereigns. But what was accomplished in the North is now being carried out in the South. The young king of Naples has been compelled to make concessions which will sooner or later bring on his downfall and his kingdom will be annexed to Piedmont like the rest of Italy. Sicily which has no sympathy for Piedmont will equally vote for annexation under the influence of foreign agents after having fallen to Garibaldi through the treachery of the Neapolitan generals who were largely bribed with foreign gold. . . .'

I replied that from all I had heard and seen I believed the present movement to be the effect of a deeply rooted desire of the Italians for national administrations. Had it been frankly met and guided by their Sovereigns they might easily have been satisfied with a Confederation, but the opposition thrown in their way and the tendency of their Rulers to call in foreign assistance against their subjects had forcibly produced a desire for unity under one Sovereign as the only manner in which they could resist foreign aggression and establish a free and powerful Italy.

'*Figlio mio*,' the Pope replied, 'you speak in ignorance of past events. I tried to give national liberties to my subjects and they murdered my Minister[1] and forced me to fly. The Grand Duke of Tuscany's government was universally admitted to be good and yet he was driven away. The Romagnoles are devoted to the Papacy, and yet a small and criminal minority was sufficient to terrorize even the better people into voting for annexation to Piedmont. As I said before, the Italians are not bad. See only how they attend the procession of the Holy Virgin in Rome. But they are timid and easily led astray. They can never govern themselves, they require a firm hand to guide and govern them. As to my Government it belongs to the Catholic world and not to Italy alone and those who serve it cease to have a nationality of their own. They serve God and Christianity, and General de Lamoricière whose devotion is so great will be rewarded in Heaven for it. God has fought ere this for His chosen people.'

Then laughing good humouredly the Pope continued: 'The Emperor wants to make a gardener of me, and leave me the Vatican and a garden only, instead of my present dominions, but in the end the Pope will be in possession of his eternal power when perhaps neither His Majesty nor his ally King Victor Emmanuel will have a throne to rest upon. The Popes are gardeners in one sense but they have been soldiers too.'

His Holiness then proceeded to describe the fortifications of Civita Vecchia and Ancona with which he seemed much satisfied, and he dwelt on the advantage of good roads which he intended to have executed under General de Lamoricière's directions in the Marches, if 'Monsieur Cavour' allowed him the necessary time to do so. His Holiness appeared deeply convinced that a general war would restore things to

[1] Pellegrino Rossi was assassinated on 15 November 1848.

their former state and that the duty of the Papacy was to wait and protest against every change that occurred. Returning to the subject of the
Volunteer movement in England for which he again expressed his
admiration, the Pope asked me whether I thought the Emperor would
be able to hold England for any length of time, after he had invaded it.
I replied that he could not, but in the first instance I did not believe that
any invasion was contemplated by our ally.

'Then you do not know,' His Holiness continued, 'that the question
was discussed by the German Sovereigns with the Emperor at the Conference of Baden and that the Emperor said he could attack and invade
England with ease, but that he could not engage to maintain his possession long against a hostile population.'

I begged for some explanation but His Holiness merely answered
that the revolutionary policy of England had rendered all the Governments of Europe hostile to her and that she could not reckon on friends
or allies if ever she were attacked. 'It would be more easy,' he concluded,
'for France to form a Coalition against England than for England to
form a Coalition against France, for after all the Emperor Napoleon is
at present the Master of Europe.'

After some further conversation the Pope invited me to wait on him
again whenever I felt inclined to do so and dismissed me with his customary blessing. If I have dwelt so long and in such detail on a private
conversation of no public importance in itself, it is chiefly to show your
Lordship that the mind of Pope Pius IX is not of a nature to grapple
effectively with the difficulties that threaten the Holy See.

122 [P.R.O. 30/22/75]   *Naples, 28 July 1860*

Private
O.R. to Lord J.R.

Your last speech on non-intervention in Italian affairs has created a
burst of enthusiasm in Naples. Foreign intervention can impose any
form of Government here. If left to themselves the Neapolitans will
unite with Northern Italy, for Italy is deeply imbued with the spirit of
Gioberti's writings. Some people look upon the present cry for annexation as the result of a strong anti-dynastic feeling and think that if
the Bourbons were removed and a more popular King placed on the
throne of Naples the Neapolitans would be satisfied with an Italian
Confederation.

My observations lead me to think that this is not the case, and that experience will prove that *Unity under one Sceptre* is the real and deeply rooted wish of Italy. *Vedremo.* I may be mistaken, but as far as the Roman States are concerned I will answer for the most anxious desire of the Pope's subjects to send His Holiness to Jerusalem.

123 [P.R.O. 30/22/111]   *F.O. 6 August 1860*

Private
Lord J.R. to O.R.

The spectacle of the Papacy with Victor Emmanuel on one side and Garibaldi on the other will be very curious. I conclude with you that the unity of Italy under one sceptre will come to pass. But I hope the Italians will stop short at Mantua. If they attack the white uniforms, they may find themselves driven back to the Ticino. . . .

124 [F.O. 43/77]   *Rome, 14 August 1860*

No. 106
O.R. to Lord J.R.

. . . The French Ambassador and Cardinal Antonelli inform me that all idea of withdrawing the French army from Rome has for the present been given up. . . .

125 [P.R.O. 30/22/75]   *Rome, 21 August 1860*

Private
O.R. to Lord J.R.

. . . I am convinced that the Unionist Party will prove to be immense in the Kingdom of Naples, as it is in the Papal States, and that the annexation will be accomplished either through Garibaldi or through the first Neapolitan parliament, according to circumstances. Certainly, I should prefer to see Garibaldi where he is and rest on his past glory, and Naples allowed a more organic development, as was the case in Tuscany, for progress is fraught with danger. An attack on the Holy See and Venetia may serve as the excuse for Austrian intervention and then *Good night* to Italian independence for years to come. . . .

Private

O.R. to Lord J.R.

I have been spending a few days here at Villa Falconieri with the Gramonts who are always most exceedingly kind to me. He is a very amiable host and his conversation is clever, witty and instructive for he takes interest in everything. The Duc de Gramont has fully confirmed to me what I reported to you in my despatches – namely that the occupation of Rome by French troops must now continue indefinitely as the Emperor could not take upon himself to give up the Pope to the Revolution, and he also asserts that the temporal power of the Pope in Italy depends solely on the presence of a foreign force, and as an attack on Venetia by Garibaldi may result in the occupation of all Italy by the Austrians, it becomes the duty of France to keep the Pope to herself. General de Noue is to have the chief command of the garrison of Rome which is to be immediately increased by a third Regiment of about two thousand men. This measure will greatly please Cardinal Antonelli, whose tenure of office thereby becomes safer than ever and which may now last as long as he or the Pope live on earth, to the detriment of the Romans. The French army will however not stir out of Rome whatever Garibaldi may do with Lamoricière, the Marches or Umbria. But woe to Garibaldi if he should take it into his head to march upon Rome. Lamoricière is preparing for defence, he has now about thirty thousand men, ten thousand of which are good Austrian troops who have served in Italy before, and who are commanded by their own officers. About one hundred and twenty arrive every week from Austria, and are at once incorporated in special Austrian Corps, and General Lamoricière looks upon them as his best troops. The Italian officers have now almost all been dismissed and replaced by Germans, Belgians and Swiss, but the Italian soldiers cannot be relied on. Desertion is more frequent than ever, especially among the Swiss. The other night forty of them left in a body and crossed the Tuscan frontier. The Papal Government look on and seem to have plenty of money at their disposal, while the people sigh for Garibaldi and United Italy. It is extraordinary what sacrifices in money the poorest subjects of the Pope are making to assist Garibaldi. Families of labourers who have scarcely enough to buy bread, manage to lay by a few *bajocks* every week which they give to

Garibaldi's agents in Rome with a prayer to the Madonna that they may be delivered of the *Maledetti Preti*.

[*On 19 August Garibaldi had landed in Calabria. He advanced rapidly on Naples which he entered on 7 September. The King of Naples had retired to Gaeta.*]

127   [P.R.O. 30/22/75]   *Rome, 4 September 1860*

Private
O.R. to Lord J.R.

... Gramont is the most amiable of hosts and is really *charmant* with me, but unfortunately he cannot speak the truth, so that his statements are not worth much. It is difficult to be more agreeable and less truthful than he is, in short he is an amiable humbug. Like all French diplomatists in Italy, he affects the greatest contempt for Italian aspirations and liberties, and the greatest hatred of Italians, and declares he cannot take interest in a Nation who forget the laws of public and political morality. He wishes to hang Cavour, shoot Garibaldi and hand all Italy over to an everlasting Austrian occupation. But he says all this in the pleasantest possible manner, as if he were inviting you to come and dine with him. ...

128   [F.O. 43/77]   *Rome, 11 September 1860*

No. 119
O.R. to Lord J.R.

... On Monday morning, 10th instant, the Royal Sardinian steam frigate 'Tripoli' arrived at Civita Vecchia from Genoa with Count della Minerva on board on a special mission from King Victor Emmanuel to the Pope. The Count was not allowed by the police authorities to proceed to Rome but was requested to remain on board and later a message from Cardinal Antonelli invited him to make known the object of his mission either through the Papal delegate at Civita Vecchia or through the French Ambassador at Rome. The former course having been adopted, Cardinal Antonelli received through the delegate at 8 o'clock last night the despatch from Count Cavour brought by Count della Minerva in which the Turin Cabinet summon the Papal Government to dismiss all the foreign mercenary troops in the Pope's service, with as little delay as possible, or to expect the occupation of the Marches and Umbria by the troops of King Victor Emmanuel. A similar communication had been made to General de Lamoricière by General Fanti. Whilst these startling communications were reaching the Vatican, Monsieur de Gramont, the French Ambassador, arrived also from his villa with a formal message from the Emperor to the Pope, to the effect, that, while at Marseilles, his Imperial Majesty had learnt with regret in what manner the King of Sardinia intended to occupy the Papal States, and that he had at once written to His Majesty that he would oppose any aggression on the Papal Territory with the force of arms, and that orders were already given to embark several regiments at Marseilles for Civita Vecchia for the defence and protection of the Holy See. His Imperial Majesty was compelled to adopt this line of policy towards Sardinia in consequence of the breach of faith of which the Piedmontese cabinet had become guilty by threatening the Pope, after the repeated assurances given at Paris that the Papal territory would be respected by the troops of King Victor Emmanuel.

I need scarcely tell your Lordship that this communication on the part of the French Ambassador has given the greatest satisfaction to the Pope as well as to His Holiness's Government. . . .

[*On 11 September the Piedmontese forces under General Fanti invaded the Marches and Umbria.*]

129 [F.O. 43/77]   *Rome, 15 September 1860*

No. 126. Confidential
O.R. to Lord J.R.

The Duc de Gramont announceed yesterday to Cardinal Antonelli that the rupture between France and Piedmont was complete, that Monsieur Talleyrand had been recalled from Turin and the Sardinian representative at Paris had received his passports, and he repeated the assurance mentioned in my despatch of the 11th instant, that General de Goyon was expected here on the 17th with a considerable force to oppose the progress of the Piedmontese army in the Papal States. In conversation with me his Excellency added that all the representatives of foreign powers, with the exception of Sir James Hudson, had been recalled from Turin, that an Austrian intervention from Venetia was more than likely, that he had given up the protection of Piedmontese subjects for the time being, and that he knew no limit to the numbers of soldiers France would send to Rome for the protection of the Holy See. His Excellency could not, however, specify, in answer to my questions, in what manner the French army would act in the Papal States and how far they would extend their operations. He could not believe Piedmont would accept war with France and he thought a European Congress would now settle the Roman question. . . .

Meanwhile the Sardinian Army has already occupied Perugia, Pesaro, Fano, Sinigallia etc., etc., and is advancing steadily amidst the enthusiasm of the population, while General de Lamoricière, who reports that he is highly satisfied with the spirit of his troops, has started from Spoleto at the head of ten thousand men to reach Ancona in forced marches before that fortress falls to the Piedmontese. The result of all this is that the first joyful impression has vanished and a feeling of insecurity has crept over the inmates of the Vatican who begin to fear that the zeal and devotion of the French Ambassador for the Pope and the implacable hatred he professes to the Italians and their aspirations, may have led His Excellency to use language indicating more his own feelings than the future policy of his Government with which he is as yet but imperfectly acquainted. It is, however, difficult to believe that a man of high qualifications and brilliant abilities like the Duc de Gramont could have spoken as he did without authority. On the other hand the National Party, who seem to have been well acquainted with the intentions of Piedmont, are carried away by an indescribable enthusiasm at the idea that their long political sufferings are drawing to a close. . . .

130 [F.O. 43/77]   *Rome, 16 September 1860*

No. 129. Confidential
O.R. to Lord J.R.

I mentioned to your Lordship in my despatch of the 15th instant that Cardinal Antonelli had often expressed his conviction that Austria would involve herself in European difficulties of such magnitude if she attempted any armed intervention in Italy that he could not in conscience wish to see her run the risk at present. The crisis in Italy, he says, is a hail storm and it is best to wait patiently without stirring until it has blown over. Pope Pius IX does not share the views of his Secretary of State on this point. It is a matter of painful surprise to him that Austria has not yet come to the rescue of the Holy See, and in his last conversation, some days since, with Baron de Bach His Holiness expressed himself in strong and bitter terms of reproach, regret and condemnation at the policy of non-intervention pursued up to this day by the Cabinet of Vienna, and the Pope ended by reminding the Ambassador that such policy could not in the long run prove beneficial to the soul of his Imperial Master.

131 [F.O. 43/77]   *Rome, 17 September 1860*

No. 131
O.R. to Lord J.R.

... The feeling of the great majority [in Rome] is entirely for a United Italy under King Victor Emmanuel and it is curious to witness the intense joy and gratitude with which the advance of Piedmont is hailed. The intellect and energy of the population is chiefly to be found in the middle classes and they are all with Piedmont. The aristocracy with all the amiable qualities that characterize them, do not appear to have the courage to stand by their opinions or the energy of action. They are as distant from the throne as all the other lay subjects of the Sovereign Pontiff, and the majority of them are Italian in their sympathies. The Pope has long ceased to consult the Sacred College of Cardinals, dismissed the financial *Consulta* and governed his States despotically with the aid of Cardinal Antonelli, and the minor Italian clergy now begin to give vent to their feelings and complain that his Eminence by substituting illegally his own advice for that of the Cardinals has brought on many of the present misfortunes of the Church. The Cardinals grumble but do not speak out. The result is that the national movement has adherents even in the lower ranks of the Roman Clergy who have long viewed with jealousy the favors bestowed by the Pope on the foreign prelates who surround his throne. No one has questioned the ability, energy and excellent intentions of General de Lamoricière, but both he and his army are distasteful to the Romans. The violence of opinion of the French Legitimists who came with him alarmed all classes. The Austrians and Swiss were old enemies. Strange to say, the solemn declarations and promises of the French Ambassador, which had been so gratefully received at the Vatican a week ago, regarding the defence of the Holy See by a large army about to sail from France under General de Goyon's orders, and the rupture of diplomatic relations between

Paris and Turin, has not shaken the conviction of the National Party in Rome that the Emperor Napoleon is their truest friend and that he sceretly favors their ardent wish for a United Italy. Wherever one looks, contempt for the administration by the priests stares one in the face and a deəp anxious national desire for the success of Piedmont transpires in every word and gesture. The absence of newspapers and the presence of spies renders intelligence from liberated Italy doubly sweet and discussion dangerous. It has the attraction of forbidden fruit and the charm of mystery. Distance also lends enchantment to the joyful tidings of freedom that secretly find their way into the Papal States from the south and from the north. They are sunbeams through the thick *malaria* that hangs around the Vatican and weighs heavily on every breast. In short polytheism has ever been the religion of Italy, and Victor Emmanuel, Cavour and Garibaldi appear to be the demi-gods of modern Rome.

132 [F.O. 43/77]   *Rome, 18 September 1860*

No. 134. Confidential
O.R. to Lord J.R.

Ever since I had the honour to know Cardinal Antonelli I have never seen His Eminence in a more painful state of dejection than this morning. All was over, he said, it had pleased God to allow his Church to be visited by severe trials and the Papacy was in the position of an unarmed man attacked by a legion of assassins. No news had reached Rome from General de Lamoricière since Saturday 15th instant, when he was still at Macerata with eight thousand men and in all probability his communications with Rome had been cut off by the Piedmontese. He begged I would inform Her Majesty's Government that the population of the Marches and Umbria had been perfectly tranquil and satisfied with their fate and had not moved or shown symptoms of dissatisfaction until armed bands of volunteers from Tuscany had come to rouse and force them to acts of rebellion. The new principles of international Law introduced by Piedmont and not as yet combatted by Europe would soon lead to communism and the total destruction of social order. God alone by a miracle could arrest the misfortunes which threatened the world.

The promises of assistance and intervention on the part of the Emperor Napoleon conveyed to the Pope by the Duc de Gramont had not yet been followed up by any very energetic acts. He hoped for the best, but meanwhile the forces of Piedmont would occupy the Adriatic provinces and the Papal army, too weak to resist invasion from without, would have to yield to overwhelming numbers. He really knew not what France intended to do then, but it appeared to him that Cavour and Garibaldi were better informed than the Papal Government of the true policy of the Emperor Napoleon.

[*On 18 September Lamoricière's army was dispersed by the Piedmontese at the battle of Castefidardo.*]

133 [F.O. 43/77] *Rome, 22 September 1860*

No. 140. Confidential
O.R. to Lord J.R.

The Duc de Gramont informs me that the Pope did not receive General de Goyon well and used hard and unjust language in his presence about the present policy of the Emperor Napoleon, so much so that Cardinal Antonelli made a sort of apology and explained to the French Ambassador that the Pope who had suffered formerly from epilepsy, when threatened with an attack of that disease could not be held responsible for all he said; that the approaching symptoms of the attack were visible in the eyes and hands, and that when he, Cardinal Antonelli, perceived them he avoided many subjects in conversation with His Holiness, which he knew by a long experience were liable to hasten the crisis. At present the Pope's excitement was caused by the slowness of the movements of the French Army. He had been led to expect by Monsieur de Gramont that the Emperor Napoleon was going to war with the King of Sardinia for the purpose of driving the Piedmontese troops out of the Holy See and he was now beginning to fear for many reasons that the Emperor would not fulfil his promise. Under those circumstances the Cardinal had intimated to the Ambassador that the Pope would be compelled to leave Rome and seek an asylum in Spain or Bavaria, and in consequence Monsieur de Gramont had decided to send his Secretary of Embassy, the Marquis de Cadore, in a French man of war 'Yonne' at once to Marseilles to meet the Emperor, on his return from Algiers, for the purpose of explaining the painful impression produced on the mind of His Holiness by the apparent hesitation of his Majesty in the accomplishment of the promises of protection conveyed to the Vatican by the order of Monsieur Thouvenel through the Duc de Gramont. The Marquis de Cadore had sailed yesterday for Marseilles and the Pope had agreed to await the result of his mission. The Duke, who deplores these events most sincerely, seems to expect that the Emperor on learning the state of affairs in Rome will take immediate steps to restore the Marches and Umbria to His Holiness, but I must in truth observe that no one in Rome shares His Excellency's hopes or expectations.

There is a large party of foreign prelates who urge the Pope to leave Rome and appeal to the Catholic world for assistance and protection, but I do not believe Cardinal Antonelli shares their views. My own impression is that His Eminence's influence will prevail in the end and that the Pope will remain at Rome under all circumstances.

General de Goyon has orders to repulse any attack on the part of Garibaldi, and in all probability the Piedmontese army will have arrested his progress before he can march upon Rome. . . .

134 [P.R.O. 30/22/75]   *Rome, 25 September 1860*

Private
O.R. to Lord J.R.

Gramont's position is painfully awkward! His colleagues here fancy that his extreme desire to interfere in Italy and crush Piedmont and the whole Italian movement made him believe what he *hoped* and *promised* the Pope in the name of the Emperor, namely that an army of from 50 to 100,000 men would be sent into the heart of Italy to drive Piedmont out of the Papal States and as I have since learnt he added that the stipulation of Villa Franca would then be carried out by the combined armies of France and Austria. No wonder that after all these fine promises the Pope should be in a towering passion. He says that his army being completely destroyed without one French soldier having been sent to the rescue, if the Emperor Napoleon does not at once go to war and restore his lost provinces unconditionally to him, he will leave Rome and seek protection in Spain or Bavaria. I saw Gramont today. He is profoundly annoyed. He says the Pope is really preparing for departure, but he flatters himself that His Holiness will be stopped by the answer which Monsr de Cadore will bring from the Emperor. . . .

Baron Bach does not believe in Austrian intervention just now. He agrees with Cardinal Antonelli that it would be too early and that it is desirable that the Italians should commit many excesses so as to render the intervention more sweeping when it does come. He therefore desires the departure of the Pope as he hopes it may be followed by popular excesses and then by a general Catholic intervention. Poor Italy! The Barbarians will not let her alone. . . .

The enthusiasm produced in the masses by the policy of Piedmont amounts to madness and the departure of the Pope is looked forward to with the burning anxiety of secret delight. The Roman Princes fear the anarchy that might follow, but they have no great attachment for their sovereign. His late obstinacy, his foreign army under Lamoricière and the attempt to make a Military Power of the Holy See; his belief in the obnoxious Antonelli, his neglect and contempt of the Sacred College, his preference for crazy foreign prelates such as Mérode and Talbot etc, have tended to render him more an object of contempt and pity than anything else. Among the clergy even I hear him and Antonelli loudly condemned as the authors of the present misfortunes of the Church. Some of the more powerful religious orders, such as the Benedictines and Jesuits, have shewn symptoms of mutiny and have said that they could not allow the interests of the Church to be sacrificed to Pope Pius's obstinate fancy for Cardinal Antonelli. In fact there are strange signs of discontent in the Church, and if the Pope runs away from Rome it has been whispered by wise men that we might possibly enjoy the spectacle of seeing Pope and Anti-Pope excommunicating each other as in days of old. It is certainly quite impossible to live in more interesting times than these.

135 [F.O. 43/77]   *Rome, 29 September 1860*

No. 145. Confidential
O.R. to Lord J.R.

I asked Cardinal Antonelli yesterday what truth there was in the report of the Pope's intention to leave Rome. His Eminence replied that circumstances might certainly occur which might compel the Holy Father to seek protection in some foreign country, but that there could be no question of his doing so at present since the French Emperor had guaranteed the undisturbed possession of Rome and Civita Vecchia to His Holiness. . . . There could be no doubt that the Emperor was endeavouring to realize the principles laid down in the pamphlet 'The Pope and the Congress' and the Papal Government had not the power to resist violence. All they could do was to wait until Europe was able to do them justice. The last communications received from France were as follows: The Duc de Gramont had received some despatches and a private letter from Monsieur Thouvenel in which the Emperor's deep regret, surprize and indignation at the conduct of Piedmont was expressed. He had in consequence broken off diplomatic relations with that country and would add ten thousand men to his garrison for the protection of Rome and of the Pope, but that was all he could do. Monsieur Thouvenel at the end of his letter explained to the French Ambassador that he had misunderstood or misinterpreted what his Imperial Master *could* do, he was obliged to adhere to the policy of non-intervention in Italy, and when he said he would oppose the plans of King Victor Emmanuel he meant that he would oppose any attempt on Rome, he could not go beyond that....

136 [F.O. 43/78]   *Rome, 2 October 1860*

No. 147. Secret
O.R. to Lord J.R.

It is a matter of general surprize that the French Ambassador has not preferred to resign his post than to continue in the painful position he now holds in Rome. After solemnly promising the Pope that France would drive the Piedmontese out of the Holy See and return the Marches and Umbria to His Holiness; after publickly announcing at the railway station that war was declared between France and Sardinia; after renewing these assurances in the strongest language both in writing and in conversation with his colleagues, the Imperial Government have not seen fit to back up the promises they had authorized his Excellency to make and his position has become as false as it is painful. To that must also be added the excessive violence of the language used by the Papal authorities against him. He is most unjustly accused by them of having been instrumental in the destruction of the Papal army, for General de Lamoricière would not have advanced had he not been led to expect that the French army would follow and cover his retreat upon Spoleto or Rome if beaten by Cialdini. Monsignor de Mérode, for instance, told Monsieur de Gramont among other things I will not repeat, that 'he was the faithful lackey of his lying master'. Being a priest, the Ambassador could only decline to transact business any further with him. The Pope told General de Goyon in a fit of ill-

humour that the Emperor was a traitor and a knave and Goyon a fool
to serve him, and when speaking of the Duc de Gramont the Holy
Father has repeatedly called his Excellency 'that Legitimist, who after
selling himself to Monsieur Napoleon has himself become a merchant
of lies'. . . .

137 [P.R.O. 30/22/75]   *Rome, 5 October 1860*

Private
O.R. to Lord J.R.

This Papacy costs much blood and money, and twenty thousand
French soldiers to impose it upon Italy. General Goyon talks of occupying Viterbo, Orvieto, Tivoli, Albano, Velletri and Frosinone and
re-establishing the Papal authority with their gendarmes. I regret this
measure at present which will only exasperate the unfortunate subjects
of the Pope still more, who have just tasted a few days of independence
and who will be thus exposed to the vengeance of the *Neri*. The French
occupation of Rome thereby also assumes the character of a direct
intervention in Italian affairs and indicates a change in the policy of
France. . . . The Pope has recommended recruiting, buying horses,
ordering military stores and forming an army. Four thousand French
troops arrived yesterday at Civita Vecchia. . . . The Pope has still
plenty of money, but sooner or later his resources being now cut
off, he will have none, and then it will be curious to see what the Catholic world will be prepared to do for him. . . .

138 [P.R.O. 30/22/75]   *Rome, 13 October 1860*

Private
O.R. to Lord J.R.

The French troops have met with great moral opposition in occupying
Viterbo and Civita Castellana and the smaller places that had proclaimed King Victor Emmanuel. The village of Campagnano was the
only place where they were well received. The public mind is dreadfully alarmed and painfully distressed at the French intervention, and
the constant arrival of fresh troops and munitions of war keeps up a
state of feverish excitement. Gramont keeps up the spirits of the Vatican by telling them that a Congress is about to meet at the end of the
month at Paris which will settle the Pope's difficulties to His Holiness's

entire satisfaction. The Pope wants Lamoricière to return to Rome to give him the direction of the War Department and make a Roman Prince of him, but I doubt that he will be able to carry out this plan. One of the most striking illustrations of the Pope's obstinacy is the fact that he has not only given orders for the formation of a new army but that he even insists on re-enlisting Irishmen although the late experiment turned out so disastrous. . . .

139 [F.O. 519/205] Cowley Papers   *Rome, 16 October 1860*

O.R. to Earl Cowley [Ambassador in Paris]

. . . I am satisfied that [Gramont] was perfectly sincere in believing that France and Piedmont were going to war about the Pope. Gramont has a happy disposition, he believes what he hopes. At present he believes in a Congress and that he is shortly to replace Thouvenel at the French Foreign Office!

Ld Malmesbury used to keep me well informed of all that was doing, but since Ld John is in power I have not received a scrap of information beyond blue books. If it were not for you and Sir James Hudson I should not know even of the existence of Her Majesty's Government. Ld John occasionally writes me a private letter, but it seldom contains anything to guide or instruct me. I get mutilated accounts of *our* policy from my colleagues, and I correct them instinctively as best I can. . . .

140 [F.O. 519/205]   *Rome, 30 October 1860*

O.R. to Earl Cowley

You wish to know the true history of Gramont's assurances and promises of French intervention in the Marches and Umbria? The mystery is not easily solved, but you will have seen from my dispatch No. 161 containing Gramont's letter to Antonelli that he now denies ever having announced war between France and Piedmont, although he cannot deny his telegram to the consul at Ancona. Antonelli has not yet answered Gramont's letter and it remains therefore to be seen whether he will have the pluck to convict His Excellency of lying or not.

My impression is that Monsr Thouvenel's statement reported in your No. 1257 of 26 September is perfectly correct and that Gramont's intense hatred of Cavour, Piedmont and the Italian movement in general, led him to hope and believe that when Monsr Thou-

venel telegraphed to say that the Emperor would oppose the policy of
Piedmont in the Papal States and would break off diplomatic relations
with Turin, he meant a *bona fide* war with Sardinia. Wishing to give
himself importance he exaggerated in words what he hoped and believed, and I cannot but think that his language was perfectly sincere.
After committing himself in conversation with everybody he met, he
discovered that he had made a serious mistake and hoping to induce the
Emperor to back him up in the promises he had made so rashly to the
Pope, he sent Cadore to Paris with a letter to the Emperor to entreat of
him to come to the Pope's assistance and he fully believed the Emperor
would be persuaded by his eloquence. He failed as you know and then
it was that he wrote again to Paris to insist on the necessity of extending
the occupation of Rome to the Patrimony of St Peter [*i.e. the strip
of the Papal State, of an average depth of about forty miles, on the
Tyrrhenian Coast*], Viterbo and Velletri etc., etc.

The War Dept at Paris followed his advice or rather his entreaties
by which he hoped to conciliate the infuriated Pope and never did they
make a greater mistake for they have found the populations turn against
them in silent, dogged opposition and the best families emigrate to
Tuscany so that the French Regiments are exactly in the position in
which the Austrians were in Lombardy or in Romagna before the war,
and they all most heartily wish themselves out of it. . . .

141 [P.R.O. 30/22/75]   *Rome, 6 November 1860*

Private
O.R. to Lord J.R.

I told Cardinal Antonelli that Naples being as good as annexed I expected to be attached to the only Mission we had left in Italy, namely
Turin. His Eminence grinned, looked embarrassed and then squeezing
my knees between his fingers and thumb with affectionate gesticula-
tions said: '*Caro mio*, could you not explain to your respected *Zio* with
my respects that the Pope would feel much annoyed at having a diplomatic agent in Rome in any way connected with a Government with
which he has been and ever will be at war, and with a King and a
minister who have incurred the censure of the Holy Roman Church.
We have in every way broken with Turin and if you are now to be
attached to Sir James Hudson it will be very awkward for us and
awkward for you and will give rise to unpleasant insinuations and

questions and place us and you and Her Majesty's Government in a most embarrassing position which might easily be avoided.' I replied that I understood what he meant, but what was to be done since I must be attached to some Legation according to usage? His Eminence then said, that they wished to keep me in Rome as long as possible and that no doubt H.M. Government were at liberty to do as they pleased but he felt convinced that H.M. Govt. could have no wish to annoy the Pope in the midst of his present misfortunes and afflictions, nor could they desire to embarrass His Holiness's Govt., and that as my being attached to one of our Legations was a mere form it could not be a matter of any very great importance to H.M. Govt. what Legation I belonged to. In fact, he continued, he would greatly prefer my being attached to no Legation at all than to have me here residing in Rome and in official connection with Turin. I might merely be detached from the Foreign Office, or what would be still better, I might belong to the Embassy at Paris. There would even be a good excuse for that. The French Emperor sent an army to protect Rome, why should not the English Ambassador send an Attaché from Paris to watch that army and report upon French proceedings in Rome for the information of Lord Cowley and of Her Majesty's Government? Cardinal Antonelli evidently thought this last part of his speech a capital joke, for he laughed ready to kill himself and then requested me to write to you, present you his compliments and beg that you would take the Pope's feelings into consideration and if possible not place His Eminence and the Vatican in general, in the embarrassing position of having to harbour a semi-official link with the hated, dreaded and excommunicated Government of Turin in the very bosom of the Holy Roman See. I always expected the Vatican would object to a Turin Attaché at Rome and the possibility of my being attached to Paris had already occurred to me. I suppose it will be all the same to Her Majesty's Government whether I am attached to Paris or Turin and I suppose also that you will prefer not to give unnecessary pain and annoyance to the Pope in the last days of his temporal existence, poor dear old man. . . . I hope therefore that you will see no objection to meeting the wishes of Pope and Cardinal and that you will have me attached to my dear and excellent Chief[1] of former days, to whom I am indebted for so much kindness and good advice.

Lord Cowley still continues to write, encourage and enlighten me

[1] i.e. Lord Cowley.

THE ROMAN QUESTION 137

and I am sincerely grateful to him for it. . . . I am very much obliged to you for the handsome offer of an Attaché; if you send me one I shall be delighted to turn him to account, if you don't I shall be equally *pleased*, for I confess I take a quiet little pride of my own in trying to accomplish my task here quite alone as did my predecessor Lord Lyons. Perhaps this is foolish on my part, but nevertheless such is my feeling. . . .

142 [F.O. 43/78]   *Rome, 11 November 1860*

No. 170
O.R. to Lord J.R.

Your Lordship has probably known the result of the vote for annexation in the Marches and Umbria long before it was whispered from ear to ear in Rome. I have spoken to four English tourists who have passed through Rome after travelling in those provinces, and they report that the enthusiasm for Unity and Victor Emmanuel has perhaps been even greater there than in any other portion of Italy. Even the peasants led by their parish priests, on whose fidelity the Vatican placed almost implicit reliance, voted against the temporal rule of the Popes and the inhabitants of the province of Viterbo also found means to vote, notwithstanding the presence of the French garrison. I have had occasion before this to point to the growing national sympathies of the lower clergy in Italy and I am now happy to perceive that those sympathies are gradually kindling in the breasts of the more enlightened and humane Cardinals, Bishops and Generals of monastic orders. They now admit that the Church will have to yield to the great national movement and to necessity. I have more than once sought to discuss this new feeling of the Clergy with Cardinal Antonelli, but his Eminence has invariably asserted his conviction that the laws of the Church being eternal they cannot be subject to political necessity, and that before Pius IX can yield one jot of the rights of the Vicar of Christ on Earth, it will be his duty before the Almighty to seek, like four of his predecessors, some other Avignon in a neutral portion of Europe.

143 [F.O. 43/78]   *Rome, 17 November 1860*

No. 172
O.R. to Lord J.R.

I have the honour to enclose the whole of General de Lamoricière's report to the Pro-Minister of Arms, Monsignor de Mérode, respecting the defeat of the Pope's army under his commands, by the army of King Victor Emmanuel. While Her Majesty's Consul Mr Newton is preparing a translation of this lengthy and elaborate statement I will submit a few observations to Your Lordship on the impression it has produced in Rome. In glancing over the enclosed report your Lordship will perceive that General de Lamoricière blames everyone but himself for the defeat of the Papal army. He blames France for not keeping her promise to oppose the invasion of the Pontifical States by the Piedmontese Army. He blames Cardinal Antonelli for not having been better informed as to the real intentions of Sardinia. He blames Austria for having weakened the spirit of the Pope's Austrian soldiers by promising to re-enlist them for the Imperial Army in the event of the revolution triumphing over the forces of His Holiness, a measure which led them to believe that their defeat was looked upon as inevitable by the Austrian Government. He blames the Emperor Francis Joseph for not having sent his fleet to save Ancona. He blames the Papal Government for administrative inefficiency in regard to the assistance required by the commissariat. He blames the Pope's subjects for want of intelligence, his Swiss regiments for want of courage, and his foreign soldiers in general for apathy. And finally he blames the Catholic Powers of Europe for not coming to his rescue when the bombardment of Ancona was heard on the coast of Dalmatia, at Venice and at Trieste. He finds scarcely a word of regret for the amiable and chivalrous Pimodan and he excuses his own abandonment of the army during the battle of Castelfidardo by his desire to save two millions of *scudi* sent to him by the Pope to be lodged in the fortress of Ancona, and by his desire to reach that citadel which might yet have been saved, he thought, through foreign intervention. He commends many of his officers and lauds the Franco-Belgian legion in general. He casts no blame on the Irish Brigade, which though unarmed, seems to have done him good service. It is thought in Rome that General de Lamoricière proves too much. Without entering into the military and strategical merits of his report it is quite clear that the Papal army might easily have been saved without even the loss of military honour. If instead of accepting the unequal conflict, with the daring bravery of a French soldier, General de Lamoricière had declared that it would be as unreasonable as it was inhumane to send a few newly raised regiments against overwhelming odds, tried soldiers, distinguished generals, and a hostile and insurgent population, whose ultimate success could not for one moment be doubted, and if General de Lamoricière had fallen back upon the *Campagna* of Rome where a French army was ready to protect his men, he might to this day have preserved the Pontifical army, effected a junction with the Neapolitan army at Gaeta and met King Victor Emmanuel in Central Italy at the head of eighty thousand men, backed by the French Garrison of Rome.

Happily for Italy and the peace of Europe, all this did not occur and the Pope's mercenaries were dispersed. General de Lamoricière has offended the susceptibilities of everyone by his report, with the exception of Admiral Persano, on whom he bestows the highest praise for his conduct and gallantry at the seige of Ancona. Your Lordship is already in possession of the French Ambassador's protest against the publication and falsification of his telegrams in the *Giornale di Roma* and which are now repeated in the General's report. I also learn that some of the foreign ministers complain of the disparaging tone in which he speaks of their countrymen under his command. The Austrian Ambassador has objected to the blame cast upon the policy of his Emperor, but it appears that Cardinal Antonelli's prudent counsels were overruled by the growing influence of the extreme Catholic party, and that General de Lamoricière's report was published by the express order of the Pope and without the knowledge of His Eminence, who declares that he saw and read it for the first time in the *Giornale di Roma* of the 12th and 13th instant.

144 [F.O. 43/78]   *Rome, 24 November 1860*

No. 177
O.R. to Lord J.R.

... Monsignor de Mérode has obtained permission from the Pope to re-enlist all the soldiers whom the late conflicts had dispersed and who have since returned to Rome, so as to form an army of about five thousand men, to which more could be added in future. General de Lamoricière was of opinion that the Pope would do well to exclude Italians altogether from his future army, and to favour chiefly French, Belgians, Austrians, Irish and Spaniards, but not Swiss with whom he expressed himself but little satisfied and he even passed severe censure on General Schmidt of Perugian memory. Cardinal Antonelli who never approved of the military tastes and policy of Pope Pius opposes the formation of a new army and wishes to limit the enlistment solely to such individuals as have lost everything by the dissolution of the Papal army and whom it would be charitable to provide for. His Eminence thinks two thousand men for police purposes would be sufficient for the present, but his advice is no longer exclusively followed as it was in former days by the Sovereign Pontiff, who now listens with greater complacency to the ultra montane suggestions of the foreign prelates around his throne, than to the moderate and almost timid counsels of his Secretary of State. The formation of an army of foreigners is not easy at present, the Piedmontese Government having sent all the Pope's foreign mercenaries who fell into their hands out of Italy, so the starving prisoners are re-enlisted with a promise that they shall not be marched against the Piedmontese any more, but shall only serve as a constabulary in the Comarca and Patrimony of St Peter.

Captain Russell of Killeogh was sent by Monsignor de Mérode to meet the Irish Brigade as they passed through Marseilles and to invite them to re-enlist in the defence of His Holiness; but they would not be induced any longer to serve a government with which they had become personally acquainted, and Captain Russell returned to Rome with only eighteen out of six hundred men. Experience having left no doubt as to the troublesome and expensive uselessness of the Knights of St Patrick it must be supposed that the Vatican wished to keep them in Italy, fearful of the effect which the tales they would have to tell might produce in faithful Ireland. It has therefore been decided for the present to form about five thousand men into ten battalions and the War Department, Commissariat and Army Store Depot are as busily at work under the bustling superintendence of warlike priests, as they were last summer when General de Lamoricière's first order of the day announced a new crusade and a new era of military glory to a delighted, revengeful and deluded priesthood. . . .

145 [F.O. 43/78]   *Rome, 1 December 1860*

No. 180
O.R. to Lord J.R.

General de Goyon informs me that while negotiations are still pending with General Cialdini in regard to the Neapolitan regiments who fled into the Papal States, the question is settling itself by the mighty desertions of large bodies of the men to the Abruzzi, so that their numbers

are already reduced to about eight thousand. The expense and inconvenience their presence occasions in the Papal States have induced the
French military authorities not to impede their homeward flight. In the
remaining regiments there are about eighteen hundred foreigners, nine
hundred and fifty of whom are Austrian soldiers and the remainder is
composed of Prussians, Bavarians, Swiss etc. General de Goyon speaks
highly of the soldiers, who would be excellent if officered by Frenchmen, but he complains of the Neapolitan officers, of whom he has been
obliged to put several under arrest for cruelty to their men. The
General also informs me that he has had the whole of the arms belonging to the Neapolitans conveyed to the Castle of St Angelo; they are
in good condition and worth about thirty thousand pounds. . . .

146 [F.O. 43/78]   *Rome, 1 December 1860*

No. 182
O.R. to Lord J.R.

Learned divines entertain an opinion that the Pope's knowledge of
Canon Law and ecclesiastical matters is very superficial and that His
Holiness is prone to attribute larger powers to himself than are given to
the Vicar of Christ by the Roman Catholic doctrine. Some even go to
the length of maintaining that the late excommunication is theologi-
cally indefensible. Deeply distressed by the apathy with which the
Catholics have witnessed his misfortunes, the Pope called on his ultramontane advizers to draw up a kind of manifesto in order to fix the
opinions the orthodox ought to hold on the many political theories
which now agitate Europe. They submitted a draft which was enlarged,
corrected, and annotated by the Pope himself and of which fifteen
copies were secretly struck off in the presses of the propaganda. This
document assumes that Canon Law is as superior to Civil Law as the
spiritual are superior to the temporal interests of mankind, and that no
opinion can be sound, no law valid, no policy defensible if it be not
supported by the authority of Canon Law. If its schemes could be
carried out, it would realize the dreams of Gregory VII and Innocent
III, raise the impunity of Sovereigns to the dignity of a dogma and
annul the results of civilization and the existence of modern society.
This document was submitted by Cardinal Santucci, at the Pope's
request, to the critical examination of fourteen Doctors of Canon Law
and was rejected by a majority of twelve of them.

Monsignori Tirpani and Trullet alone pronounced in its favour, and at their request, it was submitted to a second test which had the same result. Cardinal Santucci has therefore advised the Pope to cast it aside.

147 [F.O. 43/78]　　　　　　　　　　*Rome, 4 December 1860*

No. 183
O.R. to Lord J.R.

I regret to inform your Lordship that the Pope has again been suffering from epileptic symptoms which greatly affect his temper although at intervals he is as cheerful and as benevolent as ever. The bitter tone in which he expatiates to strangers, who are admitted to the honour of his presence, on the conduct of their respective sovereigns, has more than once placed the Cardinal Secretary of State in a very awkward position towards the representatives of the Catholic powers. His Holiness believes that the enemies of the Church will lay violent hands on his person and that his end is nigh. He covets the palm of martyrdom which has been borne by so many of his early predecessors. He has abandoned his former plan of withdrawing to the catacombs in the hour of danger and now wishes to fall in his pontifical robes, a victim to his persecutors, on the altar of St Peter.

148 [F.O. 43/78]　　　　　　　　　　*Rome, 4 December 1860*

No. 185. Secret
O.R. to Lord J.R.

Diplomatic agents in Rome have observed that the relations between the French Ambassador and Cardinal Antonelli have become far more intimate and confidential, since the Mérode-Lamoricière and ultramontane party are in favor and His Eminence out of favor with the Pope. Wishing to clear up the matter as far as I could, I called on the Cardinal Secretary of State and engaged him in a conversation on the policy of France. I found His Eminence decidedly more favorable to the Emperor Napoleon's acts than during the past summer and as he admitted himself, for the simple reason that the Pope owed his present existence in Rome alone to His Imperial Majesty's protection, the other Catholic powers of Europe having practically abandoned the interests of the Church and allowed the Papal States to fall a prey to Piedmontese rapacity. The Emperor had guaranteed the possession of Rome to the

Pope and he had kept his promise, and so long as the French army continued in Rome there was no reason for the Pope's departure, who did best to await with patience and resignation under their protection the end of the trials with which it pleased Providence to visit him and which must sooner or later necessarily be followed by the recognition of right and justice and the restoration of his States.

I asked what importance His Eminence attached to the rumour circulating in Rome that the Emperor Napoleon now contemplated the withdrawal of his troops of occupation who would be replaced by a Piedmontese garrison? The Cardinal replied that a serious examination of the position of France in Italy convinced him that the Emperor Napoleon could not withdraw his troops from Rome and for reasons which he would submit to me in strict confidence. The withdrawal of the Emperor's troops would be followed by the departure of the Pope who would seek protection at the hands of some other Catholic sovereign, a circumstance which could only be detrimental to the interests of the Emperor in Catholic France and which could afford him no advantage whatever. On the other hand the continued protection of the head of the Roman Catholic Church against surrounding dangers and impious enemies would ever be popular with the bulk of the French nation, and offered advantages of such magnitude to His Majesty, that it appeared impossible that he could willingly relinquish them. The Governments most hostile to the Temporal Power of the Papacy could not reasonably insist on France abandoning the Pope to the tender mercies of the revolutionary party and certainly no foreign power would or could drive the French from Rome by force. The protection due to the Holy Father was therefore a sufficient pretext to enable the Emperor to keep his garrison as long as he pleased in Rome, and whatever turn the Italian revolution took, their presence would prove an advantage to the French Empire. Supposing that King Victor Emmanuel succeeded in establishing an united Kingdom of Italy of twenty-two millions of Italians, the presence of the French in Rome and Civita Vecchia would be sufficient to control their growing power, and make them mere agents in the hands of France. If on the other hand the annexation of Southern Italy failed, and this contingency was more than likely, the Emperor's army in Rome could be employed to secure the election of a Bonaparte or a Murat to the throne of Naples. Again if Garibaldi attacked Venetia next spring and the Austrians invaded Italy, the Emperor would have a basis of operation at Rome to impede the restoration of Austrian supremacy, and finally in the improbable event of the Piedmontese beating the Austrians and annexing Venetia, the possession of Rome would be material compensation to France more valuable even than Savoy and Nice. The Cardinal concluded by an earnest request that I would consider this communication of his views as strictly personal and secret.

On the following evening I called on the Duc de Gramont and found Cardinal Antonelli and General de Goyon taking tea with His Excellence. The conversation turned on the late concessions in France and the Cardinal, the General and the Ambassador cheerfully agreed that in appealing to public opinion the Emperor would find himself compelled to follow a policy more favourable to the temporal power of the Pope and to a federal instead of a united Italy.

149 [F.O. 519/205]   *Rome, 5 December 1860*

O.R. to Earl Cowley

... I believe there is no doubt that the Pope told Lamoricière when he left that any fanatic who would undertake to murder the Emperor would obtain absolution and full indulgences from the Church, and it is believed here by pious priests that the Emperor, knowing it, is about to yield to the tremendous power of the Popes.

There is not a day passed here in Rome where I don't feel the blessings of the Reformation and I thank God with all my heart that we at home have broken for ever with this infernal Papacy. ...

150 [F.O. 43/78]   *Rome, 18 December 1860*

No. 187

O.R. to Lord J.R.

The Romans have lately shown signs of impatience at the slow development of the Roman question. Were it not for the constant advice sent from Turin to have patience, abide their time and respect French authority, and were it not for the deep faith placed in Piedmont as leader of the Italian movement, a conflict between the people and the authorities might be feared notwithstanding the presence of the French army. Of late the Romans have spoken too much and in consequence the Government has had several persons arrested and the *Caffè Nuovo* in the Corso closed. After a diligent search through that vast establishment, the police discovered four national cockades. An order of the police has also been issued forbidding for the future all exaggerated marks of approbation or disapprobation in the theatres and concert rooms of Rome. On the other hand the Philharmonic Society, who were about to give a concert for the poor, were called upon to combine it with a spontaneous and loyal demonstration in favour of the Pope, an account of which would have read well in the *Giornale di Roma*. But the members of the Philharmonic Society, men and women, have declined to sing if their charitable performance is to be construed into an ovation to the temporal power of the Pope.

This morning many houses in the principal streets of Rome were placarded with printed papers containing the following words: '*Viva Vittoria Emmanuele nostro Re.*' They were at once removed by the Papal gendarmes, Franco-Belgian Zouaves and Knights of St Patrick.

151 [F.O. 43/78] *Rome, 26 December 1860*
No. 190
O.R. to Lord J.R.

After the celebration of High Mass on Christmas Day at St Peters, the Pope on reaching the Sacristry addressed a few words to the Cardinals, Bishops and Prelates there assembled. His Holiness said that after blessing the faithful, he did not wish to withhold his blessing from his enemies, as he still hoped that God might enlighten and guide them. He need not repeat what they all knew, that the Church would never yield one jot of her temporal rights and privileges, and he was happy to think that the Sacred College of Cardinals were unanimous in the support they gave him on this question. After which the Pope withdrew and the Prelates returned in silence to their respective houses. The latter portion of the Pope's speech is difficult to explain as it is but too well known that His Holiness has not consulted the Sacred College for several years. His Holiness has never invited the attendance of more than from five to eight of their Eminences, whose implicit obedience he could reckon on, those who were likely to oppose the policy of Cardinal Antonelli were always carefully excluded, and it is also well known that among the Italian Cardinals nine are in favour of a Spiritual Church under the protectorate of a United Kingdom of Italy, and in this opinion they are now supported by a large majority of the lower Italian clergy. It is therefore evident that the Pope deceives himself as to the unanimous wishes of the Roman Church.

152 [F.O. 43/78]   *Rome, 30 December 1860*

No. 195
O.R. to Lord J.R.

There is every reason to believe that the ultramontane party are hard at
work organising disturbances in the Abruzzi and it is supposed that the
disbanded soldiers of King Francis are furnished with arms and money
for that purpose before they cross the Neapolitan frontier. Certain it is
that General de Goyon's soldiers have already seized three or four boats
in the canals of the Pontine Marshes, filled with arms and ammunition
and sent from Gaeta for the use of the Royalist bands who have now
established their headquarters at Sora. Their object is to increase the
agitation in the Kingdom of Naples as much as they can and render the
task of the Piedmontese as difficult as possible, and for that purpose
Mazzinians and Papalians will readily work together. The continued
presence of the French fleet at Gaeta greatly facilitates their endeavours,
and when the country is infested with *banditti* they will be proudly
called 'Royalists' by the one and 'Republicans' by the other party.
My firm belief is that the National, Constitutional or Piedmontese Party
is so numerous, so strong and so united in Italy that these miserable
attempts at reaction will in the end only harm those who organize them
and I am deeply convinced that Italy would establish her independence
and freedom without shedding one single drop of blood, could she but
be left in reality, for three months only, to settle her own affairs, free
from all the embarrassing intervention of France at Gaeta and Rome.

153 [F.O. 43/83A]   *Rome, 1 January 1861*

No. 1
O.R. to Lord J.R.

General de Goyon, accompanied by the officers of the French garrison,
waited this morning on the Pope to offer the customary congratulations
on the first day of the year. The Pope declined to admit them to the
honor of kissing his toe, but addressed them in very complimentary
terms and ended by saying that he willingly blessed the French nation
for the true Catholic spirit they manifested, that he equally blessed the
French army for the services they were rendering Religion in Rome, in
Syria and in China, and that he joyfully blessed the French fleet for the
noble part it was now playing near at hand, in the interest of order and

11. Monsignor de Mérode

12. King Francis II of Naples

legitimate right. His Holiness then blessed General de Goyon and his army but made no allusion to the Emperor, the Empress or to his god-child, the Prince Imperial.

General de Goyon, wishing to efface the painful impression which this omission was making on his officers, then replied that he thanked His Holiness for the blessing thus awarded to, and the high opinion expressed by the Holy Father on the French nation, the army and the fleet, and that since the nation owed its present prosperous position and generous impulses to the Emperor Napoleon and that the achievements of the army in the interest of Religion in China and Syria, and the presence of the fleet at Gaeta were the result of the Emperor's highminded policy and that France, her army and her navy were instruments in His Majesty's hand, he felt proud to be able to inform His August Master of the blessing thus conferred by His Holiness on the work and policy of the Emperor Napoleon. The Pope shrugged his shoulders and replied, 'God will bless the policy of your master according to its deserts.'

General de Goyon and his officers then withdrew.

154 [F.O. 519/205]   *Rome, 8 January 1861*

O.R. to Earl Cowley

The continued presence of the French ships at Gaeta is doing a vast deal of harm to a harmless population and no good whatever to those whom they are supposed to protect. Gramont, Goyon and Co. talk greater nonsense than ever, they think the only solution possible is a confederation, with Murat at Naples, the Pope to have back the whole of his lost provinces, Venetia a Republic and Austria compensated with the Danubian Principalities. It is truly painful to see men called upon to represent a great nation make such fools of themselves as Gramont, Goyon and Co. Luckily for Europe what they say and do is of no importance whatever. We are vegetating here, the Pope prays for the death of the Emperor Napoleon, and the destruction of Great Britain and spends his Peter's Pence on his army of cut-throats. It is impossible to see a more pitiable or a more rotten state of things.

The party which opposes the Pope and Antonelli in the church is growing every day and is Piedmontese and Unitarian to the back bone. If the Pope don't take care he may see himself set aside for an Antipope.

Meanwhile the Emperor Napoleon is making himself *wonderfully unpopular* in Italy by his Anti-Union interference here and at Gaeta and I don't see what good it does him.

155 [F.O. 43/83A]   *Rome, 12 January 1861*

No. 2
O.R. to Lord J.R.

The shortsighted policy of Pius IX, which, after lowering the dignity of the Roman Catholic Church and losing with wanton obstinacy her temporal dominion now threatens to provoke schism or the establishment of national churches, has also produced an opposition party within the bosom of the Church at Rome which is rapidly recruiting its followers among the most enlightened sincere and devoted adherents of the Roman Catholic Faith. These devout men foresee the great danger to which their church is exposed by the policy of her present rulers and the great advantages she might derive by following a totally opposite course. They would like to see the Pope cease all further hostilities, 'sheathe the sword and send a message of peace to the King of Italy', admit frankly that his temporal power is irrevocably lost, invite His Majesty to negotiate and to maintain order in Rome, dismissing the French garrison with all the gratitude due to their past services, and King and Pope to live side by side in Rome in peace and amity.

The views of this party are such that they could not with personal safety to themselves advocate them openly at the Vatican, but they are working hard to obtain a hearing of the Pope when the foreign Ultramontane prelates who surround His Holiness are less watchful and will allow their Holy Father to listen once more, as he did at the commencement of his Pontificate, to the voice of his Italian children.

This party counts among its followers, Cardinals, Prelates, Benedictines, Jesuits, Capuchins, Priests etc., etc., and some of the most eminent Canonists of the day, all Italian of course. I have endeavoured to obtain an outline of their plans, and, as far as I can understand them, they are as follows:

If a pacific settlement could be effected between the Papacy and the new Kingdom of Italy, they say, the position of the Pope, once the total loss of his temporal power was frankly accepted and acknowledged, would present itself under two new aspects:

1st. as Head of the Roman Catholic Religion throughout the world,
and

2nd. as Head of the Church in Italy.

The first condition claimed by the Pope as Head of the Roman
Catholic Church is spiritual independence, and the Faithful have been
in the habit of believing that his spiritual independence rested on his
temporal power. Now that all illusions on this question have vanished
and that it has become evident that the Pope's temporal power can only
be imposed upon Italy by the intervention of a powerful foreign army,
'the theory of his independence has become a mere shadow which is no
longer capable of application'.

But even after admitting the undeniable truth of the extinction of the
temporal independence of the Papacy, the faithful observe:

'Granted, but we cannot submit to the Pope ever being the subject
of any Power.' The question is therefore how to find the means of
giving the Papacy absolute spiritual freedom since no earthly Power
can practically restore its lost temporal independence and this might
perhaps be effected as follows:

The visible Head of the Catholic Church residing in Rome should
enjoy:

1st. Nominal sovereignty and inviolability, the privilege of crowned
Heads.

2nd. Inviolability for the Pope's Nuncios, Legates etc., and all spiritual
ministers belonging to the Catholic Hierarchy.

3rd. Sovereignty and inviolability of the Conclave.

4th. A fixed income guaranteed on landed property in and out of Italy
to defray the expenses of the Church and of the Papal Court.

5th. Free communication between the Pope and the human race
throughout the world.

6th. The temporal authorities at Rome to surround the Papacy with
all the ceremonial of respect becoming the dignity of the Head of
the Church, etc., etc., etc.

Regarding the second proposition, namely the Pope's new position
as Head of the Church in Italy, it must be remembered that up to the
present day Concordats have ruled the church in the various states that
composed Italy, their sovereigns trying to curtail as far as they could

the aggressive power of the Popes and Bishops by the Leopoldine, Josephine and other laws.

The Kingdom of Italy might now afford to make vast concessions to the Church by establishing the principle of:

1st.   A free church in a free state, that is absolute spiritual freedom.

2nd.   Free election of the Bishops by the clergy without the interference of the civil power.

3rd.   Free intercourse between the Pope and the Bishops with the clergy.

4th.   Abolition of the privileges enjoyed by the King of the Two Sicilies in spiritual matters to the detriment of the church.

5th.   Abolition of all the restrictions put on the free action of the Church by the Leopoldine and Josephine Laws and other Concordats.

6th.   Freedom of association for the Church, the State however reserving its right to recognize or not the civil personality of the association and their right to hold property.

7th.   Freedom of Synods.

8th.   Abolition of the *placet* and *jus cavendi*.

9th.   Freedom of ecclesiastical instruction.

10th.   The temporalities or diocesan expenses to be defrayed by landed property on which the State would reserve the right of common taxation only.

11th.   Freedom of the Bishops in the exercise of their spiritual authority over Priests and Monastic Orders., etc., etc., etc.

These conditions which may appear exhorbitant, proceeding as they do from a defeated party, owe their principal interest to the readiness they betray in a part of the Roman Clergy to surrender the temporal power, and the value of the above outline of agreement between the new Kingdom of Italy and the Papacy rests on the fact that it is not merely the scheme of a lay pamphleteer but embodies the conditions which learned canonists and devoted churchmen are prepared to accept as being in accordance with Canon law and the doctrines of the Roman Catholic Religion. Practically speaking however they are of no value as no one can seriously entertain the hope that the Emperor Napoleon will withdraw his garrison from Rome so long as he rules in France.

156 [P.R.O. 30/22/75]   *Rome, 12 January 1861*
Private
O.R. to Lord J.R.

The announcement that the Emperor Napoleon had at last decided to
withdraw his ships from Gaeta by the 19th inst. has given great satisfaction here to the National Party and has at the same time deeply
annoyed the Vatican. Gramont, ever ready to jump at startling con-
clusions had already declared that his Imperial Master hoped to restore
the Kingdom of the two Sicilies to Francis II, but poor Gramont is no
longer believed in Rome, even when he happens to speak the truth.
Goyon in a speech to his officers had declared that the Emperor was
frankly entering into a reactionary line of policy which England would
be compelled to follow, but his officers whose constant intercourse with
the middle classes has rendered them devoted to the idea of Italian
Unity, ridiculed his speech openly, and now since the withdrawal of the
ships is announced, both Gramont and Goyon have been obliged to eat
their own hasty words. Timid politicians fear that the Emperor Napoleon wants to persuade King Francis to cede the fortress of Gaeta provisionally to France so as to keep the Piedmontese out of it. The
attempts made to form a Muratist party have signally failed and I think
that the immense efforts of the Vatican to form reactionary bands of
Neapolitan and Papal soldiers in the Abbruzzi will fail in the same
manner, the moment Gaeta is in Italian or Piedmontese hands. The
latter are now daily recruiting adherents and friends in the lower clergy
and some Italian Cardinals now no longer conceal their dissatisfaction
with the Pope's policy and show their sympathy for the cause of Italian
Unity. If French intervention could be made to cease in Rome, the
affairs of Italy would be speedily and I think satisfactorily settled. The
Pope has to choose between two modes of settlement only, a peaceful
agreement with Piedmont or a permanent French garrison in Rome. At
present all parties are in a state of inactive expectation, which I fancy
will not last very much longer once the Parliaments of England, Italy
and France have met.

157 [F.O. 43/83A]   *Rome, 16 January 1861*
No. 4
O.R. to Lord J.R.

I observe that the French diplomatic and military authorities in Rome have again taken to advocate in strong terms the Treaty of Villa Franca as the only basis on which the Italian question can be definitively settled. The idea of Italian unity is scouted as unworthy of one moment's serious consideration and is characterized as being purely of English origin and without root or foundation in Italy.

The reaction in the south against Piedmont is assumed to be general and the annexation of the Kingdom of Naples a 'discreditable piece of jugglery', while the imaginary growth of the Muratist party is mentioned with ill feigned alarm.

The contempt France entertains for the 'grasping and dishonest policy of Piedmont' is loudly proclaimed everywhere while it is whispered that the sympathies of the English Cabinet have been bought by Count Cavour with a promise of Sicily!

Of course these views are too absurd to be founded on any official instructions from Paris. Nevertheless, it is my duty to record them for Your Lordship's more complete information.

158   [F.O. 43/83A]   Rome, 16 January 1861

No. 5
O.R. to Lord J.R.

The Diplomatic Body having been admitted some days since to the honor of congratulating the Pope on the occasion of the New Year, I was equally honoured with a private audience this morning for the same purpose. With his usual benevolence and kindness the Pope spoke on many different subjects and then enquired after the health of Her Majesty. He had read in the papers that the Prince of Wales was about to become a Freemason, a circumstance he greatly regretted, if true, because he took a lively personal interest in the Prince since he had seen him in Rome, and he believed from the perusal of a little book which he had bought at Montevideo years ago, that the principles of Freemasonry were Anti-Christian.

I replied that I believed our Freemasons to be a philanthropic society, that the most respectable and high-principled persons belonged to it and that, I had heard, the present King of Prussia had for many years been Grand Master of the Prussian lodges. The Pope replied that Prince Murat[1] was also a Freemason and had gone to congratulate the

[1] Lucien Murat (1803-78), second son of Joachim, was pretender to the throne of Naples.

King of Prussia on his accession to the throne, but that that in no way changed his belief that Freemasonry was based on infidel principles.

His Holiness then dwelt at length on the absurd presumption Free-masons put forward that they owed their origin to the Temple of Solomon. Masons had existed ever since mankind began to build dwellings and why did not the Freemasons while they were about it, date their origin from the pyramids when the Jews were in bondage, or even from Noah's Ark, which had been built by his sons?

'Or from the Tower of Babel?' I suggested.

At this observation the Pope laughed immoderately and said that Babel reminded him of the present state of Italy and Europe, and he wished to know whether I had heard that Russia, indignant at the conduct of 'Monsieur Napoleon', was about to send a fleet to Messina and to Gaeta to re-establish King Francesco at Naples.

I replied that I had, but that I in no way believed the report. 'England is ever at work against us,' His Holiness continued, 'favouring and assisting revolution. Your people hate the Pope, your Parliament hates the Pope, your ministers and especially your uncle hate the Pope, and even the English Catholics who were always good, are not at present animated with a very proper spirit.'

I here explained to His Holiness as I had done on a former occasion, that I deeply regretted to see that he mis-conceived the spirit which animated the people of England and the policy of Her Majesty's Government. Although the people were Protestant and Her Majesty's Government liberal in their feelings, no personal hatred to His Holiness biased the minds of our public men; but we differed in our views on the system of administration pursued by the late sovereigns of Italy, which had been productive of discontent and revolution, while we thought a more liberal and national government might have given peace to the country.

The Pope then explained to me, as he had also done before, that the petulance of the Italian people rendered self-government impossible, and that the present movement in Italy could never succeed; we Englishmen would not understand that Italy must be ruled by strong armies and a firm hand. It would take him several hours to discuss the matter thoroughly with me and then he knew I would not believe him, because he perceived that I entertained the same ideas on matters of administration as the late Lord Minto.

I replied that those ideas were the ideas of Englishmen and that

while they were about it, date
their origin from the Pyramids
when the Jews were in bondage
or even from Noah's Ark,
which had been built by his
Sons? —

"Or from the Tower of Babel,"
I suggested.

At this observation the Pope
laughed immoderately and said
that Babel reminded him

of the present state of Italy and
Europe, and he wished to know
whether I had heard that Russia,
indignant at the conduct of
"Monsieur Napoleon" was about
to send a fleet to Messina
and to Gaeta to reestablish
King Francesco at Naples?"

I replied that I had,
but that I in no way believed
the report.

"England

*Part of despatch No. 5 of 16 January 1861. The lefthand page is
in the writing of Arthur Russell, the right in that of Odo Russell.*

without much discussion we had but to look to facts to see that Lord Minto's advice had been good. When, at the commencement of his reign, His Holiness had pursued a national policy the people of Italy had been at his feet. Since then, several years of foreign occupation had turned the national sympathies towards Piedmont, which offered Italy the realization of a dream of many centuries, Independence, Freedom and Unity.

'But Unity is impossible,' the Pope interposed, 'because the Great Powers of Europe will prevent it. They dread the formation of a sixth Great Power, and England above all dreads the future maritime greatness which Italy would acquire.'

'We do not dread a danger so remote,' I replied, 'nor can I take upon myself to explain the secret policy of the Great Powers of Europe, but I can answer for the sympathies of England represented by Her Majesty's advizers. They sincerely desire to see Italy free from that foreign interference which has been her greatest curse, and the Italians once more in possession of their native land, building up the edifice of their liberties and consolidating the work of their independence so that Italy may again become an element of order and of progress in the Great European family.'

The Pope's eyes flashed, he clenched his fist and exclaimed: 'No, they do not wish it, and you do not believe what you say! The policy of England is not so generous. She is guided by commercial interests and selfish ends, she encourages revolution and disorder abroad and her ministers enjoy no independence. They have to yield to mobs to retain their places, and now they may appear to yield to a passing popular cry, but they will be the first to prevent the unity or even the pacification of Italy!'

I replied: 'I have listened with painful surprize to Your Holiness's words, for they have again proved to me how thoroughly Your Holiness is misinformed as to English affairs. I hereby solemnly give Your Holiness my most sacred word of honor that I am speaking my innermost conviction when I say that Her Majesty's Government sincerely and honestly desire the welfare of Italy and that they think that end can best be attained by the cessation of foreign intervention and by the Italians being left to settle their own affairs – in one word Italy for the Italians. And is it not natural that we should desire to see Italy once more at peace, happy and improving, Italy to whom we owe all the greatest blessings we enjoy, Italy the cradle of our Laws, of Science, Art, Literature and I might almost say of Religion? Did we not assist Greece in obtaining her independence, did we not favor Belgium, and why should we withhold our moral support from Italy? Are her demands and wishes not just? I appeal to Your Holiness as an Italian Prince.'

The old man's Italian heart warmed as he spoke and he said: 'Do you know what Italian Unity means? It means a nation of five and twenty millions harbouring more talent, mind and energy than any nation in the world, with an army of three hundred thousand men and a fleet of three hundred ships. History proves the eminence of Italian generals and our admirals would soon command the seas. Italy left to herself would soon be the first of the Great Powers of the world and therefore the Five Powers of Europe will ever prevent her unity.'

'Your Holiness,' I replied, 'has now spoken as you did at the commencement of your reign and then all Italy was at your feet, you were the national idol. But since Your Holiness has allowed foreign bayonets to stand between yourself and your people, they have turned to the only Italian power left, to seek the realization of their wishes. But the day that Your Holiness will extend your hand to Piedmont and say: "Let all hostilities cease, there shall be peace in Italy", then the people will bless the name of Pius IX and the great work will be accomplished.'

'No, it will not,' the Pope again exclaimed, 'and you do not believe what you say!'

'And who is to prevent it,' I asked, 'if Your Holiness and Italy agree?'

'The Great Powers of Europe,' the Pope replied.

'With the Pope's blessing and England's moral support, Italy has nothing to fear from them,' I said.

'Monsieur Napoleon will prevent it,' the Pope continued, 'whatever England may wish. He wants Naples for his family.'

'And if that really were the case,' I said, 'would it not be better to save Italy for the Italians than to give time for the establishment of a French Italy? The substitution of French for Austrian supremacy can be of no advantage to your country. Your Holiness commenced the work of liberation in 1846, it rests with Your Holiness to complete and crown it in 1861 without shedding one more drop of Italian or of foreign blood. If you do not, your successor will, while Your Holiness will find no other alternative than to accept for the remainder of your reign a permanent French occupation of Rome.'

'But I have never been consulted,' the Pope said, evidently labouring under great excitement, 'I have never been consulted by the Italians for whom I then hoped to do so much. See how they have treated and abandoned me!'

'Because Your Holiness placed a hedge of foreign bayonets between them and yourself,' I replied.

'But I have never been consulted either by the Great Powers,' the Pope continued.

'Has not France,' I enquired, 'repeatedly offered Your Holiness the very best advice?'

'The Pope needs no advice, the Pope has a right to be consulted,' His Holiness replied. 'Everything that has been done has been done against me. My states have been torn from me, my former friends have looked on without assisting me, but a cry of indignation will be raised throughout the Catholic world and the Faithful will not forget their duty, nor the Pope be abandoned.'

I replied: 'The time has passed, the worst of the crisis is over, and how has the Catholic world answered Your Holiness's appeal? The Peter's Pence will not suffice to support the Holy See, and to obtain foreign soldiers Your Holiness's Government has been obliged to pay a higher premium than any Government in the world. To the support alone of France is due what remains of Your Holiness's Temporal Power, while all around the cause of Italian freedom is gaining strength. If Your Holiness has a right to be consulted, you have also a right to speak and take a generous initiative both as an Italian Prince and as Head of the Roman Catholic Church. In the miraculous course of events which all seem to turn in favor of the Italian cause, does Your Holiness not see the hand of God?'

'The hand of God is everywhere,' the Pope answered, 'He allows all that occurs, but we do not yet know what He intends.' And then His Holiness added for the third time and with great force, 'But I have never been consulted on all these matters, I have been ignored and forgotten. In England you hate the Pope, but you are enthusiastic for Garibaldi, and why do you admire Garibaldi?'

I said: 'In Garibaldi we have admired a disinterested patriot, who, without seeking one single personal advantage, has loved his country better than his life.'

'Lord John Russell,' His Holiness continued, 'you say is a friend of Italy, yet he will listen to Garibaldi, but he would never consult the Pope.'

I said: 'Our diplomatic relations with Rome have unfortunately not been what they ought to be. I speak to Your Holiness as a private individual without official authority and I must thank Your Holiness for so patiently listening to the free expression of my personal convictions, but if Lord John Russell could consult the Pope on Italian affairs, might I know what Your Holiness would reply?'

After some hesitation, the Pope said with a smile: 'I would say that Italian Unity and Independence is a great and a beautiful idea, but that it is impossible.'

'But it would become possible,' I answered, 'if Your Holiness ceased to oppose it and no longer withheld your blessing from it. Thousands of the most devout and devoted Catholics in Italy pray that the Pope may acknowledge the work of God in the late events, may treat with Piedmont, give peace to Europe and bless the cause of united Italy.'

'They pray, do they? And do you pray, for I think you Protestants do not know how to pray?' the Pope enquired. 'I will tell you how to pray. You must say at the end of all your prayers, "Father, not my will, but thine, be done". For although things may appear evident to us, we cannot fathom God's ultimate ends.'

I replied: 'We are Christians and have all learned to pray from one Master and I am sure Your Holiness also adds at the end of your prayers as we all do, "not my will but thine be done". And Your Holiness who commenced the task and who have been chosen to complete it, will not withhold your blessing from the work of God, and your memory will be blessed by your grateful country.'

'Pray, my good Russell,' the Pope said, 'pray, it will do you good. I also will pray.' And then extending his hands he wished me goodbye.

I knelt to receive the old man's blessing and said: 'Holy Father, I will pray that the next time I have the honor of being admitted to your presence, Italy and the Pope may be at peace.'

He waved his hand and smiled with strange emotion and I withdrew.

In writing the foregoing conversation I have taken great pains to give Your Lordship an accurate and conscientious account of all that passed between His Holiness and myself. The impression it has left on my mind is, that the Italian feelings of the Pope would again prevail if other and more truthful advizers surrounded his throne.

159 [P.R.O. 30/22/75]   *Rome, 19 January 1861*
Private
O.R. to Lord J.R.

The Pope and his Ministers are now spending their Peter pence in trying to get up what they call reactionary bands in the Abbruzzi. They send men and money and arms and priests to excite and revolutionize the country, but in the end they will only succeed in organizing brigandage on a large scale. Things will go better when the siege of Gaeta is at an end, and things might go quite well if the intervention of France were withdrawn and the Constitutional or Piedmontese Party were allowed to act freely in Italy. As it is, Rome will continue to be a nest of intrigue and corruption. But I don't myself share the gloomy views of many people respecting the South. I see good elements everywhere, but they require time to ripen. Rome was not built in a day, and Italian independence cannot be established in a year. . . .

160 [F.O. 43/83A]   *Rome, 27 January 1861*

No. 9
O.R. to Lord J.R.

Signor Georgi, a country gentleman who resides in the Abruzzi and who has been employed by the Papal Government in organizing and arming reactionary bands in the Abruzzi, returned some days since to Rome, and while walking down the Corso this morning was recognized by the people, followed, hooted and hissed, so that he could only escape with difficulty by running into an open house in the Via Condotti.

He has been furnished with money and further instructions by the Papal Government and returns tomorrow morning with a Signor Ricci who is equally employed on a similar mission to the Abbruzzi.

161 [F.O. 43/83A]   *Rome, 12 February 1861*

No. 13. Most Secret. [Conveyed by Mr Arthur Russell.]
O.R. to Lord J.R.

My dispatch No. 5 marked Secret, of the 16th ultimo has placed Your Lordship in possession of the conversation I had with the Pope on that day. It appears that immediately after I had left the Vatican His Holiness sent for Cardinal Antonelli and recounted to him all that had passed between us. The Cardinal lost no time in communicating the news to the French Ambassador and His Excellency at an evening party hastened to despatch one of his Secretaries to me, who made diverse attempts to find out what had passed. While we were talking the Duc de Gramont himself approached and questioned me directly on the matter.

I told His Excellency that I could have no reason to conceal the personal convictions I had taken the liberty to express as a private individual to the Pope, and I gave him a general outline of my interview with His Holiness.

The Duke, who seemed much annoyed at the freedom with which I had 'dared' to address the Pope, entirely disapproved of my conviction that an amicable settlement between the Pontiff and the King of Italy was desirable. However great the wish of England might be to destroy the Pope, France would always be ready to protect the Holy See. Unity was impossible and a Confederation the only solution to the Italian question. Even a Confederation of small republics was better for Italy and Europe than Unity.

His Excellency further complained of the Pope's hostility and ingratitude to the Emperor and of his ignorance of the temporal interests of the Church which might have been saved by confidence in the Emperor's advice before and after the Peace of Villafranca. His Excellency concluded by expressing his conviction, which he formulated into the offer of a bet, that the Pope would regain his lost Provinces, King Francesco be reinstated at Naples and King Victor Emmanuel ere long driven into exile by his present subjects.

I need scarcely remind Your Lordship that the impulsive nature of the Duc de Gramont's political feelings renders the ever-changing expression he lends to them utterly unimportant.

I replied to His Excellency that the French occupation of Rome could not be eternal, that a pacific settlement between the Pope and the King appeared to me preferable to the present impotent warfare carried on with the blood and the pence of the faithful, which could only result in useless bloodshed, discredit to the Church and the strengthening of the opposite party in the opinion of all sincerely religious men. As to the question of Unity or Confederation it appeared to me that all the efforts of the Italians since they had been left to themselves tended towards Unity, whilst the combined efforts of the Pope and King Francesco to organize a reactionary movement had proved a miserable failure, notwithstanding the presence of the French fleet at Gaeta and of the French army at Rome which might have given a semblance of protection and encouragement to the reactionary party had such a party really existed in the country. No doubt a Confederation could be forced on Italy by foreign intervention, but if the Emperor Napoleon's declared policy of non-interference were adhered to a Confederacy of Monarchies or Republics was visionary. For the great majority in Italy had given undeniable proofs that the country was at present in favor of a United Constitutional Monarchy.

As to the hostility His Excellency assumed Her Majesty's Government entertained towards the Pope, it was totally unfounded. What Her Majesty's Government really wished in the interest of the Roman Catholic Church was to see the Pope take up a respectable and independent position in the European family.

The Duc de Gramont then gave the conversation a jocular turn and we soon parted. Meanwhile the emotion felt by the Pope after the conversation I had had with him bore its fruits and Cardinal Santucci, who had for some time past endeavoured to obtain a hearing as leader of the Italian national party in the church, now found the Papal heart ripe for a more merciful policy, and after long and impassioned discussions he obtained an audience for the eminent and enlightened Professor of Canon Law, Padre Passaglia, who had been working out a plan of negotiation in an Italian sense between the Pope and the King of Italy. The general bearing of this plan will be found in my despatch to Your Lordship No. 2 of 12th ultimo.

After a good deal of hesitation on all sides and obstinate opposition on the part of Cardinal Antonelli, the Pope allowed Padre Passaglia to proceed incognito and without instructions to Turin for the purpose of sounding Count Cavour as to his general intentions in regard to Rome and the Church, and the ex-Jesuit departed on the 6th instant.

Cardinal Santucci and Padre Passaglia are sincere advocates of Unity and wish to free the Church from her temporal encumbrances, and they report that in the heat of discussion, the Pope's early Italian sympathies so entirely got the better of him that he suddenly declared that if he could believe in the possibility of a great and united Italy, with four hundred thousand men to defend her independence, he would not hesitate any longer to give her his most fervent blessing.

The departure of Padre Passaglia soon became known in Rome and created deep sensation. Diplomacy hurried to the Vatican for information and was told by Cardinal Antonelli that the learned Canonist had undertaken his journey on his own responsibility and only with the Pope's reluctant consent, since it was absurd to imagine that Rome could ever treat with Turin. The Ultramontane party however took fright at the Pope's unexpected concession to the liberal-minded Cardinal Santucci and determined to bring His Holiness to his senses. Cardinal della Genga, their leader and, they confidently asserted, their future Pope, was therefore called upon to see the Sovereign Pontiff and shew him the dangers he was courting. Cardinal della Genga, by far the most violent of the Ultramontane Prelates of the Roman Hierarchy, proceeded to the Vatican on the 9th instant and found the Pope labouring under the influence of his early patriotic feelings. A violent altercation ensued. The Cardinal returned home deeply affected by the change his Master had undergone, and, in the course of the night, died of apoplexy. His unexpected death is an incalculable loss to the Ultramontane party.

Last night I met the Duc de Gramont and asked him whether he could give me any information respecting Padre Passaglia's mission to Turin. The Duke replied that he was surprized I came to him for information about a matter in which he well knew I had taken a prominent part! He knew that I had been instructed by Her Majesty's Government to speak as I had done on the 16th ultimo to the Pope and to recommend negotiations between Rome and Turin, and he knew that I, together with Dr Pantaleoni, had worked for the last three months to bring about Padre Passaglia's mission to Count Cavour! Cardinal Antonelli was however too cunning by far to be so easily taken in, and by simply acceding to the Pope's fancy and letting Father Passaglia proceed on his own responsibility to Turin, he had struck a blow at the attempt to establish direct negotiations with Count Cavour, which would upset the whole scheme. It was a bubble without importance; the only advantage Count Cavour might derive from it was the power it gave him to silence the questions of the opposition by saying that serious negotiations were pending with the Court of Rome.

The Duke entered into a great many details with which I need not trouble Your Lordship. Although his manner towards me is always most frank and friendly, I could perceive that he was inwardly much vexed at the idea that I might have had a share in bringing about direct negotiations between the Pope and the King of Italy without his personal and public interference.

I replied, laughing, that this was not the first time I had thought His Excellency's information about Italian affairs to be at fault; this time I knew he was mistaken. I had no instructions whatever from Your Lordship, as he seemed to believe. I had spoken to the Pope as a private individual expressing his personal convictions and although I had heard much of the aspirations and proceedings of the National party in the Church, I could not unfortunately consider my influence sufficiently powerful to bring about so desirable a thing as pacific negotiations and an amicable settlement between the Church of Rome and the Kingdom of Italy.

After some further conversation the Duke begged of me to call on him as often as I could, as he wished to have more frequent opportunities of explaining his views on the Roman question to me.

I cannot say that I expect any great or immediate results from Padre Passaglia's visit to Count Cavour, but I do think that great importance attaches to the fact that the Pope has at last admitted the possibility of direct pacific negotiation with the government of King Victor Emmanuel, free from the patronage of France.

162 [P.R.O. 30/22/75]   *Rome, 16 February 1861*
Private
O.R. to Lord J.R.

King Francesco and his Queen are living at the Quirinal since Friday morning and it is believed that they intend leaving Italy in a few days for Bavaria or for Spain. But in truth nothing certain or authentic is known in Rome yet about the capitulation, the King's intentions or the state of the fortress since the last armistice. Anyhow it is a great blessing to have done with that siege and you will see, as I have before predicted, that the late Kingdom of Naples or rather Southern Italy will settle down into a state of tranquillity and satisfaction nearly equal to that of Tuscany, Romagna and the Marches. Reaction has not a leg to stand upon, and the elements of order in Italy are far greater than foreigners like to admit. Give the great National Constitutional Party a little more moral support and a few months hence it will not be an easy task to disunite Italy again, however much the hostile Powers may wish it. The desire for Unity is gaining ground in all classes. . . . The feeling of gratitude in the country towards you is deeply gratifying.

163 [F.O. 43/83A]   *Rome, 20 February 1861*
No. 17
O.R. to Lord J.R.

When the capitulation of the fortress of Gaeta became known in Rome

on 14th instant the population gave vent to their intense joy by crowd-
ing into the streets to discuss the happy event, and towards dusk the
police reported that nearly three and twenty thousand individuals were
in the Corso between the Piazza del Popolo and the Piazza di Venezia.
The crowd, though enthusiastic, was orderly, occasionally cheering
'Victor Emmanuel, United Italy and the Emperor Napoleon', and
Bengal lights, white, green and red, were burnt in various parts of the
town. General de Goyon acted with prudence and kindness. He
ordered the Pontifical Gendarmes and Zouaves to be consigned to their
barracks so as to avoid irritation and the dangers of popular vengeance,
and he sent French officers and soldiers to walk through the crowd and
beg of everyone to go home quietly. The people fraternized with the
French and after a good deal of shaking of hands, crying and em-
bracing, they good-humouredly followed the advice given them and
withdrew to their houses.

The moment the streets were empty, General de Goyon sent double
patrols all over the town and the night passed as quietly as possible.

I regret to have to add that the Pontifical Government mistaking this
spontaneous national and harmless demonstration for a conspiracy had
a large number of persons arrested on the following day whom they
accused of being the leaders of the movement. Some were again
released, some sent to prison and thirteen were exiled. I add the names
of the latter [the names are given].

164 [F.O. 43/83A]   *Rome, 25 February 1861*

No. 18
O.R. to Lord J.R.

King Francis II, the Queen and His Majesty's brothers, with a numerous suite, were received on 15th instant on arriving at the Palace of the
Quirinal from Gaeta via Terracina by Cardinal Antonelli and General
de Goyon at about one o'clock a.m. The Pope paid the first visit to his
royal guests on the following day, and a few days later the King and
Queen returned the Pope's visit at the Vatican.

The Church, the Army and Diplomacy have since claimed the
honor of paying their tribute of respect to the late King of the Two
Sicilies and His Majesty is generally reported to bear his misfortunes
with cheerful dignity. At present their Majesties indulge to a great
extent in carriage and horse exercise and are constantly to be seen in the

most populous parts of the town alone and without escort of any kind. The people bow respectfully when they pass, although the general wish is that Their Majesties may not prolong their residence in Italy....

165 [F.O. 43/83A]   *Rome, 26 February 1861*

No. 20

O.R. to Lord J.R.

It had been generally believed since September last, that the Pope would proceed to Spain or to Bavaria if the Emperor Napoleon saw fit to allow an Italian garrison to take the place of his French garrison in Rome. However, since the Pope's Italian sympathies have again influenced his thoughts, he has repeatedly declared that after all he saw no use in going away. He could protest against violence and die even better in the chair of St Peter than in Spain or Bavaria, and since late experience showed that the Catholic Powers were not inclined to offer him any efficient material assistance, he was determined not to leave Rome under any circumstances whatever....

166 [F.O. 43/83A]   *Rome, 19 March 1861*

No. 24

O.R. to Lord J.R.

General Count de Goyon has had the extreme goodness to grant the request I had long since and repeatedly addressed to His Excellency, to be furnished with a plan of the fortifications erected under his directions at Civita Vecchia. I now have the honor to transmit that plan herewith, on which as Your Lordship will perceive the General has written in his own hand some valuable notes respecting the extent of the works.

As Count de Goyon in granting me copy of this plan has made an exception in favor of Her Majesty's Government I trust Your Lordship will authorize me to express your acknowledgements of the same to the gallant and distinguished general.

[*This despatch is endorsed to the effect that the plan was forwarded on 5 April to the War Dept. It is now to be found among the archives of that department in the Public Record Office, reference M.R. 184/49 (20).*]

167 [F.O. 43/83A] *Rome, 20 March 1861*

No. 25. Confidential
O.R. to Lord J.R.

A report from Paris known to a few persons only in Rome stated that King Victor Emmanuel had sent a Marchese Vimercati to the Emperor Napoleon to endeavour to come to some understanding with His Majesty in regard to Roman affairs, and it was supposed that the Emperor in discussing Marchese Vimercati's confidential mission with a foreign Ambassador in Paris had let fall that Her Majesty's Government proposed that the Pope should be compensated for the loss of Rome by giving the island of Sardinia to His Holiness.

In talking over this report with Cardinal Antonelli I observed to His Eminence that the foreign Ambassador must have misunderstood the Emperor's words, for I felt quite convinced that Her Majesty's Government had never suggested the cession of the island of Sardinia to the Pope.

Cardinal Antonelli replied that the plan had as yet not been submitted to His Holiness's Government in any official form but that if it ever were, it would meet with the same refusal which all such plans must meet with on the part of the Sovereign Pontiff. The Pope stood on legal ground and demanded his Rights. No other settlement was possible.

168 [F.O. 43/83A] *Rome, 25 March 1861*

No. 26
O.R. to Lord J.R.

The state of things in Rome has not become more satisfactory since I last had the honor to address Your Lordship. Public feeling tends as strongly as ever towards Piedmont and the desire for Unity seems only to increase with every new difficulty and delay. The Romans look hopefully to the Italian Parliament at Turin, while the Vatican listens confidently to the debates in Paris.

As the indefinite duration of the French occupation of Rome becomes more evident, the confidence of the Ultramontane party increases and their spirits rise at the prospect of prolonged impunity. While the pecuniary contributions of the faithful in all parts of the world are swelling the Pontifical treasury, the misery of the working classes is becoming a subject of general alarm and notwithstanding an immense military force which General de Goyon is obliged to keep constantly under arms for the suppression of popular demonstrations in favor of Unity and King Victor Emmanuel, street robberies have literally become 'the order of the night'. . . .

169 [F.O. 43/83A]   *Rome, 26 March 1861*

No. 28
O.R. to Lord J.R.

It is with sincere regret that I have to inform Your Lordship that the Pope has seen fit to exile Doctor Pantaleoni from Rome. The learned doctor together with Padre Passaglia had been charged by Count Cavour with a negotiation on ecclesiastical affairs with the Court of Rome and the Sovereign Pontiff has cut the matter short by pronouncing the sentence of banishment.

It is not yet known what measures may be taken against Padre Passaglia.

Doctor Pantaleoni is compelled to start tomorrow morning for Turin, leaving his wife and three children, a very considerable number of patients and I may add a general feeling of consternation and regret in Rome among his numerous friends and acquaintances.

[*On 31 March England recognized the Kingdom of Italy.*]

170 [F.O. 43/83A]

No. 30. [Recites Telegram]
Lord J.R. to O.R.
'London Tuesday April 2nd. 2 p.m.

In answer to your dispatch No. 25 of the 20th March I have to acquaint you that Her Majesty's Government disapprove the plan of giving the island of Sardinia to the Pope.'

171 [F.O. 43/83A]   *Rome, 2 April 1861*

No. 31
O.R. to Lord J.R.

With reference to my despatch No. 28 of the 26th ultimo I now have the honor to submit to Your Lordship a more detailed account of the circumstances which led to the banishment of Dr Pantaleoni by the Papal Government. Some six or eight months ago Dr Pantaleoni drew up a paper embodying a plan of conciliation between Italy and the Holy See, which he submitted to the most intelligent, learned and pious members of the Church in Rome. He met with greater encouragement than he had expected and was urged to further action by the liberal or national party in the Church, a party which is said to number nine Cardinals among its members.

Two of the most eminent and pious men of this party, Cardinal Santucci and Padre Passaglia, offered their assistance and having communciated Dr Pantaleoni's memorandum to the Pope, who seemed to approve the spirit in which it was written, the Cardinal obtained a private audience of His Holiness for the Padre.

Padre Passaglia's great learning and powerful eloquence were not lost on Pius IX, who, after consulting Cardinal Antonelli, allowed Passaglia, at Dr Pantaleoni's suggestion, to proceed to Turin, but with a distinct understanding that he was charged with no official mission on the part of the Papal Government, and only went in his private capacity to sound the feelings of Count Cavour in regard to the possibility of an understanding between Turin and Rome.

Padre Passaglia returned well satisfied with the result of his interview with Count Cavour, who had determined to charge him and the doctor with the difficult mission of negotiating peace between Church and State. Padre Passaglia had an interview with Cardinal Antonelli soon after his return from Turin in which he is said to have advocated the policy of conciliation with extraordinary force, conviction and eloquence, declaring that the Spiritual Power of the Papacy might be elevated to new splendour and increased influence through United Italy, whilst the policy of resistance would be productive of schism and could not even save the last remnants of the Temporal Power which he considered as already practically lost.

Cardinal Antonelli is reported to have replied that he could not conceal his painful surprize at seeing a priest so distinguished for his piety and learning, become the advocate of revolutionary principles which tended to the destruction of the Roman Catholic Church, by calling upon the Pope to renounce for ever the rights which centuries had consecrated, and of which he could not dispose since he was only their guardian. The Catholic world was not Italy alone, it embraced two hundred millions of Faithful who expected the head of their religion to be independent and not merely a Piedmontese bishop, and their church to be not merely a national or Italian church, but a Universal Roman and Apostolic Church protecting all her children whatever language they spoke. If the Pope ceased to be the independent Sovereign who for centuries had reigned at Rome, and if the Catholic world saw their Sovereign Pontiff sink to the level of a mere Piedmontese Pensioner, then indeed schism might threaten the Church. But happily no such danger existed, the Sacred College as also the Bishops of the whole world, thro' the medium of their Pastoral Letters had unanimously proclaimed the absolute necessity of the Temporal Dominion of the Papacy, and when the present crisis had passed, the wicked would be punished and justice be done to the Pope.

Cardinal Antonelli's language did not however discourage Dr Pantaleoni or Padre Passaglia who founded their best hopes on the encouragement received from the liberal party in the Church and from the Pope through Cardinal Santucci, but they evidently forgot the influence of the Utramontane party and of their other political enemies in Rome, already hard at work to counteract the sympathies they had gained.

Meanwhile the 'Full Powers' announced by Count Cavour were daily and anxiously expected by Doctor Pantaleoni, but never arrived, although they had been despatched from Turin and entrusted to a priest who was going to Rome. The priest and the credentials had disappeared and the position of the two negotiators was becoming exceedingly awkward, when at last a French traveller brought a parcel mysteriously entrusted to him at Naples for Dr Pantaleoni, which was found to contain the missing papers.

It appears that the priest, who had originally brought them from Turin, was met at Civita Vecchia by a prelate of high standing in Rome, who directed him to re-embark, proceed to Naples with the papers entrusted to him by Count Cavour and remain concealed in a convent until further orders.

I give the facts as they were recounted to me on good authority, but I am unable to explain the mystery attaching to them. Certain it is, that the moment Doctor Pantaleoni was in possession of the 'Full Powers' authorizing him to open negotiations between Italy and the Pope, he received orders from the police to quit Rome, and he immediately addressed an humble petition to the Sovereign Pontiff begging to be made acquainted with the reasons for which he was suddenly to be banished after having received every encouragement to bring about an understanding between the two contending Powers, and he also enclosed a copy of his Memorandum which the Pope had formerly accepted from Cardinal Santucci and which had led to his appointment as negotiator on the part of Count Cavour.

The Pope, however, who had again fallen a victim to the evil influences of the Ultramontane party, took no notice of the Petition, which has remained unanswered, but insisted on the sentence of banishment being carried out without further delay and Dr Pantaleoni was compelled to leave Rome in 48 hours.

The Papal Government has not even condescended to explain or account for this new glaring and arbitrary act of injustice and bad faith.

172 [P.R.O. 30/22/75]   *Rome, 2 April 1861*

Private

O.R. to Lord J.R.

The Vatican and the French authorities in Rome having made up their minds that the only solution of the Roman question is a permanent French occupation, the ex-King of Naples has also made up his mind to establish himself in Rome with his Queen, his step-mother, his brothers and the rest of his family, and his former plan of going to Bavaria is given up for the present. The priests talk a great deal about a proposed occupation of Romagna by the Austrians (which would be the result of the prolonged occupation of Rome by the French) and of the final execution of the Treaty of Villa Franca, by the combined forces of France and Austria. Although these are evidently but idle reports, I must observe that they are in great measure founded on the language held here by the French civil and military authorities. I am quite aware that the language of French officials is generally founded on nothing at all, but nevertheless I mention it to you that you may know what they think it necessary to talk about in the Eternal City....

173 [F.O. 43/83A]   *Rome, 6 April 1861*

No. 32

O.R. to Lord J.R.

It is with much regret that I have to inform Your Lordship that the

Pope has been suffering from a sharp attack of fever. His Holiness caught cold during the ceremonies on Easter Sunday at St Peter's. On Monday the Sovereign Pontiff gave an early dinner to King Francesco II at the Quirinal and not feeling well he determined to walk after dinner for the benefit of his health to the church of *S. Agnese fuori le Mura* about a mile beyond the Porta Pia.

On Tuesday morning the symptoms of fever had increased but His Holiness could not be persuaded to abstain from attending Mass at the Sixtine Chapel and at about half past eleven a.m. His Holiness was observed to close his eyes and lean his head against the back of the throne on which he was seated. Ten minutes elapsed and the Pope gave no signs of recovery, so Cardinal de Pietro rose and hurried to Cardinal Antonelli's apartment for advice. Their Eminences returned at once, Mass was interrupted, the Pope, who had fainted, was lifted into a Sedan chair and carried to his bedroom and medical assistance immediately called in.

In the course of Wednesday His Holiness was able to receive and converse with the Cardinal Secretary of State and the Cardinal Vicar. On Thursday His Holiness endeavoured to get up, but the fever having slightly increased he was obliged to return to bed. I am happy to say that His Holiness's medical advisers seem satisfied with the course the fever is taking and announce a complete recovery of health and strength in a very few days.

174 [P.R.O. 30/22/75]   *Rome, 9 April 1861*
Private
O.R. to Lord J.R.

... Cardinal Antonelli has gone so far as to assure one of my friends that he means to have a Spanish garrison in Rome if the Emperor should ever see fit to withdraw his garrison. I am quite aware that Cardinal Antonelli is indulging his audience in pleasant illusions and that France is not going to march out of Italy to make room for Spain....

Cardinal Antonelli has nothing to gain by a change and his game is evidently to keep things as they are, so as to be able to put by *scudo* after *scudo* for his old age, and so long as the Pope lives and the French remain in Rome he has nothing to fear. ...

175 [F.O. 43/83A]   *Rome, 25 April 1861*

No. 41. [Recites Telegram]
O.R. to Lord J.R.

F.O. 24 April 1.35. Was the British Consulate illuminated with
coloured lanterns on the occasion of the late feast and illumination in
honor of the anniversary of the Pope's return from exile at Gaeta?
Answer immediately by telegraph.

Rome, 25 April. 1 p.m. Yes. Mr Severn told me he thought it was
customary to take part in a general illumination and that he could not
avoid doing so. I told him he had been wrong and referred him to his
instructions for the future.

176 [F.O. 43/83A]   *Rome, 30 April 1861*

No. 44
O.R. to Lord J.R.

It appears that the Spanish Government had proposed to settle the
Roman question by a Congress of the Catholic Powers, but although
this plan had at first met with the approval of the Vatican, it is now on
the contrary discouraged by the Cardinal Secretary of State, on the
following grounds:

The only settlement of the Roman question which the Pope can
accept is the entire and unconditional restoration of his lost provinces,
i.e. the *status quo ante bellum.*

Any other settlement proposed by the Congress of Catholic Powers
would have to be met by a strong protest on the part of His Holiness.
If therefore the Catholic Powers are not prepared to back up the decisions of the Pope and the requirement of the Church by a religious war,
His Holiness is of opinion that they had better not meet in Congress for
the present. . . .

177 [F.O. 43/83A]   *Rome, 30 April 1861*

No. 47
O.R. to Lord J.R.

The following circumstances give an idea of the wisdom and benevolence of the Papal administration.

Madame Pantaleoni, the wife of the learned doctor who was so suddenly banished by the Pope, because he was in favor of a peaceful
agreement between Rome and Turin, was about to follow her husband
with three young children, a governess and a maid, when she was informed by the police that she could not be permitted to go unless she
signed a declaration that she would never return to Rome. After some
useless attempts to get over this difficulty, she was obliged to go herself
to the Police Office and sign the document in question, which she did
under protest of course, the doctor having left a good deal of property
and a valuable collection of books in Rome, requiring future attendance.

The passport having then been granted, two friends of her husband,
one a priest, the other a doctor, both proposed to accompany her to
Civita Vecchia to see her and the children safely on board the steam-
packet, but on applying to the Police Office for the permission to travel
by railway to Civita Vecchia, they were informed that their intentions
were known and that by a special order from the Vatican no subject of
the Pope was to be allowed to accompany the exile's wife and children.

178 [F.O. 43/83A]   *Rome, 10 May 1861*
No. 56
O.R. to Lord J.R.

In my despatch No. 39 of 23rd April last, I mentioned to Your Lordship the existence of two addresses, one to the King of Italy and the
other to the Emperor of the French, petitioning for the withdrawal of
his troops, which were being mysteriously circulated and numerously
signed by the Romans.

Notwithstanding the immense exertions made and the sums offered
by the Pontifical Police to obtain a copy of the text, notwithstanding
domiciliary visits made by day and by night in search of them, notwithstanding the power of the confessional and notwithstanding the fact
that upwards of ten thousand persons of all classes have already signed
these petitions in the palaces, houses, taverns, coffee-houses, and shops
of Rome, the Pontifical Police has not yet been able to lay hands upon
them. Certainly a remarkable proof of the national spirit which animates the Romans, when one considers the immense personal risk
incurred by every individual who affixes his name to similar documents,
under ecclesiastical rule.

179 [F.O. 43/83A] *Rome, 16 May 1861*

No. 57

O.R. to Lord J.R.

A man named Chiavone, who appears to have money at his command, recruited a small force of four or five hundred men, with which he marched from Rome to Terracina and from thence to Postella, the former frontier village of the Kingdom of Naples. To the left of Postella is another village called Monticelli, which Chiavone attacked, and having killed the *sindaco* or city magistrate and some of the national guards he took possession and fortified the place. The next day the national guards of Fondi attacked Chiavone at Monticelli, but their numbers were too small and they were repulsed.

Chiavone and his men, probably fearing the advance of Piedmontese troops from Gaeta, next withdrew to the frontier of the Papal States and concealed themselves in the former haunts of Fra Diavolo and Gasparoni, where, by order of General de Goyon, they were sought and pursued by the French garrison of Terracina, but without effect, of course, the mountain guides of the French army being Pontifical gendarmes. Meanwhile the French military authorities captured somewhere near Valmontone two carts, in which they found, besides some letters, some thousand francs worth of Neapolitan copper coin, that is, ten Tornesi pieces, bearing the date of 1859. The carters, four in number, who were coming from Rome and going towards the Neapolitan frontier, declined to give any information whatever and were at once sent to Rome to General de Goyon, who had them, together with their carts, their money and their letters, consigned to prison in the Castle of St Angelo.

General de Goyon, with that frankness and loyalty which characterizes all his actions, at once proceeded to the Quirinal and waited on King Francesco, to whom he related all the circumstances of the capture. His Majesty thanked the General warmly for the course he had pursued and assured him that he entirely condemned the efforts made by false friends to promote reactionary movements in the late Kingdom which did his cause more harm than good. He knew nothing of the Neapolitan money just captured by the French authorities, but he would feel sincerely indebted to General de Goyon if he could clear up the mystery and punish the offenders. Chiavone who was acting entirely on his own personal responsibility had fruitlessly attempted to see His

Majesty, who had at once requested the Roman Government to have him arrested and detained in prison, but they had unfortunately not been able to succeed in doing so. His Majesty would therefore feel grateful to General de Goyon if he could destroy Chiavone's bands and put an end to proceedings which he deplored and condemned and had in vain attempted to prevent.

General de Goyon having met with similar declarations on the part of Cardinal Antonelli, has ordered a Board of Officers to investigate the matter. A third cart, equally laden with Neapolitan ten Tornesi pieces, was captured yesterday and brought to the Castle of St Angelo. The existence of this Neapolitan coin in Rome was explained to General de Goyon by the Papal authorities as follows. During the siege of Gaeta, King Francesco purchased 20,000 scudis worth of copper at Marseilles, which, with the Pope's permission he sent to the Pontifical mint at Rome to be coined with the die of the ten Tornesi pieces of 1859. Gaeta having fallen before the whole sum was spent in paying the troops, the remainder was sold cheap to the Jews of the ghetto who are now endeavouring to smuggle it into Naples on speculation.

The above details are obtained from thoroughly authentic sources.

180 [P.R.O. 30/22/75]　　　　　　　　　*Rome, 21 May 1861*

Private
O.R. to Lord J.R.

The Duc de Gramont, whose hatred of Cavour and hostility to Italy and the Italians increases every day, is furious at Goyon for his energetic pursuit of the Bourbon reactionists, and more especially at the capture of the copper coin, made in Rome, mentioned in my No. 57. Goyon tells me in confidence that Gramont is doing his utmost to quash the investigation. Poor Gramont, I pity him, his health is breaking up, and he does not give himself sufficient rest. He looks dreadfully ill, and the state of his body evidently influences his mind, otherwise his sudden changes and extreme views, which have no real foundation whatever, could not be explained. All that matters little, however, so far as the Roman question is concerned, which is no longer under diplomatic control. The apple will fall according to the laws of nature, and the Roman question will be solved by History. In all the plans of settlement that I have seen it appears to me that an essential point is ignored, namely that the temporal independence of the Popes has ceased to exist *de facto*, and that bayonets and grapeshot alone can give him that temporal dominion which the Catholic Powers think so essential to his dignity. . . .

181   [P.R.O. 30/22/75]   *Rome, 4 June 1861*
Private
O.R. to Lord J.R.

. . . General de Goyon tells me that while he gets on very well with the National Party, his position with the Priests he is here to protect becomes more odious every day, and that he feels he is protecting the Emperor's worst enemies and most cordial haters. The General assures me that he would give a great deal to get rid of his present command, which is rendered painfully difficult by the many conspiracies which surround him, conspiracies even against the Emperor's life, which he has lately discovered and disclosed to Cardinal Antonelli. . . .

Cardinal Antonelli, who is amiable as ever with me, asked me to come and see his collection of precious stones. I was a couple of hours alone with him and found him ready to talk about everything. The impression left on my mind is that he is determined to do nothing, refuse every plan of settlement and keep the French in Rome as long as he can, which is in fact his only policy if he wishes to remain in office. He also made me distinctly understand that if, by any chance, the French left and the Piedmontese garrisoned Rome, he would not let the Pope go, but would insist on His Holiness clinging fast to the Vatican and awaiting events in the chair of St Peter.

182   [F.O. 43/83B]   *Rome, 7 June 1861*
No. 66
O.R. to Lord J.R.

Cardinal Antonelli has just informed me that Count Cavour died yesterday morning.

His Eminence had no details, but expressed all the regret he felt at the idea that Cavour's sudden death might not have left him time to repent of the policy he had pursued, and the Pope had ordered Masses to be read in many churches for him. The Republican party whom Cavour had hitherto managed to keep down, would now have it all their own way and Italy would gradually break up into small Republics. Brigandage was assuming a most alarming character in the south and it would take years to suppress it. In former days, after 1815, the Papal Government had in the course of eleven years of constant warfare against the brigands of the provinces of Frosinone and Terracina spent many millions, but in the present state of things no one could say how much money and how many years it might require to pacify the country. His Eminence deplored the melancholy prospects of 'poor Italy', doomed to years of internal misery, shame and distress through the selfish policy of wicked men.

183 [P.R.O. 30/22/75]   *Rome, 8 June 1861*
Private
O.R. to Lord J.R.

Cardinal Antonelli yesterday received a telegram from Turin announcing Count Cavour's death; the Priest Party and the representatives of Powers hostile to Italy have shown a degree of indecent joy which has deeply shocked me. Yesterday the Pope was suddenly taken ill with vomiting and fever, but he is much better to-day. These frequent attacks of ill health are beginning to alarm many people in Rome and it is said His Holiness's doctors do not feel easy about him. . . . It is said that if His Holiness dies, Cardinal Antonelli will have to fly from Rome to save himself from the wrath, vengeance and hatred of his colleagues, among whom he certainly has not one single friend. Meanwhile I do not believe the Pope to be as ill as people here fancy.

184 [P.R.O. 30/22/75]   *Rome, 11 June 1861*
Private
O.R. to Lord J.R.

The Pope has taken it into his head that Her Majesty our Queen is about to turn Roman Catholic and that the Duchess of Kent was converted on her death bed. I have heard the matter discussed by several of the Pope's prelates and today Monsignor Talbot assured me that the Pope was in possession of the most positive information on the subject. These foolish priests really don't know what to invent next! They have also put about that Cavour on his death bed repented of his Italian policy, asked the Pope's forgiveness and begged of his King to return the Pope's lost provinces to him. . . .

[*Endorsed:* What inventors of Lies! P. [almerston].]

13. Theatricals in Rome. Odo Russell on left

14. Duc de Gramont

185 [F.O. 43/83B]   *Rome, 14 June 1861*

No. 68

O.R. to Lord J.R.

On Tuesday 11th instant at the Teatro Aliberti near the Piazza di
Spagna, during the performance of the ballet called 'Stella', some tricoloured bouquets having been thrown upon the stage to a dancer, the
audience which was very numerous rose like one man and cheered
King Victor Emmanuel and United Italy to their hearts' content. The
house was soon invaded by Gendarmes and the audience obliged to
withdraw.

The Teatro Aliberti has in consequence been closed by order of the
Papal Government.

186 [F.O. 43/83B]   *Rome, 14 June 1861*

No. 71

O.R. to Lord J.R.

The shock produced by the death of Count Cavour on the public mind
in Rome was perhaps heavier and more painful than in any other portion of Italy, but the National party have rallied rapidly and seem to
have perfect faith in their new leaders. Their sentiments are correctly
expressed in the enclosed Proclamation of the Roman National Committee. The Ultramontane party and the representatives of the Catholic
Powers on the other hand declare that the Pope is in possession of a
document signed by Count Cavour and brought to His Holiness by the
Count's confessor in which he solemnly retracts before death his past
acts and repents of his policy towards the Holy See, stating that he had
been compelled to act as he had done by the Emperor Napoleon and
advizing King Victor Emmanuel to return Romagna, the Marches and
Umbria to the Pope.

His Holiness is said to have declared with tears in his eyes on reading
this document that Cavour died as a true Catholic, and the whole story
which is generally believed by the pious in Rome appears to afford
them the greatest comfort and consolation. Indeed even the Duc de
Gramont and several other representatives of Catholic Powers assure
me that without full and sincere repentance of his past policy Count
Cavour could not have obtained the absolution of the Church to save

H

his soul from eternal damnation to which it was necessarily condemned through the Papal Bull of Excommunication of last year.

I submit these details to Your Lordship merely to shew how certain minds still have faith in the small pious frauds through which the Court of Rome delight to exercise their power....

187 [F.O. 43/83B]   *Rome, 18 June 1861*

No. 75. Confidential
O.R. to Lord J.R.

Cardinal Antonelli has received a telegram from Paris announcing the recognition of the Kingdom of Italy by France. His Eminence tells me that according to the text of the telegram the Emperor only recognizes the *de facto* power of King Victor Emmanuel over Italy but maintains the protests made against the usurpation by Piedmont of the Pope's provinces of Romagna, the Marches and Umbria. This mode of recognition he thought involved an evident contradiction, for France appeared to say: 'I recognize what I protest against.'

His Eminence however not having seen the official text of the act of recognition preferred for the present to withhold his judgement thereupon.

Meanwhile the prospect of a prolonged French occupation appeared to afford His Eminence as much satisfaction as it will produce irritation and disappointment among the people of Rome.

188 [P.R.O. 30/22/75]   *Rome, 22 June 1861*

Private
O.R. to Lord J.R.

The Pope is much better, but the priests seem to think that his end is approaching and they are tremendously excited at the prospect of a Conclave. Their excitement is shared by the Catholic Embassies and Legations and all speculate on the chances of a future election.

I am inclined to think as the doctors do, that the poor dear Pope will recover and live a long time yet, for his constitution is strong and his spirits still good. At the same time the recognition of Italy by France is said to have caused him deep annoyance, because he would not believe in the possibility of it. King Francesco and Monsignor de Mérode continue to organize their reactionary bands for the Abbruzzi, and their

iniquitous proceedings meet with the approval of the poor dear old
Pope, but even his blessing does not make them more successful. . . .

189 [F.O. 43/83B]   *Rome, 30 June 1861*
No. 80
O.R. to Lord J.R.

Last night during the *Girandola* and illumination in honor of St Peter
the Gendarmes perceived in the window of an unfurnished house of the
Corso an illuminated Cross of Savoy, which they proceeded to destroy
amid the hisses of the people. Without much further to do the gendarmes drew their sabres and charged the people in the Corso in their
usual brutal manner. Unfortunately the people in self-defence killed
one of the gendarmes, but happily the French military authorities
arrived in time to prevent further bloodshed.

The hatred between the people and the priests is growing to a most
alarming extent·

[*On 10 July O.R. went on leave via Turin and Paris. On 4 November he
returned to Rome.*]

190 [P.R.O. 30/22/75]   *Paris, 15 October 1861*
Private

O.R. to Earl Russell[1]

I have just returned from the Tuileries, where, together with Lord
Cowley I had an audience of the Emperor at 6 p.m. Lord Cowley first
presented me to His Majesty, who invited us to sit down and having
enquired how long I had been in Italy he at once plunged into the
Roman question. He gave a short précis of the history of the occupation, dwelt on the difficulties it had occasioned during the last twelve
years, and twice declared in animated terms that the greatest political
mistake he had committed was the consent he gave to that expedition
in 1849. It had been a source of constant trouble to him and he never
ceased to look for a solution of the question, but the more he turned it
over in his mind, the more he felt that he was in honor bound to protect
the Pope whom he could not abandon to the tender mercies of the

---

[1] Lord John had been created an Earl on 30 July 1861.

Italian revolution without such guarantees as would satisfy the Papacy as well as the Catholic world. It was indeed easy to withdraw his troops from Rome, but if anything happened, if violence was offered to the person of the Pope, the members of the Sacred College or the Priesthood, the blame would fall upon him, and the French Nation and the Catholic world would hold him responsible and would call upon him to return and occupy Rome. He had told Count Arese when he had last come from Turin that he desired nothing more than to withdraw his troops from Rome, if only the Piedmontese Government could come to some agreement with the Vatican, but what had the Piedmontese done? They had confiscated church property and abolished convents and that was not the way to gain the Pope's confidence. He well knew that the protection of the Vatican was an ungrateful task and that the services rendered by his troops were not appreciated by His Holiness but much as he wished to withdraw them and put an end to the irksome task he had undertaken during twelve years he felt it was impossible to do so honorably, without first finding a solution which could roughly satisfy all the parties concerned in it. I then replied to His Majesty in the sense you desired, telling him of all I had seen of the disposition of the Romans and of the passionate desire of other Italians to have Rome and how that desire would only increase and fret and eat into their souls more and more the longer his troops deprived them of their capital, and I added that the moral and physical sufferings of all classes in Rome under the present system were heart-rending to witness. His Majesty who seemed well acquainted with the wretched condition of the Romans questioned me a good deal about the Pope and the Cardinals who were likely to succeed him, about Padre Passaglia and others, and on the whole I thought him well up in Roman affairs. He asked me whether I had any solution to suggest, but mindful of your instructions not to enter upon that part of the Roman question I did not pretend to hear and when later he repeated the inquiry I merely said that I believed Padre Passaglia's views were in accordance with Canon Law and the true spirit of the Church, but that they had nevertheless just been condemned by the Inquisition and the Temporal Power thereby *de facto* declared a Dogma.

Again later the Emperor asked me for the third time whether I thought a solution possible and I said I believed the solution of the Roman question rested solely with His Majesty, to which he replied that no doubt it rested with him to open yonder window and throw himself into the street but that was not a sufficient reason for doing so, he was morally bound to leave the Pope unprotected. I inquired of His Majesty whether the Catholic feeling in France was really so strong as to prevent his taking the initiative in the settlement of the Roman difficulty? He replied he believed the sentiments of France were very much his own and that if a really satisfactory solution could be found, the French people and even a large portion of the clergy would be quite satisfied to see the French forces leave Rome, but it would be quite impossible for him to withdraw them if the French people thought it was not a spontaneous act and that he were yielding to the interference or dictation of any foreign Power. He alluded more particularly to Piedmont and thought Baron Ricasoli[1] was wrong in pressing the point so much, His Majesty twice repeated this observation adding that I could not but admit that this national feeling on the part of the French people was very natural. The attempts, he said, of the Vatican to form an ultra-montane party in France against him had been defeated by the good sense of the nation. He mentioned a plan lately proposed to him by Count Persigny *which would have been excellent had it not been erroneous in principle.* This plan was to take the question himself in hand, proclaim the sovereignty of the Pope in principle, and recognize the existence of the court of the Vatican, the Sacred College etc. but hand over the practical administration to the King of Italy, a plan which could not be carried out since it involved the proclamation and recognition of that which would have no real existence. He mentioned also the chirograph of the Pope, by which H.H. had expressed a wish that the Sacred College should elect his successor immediately after his death before he was buried and before the arrival of the foreign Cardinals, and his Majesty said that he had at once instructed his Ambassador to protest and declare that such illegal proceedings should be met by the immediate withdrawal of the French garrison. He questioned me about the Pope's health and I replied I had reason to know that H.H.'s health was far better than was generally supposed and his chances of life excellent. In answer to a question of Lord Cowley's he said that the death of the present Pope might greatly facilitate the solution of the Roman question. H.M. spoke also with Lord Cowley on the affairs of Naples and of Italy in general and he blamed the Turin Cabinet for their want of *savoir faire.* He gave them credit for good intentions but thought them unequal to their

[1] Prime Minister of Italy June 1861-February 1862.

task. He condemned centralization in Italy as in France, and praised our colonial administration, and he compared us to the ancient Romans whose history he loved to read. He regretted the presence of King Francesco at Rome and said that he was accused of having brought it about, but that he had on the contrary done all he could to induce the young King to leave Rome, unfortunately without success in consequence of the determination of Austria, Russia, Spain etc. to leave their diplomatic agents with His Majesty so long as he remained in Rome. Often in the course of this conversation the Emperor repeated his deep felt desire to find a solution of the Papal question so as to be able to withdraw his garrison. We were unfortunately interrupted by the arrival of the King of Holland. On leaving the room the Emperor expressed his regret at the interruption to Lord Cowley and said to me: 'If you can find the solution of this difficult question pray write it to Lord Cowley who can communicate it to me.' Before ending this letter I must add that nothing could be more natural frank and cordial than the Emperor's manner and he spoke with the most perfect appearance of sincerity and conviction; *sincerity* as to his wish to withdraw his troops and settle the Roman question, and *conviction* as to the impossibility of doing so, and I left his Majesty's presence confirmed in my sincere conviction that no representation, step or measure on our part will turn the French garrison out of Rome during the life time of Pius IX.

I have shown this letter to Lord Cowley who thinks I have correctly reported the conversation.

[*Lady Amberley records that, when O.R. was asked how he had felt during his audience with Napoleon III, he said*, 'J'ai senti comme l'Empereur que j'étais le neveu de mon oncle.' The Amberley Papers (1937), *Vol. 2, p. 548.*]

191   [P.R.O. 30/22/75]   *Paris, 17 October 1861*

Private
O.R. to Earl R.

Monsieur Thouvenel asked me to breakfast this morning. We went through the Roman question from beginning to end. He held exactly the same language as the Emperor, he showed the same anxious desire to find the solution of the Roman question and he declared his conviction that it could not yet be solved. He argued very rationally and showed with great force and fairness how difficult their position was from the French point of view. It would be an absurd and a dishonest policy to protect the Pope during 12 years and to withdraw that protection when he was most in need of it. I must have observed, he continued, how deeply the Emperor felt the awkwardness of his position and His Majesty had often said to him: '*l'occupation de Rome sera la faute de mon règne.*' Monsieur Thouvenel tried also to show the impossibility of getting the Catholic Powers to consent to the Pope becoming a subject of the King of Italy and he added that even the English Government could not view with indifference the power that would be given to the Italian Government to dictate the allocutions of the Vatican. I at once replied that if that argument were valid the objection to the Pope being a French subject was quite as great. Our Government was a strong Government. The Bulls, Encyclicals and allocutions of the Pope were a matter of supreme indifference to us and the Irish Bishops enjoyed a license of language which no Catholic Government would concede. Monsieur Thouvenel went on to say that unhappily the impatience shown by Baron Ricasoli and by our House of Commons only increased the Emperor's difficulty to withdraw from Rome as the national pride of France was naturally jealous of any appearance of foreign dictation. On the whole Monsieur Thouvenel said nothing that you have not already heard over and over again from Lord Cowley. He seemed to me very well disposed considering the great difficulties he has to contend with. . . .

192 [P.R.O. 30/22/75]   *Turin, 27 October 1861*

Private
O.R. to Earl R.

Just before leaving Paris I dined with Nigra[1] and sat beside Rattazzi.[2] Both in my conversations with the Emperor and with M. Thouvenel I could perceive a deep hatred to Ricasoli who is much too independent for them, and I suspect Rattazzi is endeavouring to make himself acceptable at Paris in the event of Ricasoli having to resign. A few hours after my arrival in Turin Ricasoli sent for me and received me most

[1] Italian representative in Paris.
[2] Rattazzi succeeded Ricasoli in March 1862 as Italian Prime Minister.

kindly. He showed me his plans with respect to Rome which had been refused at Paris and told me that Italy must now make up her mind to await the Emperor's pleasure in regard to her capital and that he should throw the responsibility of such policy upon the Government of France. Ricasoli appears to reciprocate the French Emperor's dislike and expressed deep gratitude for the support Italy derives from the policy of Her Majesty's Government. Poor Sir James[1] is laid up with an attack of gout at Baveno, so I went to see him and gave him your message about Rattazzi in which he entirely concurred. I returned to Turin and met my excellent friend Padre Passaglia who gave me an awful account of the state of Rome, of the wicked folly of the Pope and of the incapacity of the Sacred College. He is enthusiastic for the idea of 'Libera Chiesa in libero Stato' the abolition of the Temporal and the regeneration of the Spiritual Power alone. He appeared much touched at having been named by you in your late speech.

Ricasoli and Passaglia are patriots of high moral standing I think, and may be of great use to their country in the future.

I have met with great civility from everybody here which I owe to the honor of bearing your name. . . .

193 [F.O. 43/83B]   Rome, 16 November 1861
No. 86
O.R. to Earl R.

It is reported in official circles that the 'Chiavonists' have met with some military success near Sora and have also penetrated into the Pontifical territory near Veroli and Vallecorso; but details are unfortunately still wanting. Perhaps I should explain the etymology of the word 'Chiavonists' to Your Lordship, which has been coined at the Vatican for official purposes.

The words 'Brigands' and 'Brigandage' as applied to the armed bands in the Abbruzzi are too offensive to be pronounced while King Francesco dwells in Rome, and on the other hand the use of the words 'Royalists' or 'Bourbonists' is rendered impossible by the verbal declaration of His Majesty that he in no way sanctions or approves the proceedings of those armed bands, a declaration His Majesty, however, declined to put in writing for publication, when respectfully solicited to do so by General de Goyon in July last.

[1] Sir James Hudson, English Minister at Turin.

In this dilemma it became necessary to find a neutral denomination and armed bands were called after their leader, General Chiavone.

It is believed that the Chiavonists have their headquarters in the convents of Sciffelli and Casamare in the province of Frosinone between Veroli and Castelluccio, where the presence of the French troops renders them inaccessible to the Italian troops engaged in the suppression of brigandage in the Neapolitan provinces.

I find that the French Government have repeatedly counselled King Francesco to leave Rome and the Emperor Napoleon has offered His Majesty a residence at Nice, which the King has declined, saying that so long as the Pope would grant him hospitality he preferred staying in Italy. . . .

194 [F.O. 43/83B]   *Rome, 16 November 1861*

No. 88. Secret
O.R. to Earl R.

It is difficult to understand the policy of the French Government in regard to the brigandage now raging on the southern frontier of the province of Frosinone. I say brigandage, because the armed bands under the lead of Chiavone do not appear conscious of any political objects, and I say the policy of the French Government because I cannot for one moment admit that the distinguished general who commands in the Papal States could not in the space of a month root up and destroy a nest of brigands whose whereabouts he knows as well as Chiavone himself, if the War department in Paris sent him a telegram to the following effect: 'You are authorized to suppress brigandage in the Papal States.' To doubt General de Goyon's power to do so, with the gallant army he commands, would simply be to insult the French nation. But what has been done by the French authorities towards the suppression of brigandage in the Papal States, to assist General Cialdini's successful efforts in the Neapolitan provinces? They have investigated the causes of this brigandage until they have acquired a perfect knowledge of its origin, they have seen it organized and paid under their eyes, but they have concealed their knowledge, suppressed the publication of facts and blamed their officers for too much zeal in the pursuit of brigands. They have occupied Terracina, Vallecorso, Ceginano and Verol in the province of Frosinone, but they have left Alatri to the care of the Pontifical troops with a full knowledge that men and money were sent to Chiavone from Rome through Alatri. When over-zealous officers have seized Chiavone's agents and sent them to Rome, they have immediately been set at liberty at the request of the Papal authorities and of King Francesco's friends and the overzealous officers have been told not to seize or imprison Chiavone's agents any further without a special order from Rome.

Again, when brigands have fallen unawares into the hands of a French patrol, they have been sent to headquarters at Rome and there immediately handed over, men and arms, to the Pontifical authorities. Then the brigands have been conveyed to the barracks on the Piazza del Popolo and a week after they have been marched via Altari to the Neapolitan frontier and liberated within a few miles from Chiavone's headquarters. Again when the Italian troops approach too near the Pontifical frontiers in pursuit of these armed bands, the Vatican remon-strates and an angry correspondence ensues between the French military authorities and the Italian generals whose soldiers have been in fault, and again when the peaceful inhabitants petition the French authorities to rid them of the dreaded bands of Chiavone, those peti-tions are suppressed, like the petition of the Romans to the Emperor Napoleon last spring.

Some time since a French patrol near Veroli met with a band of Chiavonists in the night. The latter fired and severely wounded a French corporal, the French returned fire and secured one prisoner. His name was Ricci, and his pockets contained 3000 francs in Napo-leons and 20 scudi in Roman gold. He is now awaiting his trial in the Castle of St Angelo. Some weeks later the same patrol met another band of Chiavonists, who fired, and the French soldiers, only too anxious to avenge their wounded corporal fired also and killed a brigand. The affair was reported to Rome. The Vatican declare that from their information the Chiavonists only fired in the air to inform their comrades of approaching danger, and accuse the French officer, who allowed his men to fire at the Chiavonists, of deliberate murder, and the French General in command at once orders an investigation of the officer's conduct to be made.

Again, it must be remembered that the 25th and 40th regiments were removed this summer from Rome, where they had been quartered ten years, solely in consequence of their open sympathies with the Italian cause. . . .

195 [F.O. 43/83B]   *Rome, 19 November 1861*

No. 89
O.R. to Earl R.

I have not yet been long enough in Rome to give Your Lordship a very detailed account of the state of public feeling but I do not think that it has much changed since I left in the month of July, and the more so since the Roman police, who see an enemy in every shadow, have developed a boundless activity which is not calculated to gain either the confidence or the affections of the Pope's subjects.

The secret sources of wealth of the Vatican still continue to pour forth an abundance of money which can scarcely be accounted for by the mere collection of Peter's Pence. Nevertheless the Papal Government announce that the faithful are doing their duty all over the world and that the expenditure of the Holy See is already covered to the end of 1863. The Pope having more money at his command than he requires has ordered extensive improvements in the museums of the Vatican and the Lateran and restorations in many of the churches of Rome.

The Ultramontane party lift their head and are now full of confidence since they have been told from Paris that there is no danger of the French garrison being withdrawn during the lifetime of Pius IX. On the other hand I observe that the ideas of Passaglia are rapidly gaining adherents in the ranks of the Italian clergy. But the effect produced on the national party, which comprises the great majority of the Romans, by the avowed intention of France to hold Rome for many years to come, is curious to observe. They think it evident that the Emperor Napoleon intends to hold Rome until he has driven the Italian Government to offer the island of Sardinia for the national capital and they unfortunately begin to think the prize worth the sacrifice. 'Sardinia,' they say, 'is of no real importance to our national independence, while Italy cannot be practically united without Rome as our capital, delay may prove fatal, and from our national point of view the Turin cabinet should not hesitate to barter the island for the liberation of Rome.' I am assured by travellers that this opinion is gaining ground in the rest of Italy. Despair drove the Italians into the arms of Mazzini not many years since, and it is not impossible that time and imperial pressure may bring the party who advocate this policy into power.

196 [P.R.O. 30/22/75]   *Rome, 8 December 1861*

Private
O.R. to Earl R.

Monsieur de Lavalette,[1] although I was not acquainted with him, did me the honor of calling on me the day after his arrival in Rome, which according to diplomatic usage must be considered as *marked civility*, he being an Ambassador and I an attaché. I returned his visit. He carefully avoided all allusion to Roman affairs. . . . He hoped I would not treat him as an enemy but as a sincere friend of England and that I would look upon his house and his table as my own. . . . Goyon has called on me and I have called on Goyon, but I have not seen him yet. His present language is described to me as reactionary, and he is said to advocate a confederation, but I am also assured that he has received orders from Paris to act with more energy in the suppression of brigandage. On returning to Rome the General had an audience of the Pope and His Holiness asked him bluntly whether he had brought instructions from Paris to restore the Marches, Umbria and Romagna to the Holy See. Goyon was much embarrassed and confessed he had not, at which the Pope turned his back upon him and dismissed him. When Gramont took leave of the Pope, His Holiness gave him the Grand Cross of Pius IX telling him that by virtue of that order he was relieved of the effects of the Excommunication under which he had fallen. Gramont carefully concealed the gracious disclosures of the Sovereign Pontiff, but the Pope was less discreet and the representatives of the Catholic Powers are more than ever anxious to find favor in the Pope's eyes and become G.C.P. . . .

Antonelli has again bought two magnificent palaces through his secret agent Bussolini. They are to be made hotels of, I believe. Antonelli's private Secretary who a few years ago was but a poor Abbate has just built a fine lodging house. I suspect that the Pope and Antonelli one fine morning will have to exchange financial confessions like the Emperor Napoleon and Monsieur Fould, and then they will have to sell indulgences on a large and cheap scale. . . .

---

[1] The new French Ambassador in Rome, who had arrived on 4 November.

197 [F.O. 43/83B] *Rome, 17 December 1861*

No. 100
O.R. to Earl R.

Unusual interest has been felt at Rome in Monsieur de Lavalette's mission.

All parties seem to expect that a new Ambassador must necessarily be the representative of a new policy, and Roman affairs being in a state of transition all hoped in a change favorable to their conflicting interests. Meanwhile Monsieur de Lavalette, whose winning manners and pleasing conversation command the sympathies of all, has distinctly assured the Pope and Cardinal Antonelli that his Imperial Master in sending him to replace the Duc de Gramont at Rome in no way contemplated a change of policy towards the Holy See.

In a subsequent conversation with the Cardinal Secretary of State, the Ambassador touched on the desirability of finding a satisfactory solution to the Roman question, when His Eminence observed that that solution was already found at the Peace of Villa Franca and in the Treaty of Zurich, the execution of which would give entire satisfaction to the Holy Father. Monsieur de Lavalette replied that while he fully appreciated the value of the Treaty of Zurich he must remind Cardinal Antonelli that subsequent events had rendered its application impossible.

The Ambassador then went on to say that he could not but think the presence of King Francesco in Rome detrimental to the Papal cause, as it associated the Sovereign Pontiff with political acts that were foreign to the interests of the Church.

This opinion was combated by Cardinal Antonelli who claimed for the unfortunate young King the right of seeking the same quiet and neutral asylum in Rome which Pope Pius IX had found at Gaeta under the protection of His Majesty's father in 1849. . . .

198 [F.O. 43/83B] *Rome, 17 December 1861*

No. 102
O.R. to Earl R.

Since the arrival of Monsieur de Lavalette the French authorities in Rome have acted with more energy in the suppression of Neapolitan brigandage than heretofore. The following facts may have contributed to this change in their policy:

1st. That no respectable Neapolitans are to be found in Chiavone's ranks.

2nd. That his officers are all foreigners, Frenchmen, Belgians or Spaniards, sent by the Legitimist Committee at Marseilles, whilst his men are recruited among the lowest rabble.

3rd. That the chief agents employed to organize the Bourbon movement at Naples have returned to Rome saying that they have found it impossible to succeed among the Italians, the King having in fact no party at all in his late Kingdom, while the foreign element introduced into the country by the Legitimist Committee and which was compelled to amalgamate with common brigands to find any support at all, was more likely to injure than to benefit King Francesco's cause. . . .

199 [F.O. 43/83B]   *Rome, 31 December 1861*

No. 106
O.R. to Earl R.

I have often felt surprized during my late visit to France at the very superficial knowledge of the Roman question I have met with among Frenchmen. They appear generally to believe that Protestant England is eagerly pursuing a policy hostile to the Papacy in Italy, while Catholic France is protecting the Pope and the interests of religion against the revolutionary policy of Piedmont by maintaining a powerful army at Rome. On what facts this manner of viewing the Roman question is based, I am at a loss to comprehend.

It appears to me that the so-called hostile policy of England towards the Holy See may be summed up in a few speeches in Parliament pointing out the advantages of a good over a bad administration, and the general sympathy of the people and of the press for the cause of freedom and order in Italy.

Certain it is that England settled her differences with Rome three centuries ago, but she now gives the most entire liberty and independence at home and in her colonies to the Church of Rome and to her bishops for the free exercise of their faith, a liberty and independence no other government has yet felt strong enough to concede, least of all Catholic France, who resists and disputes the ecclesiastical nominations of Rome, subjects the pastorals of her bishops to secular censorship and

controls the exercise of all the duties belonging to their office, prose-
cutes her press, denounces and suspends her charitable societies and
handles her clergy generally as a dangerous political association.

And since our policy has been thought hostile I would fain solicit
Your Lordship's permission to examine in as few words as possible the
so-called friendly and protective influence of France at Rome and the
Emperor Napoleon's past, present and prospective policy in regard to
the Papacy.

As to the past it must be remembered that during the many years of
foreign occupation deemed necessary to maintain the temporal authority of the Popes over their subjects, the Emperor Napoleon from 18th
August 1849, when he addressed the letter to Count E. Ney, down to
the present year has never ceased to urge with perfect consistency at the
Vatican the expediency and necessity of administrative reforms. That
advice was never acted upon in Rome, perhaps because the Pontifical
Government felt that the administration of the Holy See was not of a
nature to bear the corrective effects of a free press and of representative
institutions. They preferred to adopt a temporizing policy calculated
to prolong the presence of the French garrison, and priestcraft prevailed over the warning voice of the statesmen who discussed the future
dangers of the Roman difficulty at the Congress of Paris, and over
the renewed advice of France to the Pope which followed their
deliberations.

At this time Monsieur About, the Roman correspondent of the official
Moniteur, published a series of letters, which were later collected into a
separate volume, pointing with great force to the ludicrous side of the
temporal administration of the priests. I need not remind Your Lordship of the powerful effect produced by this witty publication, which
was later published by the French Government at the request of the
Court of Rome.

When later a generous impulse led France to drive Austria out of
Lombardy and free Italy from the foreign yoke, the famous Proclamation of Milan once more led the Romans, who for years had hoped
in vain that the influence of France would procure them a more con-
genial administration from the Vatican, to believe that the day of
liberation had dawned at last for them also. But the peace of Villa
Franca shook that belief and the proposition made by the Emperor
Napoleon that all Italy should be placed under the Honorary Presidency of the Pope roused the Italians to unite and resist the common

danger they anticipated from the extension of ecclesiastical dominion.

But France, faithful to her proclaimed policy of non-intervention did not see fit to re-occupy the Romagna abandoned by Austria, and left the odium of the massacre of Perugia to the Pontifical mercenaries.

A European Congress was now proposed for the settlement of Italian affairs, but before it could assemble the Pontifical Plenipotentiaries were scared from proceeding to Paris to attend its meetings by the publication of the famous pamphlet, *Le Pape et le Congrès*. The able arguments of this publication tended to accustom France, the Papacy and the Catholic world to the expediency of limiting the temporal dominion of the Popes to Rome and the Patrimony of St Peter. But the author of the pamphlet who appeared ready to concede every rational liberty to the rest of Italy, assigned to the population of Rome as subjects of the Pope a position which appeared as odious as it was ridiculous, and the effect of which was to widen the breach that already separated the people from the Pontiff.

The Papal Government no longer finding that submissive devotion at Paris which the Church expects from Her Eldest Son, now began to grow suspicious of the protective policy of France and determined to shift for themselves. An appeal to the Catholic world for men and money was decided upon, the Church in distress could no longer rely on the sole protection of France, who had nothing but good advice to offer, and while Peter's Pence were collected all over the world, General de Lamoricière was charged with the formation of a Catholic army of Crusaders.

Upon this the French Government declared their intention to withdraw their garrison from Rome, since its services would no longer be needed and although Garibaldi had already sailed for Southern Italy, they hastened to sign a convention with the Vatican for the withdrawal of their garrison the moment the Pontifical army should be strong enough to keep down the Pope's dissatisfied subjects. No one could then foresee that the army of Crusaders, who were rapidly assuming the character of an army of Legitimacy, would be so suddenly destroyed at Castelfidardo by General Cialdini.

Avowedly indignant at what it considered the aggressive policy of Piedmont, the French Government had declared to the Pope through their Ambassador that they would oppose Count Cavour's policy, that they would break off diplomatic relations with Turin and that General de Goyon, then on leave in France, had received orders to embark without delay at the head of 10,000 additional troops and to hasten to Rome for the protection of the Pope. Unfortunately the French Ambassador's language was misinterpreted at the Vatican and it was understood that by protecting the Pope with 10,000 additional men, His Excellency meant that General de Goyon was to oppose the advance of the Piedmontese army. This unfortunate mistake was the more to be deplored as it caused the annihilation of the Pope's army and the death of many good and zealous men, and the Marches and Umbria no longer under foreign military rule hastened to annex themselves to Italy.

The Ultramontane party now deeming the protection offered by France to the Pope to be insufficient and insincere urged His Holiness to make a declaration to that effect with an appeal to the sense of justice of the Catholic world and to leave Rome and seek an asylum in Spain or Bavaria. The French Government hastened to use every exertion to counteract their plans by at once increasing their garrison to 20,000 men and extending their occupation to the provinces of Viterbo and Frosinone, and the Pope was persuaded and content to remain in Rome. France hereby rendered an essential service to Italy by effectually arresting all pretence on the part of the Catholic Powers for that active interference in favor of the Pope, which the Holy Father as a homeless wanderer might have solicited and possibly obtained.

We now come to the siege of Gaeta. The French Government by the presence of their fleet contributed largely towards inducing King Francesco to prolong a useless resistance. When the long and tedious siege works of the Piedmontese were finished and their batteries ready, the French Government once more proffered their best advice and then withdrew their fleet. Thereupon the Piedmontese opened fire and in eighteen days the fortress was taken and more than half the King's army which had fled into the Pontine Marshes was disarmed and disbanded by the French authorities at Rome. The unfortunate young King and his Court sought an asylum in Rome and the French Government discovered but too late that in extending their protection to His Majesty they had for ever associated the venerable name of the Pope with the arming of brigands and with the greatest of evils – civil war.

It is easy to criticize the past, and these events were perhaps beyond the control of the French Government, but it must not be forgotten that the true friends of the Roman Catholic Church all along deplored that the French Government did not beseech the Pope's Government to avoid the ill-advised step of seeking to become a military power and to avoid so ruinous an expenditure and a policy so evidently suicidal, by endeavouring rather to conciliate than to coerce his subjects.

And it must also in truth be said that the policy of the Vatican has been from beginning to end inexplicable. What would the position of the Pope have been and what the obligations of France towards His Holiness, Italy and Europe had the pontiff instead of recruiting useless and expensive armies and instead of hurling excommunication at his protectors, simply dismissed his mercenaries and said to those who had maintained him for twelve years on his throne: 'I am a weak old man and cannot defend myself for I am not a military prince. I place the Church with perfect confidence under the sole protection of her Eldest Son, and while he with his good sword protects the material interests of the Holy See, I will pray to God to forgive mine enemies.'

But, as the events reviewed above show, neither the Pope nor the Emperor seem to have understood each other or the question in which they were the principal actors. The Pope became suspicious of his sole protector because he advocated the expediency of improving an administration which the Pontiff considered to be perfect, and the Emperor seems unhappily to have lulled himself into the belief that time and a French garrison would in the end be an equivalent to good government. Thanks to the want of confidence of the one and thanks to the want of foresight of the other, the Holy See is at present socially, politically and financially in a worse condition than when France undertook the mission twelve years ago of protecting the Pope and the interests of religion, and seventy millions of francs expended on a garrison of 128,000 men have neither improved the administration nor the finances nor the prospects of the Papacy, nor even the diplomatic relations between the Vatican and the Tuileries.

Assuming that France is aware of the disastrous results of her protectorate, it is but natural to suppose that she must be now desirous to remedy the evil and obtain for the Pontiff that position which is due to the Head of the Roman Catholic Church in the world, and I will now endeavour to estimate her present policy in Rome. I need not enumerate all the ingenious solutions of the Roman question which have been debated and rejected by France. Essentially these are but three: 1st. Either the whole of the lost provinces of the Holy See are reconquered and held by foreign troops for the Pope as they were since 1849, or

2nd. The total loss of the temporal dominion is acknowledged and the principle of a free church in a free state is adopted, or

3rd. A portion only of the territory surrounding Rome is assigned to the Pope, and must equally be held by foreign troops as is now the case.

Of these three solutions the Pope will only admit the first, the Italian Government has proposed the second, and France is practically carrying out the third. France has declared that her honor is engaged, that she is bound to protect and cannot abandon the Pope to the tender mercies of Italy, and that she must continue to protect His Holiness and the interests of religion as heretofore.

In what manner then will the prolonged occupation of Rome save the honor of France and the interests of the Papacy? We can only judge by the past, and judging by that standard it will:

1st. Widen the breach between governed and government and render conciliation impossible.

2nd. It will destroy the financial resources of the Church and exhaust the purses of the faithful.

3rd. It will give time to the Pontifical authorities to add, with continued impunity to themselves, another series of blunders to those of the past.

4th. It will accustom France, Europe and the Catholic world to the administrative incapacity of the priests.

5th. It will strengthen that party in the clergy who desire Church Reform in temporal matters and may possibly encourage schism in the national churches.

6th. It will associate the name of the Papacy in the midst of a great national movement with an anti-national and illiberal policy lowering to the dignity of the Pontiff, and

7th. It will contribute to confound the pure spiritual interests of the Church with temporal impurities and breed discord among the clergy.

And every day and every year will add to these evils until Rome becomes practically a French dependency and the Pope a French bishop. Then the Catholic powers will ask themselves: 'Where is the temporal independence of the Pope, without which we have declared that the Roman Catholic Church cannot exist?' And then they will perceive that that temporal independence had long since died of inanition and that it cannot be revived either by a French or an Italian garrison, or a joint occupation of the Catholic powers, or even by a Catholic army of Crusaders, for the spiritual power of the Papacy,

which retains all its vigour, has no choice left between the total abandonment of its temporal dominion or a permanent foreign armed
protectorate.

To England it matters little or nothing whether the Pope be a
French or an Italian bishop. Not so to Italy, to whom it cannot be indifferent to harbour in her bosom a clergy ever ready to open a door to
foreign intervention. But can we in justice to France suspect her of
intending to incorporate Rome as a new permanent French possession
like Savoy, Nice or Algeria? The honesty and good sense of France
forbid such an assumption.

When therefore France becomes conscious of the harm she is inflict-
ing on the Papacy by her well-meant but ill-judged protectorate, she
will in all probability seek in earnest to exert her powerful influence to
conciliate the Papacy and Italy, since the true independence of the
Popes rests solely on the mutual confidence which ought to exist
between the Church and the laity. And while the French Government
lose time and money in the fruitless struggle to protect a hostile church,
Italy, notwithstanding her impatience to see the question settled, will
be a gainer in the end.

So long as France holds Rome, the armed interference of other
Catholic powers in Roman or Italian affairs becomes impossible and
Italy, thanks to the attitude of France, is able internally to constitute,
organize and establish herself and carry the work of unity to completion. By the time France awakens to the fact that she has accomplished
nothing in aid of the Pope by her protectorate, Italy will have become
ready to receive the prostrate and exhausted Papacy and elevate it to
that position which as an organ of moral and spiritual government it is
entitled to claim.

If France after driving Austria out of Lombardy and giving Italy
to the Italians had handed over Rome and the Church at once to them,
their difficulties might have proved insurmountable. For over and
above the arduous task of organizing the administration of the country,
the Italian government would have had to deal with the full unbroken
force of a clergy then still uncompromisingly hostile, and with the
dangers which might have been entailed by the demands, expectations
and possible interference of Catholic powers, then neither awakened to
a sense of their own weakness, nor as yet brought by experience to a
conviction of the true state of the Papacy.

Whilst professing to protect the Church against Italy, France in truth has protected Italy against the Church and her foreign allies. The occupation of Rome will therefore practically prove to be the completion of the liberation of Italy commenced by France in Lombardy and foreshadowed in the proclamation of Milan, and by holding the Papacy by the head with a French army, enabling Italy to cut off her limbs one by one with impunity, France is rendering a greater service to Italy than by any previous act of her generous policy, and nothing can lessen the magnitude of that service, not even if the unity of Italy should fail and two or several governments divide the Peninsula.

Whether the French Government be conscious or not of the ultimate effects of their Roman policy it is not for me to decide, but it is certainly significant that while they have repudiated all interference and maintained a strict neutrality in Italian affairs ever since the war in Lombardy, they have made one exception and have broken through the principle of non-intervention in favor of Rome to maintain their disastrous protectorate of the Pope.

In all these acts of her ally England has had no active share, and it is for that reason that I am at a loss to comprehend why the people of France imagine that Protestant England is pursuing a policy hostile to the Papacy in Italy, while Catholic France is supposed to be protecting the Pope and the interests of religion against the revolutionary policy of Italy by maintaining a powerful army at Rome.

200 [P.R.O. 30/22/76]   *Rome, 5 January 1862*

Private
O.R. to Earl R.

. . . The orders for the suppression of brigandage must come from Paris. Here in Rome Monsieur de Lavalette's humane and enlightened attempts to put a stop to bloodshed and murder will fail so long as General de Goyon is not furnished with complete instructions by the War Department in Paris to carry out the Ambassador's suggestions. Goyon's feelings are at present anti-Italian and his sympathies are all with the Pope and Francesco II, so that he declines to listen to Lavalette's advice and screens his inaction behind the incompleteness of his instructions. Lavalette, however, seems determined to get the better of him, and the struggle between the civil and military authority in Rome will be interesting to witness. I am well pleased with Monsieur de Lavalette's views, and only hope he may stick to them. He is a great improvement on Gramont. The Pope and Antonelli find him rather too positive and peremptory in the transaction of business and complain that he is always ready with an answer to their objections, which is against the etiquette of the Vatican where humility and submission is expected from the Faithful. They say that he is evidently more accustomed to deal with Turks than with Christians, but they hope that he will mend his manners in course of time. He is also accused of not having performed a sufficient number of genuflections on Christmas Day at St Peter's. But this is a calumny of the Ultramontane party....

201 [F.O. 43/86A]   *Rome, 6 January 1862*

No. 3
O.R. to Earl R.

I learn on good authority that the Spaniard Tristani, who was appointed a general in the Bourbon army by King Francesco about 6 months ago, has now been entrusted with the command of an expedition which is to sail from Trieste, Malta and Marseilles, meet somewhere on the coast of Dalmatia and land somewhere on the opposite coast of Italy, perhaps San Benedetto, and from thence effect a junction with Chiavone's bands for the purpose of reconquering the lost kingdom of King Francesco....

202 [F.O. 43/86A]   *Rome, 18 January 1862*

No. 7
O.R. to Earl R.

Thanks to the enlightened and humane policy of the Marquis de Lavalette, Alatri has at last been occupied by the French troops. I mentioned the importance of this position to Your Lordship in my despatch No. 88 of 16 November 1861 and everybody at all acquainted with the manner in which Chiavone was supplied with men and money from Rome through the village of Alatri, which was occupied by the Pontifical zouaves and therefore not under immediate French control, has wondered why the French authorities allowed themselves to be befooled so long by the legitimist committee in all that concerned Alatri.

Monsieur de Lavalette, whose admirable advice to King Francesco in regard to His Majesty's prospects, interests and residence in Rome had not been listened to, soon perceived the necessity of striking a blow at brigandage, and although every difficulty was thrown in the way of his judicious intentions and although the Pontifical authorities declared their inability to withdraw their own garrison from Alatri in the present season of the year, the frontier village was yesterday occupied by a French detachment.

The immediate result of this measure has been the capture of eleven of Chiavone's officers who, as usual, proved to be Frenchmen, Belgians, Germans and Spaniards, but *no* Italians were found among them, an additional proof of the preponderance of the foreign element in what is called the Neapolitan reaction.

It is also reported that a letter of General Tristani's was found, dated from Rome and warning these men of the coming danger of a French occupation of Alatri. Certain it is that this measure has deeply disconcerted the legitimist party in Rome Although the Papal Government assumed that their garrison of Alatri amounted to 400 men, the French authorities were not able to find more than 60 there altogether.

Since General de Goyon has issued orders for the capture of Chiavone's men found within the Papal territory, upwards of 900 have been taken, but as I mentioned in my despatch No. 88 they have been invariably handed over to the Pontifical authorities, who have sent them back to Alatri and set them free. General de Goyon tells me that he cannot deal otherwise with them, because he has neither means nor money to provide for their confinement and Monsieur de Lavalette informs me that they cannot be handed over to the Italian authorities, because the Pope has no treaty of extradition with the Piedmontese Government.

Under these circumstances the suppression of brigandage becomes much like the attempt to fill a sieve with water, but I have no doubt that Monsieur de Lavalette will in due course of time find means of overcoming all the difficulties he has still to contend with.

203 [F.O. 43/86A]   *Rome, 21 January 1862*

No. 10. Secret
O.R. to Earl R.

On 17th instant the French Ambassador communicated to Cardinal Antonelli a note from Monsieur Thouvenel inviting His Eminence once more to reconsider the expediency of settling the Roman question and recommending that he should do so on the basis of existing facts (*sur la base de faits accomplis*). Cardinal Antonelli replied as he has often done before, that there was but one settlement possible, that which is founded on Right and Justice, namely the total and unconditional restitution to the Pope of his lost provinces. The French Ambassador having proceeded to argue the question, the Cardinal put an end to all further discussion by observing that if he was to understand that the French Government wished to withdraw their garrison from Rome he could only say that they were at liberty to do so, no attempt should be made to retain them, but of course the Pope would then also leave Rome and seek the protection of some other Government.

That is all I have yet been able to learn from authentic sources of this important conversation. I may add in strict confidence that Cardinal Antonelli is under an impression that this move on the part of the French Government as well as that of inviting King Francesco to leave Rome, have been merely undertaken as political demonstrations for publication in the French official Yellow Book, which is to be shortly presented to the legislative body in Paris. His Eminence does not believe in any serious intention on the part of the Emperor Napoleon to withdraw his troops from Rome. I will also venture to add that the Pope's age, habits, affections and infirmities lead me to the conviction that Pius IX *will under no circumstances whatever* carry out the Cardinal's threat of leaving Rome.

204 [P.R.O. 30/22/76]   *Rome, 25 January 1862*

Private
O.R. to Earl R.

I want to ask you a great favor; it is to allow my despatch No. 106 of the 31st December 1861 to be printed and published *in extenso* in your next Italian Blue Book. If you will take the trouble to run your eye over it you will at once perceive my object. It is to show the French that their *attitude* in Rome is not quite as glorious as they have been told to believe, and to meet the arguments of the Guizot, Thiers, Montalembert school which is said to impede the Emperor's desire to withdraw his garrison from Rome. I fancy that if it were published as coming from the British Agent in Rome it might possibly excite some controversy in the French Press and perhaps do some good to the poor Romans and their eternal question. I mentioned the views I have now put on paper to you at Pembroke Lodge.[1] They are my convictions. If you don't agree with me you might say so in a despatch to be printed along side of it, but do please leave me the pleasure of being abused by the French Press as it is sure to do me good privately and professionally. I hope you won't think I am asking too much.

205 [P.R.O. 30/22/76]   *12 February 1862*

Viscount Palmerston to Earl R.

There is much in this long despatch of Odo's that is true, but there is also much which is disputable. But it is more like an essay for the Edinburgh Review than an official despatch. There is much in it which we could not adopt, by publishing it, without giving unnecessary offence to the French Government; and if it were to be published, it would require much cutting and trimming. But I think we cannot yield to Odo's pathetic intreaties that it may be published.

206 [F.O. 43/86A]   *Rome, 11 February 1862*

No. 16
O.R. to Earl R.

As an instance of the interference which the Court of Rome attempts to exercise in the internal administration of Roman Catholic States, it may not be uninteresting to Your Lordship to learn that Monsignor Chigi, the newly accredited Nuncio at Paris, has objected to the nomination of the learned orientalist, Monsieur Renan, to the vacant professorship of Hebrew at the College de France in consequence of the unorthodox opinions put forth in some of his works.

I see however that the Nuncio's objections have had no effect and Monsieur Renan's appointment has been gazetted in the *Moniteur*.

207 [F.O. 43/86A]   *Rome, 15 February 1862*

No. 17
O.R. to Earl R.

The National Party in Rome have lately made several attempts at

---
[1] Earl Russell's house in Richmond Park.

public demonstrations, the purpose of which appeared to be to show, that while they object to the temporal administration of their priests and while they desire Rome to be the capital of Italy, they at the same time respect the Pope as the head of their religion and desire him to reside as such in Rome together with the King of Italy. In short, they desire to show that they know how to separate the spiritual from the temporal power and that the Pope personally has nothing to fear from them, whether he be under the protection of France or of Italy. Thanks to the vigilance of the French and Pontifical authorities, these demonstrations have been prevented or suppressed.

One of them was attempted on the day of Cathedra Petri, 18 January, another immediately after the publication of Monsieur Thouvenel and the Marquis de Lavalette's official correspondence, another on 6 February, another on the anniversary of the fall of Gaeta, but all, as I have said above, were frustrated, thanks to the foresight and energy of General Count de Goyon. The objects seized, with which these demonstrations were to have been effected consisted of proclamations, small flags combining the colours of Italy with those of the Pope and handbills containing these words: *Viva il Pontefice non Re! Viva Vittorio Emmanuele II Re d'Italia!* The Romans, as far as I can understand, have undertaken these demonstrations of combined spiritual loyalty to the King of Italy to meet the last excuse put forward by the French Government for holding their capital, namely the necessity of protecting the Pope's sacred person against the animosity of the Roman people.

[*Two proclamations are enclosed.*]

208 [F.O. 43/86A]   *Rome, 19 February 1862*

No. 23
O.R. to Earl R.

[Bishops of Roman Catholic Christendom have been invited to attend canonization of 23 Martyrs of Japan on Whit Sunday. Italian bishops excused]. . . . To a person uninitiated in the secret tactics of the Roman Church this invitation to the bishops to witness the elevation of 23 martyrs to higher rank in the Celestial Peerage (for they have already been beatified) might appear simply an ecclesiastical ceremony and nothing else, but to judge by the concern shewn by the French authorities and the exulting confidence of the Ultramontane Party, it would appear to conceal a double object.

The French authorities, I understand, fear that the Pope may turn the presence of the assembled bishops to account and commit them, *in corpore*, to a solemn condemnation of the Emperor's policy. They think it not impossible that the Pope may overcome his antipathy to parliamentary assemblies, suddenly convert the meeting into an oecumenic Council and extract resolutions from it, which might raise the question of his temporal power to the dignity of a new dogma.

The leave of absence which His Holiness grants to the Italian bishops is looked upon as especially ominous, as it is believed that the patriotism of many might disturb the unanimity of the council and that they do not at all share the Ultramontane doctrine, that Central Italy namely does not belong to the Italians but forms an estate vested in the Catholics of the whole world, who are free to have it administered by their clergy as they see fit.

The French authorities appear further to apprehend that the bishops, invigorated by the blessing of the Pope and by the admonitions of the Sacred College, elated by the splendours of the Vatican and the vision of the Holy City, will return to their dioceses less docile than when they left them and brandish their croziers in defiance of the civil authorities. To me these fears seem exaggerated.

From the Papal point of view, a canonization is a ceremony of sufficient importance to warrant the convocation of the bishops, whose declarations as to the necessity of the temporal power of the Popes have already been published in Pastoral Letters and printed in many volumes by the *Stamperia Camerale*.

The canonization will be celebrated with great pomp and magnificence, thousands of wax candles to light up the interior of St Peter's have already been ordered and the enormous expense of the pageant will be borne by the monastic orders of which the martyred missionaries were members.

P.S. 25 February

I open this despatch to add that I see by the *Moniteur* of 20th instant received today that the alarm felt by the French Government has been sufficiently great to induce them to invite their bishops not to obey the wishes of the Pope.

209 [F.O. 43/86A]   *Rome, 19 February 1862*

No. 24
O.R. to Earl R.

The resistance offered by the Pontifical authorities to the occupation of Alatri by the French troops sufficiently betrayed the importance they attached to the undivided possession of that outpost, and the wisdom of Monsieur de Lavalette's policy, who full well recognized the necessity of holding Alatri and who carried his point against the will of the Papal Government is now clearly established. . . .

210 [F.O. 43/86A]   *Rome, 19 February 1862*

No. 29
O.R. to Earl R.

[Transmits an address of condolence to Her Majesty on the death of the Prince Consort, signed by Her Majesty's subjects residing at Rome. Two large parchment sheets, containing 195 signatures.]

211 [F.O. 43/86A]   *Rome, 1 March 1862*

No. 35
O.R. to Earl R.

The Roman National Committee issued a short handbill some days since reminding the Romans 'that all participation in the mummeries of the Carnival would be unworthy of them in the present state of the Roman question, that the Papal Government would be of course anxious to show the foreigners assembled here how merry and contented the people were under their paternal rule but that the Romans should not forget what Italy expected of them. They should abstain from the tomfooleries of the Corso and take their afternoon walk on the Forum, where they would remember the greatness of their ancestors.'

In consequence a great crowd quietly assembled on Thursday afternoon between the Capitol and the Coliseum. Their number was estimated at 12,000 in the report of the French gendarmerie. Pickets of French soldiers were stationed in some places but did not in any way interfere with the free circulation of the people.

I am assured on the other hand that the masquerade on the Corso was principally kept up by foreigners and members of the Franco-Belgian Legion.

But on Friday afternoon there being no Carnival and the streets to all appearance quiet, the French troops suddenly occupied the principal places of Rome, marched down the Corso and closed the great thoroughfares of the city. I went out to enquire what had happened and was told that popular demonstrations were expected which it was necessary to suppress. I learnt that the Papal troops had been consigned to barracks and I saw General de Goyon in a carriage, accompanied by General de Girandon driving down the Corso, addressing the troops and giving his orders personally to his officers. The population appeared quiet and amused.

Unable to clear up what had rendered these extraordinary measures necessary and wondering against whom, in the midst of an unarmed population, this enormous development of forces could be directed, I called on the French Ambassador and begged him to tell me what had passed. From His Excellency I learnt that the Roman police had informed General de Goyon that the people intended quietly to perambulate the Corso, there being no Carnival on Friday, as they had done the Forum the day before, that the Government was not going to tolerate these revolutionary demonstrations any longer and that positive orders had been issued from the Vatican to disperse the crowd by force of arms. The co-operation of General de Goyon was invited. The General had very properly answered that he did not feel justified in suppressing so pacific a demonstration by measures so violent and he requested the Papal authorities to forbear from unnecessary bloodshed. The Minister of Police at once drove to the Vatican with General de Goyon's message and after several hours conference there, he returned saying that his instructions were positive and that the Papal troops were to charge the people.

On hearing this the General, with Perugia fresh in his memory, had been compelled to turn out the garrison, have the Papal troops consigned to barracks and had by this prompt action saved Rome from a repetition of the bloody scenes of 19 March 1860 when the Papal gendarmes charged the people walking in the Corso, as Your Lordship may recollect. I must therefore conclude that the French garrison was, in fact, called under arms, not to protect the Pope against his people, but to protect the people against the Pope.

The Roman people really owe a large debt of gratitude to General de Goyon who has many a time stood between them and the Papal Government and saved them from ecclesiastical violence. It is much to be regretted that the General has no power of control over the Pontifical prisons, which are now filled with political prisoners of a most harmless description, who are entirely at the mercy of the priests who imprison them, and who can neither obtain trial or freedom even through the intercession of General de Goyon or the French Ambassador.

As it is now understood that the French occupation of Rome is to last many years longer, it would be a desirable and humane measure to transfer the direction of the Roman police from the ecclesiastical to the French military authority, so that General de Goyon might bring the same high spirit of equity, honor and humanity to bear upon the administration of the police of Rome, which has characterized the whole of his military command.

212 [P.R.O. 30/22/76]   *Rome, 4 March 1862*

Private
O.R. to Earl R.

In your letter of the 17th ult. you say that 'it appears the Emperor has given some sort of promise to the Pope to protect him during his life in possession of his present limited territory' and you direct me to enquire into the nature of this engagement. Now the Emperor has over and over again sent messages to the Pope through Gramont, Goyon, Zaccone, Chigi and other persons to say that he would never abandon him and never withdraw his garrison from Rome. . . . Indeed the Pope maintains that he is in possession of autograph letters from the Emperor containing those promises black upon white, which he occasionally threatens to print and publish and he insinuated as much in his speech to General Goyon on 1st January 1861. . . .

Cardinal Grasselini, who passed last summer in France and saw the Emperor and Thouvenel, told a friend of mine that he *knew* that the troops were not to leave Rome during the lifetime of *the Emperor*, nor of Pius IX. And it is those promises and the conviction that the garrison will never leave that make the Pope and Cardinal Antonelli so cock-a-hoop and obstinate; they have nothing to fear and love irresponsible and absolute power. The Emperor has nothing on earth to gain from withdrawing his garrison from Rome and, as Lord Cowley truly observes, his policy must be judged by his private interest in France. Why then should he not leave the settlement of the Roman question to his successor, whoever he may be?

In my despatch No. 106 of last year I endeavoured to show how little the Emperor cared for the true interests of the Roman Church and how disastrous the effects of his Protectorate were and would be.

I was very sorry to hear from Mr Layard[1] that you did not think that despatch could be printed, because I fancied I had almost put the question in its true light, but I feel sure you have good reasons for thinking so and submit cheerfully and gratefully to your advice. The more I see of Lavalette the better I like him. He appears to have entered on the duties of his Embassy with a liberal, humane and enlightened spirit and I hope he may do some good but he is already so hated by the priests that they talk of nothing but getting rid of him as soon as possible and they now deeply regret the loss of Gramont, whose virtues they have learnt to appreciate. I did not like to say so in my despatch about Goyon's military demonstration but it was the Pope himself who insisted on having the people in the Corso dispersed by force of arms as he did last year, and His Holiness has been very angry at finding himself disappointed in the satisfaction he anticipated from this massacre of his unarmed subjects. It is really hard to say so, but all those who know the Pope well agree that he is a vindictive and blood-thirsty old man. Charitable people say he has been affected by his epileptic fits. . . . Lavalette tells me that Goyon holds language so contrary to his own that he paralyses the influence of the Embassy. Goyon tells me that: '*Lavalette est tout aussi Piedmontais, que je suis Papalin.*' . . .

213 [F.O. 43/86A]   *Rome, 7 March 1862*

No. 37. Secret
O.R. to Earl R.

[Earl R. has asked whether O.R. believes Antonelli threatened the French Ambassador that the Pope would leave Rome if the French garrison withdrew.]
. . . Feeling that I could only ascertain the authenticity of this report from the Cardinal himself, I called this morning on His Eminence and

---

[1] Henry Layard (1817-94), excavator of Nineveh. From 1861 to 1866 he was Under Secretary for Foreign Affairs.

asked him whether I had been correctly informed or not. Cardinal Antonelli began as usual by saying that he was always glad to communicate privately and confidentially with me, but that he begged I would not allow his conversations with me to become public property. He had not threatened the French Ambassador, that was not necessary, he had merely incidentally observed, that if any unforeseen circumstances compelled the Emperor to withdraw the garrison so that Rome became an easy prey to the Piedmontese the Pope would not consider himself sufficiently independent to guard the interests of the Church and to fulfil the duties which his sacred office imposed upon him and His Holiness would be compelled to seek protection and a safe asylum in some foreign Roman Catholic country. This would be the Pope's duty to the Church and neither age nor infirmities could stand in the way of the performance of his duty, however painful and arduous it might be. The policy of the Piedmontese had rendered all intercourse with them impossible, and the Head of Christianity, who was the guardian of morality on earth, could not by any act of his own, or even by passive submission, sanction, or appear to sanction, a policy which violated the most sacred laws and trampled underfoot the most holy obligations of nations and of neighbours. In one word, the Pope as an honest man could not lend his hand to a thief and an assassin.

These remarks and many more he had made to Monsieur de Lavalette did not appear in His Excellency's despatch to Monsieur Thouvenel of 18 January, but His Eminence wished me to understand distinctly that if I asked him whether that despatch represented faithfully the answer he had given to the one distinct question it contained, he was bound to answer that it did, and that he subscribed to it, but if I asked him whether it represented all that had passed between him and the French Ambassador in that same conversation, he was bound to say: No, that it did not.

His Eminence regretted that subjects of such importance were treated in conversations only, he would prefer diplomatic notes and written instruments. Monsieur de Lavalette, he continued, was a very able and agreeable man, but like many of the Emperor's agents he did not appear thoroughly initiated into his Imperial Master's secret thoughts and policy. For instance, he seemed to attach importance to the discussions of the French senate and did not appear aware that the Emperor would never let himself be influenced by their deliberations. He seemed to believe in the possibility of the withdrawal of the French

15. General de Goyon

16. Odo Russell on the Pincio. Painting by Leopold Güterbock

garrison from Rome and did not seem aware that nothing was further from the Emperor's intentions.

I asked His Eminence whether he had any objection to tell me on what he founded his conviction that the occupation of Rome was likely to be permanent.

'My friend,' the Cardinal said, 'the reasons are self-evident and I wonder you should ask me what you know as well as I do. I indulge in no illusions on the subject, the Emperor does not hold Rome and protect the Pope for our sakes (*pour nos beaux yeux*) or because he has the interests of religion at heart. No, he holds Rome because it serves his own personal and dynastic interests to do so, because he would incur a vast amount of unpopularity in France if he abandoned the Pope, which he can easily avoid by leaving things as they are; because Rome is an invaluable strategical point in the event of a European war; because he holds Austria in check so long as he holds Rome; because he does not intend and never intended to allow Italy to unite; and because he intends a portion of the future Italian Confederation to be governed by a Member of his family. His Majesty has already upset the Ricasoli administration and has brought Rattazzi into power who will convulse Italy by favouring the Republican party, and out of the disorder which must necessarily ensue, the Emperor will know how to secure his advantage. These are my impressions, time will show whether I am mistaken.'

When I took my leave, His Eminence said once more: 'Pray keep what I have said to yourself.'

I may here repeat what I have already said, that everyone who is well acquainted with Cardinal Antonelli has been struck by the change that has come over him, and the calm and cheerful confidence with which His Eminence now looks forward to the future.

214 [F.O. 43/86A]   *Rome, 7 March 1862*
No. 38
O.R. to Earl R.

A considerable number of arrests have lately taken place in Rome, the vast prisons of San Michele are overfilled and the *Carcere Nuove* have been made use of to supply the want of space. These arrests are not ordered by the Roman police, but by Monsignor de Mérode, the Pro-Minister of Arms, who has the Pope's authority for undertaking part of their duties. [Instances of arrests are given.]

I

215 [F.O. 43/86A]   *Rome, 18 March 1862*

No. 42. Confidential
O.R. to Earl R.

With reference to my despatch of 28 February stating that the Pope
had received very gratifying messages from the Emperor Napoleon
through Monsignor Chigi, the new Papal Nuncio, I now have the
honor to add that a person who saw Monsignor Chigi's report has
given me the text of one of the Emperor's thrice repeated messages to
His Holiness. It runs as follows:

*Dites au St. Perè, que l'unité Italienne est impossible, c'est une Utopie,
mais que je ne puis pas en opposer l'expérience. . . .*

216 [F.O. 43/86A]   *Rome, 22 March 1862*

No. 44. Secret
O.R. to Earl R.

When Monsieur de Lavalette presented his credentials to the Pope on
10th instant, His Excellency sought an opportunity of urging the
necessity upon His Holiness of allowing him to open a discussion with
a view to settle the Roman question, which could not permanently be
left unsettled, and the Pope taken by surprise expressed his willingness
to listen to the propositions of the French Government.

The Ambassador hastened to inform his Government that he had
obtained the Pope's consent to treat and on Tuesday night His Excellency received a telegram from Monsieur Thouvenel summoning him
to Paris to receive the Emperor's instructions.

Cardinal Antonelli, on learning what had passed between the Pope
and the Ambassador, was deeply annoyed at His Holiness's indiscretion
and sought to dispel the Ambassador's illusions by reminding him that
the principles of the Church had over and over again been laid down
in former discussions, that the only settlement possible was the settlement accepted by Austria at Villa Franca, and that any new proposals
made by France which did not replace the Pope's lost provinces unconditionally under his authority must necessarily share the fate of all their
former proposals. . . .

Cardinal Antonelli, who is seriously distressed at the event, is under
an impression that the new proposition of France will be to guarantee
the Pope's present territory to the Church and to obtain a compen-

sation in money from the Italian Government for Romagna, the Marches and Umbria.

I need scarcely tell Your Lordship that the Pope will accept no transaction of this kind whatever and that this new attempt on the part of the French Government to negotiate with the Vatican is doomed to failure.

217 [F.O. 519/205]   *Rome, 22 March 1862*

O.R. to Earl Cowley

... Clever and agreeable as Lavalette is, he will find it impossible ever to negotiate with these priests. Prince Napoleon was quite right when he said 'You will obtain nothing by negotiation.' ...

I hope Lavalette will soon return for I think him charming and delight in him and his offhand manner of dealing with the priests. He will do them a vast deal of good in the end I am sure.

218 [F.O. 43/86A]   *Rome, 23 March 1862*

No. 45
O.R. to Earl R.

Since writing my despatch No. 44 of yesterday's date respecting the departure of the French Ambassador for Paris for the purpose of discussing some new settlement of the Roman question with Monsr Thouvenel, I learn that the Marquis de Lavalette has also another object in view, namely to explain to the Emperor the difficulties thrown in his way by General de Goyon's position and language in Rome. On Monday last it appears that the Ambassador called on the General and explained to him in the most courteous terms the difficulty he encountered in the transaction of business owing to the difference of opinion prevailing between them, the fatal effect of which was to lead the Papal authorities to believe that either or both of them spoke without authority from Paris or that the Imperial Government pursued two different lines of policy in Rome. Thus the language he held as French Ambassador to the Papal authorities carried no weight with it and the policy he advocated at the Vatican in the name of the Emperor was completely paralysed.

He could not under such conditions continue to hold his Embassy, and he was therefore about to solicit of the Emperor's Government that the General's communications with the Pontifical authorities should be limited to military subjects exclusively and that political questions should be entrusted exclusively to himself.

General de Goyon is reported to have expressed his regret that such differences should have arisen between himself and the Embassy, that he should as he had ever done before abide by the instructions he received from the Emperor, and that he was satisfied that the question should be referred to His Majesty at Paris.

The Marquis de Lavalette and General de Goyon are said to have then parted on very good terms.

The Ambassador's departure has given rise to many comments in Rome, the real objects of his visit to Paris not having yet transpired. It is very generally believed that he has gone to Paris to advocate the absolute necessity of persuading King Francesco to desist from his present policy by leaving Rome.

219 [F.O. 43/86A]   *Rome, 23 March 1862*

No. 47
O.R. to Earl R.

The frequent ailments of the Pope have led the Catholic Governments to enquire of their representatives in Rome what the probable results of a Conclave would be.

It has at all times been difficult to the most experienced Romans to point out, even at the death of a Pope, with any degree of certainty which member of the Sacred College was likely to succeed to the Chair of St Peter. Under the present circumstances the difficulty will be greater than ever for the Conclave will meet under entirely new conditions. In a few hours the Pope's death will be known by telegraph all over Europe, and the railways which have been completed during the reign of the present Pontiff will bring the foreign cardinals to Rome within the nine days which precede the closing of the Conclave so that the Italian cardinals residing in Rome who could formerly settle the election amongst themselves will this time have to contend with a foreign element unknown to them before.

It appears also that the Catholic Governments, with the sole exception of France, have requested their Cardinals to hasten to the next Conclave and there can be no doubt that this prospect alarms the

Roman cardinals, who are said to have held private meetings to decide on their future line of conduct.

The Pope himself, who foresees the difficulties, dissensions and dangers to which the Sacred College will be a prey, is said to have adopted a most unusual course and to have prepared a secret 'chirograph' by which he calls upon the Roman cardinals to unite at once after his death and elect, during the three days that must precede his burial, one of the three cardinals he considers most worthy to succeed him, namely Cardinal Patrizi, his Vicar General, Cardinal Barnabo, of the Propaganda, and Cardinal Bofondi, President of the Congregation of the Census. The legality of this proceeding is questioned by the Sacred College who moreover consider the three favorites of His Holiness as dangerously zealous, and the existence of the chirograph is denied by Cardinal Antonelli. . . .

220 [P.R.O. 30/22/76]   *Rome, 25 March 1862*

Private
O.R. to Earl R.

I think your plan of provisional settlement excellent and I have no doubt it would work perfectly. The Pope and his French protectors would have the Vatican, the Leonine City, Monte Mario and Civita Vecchia, the frontier line might be the Tiber from Ostia to Ponte Molle and might then follow the Florence post road and strike off at Bracciano and end at Corneto and St Stefano, opposite Elba. The Italian Government would have the Capitol and Quirinal and there is no reason why the French and Italian troops should in any way interfere with each other. But if I am not strongly mistaken the French Government will tell you such an arrangement is *impossible*, because then the Pope would leave Rome and seek the protection of some other Power. I don't believe he would, because he loves Rome better than his life and has repeatedly told his friends that he would prefer martyrdom to leaving the Eternal City, which he feels he would never see again. But the French Government are sure to tell you that they know positively he would go, and no doubt the Ultramontane party would strongly urge him to do so. If however Lord Cowley can persuade the Emperor to adopt your plan it would really be a good thing. For my part I am persuaded that it will meet with a positive refusal, because I don't

believe the Emperor has the remotest intention of withdrawing his
troops from the Pope's present possessions and because he is on the
contrary increasing their numbers quietly but steadily. . . .

221 [F.O. 519/205]   *Rome, 25 March 1862*

O.R. to Earl Cowley

I am glad to see we agree about the benefit Italy will in the end derive
from the prolonged occupation, if not prolonged beyond the life of
Pius IX, which is what I expect and fear.

At present it inflicts an immense amount of individual suffering on
those who live in Rome and will do France and the Pope no good in the
end. But people are blind about it. . . .

Pray make any and every use of my despatches. I am delighted to
have them tested and verified and regret they are not printed so that I
might have the advantage of being abused by the Press. Only I constantly remind H.M. Government not to put them in the Blue Book
otherwise I shall lose Antonelli as a source of information and he is at
present well disposed and communicative. So pray read them to Thouvenel, to Metternich and to anybody you please.

I am scrupulously conscientious about everything I write home, and
can produce my proofs of everything I put forward, but I never name
my sources for I should lose them if I played them the trick of exposing
them to the Blue Book. Antonelli I am obliged to name.

After all, I am but *a private individual* in Rome and even the small
extracts of my correspondence published in the Blue Book were detrimental to my utility for many months. I regret all this, as my wish
would be to appear as much as possible before the H. of C. and the
British Public.

I hope you will let me know what Lavalette is really about in Paris.
I fancy he won't succeed in turning out Goyon.

222 [F.O. 43/86A]   *Rome, 26 March 1862*

No. 52
O.R. to Earl R.

[Encloses an extract from the *Giornale di Roma* of 26 March, containing
a speech of the Pope at *Santa Maria sopra Minerva* which is considered
of some importance as the Pope distinctly declares therein that 'the

Temporal Power is not a Dogma but that it is necessary and indispensable to the Church as long as Providence maintains the present order of things'. O.R. gives a short analysis of the speech.]

223 [F.O. 43/86A]   *Rome, 26 March 1862*

No. 53
O.R. to Earl R.

The recent debates on the Roman question in the French Chambers have been read with deep interest in Rome. The Papal Government and their adherents naturally regret that Monsieur Billault should have coupled the assurances so gratifying to them of the continuance of the Imperial Protectorate with such severe censure of their past and present administration, and the National party regret the indefinite postponement of the fulfilment of their wishes.

To the impartial friends of the Roman Church and of the cause of order in Europe, it is a matter of surprize that a great Catholic Power should consent to continue a protectorate so disastrous in its results to the Papacy and the true interests of religion. If we may judge by the Emperor's declaration through Monsieur Billault and by the Pope's reply at Santa Maria sopra Minerva, the respective position of the contending parties is, to say the least of it, very strange.

On the one hand the Pope, after repeatedly declining to adopt any measure whatever which could in any way tend to solve the difficult position in which he is involved, declares that the temporal independence (which he has long lost) is an absolute necessity to the existence of the Church so long as Providence maintains the present order of things, the present order of things being the loss of that independence which he declares to be indispensable to the existence of the Church, but which he will by no act of his own endeavour to regain.

On the other hand Monsieur Billault in his speech declares in the Emperor's name that the French Government will continue to protect that which they entirely condemn and will maintain by force of arms the difficulties in which the Vicar of Christ has involved himself, through his own fault, notwithstanding their warnings and their advice, until Providence (whose aid and assistance the Pope likewise invokes) will solve the confusion which they, the French Government, prolong, deplore, protect and condemn.

224 [F.O. 43/86A]   *Rome, 10 April 1862*

No. 58. Confidential
O.R. to Earl R.

I have always met with great civility from the Neapolitan emigrants
who have followed the fortunes of King Francesco, but I have thought
it best not to follow the example of the Diplomatic Body in Rome who
have solicited the honor of being presented to His Majesty. Some days
since, however, in conversation with a Neapolitan gentleman, I was
asked incidentally why I had never been presented to King Francesco
like the representatives of foreign powers in Rome and I was later told
that His Majesty had observed upon my conduct and expressed some
surprize.

I replied that my position in Rome was unofficial and not such as to
necessitate my soliciting that honor.

The day before yesterday I received a note from the prince of
Ruffano, His Majesty's maggiordomo, informing me that the King
would receive me on 10th instant, and in obedience to His Majesty's
invitation I went to the Palace of the Quirinal this day at 1 o'clock p.m.

His Majesty, who was alone, received me with marked cordiality and
detained me in conversation for an hour and a quarter. He touched on
many subjects and spoke with perfect freedom on past and present
events relating to his own interests. He spoke with affectionate respect
of his father. He deplored his youth and inexperience, to which he
attributed most of his misfortunes and the loss of his throne. He reviewed his own conduct with impartiality, intelligence and modesty,
and the thoughts and feelings he expressed shewed that he had gained
experience and knowledge from past events.

His Majesty then spoke of the policy he intended to pursue when he
had regained his lost Kingdom. The principles he laid down were
sound and liberal and he ended by expressing a hope that they were
such as would meet with the sympathy and approval of Her Majesty's
Government. I replied that His Majesty had formerly been made
acquainted with the views and policy of Her Majesty's Government
through Mr Elliot, that subsequent events had led to the recognition of
the United Kingdom of Italy and that Her Majesty's Government now
hoped to see Italy united under the government of her own choice
become an element of order and progress in Europe.

The King replied that he cherished the highest opinion of Mr Elliot and he now felt that he would have done well had he followed his advice from the beginning, but he was young and inexperienced and knew not which advice was best; surrounded as he was by so many advizers he had naturally followed those recommended to him by his father. Since then he had learnt that times had changed and liberal institutions were a necessary condition of government. But he thought that Her Majesty's Government would find themselves mistaken if they believed in the success of Italian unity and he entered into a long argument about the difference of races and interests and the administrative blunders of the Piedmontese, which would sooner or later break up the present Kingdom, and then, he continued, his party would re-instate him and he would be able to give freedom to his people and seek a close alliance with England.

I replied that the Italian people were already enjoying the blessings of freedom under the Government of King Victor Emmanuel, which Her Majesty's Government had recognized, and although they had, no doubt, many difficulties and trials yet to encounter and much to learn, I believed that every coming day would lessen the desire of the nation for the change and would consolidate the unity. At the same time the lawless bands that were being organized in His Majesty's name would scarcely contribute to increase his party in the Neapolitan provinces. Indeed I had observed that all those who took an impartial interest in His Majesty's personal welfare deplored that by his presence in Rome he countenanced the formation of those bands who made use of his name to burn and pillage.

The King replied that he had never encouraged the formation of those bands which were organized by his adherents out of Rome, but at the same time he could not well discourage those who chose to risk their lives and property in his interest and that he could not refuse to reward their loyalty when he returned to Naples and had the means which were now totally wanting.

I enquired whether His Majesty really believed he could reconquer his lost Kingdom at the rear of lawless bands which were composed of low rabble and officered by foreign adventurers and which did not count one single respectable Neapolitan name in their ranks. His Majesty replied that he indulged in no illusions on that subject and well knew that those brigands, for they were at present unfortunately nothing else, could not bring him back to Naples, but that in course of time his adherents would organize a guerilla war in the mountains which, if only supported by 8,000 men, would be sufficient to render the establishment of the Piedmontese terrorism impossible.

I replied simply that I could not share His Majesty's views and that I believed he had obtained the best and most disinterested advice from the French Government through Monsieur de Lavalette. The King then entered into the arguments he had put forward to the French Ambassador to shew why he remained in Rome and ended by saying that his presence here was no doubt inconvenient to the French Government and that this led him to the subject he desired to communicate to me for the information of Her Majesty's Government, although he earnestly requested me to consider what he was going to say as a secret for everyone in Rome. It was erroneous to suppose that the Emperor Napoleon desired to establish any relation of his own on the throne of Naples. He was far too prudent and well knew that was almost impossible, but he was aiming at the establishment of a separate Kingdom of Sicily under a prince of the Bonaparte family. The Sicilians were an independent people who disliked the Neapolitans quite as much as they now disliked the Piedmontese, and agents were busy in the island urging the people to proclaim the independence of Sicily.

Having expressed some doubt and surprize, I enquired what proofs His Majesty could give me. The King said that for the present I must be content with his word and the assurance that he knew what he asserted. In 1848, he continued, the Sicilians wishing to establish their independence sought a King both at Florence and at Turin and Prince Louis Napoleon offered himself as a candidate for that throne, but was objected to by Lord Palmerston. As the establishment of an independent Kingdom of Sicily under a Bonaparte could as little suit Her Majesty's Government as it would suit himself, he had desired to lose no time in making known his discovery to them under the seal of secrecy.

I replied that the intimate relations which existed between the allied governments of England and France inclined me to think that His Majesty must have been misinformed.

After some further observations His Majesty dismissed me, graciously expressing regrets at having put me to inconvenience etc., etc.

I have given Your Lordship as short and as accurate a summary as I possibly could of this long conversation. I had always avoided being presented to the King during the year he has passed in Rome, but on this occasion I could not well decline to accept the royal invitation without disrespect.

225 [F.O. 43/86A]   *Rome, 11 April 1862*

No. 59. Confidential
O.R. to Earl R.

In my preceding despatch I recounted the interview I had yesterday with King Francesco to Your Lordship. This morning I called on Cardinal Antonelli and told him that I had seen the King. His Eminence replied that he knew it and after praising His Majesty's intelligence, pleasing manners and modesty he expressed his regrets that he could not say much in favor of those who surrounded the King and who unwisely and wrongly in their language connected His Majesty's name with the brigandage in the Neapolitan states, but beyond that did nothing towards serving his cause.

His Eminence condemned in strong terms those who organized the brigandage and thereby harmed the King whom they wished to serve. He could well understand an expedition of Royalists headed by the King or the Royal Princes in a rightful cause, and the day would come when such such an expedition would succeed. Cardinal Ruffo had taken Naples with 4,000 men only, but then he had plenty of money and with money Naples could always be taken, and when the Piedmontese had ruined the country a little more the Neapolitans would receive King Francesco with acclamations. Then, as he had often told His Majesty, his best policy would be liberal institutions and a close alliance with England founded on commercial treaties.

I observed that His Eminence's advice came a little too late since the King had lost his Kingdom and England had recognized United Italy. His Eminence replied that United Italy was a dream and would not last much longer, and that when it broke up and new sovereigns were proposed for the south, England and France must needs quarrel, for the Emperor's candidate could not possibly be the candidate of Her Majesty's Government and then King Francesco might find the support in England that would fail him in France. I replied that the Anglo-French alliance was a reality and that those who reckoned on promoting their interests in a quarrel between the two governments would find themselves sorely mistaken. . . .

226 [F.O. 43/86A]   *Rome, 21 April 1862*

No. 62
O.R. to Earl R.

General de Goyon's late measures towards the suppression of brigandage have proved very successful. . . . [Details given.]

227 [P.R.O. 30/22/76]   *Rome, 23 April 1862*

Private
O.R. to Earl R.

Lord Cowley must now perceive that I was not so wrong when I
suspected the Emperor of intending to hold Rome for many years to
come. My belief is now that Goyon will be appointed Ambassador,
and his wife, who is a very clever woman, is working to that end in
Paris. The appointment would please the Vatican and the Emperor
has now so entangled himself in the nets of the Church that he will find
it impossible to extricate himself from them. Some years hence there
will be a grand financial crash in the Holy See, then the Emperor will
pay the Pope's debts and buy the Papacy out and out. Then the Catholic Powers will begin to perceive that the Pope has practically become
a French bishop. The effect of Lord Palmerston's admirable speech on
Rome has been immense and the joy and enthusiasm of the Liberals and
the impotent rage of the Clericals is not to be described. I am deeply
convinced that the only arms to combat French policy in Rome, are
those employed by Lord Palmerston in his speech. Shew the French
nation that the policy of their Governments is shortsighted and ridiculous in Italy and you will win the day. That was what I meant when I
humbly asked you to publish my despatch reviewing French policy in
Rome No. 106 of last year. I wanted to shew that Protestant England
was the true friend and Catholic France the real enemy of the Pope.
The French press would have taken it up and the Emperor would have
found himself perhaps a little bothered by their attacks. Happily Lord
Palmerston has thrown out that idea, the Press has taken it up and the
shortsighted policy of France will be generally discussed. I think Lord
Palmerston has done the cause great good. The French having adopted
a policy of intervention as regards Rome in Italian affairs, would that
not justify H.M. Government in lending their fullest support to the
Italians if Italian unity were in danger through French intervention?

I was much annoyed the other day at having to go and see King Francesco, but I could not do otherwise without very great incivility. I hope you will not have reason to find fault with me about it. The King entreated of me in the strongest terms to come and see him whenever I pleased, which I shall, of course, never do. He appears to be a pleasing, intelligent and very cunning young man like most Neapolitans, without energy, very awkward and miserably surrounded and advized. It is a pity he won't go to Bavaria for his own sake.

228   [F.O. 43/86A]   *Rome, 26 April 1862*

No. 65
O.R. to Earl R.

. . . Although, as Your Lordship may recollect I have never doubted that the Emperor would not withdraw his garrison for an indefinite number of years from Rome, yet I cannot but feel the importance of Monsieur Thouvenel's declarations to Earl Cowley by which he has plainly and openly added the Emperor's *Nolumus* to the Pope's *Non Possumus* and Earl Cowley concludes with great truth that the course the Emperor is resolved to pursue with regard to the Papal question can now scarcely be modified by discussion or remonstrance. Nevertheless, I would willingly with Your Lordship's permission offer a few remarks upon some of Monsieur Thouvenel's declarations and in doing so I will confine my observations to the Roman Catholic point of view invoked by His Excellency.

Monsieur Thouvenel says that: 'Anyone who is at all conversant with the public opinion of France must see that the great majority of the more enlightened classes of the nation entertain the conviction that the spiritual independence of the Pontiff is closely connected with some measure of temporal authority and that without that authority the power of concordats, the privilege of being represented at foreign courts as a sovereign and other attributes of royalty would be of no use or value to him. Equally were they convinced that these attributes would not survive any settlement made without the Pope's sanction and no doubt many deplored the obstinacy which prompts His Holiness to refuse every attempt at negotiation and would gladly see the troops of France replaced by those of Italy if done with His Holiness's consent, but any arrangement forced upon him would create a general feeling of indignation which it is not the Emperor's interest to excite.'

If the majority of the more enlightened classes of France entertain the conviction that the spiritual independence of the Pontiff is closely connected with some measure of temporal authority, the enlightened classes of Catholic Italy know the contrary to be the case. But we cannot wonder at the confusion which prevails in the public opinion of France on the separation of the spiritual from the temporal power when we see that thinkers and statesmen of the intellectual power of Guizot, Thiers, Albert Broglie, Villemain, Montalembert and Cousin seem scarcely capable of realizing a distinction which to the Italians seems so evident. They do not seem to be aware that the temporal independence of the Popes has ceased to exist, and that the temporal authority of the Popes can only be upheld by foreign bayonets.

If it be therefore true that without temporal authority the power of making Concordats, the privilege of being represented at foreign courts as a sovereign and other attributes of royalty would be of no use or value to the Popes, and if France undertakes in the name of Roman Catholic Christendom the heavy responsibility of providing the Popes with this necessary temporal authority, it is self-evident that henceforward Concordats will have to be enforced in foreign countries by France and Papal Nuncios will become attached and subordinate to French Embassies and Legations.

The Austrian Concordat is now a dead letter. Will it be the duty of France to enforce its provisions if the Pope complains that he has not the power to get them respected? And who will then guarantee the Concordats of France with Rome? And if the Pope's sanction be necessary to a final settlement of the Roman question, then the Emperor's Italian policy must be undone and the *status quo ante bellum* must be re-established. And if it be not the Emperor's interest to excite a general feeling of indignation in France which the settlement of the Roman question would create, then Rome must evidently remain a French dependency.

Monsieur Thouvenel went on to say that 'among the masses there was great apathy respecting the Roman question because the churches were open, the priests officiated and the public worship was carried on without let or hindrance. But how would it be if the Pope were to be deserted by France and were to leave Rome and in a moment of irritation were to order the churches to be closed or to take other measures of that nature? The Pope was capable of doing so and what might not be the consequences to the Emperor?'

Surely, if Monsieur Thouvenel is the Catholic Minister of a Catholic country he represents himself to be, he might know that the Pope cannot legally use spiritual weapons against temporal offences. He might recollect that the late excommunication of King Victor Emmanuel was illegal at Canon Law, that the effects of that excommunication were null and void, that not one single church in Italy was closed or one single priest ceased to officiate in consequence and that public worship continued and still continues without let or hindrance.

Surely Monsieur Thouvenel must admit that what a small power like Piedmont was able to do for the good of the nation, a strong country like France might risk for the good of the church. Surely the Government of the Emperor cannot be as weak as Monsieur Thouvenel would represent it to be? But Monsieur Thouvenel quite understood 'that Your Lordship as the Minister of a Protestant country should persist in the opinions you had advocated from the commencement of the Italian question and that you should not comprehend the difficulties with which the Minister of a Roman Catholic state had to contend when dealing with the Church of Rome. It was impossible for the Imperial Government to put into execution any arrangement with regard to Rome whether temporary or final which had not the Pope's free consent. This was the pivot on which the policy of France must turn. So long as France was obliged to choose between the Pope and the King of Italy and that they could not arrive at some common understanding in regard to their future relations France must side with the Pope.'

Surely Monsieur Thouvenel as a Catholic Minister might know that the present arrangement with regard to Rome, which has been created and prolonged and is now to be upheld by the Imperial Government, is far from having the Pope's free consent and that therefore the Imperial Government by upholding it is putting into execution the very thing which he declares to be impossible, and that far from siding with the Pope, the pivot on which the policy of France is in reality turning has been condemned by the Pope himself in the illegal excommunication of 1860, without producing any of the effects Monsieur Thouvenel dreads with respect to the churches and public worship in France.

I cannot refrain from expressing my surprise that the Catholic Minister of a Catholic state should not be better acquainted with the late history and policy of his church and with the true state of the Roman question.

[*O.R. is surely here indicating how much M. Thouvenel would have benefited had he read O.R.'s despatch No. 106 of 1861.*]

229   [P.R.O. 30/22/76]   *Rome, 6 May 1862*

Private
O.R. to Earl R.

Sir James Hudson arrived here on the 4th and left this morning for Naples. His accounts of Ancona and the Marches were good. He would not let me introduce any of the authorities to him here, although many people seemed anxious to know him. He has been strictly watched by the Pontifical police, the French police and Monsignor de Mérode's extra military police. I am sorry he would not remain longer in Rome as I hoped to learn much from his conversation and experience. . . .

230   [F.O. 43/86B]   *Rome, 17 June 1862*

No. 75. Confidential
O.R. to Earl R.

. . . On 11th instant the French Ambassador called on Cardinal Antonelli and read him a despatch from Monsieur Thouvenel proposing the following solution of the Roman question to the Pope in the name of the Emperor.

1. The Emperor ventured to hope that the Pope would resign himself (*se résignerait*) to the loss of the Marches and Umbria and be content to keep Rome and the provinces still held in his name by the French army.

2. In return for this concession the Emperor would persuade the cabinet of Turin to give up their present *pretensions* to Rome as the future capital of Italy.

3. The Emperor would further obtain from the cabinet of Turin, as well as from the powers of Europe who signed the Treaty of Vienna, the necessary guarantees to ensure the possession of Rome and the provinces still held by France to the Pope and his successors.

4. The Emperor would further engage to make the cabinet of Turin accept a portion of the public debt of the Holy See and take it off the hands of the Papal Government.

5. The Emperor would further engage to obtain from the Catholic Powers the necessary subsidies for the Civil List of the Sovereign

Pontiff and would himself contribute either the sum of sixty millions or the interest thereof at 3 millions of francs per annum, with every security and the titles to be deposited in the hands of His Holiness.

Monsieur Thouvenel winds up by saying that in the event of a refusal on the part of the Pope, the Imperial Government would be compelled to seek some means (*aviser aux moyens*) of diminishing the weight of the responsibility which their present protectorate of the Pope imposed upon them. Cardinal Antonelli replied that while the Pope was unhappily compelled to suffer the violence of his enemies, he could surely not be expected to acquiesce in or approve the spoliation of the Holy Church, nor could he be expected to put much faith in the strength of treaties since the treaty of Villa Franca; that while the Pope could accept the humble offering of the beggar in the street or even beg himself if need be, he could never accept the salary of any government on the face of the earth, and that as regarded the public debt of the Holy See the Pope was still able to pay it thanks to the dutiful devotion of the faithful all over the world. His Eminence ended by saying that if the weight of responsibility imposed on the Imperial Government through their protectorate of the Pope was too heavy for them to bear, the Holy Father was quite prepared to accept the consequences of the departure of the French garrison and die the death of a martyr if necessary.

The French Ambassador then assured Cardinal Antonelli that the Emperor had not the remotest intention of withdrawing his garrison from Rome, but anxiously desired the Pope's co-operation to find a satisfactory solution of the Roman question, etc., etc. . . .

231 [F.O. 519/205]   *Rome, 17 June 1862*

O.R. to Earl Cowley

You will see the nature of Monsr Thouvenel's instructions to Lavalette in my No. 75. I don't in the least wonder at his concealing them from you nor do I wonder at Lavalette not alluding to them in conversation with me. But I do wonder at the French Govt. proposing things which neither the Pope nor Italy can accept.

I should feel inclined to say to Thouvenel what he said to me about the govt. of Italy: *Le Gouvernement français n'est pas un gouvernement sérieux vis à vis du Pape!*

I shall indeed be curious to hear from you what Thouvenel tells you about these strange propositions, and what he intends to do next to diminish the weight of the responsibility of France.

Thouvenel appears to have communicated my conversation with Francis II (communicated to him through Lord Russell) to Metternich who sent it to Rechberg who sent it back to Rome where it has caused considerable mischief. . . .

232   [F.O. 43/86B]   Rome, 18 June 1862
No. 78
O.R. to Earl R.

It is generally assumed by the faithful that the cause of King Francesco II is closely connected with the cause of religion and of the Pope. His Majesty has therefore received the ovations of the foreign bishops and of the pilgrims assembled in Rome and to all he has given the solemn assurance that he will never leave Rome or abandon the Pope. . . .

233   [F.O. 43/86B]   Rome, 26 June 1862
No. 79
O.R. to Earl R.

Notwithstanding the desire of the French Government to suppress brigandage on the Neapolitan frontier the presence near Veroli of the bands of Chiavone, Tristani and Kalkreuth, who draw their supplies of men, money, arms, accoutrements and provisions from Rome, sufficiently proves that the efforts of the French military authorities have not yet been thoroughly successful. It now remains to be seen what new system of suppression will be adopted by General de Montebello[1] under the guidance and advice of the Marquis de Lavalette.

For my part, I think that so long as the brigands who are taken prisoners are handed over to the Pontifical authorities and allowed to return to the frontier, brigandage is likely to last as long as the French occupation of Rome. General de Goyon once told me that he had taken the same brigands four times over, and that out of upwards of 1,000 prisoners consigned to the Pontifical authorities he had handed over three or four only, who had been convicted of murder, to the Italian authorities.

Brigandage being organized in Rome, it is self-evident that this

[1] General de Goyon had been replaced by General de Montebello.

French system is practically the best security the brigands can have for the continuance of their work, since they are always sure to be able to return to their companions on the frontier with additional experience, further means and fresh instructions from their employers. And it is therefore equally self-evident that brigandage would cease in a very short time if the prisoners made by the French authorities, instead of being periodically brought to Rome and let loose again to return to their avocations, were simply delivered over to the Italian authorities on the other side of the frontier. Whenever I have suggested this simple expedient I have been told that the French Government being only the protectors and not the masters of Rome, they could not negotiate a treaty of extradition with Piedmont without the Pope's consent, which could of course never be obtained. . . .

234 [F.O. 43/86B]   *Rome, 28 June 1862*

No. 83. Confidential
O.R. to Earl R.

. . . The French Ambassador had an audience of the Pope on 20th instant and submitted the Emperor's plan to His Holiness which he respectfully urged the Sovereign Pontiff to accept. The Pope referred the French Ambassador to his former declarations and allocutions and to the late address of the bishops and finally in clear and positive language declined to entertain any propositions whatever for the settlement of the Roman question.

Monsieur de Lavalette went on to show the necessity of at least reforming some of the abuses in the Pontifical administration, but the Pope declared once and for all that he would make no concessions and would grant no administrative reforms until his lost provinces were restored to him. The audience lasted one hour and a quarter.

Monsieur de Lavalette next sought another interview with Cardinal Antonelli and having again read Monsieur Thouvenel's instructions on the subject to him (copy of which he however declined to leave with His Eminence) he proceeded to take down the Cardinal's answers and refusal in writing which he subsequently requested His Eminence to read over and verify. They are in substance the same I have already reported to Your Lordship in my despatch No. 75.

On 25th instant the Marquis de Lavalette presented General Count de Montebello to the Pope, and on this occasion submitted Cardinal

Antonelli's written answers to His Holiness soliciting the favor of any further remarks the Pope might have to add to them. The Pope replied that the Cardinal's answers were in perfect accordance with his own feelings and that he could only confirm them. He wondered why the Emperor Napoleon asked him to solve the Roman question. He had not been the aggressor. It was the Piedmontese Government who had robbed the Church of her lawful dominions, and at Turin, not at Rome, the Emperor should seek the solution of the Roman question, which consisted in restoring to the Church what had been taken from the Church.

After a good deal of further discussion it appears that the French Ambassador said to the Pope that if His Holiness could give him no other message to the Emperor he had nothing left but to take his leave and go to Paris never to return again to Rome. To this the Pope gave no reply at all, and a long and awkward silence ensued.

Finally Monsieur de Lavalette having once more supplicated His Holiness to grant him a more satisfactory answer to return to the Emperor, the Pope said that he might remind His Majesty that there was at present no better solution to the Roman and Italian questions than the execution of the Treaty of Villa Franca, which had been ratified at Zurich, and which he, the Pope, was quite ready to accept whenever His Majesty and the Emperor of Austria chose to carry it out.

The preceding account has been obtained at the Vatican. Monsieur de Lavalette has mentioned his instructions to me in general terms, adding that although the conditions he had offered the Pope were excellent, he had met with an obstinate though courteous refusal.

235   [F.O. 519/205]   *Rome, 2 July 1862*

O.R. to Earl Cowley

It is Antonelli and the Pope who represent Lavalette's instructions as stringent. I have merely repeated what His Eminence told me and on comparing notes with my colleagues I find that he has communicated exactly the same thing to them all, and all are surprised at finding Thouvenel answering for the assent of the other Powers to his proposals. The Pope has also said the same thing to some of his Monsignori. But their hatred to poor Lavalette is such that they may exaggerate for the purpose of doing him injury.

One thing is very clear to me, namely, that neither Thouvenel nor

Lavalette clearly understand the position and the rights of the Roman population both as regards Italy and as regards the Pope. The condition of the people is heartrending. I mean to write a despatch on the subject.

236 [F.O. 43/86B]   *Rome, 5 July 1862*

No. 86
O.R. to Earl R.

If I may judge from the altered tone of the French authorities in Rome, the Imperial Government is about to adopt a clearer and more positive line of policy than heretofore in regard to the Holy See, and the principles laid down in the famous pamphlet, *Le Pape et le Congrès*, are to be carried into effect. The principle of the necessity of the temporal power of the Popes, proclaimed by Pius IX and his bishops in Council assembled, will be adopted by the French Government and the European powers will be invited to guarantee Rome and the territory still occupied by the French troops, with its 600,000 inhabitants, to the Pope and his successors.

The Governments of Russia, Prussia and Austria have, I am told, already been informed of the course France proposes to adopt. The Government of Italy will be advised to accept or submit and the Pope having already refused will perhaps no longer be consulted. His Holiness will no doubt protest, but the state of his health will scarcely admit of his leaving Rome.

With an army like that of France this solution of the Roman question can easily be imposed upon Italy for the time being and the Pope remain the nominal sovereign of Rome and the Patrimony of St Peter. But notwithstanding governments, armies and bishops, the *temporal independence* of the Papacy is nevertheless for ever lost.

237 [F.O. 519/205]   *Rome, 5 July 1862*

O.R. to Earl Cowley

Whatever Monsr Thouvenel's instructions may have been, stringent or general, there can be no doubt as to the manner in which Lavalette interpreted them here, and I can answer for the correctness of my reports for I have now compared notes with all the best authorities I could get hold of. It is believed here that the French Govt. expected the refusal they met with, but Lavalette appears to me sincerely surprized at not having succeeded.

As you will see by my No. 86 the French here are all coming round to the necessity of the Temporal Power and so I see no help for it, Italy will have to do without Rome as best she can, for if the Temporal Power is to be kept up, it can only be done by the presence of a French army. . . .

238 [F.O. 43/86B]   *Rome, 15 July 1862*

No. 95
O.R. to Earl R.

After the exaggerated hopes which the Pope and his followers had founded on the universal effects of the late address of the bishops assembled in Rome, the recognition of the Kingdom of Italy by Russia and Prussia and the marriage of the King of Portugal with a daughter of King Victor Emmanuel has proved an unexpected and tremendous shock to the Papal party.

On the one hand the Pope sees with amazement that the declaration of his bishops has passed unnoticed by the Governments of Europe, and on the other he perceives with deep sorrow that the excommunication hurled at Piedmont in 1860 does not prevent a Catholic prince from marrying the daughter of an excommunicated sovereign. I do not recollect ever seeing the Papal party more completely unnerved than at the present moment.

239 [P.R.O. 30/22/76]   *Rome, 15 July 1862*

Private
O.R. to Earl R.

. . . Cardinal Antonelli is completely upset by the Russian recognition of Italy. He says that six weeks ago he had the most positive assurances that Russia would never recognise Italy. He attributes the change of policy to France and says that England will suffer for it in the East, but he hopes it may have the effect of bringing about an alliance between England and Austria which he ardently desires. He thinks Russia is going to break up and he hopes for a European war which will end by driving Louis Napoleon out of France and bringing back things to what he calls their normal state. The French disasters in Mexico delight

him, he chuckles and rubs his hands and says it was a wonderful stroke
of policy on your part getting them into that mess which he prays may
bring about a war between France and the United States of America.
In short he looks for the salvation of the Holy See in a general war.
His horror of Lavalette is most amusing and he is straining every nerve
to turn him out and get back Goyon or Gramont or the like. His
Eminence is of opinion that Garibaldi is going to Greece and throws
out hints that Her Majesty's Government must know more about it
than anybody else. Cardinal Antonelli's views on foreign policy are so
childish and ridiculous that he certainly could not retain his post as
Prime Minister to the Pope for one single hour if he had not a French
army to back him and keep him in office. Yet there are many people
who want to make him out a great statesman, and our Diplomatic Body
here believe in him even more than in the Pope! Lavalette is charming,
he quite overwhelms me with hospitality and kindness of every description, but I find him rather reserved when I attempt to discuss the future
of the Roman question with him. The other day I pressed him hard and
then he confessed to me that he was rather afraid of our Blue Books. I
think if he had it all his own way here he would do a vast deal of good,
but he is evidently not sure of the Emperor and never knows whether
he will be backed up in Paris or not. He seems to be a warm partizan
of the Unity of Italy as far as I can judge. . . .

Montebello and his wife are at present more reactionary and Pontifical than Goyon ever was before them, but they seem to get on admirably with Lavalette. Their suppression of brigandage is all humbug,
they cannot be in earnest about it for their mode of proceeding is too
clumsy. I observe that everybody in Rome who has an opinion of any
value on the matter thinks they wish to keep up brigandage indefinitely. . . . Monsieur de Lavalette is entirely in the wrong when he tells
Thouvenel that Francesco II is likely to leave Rome. His Majesty is
more than ever determined to remain and the Pope attaches the greatest
importance to his presence here. When you communicated my conversation with the King to Thouvenel, Thouvenel gave it to Metternich
who sent it to Rechberg who sent it to Rome back to the King who
told his courtiers what had passed and then the Diplomatic Body in
general got hold of the story.

Notwithstanding, the King has made several attempts to get me to
call on him again, which I have carefully avoided mindful of your
advice.

240 [F.O. 43/86B]   *Rome, 26 July 1862*

No. 100
O.R. to Earl R.

Last night I received rather unexpectedly from the Vatican a written information that the Pope would receive me today at 12 o'clock. I found His Holiness alone reading Sir James Hudson's despatch in a newspaper respecting his journey through the Papal States to Naples. His Holiness complained that Sir James Hudson did him injustice when he said that the only improvements he had seen in Rome were the introduction of gas and public carriages. He wondered I had not shewn Sir James the churches built and repaired and the public works of general utility executed during his reign.

I replied that the improvements Sir James Hudson sought and thought necessary for the good of the country were of a different nature. His Holiness said that Sir James Hudson seemed to think that all the agricultural improvements he had seen in the Marches were the work of the last two years only, and he added laughing that in his opinion Sir James had not contributed to the wonderful agricultural improvements described by thus planting carrots (*piantar carote* in Italian means to exaggerate).

After a few words on my part in defence of Sir James Hudson's views, His Holiness interrupted me to say that he had heard I was going to England on leave of absence and that he had sent for me to wish me a pleasant journey and to ask when I should return to Rome. He then went on to speak of my mother's late illness and observed that 'since I had done so much for *la madre* in Rome, could I not do something for *il Papa* in London?' I replied that I should be happy to serve His Holiness in any way I could but that I did not well understand what he meant.

The Pope said he was now forsaken by every Government in Europe, all were against him, and probably even Spain would recognize the Kingdom of Italy. The recognition of Italy by Russia was the work of France. He had received several very curious letters from St Petersburg on the subject which left no doubt in his mind that prince Gortchakoff's new Italian policy was the price paid for certain concessions on the part of France in the east. Those concessions were contrary to British interests, and England, forsaken by her present ally, would have to re-establish her old alliance with Austria, an alliance which would meet with his full sympathies. I might object that the Pope, being the weakest sovereign in the world, his sympathy was of no great weight or value, but he would remind me that the progress made by the Latin Church in the east was such as to become a serious cause of alarm to the Russian Government and that the Latin Church was the most formidable enemy Russian policy would have to encounter in the east. Under such circumstances he regretted much that Your Lordship and Her Majesty's Government should be so hostile to the Papacy.

I here explained to His Holiness as I had done before that Her Majesty's advizers were not hostile to the Papacy, but that they considered the Pope's temporal independence to be lost since His Holiness had refused to introduce those administrative reforms which were necessary for the re-establishment of confidence between the people and their sovereign and had preferred the presence of a foreign army to the confidence and attachment of his subjects.

The Pope replied that I was mistaken, that he was beloved by his subjects, who were content and happy and that the demonstrations made against his Government were the work of Piedmontese agents, who paid some poor devils five bajocks a head to cheer King Victor Emmanuel and fire tricoloured Bengal lights, but he did not wish to discuss that question at present. He wished rather to ask me a question. The French Emperor, he continued, after making the late extraordinary and unacceptable propositions to him through Monsieur de Lavalette, had evidently organized the present Garibaldian movement with the cabinet of Turin to establish the basis of an excuse for handing over Rome to the Piedmontese. The whole of Monsieur de Lavalette's and Monsieur de Montebello's proceedings for the defence of Civita Vecchia, the last place Garibaldi would think of attacking, were a farce (*une comédie*). It might therefore become the Pope's duty to leave the Holy See, and it was evident he could not seek protection from the Catholic countries, who, notwithstanding the proclaimed principles of the Church, had recognized the Kingdom of Italy. Spain was likely to follow their example, Austria there were other objections to. Did I, under these circumstances think that he could go and live in peace in England? I replied that in England the rights of hospitality were sacred.

But would he not, His Holiness continued, be molested or insulted by those violent protestants whose speeches he read in the newspapers, and could he attend to his duties as Pope (*faire le Pape*) without meeting with serious impediments on the part of the English Government?

I replied that so long as he submitted to the laws of the land, he could enjoy that national hospitality and protection England extended to those who sought refuge within her realms, but at the same time I trusted His Holiness would never have to resort to so extreme a measure and would rather make peace with Italy than abandon Rome. The Pope shook his head mournfully and asked me whether I had read the late declaration of the Bishops and whether I had ever taken the trouble to study the Roman Catholic religion.

I replied that I had, but that neither the declaration of the bishops nor the principles of the Catholic Church had convinced me of the necessity of the Temporal Power. I believed on the contrary that the Spiritual Power would be far stronger without that temporal millstone round the neck of the Papacy which required the support of a foreign army to impose it upon Italy. Indeed the Temporal Power as it now existed appeared to me a serious impediment to the free exercise of the Spiritual Power and I wondered he had not cast it away since it was now evident that it could not be upheld many years longer without endangering the peace of Europe and the unity of the Roman Church.

'My son,' the Pope said, 'the Temporal Dominion was given by God to his Vicar upon Earth. God alone can take it from him. The Lord's will be done.' 'And if events,' I continued, 'deprive Your Holiness of the Temporal Dominion, what then?' 'Then,' the Pope replied, 'I must submit to God's will, but I cannot by any act of my own give up the States of the Church which I hold in trust. They are not my property, I cannot dispose of them, God must decide whether his Vicar on Earth is to be a temporal sovereign or not.'

Then, changing the subject, His Holiness entered into a religious discussion, expressed his regrets that the late Duke of Norfolk had turned Protestant on his deathbed and finally asked me whether I felt no desire to become a Roman Catholic. I replied that I did not. I was born a Protestant and should die a Protestant.

'You are a Protestant,' the Pope said, laughing, 'like Lord Russell who wants to destroy my Temporal Dominion. He was the first to recognize the Piedmontese spoliations of the Church.' 'And his policy,' I added, 'has been followed by almost all the powers of Europe, notwithstanding their previous objections, which is a proof that Lord Russell inaugurated a true, a good and a great policy.'

'Notwithstanding your opinions,' the Pope observed good-humouredly, 'I shall expect you to protect me if I go to England. *Io vi benedico* and if you think the Pope's blessing would be acceptable to your mother and brother, I give it them with all my heart.'

In the Pontifical antechamber I met Monsignor de Mérode who held similar language to me, adding that he was a prophet and foresaw that England in the end would act towards Pius IX as she had acted towards Pius VII. Having discouraged his hopes, I called according to custom on Cardinal Antonelli whom I found equally disposed to expect great things from England in consequence of the supposed Franco-Russian alliance for eastern affairs.

I told him that I thought the best chances for the Papacy were to be sought in a cordial understanding between the Pope and the King of Italy and not in an imaginary war between France and England. I need scarcely add that there is no prospect whatever of the Pope ever carrying out his threat of going to England. The Garibaldian movement may serve as a pretext to increase the French garrison at Rome, but not to withdraw it.

In all probability the Pope's intention is that I should report what he has said and that the French Government should feel the necessity of taking measures to ensure his remaining in Rome, as his flight to England would have a bad effect in France. I have therefore not mentioned the Pope's conversation with me to anyone.

241 [P.R.O. 30/22/76]   *Paris, 22 August 1862*

Private
O.R. to Earl R.

My journey has been pleasant and interesting and I shall have much to tell you when I get home. I remain a few days in Paris to dine with Thouvenel and Metternich and to see Nigra and others from whom I hope to gather some new ideas. . . .

242 [P.R.O. 30/22/76]   *Paris, 30 October 1862*

Private
O.R. to Earl R.

Monsieur Drouyn de Lhuys[1] received me this morning with much

---
[1] The new French Foreign Secretary.

kindness and civility and was pleased to remember a walk we had taken together at Broadlands ten years ago. He spoke a great deal about you and begged of me to tell you *'avec mille compliments affectueux, que j'ai gardé un souvenir bien doux des relations intimes et sincères établies entre Monsieur votre oncle et moi lors de notre séjour à Vienne et que mon plus beau souvenir est d'avoir contribué à l'oeuvre de l'alliance Anglo-Française etc. etc.'* En un mot he loaded me with messages of friendship and admiration for you which had every appearance of being perfectly sincere and he wound up by expressing an anxious desire that those relations of the past might continue in the future, and he added that as far as he was concerned he had no doubt they would. He next proceeded to the Roman question and spoke for rather more than half an hour without interruption, and in the end he succeeded in convincing me that he knew little or nothing about it. After repeating to me all he had said on the subject the other night to Lord Cowley, he contended that there were no abuses worth mentioning in the Papal administration, which he believed to be much better than the administration of the Turkish Empire, and that if any abuses really existed *'les conseils calmes et sérieux de la France'* would soon remove them. He believed that the subjects of the Pope were in reality devoted to their Sovereign and that the enemies of the Temporal Power were foreigners and Piedmontese agents. These questions, he said, would be impartially examined by the new French Ambassador[1] and in course of time the Emperor would find a solution which would enable him to withdraw his garrison from Rome. Monsieur Drouyn de Lhuys only hoped that Her Majesty's Government would meanwhile have patience and confidence etc. I endeavoured to answer Monsieur Drouyn de Lhuys in the same sense in which I knew Lord Cowley had answered him and when I left him he accompanied me to the door to repeat all his civil and friendly messages to you and *Madame votre tante*. Now it appears that Monsieur Drouyn de Lhuys will soon find out that he is but very superficially acquainted with the true state of the Papacy, and of the Romans, and with public feeling in Italy in regard to the Roman question and that *'les conseils calmes et sérieux de la France'* will meet with no success at the Vatican. The Pope will treat on no other basis than the *Status quo ante bellum* and Monsieur Drouyn de Lhuys will not be able to accept his conditions which will be pressed on the French Government with an obstinacy he little expects.

[1] Prince de la Tour d'Auvergne.

243 [F.O. 43/86B]   *Rome, 7 November 1862*

No. 104

O.R. to Earl R.

I have the honor to inform Your Lordship that I arrived in Rome on Wednesday night 5th inst. and that I called this morning at the Vatican to pay my respects to the Cardinal Secretary of State. His Eminence received me most cordially and in the course of conversation expressed in warm and grateful terms his high sense of the straightforward, honest and sincere manner in which Monsieur de Lavalette had acted during the whole period of his late embassy in Rome.

Talking of Italy, Cardinal Antonelli expressed a deep conviction that the Italian people, in whom the elements of unity were, in his opinion, totally wanting, would of their own accord in the end abandon their present dream of unity to return to the idea of a confederation which he believed to be the only solution to the Italian question.

Our conversation was interrupted by the arrival of the new French *chargé d'affaires*, Count de Tallemand.

[*This despatch, and most of those which follow, are endorsed: For the Queen. In November 1862 O.R. became 2nd Secretary in the Diplomatic Service.*]

244 [F.O. 43/86B]   *Rome, 11 November 1862*

No. 108

O.R. to Earl R.

In obedience to Your Lordship's instructions I called this morning on the Cardinal Secretary of State at the Vatican and told him that Her Majesty's Government had observed with great interest the correspondence respecting Rome which had been published in the *Moniteur* of 25 September last, and that I would, with His Eminence's permission, communicate a despatch to him which I had received from Your Lordship on the subject.

I then read Your Lordship's despatch of 25 October to Cardinal Antonelli, who listened with great attention and when I had done said he thought Your Lordship could scarcely be more anxious than he was that Rome should not be the seat of a perpetual foreign occupation. He ardently desired to see the Pope in the full possession of that independence which became the Sovereign Pontiff, the visible head of the Roman Catholic Church, independent of enemies who persecuted the Church and independent of friends whose protection could not unhappily yet be dispensed with. But since the enemies of order and legitimate right in Italy had been encouraged in their reckless and immoral course and since the Pope had not the means to protect the temporal interests of the Church against their violence and rapacity without foreign assistance, he was compelled to accept the protection afforded him by the presence of a French garrison in Rome.

Your Lordship observed truly that this melancholy state of things in Italy wounded the kind heart and harrowed the paternal feelings of His Holiness, and you were equally right in concluding that the conscientious feelings of duty of the Pope would always oblige him to refuse any terms of accommodation, whether recommended by the Emperor of the French or by any other power, which should leave him with less than his former territory. The reasons which prompted this course of action were obvious: the Pope did not hold the States of the Church as an inheritance from his ancestors and could not dispose of them at his will either before or after death. As Vicar of Christ he held them in trust from God for the Catholic World, and as he received them, so he had to leave them to his successor according to the oath taken by the Pontiffs on ascending the throne of St Peter. And again, the Pope as Vicar of Christ and therefore as the Guardian of Religion and Morality on Earth could not give his sanction to acts which violated every law of public morality and of legitimate right, and however much his heart might bleed at the sad conflict around him he had a duty, as head of the Catholic Church, to perform for which he was answerable to God alone in heaven and not to man upon earth.

This conscientious policy pursued by the Pope had been publickly and unanimously approved by the whole of the bishops of Catholic Christendom, and while His Holiness could fulfil the sacred duties of his office in any portion of the Holy See, however small and limited, with freedom and independence it was his duty to assert the temporal rights of the Church by remaining in it, until violently driven away by the enemies of religion.

Now Your Lordship, animated by a friendly feeling to both parties, suggested that the Pope should retire from the conflict and expect in tranquillity the issue which in the order of Providence might await the Papacy and determine the fate of Italy. But the abandonment of Rome, so long as its possession was guaranteed by France, would be tantamount to that very abdication of temporal rights which the conscientious feelings of duty of the Sovereign Pontiff for ever precluded. If the Pope left Rome, the Emperor of the French would naturally recall his troops to France, and Rome would be invaded by the enemies of the Church, a contingency towards which the Pope in his conscience could never contribute by any voluntary act of his own so long as he could there freely exercise the spiritual and temporal duties of his office. On the other hand, should it ever so please Providence in the course of events to allow the French protecting forces to be withdrawn and the Piedmontese to invade Rome, and should the free exercise of the Pontiff's spiritual duties thereby be endangered, then, and not till then, would it become the Pope's paramount duty to seek protection for the independence of the Church in some foreign land and the generous offers of hospitality now made by Her Majesty's Government might be gratefully accepted.[1]

Cardinal Antonelli then requested me to thank Your Lordship in the warmest terms for the communication I had made to him and asked me for a copy of your despatch which he said he would submit to the Pope.

Without renewing a useless discussion I replied to Cardinal Antonelli that while I respected the conscientious motives which dictated the policy of the Sovereign Pontiff, I could not for my part, as he well knew, see any but the most disastrous consequences to the temporal interests of the Papacy from the maintenance of the *status quo* in Rome, and I felt sure that the day would come when the immense advantages to be derived by the Roman Catholic Church from the hospitality and protection on neutral ground now offered in a friendly and impartial spirit to the Pope by Your Lordship, would be acknowledged by the whole Catholic world.

245 [P.R.O. 30/22/76]   *Rome, 19 November 1862*
Private
O.R. to Earl R.

The communication of your despatch to Cardinal Antonelli seemed to please him immensely, and he snatched the copy out of my hands and crammed it into his bosom and buttoned it up as if it had been a bag of golden *scudi*. I have given you his answer word for word in my

[1] In this despatch Lord Russell offered the Pope asylum in Malta (F.O. 43/85 No. 46). It is printed in H. of C. Accounts and Papers, 1863, Vol. LXXV.

despatch No. 108. The more I think over the measure and the more I read your despatch the more I feel it was a good move in every respect, and if the Pope had accepted it it would also have been the best thing he could do for the Roman Catholic Church. The maintenance of the *Status quo* will reduce him and his interests to a mere shadow and will discredit the Roman Government and the Emperor of the French. . . .

I was sorry the Prince of Wales was not allowed to accept the visit of King Francis II, for the incivility was great and was much felt by the unhappy Monarch who is really more to be pitied than condemned.[1] . . .

246 [F.O. 43/86B]   *Rome, 24 November 1862*

No. 115
O.R. to Earl R.

The Bourbon Committee have lately sent a further detachment of 260 men to join Tristani's band on the frontier. They were well armed and wore blue overcoats and red trousers so as to look like French soldiers at a distance and thereby deceive the Italian outposts and patrols. The men enlisted are chiefly Bavarians, Belgians and Spaniards. Tristani's headquarters are, according to circumstances, either at Santa Francesca or at Strangolagalli, and he draws his rations and supplies from Veroli.

It is difficult to understand for what object the Bourbon Committee continue to keep up and organize these useless bands of foreigners, who, beyond annoying the inhabitants of the Neapolitan frontiers, have achieved no other result than to discredit the cause of King Francis II.

Can it be for that reason that the French Government have not seen fit to put them down by striking a decisive blow at the root of the evil in Rome?

247 [F.O. 43/86B]   *Rome, 28 November 1862*

No. 118. Confidential
O.R. to Earl R.

With reference to Your Lordship's despatch No. 46 of 25 October and

[1] The Prince of Wales had arrived in Rome. The Queen thought it unsuitable that he should meet Francis II.

17. Signor Alari's music class. Odo Russell third from left

18. Charles Newton, consul. Drawing, probably by G. F. Watts

to my reply of 11 November, I have the honor to state that I asked
Cardinal Antonelli this morning whether he had submitted to the Pope
the reasons for which Your Lordship thought that it would become
His Holiness to retire from the present conflict and expect in tranquillity the issue which in the order of Providence might await the Papacy
and determine the fate of Italy, and I further inquired how His Holiness
had taken the offers of hospitality made to him in consequence by Her
Majesty's Government.

Cardinal Antonelli replied that he had communicated Your Lordship's despatch to the Pope the day after I had given him a copy of it
and that His Holiness had fully acknowledged the friendly spirit in
which that communication had been made, but that since it was his
manifest duty to remain in Rome so long as he could do so with
advantage to the spiritual interests of the Church, he could but thank
Her Majesty's Government for their intentions but he could not share
their opinions nor could he avail himself of their hospitable offers at
present.

I said I thought the great advantages of those offers would be better
felt in the future as things grew worse in Rome and better in Italy and
I enquired whether His Eminence thought that the new French Ambassador, Monsieur de La Tour d'Auvergne would be the bearer of any
acceptable propositions on the part of Monsieur Drouyn de Lhuys for
the settlement of the Roman question. Cardinal Antonelli replied as
usual that no settlement could be acceptable to the Pope which was not
based on the principle of the unconditional surrender to their lawful
sovereign of the provinces of Romagna, the Marches and Umbria, of
which the Holy Church had been despoiled by the Piedmontese
brigands, but that he had reason to think Monsieur Drouyn de Lhuys
would make no propositions at present and that things would therefore
remain as they were. . . .

248 [F.O. 43/86B]   *Rome, 2 December 1862*

No. 121
O.R. to Earl R.

With reference to Your Lordship's despatch No. 44 of 4 October
directing me to procure photographic facsimiles of certain pages of the
Codex Vaticanus for the Master of Balliol College, Oxford, I regret to
say that the Cardinal Secretary of State has not been able to grant Dr

K

Scott's request in consequence of an order from the Pope that no copies shall be taken by means of photography of any portion of the *Codex Vaticanus.*

249 [F.O. 43/86B]   *Rome, 3 December 1862*

No. 122
O.R. to Earl R.

Monsieur Thouvenel and Monsieur de Lavalette having been removed from office and Monsieur Drouyn de Lhuys and Prince de la Tour d'Auvergne appointed to their respective places to satisfy the exigencies of the Court of Rome, it is but natural on the part of the French Government to expect that the Pope will meet the Emperor Napoleon's concessions in a more friendly and encouraging spirit than has hitherto been the case, and thereby facilitate His Majesty's efforts in favor of the Pope's temporal sovereignty.

Cardinal Mathieu, archbishop of Besançon, who was sent here for the purpose of revising the French Breviary is said to have spoken in this sense at the Vatican in the name of the French clergy. Count de Tallemand, the French *Chargé d'Affaires*, appears also to have urged on the Cardinal Secretary of State the necessity of seconding the Emperor's policy by the adoption of some measures calculated to gratify public opinion in France, such as the application of the administrative reforms granted in the *Motu Proprio* of Gaeta, and a general amnesty.

Notwithstanding the long and obstinate resistance hitherto opposed by the Pope to the advice of the Emperor it is now not impossible that His Holiness may be induced to make some concessions to his subjects so as to meet the wishes of his supporters in France and thereby endeavour to strengthen the hands and lengthen the tenure of office of His Imperial Majesty's present advizers.

250 [F.O. 43/86B]   *Rome, 16 December 1862*

No. 124
O.R. to Earl R.

The new French Ambassador, Prince de la Tour d'Auvergne, arrived here on the afternoon of 11th instant and called on the following morning on the Cardinal Secretary of State and on 15th instant His Excellency delivered his credentials to the Pope. The Prince having been Secretary of Embassy in Rome for several years is well acquainted with Cardinal Antonelli and Roman society in general and was universally liked and respected so that his appointment has given great satisfaction. . . .

251 [P.R.O. 30/22/76]   *Rome, 16 December 1862*

Private
O.R. to Earl R.

Cardinal Antonelli told me the other day that he intended to make a secret of your despatch offering hospitality to the Pope at Malta and that he had not communicated it to anybody. I naturally concluded from this declaration that he must have given a copy of it to some friend or other, but the only one I could think of was the Austrian Ambassador. I next proceeded to investigate the matter and finally discovered that His Eminence had given a copy of the despatch, together with an Italian translation, to Baron Bach who had sent a special messenger with it to Vienna via Paris so that it might be read by Prince Metternich. I also discovered that the two Pontifical Under-Secretaries of State, political and ecclesiastical, had found fault with His Eminence for having accepted a copy of it from me because they thought some of your allusions to brigandage were not respectful to the Holy Father. But Cardinal Antonelli explained to them that he could not refuse to accept a document which might some day prove most useful to them all, and that he had on the contrary asked for a copy of it. To the Austrian Ambassador, Cardinal Antonelli said the same thing, adding that although the Pope could not accept English hospitality at present he might stand in need of it in the future. Baron Bach asked Antonelli how he explained this sudden fit of hospitality on the part of H.M. Government. His Eminence then told him that he explained it as follows: that last summer when the Pope fancied Garibaldi was acting in concert with the Emperor Napoleon, His Holiness had said to me he would ask England to protect him if he was driven away from Rome, that I had probably reported the Pope's words to you and that you had replied by the despatch in question.

As all this was confided to me in the strictest confidence I must beg of you not to shew me or my informant up. The Austrian Government will of course advize the Pope to die the death of ten thousand martyrs rather than abandon Rome. Prince de la Tour d'Auvergne, the new

French Ambassador, is going to insist on administrative reforms I fancy, and Monsignor Chigi, the Nuncio in Paris, writes to Antonelli that the Empress is working to get the Emperor, in return for such reforms, to occupy the Marches and Umbria and gradually re-establish the Pope's authority there, but he fears there is no hope now of ever recovering Romagna. Monsignor di Lucca, the Nuncio at Vienna, writes in the same sense on the authority of Count Rechberg. Much as I believe the Emperor Napoleon's intention of keeping Rome during his lifetime, yet I cannot believe that he would extend his occupation beyond its present limits, unless he can succeed in breaking up Italy into a Confederation which appears to be the wish of every Frenchman I have spoken to. The Pope, Antonelli, Chigi, di Lucca and all the rest of them have a plan by which they hope to bribe France, or later the Emperor, into imposing a Confederation on Italy. It is this: As Austria, they say, would be a member of the Italian Confederation by virtue of Venice, so should France equally be admitted as a member to share equal honors, equal influence and an equal number of votes by virtue of her Italian possessions, Nice and Corsica. This patriotic plan is to be pressed upon La Tour d'Auvergne whose devotion to the Pope inspires the Vatican with confidence and hope.

All the members of the French Embassy have been changed and a new set of Secretaries and attachés sent here who have been selected for their devotion to Pope and Church and their implicit belief in the absolute necessity of the Temporal Power. . . .

252 [F.O. 43/86B]   *Rome, 26 December 1862*

No. 128
O.R. to Earl R.

Prince de la Tour d'Auvergne told me this morning that Lord Cowley had communicated a despatch of mine on the subject of brigandage to Monsieur Drouyn de Lhuys in which I informed Your Lordship that a body of five or six hundred men well armed and equipped had been sent by the Legitimist Committee from Rome to join Tristani's band on the Neapolitan frontier; that he had in consequence at once instituted a searching enquiry into the matter, and that both General Count de Montebello and Monsieur Mangin, the French Prefect of Police, had assured him that no such force could have left Rome without their knowledge or have crossed the frontier unperceived by the French patrols; that the Pontifical Government who were as anxious as the French Government to put down brigandage equally denied the accuracy of my facts and that he had therefore written to Monsieur Drouyn de Lhuys to say that he was convinced I had been misinformed. His Excellency added that he was happy to learn that Tristani's band was now reduced to 61 men only.

I thanked the Ambassador for this communication and explained that the number of men mentioned by me was 260 and not five or six hundred as reported to him, but that I would hasten to inform Your Lordship of the result of his enquiries.

Last week about 20 of Tristani's men with two officers in blue overcoats and red trowsers tucked into high shooting boots arrived at the railway station of Ceprano, took their places and proceeded to Rome, thus returning whence they had gone. This fact has also escaped the vigilance of the French civil and military authorities in Rome.

253 [F.O. 43/89B]   *Rome, 7 January 1863*
No. 5
O.R. to Earl R.

I had the honor to be admitted to an audience of the Pope this morning and to wish His Holiness a happy New Year. The Pope who was looking remarkably well and who was as ever full of benevolent kindness, thanked me and said he thought the New Year was beginning better than the past year, a better feeling existed towards him in France and in England and it seemed as if Providence was about to open the eyes of the enemies of the Church. He had been gratified by the offers of hospitality made to him by Her Majesty's Government and he requested me to thank Your Lordship for the despatch I had communicated to Cardinal Antonelli offering him a palace at Malta. The Maltese, he said, were good Catholics and he knew he would there be surrounded by a population as devoted and respectful as his own subjects might be at Viterbo – he could no longer say Bologna – but so long as he was protected by France he would not avail himself of the protection of England. Nevertheless, he desired to thank Her Majesty's Government for their good intentions.

His Holiness went on to enquire after the health of Her Majesty the

Queen and he dwelt on the pleasure it had given him to see the Prince of Wales again in Rome and to make the acquaintance of the Crown Princess of Prussia of whom he spoke in terms of the highest admiration. He also said he had been gratified to learn that no impediment had been thrown in the way of a lecture which Cardinal Wiseman was about to deliver at the Royal Institution.

His Holiness next asked me whether I had seen a new pamphlet which he had received from Paris called *L'Union Italienne* and which he had read with great interest. It had been attributed to Messieurs de Bourguency, de Laguerronnière and Baron Brenier and others, but he did not know the real author. This pamphlet, after proving the impossibility of a United Italy and shewing the advantages of a Confederation, suggested, to satisfy all parties, that the principle laid down at Zurich by which Austria became an Italian power through her Venetian possessions should be extended to England and France who by virtue of their possession of the islands of Malta and Corsica would equally become members of the Italian Confederation. Now His Holiness agreed in thinking a Confederation the only possible solution to the Italian difficulty, but how could his representatives and the representatives of England sit together in the Confederate Council of Italy, divided as they would be by adverse principles? England, for instance, would probably advocate the liberty of the press, an institution he could not consider consistent with the laws of the Church, which required to guide public opinion and inculcate morality on the minds and in the habits of the people. The uncontrolled press produced a contrary effect and he wondered how in England we could tolerate such a power in the state as the *Times* newspaper had become. The Pope, he continued, could never allow the press to be free in the States of the Church, morality forbade it.

After some general conversation, the Pope asked me, with a smile, whether his friend Sir James Hudson and I still persisted in believing in the Unity of Italy. I said I did, and it appeared to me that considering the immense changes that had taken place, things were going on well enough in Italy. The Pope laughed and said, '*si, la cosa va, ma va a rotta di collo.*' He wondered at the blindness of Englishmen who did not appear to notice the awful state of Italy which had become a prey to anarchy, party hatred and foreign revolutionary agents, but he trusted in Providence to bring matters round again and give peace and repose to poor Italy when her present trials were over. . . .

254 [F.O. 43/89B]   *Rome, 14 January 1863*

No. 7
O.R. to Earl R.

[Concerning the 260 brigands mentioned in his despatch No. 115 of
24 Nov. last].

. . . Reliable as my informants appeared to me to be, I must now
suppose that they were in this case themselves deceived and I regret to
have unwittingly sent incorrect information to Your Lordship. I also
regret to say that I found General de Montebello somewhat annoyed
at the occurrence. He said that by supposing that men could be armed
and equipped in Rome and sent to the frontier without his knowledge
I had blamed his military administration of Rome, but that criticism
was a matter of indifference to him so long as his own conscience and
sense of duty were satisfied.

I told the General how much I regretted that any statements of mine
should have been a cause of annoyance to him, that I had made them
on what I considered good authority and that similar statements formerly made by me had been entirely confirmed by his predecessor
General de Goyon. The means employed, I said, by the Legitimist
Committee to send men and arms to the frontier had formerly been as
follows: The men were sent singly on foot to certain convents on the
frontier, while old French uniforms were bought from the Jews in the
Ghetto and as well as arms and other equipments carried bit by bit to
isolated *vignas* in the Campagna and at night packed in old herring
casks and gradually conveyed to the frontier where they were distributed to the men already there assembled.

The General said he had entirely put an end to such proceedings,
besides which he now had the full co-operation of the Papal Government to put down brigandage and that he could assure me on his honour
that armed men could no longer leave Rome and proceed to the
frontier without his knowledge and that I had therefore been misinformed and the statements sent home by me and communicated by
Earl Cowley to Monsieur Drouyn de Lhuys would prove to be incorrect.

I replied that I was glad to hear from him that he was so successful
in putting down brigandage and I hoped he would occasionally give
me some correct information on these subjects as his predecessor
General de Goyon had done. Count de Montebello replied that he

would do so and that for the present he could tell me that Tristani's band was reduced to about 60 men and would probably soon be altogether disbanded and destroyed; that in Rome he had put a stop to all communication between Tristani and his employers, and that he had lately seized and confiscated, in a Roman printing establishment about 2000 copies of a printed proclamation calling upon the Neapolitans to rise and join their legitimate sovereign, King Francis II.

255 [F.O. 43/89B]   *Rome, 20 January 1863*

No. 10. [Recites telegrams]
O.R. to Earl R.
London, 19 January. Earl R. to O.R.

Is it true that at Christmas you made a further communication to Antonelli founded on a private letter from me expressing regret that the Pope had not availed himself of the offer of an asylum in Malta, and adding that the Pope would be obliged to have recourse to this (Govt.)?

O.R. to Earl R.   *Rome, 20 January*

No, you never wrote to me to that effect, so I could not make the communication in question.

256 [P.R.O. 30/22/76]   *Rome, 21 January 1863*

Private
O.R. to Earl R.

I am at a loss to comprehend what has happened, but I conclude from the telegrams received yesterday from you that there must be some document published in the new French Blue or rather Yellow Book which requires comment or explanation. I confess I am the more curious to know what it can be because Cardinal Antonelli told me some time since that he heard from Monsignor Chigi that the French Government were deeply annoyed at your Malta despatch and equally annoyed at my having been the instrument wherewith you presented it. He also told me with a chuckle that Prince de la Tour d'Auvergne appeared personally deeply annoyed at the whole transaction. A colleague told me also in confidence that the French Ambassador and some of the members of his Embassy appeared ill disposed towards me, but this I can scarcely believe for I find them all most civil and Prince de la Tour d'Auvergne as cordial and friendly as possible and has already taken the trouble to call three times on me and to express the warmest regrets when I appeared to be out. As I see the offer of Malta has got into the papers I suppose there will be a row about it, but the more I think the measure over the more I convince myself that it will in the end prove to have been good policy, one of these days I will write you '*mes idées là-dessus*'. Meanwhile the French Government must be much annoyed at it and the more so as the Pope, it appears, talks about it to everybody and appears gratified at the course followed by you in the matter. Here the French reaction is complete. All the officers or officials who served Lavalette and shared his views are gradually being removed to France and their places are filled up by men who believe in the Temporal Power and an Italian Confederation.

La Tour d'Auvergne and Montebello laugh at Lavalette and declare the Papal Government is not so bad, that France will remain at Rome until Italy has acknowledged the necessity of the Pope's Temporal Power and that the only solution to the Italian question is a Confederation. The tendency of the French Ambassador and of General de Montebello is to make out that all the past accusations of bad Government brought against the Pope were exaggerated, that brigandage never was seriously organized or connived at in Rome and that the Romans are the most loyal subjects of His Holiness.

257 [F.O. 43/89B]   *Rome, 22 January 1863*

No. 11. [Recites telegram]
Earl R. to O.R.   F.O. 21 January

You will get all the information you can respecting the encouragement given in the Roman territory to brigands acting against the Southern Italian dominions; and if you think that a little money may assist your enquiries you may draw for what you may spend for the purpose on Her Majesty's Secretary of State for Foreign Affairs at 30 days sight.

258 [F.O. 43/89B]   *Rome, 26 January 1863*

No. 13
O.R. to Earl R.

The French Ambassador has kindly promised to lend me the official

Documents Diplomatiques lately published in Paris, but I have meanwhile read some extracts from them in the *Journal des Débats* of 22nd inst. and I beg to offer Your Lordship a few observations on those passages in which my name is mentioned by Monsieur Drouyn de Lhuys and Prince de la Tour d'Auvergne.

In an extract dated Paris 20 December the French Foreign Secretary informs the French Ambassador in Rome 'that having been received by the Pope, I had advized His Holiness in Your Lordship's name to leave Italy, adding that Her Majesty's Government would in such case willingly offer him Malta as a residence, that English ships would be placed at his disposal and that the Pope could reckon on the readiness of England to secure an asylum to him worthy of himself. These proposals had been made in an official form, adopted for the first time in the relations entertained by me with the Holy See.'

I need not point out the inaccuracy of Monsieur Drouyn de Lhuys' information since Prince de la Tour d'Auvergne does so for me in a despatch dated, Rome, 27 December, in which he 'hastens to transmit the information he has collected and which he has reason to think correct'. Unfortunately this is not the case and the new version of my proceedings at the Vatican is scarcely more correct than the former.

In his despatch of 27 December the French Ambassador describes the Pope as uttering sentiments to which he attaches no importance and attributes rather a weak, silly and undignified part to His Holiness in conversation with me. Now, anyone who knows Pope Pius IX, however much he may differ in opinions, must admit that his character is firm and independent, his heart charitable and benevolent and his mind clear and logical and that he means what he says. For my part I cannot give Your Lordship a more correct and conscientious account of what really passed between the Sovereign Pontiff and myself than the one I wrote down almost immediately after the audience.

My subsequent conversations with the Cardinal Secretary of State on returning to Rome from England are faithfully recorded in my despatches No. 108 and No. 118 of 28 November. I have nothing to add to them.

Prince de la Tour d'Auvergne goes on to say that Cardinal Antonelli wished to keep the secret 'but that ere long the Vatican learnt that I had spoken myself on the subject to one of the diplomatic envoys accredited to the Holy See'. The truth is this: I never made the slightest allusion to the subject of Your Lordship's despatch of 25 October to anyone and conscientiously kept the 'secret'. But one day a foreign diplomatist called on me and told me in confidence that the matter was known, and about a fortnight later an Italian gentlemen told me that the 'secret', as it was called, had oozed out of the Vatican and had been whispered in ecclesiastical circles. I added nothing whatsoever to the information they had obtained in other quarters.

The story that I had at Christmas made a further communication to Cardinal Antonelli founded on a private letter from Your Lordship expressing regret that the Pope had not availed himself of the offer of an asylum in Malta and adding that the Pope would soon be obliged to have recourse to it, is unfounded. Your Lordship never wrote to me either privately or officially to that effect and I could therefore not make the communication in question.

Finally Prince de la Tour d'Auvergne states that Cardinal Antonelli abstained from giving me any answer whatever to his imaginary communication. Among other qualities Cardinal Antonelli is possessed of eminently courteous and pleasing manners and I am surprized the French Ambassador should think His Eminence capable of an act of uncivility.

259   [F.O. 43/89B]   *Rome, 26 January 1863*

No. 14
O.R. to Earl R.

I have read in the *Journal des Débats* of 22nd inst. the official correspondence which passed between Monsieur Drouyn de Lhuys and Prince de la Tour d'Auvergne on the subject of brigandage in the Papal States called forth by a statement I made to the effect that 260 men in blue overcoats and red trowsers and well armed had been sent by the Bourbon Committee to join Tristani's band on the Neapolitan frontier. In Monsieur Drouyn de Lhuys' first despatch on the subject the number of men mentioned by me has been increased to 5 or 600.

In my despatches of 29 December and 14 January I had already informed Your Lordship that Prince de la Tour d'Auvergne, General Count de Montebello and Monsieur Mangin, the French Prefect of Police in Rome, had declared their conviction that I had been misinformed. Reliable as my informants appeared to me to be, I said they must in this case have been themselves deceived and I regretted to have unwittingly sent incorrect information to Your Lordship, and I said further that I was glad to learn from General de Montebello himself that he was so successfully putting down brigandage. The responsibility of the mistake I made must rest on my shoulders as I have no intention of disclosing the names of the persons on whose authority I thought I could safely rely. I have never known them to deceive themselves before, and at the time General de Goyon between 10 and 20 April last made the important seizure of 470 old uniforms and over 100,000 cartridges which had been successfully conveyed from Rome to Palliano and Ceprano, and on other similar occasions, I found their information coincided in every single detail with that given me by the General himself. And one of them whom I saw today still maintains that the 260 men safely reached the frontier notwithstanding the vigilance of the French authorities. But when I consider the extraordinary means of information which the French authorities in Rome can command, I cannot but conclude he has this time been deceived, and above all when a French Ambassador, a French General and a French Prefect of Police declare to me on their honor that my informants have been deceived, I am bound to believe them.

260 [F.O. 43/89B] *Rome, 27 January 1863*

No. 15
O.R. to Earl R.

Since writing my despatch No. 13 I have seen Cardinal Antonelli about an hour ago. I asked His Eminence who could have made Prince de la Tour d'Auvergne believe that I had called at Christmas on His Eminence and made a further communication to him founded on a private letter from Your Lordship expressing regret that the Pope had not availed himself of the offer of an asylum in Malta and adding that His Holiness would soon be obliged to have recourse to it.

Cardinal Antonelli's memory is generally so good that I confess I was surprized when His Eminence told me he was under the impression that I had done so, and that he had himself mentioned it to Prince de la Tour d'Auvergne. I begged he would recall all the circumstances to me as he recollected them.

His Eminence replied that I had called and spoken of a private letter of Your Lordship written in the sense above mentioned, but the circumstances he described were unknown to me beyond the fact that I had called on him on 26 December and that he seemed to be suffering from a bad cold in the head. I replied that not having received a letter from Your Lordship to that effect I was conscious that I had not made the communication in question. The Cardinal said his impressions had been different but that he would with pleasure rectify the statement on my present declaration if I wished it.

We then talked of other things, and His Eminence gave me an interesting account of the difficulties the Papal Govt. had experienced after the Napoleonic Wars in the suppression of brigandage whic᾽ had taken 10 years and cost 2,000,000 scudi. He said that in the present disturbed state of Italy brigandage might last many years notwithstanding the combined efforts of the French and Pontifical troops in the Papal States, and of the Piedmontese troops in Southern Italy to put it down.

261   [F.O. 43/89B]   *Rome, 28 January 1863*

No. 16. [Recites Telegram]
O.R. to Earl R.

                                        Rome, Tuesday

Messenger just arrived. Publish anything you please and never mind me, but leave out the Pope's blessing to myself, my mother and my brothers.

You must expect the Pope to complain of breach of confidence. I will send explanations by the messenger.

262   [F.O. 519/205]   *Rome, 30 January 1863*

O.R. to Earl Cowley

Monsignor Chigi's story about me *is not true*, but I suspect he is speaking under instructions from Rome. You may well suppose that I never alluded to the Malta despatch to anyone until the French publication. Baron Bach's secretary, Baron Ottenfels, whom you know, an old friend of mine, called on me one day and told me in strict confidence that Bach was in possession of Lord Russell's Malta despatch, both the copy in my hand made for Antonelli and an Italian translation of it. *I said I could tell him nothing about it and that he must get all his information from the Vatican on the subject, and there the matter rested.*

Then came Metternich's blabbery which I really cannot blame him for. La Tour d'Auvergne asked Antonelli, *who denied on his honour* ever having communicated the despatch to Bach. But, said La Tour d'A, how did Bach get it to send it to Metternich? Oh, said Antonelli, probably through Bach's secretary, Baron Ottenfels, who is Mr Russell's particular friend. La Tour d'Auvergne at once put about that I had communicated Lord Russell's despatch to Bach through Ottenfels.

I agree with you, there is no use in complicating matters and I have promised not to betray Ottenfels, so pray keep this to yourself and time will pass over it and wipe it out. After that the Pope himself blabbed and the matter was discussed in the Papal antechamber by the Chamberlains, Monsignori and even the 'Guardie Nobili' of H.H.

But all this I cannot put into despatches and letters which may be published and would only make matters worse.

The general impression here is that the French intend to oust me from Rome, because I am inconvenient to them.

263 [P.R.O. 30/22/76]   *Rome, 31 January 1863*

Private
O.R. to Earl R.

. . . The Pope I am told is delighted with you and I also came in for good wishes on his part. But the French appear to be frantic. Antonelli has told two fibs. 1st. That he did not give Baron Bach a copy of your Malta despatch. 2nd. That I made a renewed communication at Christmas to him. The first fib was told to please the Austrian Ambassador, the second to please the French Ambassador. He not only gave Bach a copy, but he added an Italian translation to it, as Count Rechberg can tell you. He was much embarrassed when I asked him about the renewed communication at Christmas and immediately offered to rectify the statement with all sorts of assurances of friendship. These priests and French diplomatists are a sad lot. . . .

264 [F.O. 43/89B]   *Rome, 4 February 1863*

No. 18. [Recites Telegram]
O.R. to Earl R.

It appears from further investigation that the fact I reported of the 260 brigands was correct, but I am unable to prove it yet.

265 [F.O. 43/89B]   *Rome, 4 February 1863*

No. 19. [Recites Telegrams]
O.R. to Earl R.
Earl R. to O.R.   F.O.

Have you anything to say against the publication of your despatch
No. 115 of 24 November and No. 7 of 14 January. Answer immediately.

O.R. to Earl R.   *Rome, 4 February*

Publish anything you please.

266 [F.O. 43/89B]   *Rome, 4 February 1863*

No. 20. [Recites Telegrams]

Please publish also my despatch No. 106 of 31 December 1861.

Earl R. to O.R.   F.O.

We cannot publish your despatch No. 106 at present. It would create
great irritation.

267 [F.O. 43/89B]   *Rome, 13 February 1863*

No. 24
O.R. to Earl R.

I asked Cardinal Antonelli this morning whether it was true that he
had addressed a despatch to the Papal Nuncio at Paris on 30 January
last in which he adhered to the French Ambassador's account of what
had passed with me respecting the withdrawal of the Pope from Rome
and in which he stated that the audience granted to me on 26 July last
was at my request. Cardinal Antonelli, who was most friendly in his
manner towards me, said that when Monsieur Drouyn de Lhuys had
spoken to Monsignor Chigi on that subject the Nuncio, to whom it
was unknown, had written to Rome for further information and he had
then sent His Excellency towards the end of December the despatch I
was alluding to. He could not assume any responsibility with respect
to the manner in which foreign diplomatists imparted the information
they collected to their governments and to the public, but the facts

reported by himself to Monsignor Chigi were the same as those reported by Prince de la Tour d'Auvergne to Monsieur Drouyn de Lhuys, namely, that the Pope had said to me on 26 July at an audience solicited by myself without intending to attach much importance to his words that he might perhaps some day be compelled to ask England for hospitality, that this observation was made at the moment when I was leaving His Holiness's room, that I had perhaps attached undue importance to it and that I had shortly afterwards received a telegram from Your Lordship directing me to return to England. That in November I had presented Your Lordship's despatch No. 46 of 25 October to him, which he had desired to keep secret and that although he had had it translated into Italian he had not communicated it to anyone and had always kept it in his room, and that at Christmas I had spoken to him of a private letter from Your Lordship in which you expressed regret that the Pope had not accepted your proposal and that you thought His Holiness would soon be obliged to avail himself of it.

These were his impressions and recollections of the case as he had stated them to Prince de la Tour d'Auvergne and to Monsignor Chigi. Mine he knew were different, but in the long intercourse he had had with foreign diplomatists he had often observed how different were the impressions produced by one and the same event or occurrence on the minds of men belonging to different nations.

He had just read the debate in the English Parliament on this affair and there was a statement made by Lord Palmerston which he would wish me to rectify in writing to Your Lordship, namely, Lord Palmerston said that I had not asked for an audience of the Pope, but the Pope had sent for me in July last. This was not correct. The Pope never sent for anyone, and the audience had been granted to me at my request after the feast of St Peter according to established usage.

I replied that Lord Palmerston's statement had been made on my authority as I was under the impression that the initiative had been taken at the Vatican, the intimation that the Pope would receive me on 26 July having reached me unexpectedly on the night of 25 July. I considered the intimation as unexpected for the following reasons:

According to custom, I, and my predecessors had been admitted to the honor of an audience of the Pope on the first days of every New Year and on the occasion of the feast of St Peter (29 June) a few days after the audience of the Diplomatic Body. On 16 January 1861 I had been admitted for the last time to that honor. About 29 June 1861 I applied as usual to His Eminence for the customary audience, who replied that he would take the Pope's commands and would let me know the day appointed through the Pontifical Chamberlain. A fortnight later the Cardinal very civilly expressed regret that my request had escaped his memory.

Six months later on the first days of January 1862 in accordance with my duties I asked Cardinal Antonelli whether he thought the Pope would receive me on the occasion of the New Year and His Eminence at once replied, Certainly, and that he would let me know what day His Holiness might appoint.

As on these two occasions I heard no more of my request I naturally concluded that the former privilege we had enjoyed of seeing the Sovereign Pontiff twice a year was to be discontinued. Nevertheless, after a further lapse of six months, in June 1862, on the occasion of the feast of St Peter, I thought it would not be respectful on my part to omit the customary request and it was received by Cardinal Antonelli with his usual kindness and courtesy, and then not alluded to again.

One month later, on 25 July following, on returning home at night I found the information from the Pontifical Chamberlain stating that the Pope would deign to admit me to an audience on the day following at 12 o'clock. I was taken by surprize and as I drove to the Vatican on the following day I confess I still wondered to what favorable change of circumstances I owed this unexpected honor which had not been conceded to me for eighteen months.

The language of the Sovereign Pontiff, which I carefully wrote down on the very same day, the questions His Holiness put to me, and the words: '*I sent for you to . . .*' distinctly pronounced by the Pope, left no doubt in my mind that the audience had not been granted to me in consequence of my past applications which had not been attended to for a year and a half by Cardinal Antonelli, but for a special purpose and I therefore concluded that I had been sent for by the Pope. I thought His Eminence would admit that my impressions were not unfounded.

Cardinal Antonelli replied that he recollected the circumstances I mentioned but that the long delay in granting me the customary audience I had solicited had been owing to the Pope's health which had not allowed of his receiving me before and that a reference to the Pontifical Audience Register proved that the audience in question had been granted to me at my request. The result of His Eminence's present rectification, which I hasten to submit to Your Lordship, is therefore that it was not the Pope but Cardinal Antonelli himself who directed the Papal Chamberlain to send me the intimation that the Pope would receive me on the following day at my previous request.

Cardinal Antonelli proceeded to explain that Prince de la Tour d'Auvergne's account of my interview with His Holiness had been communicated to the Ambassador by the Pope himself shortly after His Excellency's arrival in Rome in December last. I will therefore only observe that my account which Your Lordship has read in my despatch No. 100 of 26 July was written immediately after the audience and is therefore naturally more circumstantial.

With respect to the French Ambassador's opinion that I had given too much importance to the Pope's words, I said to Cardinal Antonelli, as I had said on a previous occasion to Prince de la Tour d'Auvergne, that I did not attach undue importance to them for the simple reason that I never believed in the withdrawal of the French garrison from Rome and therefore never believed the Pope would leave Rome, as a reference to my despatches will easily prove. On the other hand the French Ambassador thinks that the Pope spoke to me without attaching the slightest importance to what he said. Here again I differ in opinion from the French Ambassador, for while I did not exaggerate or attach undue importance to the Pope's words for the reasons stated above, I could not but be impressed by the earnest appearance of Pius IX and it never occurred to my mind that the spiritual independence of the Roman Catholic Church was a subject with which the Pope would trifle in conversation with anyone.

Cardinal Antonelli told Prince de la Tour d'Auvergne that he remembered my receiving a telegraphic order from Your Lordship directing me to proceed to London and telling me that my travelling expenses would be paid for reasons I had not explained, and from which he had later concluded in November that my journey home in August had been connected with the Pope's conversation in July to which I had attached undue importance.

Your Lordship will recollect better than anyone why you directed me to return to England on leave of absence at a period when my report on the Pope's conversation had not yet reached the Foreign Office.

With regard to the French Ambassador's statement that I had spoken to a diplomatic envoy on the subject of Your Lordship's despatch No. 46 of 25 October, I have already told Your Lordship that I never made the slightest allusion to the subject of that despatch to anyone and conscientiously kept the secret; that a diplomatist and an Italian gentleman had confided to me that the matter was known, but that I had added nothing to the information they had obtained in other quarters. Cardinal Antonelli gave me the most solemn assurances that he had equally not communicated it to anyone, and he wished to keep the secret, although he had had it translated into Italian. The indiscretion must therefore have been committed by a third party.

Cardinal Antonelli is still convinced that I called at Christmas on him and made a further communication to him founded on a private letter from Your Lordship, expressing regret that the Pope had not availed himself of the offer of an asylum in Malta and that His Holiness would soon be obliged to have recourse to it. I am certain I never received any letter to that effect from Your Lordship and I have no recollection of the communication made by me at Christmas His Eminence alludes to. I am therefore at a loss to know what I can have said or done to convey this impression to His Eminence's mind. The Cardinal having exchanged the most cordial expressions of regret with me that our impressions should be at variance on these past events, we proceeded to talk on other subjects.

His Eminence expressed surprize at the statement made by Lord Palmerston in the debate of the 5th that I was attached to our Mission at Turin. I explained that I was not attached to any mission at present, for when our mission was withdrawn from Naples I had remained in Rome on special service and unattached. His Eminence appeared pleased to hear that I was not connected with Turin.

14 February. Since writing the above I have called on Prince de la Tour d'Auvergne who had been unwell. I thought he might like to know the substance of my conversation of yesterday morning with Cardinal Antonelli, but I found he had already been able himself to call on His Eminence and was acquainted with it. The Prince told me he was writing to Paris and argued against my impressions on these past events in the same manner as Cardinal Antonelli.

As the Prince's despatches will in all probability be published as communciated to Your Lordship, I leave him to recount his own impressions, and I will only observe that neither the Ambassador's arguments nor the Cardinal's recollections have shaken my faith in the first impressions produced on my mind by the circumstances I reported to Your Lordship at the time they occurred. No doubt, I am liable to be mistaken, but up to the present moment instead of undergoing any modifications those first impressions still remain convictions.

268 [F.O. 43/89B]   *Rome, 14 February 1863*

No. 25. Secret
O.R. to Earl R.

In my preceding despatch Your Lordship has seen that Cardinal Antonelli at the instigation of Prince de la Tour d'Auvergne is obliged to deny that the Pope sent for me in July last and declares that the audience was granted to me at my request, which he proves by a reference to the Pontifical Audience Register. I have also explained the circumstances which led me to think that the Pope had sent for me for a special purpose. I will now explain the circumstances which induced the Pope to send for me in July last and grant me an audience after a lapse of one year and a half.

1st. Garibaldi was in Sicily preparing to march upon Rome.
2nd. The French Government had sent six men of war to cruize before Civita Vecchia, and General de Montebello had concentrated his troops in Rome and was making great preparations to defend Civita Vecchia, while he had withdrawn his troops from the Neapolitan frontier and left the mountain passes of the Abruzzi free so that Garibaldi's army might have invaded the Campagna of Rome without meeting any obstacle or resistance. In consequence the Papal Government had been obliged to complain, because they said, if Garibaldi comes he will march through Southern Italy and collect men on his way and in the Abruzzi, and he will not attempt to land at Civita Vecchia.
3rd. These circumstances and military measures naturally reminded the Papal Government of the declarations and promises of the French Government which preceded the invasion of the Marches and Umbria by General Cialdini and the destruction of General Lamoricière's army at Castelfidardo, as well as the seige of Gaeta. They thought the French Government might be later induced to impose conditions on the Papacy for the general pacification of Italy. The policy of Monsieur Thouvenel and Marquis de Lavalette confirmed their apprehensions, and they foresaw that if those conditions should prove to be unacceptable the Pope might be compelled to declare French protection insufficient and seek asylum in some foreign country.

4. At the same moment great irritation prevailed at the Vatican against the Emperor Napoleon for having obtained the recognition of the Kingdom of Italy by Russia, Prussia and Portugal.

5. The question next arose as to where the Pope should go if he had to leave Rome. Austria, Spain and Bavaria were proposed. It was soon ascertained that Austria and Spain might be seriously embarrassed in the relations with powerful France if they received the fugitive Pope, and His Holiness was asked to think twice before he exposed his best friends to such a contingency. Würzburg in Bavaria was recommended, but how to reach it without passing through Austria, Northern Italy or France? Two other governments only remained to be appealed to in case of need, England and Turkey. The Pope could not well ask the Sultan for protection. England alone remained, England who was strong enough to meet the displeasure of Catholic France.

In the midst of this crisis it became known that I was going to London on leave of absence, for I had already taken leave of some of my friends. I was the only connecting link between the two Governments, time pressed, for once I was gone, whom could they employ to sound Her Majesty's Government without awakening suspicions? It was necessary therefore to take an immediate decision, and I was sent for.

But as matters stand now the Pope and Cardinal Antonelli cannot admit that they did so. France would never forgive them, and they must get out of their difficulty by saying that which the French Government wish them to say.

269 [P.R.O. 30/22/76]   *Rome, 16 February 1863*

Private
O.R. to Earl R.

I have just seen Cardinal Antonelli who is so charming and amiable and affectionate that one cannot be angry with him even when he tells lies. . . . He was glad you had had the discretion not to publish the Pope's conversation with me. The Pope would have been hurt, and his health was now very precarious, *this however was a secret*. He earnestly hoped the present affair would be allowed to drop and that considering the privacy of my non-official position, my despatches would not be published. He also hoped I would take his observations in a friendly spirit and not be offended by them. All this is very true, for we have no official relations with Rome, and I am here only on

sufferance after all. .... I stand quite *alone* here among powerful enemies
and my friends and well wishers belong to the oppressed.

270 [F.O. 43/89B]   *Rome, 17 February 1863*
No. 26. [Recites Telegram]
O.R. to Earl R.   Tuesday
Do not publish any further despatches of mine until you hear from me.

271 [P.R.O. 30/22/76]   *Rome, 17 February 1863*
Private
O.R. to Earl R.

The French Ambassador will not allow you to deny the truth of his
reports, so he wants to convict me of lying and he has bullied Antonelli
into taking his part. Antonelli, who cannot help himself and must agree
with the more powerful French Ambassador, overwhelms me with
civilities, shrugs his shoulders, says he knew nothing about it all, the
Pope himself told the French Ambassador, so that the French account
must be correct, and begs and entreats the matter may be allowed to
drop as soon as possible. I send you what I call a satisfactory explanation, because once it comes to this sort of downright and wholesale
lying and misrepresenting, at least you know what it means. I confess
I feel stunned by the violence of the attack as it is the first I have yet
encountered. The great object of the French Ambassador is to prove
that we took the initiative and that the Pope never thought of asking
for our protection and hospitality, since he has full confidence in, and
loves the Emperor Napoleon. The Pope who hated Thouvenel and
Lavalette, and who now has Drouyn de Lhuys in whom he has more
confidence would willingly hush up the past terrors he underwent
when Garibaldi was approaching. So little did I solicit the audience of
the Pope in July that I felt horribly bored and put out when I received
the order to go to him and would have got off if possible, for the heat
was intense and the prospect of a uniform at 12 o'clock in the day was
most unpleasant to me. The Pope himself used the words '*I sent for
you*', and his whole conversation proved it without his even saying it.
I had not been admitted to the Pope's presence for a year and a half
because at my last interview with him on the 16th January 1861 his old
sympathies for Italy had been roused and as you may possibly remember, the French Embassy had complained of the freedom of my lan-

guage to His Holiness. I am now very glad you did not publish the Pope's conversation as it would vex him horribly and make matters more disagreeable. Besides his health is beginning to fail. Antonelli simply denies on his honor ever having given your despatch to the Austrian Ambassador. This is a lie. I *know* that he gave the copy to Bach, who sent it to Metternich at Paris. Of course I never mentioned it because I know my duties. Another lie is the renewed communication I made at Christmas. Why, you know you never wrote me any such letter and I know I never made any such communication. The importance Antonelli attaches to the fact that you ordered me home by telegraph on leave of absence proves that his mind was full of what the Pope had said to me and that he was watching the result with anxious interest. Now he denies ever having known anything at all about it! Well, the priest and the Frenchman may lie till they are blue in the face, they cannot deny that the Pope spoke of English protection, and that he and his Minister accepted, and thanked me for your despatch. My position is most difficult, for all these people are lying and I must be civil and hold my own ground without simply saying to them *'You lie!'* I must say that Society show me the greatest sympathy and go out of their way to be civil to me. On the whole I think the less you publish of my despatches the better, because my public position here is really so delicate and undefined that they really have every right to complain and it becomes extremely difficult for me to steer among all parties without giving offence as I have hitherto been able to do. Of course you must publish all that is necessary for yourself. The whole affair is of no further importance to anyone but myself, as I am accused of lying, which God knows I have not done. And to the evidence brought against me by a Pope, a Cardinal and an Ambassador I have nothing to oppose but my single, simple, and isolated word of honor. I was delighted with the Debate and your defence of me, and here your speech has produced an excellent impression while it has deeply irritated the French Ambassador. Give me another year and I shall get the better of my enemies.

272 [F.O. 43/89B]   *Rome, 18 February 1863*

No. 29. Secret
O.R. to Earl R.

The publication in the French *Documents Diplomatiques* of the Pope's

conversation with Prince de la Tour d'Auvergne has been a subject of
deep annoyance to His Holiness who declares the publication of the
conversation of a Sovereign to be an unjustifiable breach of confidence
and of respect, and His Holiness loses no opportunity of saying that
since the French Ambassador not only publishes his conversations, but
does not even scruple to make him (the Pope) say that which happens
to suit the Emperor's policy of the moment, he is determined never to
speak to him when he is obliged to receive him but of 'rain and sun-
shine' (*de la pluie et du beau temps*).

If the French Government thus take upon themselves to speak for
the Papal Government, as for instance they do about reforms etc., the
independence of the Papacy will cease to exist.

273 [P.R.O. 30/22/76]   *Rome, 25 February 1863*

O.R. to Earl R.

... The Pope had another fainting fit but somehow he manages to get
well in twenty-four hours and goes out driving; his doctors think the
repeated attacks, which I suppose are epileptic, will kill him. They
have become more frequent since the death of his eldest brother. In
the event of his death you will see some obscure old Cardinal selected
immediately and things will remain under the new Pope as they are
under the present one. The French Ambassador is also always ill, and
I fancy, feels already that he is losing ground every day, for the expectation he had raised on arriving cannot possibly be realized either here
or in Paris. The reforms he announced in Paris which so completely
satisfied the Senate are moonshine, the promises and assurances he
brought from Paris to Rome will not be followed up by facts and in
the end nothing will be done for the poor Romans. Prince de la Tour
d'Auvergne and his Secretary Baron de Bode have taken great pains
to run me down in conversation with the rest of the Diplomatic Body.
They say I am a spy, a liar and an enemy of the Pope and that I ought
to be made to go away. As I am on very good terms with the whole of
the Diplomatic Body, who look upon me as a harmless and inoffensive
Agent, they have mostly taken my part and told the Frenchmen that
when they have been here a little longer and know me a little better
they will alter their present opinion. Cardinal Antonelli goes out of
his way to overwhelm me with kindness and civility, he tells all the
Dips and others that he has the greatest friendship and regard for me

and that the Pope has quite a weakness for me. This last assurance
appears to irritate the French beyond measure. The Roman Society
have been so wonderfully demonstrative in their civilities to me, that
I can only account for it by their hatred of the French, and they are
cordially hated I can assure you. The Priests are very much pleased
with your Malta despatch and with your speech about the Pope. You
had been so calumniated as a hater of the Catholic religion that they
fancied your policy was based on common hatred and nothing else.
Your speech has explained matters. The passage in your Malta despatch
which seems to have caught Cardinal Antonelli's fancy is the one where
you say that the Pope might return to Rome owing his power to the
love and respect of his subjects. When La Tour d'Auvergne blew up
Antonelli for asking for a copy of the despatch, His Eminence pointed
to that passage and said: 'Lord Russell writes from his point of view
and not from ours, but he admits that the Pope might return to Rome
when called back by his subjects, a principle we like, whilst your
Government has allowed the Piedmontese to conquer the Marches and
Umbria against the will of their inhabitants who were attached to the
Pope and who would gladly return to him if they dared.' It is very odd,
that conviction of the Pope and of Antonelli that their Government is
beloved by the inhabitants of the Holy See....

274 [F.O. 43/89B]   *Rome, 10 March 1863*

No. 31
O.R. to Earl R.

While the commission sent by the Italian Parliament to investigate the
causes of the brigandage in the Southern provinces is inspecting Sora
and the frontier of the Pontifical States, Tristani is said to have thought
it more prudent to abandon his past haunts in the province of Frosinone and to seek a safe retreat in the forests of Conca in the province
of Velletri.

If your Lordship will glance at the map of the present Pontifical
dominions I lately had the honor to send to the Foreign Office, you
will find Conca at a short distance north east from Porto d'Anzio and
Nettuno. The forests of Conca belong, I think, to the convent of San
Spirito and are said to be so vast and dense as to enable Tristani and
his men easily to defy pursuit.

Tristani, who boasts that he lately succeeded in paying a visit to his friends in Rome, declares his band to number over 300 men. They are described as now wearing the ordinary dress of the peasants of the Campagna and their French uniforms are said to have been concealed by them before leaving the province of Frosinone.

The above details have been given to me by persons living in the provinces who believe themselves to be well informed, but as these details are not believed by the French authorities, they require further investigation and confirmation.

275 [F.O. 43/89B]   *Rome, 10 March 1863*

No. 33
O.R. to Earl R.

Signor Fausti, a gentleman belonging to Cardinal Antonelli's household as *Gentiluomo* or Chamberlain to His Eminence, and also employed in the office of the Dateria, was arrested on suspicion of liberal opinions by order of Monsignor Pila, the Minister of the Interior, on 22 February last. This was done without Cardinal Antonelli's knowledge.

Monsignor Pila had called on His Eminence on the morning of 22 February but had not intimated any intention of arresting one of his servants, and the Cardinal Secretary of State considered that the Minister of the Interior had been wanting in respect towards him, and the more so as the families of Fausti and Antonelli have long been connected in friendship together. Cardinal Antonelli complained to the Pope.

The Pope considered that the Minister of the Interior could arrest whom he pleased without previous reference to the Cardinal Secretary of State and the more so as His Holiness had sanctioned the arrest of Signor Fausti, Cardinal Antonelli resigned his post. The Pope declined to accept his resignation, sent for Monsignor Pila and directed him to call on Cardinal Antonelli and apologize. Monsignor Pila did so.

Cardinal Antonelli accepted the apology but declared that he should in future expect respect and obedience from the Home Office and that when Signor Fausti's trial was over he should recommend the Pope to appoint another Minister of the Interior. Monsignor Pila complained of Cardinal Antonelli's threat to the Pope. The Pope notified to Cardinal Antonelli that he was carrying matters too far, that Monsignor Pila's apology was sufficient satisfaction and that he wished the ques-

tion to be dropped. At the same time he commanded Cardinal Antonelli to withdraw his resignation and continue to attend to the duties
of his office as heretofore.

Cardinal Antonelli obeyed, but said he could only hold his post
provisionally until Fausti's trial was over when he should return to the
subject and insist on the dismissal of the Minister of the Interior. The
Pope is displeased with Cardinal Antonelli's obstinacy, but cannot do
without him, and the Cardinal knows it. The matter has been much
discussed in Rome and has been called a ministerial crisis. There are
two opinions on the subject, one, that Cardinal Antonelli is tired of
office and thinks it would be to his advantage to retire before the Pope's
death, the other, that wishing on the contrary to continue in office and
strengthen his power, he thinks it necessary to remove some of his
colleagues whose growing influence with the Pope is inconvenient to
him.

This first attempt has failed. His chief opponents in the Ministry are
Monsignor Pila and Monsignor de Mérode. But if the Pope had accepted his resignation, Cardinal Altieri would have been his successor.

The public press has in general attached too much importance to
this crisis and has exaggerated its consequences. I am inclined to think
that Cardinal Antonelli wishes to remain in office and that he will find
no difficulty in holding his present post of Secretary of State during
the lifetime of Pius IX.

276 [P.R.O. 30/22/76]   *Rome, 11 March 1863*

Private
O.R. to Earl R.

I am very much obliged to you for your letters of Feb. 16 and March
2nd, they have been a great comfort to me. The last time I wrote to you
I fear I was under the influence of great irritation for it was the first
time I found myself suspected or accused of fibbing. The tide has
turned in my favour, and here in Rome the Diplomatic Body, the
Roman and foreign society and the Church overwhelm me with practical demonstrations of sympathy and kindness, and my position is
much pleasanter than ever before. My enemy the French Ambassador
has met with no sympathy amongst his colleagues by abusing me and
saying that you were going to recall me etc. (in short the language
later published in the Paris papers), and in fact now he has be-

come somewhat ridiculous and I hope he feels it. As to Cardinal
Antonelli, poor devil, he could not help himself, for he must do something in return for twenty thousand French soldiers who keep him
in office. I forgive and despise him, but I shall not let off La Tour
d'Auvergne so cheap and I hope to see him go as I saw Gramont
and Lavalette go.

A thousand thanks for leaving me here. I should have been very
sorry if the French had been able to say they had turned me out of
Rome! I hope and pray you will be able to put off the evil hour of
appointing me Secretary of Embassy. I don't care being thrown back
a few years in my profession, I don't ask for money or for rank, but I
do beg and pray not to be taken from a mission full of historical interest
and useful labour during a period when the Roman question is uppermost in men's minds, and for the loss of which no secretaryship of
Embassy, small mission or thousands of pounds could compensate me.
To money and promotion I infinitely prefer my present interesting and
to me useful life. I am in nobody's way, since I interfere with nobody's
promotion in the profession, and I ask for nothing but what I already
have.

So pray, my dear Uncle, leave me here as long as you possibly can!

277 [P.R.O. 30/22/111]   *16 March 1863*
Private
Earl R. to O.R.

You have done beautifully, shewn a little too much charity to Antonelli
perhaps, but I suppose his cloth justifies that forbearance. . . .

278 [P.R.O. 30/22/76]   *Rome, 24 March 1863*
Private
O.R. to Earl R.

. . . My friend the Russian Minister, Monsieur Kisseleff, wishing to
break the ice which the 'incident Odo Russell' had produced between
me and Prince de la Tour d'Auvergne, asked us both to a small dinner,
without letting us know beforehand that we were to meet and so
managed that we had to sit beside each other. The French Ambassador
was exceedingly civil and awkward, I was exceedingly civil and cold
and it all did very well and the Russian Minister was delighted at the
Peace Policy he had inaugurated.

279 [F.O. 43/89B]   *Rome, 5 April 1863*

No. 40

O.R. to Earl R.

Notwithstanding the opinion of the Pope's medical advizers that His Holiness would not be able to bear the fatigue of the ceremonies of the Holy Week, the Sovereign Pontiff has attended to all his religious duties without omission, and has this morning pronounced the Paschal Benediction *Urbi et Orbi* from St Peter's in a clear and powerful voice which was heard far and wide over the Place.

The general appearance and bearing of the Pope being at variance with the apprehensions entertained by his doctors, I have endeavoured to ascertain on what symptoms they are founded and I have learnt that the chief danger is thought to be this: the fontanel opened more than a year ago in the Pope's leg to facilitate the discharge of matter threatens occasionally to close so that the erysipelas from which he suffers might suddenly attack the vital organs of the body and a most dangerous complication ensue. The syncopes are becoming more frequent and are sometimes of several hours duration and they are followed by a feeling of extreme weakness and loss of memory. In these and many other symptoms the Pope's physicians think they recognize an approaching dissolution of the system.

Be that as it may, the secret activity of the College of Cardinals indicates that they accept the opinion of the Pope's physicians and are preparing for the eventuality of a Conclave. Their conferences are of course enveloped in mystery and as I had the honor to inform Your Lordship in my despatch No. 30, it is believed that they have agreed to elect an aged Cardinal whose past opinions will ensure a continuance of the present policy of Pius IX and give them time to see what turn affairs may take in Italy, before they resign themselves to the loss of the Temporal Dominion of the Church. . . .

280 [P.R.O. 30/22/76]   *Rome, 22 April 1863*

Private

O.R. to Earl R.

. . . The growing influence of Mérode, the declining power of Antonelli, the false position of France, the increasing strength of United Italy, the neutrality of Austria, the follies of the Bourbons, and the illness of the Pope are undoubtedly producing more distinct parties in the Church, and those parties may sooner or later exercise some influence on the solution of the Roman question. I am therefore making myself gradually acquainted with the leading Cardinals, who since your Malta despatch have much greater confidence in the English Government than in the Emperor Napoleon and Monsieur Drouyn de Lhuys, and seem anxious to be civil to me, and I think I shall soon be able to give you some curious accounts of the changes I see. So long as the Sacred College fancied the Emperor Napoleon might impose some sort of solution or arrangement on the Pope they kept very quiet, but now that they see that the only result of the Emperor's policy is to keep Antonelli in office, and that the only result of Antonelli's policy is to lay by money for himself and his family, they are disappointed and jealous and they whisper to each other 'This cannot be allowed to last.'

I saw Antonelli this morning. He looked bilious and humble. . . .

281 [F.O. 519/205]   *Rome, 22 April 1863*

O.R. to Earl Cowley

. . . Madame de Montebello returns to Paris next Sunday. Strange to say that civil and pretty and pleasant as she is, she has had no success with the Romans who find her affected and bigoted, and even her own party, the Ultramontane, reactionary and pontifically pious Borgheses, Salviatis and Aldobrandinis etc. etc. complain that she shows her beautiful shoulders more than is necessary and want the Pope to order her to wear higher gowns, which she won't do.

282 [F.O. 43/89B]   *Rome, 17 May 1863*

No. 49
O.R. to Earl R.

I see by the 'Parliamentary Intelligence' of the *Times* newspaper of 9th inst. that the accuracy of my reports respecting brigandage has been called in question and General de Montebello accused of a want of good breeding. In justice to the gallant officer who commands the French forces in Rome I must beg leave to add my testimony to that of Lord Palmerston and declare that General de Montebello's character combines the greatest courtesy with the highest sense of honor.

That the General should have been surprized and annoyed at the intelligence I was supposed to have sent to the Foreign Office was natural enough, since he derived his first knowledge of it from the French Yellow Book, in which the sense of my despatch had been somewhat distorted. I was myself as much surprized as the General could be at the inaccuracy of the information which that official Yellow Book contained. But that was not a reason for uncivil words on either side, and far from shewing any want of courtesy the General discussed the matter with me with that perfect good breeding which is peculiar to him, and gave me every assistance in his power by rectifying and adding to the information I had received, as may be seen by my published despatch of 14 January last. [Various facts and figures given.]

I feel convinced that if Your Lordship will cause an enquiry to be made at Paris the French Minister of War could confirm through his official reports received from Rome the facts I have brought forward, namely: that a committee for the enlistment of brigands exists in Rome, that Tristani's band now amounts to 300 and no longer to 60 men as before, and that the use of old French uniforms by them was already known and reported by General Count de Goyon a year ago.

[*The arrest of Tristani by the French authorities in Rome was reported by O.R. in a telegram in June.*]

283 [F.O. 519/205]   *Rome, 18 May 1863*

O.R. to Earl Cowley

I enclose for your information copy of a letter I have written to Sir George Bowyer to put a stop to his calumnies of General de Montebello, who has always been most civil and kind to me.

We had some warm discussions, but I never knew him to be wanting in civility or good breeding towards me and I feel it my duty to take his part against Sir George Bowyer.

The Enclosure

Dear Sir George Bowyer,

You are reported in the 'Times' of May 9th to have given an account of a conversation between myself and General de Montebello which is incorrect. General de Montebello's character combines

the greatest courtesy with the highest sense of honour. I feel assured
that you will take the earliest opportunity of publickly contradicting
your statement on receiving intelligence that you have been misinformed. General de Montebello is not at present in Rome.

Believe etc.   Odo Russell

284 [P.R.O. 30/22/76]   *Rome, 19 May 1863*

Private
O.R. to Earl R.

You are quite right about the crisis at the Vatican. It is all over and
Antonelli, Mérode, Pila and Sagretti notwithstanding their mutual
hatred and abuse of each other to the Pope, all remain at their respective
places like the Happy Family, but each intending to destroy the other
by calumny at the very first occasion. The Pope has had his own way
and has been to the Convents of Casamare, Trisulti etc. to bless the
monks who have so successfully protected the brigands against their
enemies. Mérode pushed him to go there, but Antonelli feared the bad
effect it might have on prejudiced minds and did his best to prevent it.
However the whole affair will probably simply be denied by the
French. My views on humanity are undergoing considerable changes
since I have learnt by experience to what extent Frenchmen and priests
can lie. When you compare the reality of things in Rome with their
account of them you cannot but look forward to a second deluge. I
have endeavoured to be fair, just and truthful. I have carefully avoided
exaggeration and abuse, and yet the French Government, the correspondents of ecclesiastical newspapers and Sir George Bowyer want to
turn me out of my humble, unofficial, unaccredited position! Why?
Because I will not approve of this rotten administration and admit the
necessity of imposing it by force on a suffering, bleeding, prostrate
nation. I have quite got over the first unpleasant sensation of public
abuse and at present I rather enjoy it than not. Nevertheless I thought
it as well to check my friend Bowyer and I have written him a short
note requesting him to contradict his anecdote about Montebello and
myself. Lord Palmerston's generous defence of me I have read with
deep emotion.[1] Lord Palmerston's last Italian speech is in everyone's
heart and mouth at present. It is a curious fact, but it appears that the

[1] *Hansard*[1], 12 May.

19. Joseph Severn, consul. Painting by Mary Severn

20a. Marquis de Lavalette

20b. Comte de Sartiges

National Committee who have single copies printed off on very thin paper of good and encouraging news such as Lord Palmerston's speech, manage to smuggle them into the prisons by bribing the turn-keys, the bakers and the Capucins, so as to give comfort to the poor political prisoners. I have lately spoken to some of the prisoners who have been released and they told me in confidence that the scraps of news from a better world were the only thing that kept them from going mad. My friend the liberal Cardinal, who does not wish to be named, again assures me that the enlistments for the reaction are carried on with fresh vigor in Rome, and asked me to tell you so and to warn the Government at Turin. I told His Eminence that I would not take any notice of his news until he could furnish me with proofs and documentary evidence of his assertions. He said he would try to do so. Everyone here and more especially everyone in the provinces knows the encouragement given to the enlistment of men for King Francesco's bands. If I could give up my authorities, such as govern-ment *employés*, railway directors, liberal Monsignores, men employed in the reaction, bankers who pay the officers, and even the officers themselves who like to talk German with me, even French officers employed on the frontier, *I could prove* many curious things, but my informants would be sacrificed and become victims of the Church and of her Eldest Son. Patience. I'll get the better of my enemies yet! ...

285 [P.R.O. 30/22/76]   *Rome, 16 June 1863*

Private
O.R. to Earl R.

... Monsignor de Mérode and his party are all activity and bustle, arresting everybody they can and filling the prisons to the Pope's infinite pleasure and satisfaction. The two political prisoners Fausti and Venanzi have been condemned to twenty years hard labour each, but further accusations are now to be brought against them so as to con-demn them to hard labour for life. The public at large believe them to be innocent, but no one dares to speak openly about it for fear of being thrown into prison *for opposition to the government.* ...

The odd thing is that Cardinal Antonelli still believes in the inno-cence of Fausti, but cannot interfere and does not interfere because the Mérode party, who obtained the Pope's sanction for the arrest of Fausti is at present too strong for him, and he fears their influence with

L

the Pope if he said or did anything in favor of his old friend Fausti. In fact he allows the innocent man to be condemned to save his own skin. A more corrupt state of things than now exists in Rome cannot well be imagined. . . .

286   [P.R.O. 30/22/76]   *L'Ariccia, 10 July 1863*
Private
O.R. to Earl R.
'*Egressum magna me accepit Aricia Roma Hospitio modico.*'
My Hospitio modico is a lovely Casino belonging to Prince Chigi with a view over the Alban hills, the Campagna and the Mediterranean, a dark wood at the back, the lake of Albano to the right and the lake of Nemi to the left. Sea breezes and cool nights. I enjoy my existence, walk, sleep, read, and feel uncommonly happy. My neighbours are the Austrian Ambassador, the Brazilian Minister, the Spanish Chargé d'Affaires and the Central American Consul General, Padre Curci and two Cardinals, d'Andrea and Villefort, a third, De Pietro, is expected.
    Yesterday I took a drive with the Austrian Ambassador after an early dinner with him. We compared notes and found we had nothing to write about. . . .

287   [F.O. 519/205]   *Rome, 14 July 1863*
O.R. to Earl Cowley
General Montebello is acting with great energy and arresting all the Reactionists and Brigands he can lay hands on, which proves to me how easily it might have been done a year ago. Where there's a will there's a way.
    I took a walk the other day in the Villa Borghese with Montebello and Kisseleff and found the former most amusing and pleasant. . . .
    The change which has come over the French in their Brigandage policy is a matter of surprize to everyone. I hope it may continue.
    Poor Latour d'Auvergne has been horribly ill with spasms in the bowels. He has gone to France for his health. He has certainly been most unlucky in Rome. The reforms he announced in his Yellow Book have remained a dead letter and the priests have taken a dislike to him because he has not done enough for them. They say they prefer an enemy like Lavalette to a friend like Latour d'Auvergne. So much for the ingratitude of the Church! . . .

288 [F.O. 43/89B]   *Rome, 11 December 1863*
No. 68. Confidential
O.R. to Earl R.

I called this morning on the Cardinal Secretary of State who received
me with the greatest cordiality and was pleased to express his satisfaction at my return to Rome. After some general conversation His
Eminence asked me whether I had nothing to tell him about the
Congress. . . .

I enquired how the Papal Government, as a conservative power,
could take part in a Congress that would in all probability, if it ever
met, confirm many important changes in Europe. Cardinal Antonelli
replied that I was not the first who had expressed surprize at the Pope's
acceptance of the proposed Congress, but that when I knew the principles on which His Holiness's acceptance was based I would at once
perceive that the Papal Government had not swerved from the conservative principles that animated them. The Pope had by his letter
promised his moral support only to a Congress for the re-establishment
of justice and legality in Europe and of those rights which had been
violated by the Revolution. Based on those principles a Congress
would be a convenient and desirable mode of settling the affairs of
Europe and would meet with the full moral support of His Holiness's
Government, but unless those principles were distinctly accepted by
the powers of Europe before the meeting of their plenipotentiaries in
Paris, the Congress would lead to no good.

289 [P.R.O. 30/22/76]   *Rome, 29 December 1863*
O.R. to Earl R.

Many happy new years to you and yours and health and prosperity to
enjoy them as much as I enjoy my happy existence in the Eternal City.
I cannot say more, for I doubt whether anybody enjoys life more than
I do, and have done, in Rome.

My visit to Turin interested me very much. I learnt much that was
new to me from Elliot,[1] and I felt well pleased with the safe and sound
progress, I fancy, Italy is making. My impressions were confirmed by
a short stay at Genoa, Leghorn and Pisa and amidst the immense
difficulties which the regeneration of Italy must call forth I only wondered I could find none of a really dangerous and threatening nature.

[1] Henry Elliot had succeeded Hudson at Turin on 12 September 1863.

In Rome I found things unchanged, the French still imposing by force of arms a rotten government on a hostile and suffering population and a Pope organizing an army wherewith to shoot his subjects, and invoking the interference of Providence to assist in the work of destruction. And Providence has at last interfered in an indirect manner the Pope thinks, by dictating your refusal of the Congress. He and Cardinal Antonelli argue thus: 'If England stands up for the Treaties of 1815 and declines to attend a Congress that might confirm the Unity of Italy, it is a clear proof that England does not intend Italy to unite. Why? Because England is afraid to lose Malta and anxious to acquire Sicily. England has offended France, a war is inevitable, in the long run England will beat France and then, as in the days of Pius VII re-establish Pius IX and occupy the Castle of St Angelo!' Never do I recollect Cardinal Antonelli more devoted and affectionate to me than he is now. He fondly compares your despatch refusing to attend the Congress to the Pope's letter dictating the conditions of his acceptance to the Emperor. 'Of all the letters respecting Congress sent to Paris,' His Eminence says, 'there are but two equal in straightforwardness, clearness, sincerity and similarity of purpose, the Pope's and Lord Russell's, all the others are timid and obscure. Providence has permitted that we should agree about the Congress, who knows whether Providence may not some day permit that we should agree about Italy?' The Pope's letter to the Emperor has been erroneously described as accepting the Congress, whilst in reality his conditions are tantamount to a refusal, a fact which the French newspapers have carefully concealed. The Pope says clearly in his letter: 'I will give my moral support to your Congress if you will give me back what I have lost, and I won't if you don't, but I cannot doubt that you will, for you have often promised me that you would.' The letter is said to have been composed by the Pope himself and very proud he is of his composition. My old friend Sartiges, the new French Ambassador, is very civil to me. He has taken up a conciliatory position and has made peace between General Montebello and Monsignor de Mérode, but how long will it last?

Sartiges does not appear to have any new instructions, beyond inviting the Pope to go to Paris. '*Je veux faire le bien en détail*,' he says, but up to the present day he has done nothing. General Montebello is also very civil to me. He is popular with the army but detested at the Vatican for his late anti-brigandage policy. Rome is full of *forestieri* who spend money, so the population is quiet enough, but all classes

from the Vatican to the Piazza Montanara are heartily tired of the
French occupation. The *Osservatore Romano* says in a leading article
that when you heard that the French Emperor had decided that the Pope
was to preside over the Congress: '*Lord Russell è rimasto spaventato!*'

[*Count Sartiges had been French Minister in Washington in 1857 when
O.R. was there. Sartiges, Arthur Russell recounts, one day expounding
to O.R. in Rome the policy of his Master and the impossibility of withdrawing the French army's protection, said:* 'L'Église Catholique durera
toujours, car elle est fondée sur l'Absurde – vous n'allez pas répéter,
mon cher, ce qui vient de m'échapper la!']

290 [F.O. 43/91A]   *Rome, 7 January 1864*
No. 5. Secret
O.R. to Earl R.

Some days since the French Ambassador, Count de Sartiges, told
Cardinal Antonelli that he did not intend to renew personally the
advice given by his predecessors to the ex-King of Naples, although he
thought it would be advantageous both to His Majesty and to the Pope
if King Francis II could be induced to leave Rome. 'Notwithstanding
this opinion,' Monsieur de Sartiges added playfully (*scherzando*) 'I need
not assure Your Eminence that I do not intend to send the King over
the frontier escorted by French gendarmes.'

'Nor indeed by Pontifical gendarmes,' the Cardinal replied angrily.
Count de Sartiges paid no attention to this answer and went on to say
that having come from Turin he knew how much the Italian Government wished King Francis to leave Rome, and he even thought they
could be induced to make certain concessions to the Papal Government
to obtain that end. For instance, if the King really left Rome, the Turin
cabinet might in return accept the bishops lately appointed by the Pope
to the vacant sees in Italy. Cardinal Antonelli having explained that he
could not listen to such propositions, the question was allowed to
drop. . . .

291 [F.O. 43/91A]   *Rome, 15 January 1864*
No. 8. Secret
O.R. to Earl R.

I had the honor to be received this morning by the Pope at a private audience. His Holiness welcomed me with even more than his usual benevolent kindness. I told the Sovereign Pontiff that I had had the honor of being admitted to the presence of Her Majesty the Queen before leaving England and that Her Majesty had been pleased to enquire after His Holiness's health with interest. I also added that their Royal Highnesses the Prince of Wales and the Princess Royal had directed me to repeat their thanks to His Holiness for his reception of them on the occasion of their late visit to Rome, and at the request of His Royal Highness the Prince of Wales, I recounted that I had seen at Marlborough House the mosaic picture of St George and the Dragon which His Holiness had given to the Prince in 1859.

The Pope seemed much gratified and said that he deeply venerated the high public and private virtues of Her Majesty the Queen, and that no Sovereign in the world inspired him with more admiration, sympathy and respect, and that he felt sure Her Majesty understood his position and pitied his misfortunes more, he added with a smile, than Her Majesty's Ministers, who would willingly see him deprived of his temporal power. He was an old man, but in the whole course of his long life he had never been more favorably impressed by anyone than by Her Royal Highness the Crown Princess of Prussia. He dwelt a long time on the impressions Her Royal Highness had left on his mind, and then speaking of the Prince of Wales said that although His Royal Highness was still very young, his animated conversation, his frank and amiable manners, gave many proofs of innate sterling qualities. The Prince had won his heart and he would be glad to see him with the Princess of Wales in Rome again. His Holiness then questioned me a good deal about Her Royal Highness the Princess of Wales and expressed the pleasure he had felt at the birth of the young Prince on 8th inst. . . .

I next told His Holiness that I had been directed by Lord Palmerston to say that His Lordship had been gratified by the messages sent to him by His Holiness through Mr William Cowper last autumn, and that he regretted he had never had an opportunity of becoming personally acquainted with His Holiness. 'I too regret it,' the Pope exclaimed with great animation, 'and I should like to see Lord Palmerston sitting in that chair before me to have a discussion on Italian affairs with him, although I well know we could never agree. But I see no hope of it, for while he is in office he cannot but live in England, and when he is out of office he will probably not come to Rome. I liked Mr William

Cowper, 'è un vero gentleman', and I hope he will not turn against us as Lord Granville did in 1859. But you Englishmen are so apt to believe the revolutionary party rather than ourselves.

'I do not think I could discuss with Lord Russell, he is too much of a Protestant for me, but I could with Lord Palmerston. He has done several things for us Catholics that have pleased me, and I was again lately gratified by the appointment of Mr Justice Shee. My position is a very simple one, and easy to understand. I represent moral order and legitimate right in the world. I am bound by my engagements and I cannot act in two different ways. As to Italy, I am an Italian at heart and love my country, but I cannot countenance the atrocities that have been committed in the name of unity. And now see the state of poor Italy. A financial crisis is at hand, the advanced party preparing to attack Austria in the north, while the south cannot even be pacified. And in the midst of all this confusion Italy has not even a man of talent at Turin able to master the situation. . . .

'The example of Italy will be the ruin of the smaller Princes of Germany,' the Pope continued, 'and I think very ill of the condition of that country. Each of the smaller Sovereigns hopes to aggrandise his Kingdom at the expense of his neighbour and all will be swept away like the Grand Dukes of Tuscany, Modena and Parma were in Italy. The King of Bavaria was here and I did what I could to convince him that he was running great risks but he could not see it. His idea is that the House of Wittelsbach should be as powerful as the Houses of Hapsburg and of Hohenzollern, and if he had his own way he would begin by annexing Baden and Würtemberg to Bavaria. I daresay my protector in Paris is not at all displeased at the state of Germany, but I hear that he did not like Lord Russell's answer about his Congress. I thought that despatch quite unanswerable and that is why it gave offence. A quarrel between your Government and my protector might be a good thing for me. Did Lord Russell write that answer himself? You saw my answer, I wrote it myself too and I consider it to be quite unanswerable as Lord Russell's. In fact, of all the answers returned to the Emperor's invitation to a Congress, Lord Russell's and mine were the only two clear straightforward and unmistakeable answers, each from a different point of view, but both tending to the same end. I said I would go to the Congress, but only if it were previously understood that Legitimate Right should be the basis of negotiation. A limited Congress has since been proposed, but I said I would only join it if all the Catholic Powers were represented, and I do not expect it can succeed after Lord Russell's despatch. There is a very bad newspaper published at Turin, called the *Fischietto*, but bad as it is the caricatures in it amuse me and the other day I saw a picture in it that made me laugh. The Emperor Napoleon is represented surrounded by the representatives of the different nations he has invited to the Congress, and the Englishman holds a box in his hand out of which springs a little devil, who is doing so to the Emperor Napoleon.'

Here the Pope placed one of his thumbs on his nose and spread out his fingers like a fan, and then added the thumb of the other hand equally spread out, at the end of the little finger of the former hand, and laughed most heartily for a long time. His Holiness went on to relate various anecdotes and question me about things and people and seemed unusually cheerful. His Holiness also questioned me about Your Lordship's family and seemed much interested, when, among other facts I told him that one of Your Lordship's ancestors, Sir John Russell, had been sent to Rome by Cardinal Wolsey on a mission to Clement VII in the year 1527 to bring His Holiness the sum of 30,000 ducats.

'Lord Russell's ancestors were good Catholics in those days,' the Pope said, 'but since then the family has been enriched by confiscated church property, as I have been told. The Piedmontese are confiscating all our church property now, but they will not know how to keep it as your English families have done. All will return to the church in the course of time.'

After a good deal of conversation the Pope said he hoped I was going to remain in Rome and then dismissed me with the following characteristic words: '*Viva il nostro Odo Russell, io vi benedico!*'

292 [P.R.O. 30/22/77]   *Rome, 16 February 1864*

Private
O.R. to Earl R.

All parties in Rome seem to have accepted their relative positions for the present, positions imposed upon them by the force of events. The Pope and his friends await the interference of Providence to save them from their own blunders and piously pray for the destruction of their opponents. The National party bow their heads in silence before the will of the Emperor Napoleon and his fifteen thousand bayonets in Rome. General de Montebello abuses the Pontifical Government for their inept ingratitude, and the National party for their Italian sympathies. Count de Sartiges does nothing but laugh at everybody and everything like an old Voltairian of bygone days. He tells me he wishes to serve for his pension in peace, and then be made a Senator '*à cause des 30,000 francs qui me seront utiles à Paris*'. He lives on the best possible terms with General de Montebello and both have made peace with Monsignor de Mérode. The Pope is in excellent health and boisterous spirits. He never was gayer or happier than he is at present, and the refusal of the French Chamber to discuss the Roman question has greatly contributed towards this happy state of things. Roman society however is torn asunder by party feelings. The *Italianissimi* or *bianchi* won't attend the Carnival and won't dance, whilst the *Papalini* or *neri* dance frantically to show their devotion to the Pope because His Holiness told some old princesses that he wished the faithful to be gay and happy. In consequence we saw this winter at the balls given by the pious *Papalini* the oldest dowagers attempting to be frolicsome, and old Princess Borghese, who has scarcely been able to walk for the last half century, hobbled through a quadrille with Field Marshal Duke Saldanha who had not danced since the Congress of Vienna, and all this in the name of religion! The Cardinal Vicar complains bitterly of the Neapolitan emigration, because he says, they ruin the morals of Rome and seduce the young Romans by their bad example. The poor young Queen of Naples and her pretty sister the Countess of Trani have taken a deep horror and disgust to their husbands and have fled to Albano where they live together attended by Bavarian servants, while their gay husbands and their followers indulge their low tastes in Rome. I think Montebello, who has really acted with great energy since the publication of your despatches on brigandage last year, has succeeded in putting a stop to the organization of brigandage in Rome. He tells me he was obliged to act in a most arbitrary manner to lay hands on and arrest and banish the Spaniards and foreigners who were enlisting and organizing bands, and that he could get no support from the Pontifical authorities, but that now he has completely crushed the Bourbon Committee and made himself odious to the *Papalini* in so doing. Those who declared that I had overstated the progress of brigandage last year, are furious to see Montebello go far beyond what I had recommended by way of suppressing it, this year, after having himself doubted the accuracy of my reports. The confirmation of my statements, the grand diplomatic *fiasco* of Latour d'Auvergne at Rome after having vowed that I should leave Rome before him, the civilities of the Pope and Cardinal Antonelli, and the perfect independence I enjoy toward all parties, have made my humble position in Rome even better than it was before. You call La tour d'Auvergne *'my friend and enemy'* in your last letter. He is, as I told you a most agreeable man, and universally popular for his charming manners in the transaction of business. Indeed I have found him to be equally popular at Rome as at Turin with all those who knew him, and I sometimes suspect he is like the Traveller in the fable, whom the Satyr objected to because he blew on his soup to cool it, and on his fingers to warm them. Last year, while writing against me and talking to his colleagues against me, he called four times at my house, asked me to dinner and professed feelings of friendship which I was at a loss to account for, until the Yellow Book was published. I like Sartiges and Montebello very much because they are so straightforward and honest in their dealings. There is no diplomatic nonsense about them, they admit and invite discussion and hold their own ground with perfect freedom. The most interesting piece of news I can communicate to you, is the expected visit of the Archduke Maximilian who is coming to Rome to obtain the Pope's blessing before starting for Mexico and at the same time to solicit certain concessions with respect to Church property in Mexico, part of which he wants to have the enjoyment and revenue of. The Pope will give the new Emperor the blessing, but not the money, my Spanish colleague informs me.

293 [F.O. 43/91A]   *Rome, 5 March 1864*

No. 17
O.R. to Earl R.

Several foul murders and many robberies have been lately committed in the streets of Rome, which the Pontifical party attribute to the Piedmontese, and which the National party attribute to the Neapolitan Reactionists, but which I believe are simply to be attributed to the desire of a set of ruffians to obtain money. The Roman police are so intent on the pursuit of dangerous political characters that they find little time to attend to thieves and assassins, and although many persons have been imprisoned on suspicion, the real perpetrators of these crimes have as yet neither been arrested nor even traced. The alarm which this state of things, the insecurity of the streets and the inefficacy of the police, has produced on the Romans has been described by the National Committee in a letter to General Count de Montebello of which I enclose a copy. General de Montebello who has been most energetic and successful in the suppression of brigandage on the frontier since last August has no power to interfere with the police regulations of the city of Rome, and unhappily considerable jealousy has lately existed between the French and Pontifical authorities. So much so that on the evenings of last 3 March, French and Pontifical soldiers actually took to fighting on the Forum, the Piazza Barberini and the Piazza di Trevi, and some 6 or 7 men were wounded on both sides. But thanks to the prompt and conciliatory measures taken by the General and by Monsignor de Mérode, these disturbances are not likely to have any further consequences. . . .

294 [P.R.O. 30/22/77]   *Rome, 27 April 1864*

Private
O.R. to Earl R.

Last night I had a good deal of conversation with General de Montebello on Roman affairs. He spoke most sensibly and showed that all his past illusions had vanished with respect to the priests. But like all Frenchmen I have ever known, he advocated the division of Italy into three separate Kingdoms as the only possible solution to the Italian question. Sartiges has held the same language to me, to Baron Bach and to Cardinal Antonelli in private conversation, and I have not found a Frenchman in office yet who has not spoken to me in that sense.

Garibaldi's reception has offended everybody in Rome, but his friends in the lower classes, and they don't like his visit to Mazzini whom they really dislike and fear. The moderate majority in Italy were glad Garibaldi had been shelved at Aspromonte, and they now fear that after his glorious reception in England, he may get up another expedition and disturb the quiet, which Italy needs and at present enjoys.

[*Garibaldi had been spending April in England where he had been received with the greatest enthusiasm.*]

295 [P.R.O. 30/22/77]   *Rome, 11 May 1864*

Private
O.R. to Earl R.

I scarcely know how to thank you for your very kind letter. The
manner in which you consult my wishes gratifies me even more than
the offer itself of a post I have often longed for in former years. But all
things well considered I prefer remaining in Rome as long as you will
allow me to do so.

1st. Because I am so happy here, so well occupied and so much interested in Roman affairs that I should be a fool to give up positive happiness for experimental happiness!

2nd. Because there is reason to expect an interesting crisis in this great
question if the Pope's doctors are correct in their forebodings, and if
the poor old man is to die I should be very sorry not to be present at
the events which will attend a Conclave.

3rd. Besides all the happiness I enjoy here I am within easy reach of
London, and should be sorry to give up so great an advantage at
present for my mother's sake. I cheerfully leave the pleasures of promotion to my colleagues in exchange for the perfect happiness I enjoy in
Rome.

[*Endorsed:* declining secretaryship at Constantinople.]

296 [P.R.O. 30/22/77]   *Rome, 24 May 1864*

Private
O.R. to Earl R.

The Pope has been very ill again with erysipelas, but has so far
recovered that he can go out. He is weak and irritable and his doctors
persist in thinking he cannot last many months. The Cardinals are
actively intriguing amongst each other so as to be prepared, and sim-
plify the work of the Conclave. . . . The most stringent measures will be
taken to prevent a popular rising, an invasion from Italy, a plebiscite
or any expression of public opinion. Nevertheless there will be a row,
for the impatience of the people for the Pope's death is becoming
feverish and the National Party whisper amongst each other that blood
must flow. To prevent a conflict the French Government favors the
plan of some of the Cardinals which is to elect the new Pope with a
Conclave on the death bed of Pius IX, *presente cadavere* as they call it,

and it appears that a secret Papal Chirograph would enable them to do so legally. None of the Catholic Powers would raise an objection to this mode of election for the sake of avoiding ecclesiastical scandal in the Church. It is asserted that the public will learn the name of the new Pope before they know that Pio Nono is dead. . . .

297 [P.R.O. 30/22/77]   *Rome, 20 July 1864*

Private
O.R. to Earl R.

. . . The Emperor Napoleon is in great favour with the Pope just at present, first, because he has ousted the infidel Renan, and second, because he has promised the Nuncio, Monsignor Chigi, to appoint a Commission for the revision of the Concordat of 1802 according to the often expressed wish of Pius IX. Through this concession the Vatican hopes to get a wedge into the liberties of the Gallican Church and gradually upset them altogether. France has become so Ultramontane that they won't care for the loss of those liberties they were once so proud of. Meanwhile the Eldest Son of the Church is obtaining all the blessings of the Holy Father; the Apostolic Son, Francis Joseph, Emperor of Austria, is getting the curses. This bad and disobedient son is neglecting to enforce the stipulations of the Austrian concordat. It has become a dead letter and the Plenipotentiary who is here to revise it, asks for more concessions and liberties than Rome will ever give. Then again the Emperor Francis Joseph, who said he was unable to fight for the Pope against his oppressors in 1860, flew to the rescue of oppressed German Nationality and fought the Danes, instead of flying to the rescue of Romagna, Tuscany and Naples oppressed by the Piedmontese. All this and the anti-ultramontane feelings of the German Catholic clergy in general, have made the heart of Pio Nono incline gradually more towards France and his Eldest Son at Paris. His Holiness has left for the country and is enjoying the cool breezes on the Alban hills at Castel Gandolfo. Cardinal Antonelli has accompanied him, and then proceeds to the Quirinal for change of air in a day or two. The Cardinal seems to believe in the Holy Alliance and cannot conceal his joy at it, much to the vexation of the French Ambassador. The hot pleasant days have set in and everybody who can has fled to the country so that business of every kind has come to an end and all parties unite for the moment in *dolce far niente*. . . .

298 [F.O. 43/91B]   *L'Ariccia near Rome, 30 July 1864*

No. 59. Confidential
O.R. to Earl R.

I had the honour to be received at a private audience by the Pope this morning at his summer residence, Castel Gandolfo. I was gratified both by the great improvement I noticed in the Pope's health and by the kind, cheerful and benevolent reception the Holy Father deigned to grant me.

The audience was long and His Holiness was pleased to touch on an innumerable variety of subjects, so that I will merely give Your Lordship the general results of his remarks on subjects of public interest. Talking of Russia and Poland, the Pope strongly condemned both the religious persecutions of the Emperor and the revolutionary spirit of many of the Poles, tainted, he feared, by 'Mazzinianism'. Entire liberty for the church of Rome was, he thought, the best if not the only means of restoring peace and happiness to Poland.

With regard to Germany and Austria, His Holiness seemed to fear a general revolution as a natural consequence of the constitutional liberties conceded to the people by timid and imprudent sovereigns, and he deplored and condemned the philosophic tendencies of the Roman Catholic clergy in Germany.

Of the increasing Catholic spirit in France the Pope spoke in laudatory and grateful terms. He saw a similar spirit growing in England among the faithful and although it might take more than a century, he felt confident that England would ultimately return to his flock.

Turning to America the Pope expressed his deep regret that he could do nothing towards the re-establishment of peace between the Federals and the Confederates. He had written to both Presidents Lincoln and Davis, but without success. At the same time he would not conceal from me that all his sympathies were with the Southern Confederacy and he wished them all success. There were, His Holiness added, far more conversions to Catholicism in the South than in the North.

The Pope desired me most particularly to tell Your Lordship that the story circulated in the newspapers respecting two Monsignori sent by him to influence the vote of the Roman Catholic members of Parliament in the Schleswig-Holstein question was utterly unfounded and an invention from beginning to end. He had never and would never interfere in such matters and Monsignori Talbot and Howard had gone to England for private business only.

The Pope again expressed his deep-felt sympathy for Her Majesty the Queen, the Princess Royal and the Prince of Wales, and repeated his hope to see the Princess of Wales in Rome before he died.

299 [P.R.O. 30/22/77]   *Turin, 29 October 1864*
Private
O.R. to Earl R.

The sea was so stormy at Folkestone that the steamer could not get out of the harbour, so I tried Dover and got across the Channel, but do not ask me how!!! On Mount Cenis I found so much snow that I slept at Lanslebourg and crossed the Alps in a snowstorm with the help of horses, mules and men the following day. Here I am at last at Turin, but Elliot is still at Belgirate and I cannot hope to see him before Monday or Tuesday next, when he leaves the country altogether and settles down at Turin for the winter.

I have seen a great number of people of all kinds and colours, who, while they all complain of the manner in which the Convention of 15 Sept. was made, inform me that it has been perfectly understood by the nation at large and that it will be accepted by a very large majority in both Houses of Parliament next week, and that the people of Italy have perfectly understood that it must be carried out to the letter, so that France may have no subject of complaint and that the Emperor Napoleon may recall his troops from Rome in peace and quiet. This to my mind is a great fact and gives me immense pleasure as it will ensure the complete success of Italy as a nation.

I shall stay here to attend the debates for a week or ten days.

[*By the Franco-Italian convention of 15 Sept. Italy undertook to protect the then Papal frontier from external attack, France to evacuate the States of the Church within two years. The Italian capital would be moved to Florence.*]

300 [F.O. 43/91B]   *Rome, 7 November 1864*
No. 66
O.R. to Earl R.

Count de Sartiges, the French Ambassador, informs me that after the first painful surprize caused by the sudden communication to the Vatican of the Franco-Italian convention of 15 September, an encouraging reaction has set in, which leads him to hope that the Papal Government will gradually submit to the stipulations of that convention without, however, accepting them openly.

His Excellency sees every hope of obtaining certain concessions from the Papal authorities which will tend to render the attitude of the Pontifical and Italian Governments less hostile, such as the surrender of prisoners, late subjects of the Pope and now subjects of the King of Italy, who had been detained in Rome, as well as the appointment of plenipotentiaries to treat of the regulation and settlement of ecclesiastical affairs in the Italian provinces.

The mediation of the Imperial Government between the hostile parties which His Excellency has been instructed to offer, will facilitate the settlement of many indispensable measures before the final evacuation of Rome by the French troops and although the Papal Government still hesitate to accept the proffered hand of France, the Ambassador foresees that they will allow matters to be settled for them, which they will not consent to settle for themselves.

His Excellency frequently observes that the convention cannot be considered a settlement of the Roman question; it merely puts a term to the French occupation of Rome. The settlement of the Roman question in all its bearings will still be left to the consideration of the Catholic world. Both Count de Sartiges and General de Montebello constantly remind the Papal authorities that days are passing and time is fleeting and that they had better not lose the two years of Foreign Protectorate granted to them by the convention. But the Papal authorities still listen and do not respond to the friendly warning of their protectors.

Notwithstanding, Monsieur de Sartiges perceives symptoms of a favorable change within the last few days and thinks that his unremitting efforts to conciliate and persuade the Pope to let the Emperor treat in his name with the King of Italy may yet be crowned with success. Monsieur de Sartiges deserves the highest credit for the ability and forebearance with which he is carrying out his difficult and painful instructions from Paris.

301 [F.O. 43/91B]   *Rome, 8 November 1864*

No. 67. Confidential
O.R. to Earl R.

I called this morning on the Cardinal Secretary of State, who received me with the utmost kindness, and in reply to his enquiries I told His Eminence that the Franco-Italian Convention had met with the approval of Her Majesty's Government who saw therein a step towards the settlement of the important questions which agitate Italy and the Holy See, and who also perceived many circumstances which combined to render Florence eligible as the Capital of Italy.

In passing through Turin I had observed that the Government and the representatives of the people of Italy fully understood and acknowledged the value of the Convention and I foresaw that it would be carried by a large majority in the Italian Parliament. Cardinal Antonelli said that the transfer of the capital to Florence was a measure of greater magnitude and difficulty than the French and Piedmontese Governments seemed to think, but that was their affair and did not in any way concern the Papal Government any more than the Convention itself which had been concluded by those two powers without the knowledge or consent of the Sovereign Pontiff. Indeed the Convention had never been notified to the Government of His Holiness by any official communication on the part of the French Government so that he was not in any way bound to take notice of, or answer officially, a document which had never been officially communicated to him.

Count de Sartiges had read him Monsieur Drouyn de Lhuys' despatch of 12 September which he had since read in the newspapers together with the text of the Convention of 15 September, and to Monsieur Drouyn de Lhuys' despatch he might possibly offer some observations in writing to the Nuncio at Paris, observations he had already offered verbally to the French Ambassador. For instance, he had observed to His Excellency that he was surprized to find the French Government binding themselves by a Convention to evacuate Rome in two years, when in fact it depended on their own free will to go whenever they pleased. The Pope gratefully acknowledged the services rendered to the church by the presence of a French army, but he also fully admitted the Emperor's right to withdraw his troops from Rome whenever he thought it fit to do so. Why His Majesty should bind himself to a fixed date in virtue of a Convention with Piedmont, who had not been a party to the occupation of Rome in 1849, which had been the result of an understanding come to at Gaeta by the great Catholic powers with the declared object of protecting the Pope's dominions and rights against the revolution, he owned filled him with surprize.

But when he found Monsieur Drouyn de Lhuys declaring to the Ambassador that the French Government had resolved not to withdraw their troops from Rome until the occupation had fulfilled its object, his surprize grew even greater, as he could not forget that during the protectorate of France the Pope had been despoiled of two thirds of his dominions by the Piedmontese. There were many other passages in the French Foreign Secretary's despatch he intended to analyze.

His Eminence went on to say that two articles in the Convention had especial reference to the Government of His Holiness. Article II suggested the organization of a Pontifical army. The Pope had at present between six and seven thousand men, sufficient for all police purposes with a population reduced to 600,000. But if the Pope was expected to form an army of defence against his enemies, 100,000 men would not suffice, since they could be crushed any day by the overwhelming numbers who surround the Holy See, as General de Lamoricière's army had been destroyed at Castelfidardo, by the Piedmontese. The Pope was not a military prince. It would be folly to renew an experiment which recent experience taught could end so fatally, and the Pope was therefore resolved not to add a soldier to his present army.

Article 4 of the Convention declared that the Piedmontese Government were ready to enter into some arrangement to take a share of the public debt of the Holy See. To that he must reply that the Pope had never asked anyone to pay his debts for him, but had on the contrary faithfully and honestly paid his creditors up to the present hour, notwithstanding the grievous spoliations the church had been subjected to. If ever a day came when he could no longer pay them, the Pope could tell his creditors so, without the uninvited interference of any foreign power.

Within the last few days it had become evident that the Convention was capable of two constructions, a French and a Piedmontese interpretation. The Papal Government accepted neither and the Pope would act according to the dictates of his conscience and ignore a public act which violated the sacred rights of the church and to which he was not and never could be a party.

Throughout this conversation Cardinal Antonelli's language was firm, calm and dignified. Your Lordship will perceive that the Pope even at this important conjuncture adheres unmoved to the *Non pos-*

sumus policy of the past, and the Papal policy of the future may be summed up in recent words attributed by the faithful to Pope Pius IX: 'Before I swerve from the dictates of my conscience or submit to any transaction contrary to the oath I have taken before God and His Holy Church entrusted to my care, I will cheerfully accept the pilgrim's staff, the prisoner's chains or the martyr's death. Forty-four Popes have been driven from Rome. I may be the forty-fifth, but if I die in exile my successors will return to Rome.'

302 [F.O. 43/91B]   *Rome, 8 November 1864*

No. 68

O.R. to Earl R.

Public opinion in Rome is strangely divided as to the probable consequences of the Franco-Italian Convention. The small Mazzinian faction are unsettled and as yet without instructions from their leaders. The great National Italian party believe in the faithful execution of the Convention and are willing to follow the advice they receive from the true friends of Italy, who counsel them to observe a passive and tranquil attitude until further notice. The pious have been instructed by their confessors to abstain from all premature discussion of the question. The wealthy conservatives who cautiously abstain from active public life and claim to be called 'the party of Order', fondly hope that the French troops may not leave Rome during their lifetime, but should they be mistaken and their Sovereign, their Church and their Country be exposed to danger, declare their firm determination of running away.

The Ultramontane Church party, who govern the state, after recovering from the first shock caused by the prospect of the departure of the French garrison, have also recovered their spirits and lulled themselves into a comfortable conviction that the Convention does not in truth concern the Pope, but is intended as a slap in the face to the northern powers, for which they adduce a series of incomprehensible proofs, whilst they declare Rome to be far too valuable a position to be thoughtlessly abandoned by France and meet the earnest warnings of the French authorities, that in two years the occupation will cease, with peals of laughter.

303 [P.R.O. 30/22/77]   *Rome, Palazzo Chigi*
                                          14 November 1864

Private
O.R. to Earl R.

My new house is charming and I feel happier than ever at being again
in Rome. . . . Cardinal Antonelli appeared delighted at my return to
Rome and desired me to tell him all about you and your health etc. He
listened with interest and then asked if he might send you his compliments although he had not the honor of knowing you personally. As
to the Convention he does no more believe in its execution than any of
the priests in office, and His Eminence, Mérode, Matteucci and all of
them laugh in anybody's face who mentions the departure of the
French troops from Rome. It is a strange state of mind they are in, an
unaccountable state of bumptious security and faith in their own infallibility. I recollect well that they did not more believe in the loss of
Lombardy, the success of Garibaldi, the fall of Gaeta, the recognition
of the Kingdom of Italy and quite recently in the cession of the Ionian
Islands to Greece. But when they are mildly reminded of these facts,
they simply reply: 'The Convention of the 15 September will be a dead
letter like the Treaty of Villa Franca!' If the Pope does nothing at all,
the Emperor cannot abandon him in a helpless condition to the Piedmontese and the tender mercies of his subjects, the Catholics of France
and of the whole world will not stand it, nor will he give up the commanding position he holds at Rome etc., etc. No doubt it will be very
difficult for the Emperor to abandon the Pope in the helpless condition
in which His Holiness thinks it wise policy to be, two years hence, but
then His Majesty has not been taken by surprize, the convention is the
result of mature reflection and he will find it almost as difficult not to
carry it out as to execute his self-imposed obligations. I cannot fancy
a more deeply interesting moment in the history of the Papacy than
this, for whether the French protectors go or stay a few years longer
is not to my mind the danger that threatens them. The real danger,
the sword that hangs over them, is the immense moral pressure which
Florence as the capital of Italy will exercise on this rotten nest of knaves
and fools into whose hands the management of that wonderful corpora-
tion called 'the Church of Rome' has fallen, which was once governed
by great and able men. . . .

304 [F.O. 43/91B]   *Rome, 20 November 1864*

No. 74. Secret.
O.R. to Earl R.

While the Emperor Napoleon III is imposing a capital on the people
of Italy against their will, but which necessity induces their Parliament
to accept at his hands, and while His Majesty is deciding the future
destinies of the Holy See against the will of the Pope and against the
wishes of his subjects, a large National party exists in Rome whose
voice has been crushed by the Government imposed on them by
France, but who have ever sought to express their aspirations by
popular and unexpected demonstrations and often at the risk of exile
and imprisonment.

That party, which embraces the great majority of the Pope's
subjects, after waiting impatiently for the day of liberation while their
luckier neighbours threw off the foreign yoke and united to form a
nation, of which they hoped to become the head, that party have now
been informed by their leaders at Turin that the interests of Italy
require the frank and honest acceptation of the Convention of
15 September by the Italians and consequently the abandonment of
Rome as the capital of Italy.

Now the National Party in Rome have thoroughly understood the
dire necessity imposed upon them by Turin and Paris, but they cannot
resign themselves to their fate without seeking some means of expressing their wishes in a quiet and respectful manner which would in no
way infringe upon the stipulations of the Convention imposed on
them by France. In recording their plans in this despatch I must most
earnestly request Your Lordship to keep their secret.

To express therefore their national aspirations at a moment and in
a manner which has not been foreseen or provided against by the
negotiators of the Convention, they have hit upon the following ingenious device: The moment the death of Pius IX becomes known the
people will proceed to vote the annexation of the Papal territory to the
Kingdom of Italy, by public voting in those towns and villages where
there is no French garrison, and in Rome itself and those towns garrisoned by the French, before public notaries who will be prepared to
register the votes of the people in their private offices in a quiet and
orderly manner and without any kind of public disturbance in the
streets.

This demonstration will probably share the fate of the address of the Romans to the Emperor of the French in 1861 and of all their other demonstrations, but it will serve to show France the true nature of the National aspirations alluded to in Monsieur de Nigra's despatch which so greatly puzzled Monsieur Drouyn de Lhuys and necessitated explanations on 1 November in the presence of the Emperor Napoleon himself.

305 [F.O. 43/91B]   *Rome, 22 November 1864*

No. 76. Secret
O.R. to Earl R.

I called this morning on Cardinal Antonelli for the purpose of learning what impression the language held by the Austrian Ambassador in regard to the Convention had made on His Eminence. The Cardinal Secretary of State said that on the whole the Austrian Ambassador approved the policy of the Papal Government, as he well knew that the Pope could only follow one straight line dictated to him by his conscience and a high sense of his duty towards the Catholic World. . . . The Cardinal took my hand and said: 'I will speak to you in strict confidence and tell you a secret. After the unexampled explanations called forth by Monsieur de Nigra's and Monsieur de Lhuys' despatches about the Convention in the presence of the Emperor Napoleon on 1 November, Monsignor Chigi, our Nuncio at Paris, had a confidential conversation with the Emperor about them and His Majesty said to him: "These international discussions have greatly displeased me, but I have thought it best to allow them to drop for the present (*de ne pas les relever*) and I shall reserve to myself the right of acting as I think best when the moment comes. Tell the Pope to be calm (*d'être tranquille*), to trust in me and to judge me by my deeds and not by my words."

'From these words of the Emperor and from the explanations between Monsieur Drouyn de Lhuys and Monsieur de Nigra, and other things reported to me by the Nuncio at Paris, it has become evident that the Convention of 15 September has several meanings, one put upon it at Turin and the other at Paris publicly and officially, whilst a third interpretation, and the only correct one, exists in the Emperor

Napoleon's mind. Much as I have thought about it, I know not what His Majesty's ultimate plans may be, nor do I clearly see whether the reward he contemplates will be Genoa, Sardinia or Sicily. But one thing becomes clearer than it ever was before to my mind, namely that he does not intend Italy to unite.'

I interrupted His Eminence to observe that if we judged the Emperor Napoleon's policy from his acts and not by his words, we must come to the conclusion that he favored the unity of Italy and that the Convention was a further act in support of my view.

'So it appears at first sight,' the Cardinal continued with unusual eagerness, 'and his agents seem to think so too, but let us examine the effects of the Convention and you will see what I mean. First of all the Convention contains in itself the destruction of the unity of Italy, for it reserves the Temporal Power to the Pope and deprives Italy of Rome, and Italy can never be a united nation without Rome. Secondly, the Convention declares Florence to be the future capital of Italy, that is, it forms the great political centre of Italy in the north. Now the north did not require any other capital than Turin while it waited for Rome. The danger to unity is in the south. The south had to be conciliated, and had Naples been declared the Capital, the north of Italy might have submitted and the south have been compelled to submit to the rule of the north, but instead of that the Convention leaves the south free to fall off, separate and constitute a southern Kingdom, because the capital is placed at Florence, the true centre of northern Italy. From this it becomes evident that the Emperor Napoleon imposed Florence on the Italians as their capital, so that Naples might be free to act for herself, and Italy become a Confederation divided into three, namely a northern and a southern Kingdom and the Holy See in the centre. To make this plan acceptable to Victor Emmanuel, a prince of the House of Savoy would probably be proposed for the throne of Naples, perhaps even one of his sons.'

Having expressed my surprize to the Cardinal, I begged of him to tell me whether he had any good authority for all he had told me. 'None whatever,' he replied, 'these are merely my own speculations in trying to read the Emperor's secret intentions in making the Convention. The Nuncio is much better pleased with his relations with the Emperor since the conversation I confided to you. But pray do not betray me, I confide these things to you for your own personal guidance. . . . Meanwhile the French Ambassador continues in the name of Monsieur

Drouyn de Lhuys to press the acceptance of the Convention upon us and says: "The Emperor by this Convention offers you the means of prolonging the temporal existence of the Papacy, *acceptez, tâchez de vivre!*" But I reply: "In two years many things may happen in France, *tâchez de vivre vous mêmes!*" But all I have told you about my own thoughts and the Emperor Napoleon's double policy cannot in any way influence the conduct of the Pope. He has but one course to follow, you know it. He cannot change, *le Pape ne transigera jamais*, he is bound by his oath and by the eternal laws of honesty and international morality. In the coming struggle, we may be beaten and submerged. I am the first to admit that it is possible, nay, I will say even probable, but we will do our duty towards the Holy Church like honest men knowing that when God in his mercy allows these trials to pass His Church will rise again as she has ever done before and her enemies will be dispersed and confounded.'

Many persons were waiting to see Cardinal Antonelli and we could not prolong the conversation. I left His Eminence under the impression that he had told me what he really thought and believed, and that his cordial and confidential manner shewed his desire to keep on good terms with Her Majesty's Government. When speaking under excitement Cardinal Antonelli can scarcely conceal his abhorrence of the Emperor Napoleon, and this feeling is no doubt strengthened by the knowledge that his own tenure of office in Rome depends upon His Majesty's will and may be cut short by the withdrawal of the French garrison.

As I left the Vatican, I fell in with Prince Altomonte, the ex-King of Naples' Minister to the Court of Rome. The prince is a clever, honest man, who has loyally served his King in adversity. I questioned him as to the impression produced by the Convention on the Bourbon party which he represents officially in Rome. He put the very same interpretation upon it that the Cardinal had an hour before, namely, that it was well known the Emperor Napoleon did not desire Italy to unite, and that the Convention by securing the Pope's Temporal Dominion over Rome and imposing Florence as the capital of Northern Italy upon the Italians, left Naples free to secede and restore her autonomy under a prince of the House of Savoy.

P.S. 5 December.
Since writing the above report, which I was unable to send home any

sooner, I have heard the above impressions repeated and confirmed by
several of my colleagues and other enemies of Italian unity.

*[A minute by Palmerston, dated 16 December 1864: It has been evident
for a long time that the object of the Emperor as regards Italy is not its
unity but its division into separate states in accordance with the arrangements of the Treaty of Zürich.]*

306 [F.O. 43/91B]   *Rome, 21 December 1864*
No. 86
O.R. to Earl R.

I have the honour to enclose herewith an Encyclical Letter together
with a Letter Apostolic and a 'Syllabus containing the principal Errors
of our age', which have been promulgated from the Vatican. . . . Time
is wanting and I can but give Your Lordship a short *précis* of these
papers today, but I will return to the subject by next messenger.

The most unbounded pretensions to absolute control over the souls
and bodies of mankind are proclaimed and re-asserted by the Pope in
these documents.

Those are condemned who *asserere non dubitant optimam esse condi-
tionem societatis in qua Imperio non agnoscitur officium coercendi sancitis
peonis violatores Catholicae religionis, nisi quatenus pax publica postulet,*
and *erroneam illam opinionem libertatem conscientiae et cultuum esse
proprium cujuscumque hominis jus, quod lege proclamari et asseri debet
in omni recte constituta societate, et jus civibus inesse ad omnimodam libertatem nulla vel ecclesiastica vel civili auctoritate coarctandam, quo suos
conceptus quoscumque sive voce, sive typis, sive alia ratione palam publi-
ceque manifestare ac declarare valeant.* Those who think *in ordine
politico facta consummata eo ipso quod consummata sunt vim juris habere.*

*Atque silentio praeterire non possumus eorum audaciam, qui sanam non
sustinentes doctrinam contendunt illis Apostolicae Sedis judiciis et decretis,
quorum objectum ad bonum generale Ecclesiae, ejusdemque jura, ac disci-
plinam spectare declaratur, dummodo fidei morumque dogmata non attin-
gat, posse assensum et obedientiam detrectari absque peccato, et absque ulla
catholicae professionis jactura.* The strongest claim ever put forward by
Rome since the Reformation!

The appendix contains *LXXX praecipuos nostrae aetatis errores*
which the Bishops are ordered to combat by all the means in their

power. Among these 'heresies' is the principle *quod vocant de non interventu*, and also that church and state may be separated. Catholics are forbidden henceforth to discuss *de temporalis regni cum spirituali compatibilitate.* Those are condemned who think that *Protestantismus non aliud est quam diversa verae ejusdam Christianae Religionis forma in qua aeque ac in Ecclesia Catholica deo placere datum est.*

Those who hold *ecclesiastica potestas suam auctoritatem exercere non debet absque civilis gubernii venia et assensu.* Those who say that *Romanorum congregationum decreta liberum scientiae progressum impediunt.*

Socialismus, Communismus, Societates biblicae, Societates clericoliberales et ejusmodi pestes reprobantur.

Those are condemned who maintain that *obligatio, qua Catholici magistri et scriptores omnino adstringuntur, coarctatur in iis tantum, quae ab infallibili Ecclesiae judicio veluti fidei dogmata ab omnibus credenda proponuntur.* Those who say *Ecclesia non habet nativum ac legitimum ius acquirendi ac possidendi;* and *Sacri Ecclesiae ministri Romanusque Pontifex ab omni rerum temporalium cura ac dominio sunt omnino excludendi;* as well as *funestissimum errorum: ex lege tantum civili dimanare ac pendere jura omnia parentum in filios cum primis vero jus institutionis educationisque curandae.* And to conclude, all those who say *Romanus Pontifex potest ac debet cum progressu, cum liberalismo et cum recenti civilitate sese reconciliare et componere.*

All those errors and many more (*pravas opiniones*) says the Pope *auctoritate nostra apostolica reprobamus, proscribimus atque damnamus, easque ab omnibus catholicae Ecclesiae filiis, veluti reprobatas, proscriptas atque damnatas omnino haberi volumus et mandamus.*

307 [F.O. 43/91B]   *Rome, 31 December 1864*

No. 90
O.R. to Earl R.

The views I ventured to submit to Your Lordship in my despatch No. 106 of 31 December 1861 have proved correct and the Holy See is now in the position I then foreshadowed. The French occupation of Rome has proved beneficial to Italy and disastrous to the Papacy; beneficial to Italy because it has prevented foreign intervention and rendered the Papacy helpless and dependent, and disastrous to the Papacy because the presence of a powerful foreign army imposing an unpopular Government on an unwilling population, coercing the people and protecting and fostering an impotent administration, has gradually and effectively undermined the Temporal Power of the Popes.

Fifteen years of foreign occupation have widened the breach between governed and government and made conciliation almost impossible. The financial resources of the Church have been nearly exhausted and a large public debt has been contracted. The Papal Government has been enabled with impunity to add a series of blunders to those of the past. Europe and the Catholic world have had leisure to understand the administrative incapacity of the priests.

The name of the Papacy has been associated with an illiberal and anti-national policy. The pure spiritual duties of the Church have been confounded with temporal impurities and discord has been bred among the Catholic clergy. And when the time shall have come for the withdrawal of the French troops as stipulated in the Convention of 15 September, France will find the Papacy, thanks to her ill-judged protectorate, in a state of religious, social, financial and political destitution so great as to render government and independence impossible.

The reaction confidently looked forward to by the Ultramontane party seems an unlikely occurrence, yet the confidence of the Vatican is such that the withdrawal of the French troops is not believed in and the Convention is held to be a dead letter like the Treaty of Villa Franca. The Emperor of the French, it is said, cannot desire the unity of Italy and the existence of the cabinet of Turin depends on the will of His Majesty. The Ultramontane party do not seem to perceive that the Emperor of the French while he has been the so-called protector of the Papacy has also been the liberator and the founder of her independence and unity, that while he has acted the twofold part of defender of the Church and friend of Italian independence, while he has been the confidant and adviser of two hostile powers and the protector of both, while he has initiated the great questions which now divide Italy and the Pope and has influenced the destinies of both, while he has been the absolute master of the two antagonists, he has practically favoured Italy to the detriment of the Papacy.

So blind have the Ultramontane party been to the warnings of experience that they have not understood all the advantages offered to the Church of Rome by a frank full and honest acceptance of the Convention, which enabled them to secure Rome and save the now limited Temporal Power of the Church and to obtain the support of the Italian Government and the guarantee of the Catholic powers.

And instead of binding the Emperor and the King of Italy to the terms they offered, the Pope after an obstinate silence has paralyzed the well-meant efforts of his warmest supporters and answered the Franco-Italian Convention by an Encyclical Letter expanding the attributes of the Papacy into new regions and condemning the freedom of science and the liberties of mankind. Pius IX and his advizers have again thereby helped the progress of the Italian revolution.

Under these circumstances the year 1864 closes the past situation of affairs in Italy and the Roman question enters into a new phase. The Emperor has brought a protectorate of fifteen years to a close and bound himself by treaty to evacuate Rome in two years and leave the Pope to his own devices. The Pope has declined once for all to accept his protector's advice and good offices and by solemnly condemning the principles which now govern Europe has done his best to make conciliation hopeless, has thrown the gauntlet both to friend and to foe and has, if I may say so, burnt his ships.

The struggle is now no longer between the Pope and Italy alone, but between the Papacy and modern civilization. . . .

308 [F.O. 43/94A]   *Rome, 3 January 1865*
No. 2
O.R. to Earl R.

I had some conversation with Cardinal Antonelli this morning on the subject of the Encyclical Letter and 'Syllabus' of 8 December. His Eminence told me that the publication of those important documents had no reference whatever to present events but had been in course of preparation for two years. The 200 bishops who had been assembled in Rome in 1862 for the canonization of the Japanese martyrs had all asked for a document emanating from the Vatican and condemning collectively the many errors which had gradually grown around them in their respective dioceses, the condemnations of which were scattered all over an infinite number of allocutions, bulls and encyclicals, too numerous for practical application under existing circumstances. In consequence the Pope had had the 'Syllabus' drawn up, which was a mere memorandum to facilitate references to former documents condemning the errors in question. The Encyclical Letter alone contained some new points which he would explain to me. . . .

309 [F.O. 43/94A]   *Rome, 17 January 1865*

No. 4

O.R. to Earl R.

The Encyclical and Syllabus are a proof of the faith and sincerity of the Pope and his advizers. At a moment when the Holy See stands in need of all the support of the faithful, the Pope, animated by that deep zeal which proclaimed the new dogma of the Immaculate Conception of the Holy Virgin and dictated the fatal *Non possumus* policy, has seen fit to condemn the honest exertions of the ablest defenders of the Church.

The effects of this bold measure are incalculable. It has either placed the Pope at the head of a vast ecclesiastical conspiracy against the principles which govern modern society, or it must put the Catholic clergy in opposition to the Vicar of Christ whom they are bound to obey. An appeal might lie, as in the Middle Ages, *a Papa male informato ad Papam melius informandum*, but this practice would no longer be tolerated at the Vatican. If the priesthood are unable or unwilling to carry out the spiritual injunctions of the Pope, the moral influence of the Papacy will be greatly weakened. The army will have forsaken their general.

The efforts of the ablest and most eloquent defenders of the Papacy in Europe are paralyzed because they can no longer speak in her defence without being convicted of heresy. Silence and blind obedience must henceforward be their only rule of life.

The bishops are in a yet more difficult position, for they must either disregard their allegiance to their temporal or disobey the orders of their spiritual sovereign. They must enter upon a crusade against the governments that protect them and their flocks, or they must forsake the leadership of the Vicar of Christ. Weakness and confusion must ensue from so anamalous a position.

In Rome the position of the clergy is most painful. The great majority take refuge in silence to conceal their distress at a measure they feel to be fatal to the great interests of the Church. Some few who are bound by the offices they hold to defend the measures of the Vatican seek to explain the Encyclical canonically by declaring that the articles of the Syllabus do not mean what they say and that it needs deep reading in Canon Law and dogmatic theology to understand sentences that are purposely so constructed by the traditional wisdom of the

Church of Rome as to baffle the common sense interpretation put upon them by an ignorant or hostile laity.

The few members of the Ultramontane party who look upon the Encyclical as one of the grandest, ablest and boldest strokes of Pontifical policy, find no difficulty in adopting the plain sense of the articles as they are written and congratulate one another on the beneficial effects of a measure *qui va eclaircir les esprits et raffermir la foi*. The measure has been inspired by the Jesuits, the chief promoters of the present policy of the Vatican, whose influence is now paramount and supported by certain foreign prelates residing in Rome. Part of the composition of the text is said to be due to the Pope himself.

It is most interesting to watch the growing jealousy of the secular clergy as well as of the monastic orders of the power of the Jesuits, as their influence and their numbers increase. The Jesuits are masters of the situation, they have now long inspired the counsels of the Vatican, and will select and name the next Pope, whom they will choose among those Cardinals who will guarantee a continuation of the *Non possumus* policy of Pius IX. These modern Jesuits, or so-called Ultramontane party, and their tools, form a powerful body in the Catholic Church, but they are not the whole Church. There are Catholics like Broglie and Montalembert who think that their faith is disgraced by persecuting heresy, that civil liberty can only prove favourable to what they hold to be divine truth. There are Catholics like Döllinger and Acton who think that the honest study of the sciences may sometimes prove fatal to the interests of the clergy but never to the cause of true religion. But owing to the peculiar organization of the Roman Church these men are powerless to raise their voices.

The Jesuits exalt obedience above all other virtues, exact strict obedience of the outer forms and ceremonies of the Church and see in the promulgation of the dogma of the Immaculate Conception of the Holy Virgin one of the grandest achievements of modern times and the heaviest blow ever dealt by Rome at the growing infidelity of the age. This powerful and well disciplined party has now long governed and directed the Roman Church. Their baneful influence is deplored in silence by many good priests. There is a numerous Catholic party in Italy, but the Pope does not understand how to direct it. Probably the Ultramontane party will degrade the Church lower still in the estimate of good men before the inevitable reaction and reconstruction ensues. Then there will follow a change of government, so to speak. The

Roman Catholic Church will be governed and directed by another party. For it is not true that the Papacy has never accommodated herself to new conditions. But that day is distant, for the Jesuits are now strong enough to resist their increasing opponents for a long time and they have bound up the fortunes of Pius IX and of his immediate successor with their own.

310   [P.R.O. 30/22/77]   *Rome, 17 January 1865*
Private
O.R. to Earl R.

. . . Balls, operas and parties have now taken the place of politics in Rome as far as society and the Diplomatic Body are concerned. The priests who cannot share these amusements are divided into two sections; one, rejoicing over the Encyclical and the other moaning over the probable consequences of that extraordinary document. While they moan or rejoice, the National Committee have issued an address to the Romans inviting them to take part in the rejoicings of the Carnival to celebrate the Franco-Italian Convention. The National Party had abstained for the last few years from taking part in the fooleries of the Carnival to show their disapprobation of the French occupation, so that their reappearance in the Corso will be a source of annoyance and trouble to the Roman police, while the French authorities will find it difficult to interfere one way or the other.

    Cardinal Antonelli indulges me in long conversations. He does not believe in the departure of the French from Rome and thinks Italy at the eve of a great revolution while he, like the Pope, hopes in a European war to set matters right again in the Holy See! Although he attempts to defend the Encyclical by explaining it away, I am assured that he opposed its publication, but was overruled by the Pope, Mérode, and the Jesuits, who are now all powerful in Rome. The hatred of the Jesuits is increasing very much, but that will not prevent them electing the next Pope and doing a vast deal of mischief with impunity to the protectorate of France! . . .

311   [P.R.O. 30/22/77]   *Rome, 31 January 1865*
Private
O.R. to Earl R.

. . . I have called on Cardinal Antonelli and have found him anxious to get news but unable to give any. The fact is that the Pope having fired off his Encyclical has exhausted his powder for the present and is waiting to see what effect he has produced in the ranks of his enemies. He seems to expect miracles and is in great spirits. Some days ago His Holiness paid a visit in State to the Benedictines at *San Paolo fuori le mura* and there met the late Abbot of Monte Cassino, Abbate Pappalettere. 'Well,' he said to the Abbot, 'tell the Benedictines to rejoice and be happy for we are approaching the end of our troubles and all things will soon come right again!' An attempt has been made here to get the English Catholics to sign an address to the Pope thanking him for the last Encyclical and Syllabus. Lord Vaux of Harrowden and Sir John Acton have declined to sign it and have thereby thrown confusion and dismay in the ranks of the Ultramontane Party. Many absurd rumours are afloat. For instance it is said and believed that Lord Minto has frequent and secret interviews with the Pope and Cardinal Antonelli in consequence of a mission he is entrusted with by Lord Palmerston. Lord Grey is said to have given his entire approval to the Encyclical and Syllabus and to have told the Pope that it was a *'Masterstroke of Policy'*. Lord Carnarvon is said to have promised the Pope Lord Derby's full support whenever he comes into office. Neither Lord Grey nor Lord Minto nor Lord Carnarvon have ever seen the Pope to the best of my knowledge. Monseigneur Dupanloup's[1] pamphlet on the Convention and Encyclical, just published is thought a masterly production by the Catholic Embassies. . . .

[*Memorandum by Lord Palmerston: It can hardly be necessary for me to say that no communication whatever has passed between me and Ld Minto. P. 7/2/65.*]

312 [F.O. 43/94A]   *Rome, 13 February 1865*

No. 10. Confidential
O.R. to Earl R.

In consequence of an attack of influenza at the beginning of the year I could only obtain the honour of my annual audience of the Pope this morning. The Sovereign Pontiff, who is happily in the full enjoyment of excellent health, was pleased to receive me with even more than his

---

[1] Monseigneur Dupanloup, bishop of Orléans, was to play an important part as one of the leaders of the Anti-Infallibilists at the Vatican Council of 1869-70.

21. Lord Stanley

22a. Lady William Russell

22b. Lady Emily Russell

usual benevolent kindness. His Holiness inquired minutely after the health of [the royal family]. After deploring the dangerous state of health of Cardinal Wiseman and passing a high elogium on His Eminence, the Pope observed that he would be difficult to replace as he combined high virtues with deep learning which commanded the respect of all who knew him. There were, however, many good Catholic ecclesiastics in England and among them Dr Grant had all his sympathies.

After some general observations on people and things His Holiness spoke with evident satisfaction about the Encyclical and Syllabus. I told the Pope that I had carefully studied that document and had also read Mgr Dupanloup's pamphlet on the subject, but that I honestly confessed I could not reconcile the original text with the Bishop of Orléans' commentary, and I therefore humbly begged His Holiness to tell me whether I might consider the Bishop's interpretation of the original text as correct.

He replied that no one had a right to interpret the Pope's words, the plain meaning of which could be seen in the original texts of the documents, pastorals, encyclicals etc., to which the Syllabus referred and which he had ordered to be collected and printed in a separate volume.

I next asked whether I might tell H.M. Government that His Holiness accepted Mgr Dupanloup's pamphlet as an authentic interpretation of the Encyclical and Syllabus. 'Tell your Government,' the Pope replied, 'that Mgr Dupanloup's pamphlet is a beautiful thing (*une belle chose*), eloquent and clever, especially the political part, and that I have thanked him for it as I have thanked all the bishops who have written in the defence of my cause. The true meaning of my words I have *in petto*. To understand them you must read the original documents. The Principles of the Church are eternal and unchangeable. Circumstances and conditions vary – that liberty of conscience and toleration I condemn here, I claim in England and other foreign countries for the Catholic Church. There is no salvation out of the Roman Church, yet I, the Pope, do think that some Protestants may by the special grace of God be saved. I mean those Protestants who by peculiar circumstances have never been in a position to know Truth. For those who, like yourself, have lived in Rome at the very fountain of Truth and have not recognized and accepted it, there can be no salvation.'

The Pope then passed to other subjects. Talking of the Franco-Italian Convention, His Holiness said it had been negotiated and

M

ratified without his knowledge or consent and he could therefore take
no notice of it. . . . After a long and desultory conversation the Pope
dismissed me with his blessing.

313 [P.R.O. 30/22/111]   *F.O. 20 February 1865*
Private
Earl R. to O.R.

We are rather uneasy here about the succession to Cardinal Wiseman.
A very pompous announcement of a successor might raise a flame here,
and be detrimental not only to our design of doing full justice to the
Roman Catholic Church, but to the Roman Catholic Church itself.
What we should most desire would be that Dr Grant should quietly
extend his spiritual influence over London and Westminster, retaining
Southwark as his peculiar district. But I understand that three names
have been already sent to Rome as those of persons qualified to succeed
Wiseman: 1st. Dr Grant, 2nd. Dr Clifford, brother of Lord Clifford,
3rd. Dr Ullathorne, now administering the district of Birmingham. Of
these three the first is unobjectionable, nor do I know any valid objection against the second. But Dr Ullathorne of Birmingham is, I understand, a very injudicious [man], capable of putting forward claims
which would rouse resistance and indignation in every part of England.
Lord Palmerston and I are of opinion that by quietly talking to Cardinal Antonelli he would be induced to exert his great sagacity and
extensive influence in preventing the flame which burns so fiercely in
France from reaching England. Here are three courses which we think
tolerable: 1st. Status quo, 2nd. Grant, 3rd. Clifford. Any other course
may cause speedily or at a later period much dissension.

[*On 28 Feb. O.R. sent a private letter recounting a talk with Antonelli in
which O.R. had declared that Dr Ullathorne would be a most unsuitable
successor to Card. Wiseman.*]

314 [F.O. 43/94A]   *Rome, 1 March 1865*
No. 22
O.R. to Earl R.
[Concerning the succession to Cardinal Wiseman]

. . . I have heard English Catholics in Rome mention the names of Dr
Ullathorne, Dr Clifford, Dr Grant and Dr Amherst as likely candi-

dates. Dr Grant and Dr Clifford, although both in high favour with the Pope do not appear to have many adherents in Rome. Dr Clifford is thought too young to be promoted at present. Dr Amherst is seldom mentioned, but Dr Ullathorne appears to have the largest number of adherents amongst his countrymen.

Italian and foreign ecclesiastics in general look upon Dr Manning as Cardinal Wiseman's successor, but I hear on good authority that neither the Vatican nor the Propaganda nor the Chapter are either inclined or likely to promote a convert at present. Cardinal Wiseman will not be replaced by a Cardinal and the next English Cardinal nominated by the Pope is to reside in Rome.

315 [P.R.O. 30/22/15]   *6 March 1865*

Viscount Palmerston to Earl R.

Odo has executed your instructions with his usual judgement and ability and I hope we may avoid any Catholic display that would irritate Protestant feeling. . . .

316 [P.R.O. 30/22/77]   *Rome, 10 March 1865*

Private
O.R. to Earl R.

Cardinal Antonelli volunteered to tell me to-day that he had submitted to the Pope all I had said on the 28 ultimo respecting the succession to Cardinal Wiseman and the wishes of Her Majesty's Government in that respect; that the Pope had received the communication very favourably and had expressed his willingness to meet those wishes. . . .

317 [F.O. 43/94A]   *Rome, 12 April 1865*

No. 36. Secret
O.R. to Earl R.

About a month ago the Pope told one of his most devoted friends, Monsignor Stella, who acts as his private secretary and sometimes even as his confessor, that his conscience moved him of late to try and settle the ecclesiastical difficulties of Italy so as to give peace to the many suffering souls in the vacant sees so long deprived of spiritual comfort through the absence of their bishops.

Monsignor Stella, who is a good priest and a clever man, replied that

His Holiness could not err if he followed the dictates of his conscience. Upon which the Pope went to his writing table and as if by sudden inspiration, it is said, wrote a letter in his own hand to King Victor Emmanuel couched in the most paternal language and inviting His Majesty for the good of his soul to settle the ecclesiastical affairs of Italy.

As far as Piedmont and Lombardy were concerned, His Holiness wrote, he was ready to adhere to former Concordats for the appointment of bishops etc. In regard to the Pontifical States he should naturally reserve his rights and name and appoint whom he pleased, but as regarded Tuscany, Modena, Parma, the Kingdom of Naples and Sicily, he was ready to listen to the King's propositions and he should therefore be prepared to receive in Rome a lay plenipotentiary from King Victor Emmanuel to negotiate on the above basis, excluding every political question past, present and future.

This letter was at once conveyed secretly by a monk to King Victor Emmanuel and strange to say the Pope concealed what he had done from Cardinal Antonelli until he knew that the letter had reached its destination. His Eminence was much vexed and alarmed when he learnt what the Pope had done without his knowledge lest His Holiness should return to those Italian sympathies which characterized the early part of his reign.

Meanwhile the Pope's letter remained unanswered and unnoticed until Saturday last, when His Holiness at last received a confidential message to say that the King would answer his letter through the means of Signor Vegezzi (late Minister of Public Instruction and Justice under Count Cavour) who would arrive secretly in Rome immediately after Easter and furnished with the necessary full powers to negotiate on ecclesiastical affairs. . . .

318   [F.O. 43/94A]   *Rome, 14 April 1865*

No. 37. Confidential
O.R. to Earl R.

[The Duc de Persigny[1] had arrived in Rome, declaring he had no political mission]. . . . Nevertheless the Duke has made two important declarations in conversation with Cardinal Antonelli, which must have received the previous sanction of the Emperor Napoleon. After the

[1] The Comte de Persigny (1808-72) had been French Ambassador in London 1855-60 (except for a short interval in 1858-9). Returning to France he became Minister of the Interior till 1863 when on his resignation he was created a duke.

usual assurances of the Emperor's filial devotion to the Pope, the Duke stated that His Majesty, having always been in favour of the Temporal Power, had made the Convention of 15 September to save the Pope's remaining dominions from the rapacity of the Piedmontese and he would be obliged to adhere strictly to the letter of that document. Finding, however, to his regret that the Pope hesitated to accept it and form an army of his own, the Emperor to relieve His Holiness of all trouble now proposed to recruit a Papal army of four battalions in France for His Holiness which would be officered and commanded by experienced Frenchmen but would wear the Pontifical uniform and cockade, and although composed of French volunteers would form a Papal army and not a French garrison.

Cardinal Antonelli gave the usual answer that the Pope did not want an army but his lost provinces, that the Convention had been concluded without his knowledge and consent and that he therefore ignored it, and that the only solution to the Roman question was a return to the *status quo ante bellum*. If, however, the Emperor really withdrew his troops from Rome and carried out the Convention of 15 September, the Pope would protest and be reluctantly compelled to leave Rome and seek an asylum in some Catholic country until it pleased Providence to allow his Church to triumph over her enemies.

To this the Duc de Persigny replied that if the Pope abandoned Rome the Emperor would reorganize the Temporal Power according to its present limits, carry out the Convention and hold Rome until it pleased the Pope to return as on a former occasion in 1849, and favorable as he was to the temporal dominion of the Pope, he would never allow the Italians or 'the Revolution' to penetrate into or take possession of Rome.

Although I cannot exactly vouch for the accuracy of this conversation I hold it from the best possible authority and have every reason to believe it to be correct. . . .

319 [F.O. 43/94A]   *Rome, 26 April 1865*

No. 42. Confidential
O.R. to Earl R.

Signor Vegezzi, the Turin Plenipotentiary for Ecclesiastical Affairs, arrived incognito in Rome on 15th instant and had a first interview with the Pope on 20th to deliver the letter of King Victor Emmanuel in answer to the letter of the Pope of 19 March. Since then he has seen His Holiness and Cardinal Antonelli several times. He has not brought any letter to the French Ambassador and has not spoken to any member of the Diplomatic Body. His mission being purely ecclesiastical he seems to have held intercourse only with priests.

The presence of an envoy from Turin in Rome, the hopes and fears his mission awakens, and the mystery which surrounds him have produced a degree of unparalleled excitement in clerical circles. The liberal priests hope for a settlement, whilst the Ultramontane party fear it, because a settlement of the ecclesiastical affairs might bring about a gradual settlement of the political question between Rome and Turin which they do not desire. . . .

The exact nature of signor Vegezzi's instructions I know not, but the object the Pope has in view is simple enough. Between 70 and 80 bishoprics are vacant in Italy. While the unity of Italy is consolidating itself, the Church is losing ground. The Pope, who dreads the progress of religious indifferentism, feels the necessity of re-establishing a direct spiritual influence over the Italians through his bishops before the people get accustomed to their absence.

Signor Vegezzi, it is said, has declared King Victor Emmanuel's readiness to receive unconditionally the bishops appointed by the Pope to the former Pontifical Provinces, and in return for this concession to renew simply for the rest of Italy the former Concordats between the Pope and the former sovereigns. The Pope, however, hesitates because he will not recognize the sovereign rights of King Victor Emmanuel over Tuscany, Modena, Parma, Naples and Sicily. . . .

The Ultramontane party . . . feels that if the ecclesiastical difficulties between Rome and Italy are settled, the political difficulties will settle themselves by the 'irresistible logic of facts'. They see in the Pope's attempt to settle them the effects of advancing years and the decline of mental faculties, and their fears are increased by the fact that the Pope has been personally most favourably impressed by the language, manners and general bearing of signor Vegezzi. . . .

320 [F.O. 43/94A]   *Rome, 4 May 1865*

Nos. 43 to 46. [Recites Telegrams]
O.R. to Earl R

I have reason to think that Doctors Grant and Clifford have declined the Bishoprick of Westminster. The Pope wishes to appoint Dr Manning. I have remonstrated in a friendly spirit. Should I do more?

Earl R. to O.R.   *F.O. 5 May*

If Drs Grant and Clifford have declined it is difficult to do more than remonstrate in a friendly spirit. Continue to recommend that some moderate and quiet man should be appointed. Protestant opinion will otherwise be roused against the Roman Catholic Church.

O.R. to Earl R.   *Rome, 6 May*

The Propaganda having recommended Dr Ullathorne the Pope has definitively decided in favour of Dr Manning.

Earl R. to O.R.   *F.O. 6 May*

I am by no means dissatisfied with Dr Manning's nomination.

[*Two private letters of O.R., dated 5 May, deal in detail with this appointment.*]

321 [P.R.O. 30/22/111]   *F.O. 8 May 1865*

Private
Earl R. to O.R.

Palmerston does not at all like the appointment of Manning, and for good reasons, but I don't think we can overbear the Pope's will without more ostensible reasons than we have to give....

322 [F.O. 43/94A]   *Rome, 9 May 1865*

No. 48
O.R. to Earl R.

I asked Cardinal Antonelli to tell me the true state of the negotiations pending between Rome and Turin for the settlement of ecclesiastical affairs in Italy, and His Eminence told me what follows: One hundred and five bishoprics were vacant in Italy and the spiritual interests of the clergy and of the flocks were suffering from the prolonged absence of their bishops. In consequence the Pope had invited King Victor

Emmanuel to settle this difficulty and His Majesty had sent Signor Vegezzi to Rome, with whom His Holiness had been personally well pleased. Signor Vegezzi was an intelligent man who had fully entered into the true merits of the question and had returned to Turin to explain the Pope's views on the subject to the Piedmontese Government. He was expected to return in about three weeks for the final settlement. . . .

323   [F.O. 43/94A]   *Rome, 17 May 1865*

No. 51
O.R. to Earl R.
[Concerning the succession to Cardinal Wiseman]

. . . The English Roman Catholic bishops whose recommendation of Dr Errington had been so ill received by the Pope have resolved to present an humble address to His Holiness deploring the unjust and arbitrary suspension of Dr Errington in consequence of his differences with the late Cardinal Wiseman, explaining and even justifying his acts and submitting that if guilty of conduct deserving censure he had a right, *now that England has a hierarchy*, to be brought before and judged by the Roman Catholic chapter of Westminster etc.

These novel attempts at independence on the part of the English Roman Catholic bishops will not be tolerated at the Vatican and if they do not desist and do not return to the state of blind and passive obedience which the Court of Rome requires, they will sooner or later get the worst of it and be replaced by Ultramontane converts.

324   [P.R.O. 30/22/77]   *Rome, 17 May 1865*

Private
O.R. to Earl R.

I am sorry to learn by your letter of the 8th instant that Lord Palmerston does not like the appointment of Dr Manning. Drs Grant and Clifford had rendered themselves impossible in the eyes of the Pope by their independent proceedings and refusals. The Pope's choice rested between Drs Ullathorne and Manning and certainly from our point of view Dr Manning is preferable to Dr Ullathorne in every respect. Dr Manning will give the Roman Catholics far more trouble and annoyance than he can ever give H.M. Government. At present his appointment is extremely unpopular among the English Catholics who are frantic at the Pope's decision in favour of a convert, but if Her Majesty's Government opposes Dr Manning's appointment, the English Catholics will rally round him out of opposition and he will have a party in England to support him. If H.M. Government is silent and neutral, Dr Manning, backed up by the Vatican alone, will remain isolated and helpless in the midst of his flock. The Pope has committed a serious mistake in appointing an unpopular convert, snubbing the old English Catholics and overruling the rights of the Chapter of Westminster. The result will be very unfavourable to Rome, for the old English spirit of independence will be roused, the bishops will sign an address in favour of Dr Errington whom they think unjustly treated, and the Pope becoming irritably arbitrary and offensive will thereby not only lose the influence he intended to exercise over our General Elections, but also in great measure the pecuniary support he derived from England, called Peter's Pence. I cannot but think that division in the camp, differences of opinion and purpose between English Papists and the Vatican at present will prove favourable to the great cause of freedom in the future. The violent deep rooted irritation of the English Roman Catholic clergy in Rome proves that they foresee the dangers of discord which the Pope's arbitrary conduct has called forth among them and that the consequences of Dr Mannings appointment will be detrimental to popery in England. . . .

325 [F.O. 43/94B]   *Rome, 15 June 1865*

No. 60
O.R. to Earl R.

Commendatore Vegezzi has returned to Rome and the mission he is entrusted with awakens general interest. The Pope has submitted the propositions of which he is the bearer to a council of Cardinals, but the general impression is that their Eminences will find them unacceptable. The Italian Government insists on the three points which the Pope from the beginning had declared to be inadmissible.

    1st. The Episcopal Oath.

    2nd. The Royal Exequator.

    3rd. The reduction of the number of bishoprics in Italy.

. . . The extreme Ultramontane party have organized prayers in several convents for the failure of the whole undertaking. . . .

326 [P.R.O. 30/22/77]   *Rome, 15 June 1865*

Private
O.R. to Earl R.

Although Signor Vegezzi's mission is likely to fail at present, the Pope
seems reluctant to let him leave Rome before another attempt has been
made at Florence to obtain concessions from the Italian Government.
His Holiness might possibly give way on the subject of the reduction
of the number of Bishoprics in Italy but he will be tenacious as regards
the Royal Exequator and the Episcopal Oath because they almost involve a recognition of the new state of things in Italy. The French Ambassador thinks the difficulty of the Oath could be got over by finding
'*quelque petit serment qui n'engage à rien*' but even that practical proposition does not satisfy Cardinal Antonelli who won't hear of any oath
at all. In fact the Cardinal who is furious at the Pope for writing to
King Victor Emmanuel and initiating the present negotiations would be
delighted to see them fail altogether. When talking of Vegezzi's
mission to Cardinal Antonelli I asked what would happen if the negotiations were broken off? His Eminence's eyes flashed and he exclaimed
with his broad Italian accent: '*Tant mioux!*' ...

327 [F.O. 43/94B]   *Rome, 27 June 1865*

No. 66
O.R. to Earl R.

Cardinal Antonelli told me this morning that Commendatore Vegezzi
had left Rome for Florence. The Italian Government required the
Episcopal Oath, the Royal Exequator and a reduction of the number
of bishoprics in Italy, three points which the Pope from the beginning
had declared he could not concede and Commendatore Vegezzi not
having been able to obtain concessions from Florence, the negotiations
had necessarily come to an end....

328 [P.R.O. 30/22/77]   *Rome, 29 June 1865*

Private
O.R. to Earl R.

... The departure of Vegezzi has given pleasure to the fanatical Ultramontanes, but people in general feel convinced the negotiations will

soon be renewed. It is so obviously the interest of both to come to an agreement in principle that the only difficulty they have in reality to contend with is a question of form. The Italian Government would be wise to dispense with an oath, which the Pope can always dispense his bishops from keeping and might trust to the law of the land to keep the priesthood in order. The Italian Government would gain more in the end by conciliating the Church and the clergy at present than by making enemies of them through petty persecution in the future. The Roman clergy with few exceptions are inclined to be well disposed to Italy and only await the Pope's permission. The Pope's heart is melting secretly towards his early sympathies and only awaits cordial encouragement and *incense* from King Victor Emmanuel and his Government to go ahead, the moment is very favourable and if Cavour were still alive he would have carried all before him and the Pope and the King would have embraced on the Capitol ere this to the sound of Italian drums. . . .

329 [F.O. 43/94B]   *London, 2 Audley Square*
                                                                6 September 1865
No. 71
O.R. to Earl R.

[Encloses a note from Cardinal Antonelli. The Pope wishing to shew his sense of the gift of H.M. Govt. to the Vatican Library of the Records of the History of England etc. has directed him to forward for presentation to H.M. Govt. three cases of valuable books published by the Pontifical Govt. Encloses list of books. Endorsed that books to go to British Museum.]

[*Lord Palmerston died on 18 October, Lord Russell succeeded him as Prime Minister and Lord Clarendon became Foreign Secretary.*]

330 [F.O. 43/94B]   *Rome, 10 November 1865*
No. 2. Confidential
O.R. to the Earl of Clarendon

I called this morning on the Cardinal Secretary of State to announce my return to Rome from England to His Eminence and met with a most cordial and friendly reception. Cardinal Antonelli paid an eloquent and feeling tribute to the memory of Lord Palmerston, and after a long and desultory conversation, asked me whether the present changes in the Cabinet were likely to affect the policy of Her Majesty's Government.

I replied that the policy of Her Majesty's Government would remain exactly the same as under Lord Palmerston's administration, and in return I begged him to tell me whether the recent modifications in the Papal Government would in any way alter the policy of the Holy See. Cardinal Antonelli replied that the principles which actuated the Pope were immutable and that the policy of the Holy See would ever be the same, since it was founded on the eternal laws of Religion, Justice and Morality. The Pope's well known policy of the past would remain the policy of the future, whatever might be the progress of the Revolution, and however hard might be the trials with which it pleased Providence to visit His Church.

I observed that the public press of Europe had attached considerable importance to the resignation of Monsignor de Mérode and the appointment in his stead of General Kanzler to the War Office, as well as to the other changes which had taken place in the Pope's Government. Cardinal Antonelli said that he would tell me in strict confidence what had led to those changes. Monsignor de Mérode, as I knew, although a devoted son of the Church, was unfortunately of a very excitable and irritable temper, and as the French Government were about to withdraw their troops from the frontiers of the Papal States, and Pontifical troops to be substituted for them, it had become necessary to give the command of the Pope's army to an experienced soldier of a calm and conciliatory character, able to deal in a proper spirit with the many vexations to which the Piedmontese would probably endeavour to expose the Papal garrison on the frontiers, and General Kanzler had been appointed to Monsignor de Mérode's place for that reason. . . .

331   [P.R.O. 30/22/15]   *Rome, 15 November 1865*

Private
O.R. to Earl R.

As I said before I am more unhappy than words can tell at the idea that I am no longer to have the honor to be *your* most obedient humble servant and I should feel grateful if you will allow me to write to you occasionally about Roman and other affairs. The commencement of the departure of the French troops of occupation is a great fact and the Romans seem to feel it deeply, but they are so well disciplined and prudent that they observe a calm and dignified attitude and conceal their secret joy. . . .

332 [F.O. 43/94B] *Rome, 20 November 1865*
No. 8
O.R. to Earl of C.

Count de Sartiges told me today that upwards of 4,000 French troops had already been embarked for France and that the provinces of Frosinone and Velletri had been completely evacuated by the French and garrisoned by the Papal troops. . . .

333 [F.O. 43/94B] *Rome, 22 November 1865*
No. 10
O.R. to Earl of C.

After turning a deaf ear to the excellent advice of the Emperor Napoleon during 16 years, the Pope has at last been compelled on the departure of a portion of the French troops in virtue of the Convention of 15 September to take some measures for his own safety. A priest has been replaced by a soldier at the War Office and recruits are being enlisted in France, Belgium, Germany and Switzerland to occupy the provinces and towns evacuated by the French.

Although the Franco-Italian Convention does not bind the Emperor to withdraw the whole of the army of occupation for another year, it is evident that 'the Roman question enters into a new phase' the moment the Papal Government has to provide for its own safety even in a portion only of the Pontifical States. . . .

334 [P.R.O. 30/22/16] *Rome, 1 January 1866*
Private
O.R. to Earl R.

. . . At present the leading men of the National Party in Rome are most anxious to find means of strengthening the Municipality. They say, with perfect truth, that the Pope's temporal power is only kept up by artificial means and will crumble as soon as it is deprived of the foreign bayonets that have propped it up for seventeen years. When that moment comes it would be very desirable to have some authority that can take the reins of government in hand and prevent revolution, bloodshed and all that follows. The Italians of all parties have a traditional confidence in Municipalities, and the Romans of all parties would follow the lead of the Capitol when the Vatican dies of inanition. Happily the new Senator Marchese Cavaletti is a good man and the other elements composing the Municipality are equally good. So much so that the Senator and his conservators were cheered by the people last night as they went to Ara Coeli. This will be a cause of irritation at the Vatican where this institution of the Municipality has ever been an eyesore. When the Ecclesiastical Power fails the Municipality will be able to do much good and will in all probability carry out the plan you suggest of Rome and a three miles circuit for the Pope and Roman deputies to the Italian Parliament.

My mother wrote to me about your kind intentions towards me and I am grateful for them, but Rome interests me so much at present and I am so happy here that I greatly prefer to remain where I am and see the Roman question out so long as you can allow me to do so.

335   [F.O. 43/96A]   *Rome, 22 January 1866*

No. 7. Confidential
O.R. to Earl of C.

I had the honour of an audience of the Pope this morning and of offering His Holiness my best wishes for the New Year. The Sovereign Pontiff, who received me with the utmost kindness and benevolence said he needed good wishes if it were true, as people said, that the year 1866 was to be fraught with danger for the Papacy, but he placed his trust in God and did not fear the evil forebodings of men. Meanwhile the Romans were very gay and there were more balls, concerts and operas than ever, which was not the case in the other capitals of Europe where everyone felt the insecurity of all things produced by the revolutionary tendency of the age. He excepted Holland which appeared to enjoy material prosperity but her neighbour Belgium, who appeared so calm at present, harboured dangerous elements which filled him with apprehension. England had been troubled by the Fenians whose principles he had condemned in his last Encyclical against freemasons and secret societies in general, and he hoped the evil would soon be suppressed altogether.

Since the death of Lord Palmerston, Lord Russell had become Master of the Situation (*Maître de la Situation*) and he hoped His Lordship's new Reform Bill would contain further liberties for the Roman Catholics and that the question of education in Ireland would be taken into consideration. He had heard with great satisfaction that the Roman Catholic bishops had obtained a hearing from Sir George Grey and he trusted it would be followed by satisfactory results. He admired the power and energy of Englishmen in the suppression of revolutions, such as in the Ionian Islands, India and lately in Jamaica, where they hung 2,000 negroes and met with universal approval, while he could not hang one single man in the Papal States without incurring universal blame.

His Holiness here burst out laughing and repeated his last sentence several times holding up one finger as he alluded to hanging one man, so as to render the idea still more impressive. I observed that what he was saying illustrated the practical advantage of a representative form of Government and of responsible ministers who acted in the name of the people, while absolute sovereigns had to bear the undivided responsibility of their actions.

The Pope took no notice of my observation but went on to say that there was no sovereign in the world for whom he entertained higher respect or sincerer admiration than Her Majesty Queen Victoria and he questioned me at length respecting Her Majesty's health and occupations, Princess Helena's marriage, Prince Alfred, their Royal Highnesses the Prince and Princess of Wales and the Princess Royal whom he expressed a great desire to see again in Rome.

After a long desultory conversation, His Holiness inquired whether Your Lordship was likely to carry on the foreign policy of Her Majesty's Government in the same spirit as Lord Palmerston, to which I replied in the affirmative.

His Holiness then said he had heard of Mr Layard's visit to Rome and of his conversations with Cardinal Antonelli and he regretted he had not seen Mr Layard and talked with him on various subjects, among other things he would have liked also to have questioned him about Nineveh and heard his opinion of Queen Semiramis. His Holiness again burst out laughing and repeated his last sentence about Queen Semiramis four or five times evidently much amused at his own thoughts. After the customary blessing the Pope dismissed me with many kind wishes for my future welfare.

Although the Pope's health appeared excellent, I could not but be struck by a great alteration in his conversation, which bore unmistakeable signs of the approach of second childhood, and this impression, I may add, is shared by many who are in constant communication with His Holiness. At present the Pope's irritability is such that his ministers receive his orders and obey without daring to speak or discuss the subjects before them, and notwithstanding the proverbial goodness and benevolence of Pius IX he seems to inspire them with unreasonable apprehension and inexplicable terror.

336 [F.O. 43/96A]   *Rome, 8 February 1866*

No. 12

O.R. to Earl of C.

With reference to your Lordship's despatch of 18th ult. respecting a complaint made by the Revd G. J. Chester of the manner in which the Papal authorities at Civita Vecchia acted towards him in seizing a Bible and other books belonging to him and instructing me to afford Mr Chester such assistance as I can with a view to the recovery of his property, I have the honour to report that the books in question were recovered from the Pontifical authorities by Her Majesty's Consul, Mr Severn, and returned to Mr Chester in the F.O. bag conveyed from Rome on 16 ult. to London by Queen's Messenger Byng Hall.

Travellers visiting the Pope's dominions should be very careful not to bring forbidden books or Colts revolvers with them, the Custom House officers having strict orders to confiscate them and it is not always possible to recover them after the owners have left the Roman States. Forbidden books are those condemned by the Congregation of the Index, books on religion or morality in general, political and philosophical works of every description and more especially Italian religious tracts published in London, of which Mr Chester is said to have had several among the 21 works returned to him. But above all travellers should be careful not to bring English, Italian or other Bibles with them, the Bible being strictly prohibited by the Roman Church. In justice, however, to the Customs authorities, I must say that when met with practical civility or when previously applied to for a *lascia passare* through H.M. Consul, they are always ready to afford English travellers every possible assistance. . . .

337   [F.O. 43/96A]   *Rome, 26 March 1866*

No. 26
O.R. to Earl of C.

A Jubilee has been granted by the Pope for the purpose of offering a
holy violence to heaven by prayers and penitential works so as to avert
or lessen if possible the dangers which threaten the Church. This
Jubilee began on 12 inst. and ends with the Holy Week. Magnificent
processions headed by Cardinals and other high dignitaries and accompanied by representatives of all the holy orders and congregations in
Rome, bearing pictures surrounded by burning candles, have been
parading the streets while popular preachers have addressed the people
in the churches, on the public places, in the streets and from the steps
of the churches day after day. But perhaps one of the most interesting
ceremonies of the Roman Church took place yesterday evening on the
steps of San Carlo al Corso and several other churches. Books forbidden by the Congregation of the Index were publicly burnt on large
brasiers by priests attended by gendarmes, while conspirators' daggers
were destroyed in like manner at the *Consolazione* on the Forum. . . .

338   [P.R.O. 30/22/16]   *Rome, 28 March 1866*

Private
O.R. to Earl R.

I have to thank you for a very kind and interesting letter. . . .

Your impression that the Temporal Power of the Popes will gradually melt away is so correct that symptoms of decay are already visible
in every department of the State and, as I have said before, it would
crumble away without the foreign military prop that holds up the
rotten edifice artificially and despotically. I never cease to preach to the
leading men of the National Party, that violence would be fatal and that
organic development is the only safe way to arrive at a practical solution of the Roman Question, and I must say that one and all agree that
I am right. When Ricasoli was here, for three days, I got him to say the
same thing to them and his authority being venerated and respected by
the Romans, his words have been treasured up and repeated from
mouth to mouth and will do good. The dangerous people are the
Northern Italians whose impatience to get rid of the *Maledetti Preti*
may precipitate matters and create embarrassment. When Pio Nono is

no more, and the terror he inspires to the clergy has ceased to exist, I should not be surprised to see the *Maledetti Preti* become more liberal, more national, more *Italianissimi* than the Italian Government itself. I can already see the elements of the great change in the lower clergy and among those members of the higher clergy whose prospects of promotion under Pius IX have become hopeless. Indeed I do not hesitate to say that the whole of the Sacred College and *Prelatura Romana* are ripe for treason, if in kicking Cardinal Antonelli overboard, like Jonas, they could see any positive prospect of immediate personal advantage. . . .

339 [F.O. 43/96A]   *Rome, 6 April 1866*

No. 30. Secret
O.R. to Earl of C.

. . . [O.R. thanks Cardinal Antonelli for the course pursued by the Pope in regard to the Fenians, and expresses regret] that the Roman Catholic clergy in Ireland had not during the last 20 years opposed the secret societies and revolutionary organizations of part of their flock, which has at last culminated in Fenianism, the complete dissolution of all the ties by which society is held together, including the Roman Church and her priests, who unhappily have been the active apostles of disaffection and had taught the people that all the misfortunes they brought upon themselves by their own idle Catholic habits were attributable to the Government. Bad harvests, emigration, the exercise of their rights by landlords, etc., I said, had all been laid at the Government door and the people had been brought to believe that every earthly good would be enjoyed by them if they could shake off the yoke of England. The people now thought they could do it, but not intending to do things by halves they meant also to get rid of those who had preached disaffection to them, and in the end the Roman Catholic clergy now shared the dangers which threatened the very Government they had so long opposed.

Cardinal Antonelli said he could not quite admit the accuracy of my views, which he thought were extreme. The Irish clergy in reality had not been the apostles of disaffection towards the English Government — far from it — although they had many just causes of complaint, of which, no doubt, they had spoken with that freedom which the British Government allows to all her subjects. The Established Church and the question of Education were real grievances in Ireland which could not be supported by Protestant Englishmen as he had often had occasion to observe in conversation with the most distinguished Englishmen of all classes who visited Rome. He had talked the matter over with Mr Layard last November and he felt sure that the removal of those and other grievances would above all benefit the English Government.

As to the Irish clergy not opposing secret societies etc. in Ireland, he begged to refer me to the Pope's last Encyclical against Freemasonry, in which His Holiness condemned once for all every kind of secret society and revolutionary organization, as his predecessors had done before him, and obedience was one of the first principles the Roman clergy had to observe. The Pope's condemnation of Fenianism was therefore nothing new and was in accordance with the true principles of the Church and it gave him great satisfaction to think that the co-operation of the Roman Catholic clergy might prove an assistance to Her Majesty's Government in maintaining peace and order in Ireland. . . .

340 [F.O. 43/96A]   *Rome, 4 May 1866*

No. 37. Confidential
O.R. to Earl of C.

. . . Cardinal Antonelli after some hesitation said he would confide to me that he thought the Emperor Napoleon's real intention had always been to divide Italy into three parts, a northern Kingdom under the House of Savoy, a southern Kingdom under some foreign prince and the Papal States in the middle, and something for France, he added mysteriously.

'What?' I asked. His Eminence did not know, perhaps Sicily, perhaps Genoa, perhaps Sardinia. In the present state of affairs he considered the Emperor Napoleon to be on horseback (*a cavallo*) in Europe, by which he meant that according to events and circumstances he would abandon his present neutrality and side either with Austria or with Prussia according to his best chances of securing for France by treaty either the provinces of the Rhine, or some good ports in the Mediterranean. His Eminence considered that the affairs of Europe could now only be settled by and after a general war, before which a Congress had been clearly proved to be impossible, and in the settlement which would follow that inevitable war, he felt convinced the

Emperor Napoleon would know how to secure territorial aggrandizement to France either in the north or in the south of Europe. His Eminence ended by earnestly requesting me to consider all he said as private and secret.

341 [F.O. 43/96A]   *Rome, 4 May 1866*

No. 38. Secret
O.R. to Earl of C.

I called this morning on the Cardinal Secretary of State and told His Eminence that I had received reliable information according to which the priests in many places in Ireland had joined the Fenian movement and were known to receive the confessions of Fenians and to sympathize generally with them. He appeared much annoyed and said my report was difficult to believe after the clearly expressed condemnation of the movement by the Pope. Priests, however, were human beings and consequently liable to fail occasionally in the exercise of their duties and to give way sometimes to political passions, but if I would name individuals or localities he would at once see what could be done to remedy the evil. . . .

342 [F.O. 43/96A]   *Rome, 6 May 1866*

No. 39
O.R. to Earl of C.

. . . Notwithstanding the vigilance of the Papal police many Romans have already escaped and crossed the frontier to offer their services to Italy and the immense, deep and general enthusiasm of the people for the liberation of Venetia is another unmistakeable proof of the national desire for liberty, unity and independence. I say another proof, although for my part I need no further proofs of the deep-rooted longing of the Italian people for liberty, unity and independence. But in Rome, where priests and legitimists deny the very existence of a national movement in Italy and attribute the formation of the present Italian Kingdom to Piedmontese bribery and corruption, a spontaneous and general outburst of patriotism like the one that now agitates Italy is a new argument against the *Non possumus* policy of the Vatican, which owes its existence solely to the prolonged presence of foreign bayonets.

343 [F.O. 43/96A]   *Rome, 10 May 1866*

No. 42
O.R. to Earl of C.

I have the honour to enclose herewith an extract from the Roman
Gazette containing an Apostolical Brief of 13 ult. in virtue of which
Saint Catherine of Siena is appointed co-protectress of Rome. Besides
the theological interest, there is also a political interest attaching
to this appointment. For 17 centuries St Peter and St Paul had been
sole protectors of Rome until St Philip Neri, one of the greatest bene-
factors of the city, was elevated to the same dignity. Up to 30 April last,
therefore, Rome had but three protectors and it is not unnatural to
wonder what had rendered the appointment of a fourth patron necessary. A learned ecclesiastic, whom I consulted, reminded me that St
Catherine of Siena had taught that the Vicar of Christ on earth should
be an Italian, and true to that principle she had fought against French
influence to prevent the definitive establishment of the Papacy at
Avignon and had finally succeeded in persuading Gregory XI to
transfer his capital to Rome in 1377. At a moment, therefore, when
foreign influences threatened the Temporal Power and even the continued residence of the Papacy in Italy, it was natural to invoke the
intercession of St Catherine and place Rome under her more immediate protection. The Apostolical Brief of 13 April was therefore not
only a religious measure, but, he believed, also a measure of political
and national importance to Italy.

344 [F.O. 43/96A]   *Rome, 15 May 1866*

No. 45. Secret
O.R. to Earl of C.

[Concerning the Fenians]. . . . This morning Cardinal Antonelli returned to the subject himself and asked me whether I recollected that
he had felt some difficulty in admitting the authenticity of the facts I
had submitted to him. He went on to say that he had been in the wrong,
for after repeating our conversation to the Pope, His Holiness had
confirmed my statements by private letters which had just reached him
from Ireland. The evil, however, was happily limited to one or two
cases only of disobedience and the Pope had already caused the erring
priests to be reminded of their duties. . . .

345 [P.R.O. 30/22/16]   *Rome, 23 May 1866*

Private
O.R. to Earl R.

The enthusiasm in Italy for unity and independence and the readiness
with which young and old desire to fight and die for *Patria* and their
Venetian brethren moves me to the soul, and I hope and pray, so much
sound patriotism and true love of liberty may be finally rewarded with
success, and by the establishment of a free, united and prosperous
Italy. But the trials and dangers Italy will now have to encounter are
great, and although the spirit of the people is admirable and likely to
produce great and good things, the physical strength of Austria may
well crush their new army and their undisciplined volunteers. . . .

346 [P.R.O. 30/22/16] (Copy)   *Downing Street, 4 June 1866*

Earl R. to O.R.

We are not so quiet here as you are at Rome, nor is the House of
Commons so easy to manage as the Society of the Propaganda. We
have had several squalls and may now expect a hurricane. Still we 'bear
up and steer right onward'. In the expected war between Austria and
Italy we shall form pious wishes for Italy but we do not mean to mingle
in the fray.

  I dare say the Pope reckons on many of his turbulent subjects being
drowned in the Mincio. But they may in some proportion return more
turbulent than ever. We cannot guarantee the temporal power of the
Pope, neither could we propose that he should be represented in the
Conference. I hope he may rest quiet at Rome for the rest of his life,
and enjoy a *libera chiesa* while Italy possesses a *libero stato*.

347 [F.O. 43/96B]   *Rome, 19 June 1866*

No. 63. Confidential
O.R. to Earl of C.

The Emperor of Austria has asked the Pope to lend him his spiritual
support against the Emperor Napoleon in the great coming struggle
for supremacy in Italy, by some solemn public act, such as an Allocution condemning the policy of the French sovereign and compelling
the Catholic World to espouse the cause of Austria as the cause of

Religion and Moral Order in Europe, in compensation for which the lost provinces of the Roman States are to be occupied and guaranteed to His Holiness by Austria. The question is under discussion at the Vatican, but if the prudent counsels of Cardinal Antonelli prevail, a strict neutrality, spiritual and temporal, will be adopted and followed for the present.

[*Endorsed:* For the Queen. *And by Hammond:* It might be friendly to dissuade the Pope privately from committing such an act of folly. *And by Clarendon:* Better not to meddle.]

348 [P.R.O. 30/22/16]   *Rome, 3 July 1866*

Private
O.R. to Earl of C.

. . . The war absorbs every other interest, and the success of the Austrians at Custozza fills the Papal party with unbounded joy and the National Party with grief. The latter are however by no means discouraged and a fresh supply of volunteers has already started to enlist in the Italian army and fill up the gaps made by the Austrians on the 24 and 25 ultimo. They believe in ultimate success and are full of hope and courage. As I fear this will be for sometime to come, my last private letter to Your Lordship, I am anxious on taking leave to tell you how grateful I have felt for your *private letters* (which constitute the greatest happiness and consolation of H.M. Agents abroad), and for the indulgent kindness with which you have been pleased to treat my official reports.

[*On 24 June the Italians were defeated by the Austrians at Custozza near Verona and on 20 July worsted in a sea battle at Lissa off the Istrian coast. The Prussians, however, decisively beat the Austrian army at the battle of Sadowa on 4 July. Immediately after the disaster the Austrian Emperor ceded Venetia to Napoleon III, by whom at the peace it was ceded to the King of Italy.*]

349 [P.R.O. 30/22/16]   *Rome, 6 July 1866*

Private
O.R. to Earl R.

I am grieved to think that I am no longer to serve under your orders,

more grieved than I can tell, both for public and for private reasons.[1]
You have for so many pleasant years been a kind and indulgent chief,
you have written to me and guided me and taught me so many things
that I shall ever look back upon the past seven years as the happiest and
most profitable of my life. I am also grateful to you for having left me
quietly in Rome to see the end of these great questions, and I hope I
may succeed in remaining another year or so. A change of post now
would have made me miserable. A telegram received last night announced the total defeat of the Austrians by the Prussians and the cession of
Venetia by Austria to France. This last fact has thrown a gloom over
the National Party. They do not want to receive Venetia as a present
from France, they want to conquer Austria and liberate their Venetian
brethren alone and unassisted. . . .

350 [F.O. 43/96B]   *Rome, 10 July 1866*

No. 68. Secret
O.R. to Earl of C.

The unexpected victory of Prussia over Austria and subsequent appeal
of Austria to the Emperor Napoleon for assistance have destroyed the
hopes entertained, but a few days ago, by the Papal Government and
the Legitimists in Rome. They had prayed for and hailed the war as
their only salvation and had never doubted that Austrian troops would
again occupy the lost provinces of the Pope and would re-establish
Francis II on the throne of Naples.

Cardinal Antonelli had repeatedly told me that Austria, after occu-
pying Silesia and taking Berlin and Florence, would establish a Con-
federation in Italy on the basis of the treaty of Zurich, to which the
Emperor Napoleon would consent. The collapse has been tremendous.
I called again on Cardinal Antonelli this morning and found His
Eminence looking painfully ill and unusually excited.

'Good God,' he exclaimed and struck his forehead with the palms of
his hands, 'what is to become of us? The revolution triumphs again
and the enemies of order, justice and morality carry the day!' He then
went on to say that the Emperor of Austria must have lost his head. A
first defeat was not a reason to give in and cede Venetia to France and
constitute the Emperor Napoleon arbiter of the affairs of Europe.

----

[1] Earl Russell's government had fallen on 26 June, and been followed by that
of the Earl of Derby, with Lord Stanley Foreign Secretary.

Besides which the Emperor of Austria seemed to forget his allies of the German Confederation without whose consent he could not take the initiative of peace, since Prussia was originally at war with Germany and not with Austria alone. He thought the people of Austria would have reason to complain of the hasty appeal of their Government to France. Austria had vast resources and should fight for the good cause to the very last, and she would find allies who would join her before they would allow the Emperor of France to constitute himself Emperor of Europe.

His Eminence then asked me anxiously whether I did not think that a change of Government in England might prove favourable to Austria. I replied that although no Government in England could like to see the power of Austria either totally destroyed or even very much weakened, I felt convinced Her Majesty's Government would for the present, as heretofore, adhere to a policy of strict neutrality.

351 [F.O. 43/96B]   *Rome, 17 July 1866*

No. 69
O.R. to Earl of C.

. . . The Pope has taken the late events more calmly than his Government or his party and has said, 'When the Almighty allows such trials to afflict his Church, the Vicar of Christ on earth can only pray and wait in all humility.' So much resignation has alarmed the legitimists in Rome. They always fear that the Pope, who is by nature impulsive, may suddenly return to his Italian policy of 1848 and make peace with King Victor Emmanuel. My impression is that Cardinal Antonelli's influence will be strong enough to maintain the *Non possumus* policy of the Vatican so long as Pius IX lives. Another Pope and another Cardinal Secretary of State will naturally be compelled to submit to the new order of things in Italy. Meanwhile Pius IX is strong and healthy and has every prospect of a long life.

352 [F.O. 43/96B]   *Rome, 27 July 1866*

No. 71
O.R. to Lord Stanley

[Submits a short précis of the prospects of the Roman question.] After the failure of His Holiness's military policy, the Emperor proceeded to

sign the Convention of 15 September 1864 with the King of Italy (but
without the Pope's knowledge or consent), according to which those
remaining provinces of the Holy See held by French troops are to be
evacuated by 15 December, and the Pope will then be left to deal with
his subjects unassisted by foreign bayonets.

Up to the date of the battle of Sadowa the Papal Government appear
to have reckoned on a future restoration of past Governments in Italy
by Austria, and on an Austrian army to replace their French protectors
and to maintain their temporal administration of Rome, and had in
consequence done nothing whatever towards conciliating the Romans,
preferring to all appearance the prospect of coercing them by the assistance of foreign soldiers to regaining their confidence and their support
by a good and popular administration.

As now the dream on which their hopes for the future were founded
vanishes before them, the Papal party are at last awakening to a sense
of their utter helplessness, if the Emperor Napoleon cannot be prevailed
upon to set aside the Convention of 15 September and continue to
occupy Rome and defend the Temporal Power of the Pope against the
power of public opinion in Italy, which the Papalins persist in calling
'the Revolution' or 'the Piedmontese'. Should, however, the Emperor
Napoleon withdraw his troops of occupation from Rome according to
the stipulations of the hateful Convention, the advisers of the Vatican
suggest two courses of action to the Pope:

1st. to fly from Rome, seek refuge in Austria or Spain, and there
protest against the combined policy of France and Italy and call upon
the Catholic world for assistance and support, or,

2nd. imitate the late example of Austria, cede Rome to France and
charge the Emperor Napoleon as eldest son of the Church to defend
the temporal interests of the Holy See against the Revolution until
further orders.

Of these two courses I am convinced the Pope will follow neither.
His Holiness will await events at the Vatican protesting against everything that happens, until his death enables a new Pope to follow a new
policy If then, as I firmly believe, the Pope remains in Rome, two
difficulties await his Government:

1st. Either the execution of the Franco-Italian Convention is suspended
and the French Government continue as heretofore to impose a helpless
and hopeless administration on an unwilling population, or

2nd. The Convention is carried out and the Papal Government are left alone to settle old accounts with the Romans and surrounded by the Italians who for years past have wished for a day of reckoning with the Vatican.

Admitting that the Italian Government will have the strength to enforce the respect due to the Convention and prevent the people of Italy from flying to the rescue of their Roman brethren, as they flew to the rescue of their Venetian brethren, I question whether the Pope's subjects, who have never been consulted as to their own wishes and do not consider themselves bound by Conventions made by foreign powers without their consent, will long submit to a state of things they have so long objected to, and more especially when they consider that by upsetting an obnoxious Government their prospects are not merely to annex themselves and a new province to Italy like their neighbours, but actually to give the glorious capital they inhabit to a great country and thereby crown the work of Italian liberty and independence.

Unless therefore the Pope can find means of conciliating or of again coercing his subjects, his Temporal Power is at stake. According to the doctrine laid down by His Holiness and accepted by the Catholic powers, the Temporal Dominion is necessary to the free exercise of the Spiritual Power. The Roman Catholic Church cannot be independent unless the Bishop of Rome is a Temporal Sovereign. At present the Pope's temporal independence rests solely on French bayonets. After 15 December the Temporal Government will depend on the good will and patience of the Pope's subjects.

But as it will be difficult to persuade them long that they must submit to be ill governed for the glory and independence of the Roman Catholic Church, His Holiness may have to call in foreign aid again, in which case the Italian Government as the nearest would probably be the first to march across the frontier, when the Pope's Temporal Power will rest on Italian bayonets. If the Pope, forgetting and forgiving past events, is satisfied with an Italian garrison, the Roman Question may settle itself, but should His Holiness prefer a French, an Austrian, a Spanish or a mixed foreign Catholic garrison, the Roman Question will be once more forced upon the Catholic powers, who will then have to take the two following questions into consideration: 1st. whether the Pope's temporal sovereignty be necessary to the free exercise of his spiritual power and to the exercise of the Roman Catholic Church, and if so, 2nd. By what means, military and financial, it is again to be imposed on the Romans.

353   [F.O. 43/96B]   *Rome, 27 July 1866*

No. 72. Confidential
O.R. to Lord S.

[Conversation with Cardinal Antonelli who said that] the Emperor
Francis Joseph . . . ought to have preferred an honourable death before
the gates of Vienna to a suicidal peace which will reduce the old
Austrian Empire to a second rate oriental power. He spoke with great
warmth and for the first time in his life with something like contempt
of that same Austrian Government he had almost worshipped but a
few days ago.

Turning then to the speeches of Lord Derby, Mr Disraeli and Your
Lordship, he had read in the newspapers respecting the strict neutrality
Her Majesty's Government proposes to observe in the present conflict,
Cardinal Antonelli expressed regret and surprize, regret that England
should allow the power of Austria to be broken and perhaps destroyed,
and surprize that England should not apprehend danger to herself in
the future at the formation of two powerful maritime states, Prussia
and Italy, who, allied to each other or to France, could any day destroy
the naval supremacy of Great Britain.

354   [F.O. 43/96B]   *Rome, 23 August 1866*

No. 80. Confidential
O.R. to Lord S.

Since writing to Your Lordship on 8th inst. about the administrative
reforms recommended by the Emperor Napoleon to the Pope. I have
had several conversations on that subject with the Cardinal Secretary
of State and with the French Ambassador. Cardinal Antonelli told me
that Count de Sartiges had assured him that the advice he submitted to
His Eminence's consideration came from himself and that he was not
acting under special instructions from Paris, to which His Eminence
had replied to the Count that the plan of reforms he proposed could
and would never be carried out by His Holiness. The administrative
reforms needed by the Papal Government were of a very different
nature. Hitherto the machinery of state had been calculated for the
welfare of many rich provinces and a population of three millions, but
now that the temporal dominion of the Pope had been reduced to a
mere province with a population of only 600,000 inhabitants, the ad-

ministration would have gradually to be reduced from that of a Kingdom to that of a small province in accordance with the reduced revenues of the Holy See.

These statements of the Cardinal Secretary of State were afterwards confirmed to me by the French Ambassador who added that he had had an audience of the Sovereign Pontiff to thank him for the Grand Cross of Pius IX and that he had availed himself of the opportunity to implore of His Holiness to reform his administration in such manner as to regain the lost sympathies of his subjects before it was too late.

The Pope, Count de Sartiges said, had argued with his usual benevolent good humour against his well meant advice and had finally put an end to the discussion in the following humorous manner:

'*Caro Conte Mio*,' His Holiness had said, 'your advice is by no means in accordance with the views of your Imperial Master and I can prove it to you by the following passage I have found in the Life of Julius Caesar by His Majesty the Emperor Napoleon in Vol. I Chapter V p. 192: "*Dans les moments de crise extérieure tout mouvement populaire perd les états, comme en présence de l'étranger foulant le sol de la patrie tout changement politique est funeste*".'

The French Ambassador now perceives that it is hopeless to expect a policy of self preservation on the part of the Vatican and says: '*Il faudra les sauver malgré eux.*'

355 [F.O. 43/96B]   *Rome, 19 November 1866*
No. 81
O.R. to Lord S.

On reaching my post it may be as well to place on record what passed between Monsieur de Moustier, the new French Minister for Foreign Affairs, and myself on 4th inst. at Her Majesty's Embassy at Paris. Earl Cowley having presented me, His Excellency began at once by saying that he hoped H.M. Government would not increase the difficulties France was about to encounter in Rome by encouraging the Pope to leave the Vatican and by renewing to His Holiness the offer of an asylum in Malta.

I said that the aspect of affairs had much changed since that offer had been made. The prospects of Italy and Rome were uncertain and unsettled and the Pope having volunteered to ask for an asylum in case of danger Her Majesty's former advizers could not do otherwise than grant His Holiness's request. Since then the Convention of 15 September had regulated the future conduct of Italy and assured to the Pope the temporal possession of Rome by treaty, so that Her Majesty's present advizers could see no object in offering an asylum to the Pope which His Holiness no longer stood in need of. I did not believe in the Pope's departure from Rome, but if he should ever renew his request for British protection I should strongly urge his remaining at Rome and I should also make it a point to communicate at once with my French colleague and leave the matter in his hands. Monsieur de Moustier expressed great satisfaction at the language I was holding. . . .

[*Endorsed* Query, approve language. Stanley: Yes.]

[*On 27 November 1866 Arthur Russell wrote to his mother: 'It will be difficult for Odo to know how to present things to Lord Stanley so as to make him understand them. Lord Palmerston, Clarendon, Uncle J., Gladstone, all read Odo's reports with pleasure, but to Lord Stanley, the Vatican, the Sacred College, the Holy Office etc. etc., are empty sounds which convey nothing to his mind.'*]

356 [F.O. 43/96B] *Rome, 30 November 1866*

No. 86. Confidential
O.R. to Lord S.

The Earl of Clarendon left Rome this morning for Florence. I can already perceive that the language held by His Lordship in Rome at this solemn crisis in the destinies of the Roman Catholic Church, language which none but Lord Clarendon could have held, has been productive of great good. The Pope himself after a long conversation with Lord Clarendon authorized him to inform the Italian Government that he was willing to receive a negotiator from Florence.

Lord Clarendon having then spoken to Cardinal Antonelli on 24th inst. at the Vatican, His Eminence returned the visit on the following day at the Hotel de l'Europe and assured His Lordship by desire of the Pope, that His Holiness was entirely disposed to receive any proper person who might be sent to Rome by the Italian Government to treat confidentially upon ecclesiastical and other affairs. The Earl of Clarendon who did me the honour of informing me of these facts, also told me that Cardinal Antonelli appeared fully aware of the necessity of discussing and settling the future *modus vivendi* of the Pontifical Government.

In thus throwing a bridge across the gulf that separated Italy from the Papacy, Lord Clarendon has opened the way to a peaceful solution of the Roman Question and has achieved what no one else could have ventured even to attempt at a moment when political passions have smothered the voice of reason. And even if the proposed negotiations should not yet lead to final success, they will serve to shew the earnest desire of Italy to make peace with the Pope, and while they last will tend to calm the apprehensions of the Romans, of the Italians and of the Catholic world.

357 [F.O. 43/96B]   *Rome, 4 December 1866*

No. 89
O.R. to Lord S.

. . . A very general feeling of alarm prevails in all classes as to the insecurity of life and property, based on the belief that a considerable number of desperate characters flying the hands of justice in Italy have sought refuge in the town to provoke riots after the departure of the French troops with a view to rapine and pillage, and the respectable portion of the population deplore the absence of a national guard which would enable them to keep order and protect their own families and property, for little confidence is placed in the foreign portion of the Pontifical army who are to replace the French garrison in Rome.

The National Party hail the withdrawal of the French garrison as the dawn of salvation, but at the same time they appear to be quite determined to adhere strictly to the injunctions received from Florence, to respect the stipulations of the Convention and not to give the French Government any pretext for the re-occupation of the Papal States.

An advanced or Mazzinian party of action is spoken of who would fain overthrow the Papal Government at once, but, although said to be provided with arms they do not appear to be strong enough to carry out their plans.

The clergy is divided into two parties: the large majority of the lower clergy and some few members of the Sacred College would gladly see the Pope make peace with Italy and save what little the Convention has left him, whilst the higher clergy (called the Jesuit party in Rome) urge the Pope to fly from the Vatican and seek a safe asylum abroad, from whence he would call upon the Catholic Powers to protect the Holy Church against the Revolution and go to war with Italy.

Neither of these two parties, however, has sufficient moral courage to act in any other way but that which the Pope will hereafter prescribe to them, for the spirit of the Church is obedience, and the power of the Pope is absolute.

It therefore remains to be seen what the Pope will do, and on that I am, like everybody else, unable to express a positive opinion. My former impression, however, remains unchanged, namely, that His Holiness will remain at the Vatican and protest against everything that happens until his death enables a new Pope to follow a new policy, which will of course be hailed by the clergy as the true word of God. Meanwhile Pius IX, who for the present holds the destinies of the Church of Rome in his hand, has told us in two official documents what his policy is to be, first in an Allocution and secondly in an *Invito Sacro*.

According to the Allocution His Holiness declares that he will rather leave Rome than treat with the 'enemies of the Church', and in the *Invito Sacro* His Holiness invites the faithful to pray and gather round the Blessed Virgin as the people of Israel gathered round Deborah and the people of Bethulia round Judith and obtained the destruction of their enemies Sisera and Holofernes. These documents would leave no hope of a conciliatory policy if Lord Clarendon had not been authorized by the Pope to bring about negotiations with the Italian Government. On the result of those negotiations the hopes of all parties are now founded.

358 [F.O. 43/96B]   *Rome, 6 December 1866*
No. 93
O.R. to Lord S.

[Reports that brigandage has not decreased in the Southern provinces. Pontifical troops have lost 10 men killed and 2 wounded.]

359 [F.O. 43/96B]   *Rome, 15 December 1866*
No. 95
O.R. to Lord S.

The Franco-Italian Convention of 15 September has been faithfully executed. The French Military authorities have evacuated the Castle of St Angelo and the fortresses of Civita Vecchia and have handed them over to the Papal army. The French troops have been embarked

23. Lord Clarendon

24. Marquis de Banneville

at Civita Vecchia and at this moment there is not a French flag flying or a French sentry to be seen in the Pontifical dominions. The evacuation and the change of garrison have been effected with the utmost order and tranquillity and the population has hitherto been passive.

General de Montebello deserves the highest praise and credit for his command, management and administration under circumstances of extraordinary delicacy and difficulty. Never has an army of occupation, imposing an unpopular administration on an unwilling people, behaved with more order, discipline and kindness. . . .

360 [F.O. 43/96B]   *Rome, 18 December 1866*

No. 97. Confidential
O.R. to Lord S.

[Arrival of Signor Tonello, the Italian plenipotentiary. Negotiations about to begin.] . . . I enquired of the Cardinal Secretary of State whether he expected they would be successful. 'I will tell you,' he replied, 'in strict confidence what has passed. I have formally declared to Signor Tonello that if his instructions enable him to accept expedients for the appointment of 82 bishops to the 82 vacant sees in Italy and for the provisional arrangement of some other ecclesiastical matters, we should be able to meet the wishes of his Government and come to terms. But if he proposes to negotiate on the principle of the recognition of the Kingdom of Italy by us and of the sovereignty of King Victor Emmanuel over any other part of Italy than Piedmont, then it will be useless to proceed.' . . .

361 [F.O. 43/96B]   *Rome, 31 December 1866*

No. 99 Confidential
O.R. to Lord S.

[Tonello and the French Ambassador think the negotiations are going well.] . . . The Pontifical negotiators appear to consider the pretensions of the Italian Government as inadmissible and think Signor Tonello's mission will end, like Signor Vegezzi's in failure. . . .

I am more inclined to share the impressions of my ecclesiastical than of my diplomatic friends, and think with the former that there is no real disposition at the Vatican to come to an amicable understanding with the Italian Government. . . .

N

362 [F.O. 43/96B] *Rome, 31 December 1866*

No. 100
O.R. to Lord S.

Contrary to a prevalent opinion among the faithful during the year that ends today, I have repeatedly ventured to assert that the withdrawal of the French garrison would not be followed by immediate bloodshed or by the flight of the Pope from Rome. Circumstances have confirmed my opinion. The French army has departed in peace and the Pope has not carried out the threat, expressed in his last Allocution, of leaving Rome.

But although the population of Rome is quiet and the Pope unmolested at the Vatican and protected by an army of 11,000 men, and the Italian Government determined to respect the stipulations of the Convention, and the French Emperor ready to re-occupy Rome at his pleasure and to place 200,000 men at the disposal of His Holiness, according to official declarations from Paris, the Roman Question is still far from being solved.

Abandoned by his armed protectors and left to his own resources, two courses were open to the Vicar of Christ.
1st. To adopt a purely Christian policy of forgiveness and conciliation, bless his enemies and seek to convert them by his example, cut off the offending hand by renouncing the Kingdom of this world, and restore the primitive independence of a purely spiritual church, or
2nd. Follow a mediaeval Pontifical policy of spiritual welfare and damnation, hurl the major excommunication and interdict at his enemies and compel the Catholic powers to purchase their salvation by submission to his temporal will.

But Pius IX has preferred to steer between these two courses and to continue to seek his strength in the so-called *non possumus* policy, or in other words so to blend spiritual and temporal interests as to endanger the former through the latter. To this policy he has committed the whole of the Roman Catholic Episcopacy, their clergy and their flocks, so deeply as to make it very difficult for them now suddenly to eat their words. The object and result has been to render the recognition of facts and reconciliation with Italy impossible. . . .

The weakness of the Papal cause is apparent. While . . . the army of the Church . . . is denouncing from every pulpit in Roman Catholic Christendom the 'Revolution' as the work of Anti-Christ, and after the Pope has promulgated Allocutions, Pastorals and Encyclicals declaring flight and martyrdom preferable to conciliation, and threatening the enemies of the Church with excommunication, His Holiness has not acted quite consistently with the principles to which he has committed his clergy. On the one hand he has accepted the part-payment of the Pontifical debt from Italy, which *de facto* involves the recognition of the loss of a portion of the States of the Church, and on the other hand he has tacitly allowed the bishops to accept Baron Ricasoli's invitation to return to their vacant sees, which *de facto* involves the administration of those spiritual comforts excommunication is intended to withhold. The Episcopacy is thereby placed in the very awkward position of having to defend principles dictated to them by their spiritual head, but practically disregarded by him. The contradiction is fatal and a breach has thereby been laid open which must weaken the defence of the ecclesiastical garrison. Another bulwark will fall to the ground if the negotiations for the settlement of ecclesiastical questions between Rome and Florence should prove successful. . . .

Whatever way we look, the declining strength of the Temporal Papacy is evident. But in my opinion the much talked of financial embarrassments of the Court of Rome do not constitute the most serious danger in the future, as the Pope has an inexhaustible source of wealth in the purses of the faithful. A more serious danger is arising out of the disappointment and exhausted patience of the foreign Catholic clergy. In retracing in their heart of hearts to its origin their loss of influence and of wealth, the clergy cannot fail to perceive that the 'Revolution' is not alone to blame, but that they owe the change to the administrative incapacity of their Supreme Head at Rome, whose Government has lost the glorious traditions of the past. For upwards of three centuries Italian Conclaves have successfully continued to keep the supreme command of the Catholic Church all over the world in their own hands and to exclude all other nations from sharing the honours and the power of the Vicariate of Christ, with skill so consummate as to enlist a spiritual army in every foreign country ever ready to espouse the interests of Rome against those of their own country and imbued with an Ultramontane feeling so powerful as to prompt an unqualified admiration and defence of the grossest blunders of the Vatican.

As now the clergy of foreign countries gradually realize that the skill which governed the Church has died away and the blunders alone remain, to which the loss of their influence and wealth will be ascribed, a feeling of distrust in the leadership of Italian ecclesiastics will awaken a desire to deprive them of their supremacy. . . .

363   [F.O. 43/99A]   *Rome, 8 January 1867*

No. 7
O.R. to Lord S.

I have been informed on good authority that the Franciscans of Aracoeli have submitted to the Holy Father the importance of proclaiming the Assumption of the Virgin, a new dogma, with a view to invite her intercession in the present persecution of the Church and in order to stem the growing infidelity of the age. The Pope, it is said, deeply gratified by the great success of the establishment of his dogma of the Immaculate Conception and the enthusiasm with which it was received by the faithful has deigned favourably to consider the pious recommendation of the Franciscan friars and it will perhaps be submitted for ratification to the great assembly of bishops who have been invited to meet in Rome in June.

The Assumption of the Virgin Mary, that is to say the belief in her corporal presence in Heaven is not an article of faith in the Roman Catholic Church but has hitherto been only a tradition, the historical authenticity of which may be discussed and questioned by theologians without incurring loss of salvation after death. But the Church has sanctioned for centuries the celebration of the event on 15 August as one of the great festivals of the year.

I understand that the expediency of canonizing Christopher Columbus which has been eloquently advocated by Cardinal Donnet, archbishop of Bordeaux, in a letter to the Pope, is still under consideration.

364   [F.O. 43/99A]   *Rome, 15 January 1867*

No. 11
O.R. to Lord S.

Signor Tonello continues to express himself satisfied with the progress of his negotiations. . . . On the other hand it is a remarkable fact that Cardinal Antonelli avoids as much as possible to speak on the subject and on being too closely pressed, the other morning by the French Ambassador to admit the great advantages of a settlement with Italy, the discussion took so animated a turn that His Eminence, when it was over, was compelled to close his door and seek rest in his bed for the remainder of the day. . . .

365 [F.O. 519/205] *Rome, 27 March 1867*

O.R. to Earl Cowley

. . . There is nothing to say from Rome. We are quiet and expectant, a lull before a storm?

And I can only repeat that Sartiges is the best French Ambassador and best colleague I ever knew. May he be long my colleague in Rome for my sake as well as for that of the French Government and of the Emperor. . . .

366 [F.O. 43/99A] *Rome, 27 February 1867*

No. 23
O.R. to Lord S.

The hopes entertained by moderate men immediately after the evacuation of Rome by the French army, of a peaceful solution of the Roman Question, are gradually vanishing before the slow progress of Signor Tonello's negotiation and the failure of the French Government to obtain concessions and administrative reforms from the Papal Government, the irritation caused by the presence of the Zouaves and continued enlistment of foreigners for the Pontifical army, the general increase of prices and growing financial distress, and the firm determination of the Pope not to come to terms with Italy. . . .

367 [F.O. 43/99A] *Rome, 6 April 1867*

No. 33
O.R. to Lord S.

I have the honour to enclose a copy of the first Proclamation issued by the Roman Garibaldian Committee to inform the people that General Garibaldi has accepted the command of the expedition to liberate them from the yoke of the priests, and calling upon the Romans to be ready for action when their leaders call them. It is difficult to foretell how soon acts and deeds will follow words. . . .

368 [F.O. 519/205]   *Rome, 10 April 1867*
O.R. to Earl Cowley

The possibility of a war between France and Prussia and its consequences absorbs every other thought here. The Pope and his foolish
friends who have nothing to hope from peace, flatter themselves that a
European conflagration would give them what they have lost, and
therefore pray for war.

The National Party who dread that Italy, instead of sweeping her
new house clean, may be dragged by France or Prussia into the conflict,
pray for peace. Much as the clerical party detest the Emperor Napoleon,
they do equally detest the idea of a powerful Protestant Prussia and a
free Italy, and Christian Love and Charity have long been banished
from the councils of the Vatican.

Sartiges sees all in black in the East and North, and takes what
Frenchmen call the present humiliation of France deeply to heart. He
and every other Frenchman I speak to in Rome say that if they do not
fight and beat the Prussians at once, France will be reduced to the
position of Belgium or Holland. . . .

369 [F.O. 43/99A]   *Rome, 24 April 1867*

No. 35
O.R. to Lord S.

[The Easter ceremonies over], the whole attention of the Government
will be devoted to the preparations necessary for the Jubilee and canonization in June to which all the bishops of Roman Catholic Christendom
have been invited. It is very generally believed that the Pope intends to
avail himself of the presence of the bishops (800 in number) to form a
sort of Council and obtain from them a solemn confirmation of his
Non possumus policy. I need scarcely tell Your Lordship that the
bishops once in Rome and under the infallible influence of the Sovereign Pontiff will confirm anything His Holiness pleases, even a new
dogma. . . .

370 [F.O. 43/99B]   *Rome, 19 June 1867*

No. 51
O.R. to Lord S.

. . . It is said that the Pope in the Consistory to be held on 26th inst.

at the Vatican, will intimate the convocation of a general Council of the
Roman Church for next year. If this be true, the event is of great
importance as it involves a revision of Canon Law and of the decisions
of the Council of Trent. . . . Another report is that the doctrine of the
individual infallibility of the Pope, which was rejected by the Council
of Trent is now to be proclaimed a dogma by the projected Council.
I should scarcely have mentioned this strange report which has long
been fondly nourished by ultramontane ecclesiastics, had it not now
been powerfully advocated by the Jesuits in their last number of the
Civiltà Cattolica.[1] . . .

It is a matter of bitter disappointment to the Court of Rome that so
many Sovereigns have visited the Paris Exhibition and been the guests
of the Emperor Napoleon, and that none have made the centenary of
St Peter an excuse for paying homage to the Pope.

[*In October Garibaldi invaded the Papal State. The French Emperor
sent an expeditionary force which joined the Papal troops to defeat the
invaders at Mentana on 3 November.*]

371 [F.O. 43/99B]   *Rome, 13 November 1867*
No. 62
O.R. to Lord S.

I left Florence yesterday and reached Rome early this morning, when
I was informed by my servants that on Saturday, 9th inst., a perquisition had been made in my apartment in the Palazzo Chigi by the Pontifical police. An officer and about 30 men in plain clothes had called at
about 12 p.m. and after penetrating into Prince Chigi's cellars and
visiting those parts of his palace nearest to the Monte Citorio or
Ministry of Police, in search, they said, of a mine or of Garibaldian
arms supposed to be concealed there, about half a dozen of them proceeded to my apartment on the second floor and continued their
perquisition in my rooms.

My servant tells me that they looked everywhere, over and under
the furniture, but that they respected my archive presses, my papers
and my books and carried nothing away. They behaved civilly to him
and asked him to call at the police office next door, which he accord-

---

[1] The organ of the Jesuits in Rome.

ingly did, but after waiting for a quarter of an hour he was told that he was not wanted and might go away. . . . [Has addressed a note, endorsed, to Cardinal Antonelli on the subject.]

372   [F.O. 43/99B]   *Rome, 15 November 1867*

No. 64
O.R. to Lord S.

[He had received a letter of explanation from Cardinal Antonelli.] I called this morning on the Cardinal Secretary of State and told him that I had sent Your Lordship a copy of his note explaining the motives which had led to the perquisition. . . . Cardinal Antonelli who welcomed me with the greatest cordiality told me how much he regretted that the late Roman insurrection should have rendered these extraordinary measures and precautions necessary on the part of the police and that the circumstances which had led to those researches . . . were as follows: a plan of Rome had been found on one of the Garibaldian chiefs killed in the insurrection, indicating where arms had been concealed and the public buildings undermined, like the Seristori barracks, the blowing up of which had destroyed thirty lives and much valuable property. Most of the indications on this map had proved to be correct and had led to the discovery of several mines, large deposits of arms of every description, including hatchets, and of more than 100 so-called Orsini Bombs. Cardinal Antonelli proceeded to shew me one of these deadly weapons of conspiracy. They are the size of a large orange and so covered with copper caps as to blow up wherever they fall. About 30 of them were actually thrown in the streets of Rome, killing and wounding many people. The hospitals were filled with the innocent victims of the Garibaldian conspiracy, for His Eminence was happy to think that the Romans themselves had taken no part in the outbreak and had either been passive or loyal throughout the insurrection.

Monsignor Randi, the Governor of Rome, received an anonymous letter telling him that the Palace of Monte Citorio in which he resides and the adjacent Palazzo Chigi in which I live were undermined so that no time could be lost in giving orders to the police to search these palaces from the cellars to the roof, but in so doing the strictest orders had also been given them to respect my archives and personal property. This order was strictly obeyed and nothing belonging to me was either touched or removed.

373 [F.O. 43/99B]   *Rome, 22 November 1867*

No. 68
O.R. to Lord S.

Cardinal Antonelli told me this morning that the Pope had accepted the invitation of the Emperor Napoleon to take part in a Conference for the settlement of the Italian Question on a distinct understanding that the only principle on which the Sovereign Pontiff could consent to be represented at those Conferences was the Principle of legitimate right and justice. . . . The only solution of the Roman Question His Holiness could admit was the unconditional restitution of the provinces and property of the Holy See, of which the Church had been robbed (*volé*) by the Piedmontese Government.

374 [F.O. 43/99B]   *Rome, 23 November 1867*

No. 70
O.R. to Lord S.

. . . I have heard both from French and Pontifical officers that the Garibaldians at Mentana stood the *chassepôts*, field pieces and grapeshot so well and fought so bravely that many of the 615 killed were found to be also covered with bayonet wounds. General Kanzler told me that he had offered the prisoners taken at Mentana and elsewhere their freedom if they would sign an engagement never to take up arms again against the Pope, but one and all had refused to accept their liberty on that condition.

375 [F.O. 43/99B]   *Rome, 26 November 1867*

No. 71
O.R. to Lord S.

. . . The Pope's army is being rapidly increased, and every ship from France brings recruits for the Zouave and Antibes Legions to Civita Vecchia. The reason assigned by the Papal party for this increase of the foreign legions is that the Pope will require troops to occupy Umbria, the Marches and Romagna as soon as those provinces have been placed again under Papal rule by a decision of the Conferences about to assemble for the settlement of the Italian Question. . . .

376 [F.O. 43/99B]   *Rome, 11 December 1867*

No. 83
O.R. to Lord S.

Although the fact is not admitted at the Vatican, I am strongly inclined
to think that sooner or later we must expect a second 'Papal Agres-
sion', as the English Roman Catholic clergy are urging the Pope to
establish the Roman Catholic Hierarchy in Scotland. . . . In such
matters the Court of Rome prefers to act by surprize, and the intention
will be carefully concealed until the measure is published and applied.

377 [F.O. 43/99B]   *Rome, 19 December 1867*

No. 86
O.R. to Lord S.

Monsieur Rouher's declaration that the Emperor would maintain the
Pope in the full extent of his present dominions is considered a great
triumph of Papal policy at the Vatican. . . . On Saturday last the
French Ambassador spoke to Cardinal Antonelli about a preliminary
'exchange of ideas' before the proposed Conference and asked on what
basis he would be prepared to discuss the future *modus vivendi* of the
Papal Government. Cardinal Antonelli replied that he had nothing to
add to what he had said all along. . . . An angry conversation is said to
have ensued. Monsieur Rouher's declaration has rendered the Pope so
completely 'master of the situation' in France that the Emperor can no
longer venture to oppose the clergy without exposing himself to the
censures of the Church.

[*The new French Foreign Minister had declared in the Chamber on 5 December:* 'Nous le déclarons au nom du gouvernement français: l'Italie ne
s'emparera pas de Rome! Jamais la France ne supportera cette violence
faite à son honneur et à la catholicité.']

378 [F.O. 43/101]   *Rome, 13 January 1868*

No. 8
O.R. to Lord S.

Your Lordship will learn from the enclosed article of the official
Correspondance de Rome that the Papal Government consider Fenianism
a punishment from heaven for the revolutionary policy of Great
Britain on the Continent!

379 [F.O. 43/101] *Rome, 16 January 1868*

No. 9
O.R. to Lord S.

. . . The French Government have advized the Pope to increase his army very considerably and Her Majesty's Vice Consul at Civita Vecchia tells me that since 15th ult. they have sent 1076 soldiers from Toulon and Marseilles to enlist in the Antibes Legion, and continue to send more by every steamer from France.

Besides French soldiers, recruits from Ireland, Holland, Belgium, Switzerland, Germany, Spain, are enlisted by their bishops and sent to Rome at the expense of the Papal Government. The Pope's army is said to number nearly 16,000 men. Another curious fact is the construction of defences and earthworks, by the advice of the French Government, outside the walls of Rome, as well as the landing at Civita Vecchia of mortars, artillery of heavy calibre, ammunition and material of war from Toulon. . . .

In short, the influence of France tends to make of Rome a fortified city and of the Pope a military despot, and the clerical party who rejoice with great joy in their present turn of fortune and believe in their future triumph, pray devoutly that general European war may soon divide and break up Italy, arrest the progress of Protestant Prussia in the north and of schismatic Russia in the east, unite the Latin race and Catholic powers in the name of the Holy Roman Church, and establish the supremacy of the Pope over Europe and the world.

380 [F.O. 43/101] *Rome, 21 January 1868*

No. 14
O.R. to Lord S.

I called this morning on the Cardinal Secretary of State and told His Eminence that I had heard with regret that the Pope was being urged to erect a Roman Catholic Hierarchy in Scotland. . . .

I reminded His Eminence of the evil consequences of the 'Papal Aggression' and said that in speaking as strongly to him as I did I was solely animated by an earnest and anxious desire for the maintenance of peace in religious questions and that in whatever light Her Majesty's Government might hereafter regard the matter, it could not fail to excite in Scotland, and among the English also, a bitter anti-Catholic feeling. The present, I added, was the worst possible time to set about creating such a feeling, inasmuch as there was among all classes a sincere desire to conciliate the Catholic Irish, and the Fenian danger had made everyone anxious to give the Catholic clergy, who could do so much to encourage or repress it, fair play and whatever they could reasonably ask.

[*This despatch obtained an answer from the F.O. approving the language used by O.R.*]

381 [F.O. 43/101]   *Rome, 22 February 1868*

No. 22
O.R. to Lord S.

[Concerning the progress of French armaments in Rome and Civita Vecchia. The difficulty of obtaining precise statistics]. . . . The Papal army is said to number 20,000 men at present. . . . At Rome the French have insisted on the construction of defences and batteries on most of the points commanding the gates or the town itself, and the Castle of St Angelo has undergone all the most necessary repairs to sustain a prolonged siege or bombard the town of Rome. As far as I can judge these strategical precautions appear more calculated to suppress a revolutionary movement than to resist a foreign invasion. . . .

On landing at Civita Vecchia in October last, the French military authorities brought the conviction with them that the Garibaldian movement would be followed by a general revolution in Italy against the so-called tyranny of the Piedmontese and they hoped and believed that they would be called upon to reinstate the Pope and establish an Italian Confederation which would practically destroy the alliance they feared then existed between united Italy and Prussia. . . .

382 [F.O. 43/101]   *Rome, 10 March 1868*

No. 24
O.R. to Lord S.

Having every reason to hope that my marriage can take place towards the end of April, I trust Your Lordship will see no objection to granting me the necessary leave to absent myself from my post in the course of next month.

383   [F.O. 43/101]   *Rome, 26 March 1868*

No. 32. Secret
O.R. to Lord S.

I had the honour of an audience of the Pope this morning, who was
pleased to express the most benevolent interest in my approaching
marriage and a wish that I should present my wife to him immediately
after our return to Rome. He had seen Lady Emily last year with Lord
Clarendon whose conversations had charmed and interested him
deeply, although it had been a matter of regret to him to find that His
Lordship did not approve of Cardinal Cullen.[1] ... Yet Cardinal Cullen
had assisted Her Majesty's Government in the suppression of Fenianism and would continue to do so, His Holiness having condemned
the Fenians, whom he called 'the Garibaldians of England'. Garibaldi had compelled him to become a military prince and he now
had, in proportion to the 600,000 subjects the Piedmontese had left
him, a larger army than any other sovereign in the world and all his
soldiers were animated with the true spirit of crusaders. . . . If the
interests of the Church ever required it, His Holiness added, laughing
loudly, he would even buckle on a sword, mount a horse, and take
command of his army himself like Julius II. But on the whole he was
satisfied with the present state of Rome and the prospects of the
Church. . . .

The Pope then questioned me a good deal about the state of parties
in England and said with great warmth that he hoped Mr Disraeli
would employ the genius God had given him and the power the Queen
had invested him with to improve the condition of Ireland. . . . He
added '*Caro Russell mio*, if you see no objection, I should like Her
Majesty the Queen to be informed that the Pope entertains the highest
respect for Her Majesty.' . . .

I never saw His Holiness in better health or spirits or more benevolent in language and manner.

384   [F.O. 43/101]   *Rome, 25 October 1868*

No. 40. Confidential
O.R. to Lord S.

The Pope was pleased to receive me and my wife with his wonted

[1] Cardinal Paul Cullen, archbishop of Dublin.

benevolence and give her a mosaic paperweight as a wedding present this morning at a private audience in the palace of the Vatican. His Holiness inquired with great interest after the health of Her Majesty the Queen and again expressed his regrets at not seeing the Prince and Princess of Wales at Rome as on former occasions.

After some general conversation, His Holiness expressed an earnest desire that the public press should cease to misinterpret his words in regard to the Oecumenical Council next year and that Protestant divines would receive his invitation in a Christian spirit and come to Rome to listen to the voice of truth and reconciliation.

His Holiness, who was throughout most gracious, appeared to be in excellent health and spirits and dismissed us with his blessing.

Before closing this report I may as well explain that the Pope believes his Oecumenical Council to be the result of divine inspiration and that he is chosen to become the shepherd of the one single united Christian flock of the future.

385 [F.O. 43/101]   *Rome, 3 November 1868*

No. 44
O.R. to Lord S.

Today is the anniversary of the battle of Mentana, and I think that a short Memorandum on the advantages which the Papacy has derived in one single year from that victory may not be unacceptable to Your Lordship. Left to deal single-handed with Italy, the Temporal Power of the Popes was manifestly doomed to succumb in the struggle for liberty and nationality, had not the 'wondrous' intervention of French *chassepôts* at Mentana saved the Papal dominions from annexation to Italy, and the feeling of triumphant security which the victory of Mentana and the re-occupation of Rome by French troops gave the Vatican at once strengthened the spiritual influence of the Roman clergy all over the Catholic world. That influence was speedily exerted to bring about the failure of the proposed Paris Conference for the settlement of the relations of Rome with Italy, and the reluctance of both Protestant and Catholic powers to attend those Conferences, shewed how clerical influence had established a belief that any interference with the future *modus vivendi* of the Papacy might offend the religious feelings of the Roman Catholic subjects of those Governments.

The next achievement of the clerical party was to compel M. Rouher to declare, in the name of the Emperor's Government, that the French Protectorate of Rome would '*never*' cease. Having thus secured the existence of the Temporal Power, the influence of the clergy was successfully exerted all over the Catholic world to command an un-limited supply of Catholic Crusaders for the Papal army, and an unlimited supply of Peter's Pence for the Papal Exchequer. . . .

Nor are these results as precarious as they appear at first sight. By placing himself at the head of the Legitimist and Clerical Parties and calling upon them to crush indiscriminate Liberty, Progress or Revo-lution, the (so-called) common enemies of the Church, the Pope has created a *Political Catholic Party* all over the world, a legion of men and women disciplined and commanded by the clergy . . . who will fight or pay for a cause they are . . . persuaded to be their own, whilst France will feel the advantage of prolonging indefinitely an armed protectorate, which conciliates the clergy and insures their votes at the elections in France while it divides, commands and neutralizes Italy strategically in the event of war with Prussia. . . .

386 [F.O. 43/101]   *Rome, 16 November 1868*

No. 45. Secret
O.R. to Lord S.

[Concerning French armaments in Rome, which has become a kind of *tête de pont* against Italy.] . . . Marshel Niel is incessantly urging the Papal Government 'to lose no time in completing their armaments and placing their army on a war footing so as to be able to leave Rome and be ready to take the field at any season of the year'. The Papal army at present number 16,405 men and 1168 horses. . . . The Papal army would offer a contingent of 12,000 men to the French army of occu-pation in the event of a campaign, and the fortifications have been so constructed by General Prudon as to require but a very small number of men for the defence of the town of Rome against attack or insur-rection. . . .

General Prudon assumes that after a siege of ten days the garrison would probably have to fall back upon the right bank and blow up the bridges across the river and seek shelter in the Leonine City and Trastevere where the Castle of St Angelo and powerful defences of the Mons Vaticanus and Janiculum would enable them to resist a besieging army for more than a month, a period, he says, which would give ample time for the arrival of relief from France or elsewhere. . . . [Arrivals of French arms at Civita Vecchia are reported in subsequent paragraphs.]

[*Bodleian Library, Clarendon Papers, C. 475(4)*]

387   *F.O. 14 December 1868*

Private
Earl of Clarendon to O.R.

. . . I send you a few lines of observation on what Antonelli said – they are not of much practical utility. Mr Gladstone suggested them. Will you present my respects to His Eminence and tell him I hope with your assistance to maintain very friendly relations with Rome. You can also say from me how very ill-advized he will be if he attempts to establish a Hierarchy in Scotland just after the stout manifestations of Protestantism that the Elections have elicited. It would really look like defiance.

You might also hint that the daily prayers put up at Rome for war are not likely to be heard just at present, and that any policy founded on that benevolent desire has a chance of coming to grief. . . .

[*With the fall of the Conservative Government, Lord Clarendon had returned to the Foreign Office on 9 December.*]

388   [Clarendon Papers, C. 487]   *Rome, 16 December 1868*

Private
O.R. to Earl of C.

. . . The convocation of this Council is certainly a very popular measure in the Clergy who flatter themselves generally that they are to have an Ecclesiastical Parliament for the discussion of their local grievances and the promotion of their private interests, whilst the French Bishops in particular, who think the Papal Government too exclusively Italian, hope through their eloquence to obtain office in Rome. And no one seems yet to realize that the Pope merely intends the Council to be a grand Ceremony in St Peters for his own glorification and the formal confirmation of his Syllabus doctrines, his temporal Dominion and his Ex-Cathedra infallibility. *De part et d'autre il-y-aura des surprises!* Whatever may be said to the contrary on high Authority, I do not myself believe that any single Bishop or any number of conspiring Bishops can sustain an individual or inde-pendent opinion under the paternal wings of the Vatican if the Pope commands obedience. . . .

389   [Clarendon Papers, C. 475(4)]   *The Grove,*
27 December 1868

Private
Earl of C. to O.R.

. . . I was very glad that you had referred me to certain dispatches of yours to Stanley as I might not otherwise have seen them. I never, even of yours, read any that interested me more. The state of things you describe is exactly that which was establishing itself when I left Rome and which has been confirmed and developed in the 10 months that have since passed. I have sent your No. 44 to your illustrious Uncle John. It may disturb his general belief in the expediency and fitness of anything undertaken by Garibaldi.

I quite agree with you that although many Bishops will arrive at Rome in the belief that they are about to enjoy privileges of Parlt. and that before votes are taken grievances will be redressed, yet that the *genius loci* will overawe them and that not one will dare speak when the Holy Father demands silent assent. The Council conducted and concluded as it probably will be must I think be regarded as a monster glove thrown down not alone to the spirit of the age but to the common sense of mankind, and good may come out of it. . . .

390   [Clarendon Papers, C. 487]   *Rome, 30 December 1868*
Private
O.R. to Earl of C.

. . . The new Austrian Ambassador Count Trautmansdorff had been very cordially received by Pope and Cardinal, but when he proceeded to business and begged of them to moderate the hostile attitude of the Austrian Clergy in political matters, he preached in vain to deaf ears. The Vatican cannot afford '*pour les beaux yeux de Beust*'[1] to disavow their Bishops who squeeze ever so many more Peter's pence out of their

[1] The Austrian Chancellor, a Protestant.

flocks, if they can but persuade them that the Church is persecuted and
Religion in danger. Governments, who still attempt to reason with the
Pope, evidently forget that the French protectorate of Rome enables
His Holiness to do just as he pleases with perfect impunity. The
Austrian clergy have been instructed to form a 'Catholic party', as in
France and several lay leaders are now in Rome learning their new
policital creed and abusing Beust. . . .

I hope Mr Hammond will be satisfied with the handwriting of my
new Secretary.

391   [F.O. 43/101B]   *Rome, 1 January 1869*
No. 1.
O.R. to Earl of C.

[Concerning the proposed Scottish Hierarchy]. . . . I have spoken to
Archbishop Manning on the subject and he has entirely confirmed
Cardinal Antonelli's assurances to me that the report in question is
unfounded. He admitted that a Hierarchy for Scotland had been under
discussion at the Propaganda, but on mature reflection had been given
up for various reasons, and the Scotch Vicars Apostolic Drs Eyre and
Macdonald appointed Bishops *in partibus* instead, a *mezzo termine* which
was in all respects preferable.[1]

I was glad to hear the Archbishop say that the present friendly
relations existing between Her Majesty's Government and the Roman
Catholic clergy in England precluded the adoption of a measure of so
much importance as the creation of a Hierarchy in Scotland without
previous notice or understanding.

I have every reason to think that the 'mature reflections' which led
to the present change of policy at the Vatican in regard to the Scotch
Hierarchy are due to Your Lordship's conversation on the subject with
the Pope and reported this day last year in my despatch No. 1 to Lord
Stanley.

392   [P.R.O. 30/22/16]   *Rome, January 1869*
O.R. to Earl R.

. . . The Pope is in excellent health and looking forward to his Oecumenical Council with religious delight. It will all be so organized and
managed as to render the expression of any individual and independent

[1] The Catholic Hierarchy was established in Scotland on 4 March 1878.

opinion on the part of the foreign bishops quite impossible, and they will be disagreeably surprized to find themselves compelled to sanction what they intended to condemn! . . .

393 [Clarendon Papers, C. 487]   *Rome, 13 January 1869*
Private
O.R. to Earl of C.

Archbishop Manning paid us a long and pleasant visit and all he said was satisfactory. His strongly expressed Gladstonian predilections are said by many in Rome to have alarmed ('*Spaventato*') the Vatican, but I do not believe it, for the Pope has implicit faith and confidence in him, and Cardinal Antonelli, who never liked Wiseman, speaks of Manning in the very highest terms and congratulates himself on having selected him for his present post.

394 [F.O. 43/103B]   *Rome, 24 January 1869*
No. 5
O.R. to Earl of C.

[Concerning slanderous charges made by Dr Small against Mr Severn and Mr J. H. Parker, an eminent archaeologist.] . . . Doctor Small is an Irishman who enjoys the reputation in Rome of being an able, though quarrelsome physician. His best friends . . . and others, including myself, have been subjected to his fondness for aggressive correspondence . . . his assertions of one day are not always present to his mind on the next . . . I admit that a doctor may well be indignant with a patient who does not pay him, but the doctor's indignation should not necessitate the interference of the police to protect the patient, and Your Lordship will perceive from my answers to doctor Small that I made every allowance for his 'unsubdued Irish temperament'. [Many documents accompany this despatch.]

395 [Clarendon Papers, C. 475(4)]   *F.O. 25 January 1869*
Private
Earl of C. to O.R.

. . . I am very glad that the Scotch Hierarchy is staved off for the present for, whatever Manning may say, it would have had a disastrous effect in Scotland. I wish, tho' of course in vain, that some check could

be put upon Cullen. I told the Pope that he was the bitter and per-
tinacious enemy of the English Govt. and he never misses an opportunity of doing mischief. He and others have just done all that is most
embarrassing to Gladstone by a manifesto shewing that if any consideration is shewn to the Protestant Clergy about to be turned adrift
(in the matter of glebes, parsonages, etc.) it will not be considered
satisfactory to the Catholics. I need not say that this is an enormous
triumph to the Tories and a bitter pill to Gladstone whose object is to
satisfy the Catholics. Cardinal Antonelli is the last man, I am sure, to
desire that the utmost generosity should not be shewn to a Church
about to be disestablished, and a Clergy about to be disendowed and it
is really too bad that this viper Cullen should be permitted to create
difficulties in addition to those which already exist, and Heaven knows
they are great enough. I shall be glad if in gentle language you could
convey to the Cardinal and to Manning the *utter disgust* we feel at the
conduct of Cullen and Co, who, as I need not say, give the tone to the
whole priesthood of Ireland. This conduct is as stupid as it is malignant
and ungrateful, for it gives arms to the Ultra Protestants in England
and greatly weakens the support on which Gladstone depended. . . .

396   [Clarendon Papers, C. 487]   *Rome, 27 January 1869*

Private
O.R. to Earl of C.

. . . In the afternoon I took a walk on the Pincio with Dr Manning
and found him personally and politically devoted to Mr Gladstone of
whom he spoke with the *warmest affection.* He also said twice that he
was 'sincerely glad' you had replaced Lord Stanley at the F.O. . . .

397   [F.O. 43/103B]   *Rome, 5 February 1869*

No. 8. Confidential

[Concerning the Irish Church.] . . . Cardinal Antonelli had quite
recently again discussed the question with Dr Manning and he could
not sufficiently repeat how much impressed he had been by the Archbishops' knowledge, opinions, sentiments, views and arguments and
how entirely he subscribed to them. 'Archbishop Manning with all his
devotion to religion and the Holy See,' His Eminence added, 'is an
Englishman at heart and charmed me by the love he bears to his

country and his thoroughly English character, and Lord Clarendon
cannot do better than consult him as regards our views and wishes in
Rome.'

398 [Clarendon Papers, C. 487]   *Rome, 10 February 1869*

Private

O.R. to Earl of C.

. . . If you have time to cultivate Dr Manning when he returns to
London which will be very soon, I feel sure you will like him and find
him useful.

Austere and ascetic as he appears at first sight he can be a most
agreeable companion and as cheerful as a Roman Monsignore.

He is thoroughly straightforward, knows what he wants and speaks
to the point, and his influence on the Pope and his Government as
regards the Roman Church in England is as real as it is remarkable.
None of his Brother Bishops have any, so that he is all powerful at the
Vatican and at the Propaganda, which has not made him overpopular
with his clergy in England. . . .

399 [F.O. 43/103B]   *Rome, 9 March 1869*

No. 11

O.R. to Earl of C.

Cardinal Antonelli told me this morning that he had read Mr Gladstone's speech of 1st inst. on the Irish Church with great interest and
that the plan proposed for solving that difficult question appeared to
him both prudent and wise (*aussi prudent que sage*) because it gave full
time for an equitable *rectification* of Church interests without bearing
the character of a *confiscation* of Church property, like the odious
measures adopted in Italy two years ago.

400 [F.O. 43/103B]   *Rome, 24 March 1869*

No. 14

O.R. to Earl of C.

Sir Augustus Paget[1] has very kindly allowed me to read his most
interesting report to Your Lordship of 5th inst., from which I gather
that King Victor Emmanuel is under an impression that the French

[1] English Ambassador to Italy.

troops will not remain in Rome much after the general elections in France. I humbly beg to differ from His Majesty for the following reasons:

1st. The Emperor Napoleon's position in France is not strong enough to allow of his acting against clerical opinion in regard to the Pope, even if he wished it.

2nd. Clerical opinion must insist on the continuance of the French protectorate during the whole period of the Oecumenical Council, which may last many years, and cannot allow the Pope and the 900 bishops of Roman Catholic Christendom assembled at Rome to be again abandoned to the tender mercies of the revolutionary party in Italy after the failure of the Convention of 15 September 1864.

3rd. The exclusive protectorate of the Oecumenical Council gives France through her bishops an influence at Rome and throughout the Catholic world in spiritual matters which the Eldest Son of the Church cannot afford to neglect, quarrel with, or concede to Italy.

4th. In the event of war the presence of a French army at Rome, which has been carefully fortified by French engineers, enables the Emperor Napoleon to control the alliances and secure the co-operation of Italy, while it ensures the sympathies of the clerical party and gratifies the national pride of France.

5th. The withdrawal of the French garrison from Rome, after the general elections in France, before the end of the Oecumenical Council or during an European war would tend to weaken the cause of the Emperor Napoleon spiritually and temporally both at home and abroad.

401 [F.O. 43/103B]   *Rome, 30 March 1869*

No. 15
O.R. to Earl of C.

In reading Mr Bright's great speech on the Irish Church I could not but feel, as I have often felt before, that the practical application of purely Christian principles might solve many of the questions which threaten the peace of society. How much has been said and written about the solution of the Roman question and the Pope's *Non possumus*, and yet if the 'Vicar of Christ' would turn to his Bible he would find that his Kingdom is not of this world, and that by doing unto his subjects as he would be done by instead of coercing them, and that by loving his Italian neighbours as himself instead of quarrelling with them, the Roman difficulty would solve itself in Christian principles.

Be that as it may, Pius IX now deserves the highest credit for the convocation of an Oecumenical Council, and for thus conceding an ecclesiastical Parliament to the Church at a moment when freedom of discussion may tend so largely to promote harmony and good will among Christians. . . .

402 [F.O. 43/103B]   *Rome 6 April 1869*

No. 18. Secret
O.R. to Earl of C.

Cardinal Antonelli requested me to inform Your Lordship in strict confidence that he had received intelligence of a serious and alarming nature from several Roman Catholic priests in the West Indies, that secret agents sent from Washington by President Grant at work enlisting the co-operation of the clergy to bring about the annexation of those Islands to the United States by universal suffrage. The priests had all behaved well in declaring that it would be their duty to oppose the intrigues they were asked to assist, because the principle of universal suffrage had been condemned by the Pope in his Syllabus. Their conduct had been approved and the spirit of the West Indian clergy was excellent but still the annexation of the West Indies to the United States would in his opinion be a serious embarrassment to Europe and he hoped Your Lordship would cause inquiries to be made without naming him as informant, with a view to preventing mischief if possible. . . .

403 [Clarendon Papers, C. 487]   *Rome, 7 April 1869*
Private
O.R. to Earl of C.

Cardinal Antonelli's West Indian news is unpleasant if true, and he seemed alarmed about it in real earnest, but his geography must be superficial for he could not or would not enter into any practical details and name the Islands from whence his information was derived and whenever I asked whether he did not mean Cuba he always replied: 'No, all the Islands of the West Indies.'

You probably know more about it at the F.O. than he does at the Vatican. . . .

M de Banneville[1] avoids his Colleagues and society in a manner that surprizes everybody, and Madame de Banneville lives in bed and seldom even dines with her husband whose dismal existence is as cheerless as hers. I must say that I find him cheerful enough when I meet him, but my colleagues complain of him bitterly. . . .

404 [F.O. 43/103B]   Rome, 1 May 1869

No. 30
O.R. to Earl of C.

[Concerning the Oecumenical Council.] . . . The Pope has appointed a special Congregation of Cardinals and six Committees to direct the preparatory labours. . . . The result of the labours of the Committees will be submitted to the Bishops in Council on 8th December, when the general discussion will divulge the motives which have rendered the convocation of an Oecumenical Council desirable. . . .

The other day I asked Cardinal Antonelli to tell me whether the bishops had the right of proposing reforms. His Eminence replied that they had, and that the Council was neither more nor less than an ecclesiastical Parliament, much like the English House of Lords. 'Happily,' he added, 'we have none but matters of discipline to discuss and no dogmatic question need complicate our debates.'

'According to the newspapers,' I said, 'the *ex cathedra* infallibility of the Pope will be proposed for the approval of the bishops.'

'They are misinformed,' Cardinal Antonelli replied. 'The *ex cathedra* infallibility of the Pope has ever been an article of faith with every true Catholic and therefore admits of no discussion.' 'You surprize me,' I replied, 'for I have hitherto been led to understand that the unanimity of the Pope and Bishops in Council assembled constituted the infallibility of your Church.' 'Truly,' His Eminence replied, 'but you forget that the Pope like other sovereigns has the power to veto the decisions of the Council according to the dictates of his conscience and the inspirations of the Holy Ghost.'

From this conversation I infer that the dogma of the Pope's personal

[1] The Marquis de Banneville had become French Ambassador the previous autumn.

infallibility will never be submitted to a debate, but will be presented in such form to the Council as to enable the bishops to confirm it *'nem. con.'*

To judge from the pastorals and pamphlets published by the leading bishops of the Roman Catholic world, this measure is ardently desired by them. Some few who think otherwise have published their pamphlets anonymously and they will find it difficult to hold an independent opinion once they are in Rome and under the dome of St Peter. At first their independence would be met by paternal warning, then their errors would be threatened with the censures of the Church, then they might be refused the Sacraments, and finally excommunicated, and the position of an excommunicated priest is deplorable. On the other hand, the penitent priest who submits his judgment and abjures his errors is received like a prodigal son by the Holy Father, so that obedience is not only a virtue but also the best policy a Roman priest can follow.

When therefore the bishops meet on 8 December they will find the subjects they are called upon to consider already studied and sifted by the Roman committees and all further discussion almost superfluous, and the Pope's infallibility will be established *de facto*. Some opposition, however, is expected on the part of the French bishops. . . .

405 [Clarendon Papers, C. 487]   *Rome, 5 May 1869*

Private
O.R. to Earl of C.

. . . I called yesterday on Cardinal Antonelli whom I found idle, pleasant and humorous. He asked for news, but had none to give. I then called his attention to the debate in Parliament of the 30th ultimo on the state of Ireland and asked him to explain to me how it was that the Clergy had not sufficient control over the morals and manners of the Irish peasantry to put a stop to agrarian murders and other atrocities?

Cardinal Antonelli replied that the state of Ireland filled him with horror and distress and that the Irish character was incomprehensible to him. He knew no nationality so difficult, so hopeless or so disagreeable to deal with, and one single Irish soldier gave him more trouble than a legion of other foreigners. He was, however, happy to tell me that he was pleased with the attitude Cardinal Cullen and his Clergy were about to assume and thought their efforts to prevent

crime and calm the excitement of the people would be finally crowned
with success, and the more so if the measures proposed by H.M. Govt.
to do justice to Ireland became law, and he asked me whether Mr
Gladstone's bill would pass the House of Lords?

I said, of course, that the attitude of the Clergy and the good behaviour of the peasantry and the support of the Catholics could alone
secure the reforms they desired themselves and His Eminence knew
better than I did how far the clearly expressed will of the Pope could
influence the conduct of the clergy and of their flock, and bring about
the realization of their own wish for justice and freedom. While Her
Majesty's Govt. were making enormous sacrifices, in fact a revolution,
to secure justice to Ireland, unassisted and unsupported by those they
were fighting for, the Court of Rome without effort or publicity and
by a single whisper of advice to their adherents might prevent a
revolution against the Church which would inevitably follow the loss,
through their own ill advized apathy, of those very measures they had
clamoured for for centuries. . . .

406 [F.O. 43/103B]   *Rome, 8 May 1869*

No. 31

O.R. to Earl of C.

[Concerning the attitude of the French clergy to the Council.]
. . . I do see the elements of a future struggle for power in the idea
which is taking root in the minds of the French clergy that the time
has come for them to reap the reward of their services and participate
in the temporal administration of Rome. For three centuries and a half,
since the pontificate of Adrian VI, Italian Popes, prelates and priests
have governed the Catholic world, so that the administration of the
Church has ceased to be Catholic and has assumed an exclusively
Italian character, the inconvenience of which will now be practically
felt by the clergy of other nations when the Pope imposes his reform
bill on the Council of the Vatican and the Syllabus becomes law.

The administration of the Roman Catholic Church by Italians was
convenient to the Catholic powers so long as Italy could be considered
as a mere 'geographical expression', but now that Italy has acquired a
national existence, the temporal administration of Rome may become
a national question among them. . . .

The French clergy after exchanging their Gallican liberties for

Ultramontane bondage have felt, in their closer contact with Rome, an intellectual superiority that ought to have entitled them, they think, to some influence at the Vatican, but they cannot conceal from themselves any longer that with all their virtues, their talents, their eloquence and their devotion, they are still as powerless against the Italian element that governs the Church in Rome as the Emperor Napoleon against the *Non possumus* policy of Pio Nono.

Notwithstanding his services, his embassies and his armies, the Emperor has signally failed to give France that moral ascendency in Rome which his protective policy seemed to warrant, and while the Pope can force the Emperor to protect and fight for the Papacy, the Emperor cannot persuade the Pope to listen to his advice and accept his *modus vivendi*; while the Pope can influence the elections in France, the Emperor has not a single vote in the Sacred College; while the Pope can raise loans and legions at his pleasure in France, the Emperor cannot even obtain a Cardinal's hat and stockings for his Archbishop of Paris.[1] . . .

I am for my part convinced that in the long run an Italian priest will always outwit a Frenchman and that Italians will continue to govern the Church of Rome in the name of the Catholic world as heretofore. . . .

[Quotes Grant Duff's Political Survey: 'Are the French troops really going to be used to make possible an assembly, which will be gathered together for the express purpose of damning modern civilization in general and the principles of 1789 in particular? If so, the humour of the spectacle will transcend anything that Europe has yet seen!']

407 [F.O. 43/103B]   *Rome, 8 May 1869*
No. 32
O.R. to Earl of C.

[Concerning a circular despatch addressed by the Bavarian Government to their representatives abroad on the subject of the Council.] . . . The Circular has given great offence at the Vatican, because it is not written in that submissive spirit, which the Pope expects from Roman Catholic governments. . . .

The Bavarian Government have doubtless shewn prudence in consulting other Catholic Governments, before it is too late, as to the

[1] Archbishop Georges Darboy (1813-71), leader of the Gallican clergy.

manner in which they intend to meet and deal with the decisions of
an ecclesiastical tribunal which (under the armed protectorate of
France) is about to enact irrevocable laws which will be binding on
the consciences of the clergy and of millions of their subjects.

[*The circular, drawn up by Professor Döllinger, of Munich, and sent to
the Catholic Governments of Europe, proposed a conference in order to
prepare a united front against the threat of the subjection of the civil power
to the Pope which was feared from the decisions of the Oecumenical
Council.*

*During May it was proposed to O.R. that he should undertake a
mission to the United States. For public and private reasons he declined,
and his father-in-law agreed with his decision.*]

408 [F.O. 43/103B]   *Rome, 8 June 1869*

No. 40. Confidential
O.R. to Earl of C.

The Marquis de Banneville has asked the Cardinal Secretary of State
for a statement of the subjects intended to be submitted to the Council,
but although His Excellency used every argument in his power to
prove the advantages of a friendly understanding on the subject,
Cardinal Antonelli was unable or unwilling to meet the wishes of the
French Government.

In talking over the matter myself with His Eminence this morning
I said that every Catholic Government must naturally desire to know
for what object the Council had been convoked and I should not be
surprised if a collective inquiry were made by them at Rome with
regard to the subjects bearing upon civil rights and the relations of
Church and State to which the attention of the Council might be
called.

Cardinal Antonelli replied that . . . the object of the Council had
been generally stated by the Pope in his Bull of Convocation wherein
he invited the bishops to assemble and discuss those reforms of
ecclesiastical discipline which modern times required. . . . There were
no dogmatic questions to be discussed. . . . He told me in strict confidence that in framing the Bull of Convocation the bishops alone had
been invited and the Catholic Governments left out because they
had practically ceased to be Catholic powers by neglecting their most

sacred duties towards the Church and by encouraging anti-Catholic principles which the Popes had repeatedly condemned. There was not one so-called Catholic Government that possessed moral courage enough to stem the revolutionary torrent of infidelity and immorality that threatened society. The Governments of Austria and Italy gave sad examples of such perversion.

Abandoned by those whose duty and interest it was to protect the Church, it became the sacred duty of the Pope to find means of protecting religion and moral order in the world and fulfil his divine mission on earth without the temporal support he had hitherto been able to rely on, and the convocation of an Oecumenical Council was a first step in that direction. He would frankly admit to me that the position of the Roman Catholic clergy in England and America was more satisfactory . . . than in any Catholic country at present and he would be glad to see the Roman Church as free from state interference all over the world as in England and America. . . .

409 [Clarendon Papers, C. 487]   *Rome, 16 June 1869*

Private
O.R. to Earl of C.

. . . As matters now stand I really do not believe that Bishops can hold independent opinions in Rome, and whatever their private feelings may be in their respective Sees, not one of them in Rome will venture to vote against the Infallibility and Assumption of the Virgin Dogmas, or the confirmation of the Syllabus. I hope I may be mistaken.

Three times in ten years have I seen the Bishops assembled in Rome made to sign an Address to the Pope against their inclinations and convictions by order of His Holiness.

During the 'Centenary of St Peter' an Address was crammed down their throats which virtually contained a declaration in favour of the personal infallibility of Pius IX. Some hesitated, but an order came from the Vatican which none ventured to resist.

Five hundred and sixteen Bishops signed it including those who are supposed to have an independent and rational opinion of their own such as the Archbishop of Cologne and Darboy, the Archbishop of Paris &.. &.. &...!

One single Portuguese Bishop resisted and refused to sign this address, but he died soon after this act of disobedience like Cardinal d'Andrea, and will not be available for the Council.

Again Mr Gladstone says that there might be an opportunity of helping to do what the Reformation in many things did, to save the Pope and the Roman Church from themselves.

I am afraid that to save the Pope and the Roman Church from themselves would give satisfaction but to a very limited number of rational Romanists while the enormous Catholic Party all over the World will hail any new outrage of the Papacy against human reason with unbounded enthusiasm and will meet it with increased Faith and active Fanaticism, Peter's Pence, Infallibility associations, Catholic Crusaders, religious orders, unlimited Donations &. &. as was the case in a smaller way after the proclamation of the Dogma of the Immaculate Conception of the Virgin. . . .

410 [Clarendon Papers, C. 475(4)]   *F.O. 28 June 1869*

Private
Earl of C. to O.R.

Your letters are most interesting and much appreciated by the *Chef de l'État* and her Govt.

The Council is beginning to excite much interest not to say alarm which is augmented by the secrecy observed at the Vatican.

It is curious that Pce. Hohenlohe the most ultramontane Minister of the most Catholic Kingdom in Germany should be the man to *sonner le tocsin* and to ask other powers to be as frightened as Bavaria.

For my own part I hope that the dogmas and doctrines to be propounded will be to the last degree extravagant as the common sense of mankind may thereby be awakened and, *possibly*, impelled to revolt. . . .

411 [Clarendon Papers, C. 487]   *Rome, 14 July 1869*

Private
O.R. to Earl of C.

. . . Since poor Monsignor Talbot has been shut up in a madhouse at Passy, no English Prelate has been appointed to fill his place at Court and Dr Manning enjoys in consequence the sole and undivided confidence of the Vatican. . . .

412 [F.O. 43/103B]   *Rome, 8 December 1869*

No. 58. Secret
O.R. to Earl of C.

[O.R. had arrived in Rome on 5 December. He reported the opening of the Council on 8 December with great pomp and solemnity. Between 6 and 700 bishops present.] . . . I called yesterday on Cardinal Antonelli, who received me with his wonted cordiality, and I gave him Mr Gladstone's as well as Your Lordship's friendly messages with the warmest expressions of reciprocal interest.

I then said that Mr Gladstone and Your Lordship had authorized me to assure His Eminence that while you hoped that the Oecumenical Council might prove conducive to the good of humanity, you could not conceal from him that great danger to the peaceful relations of Church and State might ensue if the exaggerated views of extreme parties prevailed in the Assembly and you therefore trusted that the Papal Government would be foremost in giving the example of enlightened moderation to the bishops in Council assembled.

Cardinal Antonelli replied that he fully shared the views I had expressed and that no one could more sincerely regret the controversy which had lately raged in the clerical press, than he did. The Pope had convoked an ecclesiastical Parliament for the free and independent discussion of Church interests by the bishops among themselves and it was deplorable to see some of them forget themselves so far as to discuss like journalists in the daily press those grave and solemn questions which an Oecumenical Council alone could consider and decide.

I said that I believed that the definition of the infallibility of the Pope, so strongly urged by the authors of the *Civiltà Cattolica*, had never been countenanced by the Papal Government. Cardinal Antonelli replied that I was correct in thinking that the definition of the dogma had not been suggested by the Pope or his Government, but that the bishops could not be prevented from taking it into consideration if so inspired during their debates. He, for one, had always believed the *ex cathedra* utterances of the Papacy to be the result of divine inspiration, for the infallibility of the Catholic Church assembled, when the bishops, away from Rome, were dispersed all over the world attending to their flocks, resided in the Pope; and even the decisions of an Oecumenical Council, before becoming law, required the final sanction of the Pope.

I asked whether His Eminence believed the dogma would be defined. Cardinal Antonelli replied that no one could foretell in what sense the Council would be inspired by the Holy Ghost. . . .

413 [Clarendon Papers, C. 487]   *Rome, 8 December 1869*

Private
O.R. to Earl of C.

I have just telegraphed to tell you that the Oecumenical Council has been opened with great pomp and solemnity, between six and seven hundred Bishops present.

On Lord Acton's[1] authority I added that: it was confidently asserted by the French that the opposition led by Monsignor Dupanloup would triumphantly carry the fallibility of the Pope. This impression I find is shared by the Laity, the Diplomatic body and the foreign Clergy generally, but Roman Ecclesiastics shake their heads and seem to think the Jesuits are not beaten yet.

Rome is running alive with newspaper correspondents who will inundate the Post Office with letters tonight from which you may learn the ecclesiastical gossip of the day. I have not yet been here long enough to know more of the truth they than do, but I advize you to take their statements *'cum grano'*. . . .

The enormous quantity of anecdotes in circulation about what the Pope said to this or that Bishop is confusing, but the sum total is that the Bishops dislike the infallibility dogma and that the Pope preaches obedience and submission to them.

The Roman, Papal, Jesuit or ultramontane party is said to be composed of the Italian, Spanish, South American, English, Irish, Belgian and half the French Bishops, whilst the other half led by Dupanloup ocmmand the votes of the Austrian, German, North American, Bohemian, Hungarian and Portuguese Bishops. The Orientals are still wavering. . . .

With all due deference to the opinion of the French Embassy and of the Liberal Catholics in general my private conviction remains unshaken that the Pope will make the Council vote as he pleases, but

[1] Lord Acton was a liberal Catholic of the Döllinger School, present in Rome during part of the Council.

25. Lord Granville

26. Cardinal Manning

I have not had time yet to see many people and to form a correct opinion of the situation of parties. . . .

414 [F.O. 43/103B]   *Rome, 11 December 1869*

No. 59
O.R. to Earl of C.

[O.R. had failed to attend the opening ceremony of the Council.] . . . Although Cardinal Antonelli had advized me to take my wife to the Diplomatic Tribune, Monsieur de Banneville, the French Ambassador, who is the *doyen* of the diplomatic body, did not think himself authorized '*de décider si des agents non reconnus officiellement par le Gouvernement Pontifical font partie à Rome du corps diplomatique et, par conséquent, s'ils peuvent être admis dans la Tribune Diplomatique etc.*'

No doubt, Monsieur de Banneville was legally right, but I have since been informed that the Cardinal Secretary of State regrets the Ambassador's decision.

[Describes some of the procedure of the Council. The Pope has appointed a commission of 24 bishops (including Cullen and Manning) to whom members of the Council will have to submit the subjects they desire to bring before the house.] . . . As most of the above-named prelates belong to the party of the *Civiltà Cattolica*, the so-called liberal Catholics, led by Monseigneur Dupanloup, protest against the Pope's selection, but I do not expect they will succeed in obtaining any alteration in their favour, as they still form but a small minority of the episcopacy. Out of 700 bishops in Rome, Monseigneur Dupanloup has not found more than 150 to support his policy and vote with him against the supporters of the Papal Government.

Another grievance has been the unexpected issue of a Papal Bull establishing the rules of procedure of the Council, which the liberal bishops had intended to make for themselves. . . . But the one great question which is now uppermost in men's minds is the definition of the *ex cathedra* infallibility of the Pope. To judge from the present language of the opposition led by the bishop of Orléans the definition of the dogma would lead to schism. And to judge from the language of the Ambassadors of France and of Austria, who ought to be well informed, the Papal Government acknowledge the danger and are preaching moderation to the Infallibilist party and recommending the indefinite postponement of the debate on that question. With all due

o

deference to the opinion of the representatives of France and of Austria in Rome, I confess my inability to share their hopes. The indefinite postponement of the definition of the Pope's infallibility would practically amount to a defeat of the Government and a victory of the opposition, and the Papal Government having a majority in their favour would scarcely like to subject themselves in the eyes of the world to a defeat, which in public opinion would be tantamount to a declaration of the Pope's fallibility.

415 [Clarendon Papers, C. 475(4)]   *The Grove,*
                                                      13 December 1869
Private

Earl of C. to O.R.

. . An *explosion d'hilarité* followed my reading to the Cabinet your telegram saying that the French hoped under the lead of Dupanloup triumphantly to establish the Pope's fallibility. Gladstone shook his head and said the French were always sanguine folk and that their expectations were too good to come true. . . .

I shall be glad to know what amount of consideration is shown to Acton and whether he is thought too black a sheep to be of service in the cause of common sense.

The curiosity, I should perhaps say interest about the Council is daily on the increase, and the Queen and her Confidential advisors are eager for your reports.

I don't know who is the correspondent of the Times but I hear that the R.C.'s are frantic at the bantering style in which he describes the *mise en scène* of the 'much ado about nothing' comedy that is now being performed in Rome.

There is an inclination to bet that the Pope will back out of his infallibility but I think he must be too far gone in obstinacy for that. . . .

416 [Clarendon Papers, C. 487]   *Rome, 16 December 1869*
Private

O.R. to Earl of C.

. . . Dr Manning called last night on Emily (to meet Acton and Amberley[1]) and told us that the result of the election of the Dogma Committee in Thursday's sitting was not yet known.

[1] Lord Amberley, Earl Russell's eldest son.

He said that the sittings would probably have to be suspended until another Council Hall could be found in which the '*Fathers*' could hear each other, which was simply impossible in St Peter's. Dr Manning believes the Pope's infallibility will be defined. . . .

417 [Clarendon Papers, C. 487] *Rome, 18 December 1869*
Private
O.R. to Earl of C.

. . . Cardinal Schwarzenberg has adhered to the Dupanloup oppositon and has brought a number of Austrian Bishops with him, but not all, for many don't like to follow the lead of a Frenchman.

Altogether the character of the struggle is becoming clearer, and I perceive a strong undercurrent of nationality in this Clerical Parliamentary Babel. We have no longer Bishop opposing Bishop, but Frenchmen against Italian, and German against Italian and Frenchman, and Englishmen against themselves and Irishmen against everybody.

Whatever wise and learned men may say to the contrary I feel convinced that the Court of Rome delight in the confusion of Bishops and know well that by waiting and gaining time the opposition will lose and the Papal Party gain in strength and that all will *infallibly* end well.

Cardinal Bonnechose has already retracted and gone over to the Infallibilists and others will follow. The Pope is as cheerful and happy and calm as possible. He is benevolent, paternal and jocular with his opponents and won't allow a word to be said against them in his presence like a man '*qui est sur de son affaire*'.

The independent Bishops have gone to him in fear and trembling prepared for attack and defence, and have come away overwhelmed with the Cordiality of His Holiness and charmed with his wit and humour.

I have established intimate relations with Lord Acton and Sir Rowland Blennerhasset and am to meet all the Irish Bishops '*a poco a poco*'. . . .

418 [F.O. 43/103B] *Rome, 19 December 1869*
No. 61
O.R. to Earl of C.

[The second general Congregation of the Council held in St Peter's on 14th inst. elected the first of the four Commissions of 24 bishops to report on matters relating to dogma.] ... From 10th to 14th considerable excitement prevailed among the bishops, who held daily meetings in various private houses, according to nationalities or 'languages', for the purpose of drawing up lists of candidates supposed to represent the two great parties in the Church of Infallibilists or Manningites and Fallibilists or Orleanists.... The result of the struggle has been the complete discomforture of the Orleanist or Fallible opposition and the complete triumph of the Infallible Government party. [List of the 24 bishops, which includes Leahy, archbishop of Cashel, and Manning.] As far as I have been able to learn everyone of the above-named dignitaries is favourable to the dogmatic definition of Papal Infallibility. ...

Still the Orleanists are not discouraged and flatter themselves that they will be stronger or better organized on 20th when they meet to elect the second Commission for question relating to discipline.

After the election of the Dogmatic Commission, a Papal Bull was distributed to the bishops limiting the ecclesiastical censures. ... The object of this Bull is a practical one. It abolishes the numberless ecclesiastical censures which had become obsolete but still existed in the Canons of the Church, and enumerates in a condensed form all those which the Pope desires to retain. The opposition bishops seemed to think that measures and reforms of this nature should not have been promulgated by the Pope without being submitted to them and some were even inclined to remonstrate, but the Pope had foreseen and provided against this contingency by article 4 in the Bull which excommunicates anyone who objects to a Pontifical order and appeals to a future Council. As an argument wherewith to combat the opposition led by Monseigneur Dupanloup this measure will prove invaluable. ...

The oath of secrecy of members renders it very difficult to know the truth about the proceedings of Council and the conflicting opinions of theologians as to the exact meaning or practical effect of Pontifical Bulls renders it equally difficult to say whether the Bull of Censures is a *de facto* excommunication or merely a paternal warning. Both interpretations have been put upon it with equal science and lucidity by the distinguished theologians I have been able to consult, whilst the Cardinal Secretary of State explains it to alarmed diplomatists as a liberal reform without practical importance. The first impression it produced on the public mind was certainly that an excommunication

of the Emperors of France and Austria, together with their Governments, was intended, but the Ambassadors of France and Austria do
not appear to attach any importance whatever to the Bull which they
tell me 'contains nothing new'. . . .

419 [Clarendon Papers, C. 487] *Rome, 22 December 1869*

Private
O.R. to Earl of C.

. . . You ask me what amount of consideration is shewn to Acton in
Rome and whether he is thought too black a sheep to be of service
to the cause of common sense? He is simply looked upon as *'un diable
dans un bénitier'* at the Vatican because of his Articles in the last 'North
British', the 'Massacre of St Bartholomew and the Pope and Council',
and his active interference to bring about an understanding between
Monseigneur Dupanloup and the German Bishops. . . .

I see a great deal of him and he is most kind and useful to me and
both he and Sir Rowland Blennerhasset promise to introduce me to the
Irish Bishops. . . .

I cannot say how deeply I admire his (Acton's) talents, virtues and
learning and how much I delight in his society and I wish I could
agree in thinking, as he does, that the enlightened opposition of the
school he belongs to, can succeed in reconciling the Church of Rome
with common sense through the Council. . . .

420 [F.O. 43/103B] *Rome, 24 December 1869*

No. 64
O.R. to Earl of C.

[The commission for discipline has been elected. All 24 (which include
Ullathorne, bishop of Birmingham) are of the Government party. The
opposition bishops have drawn up a petition asking the Pope to modify
some of the procedural rules.] . . . Although I have been repeatedly
assured by the French Ambassador that over 200 bishops had accepted
the leadership of Orléans . . . I now learn that only 14 French bishops
could be persuaded to sign the petition and about a dozen German
bishops, whilst Cardinal Schwarzenberg . . . withdrew at the last

moment from the Fallibilitarians, declined to sign the petition and joined the majority as Cardinal Bonnechose had done a few days before him. The loss of Cardinal Schwarzenberg is a serious blow to the opposition as it entails also the loss of those Austrian bishops who had accepted him as their leader. I should not, however, be surprized to see His Eminence waver more than once between the two contending parties.

Archbishop Simor, the Primate of Hungary, is, rightly or wrongly, accused by the opposition of yielding to the temptations of a Cardinal's hat, sixteen of which are now at the Pope's disposal, so that his support can no longer be reckoned on by them.

To me the position of the minority appears hopeless, and they must think so themselves, if it be true that they have appealed to the Emperor Napoleon for moral support. . . .

421 [F.O. 43/103B]   *Rome, 29 December 1869*
No. 66
O.R. to Earl of C.

[Yesterday the Commission for the reformation of regulars and monastic orders was elected. All the names belonged to the Governmental majority.] . . . After the election the Cardinal Speaker (De Luca) declared the Session open and the first debate in Council commenced on the 'Condemnation of Errors' Bill. . . . Cardinal Rauscher, who opened, spoke more than an hour and took the Council by surprise, for all his arguments were against the Government measure, which he desired to see altogether withdrawn. The six bishops who followed all spoke in the same sense, and as no one rose on the part of the Dogmatic Commission to defend the Bill, the oppostion considered this first debate as a great triumph, and the excitement of their partisans outside the Council has been boundless ever since.

Tomorrow's debate will be even more important as the Archbishop of Paris and the bishop of Orléans are expected to speak against the Bill and the Government have as yet appointed no one to speak on their side. . . .

Cardinal Antonelli is reported to have said after the debate, that judging from the length of the first six speeches, the Council might be expected to last over ten years.

422 [F.O. 43/103B] *Rome, 30 December 1869*

No. 67
O.R. to Earl of C.

[The debate on the 'Condemnation of Errors' Bill continued this morning. Vanesa, Strossmayer, Genouilhac and Caixal-y-Estrade spoke, all against the Bill.] . . . The only fact of interest that has yet transpired with respect to this debate is that bishop Strossmayer, generally said to be the best Latin orator who has yet spoken in the Council, was twice called to order by the Cardinal Speaker, but the bishop, less obedient than his predecessors, asserted his independence, repeated the sentences for which he had been reproved and completed his oration amidst the approbation of the Fathers of the opposition. . . .

423 [F.O. 43/106] *Rome, 3 January 1870*

No. 3
O.R. to Earl of C.

. . . The bishops of the opposition now regret that the Catholic Governments did not insist on being diplomatically represented at the Council as proposed by the Bavarian Government last spring. . . . But I doubt whether any of the Catholic Governments will venture, now that the labours of the bishops have commenced, to alter the decision they came to before the Council met, when Bavaria invited their co-operation in vain.

424 [F.O. 43/106] *Rome, 4 January 1870*

No. 4
O.R. to Earl of C.

[The debate on the 'Condemnation of Errors' bill continues. Speeches in favour of the bill.] . . . The leaders of the opposition, Monseigneur Darboy and Monseigneur Dupanloup, having declared to the Cardinal Speaker De Luca that if any attempt was made to carry the infallibility dogma by acclamation, they and their followers would protest and leave, not only the Council Hall but even Rome, it has been thought more prudent by the Infallibilitarians to circulate a declaration in favour of the new dogma for signature among themselves so as to ascertain their numerical strength before they proceed to action. . . .

425   [Clarendon Papers, C. 487]   *Rome, 5 January 1870*

Private
O.R. to Earl of C.

. . . I have made the acquaintance of Monseigneur Dupanloup, and he appears to me to indulge in illusions with respect to the Opposition he has undertaken to lead against the Vatican. Cardinal Antonelli holds him and his followers very cheap indeed and says that '*la furia francese*' has often been cured by a residence in the Roman atmosphere. . . .

426   [F.O. 43/106]   *Rome, 8 January 1870*

No. 8
O.R. to Earl of C.

[The debate on the 'Condemnation of Errors' bill continues.] . . . Although the bishops of the opposition flatter themselves that their arguments have demolished the Government measure, I have not the slightest doubt that the Dogmatic Commission, after modifying perhaps the wording, will send up a 'Draft' or 'Project of Condemnation' to His Holiness which will retain the spirit of the bill and will be promulgated by the Pope in the shape of an irrevocable decree to the infinite surprize of the Fallibilitarians, who may then perhaps begin to perceive that their opposition is impotent.

427   [Clarendon Papers, C. 475(4)]   *The Grove,*
10 January 1870

Private
Earl of C. to O.R.

. . . The interest here in the Council does not flag but the contrary. People were wonderstruck at the audacity of the assault on human reason, amused at Bishops being brought from the uttermost parts of the earth to be treated with less confidence than an infant school. . . .

The Pope seems quite equal to the management of that cunningly devised machine the Catholic religion and I feel sure he will have all things his own way as from the first you said he would, but I don't envy the Bishops who will return from their unavailing opposition crestfallen to their dioceses which their Holy Father will much enjoy. . . .

428 [F.O. 43/106]   *Rome, 10 January 1870*
No. 10
O.R. to Earl of C.

. . . The petition in favour of the dogmatic definition of Papal infallibility has called forth a counter petition on the part of the opposition.
. . . Cardinal Rauscher of Vienna and bishop Clifford of Clifton are
said to have joined the Fallibilists on this occasion and to have accepted
the lead of Monsgr Dupanloup who reckons on 200 signatures, whilst
the Infallibilists led by bishops Spalding of Baltimore, Mermillod of
Geneva and Archbishop Manning expect to command the votes of the
remaining 560 bishops.

The opposition bishops flatter themselves that they can prevent the
dogmatic definition of the dogma and their hopes are shared by the
representatives of the Catholic powers in Rome. To me it is difficult
to believe that the Pope can allow his authority to be doubted. He
called the Council to ratify his past policy and not to criticise it. If his
Infallibility is not confirmed, his Syllabus and his *Non possumus* policy
will die with him and he well knows that a decentralizing reaction
would follow a vote that admitted the principle of criticism to enter
the gate of the Vatican. . . .

429 [F.O. 43/106]   *Rome, 13 January 1870*
No. 13. Secret
O.R. to Earl of C.

In order to give more effect to Your Lordship's instructions respecting
Ireland, I applied for, and had the honour this morning of a private
audience of the Pope, who was pleased to receive me with the utmost
kindness and paternal benevolence.

His Holiness said he had been gratified to learn that I had declined
other diplomatic posts for the sake of being in Rome during the
Council. I explained that His Holiness had been misinformed by a
paragraph in one of the Roman papers, but that I preferred Rome to
any other post at this interesting moment although the difficulty of
getting at the truth was a serious drawback to my happiness and I
deeply regretted that His Holiness's Government did not see fit to
give authentic information to foreign representatives with regard to
the labours of the Council.

The Pope said he thought on the contrary that bishops were not sufficiently reserved and more especially French bishops who committed culpable indiscretions whenever they went to the French Embassy, to which he desired to put a stop. The result of the labours of the Council should be known when it was over, not before. In a century where railways and telegraphs had shortened time and lengthened life, where great campaigns had lasted but a few days, he had hoped to see an Oecumenical Council accomplish its task in four or five months. But he noticed with regret that bishops indulged in tiresome and never-ending orations, and wasted time to no purpose, so that the Council might last years instead of months. But he could not or rather he *ought* not to tell them so, otherwise they might complain of want of independence.

I said that independence was essential to Parliaments but that members given to verbosity were exposed to address empty benches and that bishops like members of other Parliaments would probably learn to leave the Council Hall when a tiresome orator addressed them. The Pope laughed and said they had already begun to show signs of impatience when *'certi chiacchieroni'* spoke too long. . . .

After some unimportant observations, His Holiness asked me whether I knew many bishops. There were, he added, five or six very good English bishops and the Irish were all good. I said I had endeavoured to know the Irish bishops with a view to ascertaining and consulting their wishes, because Her Majesty's Government were about to introduce important reforms in Ireland which would require their cordial and powerful co-operation, but unfortunately they were all in Rome when their presence was most needed at home to combat Fenianism, the enemy of Church and State.

The Disestablishment of the Church was an enormous measure carried at a great cost as it alienated the Protestants, but it was intended as a message of peace to Ireland and a hand cordially offered to the Roman Catholic subjects of Her Majesty. The bishops, I was happy to say, had received it in a Christian spirit and Her Majesty's Government were grateful for their support, but among the lower clergy were many who sympathized with the Fenians, denounced their bishops, criticized their theology, condemned their pastorals, encouraged disobedience, crime and sedition and undermined the spiritual authority of the Pope in Ireland. If His Holiness would consult the bishops, he would find that they needed his immediate interference to pacify Ireland and that they could do no more than they had done without his support to re-establish their authority over the lower clergy and enforce respect for law and religion among the people.

The Pope said that he pitied the bishops who in the pursuit of their calling were constantly exposed to a '*bastonata*' from the Fenians who were the Garibaldians of England.

I said that a message, a single word, from His Holiness to the Irish clergy, in support of episcopal authority, and stringent instructions to the bishops to suspend offending priests, would give the example of respect to authority so much needed at present in Ireland, and the clergy could always reckon on the cordial co-operation of the civil authorities whenever they were themselves willing to accept it. I then entered into a detailed account of the state of Ireland. . . .

The Pope deigned to listen and question with interest, and showed no signs of impatience or displeasure at my repeated and urgent appeals for some practical measures to strengthen the authority of the bishops who had admitted to me that they no longer had the power to do good where Fenianism prevailed in Ireland. Finally, after a very long conversation the Pope authorized me to tell Your Lordship that although he had already condemned Fenianism, he would again consult the Irish bishops and take such measures as might be deemed expedient by them. . . .

430 [F.O. 43/106]   *Rome, 14 January 1870*
No. 16
O.R. to Earl of C.

. . . The last of the four Commissions of 24 bishops for oriental rites was elected, and a message from the Pope to the Council was read by the Cardinal Speaker intimating that indiscretions committed by some of the Fathers compelled His Holiness to declare the violation of the secrecy he had imposed upon them by the 'Rules of the Council' to be henceforward a mortal sin.

This measure will render it more difficult than ever to get at the truth about the debates in Council.

431 [F.O. 43/106]   *Rome, 18 January 1870*
No. 18
O.R. to Earl of C.

. . . I am told on the authority of the opposition bishops that the

Archbishop of Algiers has left Rome for Paris on a mission from the Pope to the Emperor to obtain a distinct guarantee from His Majesty that the opposition bishops will not have Imperial support against any merely dogmatic decrees, and in return the Vatican will enter into engagements and make concessions about morals and politics, Syllabus and Censures. For my part, I cannot see that the opposition has yet sufficiently alarmed the Vatican to render concessions necessary on the part of the Pope to the Emperor.

432 [F.O. 43/106]   Rome, 19 January 1870

No. 19
O.R. to Earl of C.

Monsgr Darboy, the Archbishop of Paris, is said to have made a powerful speech this morning against the principle of the 'Duties of Bishops' bill and to have protested against the encroachments upon episcopal rights which the centralizing and romanizing policy of the Vatican was leading to. . . .

433 [F.O. 43/106]   Rome, 23 January 1870

No. 23
O.R. to Earl of C.

I have seen Archbishop Manning and bishop Moriarty who tell me that the Pope has authorized the condemnation of the Fenians in Ireland. Hitherto Fenianism was a sin only in as much as it implied membership of a secret society. The present document condemns the Fenians by name as the enemies of the civil power. . . .

434 [F.O. 43/106]   Rome, 23 January 1870

No. 24
O.R. to Earl of C.

. . . Six weeks have elapsed since the opening of the Council and have turned conjectures into certainties as to the true object of its convocation and the position of parties. It is now manifest that the sole object the Vatican had in view was the dogmatic definition of Papal Infallibility or the confirmation of the absolute authority of the Bishop of Rome over the episcopacy of Roman Catholic Christendom. . . .

Those who object to the definition of the dogma have proved more numerous and stronger than the Vatican expected and have been hitherto sufficiently united to prevent a definition by acclamation. Whether they will be strong enough to prevent the definition in debate remains still to be seen, though they count in their ranks many of the most learned and eminent divines in the Church.

When the Council first met the Papal party or Infallibilists were thoroughly well organized, while the independent bishops scarcely knew each other. They expected the Council to be a constituent assembly and to become better acquainted with each other while framing their rules of procedure and selecting the officers of the Council, before the debates began on the various measures they intended to propose and discuss. Great was their surprize when they found that the officers of the Council had been appointed by the Pope and that the standing orders were imposed upon by the Bull *Multiplices Inter* according to which the Pope reserved to himself the right of initiative and the veto, thereby establishing *de facto* his authority over the Council.

The publication of the Bull *Cum Romanis Pontificibus* proroguing the Council in the event of the Pope's death the Bull of Censures *Latae Sententiae*, reviving the famous Bull *In Coena Domini*, the secrecy commanded in regard to the subjects they would be ordered to discuss, the prohibition to see the official shorthand reports of their own speeches, the result of the election of the dogmatic deputation etc., very soon proved to the independent bishops that they had been summoned to Rome to confirm the Pope's authority and not to share it. Those among them who had their own independence at heart, sought and found each other under the leadership of Monsgr Dupanloup and resolved respectfully to solicit greater independence from the Pope. But finding as their numbers increased that no single nation would follow the lead of the other, they formed national committees and drew up separate addresses, which they took separately to the Pope, who received them paternally and dismissed the bearers with his blessing, but never took the slightest notice of their petitions.

Under these circumstances they sought strength in unity by forming a permanent international committee which meets every afternoon in Cardinal Rauscher's apartment and is composed of 12 bishops among whom are Schwarzenberg, Rauscher, Darboy, Dupanloup, Genouilhac of Grenoble, Strossmayer of Bosnia, Ketteler of Mayence, Haynald of

Colocsa, Connolly of Halifax, Kenrick of St Louis, Clifford of Clifton. Notwithstanding the Pope's expressed disapprobation of extra-conciliar committees, they have continued to meet and have now over 200 bishops ready to follow their lead and vote against the Pope's majority.

The Infallibilists or Definitionists as they are now called here, in order to counteract the growing opposition of this international committee, then drew up their petition in favour of the dogmatic definition of Papal infallibility . . . which, it is said, has been signed by more than 400 bishops. This demonstration was met by the international committee in their turn by a counter petition against the definition of the dogma, to which they say they have obtained nearly 200 signatures. . . . This petition has been sent to the Pope today but no one seems to know how His Holiness is likely to receive it. The majority have handed in a *postulatum* urging earnestly the definition of the dogma in Council. . . .

The majority are determined to carry the definition of the dogma as indispensable to the very existence of the Roman Catholic Church. The opposition minority are confident that they can prevent the definition of the dogma which they consider to be disastrous to the interests of religion. In private both parties speak of each other in terms of hatred and contempt, which in public are tempered by expressions of pity, sorrow and charity. . . .

The events of the last few weeks have proved the existence of parties in the Church, which the Vatican, misled by the fulsome adulation of episcopal pastorals never expected to encounter, although the careful construction of the *Regolamento* or standing orders shows that their prudence was prepared for every contingency.

I venture to think that the opposition will find that the principal mistakes they have committed were:

1. To accept Rome and the Church of St Peter as the site of the Council.

2. To accept the rules of procedure laid down in the Bull *Multiplices Inter*, which deprives them of all control over or interference in the machinery of the Council and concedes the right of veto to the Pope.

3. To accept the Bull *Latae Sententiae* which prohibits all appeal to a future Council under pain of excommunication.

By admitting those autocratic enactments they have exposed themselves to the personal influence of the Pope over the bishops, to the arbitrary authority of the Pope over the decisions of the Council, and to the impossibility of appealing to a future Council. With regard to their petition, it appears to me further that the position of the Fallibilists is illogical, because having declared that they only acknowledge the supremacy of the Council, they appeal to the Pope, when the Council is about to act, to interfere with its supremacy and the freedom of its decisions.

I am bound to add that my opinion is not shared by the members of the opposition or their friends, who now look forward with serene confidence to the final triumph of their principles.

435 [Clarendon Papers, C. 487] *Rome, 24 January 1870*

Private
O.R. to Earl of C.

... The Papal condemnation of the Fenians will be communicated by the Irish bishops in Rome to their Vicars General and will be read from the Altar by every priest in Ireland. Bishop Moriarty assures me that it is the strongest measure the Pope could take and that he expects excellent results from it. He says that all the Irish Bishops met at Cardinal Cullens' request and agreed to it but that it will certainly expose them to persecution. It extends also to the American clergy who will have to read it from the altar as in Ireland.

I am getting on much better with the Irish Bishops than I expected. At first they were shy of me, but now they come and talk and ask me to communicate their ideas to you and Mr Gladstone. [These ideas are described.]

I have told you all about the Council in a despatch and I may add here that both Dupanloup and Strossmayer admit that the Opposition could not have been organized without Lord Acton whose marvellous knowledge, honesty of purpose, clearness of mind and powers of organization have rendered possible what appeared at first impossible. The party he has so powerfully helped to create is filled with respect and admiration for him. On the other hand the Infallibilists think him the Devil!

I admire his creation, I bow before his genius and I wish the opposition all the success they have so earnestly at heart, but I adhere to my conviction that humanity will gain more in the end by the dogmatic definition of Papal Infallibility than by the contrary.

We are all very curious about the secret mission of Monseigneur Lavigerie, Archbishop of Algiers from the Pope to the Emperor and very anxious to know the truth from Lord Lyons as to its object and result. Monsieur de Banneville has given all the support of the Embassy to Monseigneur Darboy and Dupanloup and we suspect that Lavigerie is gone to enlist the Emperor's sympathies for the Papal majority or Infallibilists or Definitionists as they are now called. The Fallibilitarians have also the full support of the Austrian Embassy and Bavarian Legation.

The crisis is at hand for the Pope must soon decide between the two contending Parties in the Council.

[*In a private letter of 26 January O.R. encloses a letter from Bishop Moriarty on Irish matters.*]

436 [F.O. 43/106]   *Rome, 26 January 1870*

No. 26
O.R. to Earl of C.

The 16th and 17th General Congregation of the Council took place on Monday and Tuesday and brought the debate on the 'Duties of Bishops' bill to a close. The speech of bishop Strossmayer of Bosnia is universally said to have proved him to be the best Latinist, the ablest debater and the greatest orator of the Council. He spoke in favour of the special privileges of the episcopacy and against the spirit of centralization of the Vatican. Bishop Strossmayer may now be considered the leader of the opposition.

The more moderate Definitionists are making an attempt to bring over to the majority those among the Fallibilists who believe the dogma but doubt the '*opportuneness*' of the definition. . . .

[*On 25 January Arthur Russell who was in Rome wrote to his mother: 'I must tell you an amusing anecdote. In the debate yesterday bishop Strossmayer in the midst of his speech exclaimed "Per Deos Immortales!"'*]

437 [F.O. 43/106]   *Rome, 29 January 1870*

No. 27
O.R. to Earl of C.

. . . In about ten days or a fortnight the discussion will commence on the: *Schema Constitutionis Dogmaticae de Ecclesia Christi*. This *Schema* is simply the Syllabus turned into a dogmatic form. . . .

A glance at the Syllabus will shew Your Lordship that it is impossible to overrate the disastrous consequences of a measure that would establish a permanent conflict between Church and State. The opposition, I am happy to say, are determined not to let it pass.

438 [F.O. 43/106]   *Rome, 29 January 1870*

No. 28. [Recites Telegram]
O.R. to Earl of C.

Lord Acton wishes me to telegraph you that he is afraid that Infallibility will be voted by acclamation if the French Government does not support the opposition with all possible energy through the French Ambassador here.

439 [Clarendon Papers, C. 487]   *Rome, 30 January 1870*

Private
O.R. to Earl of C.

The opposition fears respecting a surprize and the definition of Infallibility by acclamation I believe to be unfounded. The majority, I think, will proceed systematically, organically, dogmatically, to the definition, but not until the Bills before the Council have been discussed and settled. A definition by acclamation would be no definition at all.

Acton has seen and read with his own eyes an autograph letter of Daru, the new French Foreign Secretary, to his friend Mr Du Boys who lives with Monseigneur Dupanloup here at Rome, telling him that if the Infallibility Dogma is passed the French garrison will be immediately withdrawn! I should not believe it if Acton did not say so, and I do not believe the threat can be carried out even after the dogmatization of the Syllabus. . . .

440   [F.O. 43/106]   *Rome, 4 February 1870*

No. 34
O.R. to Earl of C.

A private letter from Count Daru to Monsieur Du Boys, a French
gentleman living with the Bishop of Orléans, has been much com-
mented upon in clerical and diplomatic circles for the last few days
because the French Minister for Foreign Affairs is said therein to
declare that the Imperial troops of occupation would have to be withdrawn if the Council gave dogmatic force to the doctrine of Papal
Infallibility. I called this morning on the French Ambassador and asked
him what reliance might be placed on this important declaration.

Monsieur de Banneville assured me that he had received no instructions from his Government that could justify a belief in the authenticity
of the letter, nor did he admit that the decisions of the Council could
influence the duration of the occupation of the Holy See by French
troops, which now depended on the will of the French Parliament. He
had, however, occasionally warned Cardinal Antonelli against the
danger of theological excesses which might create a conflict between
Church and State, as for instance the Bull of Censures. But His
Eminence invariably reminded him that the Bull in question was a
beneficial reform since it had diminished the number of excommuni-
cations by several hundred and had not added a single new censure to
those already existing in the Canons; that the decisions of the Council
generally speaking concerned the Sacristy and not the State; and that
France, in common with all countries having Concordats, could not be
affected by the decisions of the Council without previous understanding and agreement with the Court of Rome, who would always adhere
faithfully to their treaty engagements.

The Ambassador . . . no longer saw reason to fear theological
excesses on the part of the Vatican for the attitude assumed by the
French bishops and their 200 followers in the Council had created an
opposing force, based on principles of moderation, good sense and
learning, strong enough at all times to prevent any serious evil or
excess on the part of the Ultramontane majority who would not
venture to oppose the clearly and firmly expressed will of Catholic
France. He did not, for instance, expect they would further attempt
to press the infallibility dogma now that they knew that 200 bishops
would vote against it, a '*tiers partie*' was already proposing compro-

mises, and of the 84 French bishops present in Rome he did not think more than 15 could be persuaded to vote for the dogma if it ever came before the Council. Even the most Ultramontane among the French bishops agreed that the Government of the Roman Catholic Church was too exclusively Italian and should be rendered really Catholic by the appointment of foreign ecclesiastics in the Roman administration before the prorogation of the Council.

On the whole I found the French Ambassador well satisfied with the prospects of the Council generally and more particularly with the position and influence of the French bishops in Rome.

441 [F.O. 43/106]   *Rome, 7 February 1870*

No. 37
O.R. to Earl of C.

The 21 Canons of the '*Schema Constitutionis Dogmaticae de Ecclesia Christi*' have been published in the *Allgemeine Zeitung*, and the painful discovery of the existence of traitors in the Council has surprized and afflicted the Pope. . . .

442 [Clarendon Papers, C. 475(4)]   *Grosvenor Crescent,*
                                                            7 February 1870

Private
Earl of C. to O.R.

I sent you a message by Emily upon the Cabinet view of your proceedings and I have not much to add to it except that you stand *very high* with them all and that there is no business however urgent that would not be suspended if I announced that I had a dispatch from O.R. to read.

Your visit to the Pope and the manner in which you conducted and reported your conversation were *chefs d'oeuvre* and it must be gratifying to you to know that the whole was appreciated as it deserved. . . .

The French Govt. wanted your assistance at Rome to make the Pope believe that a rupture with France would be dangerous to himself and to religion and we offered that you should do what little was possible but Daru on 2nd thoughts considered it unnecessary which I was glad of as we much prefer that your energies should be concentrated on Irish affairs. . . .

443 [F.O. 43/106]   *Rome, 12 February 1870*
No. 40.
O.R. to Earl of C.

[Concerning Count Daru's desire to be supported by the Governments
of Europe in his Roman policy.] . . . I was very glad to learn that Your
Lordship had pointed out to the French Foreign Secretary the delicate
and anomalous nature of our relations with the Vatican which might
render advice from us neither welcome nor useful. . . .

By excluding for the first time in the history of the Church the
representatives of foreign powers from an Oecumenical Council, the
Pope has proved that he does not intend the State to interfere with the
Church, and by the proposed dogmatization of the Syllabus His
Holiness has foreshadowed that he intends the Church to govern the
State. Any advice tendered by foreign Governments to that of the
Church must therefore of necessity be disregarded by the Sovereign
Pontiff so as to inaugurate practically the principles about to be pro-
claimed by the Council.

Your Lordship may possibly recollect how often I have called the
attention of Her Majesty's Government to the disastrous consequences
the unconditional protectorate of the Papacy by France would lead to.
Ever since his accession to the throne, and in moments of unprece-
dented danger to his temporal sovereignty, the Pope has systematically
rejected the advice of France. Why then should he listen to the advice
of Governments who have not protected him against his enemies or
his friends? . . . Why should he now listen to the advice of France
when the bishops of Roman Catholic Christendom are about to confirm those very principles for which he has suffered persecution and
combated single-handed for a quarter of a century?

444 [Clarendon Papers, C. 487]   *Rome, 12 February 1870*
Private
O.R. to Earl of C.

. . . Thank you for letting me keep Mr Harry Jervoise for a couple of
months in Rome. I know him well and like him exceedingly, he knows
Rome and Roman Society and is very popular and wishes himself to
remain. His assistance will give me the time I lack for the collection
of information, so that we are both well pleased and very much
obliged to you. . . .

The theological exasperation now raging in the bosom of the Church defies description. The opposition Bishops are triumphant at the prospect of vanquishing Romanism and Pontifical Supremacy.

The Papal Party is silent, watchful and deeply agitated.

Both Parties talk of prorogation to bury their dead.

I still believe in the final Victory of the Vatican, but my colleagues and *friends* laugh at me for it. . . .

445 [F.O. 43/106]   *Rome, 15 February 1870*

No. 41. [Recites Telegram]
O.R. to Earl of C.

I am requested to ask you to suggest to Count Beust to establish a common action with Prussia and Bavaria to support the German bishops in Rome without which they will be defeated by the Court of Rome.

446 [F.O. 43/106]   *Rome, 15 February 1870*

No. 42. Secret
O.R. to Earl of C.

. . . Monseigneur Lavigerie, Archbishop of Algiers, has returned to Rome. . . . I am assured on high authority that the Archbishop told the Cardinal Secretary of State that the Emperor Napoleon had given him the most solemn assurances of the inevitable necessity of withdrawing his troops from Rome if the Council proclaimed the personal infallibility of the Pope. Public opinion in France, His Majesty said, would not only demand the cessation of the French protectorate, but would insist on a suspension of the Concordat and a rupture of diplomatic relations with Rome; and His Majesty earnestly hoped that the Pope would listen to the advice of the French Bishops and follow it before it was too late. Cardinal Antonelli is said to have been deeply grieved by this message from the Emperor. [Encloses copy of letter of Count Daru mentioned in despatch 34.]

I am surprised that the Emperor Napoleon and Count Daru should know so little of the character of Pio IX as to suppose that advice or threats of any kind could turn him from his path of duty. Pio IX has the faith that moves mountains and believes in his divine mission. Martyrdom at the end of his Pontificate would be the reward from heaven he has prayed for all his life. His stand-point is that of a divine teacher ready to suffer and die for his faith, and he cannot yield to the advice of the temporal sovereigns of the earth to whom his life is to serve as an example. In his own opinion he has often courted martyrdom, from which the voluntary intervention of France alone has saved him, but he owes them no gratitude for it, since they merely performed a sacred duty.

But taking a more worldly view of the threat held out by the Emperor to the Pope, what does it in reality amount to? That under certain conditions the Eldest Son of the Church is to abandon the Vicar of Christ to the tender mercies of his enemies and is to look on while they despoil him of his temporal sovereignty, murder his priests, blow up his army and drive him into exile.

The Pope has not forgotten Mentana and can afford to smile at the threats of his Eldest Son.

The only demonstration that could influence the Vatican would be a protest of the 200 opposing bishops against the Oecumenicity of the Council, followed by their immediate departure from Rome.

447   [Clarendon Papers, C. 487]   *Rome, 15 February 1870*

Private
O.R. to Earl of C.

I have repeatedly asserted that many opportunists who oppose the definition of Papal Infallibility would submit their judgement once the Dogma has been decreed by the Council. As a proof of my opinion I enclose confidentially a copy of a private Letter from Dr Newman to Bishop Ullathorne, which curiously illustrates the power Rome can exercise over the minds of the faithful

[Enclosure in Private Letter of 15 February.]

28 January 1870

My dear Lord
I thank your Lordship very heartily for your most interesting and seasonable letter.

Such letters (if they could be circulated) would do much to reassure the many minds which are at present disturbed when they look towards Rome. Rome ought to be a name to lighten the heart at all times, and a Council's proper office is, when some great heresy or other evil impends, to inspire the faithful with hope and confidence. But now we have the greatest meeting which has ever been, and that in Rome, infusing into us by the accredited organs of Rome (such as the *Civiltà*, the *Armonia*, the *Univers*, and the *Tablet*) little else than fear and dismay. When we are all at rest, and have no doubts, and at least practically not to say doctrinally, hold the Holy Father to be infallible, suddenly there is thunder in the clear sky, and we are told to prepare for something, we know not what, to try our faith, we know not how. No impending danger is to be averted, but a great difficulty is to be created. Is this the proper work for an Oecumenical Council? As to myself personally, please God I do not expect any trial at all, but I cannot help suffering with the various souls who are suffering, and I look with anxiety at the prospect of having to defend decisions which may not be difficult to my private judgement, but may be most difficult to maintain logically in the face of historical facts. What have we done to be treated as the faithful never were treated before? When has Definition of Doctrine *de fide*, been a luxury of devotion, and not a stern painful necessity? Why should an aggressive insolent faction be allowed to make the hearts of the just to mourn, whom the Lord hath not made sorrowful? Why can't we be let alone when we have pursued peace and thought no evil? I assure you, my dear Lord, some of the truest minds are driven one way and another, and do not know where to rest their feet: one day determining to give up all theology as a bad job, and recklessly to believe henceforth almost that the Pope is impeccable, at another tempted to believe all the worst that a Book like Janus[1] says, another doubting about the capacity possessed by Bishops, drawn from all corners of the earth, to judge what is fitting for European Society, and then again angry with the Holy See, for listening to the flattery of a clique of Jesuits, Redemptorists and Converts. Then again think of the score of Pontifical scandals in the history of 18 centuries, which have partly been poured out and partly are still to come.

What Murphy inflicted on us in one way, M. Veuillot[2] is indirectly bringing on us in another. And then again the blight which is falling upon the multitude of Anglican Ritualists who themselves perhaps, at least their leaders, may never become Catholics, but who are

---

[1] A commentary on the Council, issued anonymously but presumed to be the work of Döllinger.

[2] Ultramontane propagandist, editor of *L'Univers*.

leavening the various English parties & denominations (far beyond their own range) with principles & sentiments tending towards their ultimate absorption in the Catholic Church.

With these thoughts before me I am continually asking myself whether I ought not to make my feelings public: but all I do is to pray those great early Doctors of the Church, whose intercession would decide the matter, Augustine & the rest, to avert so great a calamity. If it is God's will that the Pope's infallibility should be defined then is it his blessed will to throw back the times & the moments of that triumph he has destined for His Kingdom: and I shall feel I have but to bow my head to his adorable inscrutable Providence. You have not touched on the subject yourself, but I think you will allow me to express to you feelings, which for the most part I keep to myself.

                                                        John H. Newman.

448 [F.O. 43/106]   *Rome, 20 February 1870*
No. 43
O.R. to Earl of C.

. . . The relative strength of the two great divisions in the Council has been disclosed to the world by the *Postulatum* of the majority in favour of Infallibility numbering about 450 signatures, and by the petition of the minority against Infallibility numbering about 150 signatures. About 150 bishops declined to commit themselves in writing for or against the dogma before the debate.

The *Postulatum* was a legal appeal to the Council justified by the 'Rules of procedure' and has been submitted to the Congregation of 26 bishops appointed to consider the measures proposed by members of Council. The petition of the minority was an extra-Conciliar demonstration, addressed to the Pope personally, who returned it unopened and unread to the petitioners to be equally submitted by them to the above-named Congregation of 26. The action of both parties has therefore rendered a decision of the Council unavoidable, and has virtually destroyed the original question of opportuneness.

The Infallibilists have proposed various ways of wording the definition so as to divide the Opportunists among themselves and increase their own majority when a vote is taken in the Council. Sincere Opportunists will of necessity prefer to vote with the Definitionists rather than vote against the principle of Infallibility altogether, while those who on a closer examination of self and pressed to pronounce categorically have discovered themselves to be in reality against the very principle of the proposed dogma, will join the Fallibilitarians.

For instance, Mgr Dupanloup, although the most eloquent defender of the Temporal Power and of the Syllabus, headed the Opportunist Movement, but would scarcely give his vote for Papal Fallibility, whilst Mgr Strossmayer and all the pupils of Dr Döllinger of Munich will not hesitate to vote for it. The Fallibilitarians may be called the advanced party in the Church, the 'extreme left' in the Council, and in the opinion of the Ultramontane party are tainted with the venom of German philosophy. If schism, ensued the book of Janus would be their gospel and Dr Döllinger their anti-Pope, in whom they recognize the Infallibility they deny to Pius IX. . . . In his great speech of 25 January Strossmayer spoke in favour of decentralizing and de-Italianizing the administration of the Church, of periodical Councils, with public sittings as recommended in the *Decretum Perpetuum* of the Council of Constance, and of a fallible Papacy — enough to convince the Ultramontanes that the present Council will have a heretical sect to condemn.

It is difficult to judge with accuracy of the numerical strength of the Fallibilitarians. Of the 47 Austro-German bishops belonging to the opposition several have pronounced against the doctrines published by Dr Döllinger in his letters to the *Allgemeine Zeitung* of 21 and 29 January, among them the Archbishops of Munich and of Mayence.

Of the 84 French bishops not more than half will vote with the opposition and few among them are conversant with the advanced principles of the Munich school. The present leader of the French opposition is the archbishop of Paris, Mgr Darboy, and he has done much to bring about an understanding between the French and German bishops. The standpoint of the French opposition may be studied in Mgr Dupanloup's pastorals before the Council, *père* Gratry's letters to the Archbishop of Malines, and the manifesto of the Archbishop of Paris published anonymously in the *Moniteur Universel* of 14 February. It certainly is a remarkable sign of the times that some of the most eminent Roman Catholic divines of France should publish and recommend, as the latest results of science for the benefit of the Council, opinions and principles respecting Papal Fallibility, False

Decretals, fraudulent theology, corruption of the Vatican etc., which we Protestants have held for three centuries.

The courage and energy with which the independent bishops have organized their opposition and held their ground, being hitherto only 200 against 500, deserves the highest admiration. If the plan proposed by the Bavarian Government last summer for a joint action of the states of Europe to support their independent bishops against the Jesuitism of the Vatican had been adopted, the present prospects of the opposing bishops would not be as hopeless as they are. . . . The French Government alone are giving their moral support to their bishops, but the manner in which that support is given appears to me more likely to weaken than to strengthen their cause.

A joint and simultaneous declaration of the Governments of Europe to back up their independent bishops against Papal aggressions might have embarrassed the Vatican, but the Vatican have never feared a danger which they knew would be averted by the reluctance of the Governments, Catholic or Protestant, to offend the Pope and their Ultramontane subjects, the difficulty they would experience in agreeing to the form of a joint moral intervention, the embarrassment which a rupture followed by an Italian invasion of Rome would cause in Europe, and the pride Catholic France takes in the exclusive protectorate of the Papacy. . . .

449   [Clarendon Papers, C. 487]   *Rome, 20 February 1870*

Private
O.R. to Earl of C.

[Concerning Irish affairs.] I am also well satisfied with Cardinal Antonelli, notwithstanding his attempts to persuade me that Papal Infallibility would be the destruction of Fenianism! I told him that if the Pope succeeded in eradicating Fenianism from Ireland and revolutionary priests, I should perhaps begin to think that there might, under certain conditions, be something in it, but even then I should not feel quite sure, at which His Eminence patted me on the knee and said amidst peals of laughter that I was '*una cara persona*'. . . .

Lord Acton has written a letter to Mr Gladstone on the urgent necessity of assisting the Opposition Bishops which I cannot sufficiently recommend to your notice and I abstain from writing myself because I cannot say more or write better on the subject than he has done. The only difference between us is that I do not believe the Governments of Europe can be persuaded to interfere in unison at Rome. Single and separate interference would be worse than useless.

I sent you a telegram on the 15th asking you to suggest to Count Beust to establish a common action with Prussia and Bavaria to support the German Bishops in Rome which they most anxiously desire, but won't ask for themselves, and I did so to please their spokesman, but without faith in it myself.

I should be very glad to know your opinion on Lord Acton's letter to Mr Gladstone, for he inspires me with so much respect and confidence that I should like to be always of his opinion, but of course our standpoints as regards the Church of Rome cannot always be the same. . . .

450 [Clarendon Papers, C. 487] *Rome, 22 February 1870*
Private
O.R. to Earl of C.

. . . I am blamed for being a Definitionist, but I cannot help thinking that a clearly defined position between the Papacy and the Civilized World will prove more beneficial to humanity in the end than the halfmeasures of the Opportunists who wish to preserve the benefit of the doubt.

451 [F.O. 43/106] *Rome, 25 February 1870*
No. 46
O.R. to Earl of C.

[Encloses a copy of a Papal decree amending the rules of procedure.]
. . . The Cardinal Secretary of State tells me that this amendment had become necessary to enable the Fathers of the Council to come to some conclusion on the *Schemata* submitted to them. . . .

The decree enabled the bishops first to propose their amendments in writing, so that the Congregation could alter the *Schemata* accordingly and defend them in debate, and majorities decide for or against the measures under discussion. To obviate the evil of interminable debates, power had been given to divide the Council at the request of not less than ten bishops. In this manner His Eminence hoped that the Council might get through its labours in less than a year.

Your Lordship will perceive that this measure is a severe blow to the minority, for it is obvious that the majority can force a vote when it likes and carry any and every measure by three or four to one. I am assured that the opposing bishops intend to reject the measure, and that the international committee has already held a meeting to draw up a protest declaring that they cannot surrender for all times the faith and principles of the Church.

452 [F.O. 43/106]   *Rome, 27 February 1870*

No. 49
O.R. to Earl of C.

[Count Beust, the Protestant Austrian Foreign Secretary, had, according to Antonelli] warned the Papal Government that he would prohibit the publication in Austria of any Conciliar Decrees he did not consider to be in harmony with the laws of the Empire. Cardinal Antonelli had told the Austrian Ambassador that Count Beust was of course at liberty to do as he thought best, but it appeared strange that after proclaiming the establishment of religious liberty and freedom of the press in Austria, His Excellency should prohibit the publication of the Laws the Church of Rome might see fit to give Herself through an Oecumenical Council. I asked whether the French Government had not made similar representations to the Government of the Pope. He said that they had not, and that the relations existing between Rome and France were most cordial and satisfactory.

453 [F.O. 43/107]   *Rome, 1 March 1870*

No. 50. [Recites Telegram]
O.R. to Earl of C.

Lord Acton is anxious the French Government should know that further loss of time will be fatal to the bishops of the opposition.

454 [F.O. 361/1]   *F.O. 1 March 1870*

Private
Earl of C. to O.R.

... The plot seems thickening at Rome and everything tends to prove that the Pope is infallible and Odo the only true prophet. I agree with you, as I have all along, that this monstrous assault on the reason of mankind is the only chance of mankind being roused to resistance against being insolently thrust back into the darkest periods of church despotism and I cannot therefore regard the prospects of Papal triumph with the alarm of Gladstone who (strange to say) is almost exclusively occupied by it and thinks that Catholic governments will bitterly rue the day when they determined to be passive spectators of what they well knew was about to happen. . . .

I have seen Acton's very able letter to Gladstone, and think he attaches too much importance to a union between England and France, for we really can do nothing practically good or useful at Rome. Daru as you know was disposed to ask for our assistance and we could not say nay, but I convinced him that the British dwarf could be of little aid to the French giant who was responsible for there being any council at all, and who ought to bestir himself in preventing its evil effects. . . .

It is not from want of good will that we do nothing more but from positive inability and because such interference as we *could* resort to would do no good as against the Pope and might do us harm in the matters concerning which we want Papal assistance and which to us are of far more importance than defined or undefined infallibility. So I will beg you to soothe Acton as well as you can. Acton has written to Granville in the same sense as to Gladstone but ends his letter by saying not only that he was regarded as the evil one at Rome but that he might be in some personal danger and should have to rely on the protection of his Government. I suppose that expulsion from Rome is the only danger he need apprehend and you will I am sure without special instructions throw your aegis over him. It is not a wide one but you will perhaps be able to make Cardinal Antonelli understand how much more the Papal Court would lose than gain by the banishment of an English peer and a devoted Catholic because he differs with a Council at which the freest expression of opinion was promised.

Your handling of the Irish bishops has been admirable and will I hope be productive of good results, if a good result of any kind is possible in that land of demons. . . .

455   [F.O. 43/107]   *Rome, 3 March 1870*
No. 53
O.R. to Earl of C.

. . . The opposition bishops have taken a step of great importance in protesting against the Papal decree amending the Rules of Procedure,

and on the answer they receive from the five Cardinals presiding over
the Council will depend their future influence in the Church of Rome.

According to article 13 of that decree the decisions of the Council
are to be decreed according to the votes of the majority. The bishops
of the opposition could therefore be always outvoted, whilst the power
they have hitherto so successfully exercised of speaking against time,
so as to put off the decisions of the Council until the heat of summer
necessitated a prorogation, has been set at nought by article 11,
according to which ten bishops can divide the Council and appeal to
the majority to close a debate. . . .

456   [Clarendon Papers, C. 487]   *Rome, 4 March 1870*

Private
O.R. to Earl of C.

Having no private opportunity I write by post to tell you that the
French Ambassador received about the 23rd February instructions
from Paris to announce the arrival of a second French Ambassador to
be accredited to the Council. M de Banneville not thinking the policy
of his Government prudent refrained from communicating his instructions to Cardinal Antonelli and wrote to Paris to advize against the
measure.

The Opposition Bishops are said to be indignant with him, but the
Archbishop of Paris takes Monr de Banneville's part. I hear on very
high authority that the Pope would not receive a French Ambassador
accredited to the Council and so in all probability the French Govt.
will have to give way. I cannot sufficiently often repeat my conviction
that single-handed interference is useless at Rome and that collective
measures alone can make an impression on the majority of the Council.

If the Catholic Govts. acted in harmony and simultaneously at
Rome and if the Opposition Bishops had the moral courage to leave
Rome in a body and protest against the Oecumenicity of the Council,
the course of events might be altered, but everything that has hitherto
been done by Catholic Govts. and opposing Bishops is calculated to
confirm the Vatican and the majority of the Council in the policy they
are pursuing. . . .

The Opposition Bishops have not lost their time during the Carnival
Holydays and have drawn up a protest against the Decree respecting
the new 'Rules of the House'. . . .

They protest against the principle of majorities being applied to matters of Faith and against the power given to ten Bishops to divide the Council and stop a debate. They think that fifty should be the minimum in whom so great a power is vested.

Of course the Pope's answer will be that majorities cannot decide in matters of Faith, but his own infallible veto which overrules Conciliar decisions.

If the Opposition accept this answer and remain in Rome, then the Pope's infallible authority over the Church will be virtually carried. If they don't, then it will be carried without them. . . .

457 [F.O. 43/107]   *Rome, 7 March 1870*

No. 56
O.R. to Earl of R.

I have the honour to acknowledge Your Lordship's despatch of 24 February enclosing copy of Lord Bloomfield's No. 49 and asking my opinion as to the statement made to Her Majesty's Ambassador by the Austrian Under Secretary of State, Baron Aldenburg, that Cardinal Rauscher and the Austrian prelates had evinced considerable moderation and that there was much probability their opinions would ultimately prevail, for the adherents of extreme decisions were gradually falling off, but the most violent and impracticable were the English members of the Council.

I fully agree in regard to the moderation of Cardinal Rauscher and the Austrian prelates generally, who are amongst the most distinguished and independent bishops of the opposition, but I am very much surprized that he should flatter himself that their opinions would ultimately prevail, as he must have heard from the Austrian Ambassador at Rome that the position of the minority is becoming more hopeless every day, and that the adherents of extreme decisions, instead of falling off, are increasing and joining the Papal majority in the Council.

As regards Baron Aldenburg's statement that the English bishops are the most violent and impracticable members of the Council, it is not easy to give a positive opinion, because the majority of them have been hitherto very reserved and have declined to sign the petitions for and against Infallibility.

Archbishop Manning's arguments in favour of Infallibility have been

published in his pastoral on the subject, and Dr Cornthwaite of
Beverley is the only English bishop who has signed the Infallibility
petition besides Dr Manning. Dr Ullathorne's letter to the *Times* fore-
shadows his intention to adhere to the decisions of the majority, and
Dr Grant of Southwark is generally believed to hold similar opinions.

On the other hand Dr Clifford of Clifton and Dr Errington are the
only two English bishops, and Dr Moriarty and Dr Leahy the only
two Irish bishops, I am assured, who have signed the anti-infallibilist
petition. Dr Clifford is, I believe, the only English bishop who has yet
spoken in the Council, and his oratory and Latinity are universally
acknowledged to have been of the very highest order. He spoke in the
sense of the opposition. The Colonial bishops, with the exception of
Dr Connolly, archbishop of Halifax, who has hitherto acted with the
opposition, are all believed to belong to the Papal majority. Of the
North American bishops, Dr Kenrick, Archbishop of St Louis, alone
has spoken in favour of the opposition. There are at present over 100
English-speaking bishops in the Council.

I need scarcely add that whatever be the private opinions of English
bishops at present, all will submit to the decisions of the Council in the
end.

458 [F.O. 43/107]   *Rome, 7 March 1870*

No. 57. Secret
O.R. to Earl of C.

[Concerning the instructions sent by Count Daru to the Marquis de
Banneville.] . . . During the five days that followed the arrival of the
instructions from Paris and their official communication to Cardinal
Antonelli, some of the French bishops of the opposition who dreaded
the effects of delay shewed signs of great impatience, but it is said, on
the other hand that the Archbishop of Paris agreed with the French
Ambassador in the course he had pursued.

I called on Cardinal Antonelli and asked him what he thought of
the communication he had received from Paris. His Eminence told me
that he thought both the French and the Austrian Governments
were unnecessarily alarmed, because they fancied that the *Schemata*
published surreptitiously in the newspapers as having been submitted
to the Council were calculated to trench upon the domain of the civil
power, and both Count Beust and Count Daru had thought it neces-

27. Lord Acton. Drawing by Lenbach

28. Archbishop Darboy

sary to warn him that they would not allow the publication in their respective empires of the future decrees of the Council. To that His Eminence could only reply that they were masters to do just as they thought right in their own countries, and he claimed the same privilege for the Government of the Pope in the Holy See, but it appeared strange that Governments who advocated the principles of civil liberty and religious toleration should make an exception and threaten coercion in regard to the principles of the Roman Catholic Church.

The Pope was the representative of Christ on earth, the guardian of religious and moral order in the world, and although he could not compel the powers of the world to listen to the word of God, they could not prevent him from doing his duty and proclaiming divine truth for the guidance of the faithful.

I said that the communications made by Count Beust and Count Daru had been inspired by a desire to do good at Rome and prevent evil elsewhere, and that it was not surprizing to see the Governments of the world alarmed at the principles laid down in the published *Schemata* of the Council, since they were calculated to establish a permanent conflict between Church and State which it was everyone's interest to avoid.

Cardinal Antonelli replied that I was entirely mistaken; the confirmation of the principles laid down in the Syllabus by the Oecumenical Council would in no way affect or alter the relations already existing between Church and State in the world. Those principles were not new, they were those the Church had ever professed and would ever profess, and in collecting them from those ancient documents in which they had been periodically recorded, and giving them a more concise and accessible form, the Council was merely 'codifying' Canon Law, if he might use such an expression, and passing a sort of Consolidation Bill or Declaratory Act. He would give me an example of what he meant by citing the question of marriage. The Church held and would ever hold that marriage was a sacrament, but that had not prevented Governments from admitting the legality of civil marriage. The Church condemned religious toleration, but allowed us Protestants to have these places of worship at the Porta del Popolo, and one on the Capitol in the Prussian Legation. And the Jews had several synagogues in Rome and in the Papal States.

His Eminence then appealed to me to admit in justice to the Papal Government that they never sent spies into our places of worship to listen to our sermons, and never remonstrated with the Governments of England, Prussia or the U.S.A. against the principles taught by their clergy. That was practical religious toleration, which the Church of Rome could not teach but was ready to practise in exchange for the religious toleration she claimed from the Governments of the world, since exclusively Catholic Governments had virtually ceased to exist. Catholic Governments had resigned their position as such from the moment they had admitted religious toleration in their dominions, and had thereby themselves created the very conflict between Church and State they now complained of.

If Austria had not chosen to break her engagements and abolish the Concordat, her relations with Rome would still be regulated by the laws she had herself established. France had been faithful to her engagements, and the ecclesiastical relations with Rome were regulated by the Concordat of 1802, and as the Pope would always adhere faithfully to his treaty engagements, she had nothing to fear. He, Cardinal Antonelli, could therefore not understand the nature of Count Daru's apprehensions. That which the Oecumenical Council was engaged upon concerned the Church, the sacristy alone, and the Governments who professed religious toleration at home had no right to interfere and be intolerant of Rome. They could negotiate Concordats with Rome if they liked, and Rome would ever be faithful to her engagements, but they could not forbid the Pope from fulfilling his divine mission on earth according to the dictates of his conscience and the will of God.

His Eminence took this opportunity of assuring me that the Papal Government gratefully acknowledged the perfect liberty and independence enjoyed by the Roman Catholic clergy in England and America. He could not say as much of France and Austria.

I said that I had reason to know that all the leading statesmen of Europe approved of the friendly and timely warning which the Catholic Governments of France, Austria and Bavaria had respectfully submitted to His Eminence, and that it was now well known to us all that the opinions of these leading statesmen of Europe were fully shared by at least 200 of the most distinguished among the Fathers of the Council, who openly declared their conviction that the present policy of Rome would not promote peace and concord amongst Christians, either spiritually or politically.

Cardinal Antonelli replied that the newspapers had exaggerated the numbers as well as the spirit of the bishops who did not share the opinions of the immense majority in the Council, a majority that was increasing daily because time, circumstances and lay interference contributed naturally to unite the bishops and clergy under one shepherd, whatever might be the spirit of opposition that still animated some few among them.

I said I could not, of course, judge of the spirit of the opposition in the Council, but it appeared to me that in the outer world Mgr Dupanloup, *père* Gratry and Dr Döllinger had many followers among the clergy. Cardinal Antonelli replied that a very small minority of the French clergy adhered to the views of the bishop of Orléans, and that he noticed in the newspapers a daily increasing number of pastorals published by French and German bishops to express their disapproval of Gratry and Döllinger.

I asked whether the Holy Office would likewise censure the doctrines of these two celebrated theologians. He replied that the Court of Rome would abstain from censure or from promising any opinion whatever on theological publications so as to leave complete independence and freedom of thought, speech and action to the clergy in general, and to the bishops in particular, while the Council was deliberating in Rome. The letters published by the bishops in the newspapers sufficiently proved that they had no restraint to complain of.

I said at the beginning of the Council the bishops of the opposition had sent up as many as fourteen petitions detailing their grievances, and asking for leave to make their own rules of procedure, that the two last French and German petitions were protests against the amended rules of procedure decreed on 20 February which were calculated to destroy the independence of the minority altogether, and that the daily extra-Conciliar meetings of the opposition in the houses of the Archbishop of Paris, the Cardinal Archbishop of Vienna and other high dignitaries of the Church were attended by bishops who represented over ninety millions of souls.

Cardinal Antonelli answered that all I had said proved how great was the independence of the bishops since they could petition, protest, meet and publish their opinions as much as they pleased. Their petitions and protests had been referred to competent authorities and would be discussed in Council, but the amended rules of procedure some few had complained of had been drawn up by members of the Council at the request of the majority to enable the Presidents and

Congregations to report progress, which had hitherto been impossible. The facts were these: three months of Conciliar debates had shewn that the Fathers were divided into a very large united majority and a very small disunited minority, who feeling the weakness of their standpoint had resolved at least to delay if they could not prevent the adoption of the measures they opposed by speaking against time until the heat of summer should necessitate a prorogation. A few ready speakers had managed to waste three months by delivering a series of orations that were more like endless sermons than Parliamentary discussions, but which the majority had thought it their duty to listen to with conscientious and exemplary patience until they had gradually recognized that they were at the mercy of a very small but very factious minority.

To remedy this evil and enable the majority to resist the policy of procrastination of the minority, it became necessary to amend the 'Rules of procedure' and give the Presidents power to close lengthy and useless discussions at the request of a majority in the Council. At the same time three different opportunities for considering and re-considering the measures before them were given to the bishops. In the first instance the *Schemata* were to be distributed to them at least ten days before the debate and power given to send in their amendments in writing to the Legates if they chose. Then came the actual discussion which enabled them to give a second verbal opinion, and thirdly the vote, for which they could equally give a written explanation to be placed on record in the annals of the Council. The reason which made written opinions and amendments desirable was that bishops in speaking might from mistaking the exact value of a word become guilty of heresy without knowing it, whilst every word of their written opinions would be weighed and selected with the assistance of their theologians. He had appointed as many as four theologians to assist him in his Conciliar labours. His Eminence knew of no Parliament that afforded its members more independence or more opportunities of asserting their opinions than the Council of the Vatican.

I observed that the members of the opposition did not share His Eminence's views on the new *Regolamento*. He replied with a smile that minorities always thought majorities in the wrong and wished to set them aside or ignore their existence, but that the Oecumenical Council would never end if the majority were deprived by the minority of the power to express and assert their opinions as had been the case ever since 8 December. As matters now stood His Eminence had every hope of a speedy and satisfactory termination of the labours of the Council.

I then reminded Cardinal Antonelli of Count Daru's note and asked him whether he had yet answered it. He said he had not because it related to questions he was not competent to answer. He was neither responsible for the *Schemata* nor the acts and decisions of the Council respecting which Count Daru desired to be informed, and he had therefore referred the note to the Legates of the Council, and had requested them to furnish him with answers to Count Daru's questions, which he would communicate to the French Ambassador the moment he received them.

I inquired whether the Pope would receive the special Ambassador the Emperor Napoleon desired to accredit to the Council. Cardinal Antonelli said that the request came rather late and he doubted whether either the Pope or the majority of the bishops would feel inclined to receive an Ambassador specially accredited to the Council. But that was also a question he was not competent to answer until His Holiness and the Council had decided.

The French Government had also expressed a wish to be made acquainted with the *Schemata* before they were submitted to the bishops for discussion, but he did not know whether the Cardinal Legates and Congregations would object to comply with this request or not. He frankly confessed his inability to see what object the French Government had in wishing to interfere with things that did not concern them. The *Schemata* had no importance in themselves until the Council had pronounced upon them and the Pope sanctioned their promulgation, and the French Government could not expect to alter the decrees of an Oecumenical Council.

I remarked that the decrees of an Oecumenical Council could alter the peaceful relations at present existing between Church and State and Count Daru evidently wished to avert the dangers foreshadowed in his several private letters which had found their way into the newspapers, and in which he said that on the decisions of the Council might depend the movements of the French garrison. Cardinal Antonelli interposed that the movements of the French troops in Rome depended on certain treaty engagements between France and Italy to which Rome was no party and, whatever these movements might be, they could in no way prevent the Pope from fulfilling the duties of his divine mission.

I continued to say that Count Daru also appeared anxious to save the Concordat from being abrogated by the French Parliament as had been the case in Austria. Cardinal Antonelli observed that Concordats were not essential to the existence of religion, and that the abrogation of the French Concordat would injure France but not the Church. The position of the clergy was at present in many respects better in England and America than in the so-called Catholic countries that taught but did not practise toleration. Governments need not be alarmed about the future of religion or the administration of the Church which had thrived for eighteen centuries with or without their existence, for Christ would be with his Church to the end of time etc. etc. etc.

I have given but a very rough sketch of the long conversation which Cardinal Antonelli carried on in his usual cheerful, friendly and confidential manner, but, when I rose to take my leave, His Eminence begged I would consider all he had said as a strictly private communication to Your Lordship personally.

[*Endorsement by Hammond, signed by Clarendon:* This despatch has been read with the greatest interest, and the full and clear account that he has given of this conversation is highly appreciated by H.M. Govt., who approve also entirely of the part that he took in it.]

459 [Clarendon Papers, C. 487]   *Rome, 9 March 1870*
Private
O.R. to Earl of C.

... I have taken steps to protect Lord Acton but I do not apprehend that he will be molested. He is of course watched by spies but I do not for one moment believe that they will otherwise interfere with him in any other way for the present. If later he resists the Infallibility Dogma he will naturally be excommunicated, but nothing worse.

460 [F.O. 43/107]   *Rome, 13 March 1870*
No. 62
O.R. to Earl of C.

[The attempt to organize a collective step by the Catholic Powers to influence the Council had failed.] ... Austria acting alone has received a curt reply, and France has received none at all, whilst both by attempts to interfere have hastened on the publication of the Infallibility *Schema*. And if the request of the two great Catholic powers to be represented in the Council be granted, their Ambassadors will simply attend to witness the defeat of the policy of their Governments, for state interference will have the effect of uniting and increasing the Papal party. . . .

461 [Clarendon Papers in P.R.O. f.o. 361/1]

F.O. 16 March 1870

Earl of Clarendon to Lord Loftus [Ambassador in Berlin]
Private

. . . Bismarck evidently does not want to burn his fingers at Rome where, whatever he may say to the contrary, Prussia is courted and raised on the ruins of Austrian influence. . . .

I don't believe that the closer union or the most vigorous action of the Catholic powers would now arrest the steady advance of the Pope to victory over the reason of mankind. . . .

462 [f.o. 43/107]

Rome, 17 March 1870

No. 64. [Recites Telegram]
O.R. to Earl of C.

Acton wishes you to know that some English bishops will found their protest against Infallibility on the repudiation of that doctrine by their predecessors at the time of the Emancipation Act.

463 [f.o. 43/107]

Rome, 20 March 1870

No. 65
O.R. to Earl of C.

[The sittings of the Council had been suspended from 23 Feb. to 18 March.] . . . The discussion of the *Schema* on Infallibility can scarcely come on before Easter, so the bishops of the opposition have full time to organize their plan of battle. After meeting repeatedly to discuss their best mode of action, the international opposition committee drew up four petitions signed by French, German, Anglo-American and Italian bishops, asking the Cardinal Legates of the Council to grant them as much delay as possible to consider the *Schema* on Infallibility before they proceed to the Definition, and they appear satisfied that their request will be granted.

Some English and Irish bishops, but I do not think more than three or four of them, have founded their petition against Infallibility on the repeated repudiation of that doctrine by their predecessors at the time of the Emancipation Act. Mgr Dupanloup reckons on at least 120 votes against the Definition. I cannot but think he overestimates the numerical strength of his adherents. Nor can I believe that those of the opposition bishops and their adherents who talk openly of Schism will find the support they reckon on among their flocks, whilst the dissenting bishops will break down before the practical difficulties which the establishment of a new Christian sect without a leader must necessarily encounter in Europe.

464 [F.O. 43/107]   *Rome, 20 March 1870*

No. 66
O.R. to Earl of C.

Mgr de Mérode, who has had the misfortune to break his leg, and some other relations of Count de Montalembert, invited their friends to the celebration of a funeral service to his memory at the Church of Sta Maria in Ara Coeli on 17th inst. A good many bishops and French ecclesiastics assembled in the church on the day appointed and were filled with surprize and sorrow at learning that the Pope had prohibited the ceremony. No one knew the immediate cause of the prohibition, but some thought it was Count Montalembert's last letter adhering to Father Gratry's principles, and others the effect which an extra-Conciliar episcopal expression of sympathy with liberal Catholicism might produce, that had excited the Pope's anger.

The indignation of the opposition bishops was great until the following day when the official Roman Gazette announced that the Pope had proceeded in person to the church of Sta Maria Traspontina near the Vatican at an early hour on 18th inst., and had there himself ordered the celebration of a funeral Mass for Count de Montalembert. It is now asserted that the Pope, who had been deeply offended at the tone of Count Montalembert's last letter published in the newspapers approving of Father Gratry's three pamphlets, had relented on learning that Count Montalembert had four times uttered the word 'pardon' on his death bed.

I have not yet been able to ascertain the real truth about this strange story.

465 [F.O. 43/107] *Rome, 21 March 1870*

No. 67

O.R. to Earl of C.

[The Marquis de Banneville had gone to Paris at the Pope's request to explain the difficulties of following Count Daru's demands for a special Ambassador and for the submission of the *Schemata* to the French Government.] . . . This move on the part of the Papal Government is an illustration of the opinion I have repeatedly expressed in my former correspondence to the effect that an Italian priest can always in the long run get the better of a French statesman.

To Count Daru's friendly advice that moderate measures should prevail at Rome, the Pope has answered by the publication of the Infallibility dogma. To Count Daru's request to be made acquainted with the labours of the bishops, Cardinal Antonelli has replied by referring his demand to the Cardinal Legates of the Council for their consideration. And to Count Daru's petition to accredit a special French Ambassador to the Council, the Pope has replied by sending the French Ambassador to Paris to negotiate the withdrawal of Count Daru's instructions and demands.

During a period of twenty years, from the letter of the Emperor Napoleon to Count Edgar Ney in 1850 to the instructions of Count Daru to the Marquis de Banneville in 1870 the Pope has systematically disregarded and despised the advice of his protectors.

466 [Clarendon Papers, C. 487] *Rome, 21 March 1870*

Private

O.R. to Earl of C.

. . . All Lord Acton's views appear to me admirable and I am glad to hear that he writes occasionally to Mr Gladstone and Lord Granville, for his advice is excellent in every respect.

I fully agree with him that the source of all evil in Rome has been the unconditional Protectorate of France. . . .

467 [F.O. 43/107] *Rome, 24 March 1870*

No. 71

O.R. to Earl of C.

. . . The sitting of the 22nd Congregation was important. The bishops of the opposition had arranged during the debate on the *Schema de Erroribus* to bring forward the question of the amended Rules of Procedure, and the attack was led by Cardinal Prince Schwarzenberg, Archbishop of Prague, who was called to order by the Pope's five Legates presiding over the Council. Some other bishops spoke in the same sense, but the majority became very impatient and called them to order when bishop Strossmayer mounted the tribune and insisted on his right to be heard. The bishops then became quieter and listened with attention to the great orator of the opposition until he called the policy of the Vatican which tended to alienate the a-Catholic sects uncharitable, when a burst of indignation interrupted him.

Bishop Strossmayer then resumed and said it was inconsistent with true Christianity to condemn works by non-Catholic authors such as, for instance, Leibnitz, who might be read with advantage by Catholics. The name of Leibnitz not being familiar to the majority of the Fathers, a few only groaned dissent, but when Strossmayer added that another Protestant work he could commend to his co-religionists was Guizot's *Meditations*, the majority rose shouting '*Hereticus! Hereticus!*' and called upon him to desist. He found it impossible to continue in the midst of the noise which ensued and raising his hand to heaven explained with a loud voice: '*Protesto, hoc non est Concilium!*' On hearing which some 500 bishops rushed round the tribune shaking their fists at Strossmayer, yelling: '*Nos omnes te damnamus.*' Some of bishop Strossmayer's adherents shouted: '*Non omnes! Non omnes!*' while the five Cardinal Legates presiding over the Council rang their five bells and the officers of the Council proceeded to compel the orator to descend from the rostrum. Immediately after the Council broke up and the bishops dispersed.

The consequences of this incident may become very serious if cleverly handled by the opposition.

468 [F.O. 43/107]   *Rome, 24 March 1870*

No. 72 [Recites Telegram]
O.R. to Earl of C.

Acton wishes the French Government to know that Strossmayer in his last speech declared that no dogma could be proclaimed without moral unanimity among the bishops for which he was called to order.

469 [F.O. 361/1]   *Grosvenor Crescent, 28 March 1870*
Private
Earl of C. to O.R.

. . . Döllinger has written to Gladstone praying him to use strong
language of denunciation in Parliament, or in a letter that might be
published, warning Rome that perseverance in the dogmas would lead
to hostile legislation in this country against the Roman Catholics, etc.
etc. This he says would be listened to because we have great influence
at Rome on account of never menacing or interfering with Papal concerns. Yet he urges us to do the very things that would destroy the
influence he invokes. Gladstone has been much moved by these
appeals, which are those of drowning men catching at straws, and it
has not been an easy task for me to save our fingers from being thrust
into the burning fiery furnace. . . .

470 [F.O. 43/107]   *Rome, 31 March 1870*
No. 79
O.R. to Earl of C.

. . . The amended articles of the *Schema de Fide* have been unanimously
adopted by the bishops, but the preamble gave rise to vigorous opposition on the part of the Germans led by Mgr Strossmayer, who
insisted on the omission of those sentences which implied that atheism,
materialism and unbelief were the produce of Protestantism. The
prooemium was modified in consequence. . . . The bishops of the opposition consider that the concession thus made to their demands by the
Cardinal Legates is a great victory over the Ultramontane party.

It appears that the German bishops had been confidentially informed
by the Prussian Minister in Rome that his Government would resent
the adoption by them of a declaration so insulting to their Protestant
sovereign and would be followed by a rupture of diplomatic relations
with the Vatican, and might get them into trouble on returning to their
dioceses in Germany.

471 [F.O. 43/107]   *Rome, 5 April 1870*
No. 81. Secret
O.R. to Earl of C.

[In despatches of 29 March and 2 April, he had described how three

English ladies, Miss Cunliffe, Miss Greenstreet and Miss Dawkins had been ordered to leave Rome on the Pope's personal instructions. No precise reason had been given. O.R., Manning and Severn had made strong representations to the authorities. The two former ladies had left but had been told they might return. Miss Dawkins, however, had been told again to leave.] . . . Miss Dawkins in her letter of today to Your Lordship denies having circulated Bibles and tracts, or having protected Garibaldian or Mazzinian correspondences, and I am bound to believe an English lady's word, but I regret to say that English missionaries who shall be nameless have lately inundated Rome with Italian tracts, thereby exciting the suspicions of the police and the anger of the Sovereign Pontiff. Indeed, I fear that the theological excitement produced by the Council is leading English missionaries to commit acts of imprudence in Rome which must sooner or later become a source of trouble to H.M. Government.

Miss Dawkins equally declared without foundation the report of her having attempted to convert, or even having held any controversial conversation or correspondence with Roman Catholic priests. . . . But Miss Dawkins in her letter of today's date adds a third and new accusation to those already circulated against her, to the effect that 'a Roman priest had become enamoured of one of the ladies and not being discouraged, the mandate to leave Rome was issued against them'. Miss Dawkins 'can only smile at such a mode of maintaining by Government authority the virtue and purity of a spiritual celibate'.

Miss Dawkins has thereby thrown a new and important light on this mysterious affair. Ladies can be answerable for themselves but not for the sentiments they inspire in others. Miss Dawkins is possessed of high virtues and great attractions, and many Roman prelates frequented the house she occupied with her friends. The Holy Office or Inquisition thinking these receptions too attractive for ecclesiastics may have appealed to the Pope, whose unrelenting severity and rigid austerity in such matters is well known to the Roman clergy.

The 'enamoured priest' has no doubt been imprisoned in a convent where he may linger many years, and to save others from a similar fate the Pope ordered the causes of danger to be banished. This would explain the mystery with which His Holiness has seen fit to surround himself in the matter, but could in no way excuse the arbitrary proceedings of the Roman police in regard to respectable and unoffending English ladies. . . .

472 [Clarendon Papers, C. 487] *Rome, 29 March 1870*

Secret
O.R. to Earl of C.

I have spent three anxious days in trying to settle an odious affair which you will read in the accompanying despatch. But what I could not tell you in that despatch is the nature of the accusation brought against the 3 ladies and which Cardinal Antonelli has confided to me under the seal of secrecy. It appears that they had been denounced to the Holy Office for the seduction of young priests and watched until the accusation was clearly proved, when the Pope ordered them to be sent away. Cardinal Antonelli maintains that the Pope is in possession of letters they wrote to young priests inviting them to their house and that the young priests have confessed their guilt. It is difficult to believe that three maiden ladies with a very pretty ladies' maid should have been so imprudent, and I still hope to prove that they are victims of an odious calumny but Cardinal Antonelli and Monsignor Randi say the matter does not admit of a doubt.

Miss Cunliffe and Miss Greenstreet are innocent I feel sure, but Miss Dawkins is very handsome and known to be *odd*.

She is the sister of Colonel Dawkins of the Coldstream who will probably bring the matter before Parliament and we may look forward to odious newspaper articles.

Archbishop Manning was most kind and energetic and Cardinal Antonelli tells me that it is thanks to his intervention that the Pope will ultimately allow Miss Cunliffe and Miss Greenstreet to return to Rome. But for Miss Dawkins the case is different for she appears to have been so imprudent as to render the Pope's forgiveness impossible.

I write in great haste to get this off tonight and cannot say how much anxiety, annoyance, bother and misery I have undergone to try to settle this unfortunate affair. . . .

473 [F.O. 43/107] *Rome, 5 April 1870*

No. 83. Secret
O.R. to Earl of C.

[Count Daru has confidentially asked the advice of the opposition bishops who have sent him a strongly worded secret memorandum, of which O.R. cannot send a copy but quotes 'from memory and after a

single hearing'. It enumerates their complaints against the way the
Council is being conducted and recommends that a new French
Ambassador be appointed less committed to the Vatican than de
Banneville.]

. . . In conclusion the bishops recommend Count Daru to instruct
his new Ambassador to insist on the prorogation of the Council before
the definition of Papal Infallibility, so as to avoid the scandal of and the
evils consequent on a moral schism in the Church, and they think at
the same time that the Pope should be made to understand that if he
declines to adopt the advice of Count Daru, all the Governments of
Europe would support the opposition bishops in protesting against
the Oecumenicity of the Council, thereby rendering its acts to all
eternity null and void in Roman Catholic Christendom. . . . The
French opposition bishops, who appear to have lost all confidence in
the Catholic Embassies of France and Austria in Rome, have communicated this memorandum secretly to the Prussian Minister, Baron
Arnim, and have solicited the support of his Government at Paris
through Count Bismarck, and Baron Arnim, who has been authorized
by Count Bismarck to communicate direct with Baron Werther at
Paris on all questions relating to the Council, at once agreed to recommend the memorandum to Count Daru. Judging from Count Daru's
past Roman policy, I do not expect that he will venture to adopt the
bold measures now suggested to him. . . .

474 [F.O. 43/107]   *Rome, 8 April 1870*
No. 85. Secret
O.R. to Earl of C.

The Minister of Police, Marchese Pio Capranica, called on me today
with a message from Mgr Randi (Governor of Rome) to the effect that
the Pope would allow Miss Dawkins to remain in Rome if she consented to part from and dismiss her maid, Eliza Dingle, whose presence
in Rome His Holiness could no longer tolerate. If not, both Miss
Dawkins and her maid would have to leave together. I begged of
Marchese Capranica to communicate with Her Majesty's Consul and
Miss Dawkins on the subject, and shall now endeavour to bring such
influences to bear on the Pope as may induce His Holiness to withdraw
also this last sentence of banishment against Eliza Dingle.

I begged of Marchese Capranica to tell me confidentially what motives had actuated the police to persecute Miss Dawkins and her maid, but His Excellency assured me that the police were acting under the immediate orders of the Pope without any knowledge of the secret motives that had prompted His Holiness, and which he had not seen fit to disclose to his Ministers. [A protest signed by Eliza Dingle, addressed to O.R., is enclosed.]

475 [F.O. 43/107]   *Rome, 8 April 1870*

No. 86. Confidential
O.R. to Earl of C.

[Antonelli had read to O.R. his note in answer to one from Daru. ... The note ... is intended to prove that the civil power has nothing to fear from the decisions of the Council. ... Cardinal Antonelli said that he thought it had convinced Count Daru that he had been ill-advized in trying to interfere with the Council. ... I said that I did not think the opposition bishops would allow the question to drop, and that they seemed at all events determined to resist the definition of dogmas by majorities without moral unanimity in the Council. He replied that the opposition was daily decreasing and the majority increasing, and that the first votes taken on the *Schema de Fide* had all been unanimous. In regard to Papal Infallibility, he could only say that 600 bishops had signified their intention to vote for it, and those did not include the 40 who had been in favour of the measure from the beginning.

The question of majorities was one that had been mis-represented by the Press, and bishops were quite right to say that majorities could not decide questions of faith in the Council because no decision of a Council was binding on the conscience of the faithful until it had the sanction of the Pope. The Pope could sanction a decision of a majority, or set it aside and adopt the opinion of a minority, or even with-hold his sanction from an unanimous decision of a council, or define a dogma without consulting a council at all, according to the will of God whose Vicar he was on earth.

What then, I inquired, was the use of a Council?

The use of a Council, Cardinal Antonelli replied, was to enable the Pope to ascertain with certainty what were the opinions, wishes, grievances, requirements and wants of the bishops and clergy all over the world.

And what, I further inquired, would be the fate of those among the opposition bishops who could not in conscience submit their faith, and appealed to a future Council?

They would expose themselves to the censures laid down in the Bull *Latae Sententiae*, Cardinal Antonelli replied.

476   [F.O. 43/107]   *Rome, 10 April 1870*

No. 87
O.R. to Earl of C.

. . . It is a remarkable fact that the bishops of the opposition, after their repeated protests against the old and new Rules of Procedure of the Council, which the Pope has never deigned to take the slightest notice of, should now be debating and voting in the Council Hall as if they had forgotten their protests and had accepted those very rules they declared but a month ago to be utterly inadmissible. It appears that bishops Hefele and Genouilhac have now drawn up a further protest which the bishops of the opposition desire to sign and publish in the newspapers, since the Pope will take no notice of the many protests they have sent up to the Vatican, whereby they solemnly declare their conviction that moral unanimity in an Oecumenical Council is necessary to render dogmatic definitions binding on the consciences of the faithful, and 2nd. that if the Council proceeds to the definition of dogmas by majorities only, and without moral unanimity, it will not in their consciences be accepted as Oecumenical.

477   [Clarendon Papers, C. 487]   *Rome, 10 April 1870*

Private
O.R. to Earl of C.

. . . The Irish Bishops are a hopeless set of humbugs, talking one way, writing another and acting a third, ignorant, cunning and deceitful like Neapolitans. To me their language is most satisfactory, full of praise and gratitude to H.M. Govt., but they do not act as they speak and since Bishop Furlong has published his extraordinary letter not one of them, or even of the English Bishops will in conversation with me blame, criticize or venture to disagree with a brother Bishop's published opinions!

They all express themselves delighted with the stringency of the peace preservation Law for Ireland and more particularly with the suppression of the pestilent newspapers and wish the Law to be extended to Liverpool, Glasgow &c. &c. where they fear the Fenians will now publish their papers and send them to Ireland. But who can tell whether they are sincere? . . .

In my humble opinion Daru's, Beust's and Bismarck's interference with the Council is a Godsend to the Pope and will contribute powerfully to increase the numbers and the energy of the Ultramontane fanatics. If, however you see any advantage in England making the declaration in Parliament suggested by Dr Döllinger to Mr Gladstone do not fear for one moment that it might impair my personal influence in Rome, for I have none. No Diplomatists' personal influence in Rome can obtain anything that is not strictly to the advantage of the Church, and Banneville with his army of occupation and Trauttmansdorff with his Hungarian Bishops and Arnim with all the science and theology of Germany have not more personal influence to boast of at the Vatican than Her Majesty's unofficial Agent with his Secretary Mr Jervoise! A Declaration such as Dr Döllinger suggests could in no way affect my influence as matters stand, but it would probably unite the English and Irish Bishops in favour of Papal Supremacy and in opposition to Her Majesty's Government.

If however Dr Döllinger and Lord Acton, whom I respect as the two highest and most trustworthy authorities in and out of the Church, recommend a Declaration in Parliament they must have good reasons for it, and must be better able than I am to judge of the good it will produce in the Catholic World, and I should therefore be the last person to object to it from any personal motives in Rome.

You alone in England can judge of the policy they recommend. To Lord Acton's marvellous talents, science, energy and zeal the enlightened opposition in the Council owes its present existence and strength. Without him the Germans, French, American and English could not have agreed and acted together, so different are their national theological standpoints.

Acton has done what no one else in the world could do, and deserves the highest credit for it.

Of course if I cannot always follow his able lead it is because he is a Catholic and I am a Protestant and our standpoints differ accordingly.

For my part I hold that warnings and threats of hostile legislation are welcome streams of water on the Pontifical mill, whilst neutrality, freedom, non-intervention and *indifference* are the weapons most dreaded by the Vatican, because the political power of the Roman clergy is created by persecution and crushed by Liberty.

478 [F.O. 43/107]   *Rome, 12 April 1870*

No. 90 [Recites Telegram]
O.R. to Earl of C.

Before committing Her Majesty's Government to the support of Daru's ill-advized note I venture humbly to submit to Your Lordship that it will defeat its own object and do H.M. Govt. more harm than good in the Catholick world.

479 [F.O. 43/107]   *Rome, 13 April 1870*

No. 91
O.R. to Earl of C.

. . . I should fail in my duty if I concealed from Your Lordship that after reading Count Daru's note I could not but regret that Her Majesty's Government have seen fit to depart from their former neutrality to give their moral support to a measure that will strike the independent minority of the Council so heavily by admitting and paying tribute to the Oecumenicity of the Council. I have repeatedly ventured to assert that the Papal majority is strong enough to carry its own measures, and the bishops of the minority have no other resource left them but to declare that the Oecumenical authority of the Council is in danger by reason of the intended use of that majority by the Pope.

By associating themselves with the public act of the French Government the states of Europe imply their recognition of the Oecumenical character of the Council and deprive the independent bishops of their only bases of action in the future. This explains the support which Count Daru's policy has met at the hands of his Ultramontane advizers in France, and the communication of his note by the Marquis de Banneville to the Vatican backed up by the great powers will be welcomed by the Pope as a measure calculated to encourage the majority in the course they are pursuing, as it contributes to render their decisions binding on the consciences of the minority. A telegram from Paris in today's papers announces the probable retirement from office of Count Daru, and I cannot but hope that the Marquis de

Banneville may in consequence find a telegram awaiting his arrival in Rome instructing him to suspend the execution of his instructions for the present.

480 [F.O. 43/107]   *Rome, 13 April 1870*
No. 92
O.R. to Earl of C.

I called on Miss Dawkins yesterday and was informed by her that thanks to the protection of Her Majesty's Consul Mr Severn, neither herself nor her maid Eliza Dingle had been further molested by the Roman police. . . . [O.R. will press for an explanation] immediately after Easter, when the Pope is able to attend to temporal concerns, because, as I have said before, the civil authorities being ignorant of questions appertaining to the province of the Holy Office (*Inquisition*) which is responsible only to the Pope, I conceive that I shall have to appeal to His Holiness to obtain the explanations required by Her Majesty's Government.

481 [F.O. 43/107]   *Rome, 13 April 1870*
No. 93
O.R. to Earl of C.

. . . On 12th inst. the last votes having been taken on the amendments proposed to the *Schema de Fide*, the bishops proceeded to give an open vote on the entire bill. Out of 600 bishops present, 517 voted for and 83 against the *Schema de Fide*. The opposition bishops are highly satisfied at this result of their first general open vote, because it was spontaneous. They did not expect to be called upon to vote before next week and say that they were taken by surprize. They now have every hope of increasing their numbers by careful organization and are to discuss the matter in the international committee during the Easter week. . . .

482 [F.O. 43/107]   *Rome, 13 April 1870*
No. 95
O.R. to Earl of C.

The Hungarian Government have sent a secret agent to Rome to advise their bishops to return to their respective dioceses, but the

Hungarian bishops have replied that the Hungarian Government would do better to send the bishops who have remained in their dioceses in Hungary to Rome to assist in opposing the encroachments of the Ultramontane party in the Council.

483 [F.O. 43/105]   *F.O. 15 April 1870*

No. 35 [Recites Telegram]
Earl of C. to O.R.

Our support of Count Daru's note is restricted to the expression of a hope that the Syllabus may be modified in the sense desired by the French Govt. and having promised we cannot recede but you will not enter into any argument on the subject. As Count Daru is out of office his note may perhaps not be delivered which will be fortunate as we wish to interfere as little as possible.

484 [F.O. 43/107]   *Rome, 16 April 1870*

No. 96
O.R. to Earl of C.

The *Civiltà Cattolica* has at last officially answered the attacks of the liberal Catholic press on the Rules of Procedure of the Council [*Précis* enclosed]. This controversy is doubly interesting because the attack against the Rules published in the '*Français*' of 3rd ult. is attributed to Mgr Dupanloup, whilst the answer in the *Civiltà Cattolica* is said to be written by Padre Piccirillo himself.

485 [F.O. 43/107]   *Rome, Easter Sunday*
                                                                 17 April 1870

No. 97
O.R. to Earl of C.

[De Banneville has arrived in Rome and solicited an audience of the Pope.] . . . Count Beust has addressed a despatch to the Austrian Ambassador, Count Trauttmansdorff, for communication to Cardinal Antonelli, in which he not only gives the full support of the Austrian Government to Count Daru's note, but adds that he has reason to believe that the views and wishes therein expressed are shared by the Austro-Hungarian bishops attending the Council. This is, I believe, the first time that the bishops of the opposition have been nominally supported by a Catholic power in a formal communication to the Papal Government. But I regret to say that the bishops of the opposition do not consider Count Daru's note calculated to obtain for them the support and protection they expected at the hands of their respective Governments.

The Prussian Minister, Baron Arnim, also expects to receive a despatch from Count Bismarck in support of Count Daru's note, which he will be instructed to communicate to Cardinal Antonelli when His Eminence has been placed in possession of the French despatch by the Marquis de Banneville. . . . Cardinal Antonelli told a friend of mine that he expected to receive that note from the French Ambassador on Saturday and that he had every reason to be satisfied with the manner in which the French Government had received his answer of 19 March. He was gratified to think that by not insisting on the appointment of a special Ambassador to the Council and by allowing the Marquis de Banneville to return, the French Government had paid due deference to the wishes of the Pope, but he did not know whether His Holiness would allow the French Ambassador to communicate Count Daru's note to the Council. . . .

486 [Clarendon Papers, C. 487]   *Rome, 17 April 1870*
                                                  Easter Sunday

Private
O.R. to Earl of C.

I perfectly understand the limits of your support of Count Daru's note and shall carry out your instructions faithfully, but I should have preferred strict neutrality to any interference however limited, not for the sake of my personal position in Rome, because it will interest me immensely to carry out your instructions and report the result, and can do me no harm one way or the other, but simply because our support of Daru's policy will irritate our English Catholics beyond measure in Rome and not satisfy or help the Opposition Bishops whom Daru wants to serve.

Lord Acton is in despair about it and has written to entreat of me 'to telegraph as forcibly as I can the gravity of the mistake Daru's note involves in regard to the Opposition Bishops'.

But I had done so already when his letter reached me. He wrote because I cannot call on him now while his little girl has the measles. . . .

487 [F.O. 43/107]   *Rome, 19 April 1870*

No. 98
O.R. to Earl of C.

The Cardinal Secretary of State this morning desired me to tell Your
Lordship how deeply grieved he had been at the annoyance to which
Miss Cunliffe, Miss Greenstreet and Miss Dawkins had been exposed
under circumstances over which he had no control at the time the
order for their departure was given to the police. . . . His Eminence
desired in the strongest terms to apologize and express his deep-felt
regrets at the indignity to which these English ladies had been so
unfortunately subjected, and to assure Your Lordship that he will,
after a searching investigation, visit with his displeasure and severely
punish any persons proved to have been instrumental in calumniating
them.

    The grounds on which the competent authorities had been led to
have recourse to the measures His Eminence so much deplored were
to be sought, the Cardinal explained, in the imprudent manner in
which the ladies had allowed the use of their apartment to their
servants, which had given rise to misapprehension of a distressing
character, and His Eminence sincerely hoped the ladies would be more
careful in regard to their household concerns in the future.

488 [F.O. 43/107]   *Rome, 22 April 1870*

No. 100
O.R. to Earl of C.

The French Ambassador called on me this afternoon to tell me that
he had had an audience of the Pope at 12 o'clock. . . . He had previously
given a copy of Count Daru's note to Cardinal Antonelli so that the
Pope was already acquainted with its contents, and was pleased to
enter generally into conversation with the French Ambassador on the
subject. His Holiness . . . contended that the civil power had nothing
to fear from the decisions of the Council, that the relations between
Church and State in France were regulated by a Concordat, and that
the Court of Rome had always respected their treaty engagements. . . .

    The French Ambassador explained that he had been also instructed
to communicate Count Daru's note to the Council in accordance with
the ancient usages and rights of the crown of France, and that he there-

fore humbly desired to address His Holiness both as Pontiff and as President of the Council and to solicit that His Holiness would be pleased as such to make known the contents of Count Daru's note to the bishops in Council assembled. The Pope replied that he would take this demand into consideration, but that he foresaw objections which might render it difficult for him to grant the request. ...

The Marquis de Banneville took occasion to observe that he could not conceal how painful would be the impression produced in France if the Council adopted the advice of some of the leading bishops to alter the order in which the *Schemata* were to be discussed, so as to bring a debate on the *Schema de Ecclesia* immediately after the public session of Sunday next 24th inst., and before the discussion of the other *Schemata* which had already engaged the attention of the Fathers. The very serious consequences which such a course might produce in France led the Ambassador to hope that His Holiness would not hesitate to make the bishops as soon as possible acquainted with the apprehensions his Government entertained in regard to the dogmatization of the principles laid down in the *Schema de Ecclesia*.

The Marquis de Banneville assured me that His Holiness had listened to all his remarks with that paternal benevolence which characterizes Pius IX, and that he had every reason to be gratified by the reception he had met. Having accomplished the mission with which he had been entrusted, the French Ambassador now desired to invite the representatives of those powers who had promised Count Daru their support at the Vatican to give effect to the instructions they had received from their Governments among which he was gratified to know was also the Government of Her Majesty.

I thanked the Marquis de Banneville for his visit and said I that would take the earliest opportunity of carrying out the instructions with which Your Lordship had been pleased to entrust me.

489 [F.O. 43/107]   *Rome, 25 April 1870*

No. 101
O.R. to Earl of C.

I have the honour to enclose the official account of the third public session of the Oecumenical Council as well as a copy of the *Constitutio Dogmatica de Fide Cattolica*, unanimously adopted by the bishops in Council assembled and promulgated by the Pope. 667 bishops were present and gave their *placet* to the decree. Between 30 and 40 bishops of the opposition are said to not have attended the ceremony at all. Bishop Strossmayer was conspicuous by his absence.

I beg to call Your Lordship's attention to the last paragraph of the decree beginning *quoniam vero satis non est* etc., giving dogmatic authority to the enactments of the Roman Congregations over which the Pope exercises absolute power. To my mind this paragraph is the first step taken by the Council towards the dogmatization of Papal Infallibility and tends to confirm the views I have so often ventured to submit to Your Lordship.

490 [F.O. 43/107]   *Rome, 26 April 1870*

No. 102
O.R. to Earl of C.

[Interview with Antonelli.] . . . I said that Count Daru's memorandum . . . had been communicated to Her Majesty's Government, who fully shared the apprehensions felt by that of the Emperor as to the danger of serious conflict between the civil and ecclesiastical authorities if the *Schema de Ecclesia* were enacted with the authority of the Pope and Council, and I assured His Eminence that Her Majesty's Government would learn with sincere satisfaction that the *Schema* would be modified in the sense indicated by the French Government. I desired at the same time to remind him that Her Majesty's Government, full of respect for the liberty of the Church . . . in no way pretended to interfere with the Synodical deliberations on spiritual matters, but being a Protestant power did not of course prevent our desiring peace, and doing what we could to promote goodwill among men.

Cardinal Antonelli replied that he had already explained to the French Government that their apprehensions were totally unfounded, because the competence of the civil and ecclesiastical powers being perfectly distinct and definite, the Church did not exercise a direct and absolute interference in questions relating to the constitutive principles of governments, the forms of civil institutions, the political rights of citizens, the duties of the state, etc., etc., besides which the relations between Church and State in France were already regulated by a Concordat with which the decisions of the Council could not interfere, and His Eminence noticed with satisfaction that Count Daru had fully acknowledged and done justice to those explanations in his memorandum, so much so indeed that it was a matter of surprize to him why Count Daru had thought it necessary to re-open questions which he himself admitted had been answered to the satisfaction of the Emperor's Government.

As to the *Schema de Ecclesia* His Eminence explained that all the *Schemata* so long as they had not been discussed and modified in the Council and promulgated by the Pope were in reality dead letters, as, for instance, the *Schema de Fide* which had been promulgated on Sunday last had been discussed for weeks and entirely remodelled and re-written by the Fathers themselves before they had consented to vote for it, and their vote had then been unanimous. He had no doubt the *Schema de Ecclesia* would in like manner be modified in debate, but he was of course not in a position to foretell in what sense those modifications might result.

I said I was glad to learn that the conflict between the civil and ecclesiastical authorities apprehended by the French Government would be practically avoided by the Church and that he expected the *Schema de Ecclesia* would be modified by the bishops in Council assembled. . . .

I then called on the French Ambassador and told His Excellency in what manner I had endeavoured to carry out Your Lordship's instructions in support of Count Daru's memorandum.

491 [F.O. 43/107]   *Rome, 26 April 1870*

No. 103. Secret
O.R. to Earl of C.

I have given the substance of the conversation I had with Cardinal Antonelli on the subject of Count Daru's memorandum, and I will now add a few details of a strictly confidential nature. His Eminence made the following characteristic remarks in a further conversation which followed the one already reported.

The interference of the French Government was very strange and he wondered what would be said in France if the Pope endeavoured in like manner to interfere with the Plebiscite. I said that the French Government desired to maintain peace among Christians, and that the highest authorities were of opinion that the dogmatization of the Syllabus would produce a formidable struggle in France and elsewhere, the

428 THE ROMAN QUESTION

results of which might prove very different from those which the Head of the Catholic Church must desire in the interest of religion. The Court of Rome might think that the Catholic party was strong in France, but they must also know that indifference to religion was spreading, and that if consciences were too severely tried their present indifference might at any moment assume a form of hostility.

Cardinal Antonelli replied that in France, as in every other part of the world, there were three other categories of consciences besides those who were indifferent to religion, namely, Unbelievers, Dissenters and true Catholics. Now unbelievers and those who really were indifferent could not be disturbed by the decisions of the Pope and Council if they were what they professed to be, namely faithless or indifferent. Dissenters had their own way of thinking and need not trouble their minds about the Church of Rome. There remained the fourth category, true Catholics, with whom the Church had to deal, and true Catholics derived happiness, comfort and eternal salvation from the decisions of the Pope and Council.

I said that the Council had proved the existence of divisions in the Church and that the appeal now made by the Catholic powers was dictated by a sincere religious spirit.

Cardinal Antonelli explained that the bishops had been convoked to study those divisions and rectify errors and that true Catholics would abide by the decisions of the Council whatever they were.

I said that I had also heard on high authority that another matter for serious consideration was the irritation that would be produced in France by the publication of Count Daru's note if it was accompanied by the refusal of the Pope to take into consideration the interests and wishes of France that had been set before His Holiness with so much respect, sincerity and moderation. Count Daru himself had remarked in one of his letters published by the newspapers that a responsible ministry might find it difficult to resist the pressure of public opinion in France and continue to protect Rome if the Pope and Council decreed a permanent conflict between Church and State.

Cardinal Antonelli said that the pressure of public opinion in France had already compelled Count Daru to resign. His opinions were neither shared by his colleagues nor by the majority of his countrymen who cared little for Gallicanism but very much for the personal safety of the Pope, the liberty of the Church and the honour of France.

I said that Count Daru had resigned on the question of the Plebiscite and not on that of his Roman policy, which had been adopted by the Emperor and Mr Ollivier.[1]

Cardinal Antonelli smiled and said that his information led him to think that all interference with the Council on the part of the French Government would cease with Count Daru's resignation, whose memorandum the Pope had declined to communicate to the Council, and he did not expect that the Marquis de Banneville would ever be instructed to allude to the subject again.

492   [F.O. 43/107]   Rome, 27 April 1870

No. 104
O.R. to Earl of C.

My colleagues having communicated the support of their Governments desired to give Count Daru's memorandum in writing to the Cardinal Secretary of State were anxious I should do likewise in the name of H.M. Govt. I gave three reasons for not doing so:

1st.   Because I had no instructions to that effect from Your Lordship.
2nd. Because I was not officially accredited to the Court of Rome.
3rd.   Because the Cardinal Secretary of State was not strictly bound to receive an official note from an unofficial agent.

As, however, my colleagues did not think I ought to take the responsibility on myself of declining to adhere to their request and thought it not impossible Your Lordship might see fit to write an autograph private letter for communication to the Pope, I consented to telegraph to the Foreign Office, and am now awaiting Your Lordship's reply.

493   [F.O. 43/107]   Rome, 27 April 1870

No. 105 [Recites Telegram]
O.R. to Earl of C.

My colleagues who have sent in Notes are not satisfied and are anxious I should ask you do to so likewise. If you agree with them please to send me a note as soon as possible for communication to the Pope.

[1] The French Premier.

494 [F.O. 43/105]   *F.O. 29 April 1870*
No. 43 [Recites Telegram]
Earl of C. to O.R.

Being unaccredited to the Pope and never interfering officially in
political or ecclesiastical affairs you are in a different position from the
Foreign Ministers at Rome and you may assign to them that reason
for not presenting a note and accordingly you will not present one.

495 [Clarendon Papers, C. 475(4)]   *F.O. 2 May 1870*
Private
Earl of C. to O.R.

. . . The smothered hiss of the opposition Bishops and the timid
vacillation of the Catholic Governments have made more manifest
the power of the Pope who safely reckons on the unabating ignorance
and superstition of mankind.

   You did quite right not to yield to the pressure of your colleagues
to send a note to the Cardinal in support of Daru's note. I had some
difficulty in the matter as Gladstone was for and I was against your
writing, and I was therefore obliged to circulate to the colleagues his
and my opinion and to ask for theirs which were unanimous against
a note. . . . .

   The objections raised by the opposition Bishops to the note seem
to me feeble and their reliance upon the non-oecumenicity of the
Council, which is modern, must make Pio Nono laugh. Acton & Co.
have made a gallant swim in the torrent but they have known for a
long time past that it was carrying them away and that the straws they
caught at could not prevent their being drowned. If the Govts. will
support them when they get home some evils may be prevented and
the Oecumenicity of the Council will then matter little or nothing.
The if however is important and I expect there will always be some
political or social reasons to make the Governments submit to be
kicked and to say they like it. . . .

496 [F.O. 43/108]   *Rome, 4 May 1870*
No. 108
O.R. to Earl of C.

The discussion on the *Schema, Dei Parvo Catechismo,* was terminated today. 101 bishops of the minority voted against the *Schema* (45 '*juxta modum*' and 56 '*non placet*') and 576 voted for the *Schema* which amounts to a dogmatization of the Catechism of Bellarmin.

497 [F.O. 43/108] *Rome, 4 May 1870*

No. 108
O.R. to Earl of C.

[Acknowledges despatch instructing him to ask Antonelli to make a searching inquiry into the matter of the three ladies.] . . . Before carrying out this instruction I venture to submit my impression that it would perhaps be more advantageous to the ladies if they would first institute a searching inquiry themselves into the circumstances which gave rise to the misapprehensions of the Pontifical authorities, so as to relieve their servants of all suspicion. . . .

It appears for instance that the attachment of a gentleman called Murray for the ladies' maid, Miss Dingle, was not objected to by her mistress, although it was giving rise to much idle gossip in the neighbourhood. Miss Dawkins herself in her letter of 5 April to Your Lorship alludes to the report 'that a Roman priest had become enamoured with one of the ladies and, *not being discouraged*, the mandate to leave Rome was issued against them'. This report, which has been reported all over Rome may owe its origin to the imprudence of a servant.

Your Lordship will also recollect that Miss Dawkins in her first letter of 30 March remarks that the police in searching the apartment at 11 o'clock at night looked neither at books nor papers 'but seemed in quest of some person', which leads to the inference, since we know the ladies to be entirely above all suspicion, that the imprudence of the servants might have misled the police into fancying that a person could be concealed there.

For these and other reasons, I think that in the interest of the ladies the safer course in this very delicate matter would be for them to satisfy themselves that they have really not been betrayed by their servants before a further appeal to the Papal Government revives the idle and mischievous gossip they have been victims to, and which the reversal of the order for their departure and the regrets expressed by the Papal authorities had silenced and disproved.

While awaiting Your Lordship's answer to this despatch I shall make it my business to consult the wishes of the ladies confidentially on the subject, so as to be better able to assist them later with the Cardinal Secretary of State. . . .

498 [Clarendon Papers, C. 487]   *Rome, 7 May 1870*

Private and Secret
O.R. to Earl of C.

I have availed myself of your permission not to act at once on your last instruction about the 3 ladies until I have consulted their own wishes.

In declaring them innocent Cardinal Antonelli evidently wished to avoid all further scandal, but if pushed to the wall he may be induced to make some unpleasant publication which we should all regret. Miss Cunliffe and Miss Greenstreet have parted company with Miss Dawkins and her pretty maid, Eliza Dingle, because they admit in confidence that her imprudence displeased them. They say that Miss Dawkins and her maid were in the habit of going out alone and making acquaintances with priests in the Churches, Galleries and Museums and of inviting them to the house without even knowing their names. The priests who came there were not among the most respectable.

Our clergyman *confides to me* that he was so shocked at the liberties Miss Dawkins allowed the priests to take that he would not allow his wife to frequent the house any more. The neighbours and more especially the English servants living around say that the maid's love affair with one Murray was a scandalous affair and annoyed the other inmates of the house, but Miss Dawkins sanctioned it. An American family complained.

It now appears that Miss Cunliffe and Miss Greenstreet foolishly associated with Miss Dawkins and her maid without previously knowing her and they had not the energy to quarrel and part with her when they found that her manners were unsuited to their tastes and habits because the lease of their apartment had not expired. They now live in different houses and streets.

I have of course stood up all along for the innocence of the three ladies and I believe in the respectability of Miss Cunliffe and Miss Greenstreet and I suppress all the gossip about their tea fights with priests, but a searching enquiry will only prove that Miss Dawkins and her maid had priests and lovers who slept in the house &c. &c.

&c. and Miss Cunliffe and Miss Greenstreet will then be in a worse position than before, when they stand convicted of having lived in a 'Bordello Ecclesiastico' as I told you in my first private letter on the subject. . . .

Miss Dawkins, who is not shy, intends to go to the Pope and have it out with him herself!

499 [F.O. 43/108]   Rome, 10 May 1870

No. 111
O.R. to Earl of C.

The amended Infallibility Schema was submitted to the Pope on Saturday night for his approval and has been distributed to the bishops this morning. [O.R. has seen it and encloses a copy he made of the Canons.] The discussion of this Schema is expected to begin on Friday next 13 May, and is likely to last to the end of June.

The bishops of the opposition confidently announce at least 150 votes against Papal Infallibility, but they have hitherto always over-rated their own strength. . . .

500 [F.O. 43/108]   Rome, 11 May 1870

No. 113
O.R. to Earl of C.

[Concerning the total defeat of the opposition bishops in the Council on 24 April.] . . . A careful study of the Constitutio de fide, unanimously adopted by the Council on that day, will prove that they have not the courage of their opinions in the august presence of Pius IX. [Three quotations follow.] Without being a theologian I understand the first of these quotations to confirm the ex Cathedra Infallibility of the Pope; the second the Infallibility of the Church; and the third all the past enactments of the Court of Rome including the Syllabus.

83 bishops voted against this last paragraph in the Secret Congre-gation of 19 April, but when on 24th, at the public meeting, they found themselves in the presence of the Pope, they voted against themselves and with the majority. Bishop Strossmayer himself rather than give his 'non placet' in the presence of the Pope preferred to absent himself altogether.

If I insist on these painful details it is to shew that I have not misjudged the opposition in my past correspondence as friends and colleagues have repeatedly told me.

Although the defeat of 24 April has proved the moral strength of the majority and the timidity of the minority, the leading bishops of the opposition are in no way discouraged and confidently announce a minority vote of 150 against the new *Constitutio de Ecclesia* and they even defy the Pope to venture on the promulgation of his own Infallibility without the moral unanimity of the Council. They have drawn up another protest against the priority given to the Infallibility *Schema* and the principle of majorities in dogmatic questions, but only 77 bishops could be persuaded to sign it, and only under condition that it would not be published. . . .

It must be admitted that nothing can be more satisfactory than the language and professions of the opposition bishops in regard to the vigorous resistance with which they propose to meet Infallibility and the Syllabus, and, if their votes respond to their speeches, 150 '*non placets*' may be recorded against Infallibility. But I do not expect that that would deter the Pope from promulgating the dogma since the Council unanimously gave him the power to do so on 24 April by voting their faith in the 3rd chapter '*De Fide*' quoted above. . . .

After the promulgation of the dogma, the opposition bishops have but two open courses before them, either to submit and accept or to protest against the Oecumenicity of the Council. The latter course involves excommunication according to the Bull *Latae Sententiae*. And after they have been excommunicated, what support have the excommunicated bishops to expect at the hands of their respective Governments?

501 [F.O. 43/108]   *Rome, 14 May 1870*

No. 116
O.R. to Earl of C.

The discussion on the *Constitutio Dogmatica prima de Ecclesia Christi* was opened yesterday by Mgr Pie, bishop of Poitiers, and continued this morning. . . . I have already told Your Lordship that the opposition reckoned on at least 150 votes against the definition of Papal Infallibility. Last night the leaders had collected 131 promises of support from their followers: 43 Austrian, Hungarian and German bishops, 40 American, 29 French, 10 Italian, 5 English (?), 4 Portuguese.

29. Bishop Dupanloup

30. Bishop Strossmayer. Painting by Lenbach

But as I have also said before, the opposition bishops overrate their moral strength in the Council, and once the dogmatic definition of Papal Infallibility has been promulgated by Pius IX, all, without one single exception, will accept it without a protest.

502 [Clarendon Papers, C. 487]   *Rome, 16 May 1870*

Private
O.R. to Earl of C.

. . . Lord Acton has recovered from his fever I am happy to say. He intends to send his wife and children to Germany as soon as possible and to remain here himself to assist the opposition to the end which I am very glad of for I do not know what I should do without him. You know all his marvellous talents and virtues but you cannot know the extraordinary power he has displayed here as a leader of thought, and the great resources and energies he possesses for organizing a party. If he ever turns his attention to public affairs he is certainly called upon to play a great part in the history of Europe.

You say truly in your letter of the 2nd instant that he has made a gallant swim against the torrent, but I see no symptoms on the part of France or indeed of any of the European Powers to support him and his party after their defeat in the Council or even to resent the kick Pio Nono has given our collective remonstrances at the Vatican.

I fear, as you say, that the Governments of Europe will always knock under in the end and submit to be kicked by the Pope, otherwise a sense of dignity ought to make them *all* break off diplomatic relations with Rome after the dogmatization of Syllabus and Infallibility. But they won't do it, and the Pope will be allowed to kick them to his heart's content with the full support of his French Protectors. The withdrawal of all the missions in Rome during the Lifetime of Pio Nono would be logical and dignified, but France would not consent to it.

I will seek a favourable opportunity to carry out Mr Gladstone's suggestion of signifying to Antonelli that Her Majesty's Government did not directly or indirectly enter into the question of Oecumenicity in supporting Daru's Memorandum, but that we simply viewed the Assembly in Rome under the Pope as one having *de facto* power to exercise a great influence over a large portion of the Christian World.

The question of the Oecumenicity of this Council will in my humble

Q

opinion agitate Theology and the Catholic World for centuries to come, because it involves the four greatest questions of the future, viz. The Supremacy of the Roman Pontiff, The Independence of the Episcopacy, The Nationality of Churches and The relations of Church and State all over the World. But even Opposition Bishops have not yet realized its magnitude!

503 [F.O. 43/108]   *Rome, 19 May 1870*

No. 118
O.R. to Earl of C.

The leading French bishops of the opposition, Monseigneurs Darboy and Dupanloup, and the bishop of Bayeux, Mgr Hugonin, are under an impression that Monsieur Ollivier addressed a despatch to the French Ambassador, Monsieur de Banneville on 12th inst., or thereabouts, telling him that since the Pope had rejected the friendly advice of the French Government and preferred war to peace, he foresaw that the consequent struggle would inevitably lead to the abrogation of the Concordat and the separation of Church and State in France, and the final departure of the French garrison from Rome.

Mr Ollivier desired Mr de Banneville to speak confidentially in this sense with the members of the Roman Government, but not to communicate the despatch itself to Cardinal Antonelli.

This report led me to call this morning on the Marquis de Banneville and to ask him what amount of truth there was in it. His Excellency assured me that it was unfounded and that he had, not later than 17th inst., told Cardinal Antonelli that after the total disregard shewn by the Court of Rome to the friendly warning of France he did not intend to speak to His Eminence any more about the Council at all. On the other hand, Monsieur de Banneville added, it was gratifying to see how much the opposition had gained in numbers and in moral power since Count Daru's memorandum in their behalf had become known to the bishops, and he now felt convinced that the Ultramontane party would never venture to let the Pope promulgate the dogmatic definition of his Papal Infallibility in the face of the moral forces that now threatened the Vatican.

The Austrian Ambassador, Count Trauttmansdorff, whom I called on later, holds the same opinion in regard to the power of the opposition to prevent the promulgation of the Infallibility dogma. But with

all due deference to the opinion of the representatives of the great
Catholic powers in Rome, I cannot but think that their views are
influenced by their wishes.

504 [F.O. 43/108]   *Rome, 27 May 1870*

No. 121
O.R. to Earl of C.

[Forwards a pamphlet *De l'Unanimité Morale*, drawn up by the
opposition bishops.] . . . The importance of this protest cannot be
overrated, for it is the standpoint from which the opposition can later
dispute the Oecumenicity of the Council. . . .

505 [F.O. 361/1]   *30 May 1870*

Earl of C. to O.R.

. . . The moral of the whole tale is that you have been right from the
beginning and have steadily maintained against all comers that the
Pope would have his own way. . . .

506 [F.O. 43/108]   *Rome, 31 May 1870*

No. 122
O.R. to Earl of C.

. . . Since 13th inst. the Fathers have met 13 times to consider the
Infallibility *Schema*, and have made so little progress that the discussion
is expected to last all June and a part of July. The bishops of the opposition flatter themselves that the solemn promulgation of the dogma
will then be put off until next winter and after the prorogation of the
Council which they confidently expect to obtain from the Pope. Be
that as it may, there can be no doubt that the opposition has gained in
numbers and in moral courage, and that they are now fighting the
battle of the episcopacy against the absolutism of Rome with united
energy and with all the power of the moral forces at their disposal.
    The speeches of Cardinals Schwarzenberg, Rauscher and Mathieu,
of Archbishops Darboy, McHale, Genouilhac and Simor, of Bishops
Greith, Hefele, Jussuf, Ketteler, Clifford, etc. against the definition are
said to have produced a deep impression on the assembly, whilst the
speeches of Cardinals Patrizi and Cullen, Archbishops Deschamps and

Manning, Bishops Pie, Hassoun, etc. in favour of the definition are said not to have converted a single member of the opposition. Some of these speeches have been reported in the newspapers, but the speakers themselves do not admit their authenticity. [The 6 English and Irish bishops of the opposition are Clifford, Amherst, Errington, Vaughan, Moriarty and McHale.] 109 bishops are inscribed to speak on the Infallibility *Schema*, and the opposition think that by speaking against time they may prolong the debate until the great heat of summer necessitates a prorogation of the Council, when the promulgation of the decree would be put off until the winter session. For they do not admit the definition of a new dogma without the moral unanimity of the Pope and Council, which a minority vote of 132 would render impossible. . . .

The struggle may be long and fierce, but I still cannot see that the opposition have the slightest prospect of success against the majority in the Council so long as they are not prepared to set aside the question of Opportunity and deny the very principle of Infallibility, protest against the Oecumenicity of the Council and face excommunication when it is hurled after them.

507 [F.O. 43/108]   *Rome, 4 June 1870*

No. 124
O.R. to Earl of C.

I enclose copy of a letter addressed by the Pope to M. Veuillot, the editor of the *Univers*, thanking him for the subscriptions he has collected in aid of the Council. His Holiness goes on to congratulate the clergy in France who have united in common action to assist M. Veuillot by their example, etc. This sentence is of great importance at the present moment since M. Veuillot, who is the champion of Infallibility in France, has set the clergy against those of their bishops who have joined the opposition in the Council and has encouraged them in every way to resist episcopal authority. The bishops who vote against Infallibility will therefore not only be in bad odour at Rome, but will find the insubordination of their clergy in their dioceses sanctioned by the Pope. The celebrated *Avertissement* of Mgr Dupanloup of November last to M. Veuillot has been thereby disavowed by His Holiness, and the triumph of the editor of the *Univers* over the bishop of Orléans is now complete.

Well may it be said that Pius IX after revolutionizing the state at the commencement, has revolutionized the Church at the end of his eventful and disastrous reign.

508 [F.O. 43/108]   *Rome, 4 June 1870*

No. 126
O.R. to Earl of C.

[Concerning the efforts of Baron Arnim, the Prussian Ambassador, to persuade O.R. to make a written communication to the Vatican about the Council.] . . . Baron Arnim was more anxious than his colleagues that England and Prussia should act in concert, and thought that the objections to the line of conduct he recommended came from me personally, and might be overcome by an appeal from Berlin to Your Lordship. [Such an appeal had now been made. Arnim had been given the impression by Antonelli that O.R. had not even made the verbal communication, that he had made, with regard to Daru's memorandum. The misunderstanding now apparently cleared up.]

509 [F.O. 43/108]   *Rome, 4 June 1870*

No. 127
O.R. to Earl of C.

The majority in the Council after listening to the speeches of 65 of the 109 bishops who desired to speak on the principle of the Infallibility *Schema* closed the general debate yesterday by acclamation, and called upon the Legates to let them proceed to the discussion of the Preamble and the four chapters of the *Schema* itself without further loss of time. Although not exactly unexpected, the measure seems to have taken the opposition by surprize, who had reckoned on prolonging the discussion so as to gain as much time as possible, and put off the discussion of the *Schema* itself indefinitely.

As the 109 speeches were to have lasted to 22 June they have thus lost nineteen days, and I hear that they have convoked a meeting of the opposition committees at Cardinal Rauscher's house today to concert the best means of meeting the difficulty. Had the opposition taken their stand on the 'Rules of Procedure' and declined to attend the Council until those Rules had been modified, as I have so often observed in my correspondence, they would not have been exposed to their present dilemma. But having practically accepted those Rules they will now find it very difficult to refuse to accept the decisions of the majority, unless they protest and all leave Rome, which they have not the courage to do. . . .

510 [F.O. 43/108]   *Rome, 8 June 1870*

No. 130. Confidential
O.R. to Earl of C.

I am assured on high authority that Count Beust proposed to Monsieur Ollivier not to lose the few days that must necessarily elapse between the last vote of the bishops on the Infallibility question and the solemn promulgation of the dogma by the Pope himself, and to present a collective protest of the European powers against the final definition to His Holiness, followed by a collective rupture of diplomatic relations. But Monsieur Ollivier is reported to have declined the proposition, saying that the French Government were not in a position to quarrel with the Pope.

511 [F.O. 43/108]   *Rome, 8 June 1870*

No. 131
O.R. to Earl of C.

The meeting of the opposition in Cardinal Rauscher's house has resulted in a protest against the Rules of Procedure and the vote of the majority of Friday last, and has been signed by about 80 bishops and sent to the Cardinal Legates, who will not take more notice of it than of the many other protests of the opposition since 8 December last.

Some of the leading bishops such as Strossmayer, Dupanloup, Darboy, Clifford, Kenrick, Conolly, Haynalt and others were in favour of a protest followed by the departure *en masse* of the opposition from Rome, but the majority of the opposition declined to follow them and were confirmed in their decision by the persuasive speeches of bishops Ketteler and Hefele, who warned them against a rupture with Rome which could not benefit the Catholic Church, since the history of Councils proved that the bishops who had attempted it had stood out in the cold without achieving their object in the end.

The Hungarian bishops then proposed to attend the Council and vote, but not to speak any more and by their silence to protest against the interruption of the preliminary debate by the majority. To that

Cardinal Rauscher opposed the duty of bishops to speak the truth according to the dictates of their consciences, and the Hungarian proposition was rejected both by the Germans and the French.

A proposition of the bishop of Orleans to address pastorals explaining and justifying the position of the minority bishops to their respective flocks was equally rejected by the assembly, and finally the usual protest against the Rules of Procedure was carried against every other course of action proposed.

The opposition have thus again lost a great opportunity of asserting their independence, and have once more shewn the Vatican their want of unity and organization, and the influence of nationality over theology. They will now have one last opportunity when vote is taken on Infallibility of choosing between martyrdom or submission, and they say that their numbers have increased to 150 and more since Friday last.

On 6th and 7th inst. the Council passed the Preamble and the two first chapters of the Infallibility *Schema* on the primacy and perpetuity of the Papacy without opposition. . . . Tomorrow, at the 68th General Congregation, the discussion of the third chapter on the spiritual jurisdiction of the Papacy commences, and as its object is to limit the jurisdiction and independence of the episcopacy and to abolish some of the privileges of the Oriental Church, an interesting debate of some length is expected.

512 [Clarendon Papers, C. 487] *Rome, 9 June 1870*

Private
O.R. to Earl of C.

. . . Lord Acton is going away on Saturday next and as he has been the soul of the opposition, we all expect the body to collapse the moment he goes.

Mr Gladstone, you tell me, thinks that if the opposition Bishops could join in a protest against Infallibility and leave Rome '*en masse*' it would be a great blow to Oecumenicity. I have thought so all along, but to confess the honest truth I have failed to find among the Opposition Bishops that faith and courage that makes martyrs, and doubt whether more than a dozen, if *so many*, would face excommunication and starvation, for they well know that Governments don't generally provide for suspended and censured priests.

I have said to my colleagues and others all along: it is useless to advize the Vatican and the Majority. Tell the Opposition what your Governments will do for them after the Pope has cut off their spiritual and temporal supplies 'if you want them to succeed'.

However, Acton who knows his men and is in favour of a protest and departure 'en masse' of the Opposition, still thinks it possible at the last moment, so I hope I may be mistaken in my estimate of the character of the R.C. Bishops of the Opposition.

Cardinal Antonelli is very cheerful and amiable, but Diplomatists complain of his never speaking but of 'la pluie et le beau temps'.

Banneville is a myth, no one ever sees him, and Arnim, the Prussian, has quarrelled with him about the old story of not returning cards! It is a pity the French Govt. were not represented during the Council by Sartiges, the Voltairian, rather than by Banneville the Jesuit, who has been true to the principles of St Ignatius of Loyola. . . .

513 [F.O. 43/108]   Rome, 10 June 1870
No. 133
O.R. to Earl of C.

In talking about the Council this morning with the Cardinal Secretary of State I observed that I expected after the dogmatization of Pontifical Infallibility to see a powerful party arise in the Church who would dispute the Oecumenicity of the Council. The Governments which had given their support to Count Daru's memorandum, including that of Her Majesty, had not entered directly or indirectly into that vast and grave question. They had simply viewed the assembly at Rome under the Pope as one having *de facto* powers to exercise a great influence over a large portion of the Christian world, and they might, in course of time, side morally with those bishops and that portion of the clergy who could not admit the right of majorities to decide in dogmatic questions without the moral unanimity of the Council, and who would consequently deny its Oecumenicity.

Cardinal Antonelli replied that he did not believe in the possibility of a schism, but admitting even for the sake of argument that the bishops of the opposition adopted the course I had indicated, there still remained over 900 bishops and the clergy of the Catholic World whose faith in the Oecumenicity of the Council remained unshaken. He did not however expect that a single bishop would exclude himself from the Roman Catholic community by questioning the Oecu-menicity of the Council which involved excommunication, nor did he expect that Catholic Governments would materially encourage schism in the Church.

The liberty of speech in the Council had been so great that even heretical opinions had been expounded without interference from the Legates, and he only regretted that some bishops had unnecessarily excited and misled the faithful by printing their grievances in the newspapers instead of stating them in the Council which had been convoked for the purpose of listening to their wishes, suggestions and opinions.

514 [F.O. 43/108]   *Rome, 10 June 1870*

No. 134
O.R. to Earl of C.

[Encloses correspondence with Miss Dawkins.] . . . Miss Cunliffe and Miss Greenstreet it appears have parted company from Miss Dawkins and her maid. Miss Dawkins, with that courageous spirit and love of truth that characterize her, has defended all along the character and conduct of her maid, Eliza Dingle, whose remarkable beauty had attracted the attention of the Romans. I shall return to the subject as soon as I have further information to impart.

515 [F.O. 43/108]   *Rome, 15 June 1870*

No. 135
O.R. to Earl of C.

The processions and religious ceremonies ordered by the Cardinal Vicar for the definition of Papal Infallibility by the Council have lasted a week and have been very numerous, but I cannot say that they were as well attended by the laity as the clerical newspapers seem to think. The professors and masters of the Roman University and the officials generally have been called upon to sign a petition to the Council in favour of the new dogma, and few have thought it prudent to abstain from obeying superior orders. . . . Orders have been given for a general and spontaneous illumination of Rome when the dogma shall be promulgated.

R

516 [F.O. 43/108]   *Rome, 15 June 1870*

No. 136
O.R. to Earl of C.

The first and second chapters of the Infallibility *Schema* on the primacy and perpetuity of the Papacy have been unanimously voted and adopted by the Fathers of the Council. The discussion on the 3rd chapter respecting the spiritual jurisdiction was brought to a close yesterday, but some modifications of the text are expected before the vote can be taken. The debates are described as languid and ill-attended, and several of the bishops who had put down their names to speak were not present when their turn came and had to be passed over....

Mgr Dupanloup and the other French opposition bishops spoke in favour of the first two chapters, but directed their angry attacks against the speech of the Patriarch of Jerusalem, who had endeavoured to demolish Gallicanism.

The discussion of the 4th chapter on Papal Infallibility commenced this morning and about 80 bishops are expected to take part in the debate. If all speak, the dogmatic definition could scarcely take place before 10 July which is the feast of All the Popes of Rome. But if the debate is again cut short by a vote of the majority, the promulgation might come as early as 29th inst., the feast of St Peter and St Paul. The bishops of the opposition still hold that at least 150 *non placets* will be given against the new dogma.

I shall not be surprised if they are mistaken. The dread of action which has hitherto paralyzed their oratorical achievements will paralyze the independence of their votes in the august presence of the 'Idol of the Vatican'. Ever since the opposition bishops have begun to realize that the dogmatization of Papal Infallibility is inevitable and that they will have on some given day to choose between submission or action, I hear them say that after all they will have plenty of time during the prorogation to settle in what manner they can best discredit the decision of a not Oecumenical Council, since no Conciliar decision was ever binding or had force of Canon Law so long as a Council continued its labours, and had not been definitely closed. 'Above all,' they add, 'let us avoid the fatal consequences which a rupture with Rome might entail.'

The leading bishops of the majority have it also always in their power to break up the opposition at the last moment by offering to compromise the wording of the fourth Canon on Infallibility, and I feel convinced that the smallest concession on the part of the Infallibilists would be hailed by three quarters of the opposition with triumphant submission to the inspirations of the Holy Ghost.

517 [F.O. 361/1]   *F.O. 15 June 1870*

Earl of Clarendon to Lord Lyons [Ambassador in Paris]

. . . How right Odo has been throughout in declaring that the Pope would end by having his own way in all things. He has stood alone against all the representatives of the Catholic powers and all the opposition bishops *plus* Acton who is worth them all put together. . . .

I never thought there would be energy enough in France for schism.

518 [F.O. 43/108]   *Rome, 16 June 1870*

No. 138
O.R. to Earl of C.

The French and Austrian Ambassadors and the Prussian and Bavarian Ministers have written to their Governments that they now think the dogmatic definition of Infallibility not impossible and wish for instructions. The Austrian proposes that he and his colleagues should abstain from taking part in any public rejoicings or general illuminations, and from being present in the Diplomatic Tribune on the day of the promulgation. He also suggests that they should either make a short excursion in the country or take their leave of absence a little earlier than they intended so as not to be in Rome on the day of the ceremony and thereby mark their disapprobation. . . .

Not being officially accredited, and having been in consequence excluded by the French Ambassador from the Diplomatic Tribune, I need not trouble Your Lordship in this case with a similar request for instructions which I should not be in a position to carry out, besides which I need not tell Your Lordship how deeply I should regret not being present at the great ceremony my colleagues desire to avoid.

519 [F.O. 43/108]   *Rome, 18 June 1870*

No. 140. Secret
O.R. to Earl of C.

Lord Acton left Rome for Germany and England on 11th inst. The leading bishops of the opposition acknowledge that of all the laymen present in Rome who took a real interest in the debates of the Oecumenical Council none will leave a greater name in history than Lord Acton.

The strong ties that now unite the leading theological minds of England, France, Germany, Hungary and Austria are due to Lord Acton's personal influence, profound knowledge, great talents and high virtues. Without his personal intervention the bishops of the opposition could scarcely have known each other. Without his knowledge of language and of theology the theologians of the various nations represented in the Council could not have understood each other, without his talents as a leader they could not have remained united amongst each other and without his high virtues they could not have accepted and followed the lead of a layman so much younger than any of the Fathers of the Council.

The time has not come when the manner in which Lord Acton exercised his all-important influence on the party of opposition can be recounted in detail, but Your Lordship may rest assured that whatever the Liberal Catholic party achieve in the world after the Council will be mainly due to the influential presence of Lord Acton during the Council in Rome; and I feel that it is my duty to place these facts on record in the annals of Your Lordship's office.

520 [F.O. 43/108]   *Rome, 22 June 1870*

No. 142
O.R. to Earl of C.

... The most noteworthy incident of the discussion on the 4th chapter respecting Papal Infallibility has been a speech of Cardinal Guidi's on Saturday last in favour of the principles represented by the opposition bishops. The fact of a Roman Cardinal having joined the opposition at the eleventh hour has produced great irritation at the Vatican and has more or less encouraged the minority in the course they are pursuing.

Cardinal Guidi as a Dominican only represented the traditional hostility of his order to that of the Jesuits, but the Pope sent for him after he had spoken and reproved him in the severest terms, telling him that he had forgotten his Catechism, that he should repeat, study and meditate over his profession of faith and that he was guilty of heresy.

Cardinal Guidi entreated the Pope to read his speech and point out to him which of his opinions could be called heretical. But His Holiness replied that the indignant interruptions of the majority while he spoke were sufficient proof of his errors. Cardinal Guidi endeavoured to argue with the Sovereign Pontiff that tradition was not favourable to Infallibility, but Pius IX put a stop to all further discussion by exclaiming, '*La Tradizione son io!*'

[The opposition had elected a committee to consider amendments.] . . . It strikes me that the opposition by appointing a committee to examine the amendments proposed for the definition of Infallibility have made a great and fatal concession to the majority, as they have thereby proved their readiness to vote for some sort of definition of the dogma they have hitherto opposed with so much courage and firmness. It would have been more logical on their part to have declined any and every transaction with the Definitionists or Infallibilitarians, and to have taken their stand on the definition of the Council of Florence, which having hitherto been the law of the Church might have been considered as final and immutable by the minority. As matters now stand, it will be difficult for them to give an unqualified *non placet* to any new definition of Infallibility submitted to their votes.

Bishop Ketteler of Mayence who had been reckoned among the Fallibilitarians, has published a declaration in the *Katholick* of Mayence protesting that he has always been an opportunist, but will submit in the end to any decision of the Council. His example will probably be followed by bishop Melchers of Cologne and some other German bishops, so that the Infallibilists are now sure of their power to break up the opposition by some slight concessions in the wording of the Canon on Infallibility.

Bishop Dupanloup is organizing a deputation of the opposition to the Pope to ask for a prorogation of the Council before the solemn definition, or for the privilege of secret instead of open voting. Neither will be conceded by the Pope in my humble opinion.

I cannot but think that if the opposition would act up to the principles they so eloquently, ably and courageously profess, they might still destroy the Oecumenicity of the Council, but they appear to me deplorably wanting in unity and energy of action.

521 [F.O. 43/108]   *Rome, 24 June 1870*

No. 143
O.R. to Earl of C.

Bishop Connolly of Halifax made a speech against Infallibility on 22nd
inst., but without producing the impression expected by his friends
because he omitted to protest against the principle of the dogma. On
the other hand, bishop Landriot of Reims made a most impressive and
effective speech against the principle of the dogma in yesterday's
sitting, but most unfortunately mitigated the effect produced by declaring at the end that notwithstanding the convictions he had expressed
he should submit to any decision of the Council on the great question
of Papal Infallibility.

The Austrian Ambassador tells me that a report is in circulation
among the German bishops that the Pope has consented to put off the
ceremony of the dogmatic definition of his own Infallibility after the
final vote of the bishops has been taken until the rest of the *Schema
de Ecclesia* has been discussed and voted in the course of next winter.
The Pope appears to me too old to put off the triumph of his policy
for so many months, and I fully expect the definition to follow
immediately upon the vote in the course of July.

Bishop Hefele of Rothenburg has told many of his friends in confidence that he intends to resign his bishoprick if Papal Infallibility is
dogmatized, but without leaving the Roman Catholic Church. He is
said to attribute the present critical position of the bishops of the
minority to the absence of support from their respective Governments.

522 [F.O. 43/108]   *Rome, 25 June 1870*

No. 145
O.R. to Earl of C.

99 bishops have still to speak on the chapter of Infallibility, which
amounts to 99 hours of oratory, as no bishop has yet been known to
condense his ideas in less than an hour's speech. No wonder that 40
bishops have put down their names to ask for the closing of the debate.
I should not be surprized if in the course of next week the growing
pressure of the majority compelled the Legates to put the question. . . .
The leaders of the majority have calculated correctly that time was
in their favour, for every day adds to their numbers whilst the minority

decreases and yields to the influence of the Vatican. It is naturally of vast importance to the Infallibilists to reduce the number of the opposition votes so as to render it as difficult as possible to the Fallibilitarians to dispute the Oecumenicity or Moral Unanimity of the Council in later years.

Leave of absence is therefore granted to any bishops of the opposition who apply, and I regret to say that many avail themselves of this method of evading the responsibility of a vote.

[*On 27 June Lord Clarendon died.*]

523 [F.O. 43/108]   *Rome, 1 July 1870*

No. 150
O.R. to Principal Secretary of State, F.O.

The great national loss we have sustained has met with deep and general sympathy in Rome, and all unite in feeling that the death of the Earl of Clarendon is an European calamity. I cannot resist the melancholy satisfaction of leaving a record in the annals of England of the letter I have received from Cardinal Antonelli (enclosed) on the loss of the great and good man who has passed away from among us, and who will ever live in the souls of those who knew him.

524 [F.O. 43/108]   *Rome, 1 July 1870*

No. 151
O.R. to the same

Mgr Dupanloup has just received a letter from Monsieur Émile Ollivier expressing the deep sense of his sympathy and admiration for the principles and moral courage of the bishops of the opposition, and of his entire condemnation of the errors and tactics of the Infallibilists, but he ends by deploring the inability of the French Government to assist and support the cause he has faith in.

525 [43/108]   *Rome, 1 July 1870*

No. 152
O.R. to the same

Both parties in the Council have now again reverted to the tactics of procrastination. The opposition hope thereby to obtain a prorogation of the Council before the definition of Infallibility. The majority hope to tire out their opponents and reduce their numbers by the growing tendency of the more timid portion of the Opportunists to apply for leave (which is readily granted), and return to their dioceses. Mgr Dupanloup's petition to the Pope for prorogation has not obtained a sufficient number of signatures to render it available, and the majority have meanwhile started a counter-petition asking for two sittings a day morning and evening which will certainly not meet with more success than the former, as they well know themselves.

If the leaders of the opposition were able to control the movements of their adherents and prevent their desertion the policy of procrastination would serve to prove that they possess moral influence enough to postpone the realization of the wishes of the Vatican, but as matters now stand the result will only be to diminish the number of the opposition votes against Infallibility, and give the final vote of the majority a greater appearance of moral unanimity than would have been the case if the opposition had spoken less and acted more vigorously.

The Pope has condemned Cardinal Guidi to religious exercises in his cell at the convent of the Minerva. He is not allowed to receive visitors except those who are likely to persuade him to retract the views he advocated in his great opposition speech, but he is allowed to attend the sittings of the Council.

526 [F.O. 43/108]   *Rome, 4 July 1870*

No. 155
O.R. to the same

On Friday last the Hungarian, Austrian and German bishops of the opposition met to discuss what they should do to induce their friends not to leave Rome before the final vote on Infallibility, and they decided to withdraw their names from the list of orators and ask for the closing of the debate on the 4th chapter. But the French bishops of the opposition to whom they communicated this resolution declined to adhere to it.

On Saturday the Germans, Hungarians and Austrians announced their intentions to give up their right of speaking, but the Cardinal Legates declined to divide the Council on the question of closing the debate so as not to disappoint the French bishops who still wished to speak.

Mgr Dupanloup and Mgr Darboy were still endeavouring to obtain signatures to their petition for the prorogation of the Council, but with as little success as when I last wrote.

Meanwhile a general meeting of the international opposition committee took place yesterday, Sunday, at Cardinal Rauscher's, which resulted in the adherence of the French bishops to the wishes of the rest of the Opportunists, and today, Monday, at the 85th Congregation two bishops of either side having spoken amidst general impatience, the Cardinal Legates declared the debate on the 4th chapter closed with the unanimous approbation of all the bishops present. . . .

[*Lord Granville became Foreign Secretary on 4 July.*]

527 [F.O. 43/108]   *Rome, 5 July 1870*

No. 156
O.R. to the same

The success of the policy of the Vatican which I have repeatedly ventured to foreshadow in my past correspondence is now becoming more apparent. Before the month of July is over the object for which the Council has been convoked will have been attained by the dogmatic definition of Papal Infallibility.

Six months ago the opposition party in the Council numbered over 200, many of whom represented the most important dioceses of Europe and America and altogether about 90 millions of souls. They enjoyed the sympathies of Liberal Humanity, and the moral support of the great powers, led by France, was conceded to them. A more formidable array of moral forces had never before resisted the pretentions of the Papacy. Yet the Vatican, that is a handful of Italian priests, by a steady application of the *non possumus* policy have defeated the collective interference of the great powers and reduced the 200 opposing bishops to an impotent minority in less than six months.

Prince Hohenlohe who was the first to recommend resistance to Rome was compelled by the clerical party in Bavaria to resign office and make room for a more Catholic Foreign Secretary. Count Daru, who led the attack by his able memorandum, fell a victim to clerical influence, and Monsieur Émile Ollivier who retained office withdrew from the struggle, instructing the French Ambassador in Rome on 12 May to avoid all further discussion with the Pope and his Government

on the Council, and to explain to the French bishops that 'non-intervention' was not indifference on the part of their Government but a
proof of confidence in their unsupported efforts.

Count Beust gave up the contest because he preferred to rely on the
laws of Austria for protection against Papal aggression to running the
awkward risk of a complete diplomatic rupture with Rome. Count
Bismarck declined to proceed unless the North German bishops applied
personally or in a body for the support of the Prussian Government
and disavowed the able note of sound advice addressed by the Prussian
Minister at Rome to Cardinal Antonelli. And other Governments
ceased to fight for a cause which their leaders in France had abandoned
or never seriously taken up.

Having nothing further to apprehend from State interference at
Rome, the Vatican proceeded to deal with the bishops of the opposition
by inducing the minor clergy in their respective dioceses to petition
the Pope for the very definition their bishops opposed, and His Holiness rewarded them by blessings conveyed in autograph letters and
speeches, encouraging the flocks and the clergy to rebel against their
shepherds. Many of the bishops of the opposition who reckoned on
finding in their dioceses those sympathies they had forfeited at Rome
by their independence have thus been reduced to obedience, well
knowing that a bishop whom the Vatican has denounced to his flock
has also nothing to hope from his temporal Government.

It will be curious to know, when the vote on Infallibility has been
taken, to what number the 200 bishops have been reduced. . . . As
matters now stand the leading bishops of the opposition fully expect
that their influence has been sufficiently great, notwithstanding their
many defeats, to obtain a modification of the Canon on Infallibility in
their sense, that is, an admission of the participation of the episcopacy
in the Infallible decisions of the Pope. If this really proves to be the
case, the moral forces of the opposition have not been exerted in vain.
But it still appears very doubtful to me that the Pope and his majority
will make so great a concession to the Gallicans.

[After the promulgation of Infallibility other *schemata* will be
worked out which are likely to cause opposition.] . . . But all these
elements of opposition can easily be overcome by the Vatican so long
as the presence of a French garrison practically paralyses the action of
the states of Europe on the Church of Rome and shields the Papacy
against the corrective effects of public opinion.

528 [F.O. 43/108]   *Rome, 9 July 1870*

No. 159
O.R. to the same

... Mgr Darboy has announced the intention of the French opposition bishops to re-open the debate when the amended Canon on Infallibility shall be submitted to the Council, but they will hardly be supported in this by the rest of the opposition who desire now rather to vote than to speak after the 120 speeches on both sides they have listened to on the subject of the new dogma. According to the latest calculations of the leaders of the opposition they can reckon on 97 *non placets* against the dogma. I cannot but think the opposition overestimate their forces.

The bishops of the Munich school who denied the principle of Infallibility and recommended a protest against the Oecumenicity of the Council followed by the departure of the opposition bishops in a body from Rome, are now reduced to a very small number and indeed some of them may at the decisive moment abstain from voting altogether.

The Opportunists have ceased to exist as a party, almost every one of them having finally drawn up a definition of Infallibility which he is individually prepared to vote for and anxious to get adopted by the Council, thereby practically abandoning his former standpoint of 'inopportuneness'. Granted the principle and the opportuneness, the question before them is to fix the residence of Infallibility, that is, to define whether Infallibility resides in the Pope *alone* as supreme teacher and successor of Peter, or in the Pope as head of the Church *with* the participation of the bishops.

If the definition of the majority submitted to the votes of the Council next week should prove to be too exclusive, the opposition might add a solemn protest to their *non placets* and depart, but they are unfortunately for themselves not sufficiently united to act with the energy the situation requires.

On the other hand, the Congregation of Faith has the power of dividing the opposition and of gaining over many of their votes by so wording the definition as to admit also the Infallibility of the bishops in Council assembled with the Pope. For instance, if the definition declares the Church to be infallible and the Pope by divine dispensation equally preserved from error with or without the Church according to circumstances when he acts *ex cathedra* in matters of

Faith, Morals, Discipline and Church Government as Supreme Teacher, then I think that many of the opposition would vote with the majority. The Canon added to this definition might also be rendered more acceptable by simply declaring without further specification that anyone who denies this definition is anathema.

In all this I am bound to admit that not being a theologian I may be greatly mistaken, and in thus stating my convictions which are not generally shared by others I humbly crave all the indulgence of Her Majesty's Government.

529 [P.R.O. 30/29/84]   *Rome, 12 July 1870*
Private
O.R. to Earl Granville

I begin my first private letter to you with a heavy heart for I have lost the best of fathers and the kindest of chiefs and one of the greatest enjoyments I had in life was my correspondence with Lord Clarendon.

Eleven years ago I dined with you the day of my arrival in Rome at the Hotel de Londres on 20th December 1858, and the kind advice you then gave me, when I was ignorant of the duties I had undertaken, contributed largely to the perfect happiness I have enjoyed here ever since.

I think I may fairly say that you will find our unofficial relations as satisfactory as they can well be and the Pope better disposed on the whole towards Her Majesty's Government than towards any other power in the world. That is perhaps not saying very much, but still it is better than the contrary. The Pope and Cardinal Antonelli derive all their opinions about England from Dr Manning and about Ireland from Cardinal Cullen and as long as those two prelates are satisfied we may expect peace from the Vatican. The rest of the English Catholic clergy have no real influence in Rome.

530 [F.O. 43/108]   *Rome, 12 July 1870*
No. 2
O.R. to Earl G.

I enclose herewith copy of the *Constitutio Dogmatica Prima de Ecclesia Christi* in its present amended form. From my past correspondence Your Lordship has learnt already that the preamble and the first, second and third chapters have been almost unanimously adopted by the bishops in Council. ... The amended text of the fourth chapter on

Infallibility was out to the test for the first time yesterday, and the opposition bishops say that between 90 and 100 of their side remained sitting, while about 500 bishops rose to vote in favour of it. The majority say that not more than 40 or 50 kept their seats. It is extremely difficult to ascertain the truth in these matters but I shall not be surprized to hear that the whole text of the *Schema* enclosed has been definitively adopted in tomorrow's General Congregation.

The opposition were painfully surprized yesterday to see Cardinal Guidi and bishop Senestrey of Ratisbon vote with the majority. Other similar surprizes are, I fear, in store for them tomorrow.

[The conclusion of the fourth chapter of the enclosed printed *Constitutio* is as follows: '. . . *sacro approbante Concilio, docemus et divinitus revelatum dogma esse definimus: Romanum Pontificem, cum ex Cathedra loquitur, id est, cum omnium Christianorum Pastoris et Doctoris Munere fungens, pro suprema sua Apostolica auctoritate doctrinam de fide vel moribus ab universa Ecclesia tenendam definit, per assistentiam divinam, ipsi in beato Petro promissam, ea infallibilitate pollere, qua divinus Redemptor Ecclesiam suam in definienda doctrina de fide vel moribus instructam esse voluit; ideoque ejusmodi Romani Pontificis definitiones esse ex sese irreformabiles. Si quis autem huic Nostrae definitioni contradicere, quod Deus avertat, praesumpserit, anathema sit.*']

531 [F.O. 43/108]   *Rome, 14 July 1870*

No. 4
O.R. to Earl G.

The 88th General Congregation of the Council took place yesterday and the first vote on the entire *Schema* was taken, that is, Preamble, four chapters and four Canons as a whole with the following result:

451 Placets
88 Non Placets
62 Juxta Modum
—————
Total 601

The bishops of the opposition consider the 88 *non placets* to be a great moral victory. The majority admit the opposition vote to be larger than they expected. 80 bishops are said to have abstained from attending, including Cardinals Antonelli and Berardi, but that number appears to me greatly exaggerated. The 62 *juxta modums* are to be taken into consideration and reported upon today by the Faith Congregation, and are said to have been chiefly given by members of the majority who objected to the concessions made in the amended *Schema* and wish for a more stringent definition. . . .

Although the opposition bishops who numbered 200 at the outset have dwindled down to less than half, yet the importance of the 88 *non placets* should not be under-rated, because they represent some of the largest dioceses in the world. As far as I have been able to learn they include Cardinals Rauscher, Schwarzenberg and Mathieu . . . the archbishop of Paris and about 20 French bishops, the archbishop of Milan and 5 or 6 Italian bishops, all the Hungarian and Austrian bishops, 8 or 10 Germans, 10 or 12 Americans, 2 English (Clifford and Errington) and 1 Irish bishop, Moriarty. . . .

The opposition have now another great opportunity of protesting against the Oecumenicity of the Council by leaving Rome in a body and declaring that they cannot accept or submit to the promulgation of the definition of Papal Infallibility without the moral unanimity of the Council which their vote of yesterday would appear to exclude. If on the other hand they remain in Rome and assist at the ceremony of the dogmatic definition they can no longer protest against a Conciliar decision promulgated by the Pope in person without excluding themselves altogether from the Roman Catholic Church or exposing themselves to the censures decreed in the Bull *Latae Sententiae*. . . . The bishops I have spoken to admit these apprehensions, but flatter themselves that by remaining to the end they can increase the *non placets* to 120 and thereby prevent the dogmatic definition altogether. I do not believe it and feel convinced they are again indulging in illusions, but a few days more will open their eyes, and they will recognize after the definition has been promulgated that the hierarchy has lost the last great opportunity in Rome of resisting the encroachments of the Papacy.

532   [F.O. 43/108]   *Rome, 15 July 1870*

No. 5
O.R. to Earl G.

[Gives a list of the 88 bishops so far as he has been able to ascertain them.]

533 [F.O. 43/108]   *Rome, 16 July 1870*

No. 6
O.R. to Earl G.

The international opposition committee met yesterday and determined to send a deputation to the Pope composed of Mgr Darboy, Mgr Rivet, bishop of Dijon, bishop Ketteler of Mayence and archbishop Simor, primate of Hungary, to petition His Holiness to concede the two following points to them: 1st the suppression of the sentence in the 3rd chapter of the *Constitutio de Romano Pontefice* relating to the plenitude of papal Power, and 2nd the addition of the words *consensu ecclesiarum* in the formula defining Infallibility in the 4th chapter of that *Schema*.

The Pope received them with great kindness, but said he could not interfere with the decisions of the Council. Bishop Ketteler then threw himself on his knees and implored His Holiness to listen to the warning voice of the minority. The Pope replied that if they would state their wishes in writing, he would submit them to the Cardinal Legates and the Faith Congregation.

This morning the 89th Congregation took place in St Peter's, and the written wishes of the deputation as well as all the 62 *juxta modum* amendments were taken into consideration. The result of the deliberation was an alteration in the text of the 3rd chapter, respecting the plenitude of Papal power and the insertion of the following words in the definition of Infallibility in the 4th chapter. '. . . *ejusque definitiones ex sese non autem ex consensu Ecclesiae esse irreformabiles.*' Your Lordship will perceive that the definition has therefore been strengthened by the majority, and the opposition will be called upon to give their final vote on this wording on 18th inst. in the fourth public session. . . .

The Council is not to meet until 11th of next November, so as to enable the bishops to return to their dioceses during the remainder of the summer.

534 [F.O. 43/108]   *Rome, 17 July 1870*

No. 7
O.R. to Earl G.

It is again my painful duty to repeat what I have said from the beginning in regard to the weakness of the collective action of the opposition bishops, which has never corresponded to the power and independence of their individual speeches, making them lose in practice every advantage they had gained in theory. The international opposition committee met last night. The leaders reckoned on at least 100 *non placets* on the day of the final definition vote, when the result of their last Whip proved that 16 of their bishops had left Rome since the vote of Wednesday last and that 30 other bishops declared their inability to give their *non placet* in the august presence of Pius IX.

Mgr Dupanloup then advized the venerable brethren to sign a protest against the definition of the dogma, and to abstain from attending the public session altogether. Bishop Clifford and bishop Haynald objected to this course but were outvoted and bishop Strossmayer drew up the enclosed protest which was signed by all the bishops present, with the exception of Melchers who objected to a collective protest and preferred to draw up one of his own. I am assured that they hope to get as many as 70 signatures. Last night 20 opposition bishops who had signed left Rome, among them Dupanloup, Maret, Haynald, Ketteler and Melchers. . . . By tomorrow night the whole opposition will have left Rome.

I am bound to say that all the leading opposition bishops, their lay advizers and personal friends approve this step, and think that the moral effect of their protest and departure will be beneficial to their cause. May it be so but I cannot divest myself of the conviction that the time for the opposition to protest and depart was after the promulgation of the Rules of Procedure, which they believed would destroy their independence. But having practically accepted and acted under those Rules, the time to stay, attend the Council and give a sincere, courageous and conscientious *non placet*, was before the promulgation of the dogma and in the presence of the hierarchy and of the Pope.

[*On 17 July France declared war on Prussia.*]

535   [F.O. 43/108]   *Rome, 18 July 1870*
No. 8
O.R. to Earl G.

I have the honour to enclose copy of the *Constitutio Dogmatica* adopted by the bishops, in the absence of the bishops of the opposition and in the presence of the Pope, at the 4th public session this morning

at the church of St Peter. Your Lordship will perceive that the definition
of Papal Infallibility dogmatically decreed and promulgated by the
Pope and Council this day is the strongest and most absolute that
words can express.

The independence of the Roman Catholic hierarchy has thus been
destroyed and the supreme absolutism of Rome at last been obtained,
established and dogmatized for which the Papacy has contended more
than one thousand years.

P.S.   Since writing the above, I learn that 547 bishops voted *placet*,
2 *non placet* and about 96 abstained from attending the ceremony.

536   [F.O. 43/108]   *Rome, 20 July 1870*

No. 12
O.R. to Earl G.

I beg to thank Your Lordship for the leave of absence granted me
yesterday, and have the honour to report that I intend to leave Rome
tomorrow for London via Civita Vecchia and Marseilles.

As the presence of a French garrison renders Rome an important
post of observation at this moment, I have requested Mr Jervoise to
remain here and report events to Your Lordship. Mr Jervoise is already
acquainted with the best sources of information in Rome, and my
colleagues as well as Cardinal Antonelli have promised me to lend
him every assistance, so that I feel sure that Your Lordship will derive
great advantage from his presence in Rome.

Index

Toscanella, 105

Tosti, Cardinal, 69

Trani, the Countess of, 283

Trauttmansdorff, Count, Austrian Ambassador in Rome, 355, 419, 422, 436, 445, 448

Trent, Council of, 345

Tripoli, the, Sardinian frigate, 124

Tristani, General, a Spaniard, and his band, 200–1, 228, 242, 246–7, 250, 253, 267–8, 273

Trisulti, convent of, 274

Troile family, xviii

Trullet, Monsignore, 142

Turin, O.R. at, 47, 185, 277, 289, 291

Turkey, possible asylum for Pope, 263

Tuscany, Etruria, 22, 48, 60, 71, 87, 104–5, 128, 135, 164, 310, 312
  Grand Duke of, 34, 37, 41, 47, 70, 77, 89, 120, 281
  a part of, offered to the Pope, 89
  O.R. attached to mission to, xxii
  end of mission to, 101
  English representatives in. *See* Corbett; Normanby; Scarlett

Ullathorne, Dr, Bishop of Birmingham, 72, 308–9, 313–14, 375, 392, 402

Umbria, 87, 90, 123, 125, 128, 130, 132, 134, 137, 179–80, 190, 196, 213, 226, 243, 246, 262, 267, 347

Union Italienne, L', 248

Univers, L', 393, 438

Valentano, 105–6

Vallecorso, 186–7

Valmontone, 175

Vanesa, Bishop, 377

Vatican, Council. *See* Oecumenical Council
  Library, 317
  Museum, 189

Vaughan, Bishop, 438

Vaux of Harrowden, Lord, 306

Vegezzi, Commendatore Francesco Saverio, 310–12, 314–16, 339

Velletri, xxxix, 133, 135, 319
  Conca forests in province of, belonging to convent of S. Spirito, 267

Venanzi, Giovanni, 275

Venice, Venetia, xix, 71, 98, 122–3, 125, 143–4, 246, 326, 328–30, 333

Veroli, 186–8, 228, 242

Versailles, O.R. at, ix

Veuillot, Louis, 393, 438

Viale Prela, Cardinal, formerly Nuncio in Vienna, 80, 99

Victor Emmanuel, King of Sardinia, *passim*
  letters from and to Pope, 310, 316

Victoria, Queen, 84, 178, 242, 248, 280, 321, 351–2, 372
  address of condolence to, 206
  despatches mostly endorsed for, from 239

Villafranca, Villa Franca,
  armistice (or treaty) at, 34, 63, 70, 76, 89, 130, 152, 161, 171, 191, 212, 227, 230, 294, 301

Villefort, Cardinal, 276

Villemain, François, 224

Vimercati, Marchese, 167

Viterbo, 27, 78, 105, 107, 133, 135, 137, 195, 247

Wales, Prince of (Baron Renfrew), xiv, 1, 2, 6, 152, 242, 248, 280, 289, 321, 352
  Princess of, xiv, 280, 289, 321, 352

Walewsky, Walewski, comte, French Foreign Minister, 43, 49, 60–2, 66, 75

Washington, O.R. in, ix, xi, xv

Wellington, the Duke of, ix

Werther, Baron, Prussian Minister in Paris, 416

West Indies,
  R.C. clergy in, 361
  American attempt on, 361

Westminster, Archbishopric of, 308–9, 313

Westmorland, Lord, xxi

Williamson, Rev David, xxx

Wiseman, Cardinal, Archbishop of Westminster, 4, 72, 81, 83, 248, 307–9, 314, 357
  O.R.'s interview with, 112–13

Würtemberg 281,

Xenophon, xi